ScottForesman
LITERATURE
AND INTEGRATED STUDIES

Middle School: Grade Six

Middle School: Grade Seven

Middle School: Grade Eight

Forms of Literature

World Literature

American Literature

English Literature

The cover features a detail of William Holman Hunt's *The Afterglow in Egypt,* which appears in full on this page. He began this study of a peasant woman during a visit to Egypt in 1854, complaining of "the difficulty of getting the model day by day and the horrible trials of dust and wind." Hunt's title refers to the period after sunset in which a brilliant light sometimes lingers in the western sky. *Southampton City Art Gallery*

ScottForesman
LITERATURE
AND INTEGRATED STUDIES

World Literature

Senior Consultants

Alan C. Purves
State University of New York at Albany

Carol Booth Olson
University of California, Irvine

Carlos E. Cortés
University of California, Riverside (Emeritus)

ScottForesman

Editorial Offices: Glenview, Illinois
Regional Offices: San Jose, California • Tucker, Georgia • Glenview,
Illinois • Oakland, New Jersey • Dallas, Texas

Visit ScottForesman's Home Page at http://www.scottforesman.com

ACKNOWLEDGMENTS

Texts

6 "Through The Tunnel" from *The Habit of Loving* by Doris Lessing. Copyright © 1955 by Doris Lessing. Originally appeared in *The New Yorker.* Copyright renewed. Reprinted by permission of HarperCollins Publishers, Inc. and Jonathan Clowes Ltd.

19 "Two Kinds" from *The Joy Luck Club* by Amy Tan. Copyright © 1989 by Amy Tan. Reprinted by permission of G. P. Putnam's Sons.

30 "The Censors" by Luisa Valenzuela. Reprinted by permission of Rosario Santos Literary Agent.

36 "The Voter" by Chinua Achebe. Reprinted by permission of the author.

45 "The Other Wife" from *The Other Woman* by Colette, translated from the French by Margaret Crosland. Copyright © 1971, 1972 by Peter Owen, Ltd. Reprinted by permission of Simon & Schuster, Inc. and Peter Owen Ltd. Publishers.

52 From *Mozart: A Life* by Maynard Solomon.

Copyright © 1995 by Maynard Solomon. Reprinted by permission of HarperCollins Publishers, Inc.

66 "The Monkey's Paw" from *The Lady of the Barge* by W. W. Jacobs. Reprinted by permission of The Society of Authors.

79 "The Demon Lover" from *Collected Stories* by Elizabeth Bowen. Copyright 1946 and renewed © 1974 by Elizabeth Bowen. Reprinted by permission of Alfred A. Knopf, Inc.

87 "An Astrologer's Day" from *Malagudi Days* by R. K. Narayan. Published by Viking Press. Copyright © R. K. Narayan. Reprinted by permission of the Wallace Literary Agency, Inc.

104 "The Rain Came" by Grace A. Ogot from *Land Without Thunder.* Reprinted by permission of East African Educational Publishers Ltd.

continued on page 852

Senior Consultants

Alan C. Purves

Professor of Education and Humanities, State University of New York at Albany; Director of the Center for Writing and Literacy. Dr. Purves developed the concept and philosophy of the literature lessons for the series, consulted with editors, reviewed tables of contents and lesson manuscript, wrote the Assessment Handbooks, and oversaw the development and writing of the series testing strand.

Carol Booth Olson

Director, California Writing Project, Department of Education, University of California, Irvine. Dr. Olson conceptualized and developed the integrated writing strand of the program, consulted with editors, led a team of teachers in creating literature-based Writing Workshops, and reviewed final manuscript.

Carlos E. Cortés

Professor Emeritus, History, University of California, Riverside. Dr. Cortés designed and developed the multicultural strand embedded in each unit of the series and consulted with grade-level editors to implement the concepts.

Series Consultants

Visual and Media Literacy/Speaking and Listening/Critical Thinking

Harold M. Foster. Professor of English Education and Secondary Education, The University of Akron, Akron. Dr. Foster developed and wrote the Beyond Print features for all levels of the series.

ESL and LEP Strategies

James Cummins. Professor, Modern Language Centre and Curriculum Department, Ontario Institute for Studies in Education, Toronto.

Lily Wong Fillmore. Professor, Graduate School of Education, University of California at Berkeley.

Drs. Cummins and Fillmore advised on the needs of ESL and LEP students, helped develop the Building English Proficiency model for the program, and reviewed strategies and manuscript for this strand of the program.

Fine Arts/Humanities

Neil Anstead. Coordinator of the Humanitas Program, Cleveland Humanities Magnet School, Reseda California. Mr. Anstead consulted on the fine art used in the program.

Reviewers and Contributors

Pupil and Teacher Edition

Jay Amberg, Glenbrook South High School, Glenview, Illinois **Edison Barber,** St. Anne Community High School, St. Anne, Illinois **Lois Barliant,** Albert G. Lane Technical High School, Chicago, Illinois **James Beasley,** Plant City Senior High School, Plant City, Florida **Linda Belpedio,** Oak Park/River Forest High School, Oak Park, Illinois **Richard Bruns,** Burges High School, El Paso, Texas **Kay Parks Bushman,** Ottawa High School, Ottawa, Kansas **Jesús Cardona,** John F. Kennedy High School, San Antonio, Texas **Marlene Carter,** Dorsey High School, Los Angeles, California **Patrick Cates,** Lubbock High School, Lubbock, Texas **Timothy Dohrer,** New Trier Township High School, Winnetka, Illinois **Margaret Doria,** Our Lady of Perpetual Help High School, Brooklyn, New York **Lucila Dypiangco,** Bell Senior High School, Bell, California **Judith Edminster,** Plant City High School, Plant City, Florida **Mary Alice Fite,** Columbus School for Girls, Columbus, Ohio **Montserrat Fontes,** Marshall High School, Los Angeles, California **Diane Fragos,** Turkey Creek Middle School, Plant City, Florida **Joan Greenwood,** Thornton Township High School, Harvey, Illinois **William Irvin,** Pittsfield Public Schools, Pittsfield, Massachusetts **Carleton Jordan,** Montclair High School, Montclair, New Jersey **Mark Kautz,** Chapel Hill High School, Chapel Hill, North Carolina **Elaine Kay,** Bartow High School, Bartow, Florida **Roslyn Kettering,** West Lafayette Junior/Senior High School, West Lafayette, Indiana **Kristina Kostopoulos,** Lincoln Park High School, Chicago, Illinois **Julia Lloyd,** Harwood Junior High School, Bedford, Texas **John Lord,** Ocean Township High School, Oakhurst, New Jersey **Dolores Mathews,** Bloomingdale High School, Valrico, Florida **Jim McCallum,** Milford High School, Milford, Massachusetts **Monette Mehalko,** Plant City Senior High School, Plant City, Florida **Lucia Podraza,** DuSable High School, Chicago, Illinois **Frank Pool,** Anderson High School, Austin, Texas **Alice Price,** Latin School, Chicago, Illinois **Anna J. Roseboro,** The Bishop's School, La Jolla, California **Peter Sebastian,** Granite Hills High School, El Cajon, California **Rob Slater,** East Forsyth High School, Winston Salem, North Carolina **Catherine Small,** Nicolet High School, Glendale, Wisconsin **Dennis Symkowiak,** Mundelein High School, Mundelein, Illinois **Rosetta Tetteh,** Senn High School, Chicago, Illinois **Pamela Vetters,** Harlandale High School, San Antonio, Texas **Polly Walwark,** Oak Park High School, Oak Park, Illinois **Karen Wrobleski,** San Diego High School, San Diego, California **Dru Zimmerman,** Chapel Hill High School, Chapel Hill, North Carolina

MULTICULTURAL REVIEW BOARD

Duane BigEagle, writer and teacher, Tomales, California **Maria Campanario,** Raphael Hernandez School, Stoughton, Massachusetts **Pat Canty,** Beverly Woods Middle School, Charlotte, North Carolina **Jesús Cardona,** John F. Kennedy High School, San Antonio, Texas **Diego Davalos,** Chula Vista High School, Chula Vista, California **Sandra Dickerson,** Milwaukee Public Schools, Milwaukee, Wisconsin **Lucila Dypiangco,** Bell Senior High School, Bell, California **Marion Fleming,** Roselle Junior/Senior High School, Roselle, New York **Gloria Garcia,** Madero Middle School, Chicago, Illinois **Thelma Hernandez,** Edison Junior High School, San Antonio, Texas **Yvonne Hutchinson,** Markham Intermediate School, Los Angeles, California **Narva Jackson,** Roselle Junior/Senior High School, Roselle, New York **May Lee,** Baldwin Senior High School, Baldwin, New York **Dolores Mathews,** Bloomingdale High School, Valrico, Florida **Jack Matsumoto,** Edison Regional Gifted Center, Chicago, Illinois **James Masao Mitsui,** Hazen High School, Renton, Washington **Ed Ramirez,** Wang School, Derry, New Hampshire **Mary Sasse,** consultant, Carbondale, Illinois **Harolene Steele,** Hill Middle School, Winston-Salem, North Carolina **Suthinee Suktrakul,** Norcross High School, Norcross, Georgia **Jerry Tagami,** New Harbor High School, Newport Beach, California **Barbara Wheeler,** Harford County Public Schools, Bel Air, Maryland **Raymond Zamarippa,** Bowie Junior High School, Irving, Texas

BUILDING ENGLISH PROFICIENCY (ESL / LEP)

Kata Alvidrez, Newton High School, Newton, Iowa **Judy Bebelaar,** International Studies Academy, San Francisco, California **Rebecca Benjamin,** University of New Mexico, Albuquerque, New Mexico **Ioana Cummins,** Toronto, Ontario **Doti Foster,** Lubbock Independent School District, Lubbock, Texas **Bridget Hawthorne,** Oliver Hazard Perry Middle School, Providence, Rhode Island **Sandra Huezo,** Gompers Secondary School, San Diego, California **Nancy Hykel,** Harlandale High School, San Antonio, Texas **Mary Ann Jentel,** Madonna High School for Girls, Chicago, Illinois **Nancy Duke S. Lay,** City College of New York, New York, New York **José Lebrón,** Julia De Burgos Middle School, Philadelphia, Pennsylvania **Mary Linnstaedter,** Nimitz High School, Houston, Texas **Mayra Menéndez,** School Board of Broward County, Fort Lauderdale, Florida **Sharese Tisby,** Waukegan High School, Waukegan, Illinois **Sylvia Velazquez,** Braddock Senior High School, Miami, Florida **Greta Vollmer,** International Studies Academy, San Francisco, California **Shirley Wright,** Longview Independent School District, Longview, Texas **Suzanne Zweig,** Norwood Park School, Chicago, Illinois

WRITER'S WORKSHOP PROMPT WRITERS

Bill Burns, Sonora High School, LaHabra, California **Patricia Clark,** Century High School, Santa Ana, California **Glenn Patchell,** Irvine High School, Irvine, California **Maureen Rippee,** Woodrow Wilson High School, Long Beach, California **Julie Simpson,** Sunny Hills High School, Fullerton, California

STUDENT CONTRIBUTORS

Julia Besterfeldt   Susan Biebel   Chelsea Brown   Lisa Cason   Elizabeth Ratliff   Sheila Chalegua   Brandi Cleaver   Christian DeVos   Lynn DeWitt   William Eckmann   Maggie Gorecki   Nina Grigsby   David Hardy   Melanie Jetter   Louis Kholodovsky   Charly Kittay   Michael J Kurcz   Samantha Anne La'o   Courtney Ann Lambke   William McKelphin   Karen Miramontes   Hollie Nygaard   Chinyera Osuji   Adam Peterson   Elizabeth Ratliff   Jeremy A. Redburn   Kimyona Roberts   Brendan Rose   Morgan Russell-Dempsey   Rebecca Ryan   Isaac Saposnik   Mark Sarna   Mike Uehara   Melissa Villalon   C. M. Wiggins

CONTENTS

UNIT 1

MEETING THE CHALLENGE

PART ONE: PUSHING TOWARD THE TOP

PART TWO: TRYING TO BEAT THE ODDS

EXPLORING A THEME THROUGH SEVERAL GENRES

PART THREE: DEALING WITH CONSEQUENCES

UNIT **2**

$\mathcal{M}$AKING JUDGMENTS

GENRE OVERVIEW:
READING A PLAY   **184**

PART ONE: ON TRIAL

EXPLORING A THEME THROUGH SEVERAL GENRES

PART TWO: BENEATH THE SURFACE

Literature

Integrated Studies

UNIT 3

ANSWERING THE CALL

GENRE OVERVIEW: READING
ARTHURIAN LEGENDS   336

PART ONE: ARTHURIAN LEGENDS

Literature

PART TWO: MANY KINDS OF HEROES

Literature

Integrated Studies

UNIT 4

WHAT REALLY MATTERS

GENRE OVERVIEW:
READING NONFICTION   **452**

PART ONE: WORTH FIGHTING FOR?

Part Two: Something of Value

Literature

Integrated Studies

UNIT 5

A PLACE IN THE WORLD

GENRE OVERVIEW:
READING POETRY   **548**

PART ONE: CONNECTIONS

PART TWO: REFLECTIONS

PART THREE: CULTURE CROSSROADS

Literature

UNIT 6

$\mathcal{P}$OWER PLAYS

GENRE OVERVIEW:
READING A SHAKESPEAREAN PLAY   674

THE COST OF WINNING

GLOSSARIES, HANDBOOKS, AND INDEXES

GENRE OVERVIEW

Short Stories

Poetry

Plays

Nonfiction

Legends

FEATURE OVERVIEW

Genre Overviews

Interdisciplinary Studies

Reading Mini-Lessons

Writing Workshops

Beyond Print

Model for Active Reading

Good readers read actively. They become involved in what they read, relating the characters and situations to people and events in their own lives. They question, clarify, predict, and in other ways think about the story or article they are reading. These three students agreed to let us in on their thoughts as they read "The False Gems." You might have different ideas and questions than they did about this story. However, their ways of responding will give you ideas for how you can get actively engaged as you read literature.

NINA GRIGSBY Well, I'm sixteen. I like ballet, singing—I sing in the choir, CDs. I read a lot, sometimes two books a week. The books I really like are romances. I guess you could say I read two ways: kind of casually for the romances; more deliberately for school stuff that I know I'll be tested on. I want to be a writer.

ISAAC SAPOSNIK I'm sixteen. I'm active in my youth group. Actually, I don't do much reading outside of school, but when I get time, I do a little reading—mostly low-keyed stuff. I get into details, so I have to keep in mind the big picture when I read and not get sidetracked. I'm not sure about the future, but I'd like to do something connected with education.

MIKA UEHARA Well, I'm into sports. I'm captain of the girls volleyball team. What else? I like to hang out and talk lots on the phone. Like Isaac, I don't read that much, but I do like magazines. I'd like to be a psychologist or something in the medical field.

Six Reading Strategies

Following are some of the techniques that good readers use, often without being aware of them.

Question Ask questions that arise as you read.

Example: Is Madame Lantin happy with her life? Would she be so dependent on others for her support if she lived today?

Clarify Clear up confusion and answer questions.

Example: Oh, I see what's going on. M. Lantin wasn't suspicious because he thought the gems were false.

Summarize Review what has happened so far.

Example: The Lantins seemed to have had a happy married life. After she dies, he doesn't wait long to remarry, but this time he chooses a very different woman.

Predict Use what has happened so far to make reasonable guesses about what might happen next.

Example: M. Lantin doesn't seem like the kind of person who spends money wisely. I bet he uses up his fortune quickly.

Evaluate Use your common sense and evidence in the selection to arrive at sound opinions and valid conclusions.

Example: Madame Lantin, who wanted both marital security and wealth, worked out a clever scheme to have it both ways.

Connect Compare the text with something in your own experience, with another text, or with ideas within the text.

Example: Based on stories I've read and movies or TV programs I've seen, I'd say that instant wealth usually makes people unhappy.

The False Gems

Guy de Maupassant

$\mathcal{M}$. Lantin had met the young woman at a *soirée,* at the home of the assistant chief of his bureau, and at first sight had fallen madly in love with her.

She was the daughter of a country physician who had died some months previously. She had come to live in Paris, with her mother, who visited much among her acquaintances, in the hope of making a favorable marriage for her daughter. They were poor and honest, quiet and unaffected.

The young girl was a perfect type of the virtuous woman whom every sensible young man dreams of one day winning for life. Her simple beauty had the charm of angelic modesty, and the imperceptible smile which constantly hovered about her lips seemed to be the reflection of a pure and lovely soul. Her praises resounded on every side. People never tired of saying: "Happy the man who wins her love! He could not find a better wife."

Now M. Lantin enjoyed a snug little income of $700, and, thinking he could safely assume the responsibilities of matrimony, proposed to this model young girl and was accepted.

He was unspeakably happy with her; she governed his household so cleverly and economically that they seemed to live in luxury. She lavished the most delicate attentions on her husband, coaxed and fondled him, and the charm of her presence was so great that six years after their marriage M. Lantin discovered that he loved his wife even more than during the first days of their honeymoon.

He only felt inclined to blame her for two things: her love of the theater, and a taste for false jewelry. Her friends (she was acquainted with some officers' wives) frequently procured for her a box at the theater, often for the first representations of the new plays; and her husband was obliged to accompany her, whether he willed or not, to these amusements, though they bored him excessively after a day's labor at the office.

After a time, M. Lantin begged his wife to get some lady of her acquaintance to accompany her. She was at first opposed to such an arrangement; but, after much persuasion on his part, she finally consented—to the infinite delight of her husband.

Now, with her love for the theater came also the desire to adorn her person. True, her costumes remained as before, simple, and in the most correct taste; but she soon began to ornament her ears with huge rhinestones which glittered and sparkled like real diamonds. Around her neck she wore strings of false pearls, and on her arms bracelets of imitation gold.

Madame Alphonse Daudet by Pierre Auguste Renoir (1841–1919) illustrates the artist's interest in the human figure and in rich colors and glowing light. Do you think an oil portrait like this can reveal as much about a person as a photograph would?

MIKA I remember this author from French class. (connect)

ISAAC De Maupassant has a thing about gems. In "The Necklace," the gems were false, but she thought they were real. (connect)

MIKA Interesting contrasts: She's rich in beauty and charm, and poor financially. (evaluate)

NINA I noticed adjectives like *honest, quiet, unaffected, perfect, angelic, pure, lovely.* Is she too good to be true? (question)

NINA There's a change of tone here. Maybe things aren't so perfect. (evaluate)

ISAAC *false jewelry*—It seems odd that such a pure and simple woman would be so fond of fake jewels. (evaluate)

ISAAC *infinite*—This is a strange word here. I wonder why he uses it. (question)

ISAAC *false pearls, imitation gold*—It makes them sound tacky. (evaluate)

Her husband frequently remonstrated with her, saying:

"My dear, as you cannot afford to buy real diamonds, you ought to appear adorned with your beauty and modesty alone, which are the rarest ornaments of your sex."

But she would smile sweetly, and say:

"What can I do? I am so fond of jewelry. It is my only weakness. We cannot change our natures."

Then she would roll the pearl necklaces around her fingers, and hold up the bright gems for her husband's admiration, gently coaxing him:

"Look! are they not lovely? One would swear they were real."

M. Lantin would then answer, smilingly:

"You have Bohemian tastes, my dear."

Often of an evening, when they were enjoying a tête-à-tête by the fireside, she would place on the tea table the leather box containing the "trash," as M. Lantin called it. She would examine the false gems with a passionate attention as though they were in some way connected with a deep and secret joy, and she often insisted on passing a necklace around her husband's neck, and laughing heartily would exclaim: "How droll you look!" Then she would throw herself into his arms and kiss him affectionately.

One evening in the winter she attended the opera, and on her return was chilled through and through. The next morning she coughed, and eight days later she died of inflammation of the lungs.

M. Lantin's despair was so great that his hair became white in one month. He wept unceasingly; his heart was torn with grief, and his mind was haunted by the remembrance, the smile, the voice—by every charm of his beautiful, dead wife.

Time, the healer, did not assuage his grief. Often during office hours, while his colleagues were discussing the topics of the day, his eyes would suddenly fill with tears, and he would give vent to his grief in heartrending sobs. Everything in his wife's room remained as before her decease; and here he was wont to seclude himself daily and think of her who had been his treasure—the joy of his existence.

But life soon became a struggle. His income, which in the hands of his wife had covered all household expenses, was now no longer sufficient for his own immediate wants; and he wondered how she could have managed to buy such excellent wines, and such rare delicacies, things which he could no longer procure with his modest resources.

He incurred some debts and was soon reduced to absolute

ISAAC *remonstrated*—I'm not sure about meaning. Oh, judging from what follows, it must mean "disagreed." (clarify)

ISAAC "It is my only weakness." We've been told that she's modest, but this doesn't sound very modest. (evaluate)

MIKA The "deep and secret joy" seems to foreshadow something. I wonder why these false gems mean so much to her? (question)

NINA This seems so sudden and unexpected. Only one paragraph on her death makes it sound unimportant. (evaluate)

NINA The words *torn, haunted, heartrending* seem so dramatic. So does his white hair. (evaluate)

NINA *Assuage* must mean "heal." (clarify)

MIKA I agree that time is a healer. (connect)

NINA The word *treasure* here is interesting. It suggests that she was like a gem. Gems were her treasure; she was his treasure. (connect)

MIKA Life does become a struggle when you lose a loved one. (connect)

poverty. One morning, finding himself without a cent in his pocket, he resolved to sell something, and, immediately, the thought occurred to him of disposing of his wife's paste jewels. He cherished in his heart a sort of rancor against the false gems. They had always irritated him in the past, and the very sight of them spoiled somewhat the memory of his lost darling.

To the last days of her life, she had continued to make purchases, bringing home new gems almost every evening. He decided to sell the heavy necklace which she seemed to prefer, and which, he thought, ought to be worth about six or seven francs; for although paste it was, nevertheless, of very fine workmanship.

He put it in his pocket and started out in search of a jeweler's shop. He entered the first one he saw, feeling a little ashamed to expose his misery, and also to offer such a worthless article for sale.

"Sir," said he to the merchant, "I would like to know what this is worth."

The man took the necklace, examined it, called his clerk and made some remarks in an undertone; then he put the ornament back on the counter, and looked at it from a distance to judge of the effect.

M. Lantin was annoyed by all this detail and was on the point of saying: "Oh! I know well enough it is not worth anything," when the jeweler said: "Sir, that necklace is worth from twelve to fifteen thousand francs; but I could not buy it unless you tell me now whence it comes."

The widower opened his eyes wide and remained gaping, not comprehending the merchant's meaning. Finally he stammered: "You say—are you sure?" The other replied dryly: "You can search elsewhere and see if anyone will offer you more. I consider it worth fifteen thousand at the most. Come back here if you cannot do better."

M. Lantin, beside himself with astonishment, took up the necklace and left the store. He wished time for reflection.

Once outside, he felt inclined to laugh, and said to himself: "The fool! Had I only taken him at his word! That jeweler cannot distinguish real diamonds from paste."

A few minutes after, he entered another store in the Rue de la Paix. As soon as the proprietor glanced at the necklace, he cried out:

"Ah, *parbleu!* I know it well; it was bought here."

M. Lantin was disturbed, and asked:

"How much is it worth?"

ISAAC *paste jewels*—This sounds like an arts and crafts project (evaluate)

ISAAC *Rue de la Paix*—Street of Peace. I wonder if this name is significant. Will he find peace of mind? (question)

"Well, I sold it for twenty thousand francs. I am willing to take it back for eighteen thousand when you inform me, according to our legal formality, how it came to be in your possession."

This time M. Lantin was dumbfounded. He replied:

"But—but—examine it well. Until this moment I was under the impression that it was paste."

Said the jeweler:

"What is your name, sir?"

"Lantin—I am in the employ of the Minister of the Interior. I live at No. 16 Rue des Martyrs."

The merchant looked through his books, found the entry, and said: "That necklace was sent to Mme. Lantin's address, 16 Rue des Martyrs, July 20, 1876."

The two men looked into each other's eyes—the widower speechless with astonishment, the jeweler scenting a thief. The latter broke the silence by saying:

"Will you leave this necklace here for twenty-four hours? I will give you a receipt."

"Certainly," answered M. Lantin, hastily. Then, putting the ticket in his pocket, he left the store.

He wandered aimlessly through the streets, his mind in a state of dreadful confusion. He tried to reason, to understand. His wife could not afford to purchase such a costly ornament. Certainly not. But, then, it must have been a present!—a present!—a present from whom? Why was it given her?

He stopped and remained standing in the middle of the street. A horrible doubt entered his mind—she? Then all the other gems must have been presents, too! The earth seemed to tremble beneath him—the tree before him was falling—throwing up his arms, he fell to the ground, unconscious. He recovered his senses in a pharmacy into which the passers-by had taken him, and was then taken to his home. When he arrived he shut himself up in his room and wept until nightfall. Finally, overcome with fatigue, he threw himself on the bed, where he passed an uneasy, restless night.

The following morning he arose and prepared to go to the office. It was hard to work after such a shock. He sent a letter to his employer requesting to be excused. Then he remembered that he had to return to the jeweler's. He did not like the idea; but he could not leave the necklace with that man. So he dressed and went out.

It was a lovely day; a clear blue sky smiled on the busy city below, and men of leisure were strolling about with their hands in their pockets.

Observing them, M. Lantin said to himself: "The rich, indeed, are happy. With money it is possible to forget even the deepest

---

ISAAC Why is it so important where the jewels have come from? Could the jeweler have made a mistake about their worth? (question). Or maybe he thinks this guy's a thief.

NINA *Rue des Martyrs* is a street mentioned in "The Necklace." (connect)

ISAAC I wonder if the word *Martyrs* is significant. Is someone being offered up? (connect)

MIKA How did she get the gems? from whom? (question) Everything flashes before his eyes. He is having a moment of revelation. He's very upset. (summarize)

ISAAC "The earth seemed to tremble beneath him"—Something awful occurs to him. Could she have been having an affair? (question)

ISAAC *lovely, smiled, leisure, strolling*—This sure seems like an entirely different mood. (evaluate)

NINA M. Lantin's observation here is ironic. I don't think that he'll be happy if he's rich. (predict)

sorrow. One can go where one pleases, and in travel find that distraction which is the surest cure for grief. Oh! if I were only rich!"

He began to feel hungry, but his pocket was empty. He again remembered the necklace. Eighteen thousand francs! Eighteen thousand francs! What a sum!

He soon arrived in the Rue de la Paix, opposite the jeweler's. Eighteen thousand francs! Twenty times he resolved to go in, but shame kept him back. He was hungry, however—very hungry, and had not a cent in his pocket. He decided quickly, ran across the street in order not to have time for reflection, and entered the store.

The proprietor immediately came forward and politely offered him a chair; the clerks glanced at him knowingly.

"I have made inquiries, M. Lantin," said the jeweler, "and if you are still resolved to dispose of the gems, I am ready to pay you the price I offered."

"Certainly, sir" stammered M. Lantin.

Whereupon the proprietor took from a drawer eighteen large bills, counted and handed them to M. Lantin, who signed a receipt and with a trembling hand put the money into his pocket.

As he was about to leave the store, he turned toward the merchant, who still wore the same knowing smile, and lowering his eyes, said:

"I have—I have other gems which I have received from the same source. Will you buy them also?"

The merchant bowed: "Certainly, sir."

M. Lantin said gravely: "I will bring them to you." An hour later he returned with the gems.

The large diamond earrings were worth twenty thousand francs; the bracelets thirty-five thousand; the rings, sixteen thousand; a set of emeralds and sapphires, fourteen thousand; a gold chain with solitaire pendant, forty thousand—making the sum of one hundred and forty-three thousand francs.

The jeweler remarked, jokingly:

"There was a person who invested all her earnings in precious stones."

M. Lantin replied, seriously:

"It is only another way of investing one's money."

That day he lunched at Voisin's and drank wine worth twenty francs a bottle. Then he hired a carriage and made a tour of the Bois, and as he scanned the various turn-outs with a contemptuous air he could hardly refrain from crying out to the occupants:

"I, too am rich!—I am worth two hundred thousand francs."

MIKA I think that getting rid of these gems would mean the loss of his memories of past happiness with Madame Lantin. (evaluate)

MIKA He reacts to money like most people do. I remember his wife's observation. "We cannot change our natures." (connect)

NINA I'll bet they look at him *knowingly* because they know that his wife was cheating on him. (clarify)

ISAAC He's going to be rich. I bet he'll end up spending all the money. (predict)

NINA Now that we know the gems are real, they're described in a more dignified way—as "large diamond earrings," "a set of emeralds and sapphires," "a gold chain with solitaire pendant." When they were false they sounded gaudy: *huge rhinestones, false, imitation, worthless, paste, glittered.* (evaluate)

MIKA He's already assuming the "contemptuous" air of a rich person. He'll probably become a snob. (predict)

Suddenly he thought of his employer. He drove up to the office, and entered gaily, saying:

"Sir, I have come to resign my position. I have just inherited three hundred thousand francs."

He shook hands with his former colleagues and confided to them some of his projects for the future; then he went off to dine at the Café Anglais.

He seated himself beside a gentleman of aristocratic bearing, and during the meal informed the latter confidentially that he had just inherited a fortune of four hundred thousand francs.

For the first time in his life he was not bored at the theater, and spent the remainder of the night in a gay frolic.

Six months afterward he married again. His second wife was a very virtuous woman, with a violent temper. She caused him much sorrow.

MIKA The way he exaggerates the gems' worth and mentions his inheritance suggests now that he's wealthy he has an inflated idea of himself. (evaluate)

ISAAC *Violent* and *virtuous* don't seem to mix. Rather abrupt ending. (evaluate)

Discussion After Reading

General Comments

ISAAC Is there supposed to be a moral here? Maybe "Money brings sorrow." But the wife seemed pretty happy when she had the jewels, so this moral doesn't apply. (evaluate)

After thinking about the story, I see lots of lines are ironic that I didn't think were when I first read them. Like when Madame Lantin says jewels were her only weakness. This isn't true. I think she was really good and virtuous before she met him, but her desire for money corrupted her. That's how I'd sum up the point of the story: Money corrupts. (evaluate)

ISAAC It's interesting that he goes from happy (with first wife) to sad (when she dies) to happy (when he first is rich) to sad (when he remarries.) Well, at least his new wife doesn't sound like she'll be false. (summarize)

NINA This ending seems ironic. His new wife is "virtuous" but causes him much sorrow. His first wife, who was described as "virtuous" but really wasn't, made him happy. (evaluate)

MIKA Now I get the title. She is the false gem. She's put on a false front. (clarify)

ISAAC I finally understand why he didn't originally suspect her of being unfaithful. He thought the gems were false! He would have suspected her if he had known that they were real. (clarify)

NINA This final paragraph is so compact, it reminds me of the paragraph where Madame Lantin dies. (connect)

MIKA The story is full of contrasts. The final one is his two very different wives — one who is really virtuous though violent, the other who only appears to be virtuous but is gentle and gracious. Maybe the author is saying you can't have it both ways. (summarize)

Is it sometimes difficult for you to talk about literature once you've read it? Take some cues from active readers, who reflect and respond in a variety of ways. After reading "The False Gems," these three students reveal their personal reactions (Shaping Your Response) and literary responses (Analyzing the Story), along with the connections they have made to their own experiences (Extending the Ideas). These are the types of questions you will find in this book.

Shaping Your Response

Rate Madame Lantin as a wife from 1–10 with 10 being the ideal wife.

ISAAC I'd give her a 5. I think she really loves her husband — she gives him lots of attention and she runs the house well. She's probably a good person but wanted gems and would do anything for them.

MIKA Maybe a 4 but not very high. After all, she's unfaithful.

NINA Originally I wanted to give her a 10, but once I figured out what was going on, I'd say a 1 or 2. I think that the second wife will be much better, even though she has a bad temper.

Analyzing the Story

What examples of irony can you find in the story?

MIKA First of all, there's the title. She has "false" gems that we find out are real. She's a false gem, although he thought she was true.

NINA Just about everything seems ironic when you reread the story: ". . . she governed his household so cleverly and economically that they seemed to live in luxury." Here, she's getting all this money on the side; no wonder it appears they live in luxury. All those words like *virtuous, pure,* and *perfect* are really ironic. How about "It is my only weakness"?

Extending the Ideas

What other stories, movies, TV programs, or real-life situations does this story remind you of?

ISAAC "The Necklace," also by de Maupassant. We just read *One Hundred Years of Solitude* by García Márquez, and the situations seem very similar. People will do anything for money. In the novel, Aureliano takes up with Petra so their animals will mate and they can make money.

MIKA This reminds me of the movie *Indecent Proposal.* It's also like a news story about someone winning the lottery. I wonder if instant millionaires are miserable in the end.

Meeting the Challenge

Pushing Toward the Top

Trying to Beat the Odds

Dealing with Consequences

1

Reading

When you read a short story, you get to know fictional characters and become involved in the situations and dilemmas they face. This involvement doesn't just happen by chance. Because they have to pack a lot into a few pages, short story writers must quickly engage readers, using the elements described here. At the end of this unit, you will find not only short stories, but poems and nonfiction that explore a common theme. With such a mixture, you can discover which elements are unique to short stories, and which can be found in other types of literature.

A young woman... must die so that the country may have rain.

—*Grace Ogot, "The Rain Came"*

PLOT

First comes the **plot**—the pattern of events that is the framework of a narrative. As you read, note what sets these events in motion and how one event leads to the next. The basic ingredient that energizes a plot is **conflict.** Sometimes the conflict is a struggle between the main character or characters and an adverse character, group, or outside force. At other times, the conflict is within a character. A story's conflict intensifies until it reaches a **climax,** a turning point at which the conflict is confronted head-on. The end of the conflict is called the **resolution.**

...her eyes, and her wavy golden hair, disguised her as a fragile and soulful blond.

—*Colette, "The Other Wife"*

CHARACTERS

Also central to a short story are the **characters**—the personalities that pop from the page. We get to know some fictional characters more intimately than real people because we can share their innermost thoughts. Authors have several ways of acquainting us with characters. They may depict them directly by stating the character's appearance and thoughts. At times, however, writers choose to suggest certain character traits, requiring that the reader make inferences based on what is done or said by other characters.

a Short Story

POINT OF VIEW

Just as important as the people and places in a story is the person who is telling it—the narrator who filters what is being told and seen. An author's choice of narrator dictates the **point of view.** If the narrator is a character in the story, then this first-person point of view presents a very personal and limited picture of what you learn. "Two Kinds" has a first-person narrator. But frequently, the narrator is someone outside the story—a third-person narrator, as in "Through the Tunnel" and "The Censors." In this third-person point of view, a narrator can be limited like the first-person narrator, or can be omniscient—knowing everything about the characters and their thoughts.

SETTING

Stories take readers places. The **setting** of a story—the time and place in which events occur—serves as a backdrop for characters and events. The when and where of stories in this unit range from a medieval castle to a polling booth in Nigeria and a school in Maoist China. A setting may help create the atmosphere, or **mood,** in a story. For example, an empty house during wartime London in "The Demon Lover," establishes a mood of tension and terror. Setting can also be vital to understanding characters, customs, and events, as it is in "The Rain Came."

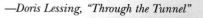

THEME

During and after reading, you will find yourself reflecting on ideas common to these stories, as well as links between the fictional characters and situations and those in the real world. These links form the theme of the story. For instance, in "Through the Tunnel," Jerry's changing relationship with his mother and his need to prove himself indicate a universal journey toward maturity. Different readers may find different themes in a story, and a single story can have several themes.

Part One

Pushing Toward the Top

You are about to meet some characters who are determined to succeed—to be the best. But although they are willing to go to great lengths to excel, not all these people come out winners in their push to the top.

Multicultural Connection **Individuality** may involve asserting oneself against group culture. As you read the following selections, decide how the pursuits of individual goals are influenced by a larger cultural context.

Before Reading

Through the Tunnel

by Doris Lessing   Great Britain

Doris Lessing
born 1919

The mission of the writer is to provide the world with a "small personal voice," according to Doris Lessing. Growing up in Southern Rhodesia (now Zimbabwe but then part of the British Empire), Lessing quit school at fourteen, began writing novels, and left the family's farm to work in the city. In 1949, after writing her first book, she moved to England where she still lives. She has written essays, short stories, a science fiction series, and many novels, including *The Golden Notebook,* a classic of feminist literature. Lessing's concerns include politics, the changing role of women in society, and the effects of technology.

Building Background

An Explosion of Light "He felt he was dying. He was no longer quite conscious. He struggled on in the darkness between lapses into unconsciousness. An immense, swelling pain filled his head, and then the darkness cracked with an explosion of green light. His hands, groping forward, met nothing." Imagine finding yourself in a situation like that described above. Where are you? How did you come to be here? What will you do to get out of this situation? Explain to a partner what you imagine. You may want to illustrate the situation. Now speculate on how this quoted description might be related to a story titled "Through the Tunnel."

Literary Focus

Theme You will often link the stories you read or movies you see with your own experiences. Jerry's experience in "Through the Tunnel" may remind you of a time you responded to a dare or of a cartoon superhero who lived up to her reputation. You might call these common links something like "improving yourself," "struggling to succeed," or "initiation." Such links are called **themes**. Not everyone finds the same theme in a work or gives it the same label, and stories may have more than one theme.

Writer's Notebook

Risky Business Before reading "Through the Tunnel," think about times in your life when you have taken risks. Were they foolish risks, or did they pay off? Zero in on a particular risk and record how you felt before, during, and after taking it. Speculate on whether or not you would do things differently now.

THROUGH the TUNNEL

Doris Lessing

Going to the shore on the first morning of the vacation, the young English boy stopped at a turning of the path and looked down at a wild and rocky bay, and then over to the crowded beach he knew so well from other years. His mother walked on in front of him, carrying a bright striped bag in one hand. Her other arm, swinging loose, was very white in the sun. The boy watched that white, naked arm, and turned his eyes, which had a frown behind them, toward the bay and back again to his mother. When she felt he was not with her, she swung around. "Oh, there you are, Jerry!" she said. She looked impatient, then smiled. "Why, darling, would you rather not come with me? Would you rather—" She frowned, conscientiously worrying over what amusements he might secretly be longing for, which she had been too busy or too careless to imagine. He was very familiar with that anxious, apologetic smile. Contrition[1] sent him running after her. And yet, as he ran, he looked back over his shoulder at the wild bay; and all morning, as he played on the safe beach, he was thinking of it.

He was very familiar with that anxious, apologetic smile. Contrition sent him running after her.

Next morning, when it was time for the routine of swimming and sunbathing, his mother said, "Are you tired of the usual beach, Jerry? Would you like to go somewhere else?"

"Oh, no!" he said quickly, smiling at her out of that unfailing impulse of contrition—a sort of chivalry. Yet, walking down the path with her, he blurted out, "I'd like to go and have a look at those rocks down there."

She gave the idea her attention. It was a wild-looking place, and there was no one there; but she said, "Of course, Jerry. When you've had enough, come to the big beach. Or just go straight back to the villa, if you like." She walked away, that bare arm, now slightly reddened from yesterday's sun, swinging. And he almost ran after her again, feeling it unbearable that she could go by herself, but he did not.

She was thinking. Of course he's old enough to be safe without me. Have I been keeping him too close? He mustn't feel he ought to be with me. I must be careful.

He was an only child, eleven years old. She was a widow. She was determined to be neither possessive nor lacking in devotion. She went worrying off to her beach.

As for Jerry, once he saw that his mother had gained her beach, he began the steep descent to the bay. From where he was, high up among red-brown rocks, it was a scoop of moving bluish green fringed with white. As he went lower, he saw that it spread among small promontories[2] and inlets of rough, sharp rock, and the crisping, lapping surface showed stains of purple and darker blue. Finally, as he ran sliding and scraping down the last few yards, he saw an edge of white surf and the shallow, luminous[3] movement of water over white sand, and beyond that, a solid, heavy blue.

He ran straight into the water and began swimming. He was a good swimmer. He went out fast over the gleaming sand, over a middle region where rocks lay like discolored monsters under the surface, and then he was in the real sea—a warm sea where irregular cold currents from the deep water shocked his limbs.

When he was so far out that he could look back not only on the little bay but past the promontory that was between it and the big beach, he floated on the buoyant surface and looked for his mother. There she was, a speck of yellow under an umbrella that looked like a slice of orange peel. He swam back to shore, relieved at being sure she was there, but all at once very lonely.

On the edge of a small cape that marked the side of the bay away from the promontory was a loose scatter of rocks. Above them, some boys

---

1. **contrition** (kən trish′ən), *n.* guilt.
2. **promontory** (prom′ən tôr′ē), *n.* high point of land extending from the coast.
3. **luminous** (lü′mə nəs) *adj.* full of light; shining.

were stripping off their clothes. They came running, naked, down to the rocks. The English boy swam toward them, but kept his distance at a stone's throw. They were of that coast; all of them were burned smooth dark brown and speaking a language he did not understand. To be with them, of them, was a craving that filled his whole body. He swam a little closer; they turned and watched him with narrowed, alert dark eyes. Then one smiled and waved. It was enough. In a minute, he had swum in and was on the rocks beside them, smiling with a desperate, nervous supplication.[4]

They shouted cheerful greetings at him; and then, as he preserved his nervous, uncomprehending smile, they understood that he was a foreigner strayed from his own beach, and they proceeded to forget him. But he was happy. He was with them.

They began diving again and again from a high point into a well of blue sea between rough, pointed rocks. After they had dived and come up, they swam around, hauled themselves up, and waited their turn to dive again. They were big boys—men, to Jerry. He dived, and they watched him; and when he swam around to take his place, they made way for him. He felt he was accepted and he dived again, carefully, proud of himself.

Soon the biggest of the boys poised himself, shot down into the water, and did not come up. The others stood about, watching. Jerry, after waiting for the sleek brown head to appear, let out a yell of warning; they looked at him idly and turned their eyes back toward the water. After a long time, the boy came up on the other side of a big dark rock, letting the air out of his lungs in a sputtering gasp and a shout of triumph. Immediately the rest of them dived in. One moment, the morning seemed full of chattering boys; the next, the

air and the surface of the water were empty. But through the heavy blue, dark shapes could be seen moving and groping.

Jerry dived, shot past the school of underwater swimmers, saw a black wall of rock looming at him, touched it, and bobbed up at once to the surface, where the wall was a low barrier he could see across. There was no one visible;

"Look at me! Look!" and he began splashing and kicking in the water like a foolish dog.

under him, in the water, the dim shapes of the swimmers had disappeared. Then one, and then another of the boys came up on the far side of the barrier of rock, and he understood that they had swum through some gap or hole in it. He plunged down again. He could see nothing through the stinging salt water but the blank rock. When he came up the boys were all on the diving rock, preparing to attempt the feat again. And now, in a panic of failure, he yelled up, in English, "Look at me! Look!" and he began splashing and kicking in the water like a foolish dog.

They looked down gravely, frowning. He knew the frown. At moments of failure, when he clowned to claim his mother's attention, it was with just this grave, embarrassed inspection that she rewarded him. Through his hot shame, feeling the pleading grin on his face like a scar that he could never remove, he looked up at the group of big brown boys on the rock and shouted, *"Bonjour! Merci! Au revoir! Monsieur, monsieur!"*[5]

---

4. **supplication** (sup′lə kā′shən), *n.* a humble and earnest prayer.
5. *"Bonjour! (bô zhür′) Merci! (mer sē′) Au revoir! (ō rə vwär′) Monsieur . . ."* (mə syər′), French terms meaning "good morning," "thank you," "good-by," and "mister" or "sir."

while he hooked his fingers round his ears and waggled them.

Water surged into his mouth; he choked, sank, came up. The rock, lately weighted with boys, seemed to rear up out of the water as their weight was removed. They were flying down past him, now, into the water; the air was full of falling bodies. Then the rock was empty in the hot sunlight. He counted one, two, three. . . .

At fifty, he was terrified. They must all be drowning beneath him, in the watery caves of the rock! At a hundred, he stared around him at the empty hillside, wondering if he should yell for help. He counted faster, faster, to hurry them up, to bring them to the surface quickly, to drown them quickly—anything rather than the terror of counting on and on into the blue emptiness of the morning. And then, at a hundred and sixty, the water beyond the rock was full of boys blowing like brown whales. They swam back to the shore without a look at him.

He climbed back to the diving rock and sat down, feeling the hot roughness of it under his thighs. The boys were gathering up their bits of clothing and running off along the shore to another promontory. They were leaving to get away from him. He cried openly, fists in his eyes. There was no one to see him, and he cried himself out.

It seemed to him that a long time had passed, and he swam out to where he could see his mother. Yes, she was still there, a yellow spot under an orange umbrella. He swam back to the big rock, climbed up, and dived into the blue pool among the fanged and angry boulders. Down he went, until he touched the wall of rock again. But the salt was so painful in his eyes that he could not see.

He came to the surface, swam to shore, and went back to the villa to wait for his mother. Soon she walked slowly up the path, swinging her striped bag, the flushed, naked arm dangling beside her. "I want some swimming goggles," he panted, defiant and beseeching.[6]

She gave him a patient inquisitive look as she said casually, "Well, of course, darling."

But now, now, now! He must have them this minute, and no other time. He nagged and pestered until she went with him to a shop. As soon as she had bought the goggles, he grabbed them from her hand as if she were going to claim them for herself, and was off, running down the steep path to the bay.

Jerry swam out to the big barrier rock, adjusted the goggles, and dived. The impact of the water broke the rubber-enclosed vacuum, and the goggles came loose. He understood that he must swim down to the base of the rock from the surface of the water. He fixed the goggles tight and firm, filled his lungs, and floated, face down, on the water. Now, he could see. It was as if he had eyes of a different kind—fish eyes that showed everything clear and delicate and wavering in the bright water.

Under him, six or seven feet down, was a floor of perfectly clean, shining white sand, rippled firm and hard by the tides. Two grayish shapes steered there, like long, rounded pieces of wood or slate. They were fish. He saw them nose toward each other, poise motionless, make a dart forward, swerve off, and come around again. It was like a water dance. A few inches above them the water sparkled as if sequins were dropping through it. Fish again—myriads[7] of minute fish, the length of his fingernail, were drifting through the water, and in a moment he could feel the innumerable tiny touches of them against his limbs. It was like swimming in flaked silver. The great rock the big boys had swum through rose sheer out of the white sand—black, tufted lightly with greenish weed. He could see no gap in it. He swam down to its base.

6. **beseeching** (bē sēch′ing), *adj.* asking earnestly; begging.
7. **myriad** (mir′ē əd), *n.* a great number.

▲ David Wojnarowicz used spray paint to construct *The Untidiness of the Ocean* in 1982. What is the most forceful image in the first panel of the painting? How does the second panel show a different balance of power?

Again and again he rose, took a big chestful of air, and went down. Again and again he groped over the surface of the rock, feeling it, almost hugging it in the desperate need to find the entrance. And then, once, while he was clinging to the black wall, his knees came up and he shot his feet out forward and they met no obstacle. He had found the hole.

He gained the surface, clambered about the stones that littered the barrier rock until he found a big one, and, with this in his arms, let himself down over the side of the rock. He dropped, with the weight, straight to the sandy floor. Clinging tight to the anchor of stone, he lay on his side and looked in under the dark shelf at the place where his feet had gone. He could see the hole. It was an irregular, dark gap; but he could not see deep into it. He let go of his anchor, clung with his hands to the edges of the hole, and tried to push himself in.

He got his head in, found his shoulders jammed, moved them in sidewise, and was inside as far as his waist. He could see nothing ahead. Something soft and clammy touched his mouth; he saw a dark frond moving against the grayish rock and panic filled him. He thought of octopuses, of clinging weed. He pushed himself out backward and caught a glimpse, as he retreated, of a harmless tentacle of seaweed drifting in the mouth of the tunnel. But it was enough. He reached the sunlight, swam to shore, and lay on the diving rock. He looked down into the blue well of water. He knew he must find his way through that cave, or hole, or tunnel, and out the other side.

First, he thought, he must learn to control his breathing. He let himself down into the water with another big stone in his arms, so that he could lie effortlessly on the bottom of the sea. He counted. One, two, three. He counted steadily. He could hear the movement of blood in his chest. Fifty-one, fifty-two . . . His chest was hurting. He let go of the rock and went up into the air. He saw that the sun was low. He rushed to the villa and found his mother at her supper. She said only "Did you enjoy yourself?" and he said "Yes."

All night the boy dreamed of the water-filled cave in the rock, and as soon as breakfast was over he went to the bay.

That night, his nose bled badly. For hours he had been underwater, learning to hold his breath, and now he felt weak and dizzy. His mother said, "I shouldn't overdo things, darling, if I were you."

...Jerry exercised his lungs as if everything, the whole of his life ... depended upon it.

That day and the next, Jerry exercised his lungs as if everything, the whole of his life, all that he would become, depended upon it. Again his nose bled at night, and his mother insisted on his coming with her the next day. It was a torment to him to waste a day of his careful self-training, but he stayed with her on the other beach, which now seemed a place for small children, a place where his mother might lie safe in the sun. It was not his beach.

He did not ask for permission, on the following day, to go to his beach. He went, before his mother could consider the complicated rights and wrongs of the matter. A day's rest, he discovered, had improved his count by ten. The big boys had made the passage while he counted a hundred and sixty. He had been counting fast, in his fright. Probably now, if he tried, he could get through that long tunnel, but he was not going to try yet. A curious, most unchildlike persistence, a controlled impatience, made him wait. In the meantime, he lay underwater on the white sand, littered now by stones he had brought down from the upper air, and studied the entrance to the tunnel. He knew every jut and corner of it, as far as it was possible to see. It was as if he already felt its sharpness about his shoulders.

He sat by the clock in the villa, when his mother was not near, and checked his time. He was incredulous[8] and then proud to find he could hold his breath without strain for two minutes. The words "two minutes," authorized by the clock, brought close the adventure that was so necessary to him.

In another four days, his mother said casually one morning, they must go home. On the day before they left, he would do it. He would do it if it killed him, he said defiantly to himself. But two days before they were to leave—a day of triumph when he increased his count by fifteen—his nose bled so badly that he turned dizzy and had to lie limply over the big rock like a bit of seaweed, watching the thick red blood flow on the rock and trickle slowly down to the sea. He was frightened. Supposing he turned dizzy in the tunnel? Supposing he died there, trapped? Supposing—his head went around, in the hot sun, and he almost gave up. He thought he would return to the house and lie down, and next summer, perhaps, when he had another year's growth in him—*then* he would go through the hole.

But even after he had made the decision, or thought he had, he found himself sitting up on the rock and looking down into the water; and he knew that now, this moment, when his nose had only just stopped bleeding, when his head was still sore and throbbing—this was the moment when he would try. If he did not do it now, he never would. He was trembling with fear that he would not go; and he was trembling with horror at that long, long tunnel under the rock, under the sea. Even in the open sunlight, the barrier rock seemed very wide and very heavy; tons of rock pressed down on where he would go. If he died there, he would lie until one day—perhaps not before next year—those big boys would swim into it and find it blocked.

He put on his goggles, fitted them tight, tested the vacuum. His hands were shaking. Then he chose the biggest stone he could carry and slipped over the edge of the rock until half of him was in the cool, enclosing water and half in the hot sun. He looked up once at the empty sky, filled his lungs once, twice, and then sank fast to the bottom with the stone. He let it go and began to count. He took the edges of the hole in his hands and drew himself into it, wriggling his shoulders in sidewise as he remembered he must, kicking himself along with his feet.

Soon he was clear inside. He was in a small rock-bound hole filled with yellowish-gray water. The water was pushing him up against the roof. The roof was sharp and pained his back. He pulled himself along with his hands—fast, fast—and used his legs as levers. His head knocked against something; a sharp pain dizzied him. Fifty, fifty-one, fifty-two . . . He was without light, and the water seemed to press upon him with the weight of rock. Seventy-one, seventy-two. . . There was no strain on his lungs. He felt like an inflated balloon, his lungs were so light and easy, but his head was pulsing.

He was being continually pressed against the sharp roof, which felt slimy as well as sharp. Again he thought of octopuses, and wondered if the tunnel might be filled with weed that could tangle him. He gave himself a panicky, convulsive kick forward, ducked his head, and swam. His feet and hands moved freely, as if in open water. The hole must have widened out. He thought he must be swimming fast, and he was frightened of banging his head if the tunnel narrowed.

A hundred, a hundred and one . . . The water paled. Victory filled him. His lungs were beginning to hurt. A few more strokes and he would be out. He was counting wildly; he said a hundred and fifteen, and then, a long time later, a hundred and fifteen again. The water was a

_____
8. **incredulous** (in krej′ə ləs), *adj.* doubting; skeptical.

clear jewel-green all around him. Then he saw, above his head, a crack running up through the rock. Sunlight was falling through it, showing the clean, dark rock of the tunnel, a single mussel shell, and darkness ahead.

He was at the end of what he could do. He looked up at the crack as if it were filled with air and not water, as if he could put his mouth to it to draw in air. A hundred and fifteen, he heard himself say inside his head—but he had said that long ago. He must go on into the blackness ahead, or he would drown. His head was swelling, his lungs cracking. A hundred and fifteen, a hundred and fifteen pounded through his head, and he feebly clutched at rocks in the dark, pulling himself forward, leaving the brief space of sunlit water behind. He felt he was dying. He was no longer quite conscious. He struggled on in the darkness between lapses into unconsciousness. An immense, swelling pain filled his head, and then the darkness cracked with an explosion of green light. His hands, groping forward, met nothing; and his feet, kicking back, propelled him out into the open sea.

He drifted to the surface, his face turned up to the air. He was gasping like a fish. He felt he would sink now and drown; he could not swim the few feet back to the rock. Then he was clutching it and pulling himself up onto it. He lay face down, gasping. He could see nothing but a red-veined, clotted dark. His eyes must have burst, he thought; they were full of blood. He tore off his goggles and a gout of blood went into the sea. His nose was bleeding and the blood had filled the goggles.

He scooped up handfuls of water from the cool, salty sea, to splash on his face, and did not know whether it was blood or salt water he tasted. After a time, his heart quieted, his eyes cleared, and he sat up. He could see the local boys diving and playing half a mile away. He did not want them. He wanted nothing but to get back home and lie down.

In a short while, Jerry swam to shore and climbed slowly up the path to the villa. He flung himself on his bed and slept, waking at the sound of feet on the path outside. His mother was coming back. He rushed to the bathroom, thinking she must not see his face with bloodstains, or tearstains, on it. He came out of the bathroom and met her as she walked into the villa, smiling, her eyes lighting up.

"Have a nice morning?" she asked, laying her hand on his warm brown shoulder a moment.

"Oh, yes, thank you," he said.

"You look a bit pale." And then, sharp and anxious, "How did you bang your head?"

"Oh, just banged it," he told her.

She looked at him closely. He was strained; his eyes were glazed looking. She was worried. And then she said to herself, Oh, don't fuss! Nothing can happen. He can swim like a fish.

They sat down to lunch together.

"Mummy," he said, "I can stay underwater for two minutes—three minutes, at least." It came bursting out of him.

"Can you, darling?" she said. "Well, I shouldn't overdo it. I don't think you ought to swim anymore today."

She was ready for a battle of wills, but he gave in at once. It was no longer of the least importance to go to the bay.

After Reading

Making Connections

Shaping Your Response

1. Draw in your notebook the spectrum below and place an **X** to show how brave or foolish you think Jerry is. Be prepared to discuss your response.

foolish ⟵⟶ brave

2. Why do you think Jerry chooses to swim through the tunnel despite his doubts?

3. If this were a video game, what could be the level before swimming through the tunnel or the next level afterwards?

Analyzing the Story

4. Describe the changing relationship between Jerry and his mother during the story. Do you think these changes reflect Jerry's growing maturity or something else? Explain.

5. Describe Jerry's external and internal **conflicts** while accomplishing his goal.

6. How does the older boys' attitude toward Jerry change during the time he is with them?

7. After swimming through the tunnel, Jerry no longer considers the bay important. In your opinion, what does this change in attitude reflect about Jerry?

Extending the Ideas

8. 🐾 Would you say that Jerry's acts are motivated by group pressure or by **individual** standards? Explain.

9. Provide examples from your experience, books, TV, or movies of both adults and children who are trying to prove themselves.

Literary Focus: Theme

One way to arrive at a **theme**, or underlying main idea, of "Through the Tunnel" is to think about why Jerry behaves as he does. Examine the following three examples. Then choose the statement you think comes closest to what you consider the theme of the story, or add your own theme statement. Explain why you chose it.

1. A young boy puts himself through strict training to swim successfully through a perilously long underwater tunnel.

2. To be treated like an adult, act like one!

3. The accomplishment of a difficult task through one's own will and effort can be an important step in growing up.

Vocabulary Study

beseeching
contrition
incredulous
luminous
myriad
promontory
supplication

Make a word web to illustrate meanings for two of the listed words. An example has been done for you.

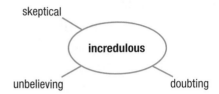

Expressing Your Ideas

Writing Choices

Writer's Notebook Update Before you read "Through the Tunnel," you wrote about a risk that you have taken and the emotions associated with it. In a paragraph, write a comparison between the risk Jerry takes and your own. How are they alike? How are they different?

On the Other Hand Just before he decides to attempt the tunnel, Jerry considers the possibility of becoming stuck in the tunnel and drowning. The prospect nearly makes him put off the swim until the following year, "when he had another year's growth in him." Write an **explanation** telling how the theme of the story would be different had Jerry delayed.

Dear Abby Worried that she is being overly protective, Jerry's mother asks an advice columnist how much freedom she should give her son during their seaside vacation. Respond to Jerry's mother as if you were writing an **advice column** that might be published in a newspaper.

Other Options

Club Med? Use the details about setting in the story plus your imagination to create a **travel brochure** describing the setting of "Through the Tunnel" as the perfect vacation place. Mention sports and activities vacationers could enjoy here, along with qualities of the landscape and water that make this an ideal spot. Remember that you are creating a persuasive piece to appeal to a wide audience.

Get the Picture After skimming the story again and checking the Glossary at the back of the book for the meaning of such words as *promontory* or *luminous,* draw a **color picture** of the setting. Decide which element of the land- or seascape should be the central focus and which should be background. Alternately, you could create a three-dimensional model of the same setting.

Brush Up Working with a partner, examine the picture on pages 10-11 and reread the caption. How does this picture make you feel? What do you think the use of color adds to the overall effect? What other details about the art do you find noteworthy? Then explain in an **art talk** whether or not you think this picture is an appropriate way to launch the theme "Pushing Toward the Top."

Before Reading

Two Kinds

by Amy Tan   USA

Amy Tan
born 1952

Amy Tan, whose Chinese name, An-mei, means "blessing from America," wrote her first novel, *The Joy Luck Club*, in order to understand her cultural heritage and the conflicts between her mother and herself. Tan was born in California, shortly after her parents emigrated from China and more than one hundred years after the first wave of Chinese immigrants came to America. Although her parents had hoped she would become a neurosurgeon, Tan majored in English in college and became a free-lance business writer before she began writing novels. For recreation, she reads, plays jazz piano, and shoots pool.

Building Background

The Need to Succeed Do you feel that young people are often pushed too hard by parents, teachers, coaches, or family members to accomplish and excel? Think about the difference between encouragement and pressure in preparation for reading "Two Kinds."

Literary Focus

Characterization Plot and setting are important, of course, but what really makes fiction come alive is people! From the moment the mother in "Two Kinds" says, "You can be best anything," readers know that she will be a **"character"** in every sense of the word. As you read this story, think about the two major characters, a mother and her daughter. Ask yourself, "What kind of people are they? Why do they act and feel as they do?"

Writer's Notebook

When Push Comes to Shove In this story, a mother is so eager for her daughter to excel that she pushes and pushes until the daughter defiantly pushes back. Jot down several motives that a parent, guardian, teacher, or coach might have for wanting a child to excel.

Two Kinds   **17**

Two Kinds

>Amy Tan<

My mother believed you could be anything you wanted to be in America. You could open a restaurant. You could work for the government and get good retirement. You could buy a house with almost no money down. You could become rich. You could become instantly famous.

"Of course you can be prodigy,[1] too," my mother told me when I was nine. "You can be best anything. What does Auntie Lindo know? Her daughter, she is only best tricky."

America was where all my mother's hopes lay. She had come here in 1949 after losing everything in China: her mother and father, her family home, her first husband, and two daughters, twin baby girls. But she never looked back with regret. There were so many ways for things to get better.

We didn't immediately pick the right kind of prodigy. At first my mother thought I could be a Chinese Shirley Temple.[2] We'd watch Shirley's old movies on TV as though they were training films. My mother would poke my arm and say, *"Ni kan"* —You watch. And I would see Shirley tapping her feet, or singing a sailor song, or pursing her lips into a very round O while saying, "Oh my goodness."

"Ni kan," said my mother as Shirley's eyes flooded with tears. "You already know how. Don't need talent for crying!"

Soon after my mother got this idea about Shirley Temple, she took me to a beauty training school in the Mission district[3] and put me in the hands of a student who could barely hold the scissors without shaking. Instead of getting big fat curls, I emerged with an

---

1. **prodigy** (prod′ə jē), *n.* person endowed with amazing brilliance or talent, especially a remarkably talented child.
2. **Shirley Temple,** popular child movie star of the 1930s and 1940s.
3. **Mission district,** a section of the city of San Francisco.

◄ Henri Matisse made the mood more important than details in this 1924 oil painting, called *La Petite Pianiste*. What does the girl in this painting seem to have in common with Jing-mei in the story?

uneven mass of crinkly black fuzz. My mother dragged me off to the bathroom and tried to wet down my hair.

"You look like Negro Chinese," she lamented, as if I had done this on purpose.

The instructor of the beauty training school had to lop off these soggy clumps to make my hair even again. "Peter Pan is very popular these days," the instructor assured my mother. I now had hair the length of a boy's, with straight-across bangs that hung at a slant two inches above my eyebrows. I liked the haircut and it made me actually look forward to my future fame.

In fact, in the beginning, I was just as excited as my mother, maybe even more so. I pictured this prodigy part of me as many different images, trying each one on for size. I was a dainty ballerina girl standing by the curtains, waiting to hear the right music that would send me floating on my tiptoes. I was like the Christ child lifted out of the straw manger, crying with holy indignity. I was Cinderella stepping from her pumpkin carriage with sparkly cartoon music filling the air.

In all of my imaginings, I was filled with a sense that I would soon become *perfect*. My mother and father would adore me. I would be beyond reproach.[4] I would never feel the need to sulk for anything.

But sometimes the prodigy in me became impatient. "If you don't hurry up and get me out of here, I'm disappearing for good," it warned. "And then you'll always be nothing."

Every night after dinner, my mother and I would sit at the Formica kitchen table. She would present new tests, taking her examples from stories of amazing children she had read in *Ripley's Believe It or Not*, or *Good Housekeeping, Reader's Digest*, and a dozen other magazines she kept in a pile in our bathroom. My mother got these magazines from people whose houses she cleaned. And since she cleaned many houses each week, we had a great assortment. She would look through them all, searching for stories about remarkable children.

The first night she brought out a story about a three-year-old boy who knew the capitals of all the states and even most of the European countries. A teacher was quoted as saying the little boy could also pronounce the names of the foreign cities correctly.

"What's the capital of Finland?" my mother asked me, looking at the magazine story.

All I knew was the capital of California, because Sacramento was the name of the street we lived on in Chinatown. "Nairobi!" I guessed, saying the most foreign word I could think of. She checked to see if that was possibly one way to pronounce "Helsinki" before showing me the answer.

The tests got harder—multiplying numbers in my head, finding the queen of hearts in a deck of cards, trying to stand on my head without using my hands, predicting the daily temperatures in Los Angeles, New York, and London.

One night I had to look at a page from the Bible for three minutes and then report everything I could remember. "Now Jehoshaphat had riches and honor in abundance and . . . that's all I remember, Ma," I said.

And after seeing my mother's disappointed face once again, something inside of me began to die. I hated the tests, the raised hopes and failed expectations. Before going to bed that night, I looked in the mirror above the bathroom sink and when I saw only my face staring back—and that it would always be this ordinary face—I began to cry. Such a sad, ugly girl! I made high-pitched noises like a crazed animal, trying to scratch out the face in the mirror.

And then I saw what seemed to be the prodigy side of me—because I had never seen that face before. I looked at my reflection, blinking so I could see more clearly. The girl staring back at me was angry, powerful. This girl and I were the same. I had new thoughts, willful thoughts, or rather thoughts filled with lots of

_____

4. **reproach** (ri prōch′), *n.* blame or disapproval.

won'ts. I won't let her change me, I promised myself. I won't be what I'm not.

So now on nights when my mother presented her tests, I performed listlessly,[5] my head propped on one arm. I pretended to be bored. And I was. I got so bored I started counting the bellows of the foghorns out on the bay while my mother drilled me in other areas. The sound was comforting and reminded me of the cow jumping over the moon. And the next day, I played a game with myself, seeing if my mother would give up on me before eight bellows. After a while I usually counted only one, maybe two bellows at most. At last she was beginning to give up hope.

Two or three months had gone by without any mention of my being a prodigy again. And then one day my mother was watching *The Ed Sullivan Show*[6] on TV. The TV was old and the sound kept shorting out. Every time my mother got halfway up from the sofa to adjust the set, the sound would go back on and Ed would be talking. As soon as she sat down, Ed would go silent again. She got up, the TV broke into loud piano music. She sat down. Silence. Up and down, back and forth, quiet and loud. It was like a stiff embraceless dance between her and the TV set. Finally she stood by the set with her hand on the sound dial.

She seemed entranced[7] by the music, a little frenzied[8] piano piece with this mesmerizing[9] quality, sort of quick passages and then teasing lilting ones before it returned to the quick playful parts.

"*Ni kan*," my mother said, calling me over with hurried hand gestures. "Look here."

I could see why my mother was fascinated by the music. It was being pounded out by a little Chinese girl, about nine years old, with a Peter Pan haircut. The girl had the sauciness of a Shirley Temple. She was proudly modest like a proper Chinese child. And she also did this fancy sweep of a curtsy, so that the fluffy skirt of her white dress cascaded slowly to the floor like the petals of a large carnation.

In spite of these warning signs, I wasn't worried. Our family had no piano and we couldn't afford to buy one, let alone reams of sheet music and piano lessons. So I could be generous in my comments when my mother bad-mouthed the little girl on TV.

"Play note right, but doesn't sound good! No singing sound," complained my mother.

"What are you picking on her for?" I said carelessly. "She's pretty good. Maybe she's not the best, but she's trying hard." I knew almost immediately I would be sorry I said that.

"Just like you," she said. "Not the best. Because you not trying." She gave a little huff as she let go of the sound dial and sat down on the sofa.

The little Chinese girl sat down also to play an encore of "Anitra's Dance" by Grieg. I remember the song, because later on I had to learn how to play it.

Three days after watching *The Ed Sullivan Show,* my mother told me what my schedule would be for piano lessons and piano practice. She had talked to Mr. Chong, who lived on the first floor of our apartment building. Mr. Chong was a retired piano teacher and my mother had traded housecleaning services for weekly lessons and a piano for me to practice on every day, two hours a day, from four until six.

When my mother told me this, I felt as though I had been sent to hell. I whined and then kicked my foot a little when I couldn't stand it anymore.

"Why don't you like me the way I am? I'm *not* a genius! I can't play the piano. And even if I could, I wouldn't go on TV if you paid me a million dollars!" I cried.

My mother slapped me. "Who ask you be

_____

5. **listlessly** (list′lis lē), *adv.* seemingly too tired to care about anything.
6. **The Ed Sullivan Show,** a weekly television variety show of the 1950s and 1960s.
7. **entranced** (en transd′), *adj.* delighted; charmed.
8. **frenzied** (fren′zēd), *adj.* greatly excited; frantic.
9. **mesmerizing** (mez′mə rī′zing), *adj.* hypnotic.

genius?" she shouted. "Only ask you be your best. For you sake. You think I want you be genius? Hnnh! What for! Who ask you!"

"So ungrateful," I heard her mutter in Chinese. "If she had as much talent as she has temper, she would be famous now."

Mr. Chong, whom I secretly nicknamed Old Chong, was very strange, always tapping his fingers to the silent music of an invisible orchestra. He looked ancient in my eyes. He had lost most of the hair on top of his head and he wore thick glasses and had eyes that always looked tired and sleepy. But he must have been younger than I thought, since he lived with his mother and was not yet married.

I met Old Lady Chong once and that was enough. She had this peculiar smell like a baby that had done something in its pants. And her fingers felt like a dead person's, like an old peach I once found in the back of the refrigerator; the skin just slid off the meat when I picked it up.

I soon found out why Old Chong had retired from teaching piano. He was deaf. "Like Beethoven!" he shouted to me. "We're both listening only in our head!" And he would start to conduct his frantic silent sonatas.

Our lessons went like this. He would open the book and point to different things, explaining their purpose: "Key! Treble! Bass! No sharps or flats! So this is C major! Listen now and play after me!"

And then he would play the C scale a few times, a simple chord, and then, as if inspired by an old, unreachable itch, he gradually added more notes and running trills and a pounding bass until the music was really something quite grand.

I would play after him, the simple scale, the simple chord, and then I just played some nonsense that sounded like a cat running up and down on top of garbage cans. Old Chong smiled and applauded and then said, "Very good! But now you must learn to keep time!"

So that's how I discovered that Old Chong's eyes were too slow to keep up with the wrong notes I was playing. He went through the motions in half-time. To help me keep rhythm, he stood behind me, pushing down on my right shoulder for every beat. He balanced pennies on top of my wrists so I would keep them still as I slowly played scales and arpeggios.[10] He had me curve my hand around an apple and keep that shape when playing chords. He marched stiffly to show me how to make each finger dance up and down, staccato like an obedient little soldier.

He taught me all these things, and that was

. . . I just played some nonsense that sounded like a cat running up and down on top of garbage cans.

how I also learned I could be lazy and get away with mistakes, lots of mistakes. If I hit the wrong notes because I hadn't practiced enough, I never corrected myself. I just kept playing in rhythm. And Old Chong kept conducting his own private reverie.[11]

So maybe I never really gave myself a fair chance. I did pick up the basics pretty quickly, and I might have become a good pianist at that young age. But I was so determined not to try, not to be anybody different that I learned to play only the most ear-splitting preludes, the most discordant[12] hymns.

Over the next year, I practiced like this, dutifully in my own way. And then one day I heard my mother and her friend Lindo Jong both talk-

---

10. **arpeggio** (är pej′ē ō), *n.* the sounding of the individual notes of a chord.
11. **reverie** (rev′ər ē), *n.* dreamy thoughts, especially of pleasant things.
12. **discordant** (dis kôrd′nt), *adj.* not in harmony.

ing in a loud bragging tone of voice so others could hear. It was after church, and I was leaning against the brick wall wearing a dress with stiff white petticoats. Auntie Lindo's daughter, Waverly, who was about my age, was standing farther down the wall about five feet away. We had grown up together and shared all the closeness of two sisters squabbling over crayons and dolls. In other words, for the most part, we hated each other. I thought she was snotty. Waverly Jong had gained a certain amount of fame as "Chinatown's Littlest Chinese Chess Champion."

"She bring home too many trophy," lamented Auntie Lindo that Sunday. "All day she play chess. All day I have no time to do nothing but dust off her winnings." She threw a scolding look at Waverly, who pretended not to see her.

"You lucky you don't have this problem," said Auntie Lindo with a sigh to my mother.

And my mother squared her shoulders and bragged: "Our problem worser than yours. If we ask Jing-mei wash dish, she hear nothing but music. It's like you can't stop this natural talent."

And right then, I was determined to put a stop to her foolish pride.

A few weeks later, Old Chong and my mother conspired to have me play in a talent show which would be held in the church hall. By then, my parents had saved up enough to buy me a secondhand piano, a black Wurlitzer spinet with a scarred bench. It was the showpiece of our living room.

For the talent show, I was to play a piece called "Pleading Child" from Schumann's *Scenes from Childhood*. It was a simple, moody piece that sounded more difficult than it was. I was supposed to memorize the whole thing, playing the repeat parts twice to make the piece sound longer. But I dawdled[13] over it, playing a few bars and then cheating, looking up to see what notes followed. I never really listened to what I was playing. I daydreamed about being somewhere else, about being someone else.

The part I liked to practice best was the fancy curtsy: right foot out, touch the rose on the carpet with a pointed foot, sweep to the side, left leg bends, look up and smile.

My parents invited all the couples from the Joy Luck Club to witness my debut. Auntie Lindo and Uncle Tin were there. Waverly and her two older brothers had also come. The first two rows were filled with children both younger and older than I was. The littlest ones got to go first. They recited simple nursery rhymes, squawked out tunes on miniature violins, twirled Hula Hoops, pranced in pink ballet tutus, and when they bowed or curtsied, the audience would sigh in unison, "Awww," and then clap enthusiastically.

When my turn came, I was very confident. I remember my childish excitement. It was as if I knew, without a doubt, that the prodigy side of me really did exist. I had no fear whatsoever, no nervousness. I remember thinking to myself, This is it! This is it! I looked out over the audience, at my mother's blank face, my father's yawn, Auntie Lindo's stiff-lipped smile, Waverly's sulky expression. I had on a white dress layered with sheets of lace, and a pink bow in my Peter Pan haircut. As I sat down I envisioned people jumping to their feet and Ed Sullivan rushing up to introduce me to everyone on TV.

And I started to play. It was so beautiful. I was so caught up in how lovely I looked that at first I didn't worry how I would sound. So it was a surprise to me when I hit the first wrong note and I realized something didn't sound quite right. And then I hit another and another followed that. A chill started at the top of my head and began to trickle down. Yet I couldn't stop playing, as though my hands were bewitched. I kept thinking my fingers would adjust themselves back, like a train switching to the right track. I played this strange jumble through two

---

13. **dawdle** (dô′dl), *v.* waste time; loiter.

repeats, the sour notes staying with me all the way to the end.

When I stood up, I discovered my legs were shaking. Maybe I had just been nervous and the audience, like Old Chong, had seen me go through the right motions and had not heard anything wrong at all. I swept my right foot out, went down on my knee, looked up and smiled. The room was quiet, except for Old Chong, who was beaming and shouting, "Bravo! Bravo! Well done!" But then I saw my mother's face, her stricken face. The audience clapped weakly, and as I walked back to my chair, with my whole face quivering as I tried not to cry, I heard a little boy whisper loudly to his mother, "That was awful," and the mother whispered back, "Well, she certainly tried."

And now I realized how many people were in the audience, the whole world it seemed. I was aware of eyes burning into my back. I felt the shame of my mother and father as they sat stiffly throughout the rest of the show.

We could have escaped during intermission. Pride and some strange sense of honor must have anchored my parents to their chairs. And so we watched it all: the eighteen-year-old boy with a fake mustache who did a magic show and juggled flaming hoops while riding a unicycle. The breasted girl with white makeup who sang from *Madame Butterfly* and got honorable mention. And the eleven-year-old boy who won first prize playing a tricky violin song that sounded like a busy bee.

After the show, the Hsus, the Jongs, and the St. Clairs from the Joy Luck Club came up to my mother and father.

"Lots of talented kids," Auntie Lindo said vaguely, smiling broadly.

"That was somethin' else," said my father, and I wondered if he was referring to me in a humorous way, or whether he even remembered what I had done.

Waverly looked at me and shrugged her shoulders. "You aren't a genius like me," she said matter-of-factly. And if I hadn't felt so bad, I would have pulled her braids and punched her stomach.

But my mother's expression was what devastated[14] me: a quiet, blank look that said she had lost everything. I felt the same way, and it seemed as if everybody were now coming up, like gawkers at the scene of an accident, to see what parts were actually missing. When we got on the bus to go home, my father was humming the busy-bee tune and my mother was silent. I kept thinking she wanted to wait until we got home before shouting at me. But when my father unlocked the door to our apartment, my mother walked in and then went to the back, into the bedroom. No accusations. No blame. And in a way, I felt disappointed. I had been waiting for her to start shouting, so I could shout back and cry and blame her for all my misery.

I assumed my talent-show fiasco[15] meant I never had to play the piano again. But two days later, after school, my mother came out of the kitchen and saw me watching TV.

"Four clock," she reminded me as if it were any other day. I was stunned, as though she were asking me to go through the talent-show torture again. I wedged myself more tightly in front of the TV.

"Turn off TV," she called from the kitchen five minutes later.

I didn't budge. And then I decided. I didn't have to do what my mother said anymore. I wasn't her slave. This wasn't China. I had listened to her before and look what happened. She was the stupid one.

She came out from the kitchen and stood in the arched entryway of the living room. "Four clock," she said once again, louder.

"I'm not going to play anymore," I said nonchalantly. "Why should I? I'm not a genius."

---

14. **devastate** (dev′ə stāt′), *v.* make desolate; destroy.
15. **fiasco** (fē as′kō), *n.* a complete or ridiculous failure; humiliating breakdown.

She walked over and stood in front of the TV. I saw her chest was heaving up and down in an angry way.

"No!" I said, and I now felt stronger, as if my true self had finally emerged. So this was what had been inside me all along.

"No! I won't!" I screamed.

She yanked me by the arm, pulled me off the floor, snapped off the TV. She was frighteningly strong, half pulling, half carrying me toward the piano as I kicked the throw rugs under my feet. She lifted me up and onto the hard bench. I was sobbing by now, looking at her bitterly. Her chest was heaving even more and her mouth was open, smiling crazily as if she were pleased I was crying.

"You want me to be someone that I'm not!" I sobbed. "I'll never be the kind of daughter you want me to be!"

"Only two kinds of daughters," she shouted in Chinese. "Those who are obedient and those who follow their own mind! Only one kind of daughter can live in this house. Obedient daughter!"

"Then I wish I wasn't your daughter. I wish you weren't my mother," I shouted. As I said these things I got scared. It felt like worms and toads and slimy things crawling out of my chest, but it also felt good, as if this awful side of me had surfaced, at last.

This papercut image from the Shanxi Province of China provides two views of a girl—a profile and a view of her full face. What similarities and differences can you find between this piece of art and the Matisse painting on page 18?

"Too late change this," said my mother shrilly.

And I could sense her anger rising to its breaking point. I wanted to see it spill over. And that's when I remembered the babies she had lost in China, the ones we never talked about. "Then I wish I'd never been born!" I shouted. "I wish I were dead! Like them."

It was as if I had said the magic words. Alakazam!—and her face went blank, her mouth closed, her arms went slack, and she backed out of the room, stunned, as if she were blowing away like a small brown leaf, thin, brittle, lifeless.

It was not the only disappointment my mother felt in me. In the years that followed, I failed her so many times, each time asserting my own will, my right to fall short of expectations. I didn't get straight A's. I didn't become class president. I didn't get into Stanford. I dropped out of college.

For unlike my mother, I did not believe I could be anything I wanted to be. I could only be me.

And for all those years, we never talked about the disaster at the recital or my terrible accusations afterward at the piano bench. All that remained unchecked, like a betrayal that was now unspeakable. So I never found a way to ask her why she had hoped for something so large that failure was inevitable.

And even worse, I never asked her what frightened me the most: Why had she given up hope?

For after our struggle at the piano, she never mentioned my playing again. The lessons stopped. The lid to the piano was closed, shutting out the dust, my misery, and her dreams.

So she surprised me. A few years ago, she offered to give me the piano, for my thirtieth birthday. I had not played in all those years. I saw the offer as a sign of forgiveness, a tremendous burden removed.

"Are you sure?" I asked shyly. "I mean, won't you and Dad miss it?"

"No, this your piano," she said firmly. "Always your piano. You only one can play."

"Well, I probably can't play anymore," I said. "It's been years."

"You pick up fast," said my mother, as if she knew this was certain. "You have natural talent. You could been genius if you want to."

"No I couldn't."

"You just not trying," said my mother. And she was neither angry nor sad. She said it as if to announce a fact that could never be disproved. "Take it," she said.

But I didn't at first. It was enough that she had offered it to me. And after that, every time I saw it in my parents' living room, standing in front of the bay windows, it made me feel proud, as if it were a shiny trophy I had won back.

Last week I sent a tuner over to my parents' apartment and had the piano reconditioned, for purely sentimental reasons. My mother had died a few months before and I had been getting things in order for my father, a little bit at a time. I put the jewelry in special silk pouches. The sweaters she had knitted in yellow, pink, bright orange—all the colors I hated—I put those in moth-proof boxes. I found some old Chinese silk dresses, the kind with little slits up the sides. I rubbed the old silk against my skin, then wrapped them in tissue and decided to take them home with me.

After I had the piano tuned, I opened the lid and touched the keys. It sounded even richer than I remembered. Really, it was a very good piano. Inside the bench were the same exercise notes with handwritten scales, the same second-hand music books with their covers held together with yellow tape.

I opened up the Schumann book to the dark little piece I had played at the recital. It was on the left-hand side of the page, "Pleading Child." It looked more difficult than I remembered. I played a few bars, surprised at how easily the notes came back to me.

And for the first time, or so it seemed, I noticed the piece on the right-hand side. It was called "Perfectly Contented." I tried to play this one as well. It had a lighter melody but the same flowing rhythm and turned out to be quite easy. "Pleading Child" was shorter but slower; "Perfectly Contented" was longer, but faster. And after I played them both a few times, I realized they were two halves of the same song.

After Reading

Making Connections

Shaping Your
Response

1. Rate Jing-mei and her mother on a scale from 1-10 with 10 being
   what you consider an ideal mother or daughter. Be ready to explain
   your ratings.

Character	Rating
Jing-mei	
Mother	

2. For which **character** do you feel more sympathy—the mother or
   Jing-mei? Why?

Analyzing the
Story

3. Do you think the mother's plan for her daughter to become a prodigy
   is unrealistic? Why or why not?

4. Reread the final paragraph of the story. What do you think Jing-mei
   has learned?

5. Why might Tan have titled her story "Two Kinds"? To what do you
   think this phrase refers?

Extending the
Ideas

6. Do you think that Jing-mei's mother is more concerned with group
   norms than with letting her daughter develop as an **individual**? Explain.

7. In your opinion, could the mother's background in China have
   influenced her to push Jing-mei? Why or why not?

8. In your opinion, is proving herself as an **individual** as important to
   Jing-mei as it is to Jerry in "Through the Tunnel"? Explain.

9. Think of people who have demonstrated notable talent or genius. To
   what extent do you think such people are born with these gifts? To
   what extent are outside influences and support responsible?

Literary Focus: Characterization

One of a fiction writer's greatest challenges involves the creation of
believable **characters**. Sometimes characters seem realistic and
complex (or three-dimensional); sometimes they may seem unrealistic
and one-dimensional. To make characters come alive, writers may
describe their physical appearance and situation; reveal their
thoughts and words; show the reactions of other characters to them.

- Find an example of each method of characterization in the story.

Vocabulary Study

arpeggio
dawdle
devastate
discordant
entranced
fiasco
frenzied
listlessly
mesmerizing
prodigy
reproach
reverie

Use eight of the vocabulary words to write about one of the following.

- a plot summary of "Two Kinds"
- a description of a frenzied prodigy
- an ad for a new miracle product

Expressing Your Ideas

Writing Choices

Writer's Notebook Update Reread the list of motives you wrote down before reading "Two Kinds." Do any of these help explain why the mother acts as she does? Write an explanation of why you think Jing-mei's mother pushes her. Cite evidence from the story to support your ideas.

Rebel with a Cause Create your own version of a Jing-mei and her mother. Write a **dialogue** between a parent and a child that reflects their different goals. Put the characters in a specific situation—for example, a shopping mall, an athletic event, a family reunion. Begin in the middle of an argument, and fill in background details. You might use vocabulary words such as *fiasco, discordant,* and *reproach* to create a mood of conflict.

Dear Jong Jing-mei's mother regularly corresponds with an older brother who lives in China, telling him about her family. Write a **letter** the mother might have written after either the talent show or the angry conversation with her daughter that made her appear "stunned, as if she were blowing away like a small brown leaf, thin, brittle, lifeless."

Other Options

Portrait Gallery Create a portrait gallery of young people who have displayed notable talent in a particular field. You may include celebrities or people you know who have not achieved fame. Draw **pictures** or use **photographs**, and write a caption beneath each one. Then find an interesting way to display your work in the classroom. You might look at the Interdisciplinary Study on pages 50–54 for inspiration.

Talent Shows Several movies of the 1990s deal with child prodigies. In *Little Man Tate,* director and star Jodie Foster—herself a prodigy—creates a realistic portrait of a youthful genius. *Searching for Bobby Fischer* and *Hoop Dreams* depict talented chess and basketball players, respectively. You might give a **report** on one of these movies or, if your teacher agrees, bring it to class for viewing. Then lead a discussion on the advantages and drawbacks that come with exceptional talent, as well as the best way to nurture such talent.

The Censors

by Luisa Valenzuela   Argentina

Luisa Valenzuela
born 1938

One of Argentina's most famous authors, Luisa Valenzuela (lü ē′sə val′ən-zwā′lə) "plays with words, turns them inside out, weaves them into sensuous webs." Born in Buenos Aires in 1938, the daughter of a physician and a well-respected writer, Valenzuela wrote and published her first story at eighteen. Many of her works deal with the harsh military rule of Argentina after the brief return of Juan Perón to the presidency in 1973. Valenzuela currently divides her time between Buenos Aires and New York City, where she teaches creative writing.

Building Background

Strange to Say Cryptographers, professional decoders of secret messages, have been asked to crack a code. The security of their nation depends on their success! What do you know about their methods? Have you ever decoded or created a secret language — something more complicated than Pig Latin? Working in small groups, try to decipher the following code: *2-5 1-12-5-18-20-5-4! BSNT XJMM BSSJWF PO BJS GPSDF POF GSJEBZ.*

In the story you are about to read, Juan, the main character, becomes so inventive at detecting messages in letters that he can find in a simple phrase a plot to overthrow the government.

Literary Focus

Satire The art of criticizing a subject by mocking it and evoking toward it an attitude of amusement, contempt, or scorn is called **satire**. The purpose of much satire is to bring about a change. What is being satirized in this cartoon?

Drawing by Lorenz; © 1977 The New Yorker Magazine, Inc.

THIS STRUCTURE WILL BE TORN DOWN AND REPLACED BY A NEW 44-STORY COOKIE

Writer's Notebook

Big Brother Is Watching You People living under a dictatorship are constantly aware that their every action is watched closely. For even the slightest offense, they might be picked up for questioning or punished. Jot down a list of ways your life would be different if you lived under this kind of government.

THE CENSORS

Luisa Valenzuela

Poor Juan! One day they caught him with his guard down before he could even realize that what he had taken as a stroke of luck was really one of fate's dirty tricks. These things happen the minute you're careless and you let down your guard, as one often does. Juancito let happiness—a feeling you can't trust—get the better of him when he received from a confidential source Mariana's new address in Paris and he knew that she hadn't forgotten him. Without thinking twice, he sat down at his table and wrote her a letter. *The* letter that keeps his mind off his job during the day and won't let him sleep at night (what had he scrawled, what had he put on that sheet of paper he sent to Mariana?).

Juan knows there won't be a problem with the letter's contents, that it's irreproachable,[1] harmless. But what about the rest? He knows that they examine, sniff, feel, and read between the lines of each and every letter, and check its tiniest comma and most accidental stain. He knows that all letters pass from hand to hand and go through all sorts of tests in the huge censorship offices and that, in the end, very few continue on their way. Usually it takes months, even years, if there aren't any snags; all this time the freedom, maybe even the life, of both sender and receiver is in jeopardy. And that's why Juan's so down in the dumps; thinking that something might happen to Mariana because of his letters. Of all people, Mariana, who must finally feel safe there where she always dreamed she'd live. But he knows that the *Censor's Secret Command* operates all over the world and cashes in on the discount in air rates; there's nothing to stop them from going as far as that hidden Paris neighborhood, kidnapping Mariana, and returning to their cozy homes, certain of having fulfilled their noble mission.

Well, you've got to beat them to the punch, do what everyone tries to do: sabotage the machinery, throw sand in its gears, get to the bottom of the problem so as to stop it.

This was Juan's sound plan when he, like many others, applied for a censor's job—not because he had a calling or needed a job: no, he applied simply to intercept his own letter, a consoling but unoriginal idea. He was hired immediately, for each day more and more censors are needed and no one would bother to check on his references.

Ulterior[2] motives couldn't be overlooked by the *Censorship Division,* but they needn't be too strict with those who applied. They knew how hard it would be for those poor guys to find the letter they wanted and even if they did, what's a letter or two when the new censor would snap up so many others? That's how Juan managed to join the *Post Office's Censorship Division,* with a certain goal in mind.

---

1. **irreproachable** (ir′i prō′chə bəl), *adj.* free from blame; faultless.
2. **ulterior** (ul tir′ē ər), *adj.* beyond what is seen or expressed; hidden.

▲ Antonio Berni constructed this collage on wood, called *Portrait of Juanito Laguna*, in 1961.
What do the fragments in the collage tell about the boy being shown? What do they
suggest about the character of Juan in the story?

The building had a festive air on the outside which contrasted with its inner staidness.[3] Little by little, Juan was absorbed by his job and he felt at peace since he was doing everything he could to get his letter for Mariana. He didn't even worry when, in his first month, he was sent to *Section K* where envelopes are very carefully screened for explosives.

It's true that on the third day, a fellow worker had his right hand blown off by a letter, but the division chief claimed it was sheer[4] negligence on the victim's part. Juan and the other employees were allowed to go back to their work, albeit[5] feeling less secure. After work, one of them tried to organize a strike to demand higher wages for unhealthy work, but Juan didn't join in; after thinking it over, he reported him to his superiors and thus got promoted.

You don't form a habit by doing something once, he told himself as he left his boss's office. And when he was transferred to *Section J,* where letters are carefully checked for poison dust, he felt he had climbed a rung in the ladder.

By working hard, he quickly reached *Section E* where the work was more interesting, for he could now read and analyze the letters' contents. Here he could even hope to get hold of his letter which, judging by the time that had elapsed,[6] had gone through the other sections and was probably floating around in this one.

Soon his work became so absorbing that his noble mission blurred in his mind. Day after day he crossed out whole paragraphs in red ink, pitilessly chucking many letters into the censored basket. These were horrible days when he was shocked by the subtle and conniving[7] ways employed by people to pass on subversive[8] messages; his instincts were so sharp that he found behind a simple "the weather's unsettled" or "prices continue to soar" the wavering hand of someone secretly scheming to overthrow the Government.

His zeal[9] brought him swift promotion. We don't know if this made him happy. Very few letters reached him in *Section B*—only a handful

passed the other hurdles—so he read them over and over again, passed them under a magnifying glass, searched for microprint with an electronic microscope, and tuned his sense of smell so that he was beat by the time he made it home. He'd barely manage to warm up his soup, eat some fruit, and fall into bed, satisfied with having done his duty. Only his darling mother worried, but she couldn't get him back on the right road. She'd say, though it wasn't always true: Lola called, she's at the bar with the girls, they miss you, they're waiting for you. Or else she'd leave a bottle of red wine on the table. But Juan wouldn't overdo it: any distraction[10] could make him lose his edge and the perfect censor had to be alert, keen, attentive, and sharp to nab cheats. He had a truly patriotic task, both self-denying and uplifting.

His basket for censored letters became the best fed as well as the most cunning basket in the whole *Censorship Division.* He was about to congratulate himself for having finally discovered his true mission, when his letter to Mariana reached his hands. Naturally, he censored it without regret. And just as naturally, he couldn't stop them from executing him the following morning, another victim of his devotion to his work.

---

3. **staidness** (stād′nes), *n.* the condition of having a settled, quiet character.
4. **sheer** (shir), *adj.* unmixed with anything else; complete.
5. **albeit** (ôl bē′it), *conj.* even though; although.
6. **elapse** (i laps′), *v.* slip away; pass.
7. **conniving** (kə nī′ving), *adj.* giving aid to wrongdoing by not telling of it or by helping it secretly.
8. **subversive** (səb vėr′siv), *adj.* tending to overthrow; causing ruin.
9. **zeal** (zēl), *n.* eager desire or effort; earnest enthusiasm.
10. **distraction** (dis trak′shən), *n.* disturbance of thought.

After Reading

Making Connections

Shaping Your Response

1. In your notebook, write three words that you think describe this story. Share your words with your classmates.

2. What advice would you have for people like Juan who get carried away with a job or goal?

3. If you had watched a film version of this story, what is the first thing you would say to a friend when it was over?

Analyzing the Story

4. What characteristics does Juan exhibit at the beginning of the story? at the end?

5. What do you think brings about the changes in Juan's **character**?

6. What does the story seem to be saying about the effect of a dictatorship on the individual?

Extending the Ideas

7. What **theme** might link this story to the first two in this group?

8. 👣 Some U.S. government employees (for example, those in security jobs) agree to sign away their right of free speech. Do you believe that a group should be able to make such demands on **individuals**? Why or why not?

9. Can you think of other forms of censorship that are practiced in your country? Do you think they are necessary? Explain.

Literary Focus: Satire

The purpose of **satire** is sometimes simply to entertain, but more frequently it is to bring about a change.

- What do you think is Valenzuela's purpose in this story?

- Do you think she is satirizing Juan's character, the political situation, or both? Explain.

Vocabulary Study

albeit
conniving
distraction
elapse
irreproachable
sheer
staidness
subversive
ulterior
zeal

Write the letter of the word that best completes each sentence.

1. The ____ with which Juan did his work pleased his boss.

   a. staidness   **b.** zeal   **c.** albeit   **d.** distraction

2. Over four months would ____ before Juan found his letter.

   a. elapse   **b.** albeit   **c.** zeal   **d.** sheer

3. No one suspected that Juan concealed a(n) ____ motive for wanting to become a censor.

   a. irreproachable   **b.** sheer   **c.** elapse   **d.** ulterior

4. After an explosion, workers went back to their jobs ____ some were frightened.

    a. zeal   **b.** albeit   **c.** staidness   **d.** conniving

5. Even though Juan was executed, no one could truly say it was because of any ____ political activities.

    a. subversive   **b.** elapse   **c.** albeit   **d.** zeal

Expressing Your Ideas

Writing Choices

Writer's Notebook Update Review the notes you made in your notebook before reading "The Censors." Compare your list of the ways your life might change under a dictatorship with the reality of Juan's life. Then write a brief explanation of how something in your daily routine (listening to TV or getting to school, for example) would change under a dictatorship.

Your Censor Is Showing Are you aware that censorship—the act of changing or suppressing speech, writing, art, or any expression that is considered damaging or subversive—exists worldwide? Consider, for example, school dress codes. Now imagine that every student could dress as he or she wanted for school, without interference. Write a **satirical description** of the scene as you walk through the halls for your first class.

Dear Mariana Draft the **letter** Juan writes to Mariana that results in his death. Be imaginative. Then take the role of censor, listing the words or phrases from the letter that seal Juan's doom and explaining why they are censored.

Other Options

XSJUF B DPEF Work with a small group to write a **message in code.** You might write a message in which only the fifth word or letter is significant, one with numbers instead of letters, or one in which each letter has been replaced by the letter that directly follows it in the alphabet (like the title above and the message in italics under Strange to Say, page 29). Exchange codes with another group and try to solve.

Stamp of Approval The Post Office in Juan's country has hired you, the country's greatest artist, to produce designs for new stamps that will represent the country's new flag or its symbolic animal. What the Post Office doesn't know  is that you are planning to flee. Your stamps will satirize, not celebrate, these subjects. Draw the **stamp**s so that your opinion of the regime is clear.

Before Reading

The Voter

by Chinua Achebe   Nigeria

Chinua Achebe
born 1930

Chinua Achebe (chin′wä′ ä chā′bā) grew up knowing two very different cultures: those of Christian Europe and traditional Africa. He was born in 1930 in Ogidi, a village of the Ibo people in Eastern Nigeria. He has been a writer, teacher, editor, and lecturer, as well as a political activist during his country's civil strife. His works describe the effects of European culture and Christianity on a vigorous, traditional African culture. In addition to his best-known novel, *Things Fall Apart,* he has written other novels, poetry, a children's book, and collections of essays and stories.

Building Background

About Nigeria "The Voter" takes place in Nigeria, a country in west Africa. You might do class research to complete the Fact Sheet on Nigeria.

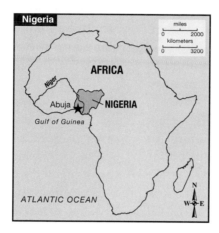

Fact Sheet

Population: about 105,000,000
Capital: Abuja
Area: 356,669 square miles
Major Ethnic Groups: Hausa, Yoruba, Ibo
Money: basic unit: Naira
Chief Products: _____
Elevation: _____
Government: _____

Literary Focus

Proverbs Brief traditional sayings containing popular wisdom are called **proverbs**. These sayings are an important component of all cultures. Be on the alert for common sayings such as "A bird in the hand is worth two in the bush" or "Early to bed, early to rise, makes a man healthy, wealthy, and wise" in conversations and writing. In west African culture, proverbs are especially important in daily speech. As you read "The Voter," note proverbs and the insights they provide into the characters and incidents.

Writer's Notebook

Look Before You Leap Think of a time that you agreed to do something and later realized you couldn't or didn't want to do it. What made you agree to do it in the first place? Why did you regret it later? Write a few sentences about your dilemma.

THE VOTER

Chinua Achebe

Rufus Okeke—Roof, for short—was a very popular man in his village. Although the villagers did not explain it in so many words Roof's popularity was a measure of their gratitude to an energetic young man who, unlike most of his fellows nowadays, had not abandoned the village in order to seek work—any work—in the towns. And Roof was not a village lout either. Everyone knew how he had spent two years as a bicycle repairer's apprentice in Port Harcourt[1] and had given up of his own free will a bright future to return to his people and guide them in these political times. Not that Umuofia needed a lot of guidance. The village already belonged *en masse*[2] to the People's Alliance Party, and its most illustrious son—Chief the Honorable Marcus Ibe—was Minister of Culture in the outgoing government (which was pretty certain to be the incoming one as well). Nobody doubted that the Honorable Minister would be re-elected in his constituency. Opposition to him was like the proverbial[3] fly trying to move a dunghill. It would have been ridiculous enough without coming, as it did now, from a complete nonentity.[4]

As was to be expected Roof was in the service of the Honorable Minister for the coming elections. He had become a real expert in election campaigning at all levels—village, local government or national. He could tell the mood and temper of the electorate[5] at any given time.

For instance he had warned the Minister months ago about the radical change that had come into the thinking of Umuofia since the last national election.

The villagers had had five years in which to see how quickly and plentifully politics brought wealth, chieftaincy titles, doctorate degrees and other honors, some of which like the last had still to be explained satisfactorily to them; for they expected a doctor to heal the sick. Anyhow, these honors had come so readily to the man they had given their votes to free of charge five years ago that they were now ready to think again.

Their point was that only the other day Marcus Ibe was a not too successful Mission-school teacher. Then politics had come to their village and he had wisely joined up, some say just in time to avoid imminent[6] dismissal arising from a female teacher's pregnancy. Today he was Chief the Honorable; he had two long cars and had just built himself the biggest house any-

---

1. **Port Harcourt,** a port city on the southern coast of Nigeria.
2. *en masse* (en mas′), in a group; all together. *[French]*
3. proverbial (prə vėr′bē əl), *adj.* relating to proverbs; commonly spoken of.
4. nonentity (non en′tə tē), *n.* a person or thing of little or no importance.
5. **electorate** (i lek′tər it), *n.* the persons having the right to vote in an election.
6. imminent (im′ə nənt), *adj.* about to occur.

one had seen in those parts. But let it be said that none of these successes had gone to Marcus's head—as they well might. He remained a man of the people. Whenever he could he left the good things of the capital and returned to his village which had neither running water nor electricity. He knew the source of his good fortune, unlike the little bird who ate and drank and went out to challenge his personal spirit.[7] Marcus had christened his new house "Umuofia Mansions" in honor of his village and slaughtered five bulls and countless goats to entertain the people on the day it was opened by the Archbishop.

EVALUATE: In your opinion, has Marcus Ibe remained "a man of the people"?

Everyone was full of praise for him. One old man said: "Our son is a good man; he is not like the mortar which as soon as food comes its way turns its back on the ground." But when the feasting was over the villagers told themselves that they had underrated the power of the ballot paper before and should not do so again. Chief the Honorable Marcus Ibe was not unprepared. He had drawn five months' salary in advance, changed a few hundred pounds into shining shillings and armed his campaign boys with eloquent little jute bags. In the day he made his speeches; at night his stalwarts[8] conducted their whispering campaign. Roof was the most trusted of these campaigners.

---

7. **personal spirit.** In Ibo tradition, each person has a personal spirit to guide him or her through life.
8. **stalwart** (stôl′wərt), *n.* person who is strong, brave, and firm.

The Nigerian painter known as Middle Art painted an enamel self-portrait on his shop door titled *The Manager in Charge* in the 1970s. 🐾 Does this manager appear to be "a man of the people," like Marcus? ➤

"We have a Minister from our village, one of our own sons," he said to a group of elders in the house of Ogbuefi Ezenwa, a man of high traditional title. "What greater honor can a village have? Do you ever stop to ask yourselves why we should be singled out for this honor? I will tell you: it is because we are favored by the leaders of PAP. Whether we cast our paper for Marcus or not PAP will continue to rule. Think of the pipe-borne water they have promised us . . ."

Besides Roof and his assistant there were five elders in the room. An old hurricane lamp with a cracked, sooty, glass chimney gave out yellowish light in their midst. The elders sat on very low stools. On the floor, directly in front of each of them, lay two shilling pieces. Outside the moon kept a straight face.

"We believe every word you say to be true," said Ezenwa. "We shall every one of us drop his paper for Marcus. Who would leave an *ozo* feast and go to a poor ritual meal? Tell Marcus he has our papers, and our wives' papers too. But what we do say is that two shillings is shameful." He brought the lamp close and tilted it at the money before him as if to make sure he had not mistaken its value. "Yes, two shillings; it is too shameful. If Marcus were a poor man—which our ancestors forbid—I should be the first to give him my paper free, as I did before. But today Marcus is a great man and does his things like a great man. We did not ask him for money yesterday; we shall not ask him tomorrow. But today is our day; we have climbed the *iroko* tree today and would be foolish not to take down all the fire-wood we need."

Roof had to agree. He had lately been taking down a lot of fire-wood himself. Only yesterday he had asked Marcus for one of his many rich robes—and had got it. Last Sunday Marcus's wife (the teacher that nearly got him

in trouble) had objected (like the woman she was) when Roof pulled out his fifth bottle of beer from the kerosene refrigerator, and was roundly and publicly rebuked[9] by her husband. To cap it all Roof had won a land case recently because, among other things, he had been chauffeur-driven to the disputed site. So he understood the elders about the fire-wood.

"All right," he said in English and then reverted to Ibo. "Let us not quarrel about small things." He stood up and adjusted his robes. Then he bent down like a priest distributing the host and gave one shilling more to every man: only he did not put it into their palms but on

> THIS **IYI** COMES FROM MBANTA. YOU KNOW WHAT THAT MEANS. SWEAR THAT YOU WILL VOTE FOR MADUKA.

the floor in front of them. The men, who had so far not deigned[10] to touch the things, looked at the floor and shook their heads. Roof got up again and gave each man another shilling.

"I am through," he said with a defiance that was no less effective for being transparently faked. The elders too knew how far to go without losing decorum.[11] So when Roof added: "Go cast your paper for the enemy if you like!" they quickly calmed him down with a suitable speech

---

9. **rebuke** (ri byük′), *v.* express disapproval of.
10. **deign** (dān), *v.* agree to; stoop or lower oneself to do something.
11. **decorum** (di kôr′əm), *n.* proper behavior; good taste in conduct, speech, or dress.

from each of them. By the time the last man had spoken it was possible—without great loss of dignity—to pick up the things from the floor.

The enemy Roof had referred to was the Progressive Organization Party (POP) which had been formed by the tribes down the coast to save themselves—as the founders of the party proclaimed—from "total political, cultural, social and religious annihilation." Although it was clear the party had no chance here it had plunged—with typical foolishness—into a straight fight with PAP, providing cars and loudspeakers to a few local rascals and thugs to go around and make a lot of noise. No one knew for certain how much money POP had let loose in Umuofia but it was said to be very considerable. Their local campaigners would end up very rich, no doubt.

Up to last night everything had been "moving according to plan"—as Roof would have put it. Then he had received a strange visit from the leader of the POP campaign team. Although he and Roof were well known to each other and might even be called friends his visit was cold and business-like. No words were wasted. He placed five pounds on the floor before Roof and said, "We want your vote." Roof got up from his chair, went to the outside door, closed it carefully and returned to his chair. The brief exercise gave him enough time to weigh the proposition. As he spoke his eyes never left the red notes on the floor.

"You know I work for Marcus," he said feebly. "It will be very bad . . ."

"Marcus will not be there when you put in your paper. We have plenty of work to do tonight; are you taking this or not?"

"It will not be heard outside this room?" asked Roof.

"We are after votes not gossip."

"All right," said Roof in English.

The man nudged his companion and he brought forward an object covered with red cloth and proceeded to remove the cover. It was a fearsome little affair contained in a clay pot with feathers stuck into it.

"This *iyi* comes from Mbanta. You know what that means. Swear that you will vote for Maduka. If you fail to do so, this *iyi* is to note."

Roof's heart had nearly flown out of his mouth when he saw the *iyi;* and indeed he knew the fame of Mbanta in these things. But he was a man of quick decision. What could a single vote cast in secret for Maduka take away from Marcus's certain victory? Nothing.

"I will cast my paper for Maduka; if not, this *iyi* take note."

"Das all," said the man as he rose with his companion, who had covered up the object again and was taking it back to their car.

"You know he has no chance against Marcus," said Roof at the door.

"It is enough that he gets a few votes now; next time he will get more. People will hear that he gives out pounds, not shillings, and they will listen."

lection morning. The great day every five years when the people exercised power—or thought they did. Weather-beaten posters on walls of houses, tree trunks and telegraph poles. The few that were still whole called out their message to those who could read. Vote for the People's Alliance Party! Vote for the Progressive Organisation Party! Vote for PAP! Vote for POP! The posters that were torn called out as much of the message as they could.

As usual Chief the Honorable Marcus Ibe was doing things in grand style. He had hired a highlife band from Umuru and stationed it at such a distance from the voting booths as just managed to be lawful. Many villagers danced to the music, their ballot papers held aloft, before proceeding to the booths. Chief the Honorable Marcus Ibe sat in the "owner's corner"[12] of his enormous green car and smiled and nodded.

---

12. **owner's corner,** the seat diagonally behind the driver, reserved for the owner of the car as a mark of respect.

One enlightened villager came up to the car, shook hands with the great man and said in advance: "Congrats!" This immediately set the pattern. Hundreds of admirers shook Marcus's hand and said "Corngrass!"

Roof and the other organizers were prancing up and down, giving last minute advice to the voters and pouring with sweat.

"Do not forget," he said again to a group of illiterate women who seemed ready to burst with enthusiasm and good humor, "our sign is the motor-car . . ."

"Like the one Marcus is sitting inside."

"Thank you, mother," said Roof. "It is the same car. The box with the car shown on its body is the box for you. Don't look at the other with the man's head: it is for those whose heads are not correct."

This was greeted with loud laughter. Roof cast a quick and busy-like glance towards the Minister and received a smile of appreciation.

"Vote for the car," he shouted, all the veins in his neck standing out. "Vote for the car and you will ride in it!"

"Or if we don't our children will," piped the same sharp old girl.

The band struck up a new number: "Why walk when you can ride?"

In spite of his apparent calm and confidence Chief the Honorable Marcus was a relentless stickler for detail. He knew he would win what the newspapers called "a landslide victory" but he did not wish even so to throw away a single vote. So as soon as the first rush of voters was over he promptly asked his campaign boys to go one at a time and put in their ballot papers.

"Roof, you had better go first," he said.

Roof's spirits fell; but he let no one see it. All morning he had masked his deep worry with a surface exertion which was unusual even for him. Now he dashed off in his springy fashion towards the booths. A policeman at the entrance searched him for illegal ballot papers and passed him. Then the electoral officer explained to him about the two boxes. By this time the spring had gone clean out of his walk. He sidled in and was confronted by the car and the head. He brought out his ballot paper from his pocket and looked at it. How could he betray Marcus even in secret? He resolved to go back to the other man and return his five pounds . . . FIVE POUNDS! He knew at once it was impossible. He had sworn on that *iyi*.

At this point he heard the muffled voice of the policeman asking the electoral officer what the man was doing inside. "Abi na pickin im de born?"[13]

Quick as lightning a thought leapt into Roof's mind. He folded the paper, tore it in two along the crease and put one half in each box. He took the precaution of putting the first half into Maduka's box and confirming the action verbally: "I vote for Maduka."

EVALUATE: Do you think that Roof has betrayed Marcus Ibe? Why or why not?

They marked his thumb with indelible purple ink to prevent his return, and he went out of the booth as jauntily as he had gone in.

---

13. **Abi na pickin im de born?,** a question in pidgin English that is commonly asked in Nigeria and means literally, "Is he giving birth to a child in there?" It can be translated, "Why is he taking so long?"

After Reading

Making Connections

Shaping Your
Response

1. Work with a partner to demonstrate for the class how you think Roof looks when he enters the voting booth and after he exits it. Have classmates guess the feelings you are trying to convey.

2. Why do you think Roof might have given up a "bright future" repairing bicycles?

3. In your opinion, does Roof have the qualities of an effective politician? Explain.

Analyzing the Story

4. What hints does Achebe provide that suggest Chief the Honorable Marcus Ibe may not be so honorable?

5. Achebe uses humor throughout "The Voter." Find examples and explain what, if anything, you think the use of humor adds to readers' feelings about Roof.

6. How would you describe Roof's **character?**

Extending the
Ideas

7. Does the practice of buying votes occur nowadays? If so, where? How? What measures are taken to prevent voting abuse?

Literary Focus: Proverbs

Working in small groups, explain what these two **proverbs** from the story mean.

1. "Opposition to him was like the proverbial fly trying to move a dunghill."

2. "But today is our day; we have climbed the *iroko* tree today and would be foolish not to take down all the fire-wood we need."

3. 👣 How do the proverbs above illustrate the needs of the **individual** within the group?

Now see if you can explain what the following African proverbs mean. Are there English language equivalents for any of these?

• "One who is overcautious of his life is always killed by the fall of a dry leaf."

• "A hen cannot lay eggs and hatch them in the same day."

• "You do not give a hyena meat to look after."

Vocabulary Study

Next to each number, write the letter of the word that best completes each sentence.

decorum
en masse
imminent
nonentity
proverbial

1. Something done *en masse* is done ____.

   a. well **b.** quickly **c.** together **d.** clumsily

2. *Proverbial* is most closely linked to the word ____.

   a. verb **b.** proverb **c.** prove **d.** rover

3. An *imminent* event is likely to happen ____.

   a. never **b.** often **c.** rarely **d.** soon

4. A *nonentity* is ____.

   a. unimportant **b.** thin **c.** loud **d.** greedy

5. *Decorum* refers to____.

   a. furniture **b.** nature **c.** behavior **d.** death

Expressing Your Ideas

Writing Choices

Writer's Notebook Update Look again at what you wrote in your notebook before reading "The Voter." Were you as resourceful as Roof in solving your problem? Build on your sentences to write a brief description of your dilemma and how you resolved it. You might want to use a vocabulary word or two.

A Stitch in Time Some proverbs have served as sources of inspiration for literary titles, musical compositions, group names, and so on. For example, "A rolling stone gathers no moss" has provided a name for songs, a musical group, and a magazine, among other things. Imagine you are starting your own business. Choose part of a proverb that would be a good name for your business and use your choice in a brief **ad**. For example, you might name your sewing service "A Stitch in Time."

Other Options

Scrollwork In ancient cultures, story pictures were sometimes drawn on long rolls, or scrolls, of papyrus or parchment. By slowly unrolling the scroll, one "read" the story, leisurely savoring each new scene and detail. Create a **scroll picture** that illustrates one of the proverbs appearing in Achebe's story, "The Voter," or another proverb of your choosing. Then reveal and explain your scroll to the class.

Pop Art Create a **poster** for PAP or POP, complete with the car or head logo, campaign slogans, and political promises that would be popular with the villagers.

More About Nigeria You might want to do additional research on Nigeria—its politics, resources, buildings, modes of transportation, and so on. **Report** your findings to the class.

The Other Wife

by Colette   France

Colette
1873–1954

Thoroughly French in every respect, Colette (Sidonie Gabrielle Claudine Colette), was born in France's Burgundy region and died in Paris. When she was twenty, Colette married Henry Gauthier-Villars, a Paris journalist, music critic, and editor, who published her early work under his own pseudonym, Willy. Later, Colette become nationally recognized under her own name with such novels as *Chéri* (1920) and *Gigi* (1944). A touring actress and lecturer as well as a writer, Colette was the first woman in France given a state funeral. She is now regarded as one of the first modern writers to focus on relationships from the female point of view.

Building Background

Slice of Life The story goes that film director Alfred Hitchcock loved to get into an elevator with a friend and silently stand there until just before arriving at his floor. As the elevator doors opened and he moved into the corridor, Hitchcock would turn to his friend and say something like, "Well, I don't care what you say. I personally think that after she cut off his head—" And the doors would close, leaving behind a group of wide-eyed eavesdroppers to speculate on the possibilities. As a reader, you too will sometimes find yourself eavesdropping on a conversation and later having to fill in puzzle pieces and make inferences. Imagine yourself seated at a table in an exclusive French restaurant. A glamorous, well-dressed couple enters and sits at the table beside you. Eavesdrop a little, and decide if you would like to change places with "The Other Wife."

Literary Focus

Point of View The author's choice of narrator for a story determines the **point of view**. This choice affects the amount of information a reader will be given, as well as the angle from which this information will be presented. Some stories have a narrator who is a character in the story. In "The Other Wife," however, the narrator is not a character but an outsider.

Writer's Notebook

Excuse Me! Few people manage to get through life without enduring an awkward or embarrassing situation—at home, in class, or somewhere else. Before reading "The Other Wife," briefly describe such a situation, one you experienced or witnessed. Note when and where it took place, why it was awkward, and how it was resolved.

▲ This 1912 work by Scottish painter William Strang shows
a young couple on holiday. In what ways is the couple
pictured both like and unlike your ideas of Alice and Marc
in the story?

The Other Wife

Colette

"For two? This way, *monsieur* and *madame*, there's still a table by the bay window, if *madame* and *monsieur* would like to enjoy the view."

Alice followed the *maître d'hôtel.*[1]

"Oh yes, come on, Marc, we'll feel we're having lunch on a boat at sea. . . ."

Her husband restrained her, passing his arm through hers.

"We'll be more comfortable there."

"There? In the middle of all those people? I'd much prefer . . ."

"Please, Alice."

He tightened his grip in so emphatic a way that she turned round.

"What's the matter with you?"

He said "shh" very quietly, looking at her intently, and drew her towards the table in the middle.

"What is it, Marc?"

"I'll tell you, darling. Let me order lunch. Would you like shrimps? Or eggs in aspic?"

"Whatever *you* like, as you know."

They smiled at each other, wasting the precious moments of an overworked, perspiring *maître d'hôtel* who stood near to them, suffering from a kind of St. Vitus' dance.[2]

"Shrimps," ordered Marc. "And then eggs and bacon. And cold chicken with cos lettuce salad. Cream cheese? *Spécialité de la maison?*[3] We'll settle for the *spécialité.* Two very strong coffees. Please give lunch to my chauffeur; we'll be leaving again at two o'clock. Cider? I don't trust it. . . . Dry champagne."

He sighed as though he had been moving a wardrobe, gazed at the pale noonday sea, the nearly white sky, then at his wife, finding her pretty in her little Mercury-type hat[4] with its long hanging veil.

"You're looking well, darling. And all this sea-blue color gives you green eyes, just imagine! And you put on weight when you travel. . . . It's

---

1. *maître d'hôtel* (me′trə dō tel′), headwaiter. *[French]*
2. **St. Vitus' dance**, a nervous disease characterized by involuntary twitching of the muscles.
3. *Spécialité de la maison* (spā syal ē tā′ də lə-mā zōn′), specialty of the house. *[French]*
4. **Mercury-type hat.** The god Mercury is characteristically pictured wearing a rounded hat with small wings.

nice, up to a point, but only up to a point!"

Her rounded bosom swelled proudly as she leaned over the table.

"Why did you stop me taking that place by the bay window?"

It did not occur to Marc Séguy to tell a lie.

"Because you'd have sat next to someone I know."

"And whom I don't know?"

"My ex-wife."

She could not find a word to say and opened her blue eyes wider.

"What of it, darling? It'll happen again. It's not important."

Alice found her tongue again and asked the inevitable questions in their logical sequence.

"Did she see you? Did she know that you'd seen her? Point her out to me."

"Don't turn round at once, I beg you; she must be looking at us. A lady with dark hair, without a hat; she must be staying at this hotel. . . . On her own, behind those children in red. . . ."

"Yes, I see."

Sheltered behind broad-brimmed seaside hats, Alice was able to look at the woman who fifteen months earlier had still been her husband's wife. "Incompatibility," Marc told her. "Oh, it was total incompatibility! We divorced like well-brought-up people, almost like friends, quietly and quickly. And I began to love you, and you were able to be happy with me. How lucky we are that in our happiness there haven't been any guilty parties or victims!"

The woman in white, with her smooth, lustrous[5] hair over which the seaside light played in blue patches, was smoking a cigarette, her eyes half closed. Alice turned back to her husband, took some shrimps and butter, and ate composedly.

o o o

Why didn't you ever tell me ... that she had blue eyes too?

o o o

"Why didn't you ever tell me," she said after a moment's silence, "that she had blue eyes too?"

"But I'd never thought about it!"

He kissed the hand that she stretched out to the bread basket and she blushed with pleasure. Dark-skinned and plump, she might have seemed slightly earthy, but the changing blue of her eyes, and her wavy golden hair, disguised her as a fragile and soulful[6] blond. She showed overwhelming gratitude to her husband. She was immodest without knowing it and her entire person revealed overconspicuous signs of extreme happiness.

They ate and drank with good appetite and each thought that the other had forgotten the woman in white. However, Alice sometimes laughed too loudly and Marc was careful of his posture, putting his shoulders back and holding his head up. They waited some time for coffee, in silence. An incandescent[7] stream, a narrow reflection of the high and invisible sun, moved slowly over the sea and shone with unbearable brilliance.

"She's still there, you know," Alice whispered suddenly.

"Does she embarrass you? Would you like to have coffee somewhere else?"

"Not at all! It's she who ought to be embarrassed! And she doesn't look as though she's having a madly gay time; if you could see her. . . ."

"It's not necessary. I know that look of hers."

"Oh, was she like that?"

He breathed smoke through his nostrils and wrinkled his brows.

---

5. **lustrous** (lus′trəs), *adj.* shining; glossy.
6. **soulful** (sōl′fəl), *adj.* full of feeling; deeply emotional.
7. **incandescent** (in′kən des′nt), *adj.* shining brightly; brilliant.

"Was she like that? No. To be frank, she wasn't happy with me."

"Well, my goodness!"

"You're delightfully generous, darling, madly generous. . . . You're an angel, you're . . . You love me. . . . I'm so proud, when I see that look in your eyes . . . yes, the look you have now. . . . She . . . No doubt I didn't succeed in making her happy. That's all there is to it, I didn't succeed."

"She's hard to please!"

Alice fanned herself irritably, and cast brief glances at the woman in white, her head leaning against the back of the cane chair, her eyes closed with an expression of satisfied lassitude.

Marc shrugged his shoulders modestly.

"That's it," he admitted. "What can one do? We have to be sorry for people who are never happy. As for us, we're so happy. . . . Aren't we, darling?"

She didn't reply. She was looking with furtive[8] attention at her husband's face, with its good color and regular shape, at his thick hair, with its occasional thread of white silk, at his small, well-cared-for hands. She felt dubious[9] for the first time, and asked herself: "What more did she want, then?"

And until they left, while Marc was paying the bill, asking about the chauffeur and the route, she continued to watch, with envious curiosity, the lady in white, that discontented, hard-to-please, superior woman. . . .

---

8. **furtive** (fėr′tiv), *adj.* done quickly and with stealth to avoid being noticed; sly.

9. **dubious** (dü′bē əs), *adj.* filled with or being in doubt; uncertain.

After Reading

Making Connections

Shaping Your Response

1. Draw a head and a thought bubble extending from it. In the bubble, write what you think is going through Alice's mind as she leaves the restaurant.

2. Do you think this couple's marriage will last? Why or why not?

Analyzing the Story

3. At the end of the story, Alice "continued to watch, with envious curiosity, the lady in white, that discontented, hard-to-please, superior woman. . . ." What do you think has happened during lunch to make her feel "dubious for the first time"?

4. Why might Marc have married Alice, who seems so different from his first wife?

5. Sometimes we can learn a great deal about a **character** who never says a word in a story. What do we learn about the first wife from the descriptions provided in the story?

6. To which of the two wives do you think the **title** of the story applies? Explain.

Extending the Ideas

7. What current social problems does the aftermath of a divorce produce for both spouses and children? Do you think it's possible for ex-husbands and ex-wives to maintain friendly relationships? Explain.

8. 👣 Alice, a character from several generations ago, finds the other woman threatening to her marriage and security. Do you think that contemporary women are more apt to be self-assured about their own **individuality** and worth outside of marriage?

Literary Focus: Point of View

Point of view refers to the perspective of the person telling a story. In this story, the narrator is not a character but an outsider, who sees events mainly through Alice's eyes. This point of view is said to be *third-person limited*. Examine the final two paragraphs of the story for insights the narrator provides about Alice.

• How do you think Alice would answer her own question, "What more did she want, then"?

• Look back at another story you have read in this group. Decide if it is told by a character in the story (*first-person point of view*) or by an outside narrator (*third-person point of view*).

Vocabulary Study

Colette chooses precise adjectives to convey her meaning. Provide one of the following synonyms for each italicized word below: sly, brilliant, uncertain, shining, deeply emotional.

dubious
furtive
incandescent
lustrous
soulful

1. "The woman in white, with her smooth, *lustrous* hair . . . was smoking a cigarette. . . ."

2. ". . . the changing blue of her eyes, and her wavy golden hair, disguised her as a fragile and *soulful* blonde."

3. "An *incandescent* stream . . . moved slowly over the sea and shone with unbearable brilliance."

4. "She was looking with *furtive* attention at her husband's face. . . ."

5. "She felt *dubious* for the first time. . . ."

Expressing Your Ideas

Writing Choices

Writer's Notebook Update Review the notes you recorded before reading "The Other Wife" about an awkward or embarrassing situation you witnessed or experienced. Now expand and rewrite your personal account using some techniques Colette uses—for example, a third-person narrator, dialogue, or powerful adjectives.

Speak Your Mind The silent first wife sitting by the bay window is well aware of the presence of her ex-husband and his new wife. Write a **monologue** that indicates what this ex-wife is thinking as she observes the pair. Limit your monologue to one of three time periods: the couple's entrance into the room, the period when they are eating lunch, or the settling of the bill and their exit from the room.

Alice's Journal Think about what Alice will write in her **journal** the evening of her encounter with Marc's first wife. Write a brief entry expressing the feelings she is experiencing.

Other Options

Face to Face Marc, Alice, and Marc's first wife meet on a **talk show** featuring ex-wives, present wives, and their husbands. In groups of four, brainstorm questions that a talk show host or hostess might ask these three characters, along with answers they might give. Then act out these four parts for the class.

What's for Lunch? Although the lunch this couple eats sounds romantic, it falls short of modern health standards. Champagne midday? Cholesterol-high foods such as eggs and bacon? Imagine the fat grams in cream cheese! In a small group, work with a health or science teacher or the school dietitian to find out the long-range effects frequent meals like this could have. Chart your findings and present them in an **oral report** to the class.

The Play's the Thing Perform "The Other Wife" as a **play** for radio, video, or the stage. If possible, incorporate music, sound effects, costumes, and simple props (stage "properties" such as glasses and plates).

Pushing Toward the Top

So Young, So Talented

Multicultural Connection

Several of the stories in this group are about young people who feel pressure to excel. Compare these fictional characters with the people pictured on these pages, who displayed talent at an early age that directed their courses in later life.

Jodie Foster appeared in her first commercial at the age of three, made her first acclaimed motion picture at twelve, and entered Yale at seventeen. This award–winning actress now directs film as well.

EARLY

Alexander the Great (356–323 B.C.), who became King of Macedonia at twenty, conquered the stretch from Asia Minor to India. This mosaic copy of the Hellenistic painting, *Battle of Issus*, by Philoxenus captures him at the most dramatic moment of the battle.

This painting was created by Wang Yani at the age of five. Born in Gongcheng, China, she now exhibits her paintings of birds, flowers, monkeys, and trees in museums in Asia, Europe, and the United States.

> In 1992, China recognized eight-year-old Ugen Thinley Dorjee as the 17th Karmapa, or Living Buddha, of Tibet. Pictured here in 1995, he is the leader of the Karma Kagyu, one of the four main sects of Tibetan Buddhism.

STARTERS

When she was five, Shirley Temple (Black) earned her first Academy Award in the special awards category. Before her tenth birthday, this actress had earned a million dollars. As an adult, she entered politics and became a U.N. delegate.

Super-prodigy of Greek mythology, Hermes was born at dawn, invented the lyre (pictured here) at noon, and stole a herd of cattle at night. As messenger of Zeus, he became the god of travel.

Mozart

THE MUSIC MAGICIAN

*The following descriptions of the young Mozart and of people's reactions who heard him and his sister play on their European tours appear in the biography **Mozart** by Maynard Solomon.*

The most famous musical prodigy in history, he was marked from the outset as the quintessential, perfect child. In an extraordinary series of triumphs, he was received, feted, and honored by the royal families of Europe—the king and queen of France, the empress of Austria and her son Emperor Joseph, the king and queen of England—and Pope Clement XIV himself. Mozart and his family were showered with money and expensive presents. He was kissed by empresses and petted by Marie Antoinette. And all because he was a gifted child, one who not only could perform wonders and miracles but was the very incarnation of a miracle, one whose small body exemplified the infinite perfectibility of the child and, by inference, of mankind....

Leopold Mozart [his father] did not exaggerate when he wrote home, "Everyone is amazed, especially at the boy, and everyone whom I have heard says that his genius is incomprehensible." Anecdotes of the visit to Schönbrunn confirm that the children put on a diverting entertainment: One of the ladies of the court assured the biographer Franz Niemetschek that both children made a "very great impression," recalling that "people could hardly believe their ears and eyes at the performance." It was said that the emperor teased the little "magician," as he was dubbed: "It is no great art to play with all your fingers; but if you could play with only one finger and on a covered keyboard, that would be something worthy of admiration." Naturally, Mozart was not fazed by this suggestion, which could not have been altogether unexpected, for he had brought along a bagful of keyboard tricks from Salzburg. He commenced "to play with one finger only, as precisely as possible; and then, he permitted the clavier keyboard to be covered and performed with marvelous dexterity, as though he had long been practicing this feat...."

But anyone who troubled to look could have perceived many early signs of Mozart's difficulty in sustaining his multiple burdens: he was quick to tears, stricken and often taken ill by the loss or absence of friends, bereft when his constant pleas to "love me" were not reciprocated. There was no indication that the child understood the extent to which he had been converted into an instrument of patriarchal ambition and subjected to the inevitable resentments that attach to a father's growing realization that he has become deeply dependent upon his little boy.

Responding

1. Who would you add to the picture gallery of talented young people? Explain your choices and provide captions.

2. Working with a partner, make a list of advantages and disadvantages to being a prodigy.

This portrait of Mozart and his father and sister is a watercolor by the French artist Louis de Carmontelle (1717-1806). What details from Solomon's biography present the young Mozart in a different light from that in the painting?

Science Connection

Excellence can take many forms. One such form is intelligence. An intelligence test is one way to measure a person's ability to solve certain kinds of problems. But a high intelligence quotient (IQ) is no guarantee of achievement, and many talented, accomplished people have IQs considered normal or lower.

MEASURING UP

A lthough there is some connection between creativity and intelligence, a "creative" test taker may fare poorly on intelligence tests. Most intelligence tests involve questions dealing with memory, reasoning, factual recall, and ability with numbers. Such tests include few questions based on mechanical skills and do not measure creativity.

An intelligence quotient, or IQ, a number used to indicate a person's intelligence, is based on a comparison of his or her score on a particular test with the scores of others taking the same test.

Psychologists who design intelligence tests try to use material with which all test takers are familiar. Nevertheless, such tests are based on culture and experience to some degree. For example, someone who has always spoken English has an advantage over someone who learned English later in school. In an effort to be culture-fair, some tests attempt to use words, symbols, ideas, and pictures that are recognized by persons of different backgrounds.

What are the IQs of some famous people? The estimated IQ of the French writer Voltaire was reported to be 170, that of Italian painter Leonardo da Vinci was 135, and that of George Washington projected at 125.

Try answering the following questions, which are typical of those appearing on IQ tests. Answers are on this page.

 If you rearrange the letters TRAACINCT, you will have the name of:
a. a color
b. an ocean
c. a food
d. an animal

 What is the missing number? 4 6 10 ? 34 66
a. 12
b. 16
c. 17
d. 18
e. 22

 Mary is smarter than John, but not as smart as Tom. Therefore, John is smarter than Tom.
a. True
b. False
c. Impossible to answer from the data given

 Which is least like the others?
a. iron
b. oxygen
c. gold
d. salt
e. nitrogen

 Which one does not belong with the others?

a.   b.   c.   d.

Responding

Do you consider questions on IQ tests too academic? What kinds of practical questions do you think people your age should be able to answer before graduating from high school? Work with a group to devise your own questions, based on real-life skills.

Answers: 1. b. Antarctic; 2. d. (Double each number and subtract 2.); 3. b; 4. d. (All the others are elements.); 5. c.

Reading Mini-Lesson

Finding Main Idea and Supporting Details

The ability to find the main idea as you read is a useful skill, especially when reading nonfiction for information. For example, when you read an article in a reference book, it is the main idea that you need to remember. The main idea gives the most important point of the whole passage and can usually be summed up in one sentence. A writer includes details to support the main idea, to clarify it, or sometimes simply to add interesting information.

One strategy to help you identify the main idea in a passage is to look for key words as you read. You might organize these key words using a pie chart. For example, if you were reading an article on the construction of the Empire State Building, your pie chart might look like this:

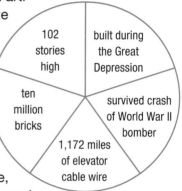

Looking at these key words and phrases, you might express the main idea of the article as "The construction of the Empire State Building was an extraordinary achievement." Remember not all details are equally important to the main idea. For example, King Kong's famous climb to the top of the building, however memorable, isn't really relevant to the main idea as expressed above.

Activity Options

1. Use a pie chart to diagram the main idea and supporting details in the passage from Maynard Solomon's biography of Mozart that appears on page 52.

2. Make a pie chart about a recent event in the news. Using the information in the chart, identify the main idea.

3. Research the careers of one of the prodigies pictured on pages 50–51. Write down at least three main ideas you discovered from your research, and list two or three supporting details for each main idea.

Writing Workshop

Challenges: Up Close and Personal

Assignment You have read stories about characters meeting challenges, some more successfully than others. Now write an essay about handling challenges in everyday life.

WRITER'S BLUEPRINT

Product   An interpretive essay

Purpose   To explore the theme of meeting challenges

Audience   People who like to read but have never read these particular stories

Specs   As the writer of a successful essay, you should:

❏ Analyze how three characters from the stories respond to challenges. Then draw conclusions from your analysis.

❏ Begin by introducing your characters and briefly summarizing the challenges that each character faces. Give your readers enough background about the plot to be able to follow your train of thought. Remember, they haven't read these stories.

❏ Go on to deal with each character in detail, one at a time. First make a general statement that analyzes his or her responses to challenges. Then cite specific examples from the stories, including quotations, to support this general statement.

❏ In your conclusion, look back at your analyses and state the lessons that can be learned from them. State these lessons in terms of *do's* and *don't's* about how to meet challenges in everyday life.

❏ Write focused paragraphs that each develop a general idea with specific examples.

❏ Follow the conventions of standard written English. Punctuate quotations from the literature correctly.

The instructions that follow are designed to lead you to a successful essay.

PREWRITING

Find challenges in the literature and make notes on the characters' responses. Organize your notes in a chart like this one:

Challenges	Responses	Specific Examples	Plan of Attack—
Jerry— "He knew he must find his way through . . . and out the other side."	—envies boys who can do it —is impatient to succeed —works to develop skills	—"a controlled impatience, made him wait" —devotes himself to "careful self-training"	always have a plan: define exactly what it is you need to do before you try to do it

LITERARY SOURCE
"He looked down into the blue well of water. He knew he must find his way through that cave, or hole, or tunnel, and out the other side."
from "Through the Tunnel" by Doris Lessing

Discuss your notes with classmates and ask for comments. If you need to explain things that are unclear to a classmate, make additional notes on those explanations. Then look back at your additional notes and revise your plan accordingly.

OR . . .
You might also talk with people who haven't read the stories before. Explaining the plots to them may help you see things from different angles.

Plan your essay. Think about what you want to say in the introduction, body, and conclusion. Organize the information in your notes in a three-part outline that reflects the Specs in the Writer's Blueprint.

I. Introduction
  A. The three characters
  B. Their challenges

II. Body
  A. First character
        1. General statement
        2. Specific examples
  B. Second character
        1. General statement
        2. Specific examples
  C. Third character
        1. General statement
        2. Specific examples

OR . . .
Turn things around in the body of your essay. Give your specific examples first for each character and follow with the general statement.

III. Conclusion
  A. Lessons Learned
  B. *Do's*
  C. *Don't's*

STEP 2 DRAFTING

Start writing. Use your writing plan and Writer's Blueprint as guides. One of these drafting strategies might help.

- If you're drafting by hand, use a separate piece of paper for each paragraph. That way you'll have lots of room to revise.

- In the body, devote one paragraph to each character.

- For your conclusion, state each *do* and *don't* in a short, catchy sentence first. Then go on to explain it.

Here is part of one student's draft.

"Through the Tunnel" tells the story of a young boy who meets his challenge by fighting his own impatience—and winning. Jerry's first impulse is to swim under, find the underwater tunnel, and quickly swim his way through—but his "most unchildlike persistence, a controlled impatience" makes him wait. Waiting is a good idea. If he had simply given in to his impulse and tried to swim the tunnel right away he would have probably drowned.

STUDENT MODEL

STEP 3 REVISING

COMPUTER TIP
Try using the Cut and Paste functions to switch your body paragraphs around as you revise. See if the body of your essay reads better with a new order.

Ask a partner to look over your draft and comment before you actually revise.

✔ Do my general statements really fit the character's responses?

✔ Do my specific examples really support my general statements?

✔ Have I written focused paragraphs?

Revising Strategy

Writing Focused Paragraphs

In a focused paragraph, the writer:

- makes a definite point—a main idea

- develops this main idea with specific details

- stays focused on this main idea

In the paragraph at the right, the narrator states her mother's belief (in America you can be anything) and gives specific examples of "anything" (entrepreneur, civil servant, homeowner, celebrity). Every sentence focuses on the main idea. Notice how the writer of the draft below used a partner's comment to delete a sentence that doesn't focus on the main idea.

LITERARY SOURCE
"My mother believed you could be anything you wanted to be in America. You could open a restaurant. You could work for the government and get good retirement. You could buy a house with almost no money down. You could become rich. You could become instantly famous."
from "Two Kinds"
by Amy Tan

Juan, the protagonist of "The Censors," fails to meet his challenge when he becomes obsessed with it. His goal is to find letters from his beloved. Juan is saddened by the fact that he has not seen or heard of his love Marianna for quite some time. He has no doubt that the government censors are keeping her letters from getting through to him. Can he prevent the censoring of her letters if he himself becomes a censor? He fails because he actually becomes the enemy he sets out to defeat—the censor. ~~Jerry in "Through the Tunnel" also wants to find~~ ~~something, but Roof in "The Voter" doesn't.~~ *Does this sentence belong here?*

STUDENT MODEL

STEP **4** EDITING

Ask a partner to review your revised draft before you actually edit it. Pay special attention to punctuating quotations from literature.

Editing Strategy

Punctuating Quotations from Literature

FOR REFERENCE. . .
More rules for punctuating quotations from literature are listed in the Language and Grammar Handbook at the back of this text.

When you edit an essay like this one, make sure you follow these rules for punctuating quotations from literature:

- Surround direct quotations with quotation marks.

- Use commas to set off words that precede or introduce a direct quotation.

- Place the end punctuation or the comma that ends the quotation inside the quotation marks.

- Begin a direct quotation that is a sentence with a capital letter.

    Amy Tan writes, "My mother believed you could be anything you wanted to be in America."

Leaving out the quotation marks can lead to confusion. Notice how the writer of the draft below fixed mistakes in punctuating quotations from literature.

The whole system has been corrupted, and the device for this corruption is money. Rufus is in the position of bribing tribal elders for their very important votes in the election. They do not refuse him, for Rufus is a convincing speaker, but they do not accept without mild protest. One elder tells Rufus "But what we do say is that two shillings is shameful" when Rufus offers him two shillings for his vote.

STUDENT MODEL

5 PRESENTING

- Read your essay aloud to a partner and discuss your *do*'s and *don't*'s.

- Create a class poster of advice on meeting challenges. Include at least one *do* or *don't* from each person in class. Donate a copy to the school library.

6 LOOKING BACK

Self-evaluate. How well does your paper meet the Specs from the Writer's Blueprint? Evaluate yourself on each point, from 6 (superior) down to 1 (inadequate).

Reflect. Think about what you learned from writing this essay.

✔ Compare your rough draft with your finished copy. Jot down comments about the kinds of changes you made. What do they tell you about your strengths and weaknesses as a writer?

✔ How could you apply some of the *do*'s and *don't*'s to challenges facing you in your life right now?

For Your Working Portfolio Add your finished paper and reflection responses to your working portfolio.

Beyond Print

Looking at Movies

Today America is a visual society that gets its information as much from images as from the printed word. Although a million people may buy a bestselling novel, many times that number could flock to see the film version. In order to become a more informed viewer of movies and TV, watch for ways (a lingering close-up, quick transitions between scenes, dissolves from one picture to the next) that the director or cameraperson tries to influence you. You might use similar techniques in your writing to appeal to your audience.

Transitions and editing Filmmakers may use special effects such as fade-outs and dissolves to represent relationships, indicate shifts in time or place, or establish contrasts. Scenes may be cut or rearranged to quicken the pace or present a flashback.

Camera angles A camera can pan a scene, linger, zoom in on important details, and make things appear important or insignificant. A camera can focus on a particular character's point of view, framing scenes according to a limited perspective.

Color Use of color can serve to develop character and mood. Note whether colors are muted or bright and whether black-and-white is used for effect. Observe how bright lighting produces a buoyant mood, while shadows can produce an ominous effect.

Music and sound effects Note whether music is used to create a mood, build tension, or signal an oncoming event.

Symbolic shots and gestures Sometimes an object or a gesture may be highlighted and invested with symbolic significance. For example, an overturned vase may suggest violence or upheaval.

Activity Options

1. Pick a scene from one of the stories in this group that lends itself to "filming." Brainstorm in groups ways that you could convert the written description into pictures, applying some of the camera techniques mentioned above. Present your ideas in the form of a few illustrated storyboards with written filming directions.

This still is from *The Joy Luck Club,* directed by Wayne Wang (Hollywood Pictures, 1993). ➤

2. Choose an item from your portfolio that could be rewritten using "camera techniques" such as close-ups, quick transitions, pans, or dissolves. You might use one of the following approaches.

- Imagine that you are behind the camera as you edit your work. Focus on details and frame your images as a film director would.

- Establish a clear point of view. Then shift your point of view at some place to lend emphasis or drama.

Camera Terms

close-up a shot taken at close range that focuses on one item or one aspect of a person and takes up almost the entire frame.

cut an immediate switch from one picture to another.

dissolve fade gradually from the screen while the succeeding picture or scene slowly appears.

fade-in/fade-out the gradual appearance or disappearance of a picture on a screen.

flashback a break in the continuous series of events to introduce some earlier event or scene.

frame a single picture or image.

pan move a camera from one side to another to take in a larger scene or to follow a moving object.

transition a change or passing from one condition, place, thing, activity, topic, etc., to another.

zoom move rapidly from one focus to another, as with a zoom lens.

Part Two

Trying to Beat the Odds

What are the odds you'll like the stories that follow? Take a chance and read them to find out. The characters you will meet here likewise take chances, many without success. But some of them do manage to succeed—through their wits or by sheer luck.

⬤ Multicultural Connection **Groups**, which supply a framework based on ethnicity, race, gender, age, religion, nationality, and other affinities, create a common thread, a unifying culture. Note the powerful influence exerted on individuals by groups in many of the following selections.

Literature

Before Reading

The Monkey's Paw

by W. W. Jacobs   Great Britain

W. W. Jacobs
1863–1943

W. W. (William Wymark) Jacobs was born in Wapping in the ship-docking section of London, England. There he got a taste of the waterfront that is reflected in many of his book titles, such as *Light Freights, The Lady of the Barge,* and *Deep Waters*, and in the plots of a number of his short stories. Jacobs worked as a civil servant until he was able to support himself by his writing. In addition to stories about life on the sea, Jacobs wrote bizarre tales and stories dealing with country life. A good example is his most famous story, "The Monkey's Paw," a classic horror tale of the supernatural.

Building Background

Your Wish Is My Command When the alarm clock sounded this morning, you may have stretched, rubbed the sleep from your eyes, and groggily mumbled, "I wish I never had to get up in the morning." Whoa! Be careful what you wish for. There might be disasterous consequences. Brainstorm with the class tales and stories you have heard where three wishes are part of the plot. What were the results of making these wishes?

Literary Focus

Plot Jacobs creates a mood of suspense that builds as the plot unfolds. **Plot** is a series of related events in a literary work. These events are organized around a *conflict* or problem, build to a *climax*, or point at which the conflict must be resolved, and finally result in a *resolution* of the conflict. As you read "The Monkey's Paw," note how each event leads to the next and how suspense mounts. The diagram below indicates plot elements.

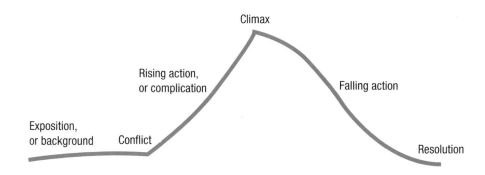

Writer's Notebook

Wishes Come in Threes Imagine you have found a magic lamp. You rub it to check its power, and WHOOSH—out comes a genie. Like most genies, this one offers you the chance to make three wishes that must be granted. What will you wish? In your notebook, write down three wishes you would want fulfilled, and explain your reasons for asking for each wish. Would you use all three wishes? Why or why not?

THE MONKEY'S PAW

W. W. Jacobs

Without, the night was cold and wet, but in the small parlor of Laburnam Villa the blinds were drawn and the fire burned brightly. Father and son were at chess, the former, who possessed ideas about the game involving radical changes, putting his king into such sharp and unnecessary perils that it even provoked comment from the white-haired old lady knitting placidly by the fire.

"Hark at the wind," said Mr. White, who, having seen a fatal mistake after it was too late, was amiably desirous of preventing his son from seeing it.

"I'm listening," said the latter, grimly surveying the board as he stretched out his hand. "Check."[1] " I should hardly think that he'd come

---

1. **check,** a call made by a chess player to warn an opponent that the opponent's king piece is in danger and must be moved. When a chess player makes the winning move that will capture the opponent's king, he or she calls "Checkmate" or "Mate."

tonight," said his father, with his hand poised over the board.

"Mate," replied the son.

"That's the worst of living so far out," bawled Mr. White, with sudden and unlooked-for violence; "of all the beastly, slushy, out-of-the-way places to live in, this is the worst. Pathway's a bog, and the road's a torrent. I don't know what people are thinking about. I suppose because only two houses in the road are let, they think it doesn't matter."

"Never mind, dear," said his wife soothingly; "perhaps you'll win the next one."

Mr. White looked up sharply, just in time to intercept a knowing glance between mother and son. The words died away on his lips, and he hid a guilty grin in his thin gray beard.

"There he is," said Herbert White, as the gate banged to loudly and heavy footsteps came toward the door.

The old man rose with hospitable haste, and opening the door, was heard condoling with the new arrival. The new arrival also condoled with himself, so that Mrs. White said, "Tut, tut!" and coughed gently as her husband entered the room, followed by a tall burly man, beady of eye and rubicund[2] of visage.

"Sergeant-Major Morris," he said, introducing him.

The sergeant-major shook hands, and, taking the proffered seat by the fire, watched contentedly while his host got out whiskey and tumblers and stood a small copper kettle on the fire.

At the third glass his eyes got brighter, and he began to talk, the little family circle regarding with eager interest this visitor from distant parts, as he squared his broad shoulders in the chair and spoke of wild scenes and doughty deeds, of wars, and plagues and strange peoples.

"Twenty-one years of it," said Mr. White, nodding at his wife and son. "When he went away he was a slip of a youth in the warehouse. Now look at him."

"He don't look to have taken much harm," said Mrs. White politely.

"I'd like to go to India myself," said the old man, "just to look round a bit, you know."

"Better where you are," said the sergeant-major, shaking his head. He put down the empty glass and, sighing softly, shook it again.

"I should like to see those old temples and fakirs and jugglers," said the old man. "What was that you started telling me the other day about a monkey's paw or something, Morris?"

"Nothing," said the soldier hastily. "Leastways, nothing worth hearing."

"Monkey's paw?" said Mrs. White curiously.

"Well, it's just a bit of what you might call magic, perhaps," said the sergeant-major offhandedly.

His three listeners leaned forward eagerly. The visitor absent-mindedly put his empty glass to his lips and then set it down again. His host filled it for him.

"To look at," said the sergeant-major, fumbling in his pocket, "it's just an ordinary little paw, dried to a mummy."

He took something out of his pocket and prof-

---

2. **rubicund** (rü′bə kund), *adj.* reddish; ruddy.

▲ Sir William Schwenk Gilbert (1836–1911), painted here by Frank Holl, is best known for his
verse collaborations with Sir Arthur Sullivan on comic operas such as *HMS Pinafore* and
The Mikado. Explain whether or not this looks like a person who would believe in magic.

fered it. Mrs. White drew back with a <u>grimace</u>,[3] but her son, taking it, examined it curiously.

"And what is there special about it?" inquired Mr. White, as he took it from his son and, having examined it, placed it upon the table.

"It had a spell put on it by an old fakir," said the sergeant-major, "a very holy man. He wanted to show that fate ruled people's lives, and that those who interfered with it did so to their sorrow. He put a spell on it so that three separate men could each have three wishes from it."

His manner was so impressive that his hearers were conscious that their light laughter jarred somewhat.

"Well, why don't you have three, sir?" said Herbert White cleverly.

The soldier regarded him in the way that

---

3. **grimace** (grə mās′, grim′is), *n.* a twisting of the face; ugly or funny smile.

middle age is wont to regard presumptuous youth. "I have," he said quietly, and his blotchy face whitened.

"And did you really have the three wishes granted?" asked Mrs. White.

"I did," said the sergeant-major, and his glass tapped against his strong teeth.

"And has anybody else wished?" persisted the old lady.

"The first man had his three wishes, yes," was the reply. "I don't know what the first two were, but the third was for death. That's how I got the paw."

His tones were so grave that a hush fell upon the group.

"If you've had your three wishes, it's no good to you now, then, Morris," said the old man at last. "What do you keep it for?"

The soldier shook his head. "Fancy, I suppose," he said slowly. "I did have some idea of selling it, but I don't think I will. It has caused enough mischief already. Besides, people won't buy. They think it's a fairy tale, some of them, and those who do think anything of it want to try it first and pay me afterward."

"If you could have another three wishes," said the old man, eyeing him keenly, "would you have them?"

"I don't know," said the other. "I don't know."

He took the paw, and dangling it between his forefinger and thumb, suddenly threw it upon the fire. White, with a slight cry, stooped down and snatched it off.

"Better let it burn," said the soldier solemnly.

"If you don't want it, Morris," said the other, "give it to me."

"I won't," said his friend doggedly.[4] "I threw it on the fire. If you keep it, don't blame me for what happens. Pitch it on the fire again, like a sensible man."

The other shook his head and examined his new possession closely. "How do you do it?" he inquired.

"Hold it up in your right hand and wish aloud," said the sergeant-major, "but I warn you of the consequences."

"Sounds like the *Arabian Nights*,"[5] said Mrs. White, as she rose and began to set the supper.

PITCH IT ON THE FIRE AGAIN, LIKE A SENSIBLE MAN.

"Don't you think you might wish for four pairs of hands for me?"

Her husband drew the <u>talisman</u>[6] from his pocket and then all three burst into laughter as the sergeant-major, with a look of alarm on his face, caught him by the arm.

"If you must wish," he said gruffly, "wish for something sensible."

Mr. White dropped it back into his pocket, and placing chairs, motioned his friend to the table. In the business of supper the talisman was partly forgotten, and afterward the three sat listening in an enthralled fashion to a second installment of the soldier's adventures in India.

"If the tale about the monkey's paw is not more truthful than those he has been telling us," said Herbert, as the door closed behind their guest, just in time for him to catch the last train, "we shan't make much out of it."

"Did you give him anything for it, Father?" inquired Mrs. White, regarding her husband closely.

"A trifle," said he, coloring slightly. "He didn't want it, but I made him take it. And he pressed me again to throw it away."

"Likely," said Herbert, with pretended horror. "Why, we're going to be rich, and famous,

---

4. **doggedly** (dô′gid lē), *adv.* not giving up; stubborn.
5. ***Arabian Nights,*** a collection of old tales from Arabia, Persia, and India, dating from the 900s.
6. **talisman** (tal′i smən, tal′iz mən), *n.* stone, ring, etc., engraved with figures or characters supposed to have magic power; charm.

and happy. Wish to be an emperor, Father, to begin with; then you can't be henpecked."

He darted round the table, pursued by the maligned[7] Mrs. White armed with an antimacassar.[8]

Mr. White took the paw from his pocket and eyed it dubiously. "I don't know what to wish for, and that's a fact," he said slowly. "It seems to me I've got all I want."

"If you only cleared the house,[9] you'd be quite happy, wouldn't you?" said Herbert, with his hand on his shoulder. "Well, wish for two hundred pounds,[10] then; that'll just do it."

His father, smiling shamefacedly at his own credulity, held up the talisman, as his son, with a solemn face somewhat marred by a wink at his mother, sat down at the piano and struck a few impressive chords.

"I wish for two hundred pounds," said the old man distinctly.

A fine crash from the piano greeted the words, interrupted by a shuddering cry from the old man. His wife and son ran toward him.

"It moved," he cried; with a glance of disgust at the object as it lay on the floor. "As I wished, it twisted in my hands like a snake."

"Well, I don't see the money," said his son, as he picked it up and placed it on the table, "and I bet I never shall."

"It must have been your fancy, Father," said his wife, regarding him anxiously.

He shook his head. "Never mind, though; there's no harm done, but it gave me a shock all the same."

They sat down by the fire again while the two men finished their pipes. Outside, the wind was higher than ever, and the old man started nervously at the sound of a door banging upstairs. A silence unusual and depressing settled upon all three, which lasted until the old couple rose to retire for the night.

"I expect you'll find the cash tied up in a big bag in the middle of your bed," said Herbert, as he bade them good night, "and something horrible squatting up on top of the wardrobe watching you as you pocket your ill-gotten gains."

He sat alone in the darkness, gazing at the dying fire, and seeing faces in it. The last face was so horrible and so simian that he gazed at it in amazement. It got so vivid that, with a little uneasy laugh, he felt on the table for a glass containing a little water to throw over it. His hand grasped the monkey's paw, and with a little shiver he wiped his hand on his coat and went up to bed.

In the brightness of the wintry sun next morning as it streamed over the breakfast table, Herbert laughed at his fears. There was an air of prosaic wholesomeness about the room which it had lacked on the previous night, and the dirty, shriveled little paw was pitched on the sideboard with a carelessness which betokened no great belief in its virtues.

"I suppose all old soldiers are the same," said Mrs. White. "The idea of our listening to such nonsense! How could wishes be granted in these days? And if they could, how could two hundred pounds hurt you, Father?"

"Might drop on his head from the sky," said the frivolous Herbert.

"Morris said the things happened so naturally," said his father, "that you might if you so wished attribute it to coincidence."

"Well, don't break into the money before I come back," said Herbert as he rose from the table. "I'm afraid it'll turn you into a mean, avaricious[11] man, and we shall have to disown you."

His mother laughed, and following him to

---

7. **maligned** (mä līnd′), *adj.* spoken against; slandered.
8. **antimacassar** (an′ti mə kas′ər), *n.* a small covering to protect the back or arms of a chair, sofa, etc., against soiling.
9. **cleared the house,** paid the debt that was still owed on the purchase of a house.
10. **two hundred pounds.** At the time of the story, this amount in British money was worth about one thousand American dollars.
11. **avaricious** (av′ə rish′əs), *adj.* greedy for wealth.

the door, watched him down the road, and returning to the breakfast table, was very happy at the expense of her husband's credulity. All of which did not prevent her from scurrying to the door at the postman's knock, nor prevent her from referring somewhat shortly to retired sergeant-majors of bibulous habits when she found that the post brought a tailor's bill.

"Herbert will have some more of his funny remarks, I expect, when he comes home," she said as they sat at dinner.

"I dare say," said Mr. White, pouring himself out some beer; "but for all that, the thing moved in my hand; that I'll swear to."

"You thought it did," said the old lady soothingly.

"I say it did," replied the other. "There was no thought about it; I had just—What's the matter?"

His wife made no reply. She was watching the mysterious movements of a man outside, who, peering in an undecided fashion at the house, appeared to be trying to make up his mind to enter. In mental connection with the two hundred pounds, she noticed that the stranger was well dressed and wore a silk hat of glossy newness. Three times he paused at the gate and then walked on again. The fourth time he stood with his hand upon it, and then with sudden resolution flung it open and walked up the path. Mrs. White at the same moment placed her hands behind her and hurriedly unfastening the strings of her apron, put that useful article of apparel beneath the cushion of her chair.

She brought the stranger, who seemed ill at ease, into the room. He gazed at her furtively, and listened in a preoccupied fashion as the old lady apologized for the appearance of the room, and her husband's coat, a garment which he usually reserved for the garden. She then waited as patiently as her sex would permit for him to broach his business, but he was at first strangely silent.

"I—was asked to call," he said at last, and stooped and picked a piece of cotton from his trousers. "I come from Maw and Meggins."

The old lady started. "Is anything the matter?" she asked breathlessly. "Has anything happened to Herbert? What is it? What is it?"

Her husband interposed. "There, there, Mother," he said hastily. "Sit down, and don't jump to conclusions. You've not brought bad news, I'm sure, sir," and he eyed the other wistfully.

"I'm sorry—" began the visitor.

"Is he hurt?" demanded the mother wildly.

The visitor bowed in assent. "Badly hurt," he said quietly, "but he is not in any pain."

"Oh, thank God!" said the old woman, clasping her hands. "Thank God for that! Thank—"

She broke off suddenly as the sinister meaning of the assurance dawned upon her and she saw the awful confirmation of her fears in the other's averted face. She caught her breath, and turning to her slower-witted husband, laid her trembling old hand upon his. There was a long silence.

"He was caught in the machinery," said the visitor at length, in a low voice.

"Caught in the machinery," repeated Mr. White, in a dazed fashion, "yes."

He sat staring blankly out at the window, and taking his wife's hand between his own, pressed it as he had been wont to do in their old courting days nearly forty years before.

"He was the only one left to us," he said, turning gently to the visitor. "It is hard."

The other coughed, and rising, walked slowly to the window. "The firm wished me to convey their sincere sympathy with you in your great loss," he said, without looking round. "I beg that you will understand I am only their servant and merely obeying orders."

There was no reply; the old woman's face was white, her eyes staring, and her breath inaudible; on the husband's face was a look such as his friend the sergeant might have carried into his first action.

"I was to say that Maw and Meggins disclaim all responsibility," continued the other. "They admit no liability at all, but in consideration of your son's services they wish to present you with a certain sum as compensation."

Mr. White dropped his wife's hand, and rising to his feet, gazed with a look of horror at his visitor. His dry lips shaped the words, "How much?"

"Two hundred pounds," was the answer.

Unconscious of his wife's shriek, the old man smiled faintly, put out his hands like a sightless man, and dropped, a senseless heap, to the floor.

In the huge new cemetery, some two miles distant, the old people buried their dead, and came back to a house steeped in shadow and silence. It was all over so quickly that at first they could hardly realize it and remained in a state of expectation as though of something else to happen—something else which was to lighten this load, too heavy for old hearts to bear.

But the days passed, and expectation gave place to resignation—the hopeless resignation of the old, sometimes miscalled apathy. Sometimes they hardly exchanged a word, for now they had nothing to talk about, and their days were long to weariness.

It was about a week after that the old man, waking suddenly in the night, stretched out his hand and found himself alone. The room was in darkness, and the sound of subdued weeping came from the window. He raised himself in bed and listened.

"Come back," he said tenderly. "You will be cold."

"It is colder for my son," said the old woman and wept afresh.

The sound of her sobs died away on his ears. The bed was warm, and his eyes heavy with sleep. He dozed fitfully, and then slept until a sudden wild cry from his wife awoke him with a start.

"The paw!" she cried wildly. "The monkey's paw!"

He started up in alarm. "Where? Where is it? What's the matter?"

She came stumbling across the room toward him. "I want it," she said quietly. "You've not destroyed it?"

"It's in the parlor, on the bracket," he replied, marveling. "Why?"

She cried and laughed together, and bending over, kissed his cheek.

"I only just thought of it," she said hysterically. "Why didn't I think of it before? Why didn't *you* think of it?"

"Think of what?" he questioned.

"The other two wishes," she replied rapidly. "We've only had one."

"Was not that enough?" he demanded fiercely.

"No," she cried triumphantly; "we'll have one more. Go down and get it quickly, and wish our boy alive again."

The man sat up in bed and flung the bedclothes from his quaking limbs. "Good God! You are mad!" he cried, aghast.

"Get it," she panted; "get it quickly, and wish—Oh my boy, my boy!"

Her husband struck a match and lit the candle. "Get back to bed," he said unsteadily. "You don't know what you are saying."

"We had the first wish granted," said the old woman feverishly; "why not the second?"

"A coincidence," stammered the old man.

"Go and get it and wish," cried his wife, quivering with excitement.

The old man turned and regarded her, and his voice shook. "He has been dead ten days, and besides he—I would not tell you else, but—I could only recognize him by his clothing. If he was too terrible for you to see then, how now?"

"Bring him back," cried the old woman, and dragged him toward the door. "Do you think I fear the child I have nursed?"

He went down in the darkness, and felt his way to the parlor, and then to the mantelpiece. The talisman was in its place, and a horrible

This illustration by Maurice Griffenhagen accompanied "The Monkey's Paw" when *Harper's* magazine published the story in 1902. What details in the illustration reinforce the mood in the story?

fear that the unspoken wish might bring his mutilated[12] son before him ere he could escape from the room seized upon him, and he caught his breath as he found that he had lost the direction of the door. His brow cold with sweat, he felt his way round the table, and groped along the wall until he found himself in the small passage with the unwholesome thing in his hand.

Even his wife's face seemed changed as he entered the room. It was white and expectant, and to his fears seemed to have an unnatural look upon it. He was afraid of her.

"*Wish!*" she cried, in a strong voice.

"It is foolish and wicked," he faltered.

"*Wish!*" repeated his wife.

He raised his hand, "I wish my son alive again."

The talisman fell to the floor, and he

---

12. **mutilated** (myŭ′tl ā′təd), *adj.* cut, torn, or broken off a limb or other important part of; maimed.

regarded it fearfully. Then he sank trembling into a chair as the old woman, with burning eyes, walked to the window and raised the blind.

He sat until he was chilled with the cold, glancing occasionally at the figure of the old woman peering through the window. The candle end, which had burned below the rim of the china candlestick, was throwing pulsating shadows on the ceiling and walls, until, with a flicker larger than the rest, it expired. The old man, with an unspeakable sense of relief at the failure of the talisman, crept back to his bed, and a minute or two afterward the old woman came silently and apathetically beside him.

Neither spoke, but both lay silently listening to the ticking of the clock. A stair creaked, and a squeaky mouse scurried noisily through the wall. The darkness was oppressive, and after lying for some time screwing up his courage, he took the box of matches and striking one went downstairs for a candle.

At the foot of the stairs the match went out, and he paused to strike another, and at the same moment a knock, so quiet and stealthy as to be scarcely audible,[13] sounded on the front door.

The matches fell from his hand and spilled in the passage. He stood motionless, his breath suspended until the knock was repeated. Then he turned and fled swiftly back to his room and closed the door behind him. A third knock sounded through the house.

"What's that?" cried the old woman, starting up.

"A rat," said the old man, in shaking tones—"a rat. It passed me on the stairs."

His wife sat up in bed listening. A loud knock resounded through the house.

"It's Herbert!" she screamed. "It's Herbert!"

She ran to the door, but her husband was before her, and catching her by the arm, held her tightly.

"What are you going to do?" he whispered hoarsely.

"It's my boy; it's Herbert!" she cried, struggling mechanically. "I forgot it was two miles away. What are you holding me for? Let go. I must open the door."

"For God's sake don't let it in," cried the old man, trembling.

"You're afraid of your own son," she cried, struggling. "Let me go. I'm coming, Herbert; I'm coming."

There was another knock, and another. The old woman with a sudden wrench broke free and ran from the room. Her husband followed to the landing, and called after her appealingly as she hurried downstairs. He heard the chain rattle back and the bottom bolt drawn slowly and stiffly from the socket. Then the old woman's voice, strained and panting.

"The bolt," she cried loudly. "Come down. I can't reach it."

But her husband was on his hands and knees groping wildly on the floor in search of the paw. If he could only find it before the thing outside got in. A perfect fusillade of knocks reverberated[14] through the house, and he heard the scraping of a chair as his wife put it down in the passage against the door. He heard the creaking of the bolt as it came slowly back, and at the same moment he found the monkey's paw and frantically breathed his third and last wish.

The knocking ceased suddenly, although the echoes of it were still in the house. He heard the chair drawn back and the door opened. A cold wind rushed up the staircase, and a long loud wail of disappointment and misery from his wife gave him courage to run down to her side, and then to the gate beyond. The street lamp flickering opposite shone on a quiet and deserted road.

---

13. **audible** (ô′də bəl), *adj.* that can be heard; loud enough to be heard.
14. **reverberate** (ri vėr′bər āt′), *v.* echo back.

After Reading

Making Connections

Shaping Your Response

1. Would you recommend "The Monkey's Paw" to a friend to read? Why or why not?

2. What do you think is Mr. White's third wish? Why do you think he makes it?

3. To what degree, if any, do you think that the Whites are responsible for the tragedy that occurs? Explain.

Analyzing the Story

4. Contrast the **setting** outside the Whites' home with the scene in the living room before the sergeant-major's arrival.

5. What does Mr. White's way of playing chess show you about his **character**?

6. What do you think is more important in this story—**characterization** or **plot**?

7. What are some ways the author builds **suspense** in this story?

Extending the Ideas

8. What stories do you know that are built on the idea that fate, rather than free will determines the outcome of events? Would you prefer to believe that you control your own destiny or that fate controls your life? Explain.

Literary Focus: Plot

A series of related events that present and resolve a conflict is a story's **plot**. Conflicts that pit characters against each other, against nature, or against the forces of society are called *external conflicts*. Conflicts within the character such as struggles between duty and desire or between opposing emotions are called *internal conflicts*. Both internal and external conflicts occur in most stories.

- Identify two conflicts in the story.
- Draw an events chain to show four events that connect with those below.

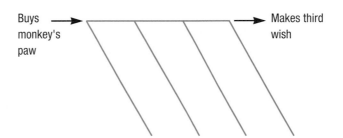

Buys monkey's paw ⟶   ⟶ Makes third wish

Vocabulary Study

On your paper, match each numbered word with the letter of its definition.

antimacassar
audible
avaricious
doggedly
grimace
maligned
mutilated
reverberate
rubicund
talisman

1. rubicund
2. antimacassar
3. avaricious
4. reverberate
5. doggedly
6. maligned
7. talisman
8. audible
9. mutilated
10. grimace

a. loud enough to be heard
b. maimed
c. echo back
d. reddish
e. a twisting of the face
f. spoken against
g. a charm
h. covering for furniture
i. greedy
j. stubbornly

Expressing Your Ideas

Writing Choices

Writer's Notebook Update Go back to your notebook and look at the wishes you wrote. Based on the outcome of the story, will you leave the wishes as written or rewrite them? Explain your thinking. Then rewrite any wishes that could be phrased in a "safer" way.

Who's That Knocking on My Door? Like other readers, you may have been disappointed not to find out who or what was outside the door. Think of a way to let the reader know these details without reducing the effectiveness of the story. Add a **new ending**, trying to maintain the level of suspense.

Fate and the Fakir The fakir who put the spell on the monkey's paw "wanted to show that fate ruled people's lives." Pretend that you are Mr. White and write a letter to Morris explaining whether the monkey's paw proved or disproved the fakir's belief.

Other Options

Put on Your Lawsuit The Whites have sued Sergeant-Major Morris for having given them the monkey's paw. Reenact a **trial** with one group representing the defense and another, the prosecution. Work up your respective cases, listing questions and anticipating questions that the other side might ask. One classmate can be Morris on trial, and another classmate can be the judge. After the case has been presented, let the rest of the class serve as jury to decide a verdict.

You As Art Critic With a partner, study the pictures that accompany this story. Ask yourselves questions about the mood and the images conveyed. Then present an **art talk** in which you describe the pictures and recommend whether or not you would keep the pictures that appear with this story or suggest new artwork.

Before Reading

The Demon Lover

by Elizabeth Bowen   Ireland

Elizabeth Bowen
1899–1973

Elizabeth Bowen's fiction focuses on themes such as growing up, social pretensions, and coping in a war-torn society. Born in Dublin, Ireland, into an upper-class Anglo-Irish family, she began to write while a teenager. In 1923, she published her first collection of stories. As her reputation grew, she became a popular hostess of the London literary world, entertaining even during nightly air raids in World War II. Dedicated to the war effort, Bowen worked for the Ministry of Information and as an air-raid warden. In 1945, she published *The Demon Lover*, a collection of stories that started as a "diary" of her reactions to the war.

Building Background

War Nerves Life in London during World War II was anything but normal. Gas masks and wailing air-raid sirens were commonplace. Driving during the blackout at night was extremely hazardous because road signs had been removed to confuse potential invaders. People's nerves were frayed in anticipation of bombing or invasion. Elizabeth Bowen's stories set at this time penetrate the anxieties that resulted from these disturbing experiences. Use these details, along with the title and art in the story, to predict what "The Demon Lover" will be about.

Literary Focus

Flashback In a **flashback**, the action of a story is interrupted to show an episode that happened at an earlier time. A flashback can fill in years of chronological time. In "The Demon Lover," you will see how Elizabeth Bowen uses flashback to inform the reader of past events and to shed light on the main character. This information will help you evaluate Mrs. Drover and her behavior.

Writer's Notebook

What's Behind That Closed Door? Writer Stephen King observed that one of the scariest things in the world is what's behind the closed door. Do you agree that things you can't see are more frightening than those you can? Think about how details such as the slightly moving curtain, the small sound, and the empty room can convey a mood of terror and suspense. As you read "The Demon Lover," jot down words and phrases that you think contribute to a mood of horror.

The Demon Lover

Elizabeth Bowen

Toward the end of her day in London Mrs. Drover went round to her shut-up house to look for several things she wanted to take away. Some belonged to herself, some to her family, who were by now used to their country life. It was late August; it had been a steamy, showery day; at the moment the trees down the pavement glittered in an escape of humid yellow afternoon sun. Against the next batch of clouds, already piling up ink-dark, broken chimneys and parapets stood out. In her once familiar street, as in any unused channel, an unfamiliar queerness had silted up; a cat wove itself in and out of railings but no human eye watched Mrs. Drover's return. Shifting some parcels under her arm, she slowly forced round her latchkey in an unwilling lock, then gave the door, which had warped, a push with her knee. Dead air came out to meet her as she went in.

The staircase window having been boarded up, no light came down into the hall. But one door, she could just see, stood ajar, so she went quickly through into the room and unshuttered the big window in there. Now the prosaic[1] woman, looking about her, was more perplexed than she knew by everything that she saw, by traces of her long former habit of life—the yellow smoke stain up the white marble mantelpiece, the ring left by a vase on the top of the escritoire; the bruise in the wallpaper where, on the door being thrown open widely, the china handle had always hit the wall. The piano, having gone away to be stored, had left what looked like claw marks on its part of the parquet. Though not much dust had seeped in, each object wore a film of another kind; and, the only ventilation being the chimney, the whole drawing room smelled of the cold hearth. Mrs. Drover put down her parcels on the escritoire and left the room to proceed upstairs; the things she wanted were in a bedroom chest.

She had been anxious to see how the house was—the part-time caretaker she shared with some neighbors was away this week on his holiday, known to be not yet back. At the best of times he did not look in often, and she was never sure that she trusted him. There were some cracks in the structure, left by the last bombing,[2] on which she was anxious to keep an eye. Not that one could do anything—

A shaft of refracted[3] daylight now lay across the hall. She stopped dead and stared at the hall table—on this lay a letter addressed to her.

She thought first—then the caretaker *must* be back. All the same, who, seeing the house shuttered, would have dropped a letter in the box? It was not a circular, it was not a bill. And the post office redirected, to the address in the country, everything for her that came through the post. The caretaker (even if he *were* back) did not know she was due in London today—her call here had been planned to be a sur-

prise—so his negligence in the manner of this letter, leaving it to wait in the dusk and the dust, annoyed her. Annoyed, she picked up the letter which bore no stamp. But it cannot be important, or they would know. . . . She took the letter rapidly upstairs with her, without a stop to look at the writing till she reached what had been her bedroom, where she let in light. The room looked over the garden and other gardens; the sun had gone in; as the clouds sharpened and lowered, the trees and rank lawns seemed already to smoke with dark. Her reluctance to look again at the letter came from the fact that she felt intruded upon—and by someone contemptuous of her ways. However, in the tenseness preceding the fall of rain she read it; it was a few lines.

Dear Kathleen,

You will not have forgotten that today is our anniversary, and the day we said. The years have gone by at once slowly and fast. In view of the fact that nothing has changed, I shall rely upon you to keep your promise. I was sorry to see you leave London, but was satisfied that you would be back in time. You may expect me, therefore, at the hour arranged.

Until then . . .
K.

Mrs. Drover looked for the date; it was today's. She dropped the letter onto the bedsprings, then picked it up to see the writing again—her lips, beneath the remains of lipstick, beginning to go white. She felt so much the change in her own face that she went to the mirror, polished a clear patch in it and looked at once urgently and stealthily in. She was confronted by a woman of forty-four, with

---

1. **prosaic** (prō zā′ik), *adj.* ordinary; not exciting.
2. **the last bombing.** The city of London was subjected to aerial bombardment many times during World War II, the time setting of the story.
3. **refracted** (ri frak′təd), *adj.* bent (a ray of light, waves, etc.) from a straight course.

eyes staring out under a hat brim that had been rather carelessly pulled down. She had not put on any more powder since she left the shop where she ate her solitary tea. The pearls her husband had given her on their marriage hung loose round her now rather thinner throat, slipping into the V of the pink wool jumper her sister knitted last autumn as they sat round the fire. Mrs. Drover's most normal expression was one of controlled worry, but of assent. Since the birth of the third of her little boys, attended by a quite serious illness, she had had an intermittent muscular flicker to the left of her mouth, but in spite of this she could always sustain a manner that was at once energetic and calm.

Turning from her own face as precipitately[4] as she had gone to meet it, she went to the chest where the things were, unlocked it, threw up the lid, and knelt to search. But as rain began to come crashing down she could not keep from looking over her shoulder at the stripped bed on which the letter lay. Behind the blanket of rain the clock of the church that still stood struck six—with rapidly heightening apprehension she counted each of the slow strokes, "The hour arranged . . . My God," she said, "*what* hour? How should I . . . ? After twenty-five years, . . ."

The young girl talking to the soldier in the garden had not ever completely seen his face. It was dark; they were saying good-by under a tree. Now and then—for it felt, from not seeing him at this intense moment, as though she had never seen him at all—she verified his presence for these few moments longer by putting out a hand, which he each time pressed, without very much kindness, and painfully, onto one of the breast buttons of his uniform. That cut of the button on the palm of her hand was, principally, what she was to carry away. This was so near the end of a leave from France that she could only wish him already gone. It was August, 1916.[5] Being not kissed, being drawn away from and looked at intimidated Kathleen till she imagined spectral glitters in the place of his eyes. Turning away, and

looking back up the lawn she saw, through branches of trees, the drawing-room window alight; she caught a breath for the moment when she could go running back there into the safe arms of her mother and sister, and cry: "What shall I do, what shall I do? He has gone."

Hearing her catch her breath, her fiancé said, without feeling, "Cold?"

"You're going away such a long way."

"Not so far as you think."

"I don't understand."

"You don't have to," he said. "You will. You know what we said."

"But that was—suppose you—I mean, suppose."

"I shall be with you," he said, "sooner or later. You won't forget that. You need do nothing but wait."

Only a little more than a minute later she was free to run up the silent lawn. Looking in through the window at her mother and sister, who did not for the moment perceive her, she already felt that unnatural promise drive down between her and the rest of all humankind. No other way of having given herself could have made her feel so apart, lost and foresworn. She could not have plighted[6] a more sinister troth.

Kathleen behaved well when, some months later, her fiancé was reported missing, presumed killed. Her family not only supported her but were able to praise her courage without stint because they could not regret, as a husband for her, the man they knew almost nothing about. They hoped she would, in a year or two, console herself—and had it been only a question of consolation things might have gone

---

4. **precipitately** (pri sip′ə tit′lē), *adv.* very hurriedly; suddenly.
5. **August, 1916,** a month during World War I, fought largely in Europe from 1914 to 1918.
6. **plight** (plīt), *v.* promise solemnly; pledge (as in marriage).

much straighter ahead. But her trouble, behind just a little grief, was a complete dislocation from everything. She did not reject other lovers, for these failed to appear; for years she failed to attract men—and with the approach of her thirties she became natural enough to share her family's anxiousness on this score. She began to put herself out, to wonder; and at thirty-two she was very greatly relieved to find herself being courted by William Drover. She married him, and the two of them settled down in this quiet, arboreal part of Kensington;[7] in this house the years piled up, her children were born and they all lived till they were driven out by the bombs of the next war. Her movements as Mrs. Drover were circumscribed, and she dismissed any idea that they were still watched.

As things were—dead or living, the letter writer sent her only a threat. Unable, for some minutes, to go on kneeling with her back exposed to the empty room, Mrs. Drover rose from the chest to sit on an upright chair whose back was firmly against the wall. The desuetude[8] of her former bedroom, her married London home's whole air of being a cracked cup from which memory, with its reassuring power, had either evaporated or leaked away, made a crisis—and at just this crisis the letter writer had, knowledgeably, struck. The hollowness of the house this evening canceled years on years of voices, habits, and steps. Through the shut windows she only heard rain fall on the roofs around. To rally herself, she said she was in a mood—and, for two or three seconds shutting her eyes, told herself that she had imagined the letter. But she opened them—there it lay on the bed.

On the supernatural side of the letter's entrance she was not permitting her mind to dwell. Who, in London, knew she meant to call at the house today? Evidently, however, this had

been known. The caretaker, *had* he come back, had had no cause to expect her: he would have taken the letter in his pocket, to forward it, at his own time, through the post. There was no other sign that the caretaker had been in—but if not? Letters dropped in at doors of deserted houses do not fly or walk to tables in halls. They do not sit on the dust of empty tables with the air of certainty that they will be found. There is needed some human hand—but nobody but the caretaker had a key. Under circumstances she did not care to consider, a house can be entered without a key. It was possible that she was not alone now. She might be waited for, downstairs. Waited for—until when? Until "the hour arranged." At least that was not six o'clock; six had struck.

She rose from the chair and went over and locked the door.

The thing was, to get out. To fly? No, not that: she had to catch her train. As a woman whose utter dependability was the keystone of her family life, she was not willing to return to the country, to her husband, her little boys and her sister, without the objects she had come to fetch.

Resuming work at the chest she set about making up a number of parcels in a rapid, fumbling-decisive way. These, with her shopping parcels, would be too much to carry; these meant a taxi—at the thought of the taxi her heart went up and her normal breathing resumed. I will ring up the taxi now; the taxi cannot come too soon: I shall hear the taxi out there running its engine, till I walk calmly down to it through the hall. I'll ring up—But no: the telephone is cut off. . . . She tugged at a knot she had tied wrong.

---

7. **Kensington,** a residential district in London.
8. **desuetude** (des′wə tüd), *n.* disuse.

The idea of flight . . . He was never kind to me, not really. I don't remember him kind at all. Mother said he never considered me. He was set on me, that was what it was—not love. Not love, not meaning a person well. What did he do, to make me promise like that? I can't remember— But she found that she could.

She remembered with such dreadful acuteness that the twenty-five years since then dissolved like smoke and she instinctively looked for the weal left by the button on the palm of her hand. She remembered not only all that he said and did, but the complete suspension of *her* existence during that August week. I was not myself—they all told me so at the time. She remembered—but with one white burning blank as where acid has been dropped on a photograph; *under no conditions* could she remember his face.

So, wherever he may be waiting I shall not know him. You have no time to run from a face you do not expect.

The thing was to get to the taxi before any clock struck what could be the hour. She would slip down the street and round the side of the square to where the square gave on the main road. She would return in the taxi, safe, to her own door, and bring the solid driver into the house with her to pick up the parcels from room to room. The idea of the taxi driver made her decisive, bold; she unlocked the door, went to the top of the staircase, and listened down.

She heard nothing—but while she was hearing nothing the *passé*[9] air of the staircase was disturbed by a draft that traveled up to her face. It emanated[10] from the basement; down there a door or window was being opened by someone who chose this moment to leave the house.

The rain had stopped; the pavements steamily shone as Mrs. Drover let herself out by inches from her own front door into the empty street. The unoccupied houses opposite continued to meet her look with their damaged stare. Making toward the thoroughfare and the taxi, she tried not to keep looking behind. Indeed, the silence was so intense—one of those creeks of London silence exaggerated this summer by the damage of war—that no tread could have gained on hers unheard. Where her street debouched on the square where people went on living she grew conscious of and checked her unnatural pace. Across the open end of the square two buses impassively passed each other; women, a perambulator, cyclists, a man wheeling a barrow signalized, once again, the ordinary flow of life.

At the square's most populous corner should be—and was—the short taxi rank.[11] This evening, only one taxi—but this, although it presented its blank rump, appeared already to be alertly waiting for her. Indeed, without looking round the driver started his engine as she panted up from behind and put her hand on the door. As she did so, the clock struck seven. The taxi faced the main road; to make the trip back to her house it would have to turn—and she settled back on the seat and the taxi *had* turned before she, surprised by its knowing movement, recollected that she had not "said where." She leaned forward to scratch at the glass panel that divided the driver's seat from her own.

The driver braked to what was almost a stop, turned round, and slid the glass panel back; the jolt of this flung Mrs. Drover forward till her face was almost into the glass. Through the aperture[12] driver and passenger, not six inches between them, remained for an eternity eye to eye. Mrs. Drover's mouth hung open for some seconds before she could issue her first scream. After that she continued to scream freely and to beat with her gloved hands on the glass all round as the taxi, accelerating without mercy, made off with her into the hinterland of deserted streets.

---

9. *passé* (pa sā′), *adj.* old, stale. [*French*]
10. **emanate** (em′ə nāt′), *v.* come forth; spread out.
11. **taxi rank**, a place for taxis to line up.
12. **aperture** (ap′ər chər), *n.* an opening; hole.

The Demon Lover   **83**

After Reading

Making Connections

Shaping Your Response

1. Do you think that Mrs. Drover might have imagined any of the events or details in this story? Explain your answer.

2. Think about the prediction you made before reading. How were the ideas similar to or different from the story?

3. In your opinion, is this a story about love, about war, or about something else? Explain.

4. What do you think happens to Mrs. Drover after the story ends?

Analyzing the Story

5. Draw a time line like the one below and add at least five events in the story **plot** that occur between the wars.

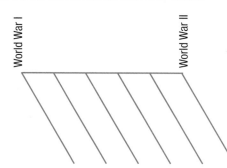

6. How would you describe the **mood** in the first two paragraphs of the story?

7. What details in the **setting** contribute to this mood?

Extending the Ideas

8. How can war affect the behavior and perspective of a **group**? In answering, consider information provided on page 77.

9. What similarities do you find between this story and "The Monkey's Paw"?

10. Why do you think people are so intrigued with elements of the supernatural in movies and books?

Literary Focus: Flashback

A **flashback** interrupts the time order of a story to present past events that shed light on current ones.

- What details in the flashback to 1916 suggest that Mrs. Drover was uncomfortable in her relationship with the young soldier?

- What information about her fiancé provides insights about his character? How does this information seem in keeping with the final scene?

Vocabulary Study

Use your Glossary, if necessary, to answer the following items.

aperture
emanate
passé
prosaic
refracted

1. The final syllable of *passé* rhymes with ____.

   a. see **b.** hay **c.** glass **d.** none of these

2. Which of the following could be *refracted*?

   a. food **b.** books **c.** light **d.** happiness

3. An *aperture* is a ____.

   a. lamp **b.** weather forecast **c.** hole **d.** bird

4. *Emanate* means to ____.

   a. spread out **b.** break **c.** lie **d.** ask

5. Someone who is *prosaic* is ____.

   a. thin **b.** odd **c.** forgetful **d.** ordinary

Expressing Your Ideas

Writing Choices

Writer's Notebook Update Compare the details you listed from the story with those of a classmate. Skim the story to find and list a few more details that establish the mood. You might use items from your list in the writing assignments that follow.

You, the Critic Do you think that this story should be interpreted in light of wartime stress and emptiness, or do you prefer to read it as simply a good ghost story that could have been set during any time period? Write a review for a literary magazine expressing your opinion.

Other Options

The Director's Chair Imagine that you are filming the end of this story. Reread the last three paragraphs. Then write **director's notes** to show how you would film this final scene (close-ups, distance shots, black/white or color), any special effects and sounds you would use, and what details you would emphasize (the clock, the street, Mrs. Drover's face, and so forth). You might want to review the article about critical viewing on pages 62–63 for ideas.

Eyewitness Reports As she enters the square near her house, Mrs. Drover notices buses, women, a baby carriage, cyclists, and a man pushing a wheelbarrow. You are a member of the police force looking into the disappearance of Mrs. Drover. Interview several people who saw her get into the taxi. In an **oral report**, identify these people, their whereabouts in the square, and any details they can provide.

Before Reading

An Astrologer's Day

by R. K. Narayan   India

R. K. Narayan
born 1906

R. K. Narayan (nä ri′yän), who once said, "Novels bore me but never people," eventually wrote his own novels that audiences have praised as anything but boring. Widely regarded as India's finest contemporary writer, Narayan often creates characters based on childhood memories of his grandmother's acquaintances, who dropped by to ask advice on subjects ranging from scorpion bites to marriage. Born in Madras, India, Narayan was an undistinguished student and taught briefly before becoming a writer. Many of his novels, which have been described as "concentrated miniatures of human experience," take place in the fictional town of Malgudi.

Building Background

What's in the Stars? Astrology is the study of how the stars, moon, sun, and planets influence life and events on earth. Some people believe that the heavenly bodies operate in patterns that reveal a person's character and future. Such people consult an astrologer, or a person who tells fortunes after studying the stars, before making important decisions. Astrologers learn about the influence of heavenly bodies by studying a horoscope, or birth chart, that shows the position of these bodies at the time of a person's birth.

Literary Focus

Dialogue A conversation that captures the exact words spoken between characters in a literary work is called **dialogue**. A writer often uses dialogue to give the reader information about the characters and to create mood. Dialogue can also help advance the plot and theme of a story. A great deal of background and information in "An Astrologer's Day" is related through dialogue.

Writer's Notebook

Our Stars or Ourselves?

> Men at some time are masters of their fates.
> The fault, dear Brutus, is not in our stars,
> But in ourselves, that we are underlings.

In these lines from Shakespeare's *Julius Caesar*, Cassius tells Brutus that people, not the stars, have the power to control their own lives. To what degree do you think you can control your destiny? To what degree do you think blind luck, fate, the stars, or other forces determine your destiny? Make a list of all the things that you think might determine what you'll be doing ten years from now. Circle those things over which you think you have some control.

An Astrologer's Day

R. K. Narayan

Punctually at midday he opened his bag and spread out his professional equipment, which consisted of a dozen cowrie shells, a square piece of cloth with obscure mystic charts on it, a notebook, and a bundle of palmyra writing. His forehead was resplendent[1] with sacred ash and vermilion, and his eyes sparkled with a sharp abnormal gleam which was really an outcome of a continual searching look for customers, but which his simple clients took to be a prophetic light and felt comforted. The power of his eyes was considerably enhanced[2] by their position—placed as they were between the painted forehead and the dark whiskers which streamed down his cheeks: even a half-wit's eyes would sparkle in such a setting. To crown the effect he wound a saffron-colored turban around his head. This color scheme never failed. People were attracted to him as bees are attracted to cosmos or

---

1. **resplendent** (ri splen′dənt), *adj.* very bright; splendid.
2. **enhance** (en hans′), *v.t.* add to; heighten.

dahlia stalks. He sat under the boughs of a spreading tamarind tree which flanked a path running through the Town Hall Park. It was a remarkable place in many ways: a surging crowd was always moving up and down this narrow road morning till night. A variety of trades and occupations was represented all along its way: medicine sellers, sellers of stolen hardware and junk, magicians, and above all, an auctioneer of cheap cloth, who created enough din all day to attract the whole town. Next to him in vociferousness[3] came a vendor of fried groundnut, who gave his ware a fancy name each day, calling it "Bombay Ice Cream" one day, and on the next "Delhi Almond," and on the third "Raja's Delicacy," and so on and so forth, and people flocked to him. A considerable portion of this crowd dallied before the astrologer too. The astrologer transacted his business by the light of a flare which crackled and smoked up above the groundnut heap nearby. Half the enchantment of the place was due to the fact that it did not have the benefit of municipal lighting. The place was lit up by shop lights. One or two had hissing gaslights, some had naked flares stuck on poles, some were lit up by old cycle lamps, and one or two, like the astrologer's, managed without lights of their own. It was a bewildering crisscross of light rays and moving shadows. This suited the astrologer very well, for the simple reason that he had not in the least intended to be an astrologer when he began life; and he knew no more of what was going to happen to others than he knew what was going to happen to himself next minute. He was as much a stranger to the stars as were his innocent customers. Yet he said things which pleased and astonished everyone: that was more a matter of study, practice, and shrewd[4] guesswork. All the same, it was as much an honest man's labor as

any other, and he deserved the wages he carried home at the end of the day.

He had left his village without any previous thought or plan. If he had continued there he would have carried on the work of his forefathers—namely, tilling the land, living, marrying, and ripening in his cornfield and ancestral home. But that was not to be. He had to leave home without telling anyone, and he could not rest till he left it behind a couple of hundred miles. To a villager it is a great deal, as if an ocean flowed between.

He had a working analysis of mankind's troubles: marriage, money, and the tangles of human ties. Long practice had sharpened his perception. Within five minutes he understood what was wrong. He charged three pice[5] per question, never opened his mouth till the other had spoken for at least ten minutes, which provided him enough stuff for a dozen answers and advices. When he told the person before him, gazing at his palm, "In many ways you are not getting the fullest results for your efforts," nine out of ten were disposed to agree with him. Or he questioned: "Is there any woman in your family, maybe even a distant relative, who is not well disposed towards you?" Or he gave an analysis of character: "Most of your troubles are due to your nature. How can you be otherwise with Saturn where he is? You have an impetuous[6] nature and a rough exterior." This endeared him to their hearts immediately, for even the mildest of us loves to think that he has a forbidding exterior.

The nuts vendor blew out his flare and rose to go home. This was a signal for the astrologer to bundle up too, since it left him in darkness

◄ This zodiac drawing of the western and eastern hemispheres accompanied a horoscope commissioned by an Indian monarch in 1840. What can you infer from this information and the picture itself about the status of astrology in Indian culture?

---

3. **vociferousness** (vō sif′ər əs nəs), *n.* noisiness; shouting.
4. **shrewd** (shrüd), *adj.* clever; keen.
5. **pice** (pīs), *n.* an Indian coin of small value. Three pice would be equal to little more than half a U.S. cent.
6. **impetuous** (im pech′ü əs), *adj.* rushing with force and violence.

except for a little shaft of green light which strayed in from somewhere and touched the ground before him. He picked up his cowrie shells and paraphernalia[7] and was putting them back into his bag when the green shaft of light was blotted out; he looked up and saw a man standing before him. He sensed a possible client and said: "You look so careworn. It will do you good to sit down for a while and chat with me." The other grumbled some reply vaguely. The astrologer pressed his invitation, whereupon the other thrust his palm under his nose, saying: "You call yourself an astrologer?" The astrologer felt challenged and said, tilting the other's palm towards the green shaft of light. "Yours is a nature. . ." "Oh stop that," the other said. "Tell me something worthwhile. . . ."

Our friend felt piqued.[8] "I charge only three pice per question, and what you get ought to be good enough for your money. . . ." At this the other withdrew his arm, took out an anna,[9] and flung it out to him saying: "I have some questions to ask. If I prove you are bluffing, you must return that anna to me with interest."

"If you find my answers satisfactory, will you give me five rupees?"[10]

"No."

"Or will you give me eight annas?"

"All right, provided you give me twice as much if you are wrong," said the stranger. This pact was accepted after a little further argument. The astrologer sent up a prayer to heaven as the other lit a cheroot. The astrologer caught a glimpse of his face by the matchlight. There was a pause as cars hooted on the road, *jutka*[11] drivers swore at their horses, and the babble of the crowd agitated the semidarkness of the park. The other sat down, sucking his cheroot, puffing out, sat there ruthlessly. The astrologer felt very uncomfortable. "Here, take your anna back. I am not used to such challenges. It is late for me today. . . ." He made preparations to bundle up. The other held his wrist and said: "You can't get out of it now. You dragged me in while I was passing." The astrologer shivered in his grip; and his voice shook and became faint. "Leave me today. I will speak to you tomorrow." The other thrust his palm in his face and said: "Challenge is challenge. Go on." The astrologer proceeded with his throat drying up: "There is a woman. . . ."

"Stop," said the other. "I don't want all that. Shall I succeed in my present search or not? Answer this and go. Otherwise I will not let you go till you disgorge all your coins." The astrologer muttered a few incantations and replied: "All right. I will speak. But will you give me a rupee if what I say is convincing? Otherwise I will not open my mouth, and you may do what you like." After a good deal of haggling[12] the other agreed. The astrologer said: "You were left for dead. Am I right?"

"Ah, tell me more."

"A knife has passed through you once?" said the astrologer.

"Good fellow!" He bared his chest to show the scar. "What else?"

"And then you were pushed into a well nearby in the field. You were left for dead."

"I should have been dead if some passer-by had not chanced to peep into the well," exclaimed the other, overwhelmed by enthusiasm.

"When shall I get at him?" he asked, clenching his fist.

"In the next world," answered the astrologer. "He died four months ago in a far-off town. You will never see any more of him."

---

7. **paraphernalia** (par′ə fər nā′lyə), *n.* personal belongings.
8. piqued (pēkd), *adj.* aroused; stirred up.
9. **anna** (an′ə), *n.* an Indian coin equal to four pice. Sixteen annas make one rupee.
10. **rupee** (rü pē′), *n.* Officially worth about thirteen U.S. cents, the rupee actually had about the same buying power in India as the dollar has in the U.S.
11. *jutka* (jüt′kə), *n.* a two-wheeled vehicle drawn by horse.
12. **haggling** (hag′ling), *n.* disputing, especially about a price or the terms of a bargain.

The other groaned on hearing it. The astrologer proceeded:

"Guru Nayak—"

"You know my name!" the other said, taken aback.

"As I know all other things. Guru Nayak, listen carefully to what I have to say. Your village is two days' journey due north of this town. Take the next train and be gone. I see once again great danger to your life if you go from home." He took out a pinch of sacred ash and held it to him. "Rub it on your forehead and go home. Never travel southward again, and you will live to be a hundred."

And then you were pushed into a well nearby in the field. You were left for dead.

"Why should I leave home again?" the other said reflectively. "I was only going away now and then to look for him and to choke out his life if I met him." He shook his head regretfully. "He has escaped my hands. I hope at least he died as he deserved."

"Yes," said the astrologer. "He was crushed under a lorry."[13] The other looked gratified to hear it.

The place was deserted by the time the astrologer picked up his articles and put them into his bag. The green shaft was also gone, leaving the place in darkness and silence. The stranger had gone off into the night, after giving the astrologer a handful of coins.

It was nearly midnight when the astrologer reached home. His wife was waiting for him at the door and demanded an explanation. He flung the coins at her and said: "Count them. One man gave all that."

"Twelve and a half annas," she said, counting. She was overjoyed. "I can buy some jaggery[14] and coconut tomorrow. The child has been asking for sweets for so many days now. I will prepare some nice stuff for her."

"The swine has cheated me! He promised me a rupee," said the astrologer. She looked up at him. "You look worried. What is wrong?"

"Nothing."

After dinner, sitting on the *pyol*,[15] he told her: "Do you know a great load is gone from me today? I thought I had the blood of a man on my hands all these years. That was the reason why I ran away from home, settled here, and married you. He is alive."

She gasped. "You tried to kill!"

"Yes, in our village, when I was a silly youngster. We drank, gambled, and quarreled badly one day—why think of it now? Time to sleep," he said, yawning, and stretched himself on the *pyol*.

---

13. **lorry** (lôr′ē), *n.* a long, flat, horse-drawn wagon without sides, set on four low wheels.
14. **jaggery** (jag′ə rē), *n.* a coarse, dark sugar made from the sap of certain palm trees.
15. *pyol* (pī′ôl), *n.* a low bench, often outdoors.

After Reading

Making Connections

Shaping Your Response

1. Would you like to have the astrologer for a friend? Why or why not?

2. How would you describe the astrologer's feelings at the end of the story?

3. Do you find this story instructive, merely entertaining, or something else? Explain.

Analyzing the Story

4. What **images** in the first paragraph help you picture the astrologer?

5. Can you **infer** why the client doesn't recognize the astrologer? Explain.

Extending the Ideas

6. How much faith would you put in an astrologer? Explain.

7. What other professions do you think require "study, practice, and shrewd guesswork"?

Literary Focus: Dialogue

The conversation between two or more people is called **dialogue**. Often dialogue in a story provides details that are crucial to the plot. Briefly recount previous events, revealed through dialogue, that enable the astrologer to give such an accurate "reading" to his client.

Vocabulary Study

On your paper, match the numbered word with the letter of its antonym.

**enhance
piqued
resplendent
shrewd
vociferousness**

1. resplendent
2. vociferousness
3. shrewd
4. enhance
5. piqued

a. lessen
b. dark; dull
c. stupid
d. calm
e. speechlessness

Expressing Your Ideas

Writing Choices

Writer's Notebook Update Examine your list and the items you circled. Then use this information to write a paragraph titled "Fate and My Future."

Astrologer for Hire The astrologer is describing the services he provides in a **classified ad**. Write the ad, complete with a catchy headline and fees you think would be appropriate in American money.

Magic or Science? Many scientists around the world denounce astrology as a great hoax consisting of nothing more than magic and superstition. Is there a scientific foundation for the belief that the forces of the stars and planets at the time of our birth can shape our futures? Do some research on astrology. Then explain your findings by writing a **science article** for readers of *Science Today*.

Sky Talk Research one of the constellations and the Greek myth that tells its story. Write a **summary** of this myth. Then tell the myth to the class.

Other Options

Starmobile Work with a group to make a **mobile** of the twelve astrological signs. Present the mobile to the rest of the class, explaining each figure and its historical or mythological significance.

Culture Note Compare astrological charts from various cultures. Explain what these charts reveal about both universal themes and specific **group** experiences.

▲ Asian lunar zodiac

Before Reading

The Masque of the Red Death

by Edgar Allan Poe   USA

Edgar Allan Poe
1809–1849

Orphaned at three, Edgar Allan Poe was raised by the wealthy Allan family, who disowned him when he decided to pursue a literary career. By 1836, when he married his thirteen-year-old cousin, Virginia Clemm, Poe was a troubled young man. Her death in 1847 plunged him deeper into despair and alcoholism. Although he eventually enjoyed fame, Poe died in poverty after he was found battered and drunk on the streets of Baltimore. His contemporaries held widely different opinions of his artistry (one dismissed him as a "jingle man"). Nevertheless, today Poe's contributions to literature are universally acknowledged.

Building Background

It's Epidemic! A dreaded epidemic disease, plague had been reported in biblical accounts. In the mid 1330s, a plague known as **The Black Death** swept across Asia and Europe, killing an estimated 40 million by 1400 in Europe alone. Spread by bacteria that live in rats and other rodents and transmitted to humans by fleas, plague can kill a victim in under five days. Although now curable by early treatment with antibiotics, it still occurs occasionally, especially in developing regions of Asia, Africa, and South America. Modern viruses, such as Ebola, which erupted in Zaire in 1976 and again in 1995, are plaguelike in their swift, deadly outbreaks.

Literary Focus

Mood Edgar Allan Poe carefully chose his words and descriptions to set the mood of his stories. **Mood** is the overall atmosphere or prevailing feeling within a work of art. Examine the web of words and phrases from the first paragraph of "The Masque of the Red Death." What feelings do the words stir in you?

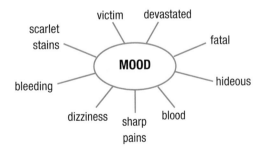

Writer's Notebook

Death Quotes Quickwrite your reactions to each of the following quotations about death.

"Death devours all lovely things. . . ."   *Edna St. Vincent Millay*

"O! death's a great disguiser."   *William Shakespeare*

"Pale Death kicks his way equally into the cottages of the poor and the castles of kings."   *Horace*

THE MASQUE OF THE RED DEATH

EDGAR ALLAN POE

he Red Death had long devastated the country. No pestilence had ever been so fatal, or so hideous. Blood was its Avatar[1] and its seal—the redness and the horror of blood. There were sharp pains, and sudden dizziness, and then profuse[2] bleeding at the pores, with dissolution. The scarlet stains upon the body and especially upon the face of the victim were the pest ban which shut him out from the aid and from the sympathy of his fellow men. And the whole seizure, progress, and termination of the disease were the incidents of half an hour.

But the Prince Prospero was happy and dauntless and sagacious.[3] When his dominions were half depopulated, he summoned to his presence a thousand hale and light-hearted friends from among the knights and dames of his court, and with these retired to the deep seclusion of one of his castellated[4] abbeys. This was an extensive and magnificent structure, the creation of the Prince's own eccentric yet august taste. A strong and lofty wall girdled it in. This wall had gates of iron. The courtiers, having entered, brought furnaces and massy hammers

---

1. **Avatar** (av′ə tär′), *n.* a sign or manifestation in bodily form; (in Hindu mythology) incarnation.
2. **profuse** (prə fyüs′), *adj.* very abundant.
3. **sagacious** (sə gā′shəs), *adj.* wise in a keen, practical way; shrewd.
4. **castellated** (kas′tl ā′tid), *adj.* built like a castle with turrets and battlements.

Like Poe's story, *The Burial of the Sardine* by Francisco Goya (1746–1828) mixes festive gaiety with gruesome horror. What effect do you think Poe and Goya intended by blending these opposing atmospheres? ➤

and welded the bolts. They resolved to leave means neither of ingress nor egress to the sudden impulses of despair or of frenzy from within. The abbey was amply provisioned. With such precautions the courtiers might bid defiance to contagion. The external world could take care of itself. In the meantime it was folly to grieve, or to think. The Prince had provided all the appliances of pleasure. There were buffoons, there were *improvisatori,*[5] there were ballet dancers, there were musicians, there was Beauty, there was wine. All these and security were within. Without was the Red Death.

It was toward the close of the fifth or sixth month of his seclusion, and while the pestilence raged most furiously abroad, that the Prince Prospero entertained his thousand friends at a masked ball of the most unusual magnificence.

It was a voluptuous[6] scene, that masquerade. But first let me tell of the rooms in which it was held. There were seven—an imperial suite. In many palaces, however, such suites form a long and straight vista, while the folding doors slide back nearly to the walls on either hand, so that the view of the whole extent is scarcely impeded. Here the case was very different, as might have been expected from the Prince's love of the bizarre. The apartments were so irregularly disposed that the vision embraced but little more than one at a time. There was a sharp turn at every twenty or thirty yards, and at each turn a novel effect. To the right and left, in the middle of each wall, a tall and narrow Gothic window looked out upon a closed corridor which pursued the windings of the suite. These windows were of stained glass whose color varied in accordance with the prevailing hue of the decorations of the chamber into which it opened. That at the eastern extremity was hung, for example, in blue—and vividly blue were its windows. The second chamber was purple in its ornaments and tapestries, and here the panes were purple. The third was green throughout, and so were the casements. The fourth was furnished and lighted with orange, the fifth with white, the sixth with violet. The seventh apartment was closely shrouded in black velvet tapestries that hung all over the ceiling and down the walls, falling in heavy folds upon a carpet of the same material and hue. But in this chamber only, the color of the windows failed to correspond with the decorations. The panes here were scarlet—a deep blood-color. Now in no one of the seven apartments was there any lamp or candelabrum, amid the profusion of golden ornaments that lay scattered to and fro or depended from the roof. There was no light of any kind emanating from lamp or candle within the suite of chambers. But in the corridors that followed the suite there stood, opposite to each window, a heavy tripod, bearing a brazier of fire, that projected its rays through the tinted glass and so glaringly illumined the room. And thus were produced a multitude of gaudy and fantastic appearances. But in the western or black chamber the effect of the firelight that streamed upon the dark hangings through the blood-tinted panes was ghastly in the extreme, and produced so wild a look upon the <u>countenances</u>[7] of those who entered that there were few of the company bold enough to set foot within its precincts at all.

CLARIFY: What do you know about the layout and lighting of these rooms?

It was in this apartment, also, that there stood against the western wall a gigantic clock of ebony. Its pendulum swung to and fro with a dull, heavy, monotonous clang; and when the

---

5. *improvisatori* (im′prō vē′zä tō′rē), *n. pl.* poets and singers of on-the-spot verses; performers who sing without rehearsal. [*Italian*]
6. **voluptuous** (və lup′chü əs), *adj.* giving pleasure to the senses.
7. countenance (koun′tə nəns), *n.* face.

minute hand made the circuit of the face, and the hour was to be stricken, there came from the brazen lungs of the clock a sound which was clear and loud and deep and exceedingly musical, but of so peculiar a note and emphasis that, at each lapse of an hour, the musicians of the orchestra were constrained to pause, momentarily, in their performance, to hearken to the sound; and thus the waltzers perforce ceased their evolutions; and there was a brief disconcert of the whole gay company; and, while the chimes of the clock yet rang, it was observed that the giddiest grew pale, and the more aged and sedate passed their hands over their brows as if in confused revery or meditation. But when the echoes had fully ceased, a light laughter at once pervaded the assembly; the musicians looked at each other and smiled as if at their own nervousness and folly, and made whispering vows, each to the other, that the next chiming of the clock should produce in them no similar emotion; and then, after the lapse of sixty minutes (which embrace three thousand and six hundred seconds of the Time that flies) there came yet another chiming of the clock, and then were the same disconcert and tremulousness and meditation as before.

But, in spite of these things, it was a gay and magnificent revel. The tastes of the Prince were peculiar. He had a fine eye for colors and effects. He disregarded the *decora*[8] of mere fashion. His plans were bold and fiery, and his conceptions glowed with barbaric luster. There are some who would have thought him mad. His followers felt that he was not. It was necessary to hear and see and touch him to be *sure* that he was not.

He had directed, in great part, the movable embellishments[9] of the seven chambers, upon occasion of this great *fête;*[10] and it was his own guiding taste which had given character to the masqueraders. Be sure they were grotesque. There were much glare and glitter and piquancy[11] and phantasm—much of what has been since seen in *Hernani.*[12] There were arabesque figures with unsuited limbs and appointments. There were delirious fancies such as the madman fashions. There was much of the beautiful, much of the wanton, much of the bizarre, something of the terrible, and not a little of that which might have excited disgust. To and fro in the seven chambers there stalked, in fact, a multitude of dreams. And these—the dreams—writhed in and about, taking hue from the rooms, and causing the wild music of the orchestra to seem as the echo of their steps. And, anon, there strikes the ebony clock which stands in the hall of the velvet. And then, for a moment, all is still, and all is silent save the voice of the clock. The dreams are stiff frozen as they stand. But the echoes of the chime die away—they have endured but an instant—and a light, half-subdued laughter floats after them as they depart. And now again the music swells, and the dreams live, and writhe to and fro more merrily than ever, taking hue from the many tinted windows through which stream the rays from the tripods. But to the chamber which lies most westwardly of the seven, there are now none of the maskers who venture; for the night is waning away, and there flows a ruddier light through the blood-colored panes; and the blackness of the sable drapery appalls; and to him whose foot falls upon the sable carpet, there comes from the near clock of ebony a muffled peal more solemnly emphatic than any which reaches *their* ears who indulge in the more remote gaieties of the other apartments.

But these other apartments were densely crowded, and in them beat feverishly the heart

---

8. ***decora*** (dā kô′rä), *n.* plural of *decorum,* thing that is proper in behavior or tasteful in dress. *[Latin]*
9. **embellishment** (em bel′ish mənt), *n.* decoration; adornment.
10. *fête* (fet), *n.* feast or festival.
11. **piquancy** (pē′kən sē), *n.* something stimulating to the mind.
12. ***Hernani*** (er nä′nē), a romantic play by the French author Victor Hugo (1802–1885).

of life. And the revel went whirling on, until at length there commenced the sounding of midnight upon the clock. And then the music ceased, as I have told; and the evolutions of the waltzers were quieted; and there was an uneasy cessation of all things as before. But now there were twelve strokes to be sounded by the bell of the clock; and thus it happened, perhaps, that more of thought crept, with more of time, into the meditations of the thoughtful among those who reveled. And thus, too, it happened, perhaps, that before the last echoes of the last chime had utterly sunk into silence, there were many individuals in the crowd who had found leisure to become aware of the presence of a masked figure which had arrested the attention of no single individual before. And the rumor of this new presence having spread itself whisperingly around, there arose at length from the whole company a buzz, or murmur, expressive of disapprobation[13] and surprise—then, finally, of terror, of horror, and of disgust.

In an assembly of phantasms such as I have painted, it may well be supposed that no ordinary appearance could have excited such sensation. In truth the masquerade license of the night was nearly unlimited; but the figure in question had out-Heroded Herod,[14] and gone beyond the bounds of even the Prince's indefinite decorum. There are chords in the hearts of the most reckless which cannot be touched without emotion. Even with the utterly lost, to whom life and death are equally jests, there are matters of which no jest can be made. The whole company, indeed, seemed now deeply to feel that in the costume and bearing of the stranger neither wit nor propriety existed. The figure was tall and gaunt, and shrouded from head to foot in the habiliments of the grave. The mask which concealed the visage was made so nearly to resemble the countenance of a stiffened corpse that the closest scrutiny must have had difficulty in detecting the cheat. And yet all this might have been

endured, if not approved, by the mad revelers around. But the mummer had gone so far as to assume the type of the Red Death. His vesture was dabbled in *blood*—and his broad brow, with all the features of the face, was besprinkled with the scarlet horror.

When the eyes of Prince Prospero fell upon this spectral image (which, with a slow and solemn movement, as if more fully to sustain its role, stalked to and fro among the waltzers) he was seen to be convulsed, in the first moment with a strong shudder either of terror or distaste; but, in the next, his brow reddened with rage.

"Who dares?" he demanded hoarsely of the courtiers who stood near him—"who dares insult us with this blasphemous[15] mockery? Seize him and unmask him—that we may know whom we have to hang at sunrise, from the battlements!"

CLARIFY: Why did the mummer's costume outrage Prince Prospero?

It was in the eastern or blue chamber in which stood the Prince Prospero as he uttered these words. They rang throughout the seven rooms loudly and clearly—for the Prince was a bold and robust man, and the music had become hushed at the waving of his hand.

It was in the blue room where stood the Prince, with a group of pale courtiers by his side. At first, as he spoke, there was a slight rushing movement of this group in the direction of the intruder, who at the moment was also near at hand, and now, with deliberate and stately

---

13. **disapprobation** (dis ap′prə bā′shən), *n.* disapproval.
14. **out-Heroded Herod** (her′əd), Herod was a tyrant depicted in medieval mystery plays. To "out-Herod" him would be to exceed him in outrageous extravagance.
15. **blasphemous** (blas′fəm əs), *adj.* speaking with abuse or contempt; profane.

step, made closer approach to the speaker. But from a certain nameless awe with which the mad assumptions of the mummer had inspired the whole party, there were found none who put forth hand to seize him; so that, unimpeded, he passed within a yard of the Prince's person; and while the vast assembly, as if with one impulse, shrank from the centers of the rooms to the walls, he made his way uninterruptedly, but with the same solemn and measured step which had distinguished him from the first, through the blue chamber to the purple—through the purple to the green—through the green to the orange—through this again to the white—and even thence to the violet, ere a decided movement had been made to arrest him. It was then, however, that the Prince Prospero, maddening with rage and the shame of his own momentary cowardice, rushed hurriedly through the six chambers, while none followed him on account of a deadly terror that had seized upon all. He bore aloft a drawn dagger, and had approached, in rapid impetuosity, to within three or four feet of the retreating figure, when the latter, having attained the extremity of the velvet apartment,

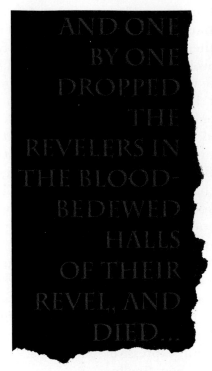

AND ONE
BY ONE
DROPPED
THE
REVELERS IN
THE BLOOD-
BEDEWED
HALLS
OF THEIR
REVEL, AND
DIED...

turned suddenly and confronted his pursuer. There was a sharp cry—and the dagger dropped gleaming upon the sable carpet, upon which, instantly afterward, fell prostrate[16] in death the Prince Prospero. Then, summoning the wild courage of despair, a throng of the revelers at once threw themselves into the black apartment, and, seizing the mummer, whose tall figure stood erect and motionless within the shadow of the ebony clock, gasped in unutterable horror at finding the grave cerements and corpselike mask, which they handled with so violent a rudeness, untenanted by any tangible form.

And now was acknowledged the presence of the Red Death. He had come like a thief in the night. And one by one dropped the revelers in the blood-bedewed halls of their revel, and died each in the despairing posture of his fall. And the life of the ebony clock went out with that of the last of the gay. And the flames of the tripods expired. And Darkness and Decay and the Red Death held illimitable dominion over all.

---

16. **prostrate** (pros′trāt), *adj.* lying flat with face downward.

After Reading

Making Connections

Shaping Your Response

1. Stories by Poe frequently appear in high school literature anthologies. Judging from this story, can you see why? Explain.

2. What three words best describe your feelings at the end of this story? Write them in your notebook.

3. Do you think that Prince Prospero and his friends deserved their fate? Why or why not?

Analyzing the Story

4. What is **ironic** about the Prince's name? about the way he meets death?

5. What do you think the ebony clock **symbolizes**, or represents?

6. What would you say is the story's **conflict?**

7. Comment on Poe's use of color in this story. For example, do you think red and black were the best colors to assign to his final, fatal room?

8. Reread Poe's biography on page 94. How might his background have influenced his writing?

Extending the Ideas

9. 👁 Discuss "The Masque of the Red Death" as a moral fable about pursuing individual gratification over **group** welfare.

Literary Focus: Mood

Mood is the feeling an author conveys to the reader through the setting, imagery, details, and descriptions in a literary work.

• Find a passage that you think strongly conveys mood and read it aloud to the class.

• Then invite classmates to supply words that describe the mood of this passage.

Vocabulary Study

Choose the letter of the word(s) that best completes or answers each item.

**castellated
countenance
embellishment
prostrate
sagacious**

1. If you were *prostrate*, you would be____.

   a. face down   **b.** far away   **c.** wealthy   **d.** overweight

2. Which of the following is most likely to cover a *countenance*?

   a. a glove   **b.** a shirt   **c.** a tablecloth   **d.** a mask

3. A *sagacious* person is ____.

   a. clumsy   **b.** wise   **c.** fearful   **d.** cautious

4. Something without *embellishment* is ____.

   a. silent   **b.** old fashioned   **c.** plain   **d.** rejected

5. Which of the following would most likely be *castellated*?

   a. an animal   **b.** a building   **c.** a dream   **d.** flowers

Expressing Your Ideas

Writing Choices

Writer's Notebook Update Which of the quotations you wrote about in your notebook do you think best expresses the theme of "The Masque of the Red Death"? Write a description of how the quotation fits the story.

'Twas a Very Bad Dream Have you ever awakened with a jolt, only to realize you were having a nightmare? "The Masque of the Red Death" has a nightmarish quality in its bizarre setting, characters, and action. Describe a **nightmare** that is real or imaginary. Use clear images to portray bizarre elements.

Noteworthy Think about ideas for your own screenplay of "The Masque of the Red Death," designed for the 21st century. Jot down **director's notes** for items such as the following: contemporary setting; musical score; special effects; casting.

Other Options

Poe on Display The library will be displaying an exhibit as a special tribute to Edgar Allan Poe. You and a partner are commissioned to design a **brochure** advertising the exhibit. Research the author and his works—poems, detective stories, short stories—to learn more about his life and writing style. Use illustrations to make your brochure convey the mood created in Poe's stories.

Architectural Nightmare You are an architect commissioned to re-create a **floor plan** of the suite of rooms in which the masquerade took place. Reread the description of the seven rooms, noting the following questions: How are the rooms laid out? Where are the corridors located in relation to each room? How are windows arranged? Where is the only source of light? Where is the ebony clock? Now draw a detailed floor plan of the seven rooms, with a direction indicator and a color key.

Before Reading

The Rain Came

by Grace Ogot   Kenya

Grace Ogot
born 1930

As a child growing up in Kenya, Grace Ogot listened to village storytellers recount native Luo folk tales and biblical stories. Years later, she recalled a story that made her cry as a child, and rewrote it as "The Rain Came." Ogot, whose works are distinguished by her Kenyan heritage, has said, "Stories of African traditional medicine and of the medicine man against the background of modern science and medicine fascinated me." Blending tradition with contemporary life, Ogot, whose bride price was twenty-five head of cattle, has worked in the Kenyan media and in politics, serving as a UN delegate and a member of parliament.

Building Background

Imagine This: The public address system in the classroom crackles with static as the principal's voice sounds: "May I have your attention please? In an effort to obtain more diverse grade distributions in this grading period, the students in each class must allot a D to three classmates and an F to two classmates—regardless of the grades earned by those students. All other students will retain the grades they have earned. Thank you, and have a nice day!"

Discuss as a class how you would choose the unlucky few to receive D's and F's. Now imagine that something more serious than grades were at stake. What if one person had to die to save an entire community? Keep this dilemma in mind as you read "The Rain Came."

Literary Focus

Setting The **setting** of a story is the time and place in which it occurs. "The Rain Came," which is based on an African folktale of the Luo tribe in Kenya, relies heavily on African traditions and surroundings. As you read this story, be aware of how the setting affects your understanding of the characters and events.

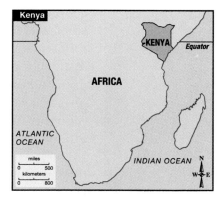

Writer's Notebook

Self-Sacrifice Throughout history people around the world have made sacrifices for the common good. Think about sacrifices that you would be willing to make on behalf of your family, friends, classmates, or community. Do you think that you have obligations to people you don't even know? Jot down your ideas on the subject.

The Rain Came

Grace Ogot

The Chief was still far from the gate when his daughter Oganda saw him. She ran to meet him. Breathlessly she asked her father, "What is the news, great Chief? Everyone in the village is anxiously waiting to hear when it will rain." Labong'o held out his hands for his daughter but he did not say a word. Puzzled by her father's cold attitude Oganda ran back to the village to warn the others that the chief was back.

The atmosphere in the village was tense and confused. Everyone moved aimlessly and fussed in the yard without actually doing any work. A young woman whispered to her co-wife, "If they have not solved this rain business today, the chief will crack." They had watched him getting thinner and thinner as the people kept on pestering him. "Our cattle lie dying in the fields," they reported. "Soon it will be our children and then ourselves. Tell us what to do to save our lives, oh great Chief." So the chief had daily prayed with the Almighty through the ancestors to deliver them from their distress.

Instead of calling the family together and giving them the news immediately, Labong'o went to his own hut, a sign that he was not to be disturbed. Having replaced the shutter, he sat in the dimly lit hut to contemplate.

It was no longer a question of being the chief of hunger-stricken people that weighed Labong'o's heart. It was the life of his only daughter that was at stake. At the time when Oganda came to meet him, he saw the glittering chain shining around her waist. The prophecy was complete. "It is Oganda, Oganda, my only daughter, who must die so young." Labong'o burst into tears before finishing the sentence. The chief must not weep. Society had declared him the bravest of men. But Labong'o did not care any more. He assumed the position of a simple father and wept bitterly. He loved his people, the Luo, but what were the Luo for him without Oganda? Her life had brought a new life in Labong'o's world and he ruled better than he could remember. How would the spirit of the village survive his beautiful daughter? "There are so many homes and so many parents who have daughters. Why choose this one? She is all I have." Labong'o spoke as if the ancestors were there in the hut and he could see them face to face. Perhaps they were there, warning him to remember his promise on the day he was enthroned when he said aloud, before the elders, "I will lay down my life, if necessary, and the life of my household, to save this tribe from the hands of the enemy." "Deny! Deny!" he could hear the voice of his forefathers mocking him.

When Labong'o was consecrated[1] chief he was only a young man. Unlike his father, he ruled for many years with only one wife. But people rebuked[2] him because his only wife did not bear him a daughter. He married a second, a third, and a fourth wife. But they all gave birth to male children. When Labong'o married a fifth wife she bore him a daughter. They called her Oganda, meaning "beans," because her skin was very fair. Out of Labong'o's twenty

---

1. **consecrate** (kon′sə krāt), *v.* set apart as sacred; make holy.
2. **rebuke** (ri byük′), *v.* express disapproval of.

This painted wooden carving attributed to the Limba people of Sierra Leone presents a figure that appears both mythic and mortal. What character traits of Chief Labong'o does the carving reflect? ➤

children, Oganda was the only girl. Though she was the chief's favorite, her mother's co-wives swallowed their jealous feelings and showered her with love. After all, they said, Oganda was a female child whose days in the royal family were numbered. She would soon marry at a tender age and leave the enviable position to someone else.

Never in his life had he been faced with such an impossible decision. Refusing to yield to the rainmaker's request would mean sacrificing the whole tribe, putting the interests of the individual above those of the society. More than that. It would mean disobeying the ancestors, and most probably wiping the Luo people from the surface of the earth. On the other hand, to let Oganda die as a ransom for the people would permanently cripple Labong'o spiritually. He knew he would never be the same chief again.

The words of Ndithi, the medicine man, still echoed in his ears. "Podho, the ancestor of the Luo, appeared to me in a dream last night, and he asked me to speak to the chief and the people," Ndithi had said to the gathering of tribesmen. "A young woman who has not known a man must die so that the country may have rain. While Podho was still talking to me, I saw a young woman standing at the lakeside, her hands raised, above her head. Her skin was as fair as the skin of young deer in the wilderness. Her tall slender figure stood like a lonely reed at the river bank. Her sleepy eyes wore a sad look like that of a bereaved[3] mother. She wore a gold ring on her left ear, and a glittering brass chain around her waist. As I still marveled at the beauty of this young woman, Podho told me, 'Out of all the women in this land, we have chosen this one. Let her offer herself a sacrifice to the lake monster! And on that day, the rain will come down in torrents. Let everyone stay at home on that day, lest he be carried away by the floods.'"

Outside there was a strange stillness, except for the thirsty birds that sang lazily on the dying trees. The blinding mid-day heat had forced the people to retire to their huts. Not far away from the chief's hut, two guards were snoring away quietly. Labong'o removed his crown and the large eagle-head that hung loosely on his shoulders. He left the hut, and instead of asking Nyabog'o the messenger to beat the drum, he went straight and beat it himself. In no time the whole household had assembled under the siala tree where he usually addressed them. He told Oganda to wait a while in her grandmother's hut.

When Labong'o stood to address his household, his voice was hoarse and the tears choked him. He started to speak, but words refused to leave his lips. His wives and sons knew there was great danger. Perhaps their enemies had declared war on them. Labong'o's eyes were red, and they could see he had been weeping. At last he told them. "One whom we love and treasure must be taken away from us. Oganda is to die." Labong'o's voice was so faint, that he could not hear it himself. But he continued, "The ancestors have chosen her to be offered as a sacrifice to the lake monster in order that we may have rain."

They were completely stunned. As a confused murmur broke out, Oganda's mother fainted and was carried off to her own hut. But the other people rejoiced. They danced around singing and chanting. "Oganda is the lucky one to die for the people. If it is to save the people, let Oganda go."

In her grandmother's hut Oganda wondered what the whole family was discussing about her that she could not hear. Her grandmother's hut was well away from the chief's court and, much as she strained her ears, she could not hear what was said. "It must be marriage," she concluded. It was an accepted custom for the family to discuss their daughter's future marriage behind her back. A faint smile played on Oganda's lips as she thought of the

---

3. **bereaved** (bi rēvd′), *adj.* deprived ruthlessly; robbed.

several young men who swallowed saliva at the mere mention of her name.

There was Kech, the son of a neighboring clan elder. Kech was very handsome. He had sweet, meek eyes and a roaring laughter. He would make a wonderful father, Oganda thought. But they would not be a good match. Kech was a bit too short to be her husband. It would humiliate her to have to look down at Kech each time she spoke to him. Then she thought of Dimo, the tall young man who had already distinguished himself as a brave warrior and an outstanding wrestler. Dimo adored Oganda, but Oganda thought he would make a cruel husband, always quarreling and ready to fight. No, she did not like him. Oganda fingered the glittering chain on her waist as she thought of Osinda. A long time ago when she was quite young Osinda had given her that chain, and instead of wearing it around her neck several times, she wore it round her waist where it could stay permanently. She heard her heart pounding so loudly as she thought of him. She whispered, "Let it be you they are discussing, Osinda, the lovely one. Come now and take me away. . . ."

The lean figure in the doorway startled Oganda who was rapt[4] in thought about the man she loved. "You have frightened me, Grandma," said Oganda laughing. "Tell me, is it my marriage you were discussing? You can take it from me that I won't marry any of them." A smile played on her lips again. She was coaxing the old lady to tell her quickly, to tell her they were pleased with Osinda.

In the open space outside the excited relatives were dancing and singing. They were coming to the hut now, each carrying a gift to put at Oganda's feet. As their singing got nearer Oganda was able to hear what they were saying: "If it is to save the people, if it is to give us rain, let Oganda go. Let Oganda die for her people, and for her ancestors." Was she mad to think that they were singing about her? How could

she die? She found the lean figure of her grandmother barring the door. She could not get out. The look on her grandmother's face warned her that there was danger around the corner. "Mother, it is not marriage then?" Oganda asked urgently. She suddenly felt panicky like a mouse cornered by a hungry cat. Forgetting that there was only one door in the hut Oganda fought desperately to find another exit. She must fight for her life. But there was none.

She closed her eyes, leapt like a wild tiger through the door, knocking her grandmother flat to the ground. There outside in mourning garments Labong'o stood motionless, his hands folded at the back. He held his daughter's hand and led her away from the excited crowd to the little red-painted hut where her mother was resting. Here he broke the news officially to his daughter.

For a long time the three souls who loved one another dearly sat in darkness. It was no good speaking. And even if they tried, the words could not have come out. In the past they had been like three cooking stones, sharing their burdens. Taking Oganda away from them would leave two useless stones which would not hold a cooking-pot.

News that the beautiful daughter of the chief was to be sacrificed to give the people rain spread across the country like wind. At sunset the chief's village was full of relatives and friends who had come to congratulate Oganda. Many more were on their way coming, carrying their gifts. They would dance till morning to keep her company. And in the morning they would prepare her a big farewell feast. All these relatives thought it a great honor to be selected by the spirits to die, in order that the society may live. "Oganda's name will always remain a living name among us," they boasted.

But was it maternal love that prevented

---

4. **rapt** (rapt), *adj.* so busy thinking of or enjoying one thing that one does not know what else is happening; distracted.

Minya from rejoicing with the other women? Was it the memory of the agony and pain of childbirth that made her feel so sorrowful? Or was it the deep warmth and understanding that passes between a suckling babe and her mother that made Oganda part of her life, her flesh? Of course it was an honor, a great honor, for her daughter to be chosen to die for the country. But what could she gain once her only daughter was blown away by the wind? There were so many other women in the land, why choose her daughter, her only child! Had human life any meaning at all—other women had houses full of children while she, Minya, had to lose her only child!

In the cloudless sky the moon shone brightly, and the numerous stars glittered with a bewitching beauty. The dancers of all age-groups assembled to dance before Oganda, who sat close to her mother, sobbing quietly. All these years she had been with her people she thought she understood them. But now she discovered that she was a stranger among them. If they loved her as they had always professed why were they not making any attempt to save her? Did her people really understand what it felt like to die young? Unable to restrain her emotions any longer, she sobbed loudly as her age-group got up to dance. They were young and beautiful and very soon they would marry and have their own children. They would have husbands to love and little huts for themselves. They would have reached maturity. Oganda touched the chain around her waist as she thought of Osinda. She wished Osinda were there too, among her friends. "Perhaps he is ill," she thought gravely. The chain comforted Oganda—she would die with it around her waist and wear it in the underground world.

In the morning a big feast was prepared for Oganda. The women prepared many different tasty dishes so that she could pick and choose.

Did her people really understand what it felt like to die young?

"People don't eat after death," they said. Delicious though the food looked, Oganda touched none of it. Let the happy people eat. She contented herself with sips of water from a little calabash.[5]

The time for her departure was drawing near, and each minute was precious. It was a day's journey to the lake. She was to walk all night, passing through the great forest. But nothing could touch her, not even the denizens[6] of the forest. She was already anointed with sacred oil. From the time Oganda received the sad news she had expected Osinda to appear any moment. But he was not there. A relative told her that Osinda was away on a private visit. Oganda realized that she would never see her beloved again.

In the afternoon the whole village stood at the gate to say goodbye and to see her for the last time. Her mother wept on her neck for a long time. The great chief in a mourning skin came to the gate barefooted, and mingled with the people—a simple father in grief. He took off his wrist bracelet and put it on his daughter's wrist saying, "You will always live among us. The spirit of our forefathers is with you."

Tongue-tied and unbelieving Oganda stood there before the people. She had nothing to say. She looked at her home once more. She could hear her heart beating so painfully within her. All her childhood plans were coming to an end. She felt like a flower nipped in the bud never to enjoy the morning

---

5. **calabash** (kal′ə bash), *n.* a gourdlike fruit whose dried shell is used to make bottles, bowls, drums, pipes, and rattles.
6. **denizen** (den′ə zən), *n.* inhabitant or occupant of a place or region.

dew again. She looked at her weeping mother and whispered, "Whenever you want to see me, always look at the sunset. I will be there."

Oganda turned southwards to start her trek to the lake. Her parents, relatives, friends, and admirers stood at the gate and watched her go.

Her beautiful slender figure grew smaller and smaller till she mingled with the thin dry trees in the forest. As Oganda walked the lonely path that wound its way in the wilderness, she sang a song, and her own voice kept her company.

The ancestors have said Oganda must die.
The daughter of the chief must be sacrificed,
When the lake monster feeds on my flesh,
The people will have rain.
Yes, the rain will come down in torrents.
And the floods will wash away the sandy beaches
When the daughter of the chief dies in the lake.
My age-group has consented
My parents have consented
So have my friends and relatives.
Let Oganda die to give us rain.
My age-group are young and ripe,
Ripe for womanhood and motherhood.
But Oganda must die young,
Oganda must sleep with the ancestors.
Yes, rain will come down in torrents.

The red rays of the setting sun embraced Oganda, and she looked like a burning candle in the wilderness.

The people who came to hear her sad song were touched by her beauty. But they all said the same thing: "If it is to save the people, if it is to give us rain, then be not afraid. Your name will forever live among us."

At midnight Oganda was tired and weary. She could walk no more. She sat under a big tree, and having sipped water from her calabash, she rested her head on the tree trunk and slept.

When Oganda woke up in the morning the sun was high in the sky. After walking for many hours, she reached the *tong'*, a strip of land that separated the inhabited part of the country from the sacred place *(kar lamo)*. No layman could enter this place and come out alive— only those who had direct contact with the spirits and the Almighty were allowed to enter this holy of holies. But Oganda had to pass through this sacred land on her way to the lake, which she had to reach at sunset.

A large crowd gathered to see her for the last time. Her voice was now hoarse and painful, but there was no need to worry anymore. Soon she would not have to sing. The crowd looked at Oganda sympathetically, mumbling words she could not hear. But none of them pleaded for life. As Oganda opened the gate, a child, a young child, broke loose from the crowd, and ran towards her. The child took a small earring from her sweaty hands and gave it to Oganda saying, "When you reach the world of the dead, give this earring to my sister. She died last week. She forgot this ring." Oganda, taken aback by the strange request, took the little ring, and handed her precious water and food to the child. She did not need them now. Oganda did not know whether to laugh or cry. She had heard mourners sending their love to their sweethearts, long dead, but this idea of sending gifts was new to her.

Oganda held her breath as she crossed the barrier to enter the sacred land. She looked appealingly at the crowd, but there was no response. Their minds were too preoccupied with their own survival. Rain was the precious medicine they were longing for, and the sooner Oganda could get to her destination the better.

A strange feeling possessed Oganda as she picked her way in the sacred land. There were strange noises that often startled her, and her first reaction was to take to her heels. But she remembered that she had to fulfill the wish of her people. She was exhausted, but the path was still winding. Then suddenly the path ended on sandy land. The water had retreated miles away from the shore leaving a wide stretch of sand. Beyond this was the vast expanse of water.

Oganda felt afraid. She wanted to picture the

◄ Like the carving on page 105, this Baule carving of the water spirit Mami Wata combines human and mythic elements. What details show Mami Wata's mythic traits? her humanity?

size and shape of the monster, but fear would not let her. The society did not talk about it, nor did the crying children who were silenced by the mention of its name. The sun was still up, but it was no longer hot. For a long time Oganda walked ankle-deep in the sand. She was exhausted and longed desperately for her calabash of water. As she moved on, she had a strange feeling that something was following her. Was it the monster? Her hair stood erect, and a cold paralyzing feeling ran along her spine. She looked behind, sideways and in front, but there was nothing except a cloud of dust.

Oganda pulled up and hurried but the feeling did not leave her, and her whole body became saturated[7] with perspiration.

The sun was going down fast and the lake shore seemed to move along with it.

Oganda started to run. She must be at the lake before sunset. As she ran she heard a noise coming from behind. She looked back sharply, and something resembling a moving bush was frantically running after her. It was about to catch up with her.

Oganda ran with all her strength. She was now determined to throw herself into the water even before sunset. She did not look back, but the creature was upon her. She made an effort to cry out, as in a nightmare, but she could not hear her own voice. The creature caught up with Oganda. In the utter confusion, as Oganda came face with the unidentified creature, a strong hand grabbed her. But she fell flat on the sand and fainted.

When the lake breeze brought her back to consciousness, a man was bending over her. "O . . .!" Oganda opened her mouth to speak, but she had lost her voice. She swallowed a mouthful of water poured into her mouth by the stranger.

"Osinda, Osinda! Please let me die. Let me run, the sun is going down. Let me die, let them have rain." Osinda fondled the glittering chain around Oganda's waist and wiped the tears from her face.

"We must escape quickly to the unknown land," Osinda said urgently. "We must run away from the wrath of the ancestors and the retaliation[8] of the monster."

"But the curse is upon me, Osinda, I am no good to you any more. And moreover the eyes of the ancestors will follow us everywhere and bad luck will befall us. Nor can we escape from the monster."

Oganda broke loose, afraid to escape, but Osinda grabbed her hands again.

"Listen to me, Oganda! Listen! Here are two coats!" He then covered the whole of Oganda's body, except her eyes, with a leafy attire made from the twigs of *Bwombwe*. "These will protect us from the eyes of the ancestors and the wrath of the monster. Now let us run out of here." He held Oganda's hand and they ran from the sacred land, avoiding the path that Oganda had followed.

The bush was thick, and the long grass entangled their feet as they ran. Halfway through the sacred land they stopped and looked back. The sun was almost touching the surface of the water. They were frightened. They continued to run, now faster, to avoid the sinking sun.

"Have faith, Oganda—that thing will not reach us."

When they reached the barrier and looked behind them trembling, only a tip of the sun could be seen above the water's surface.

"It is gone! It is gone!" Oganda wept, hiding her face in her hands.

"Weep not, daughter of the chief. Let us run, let us escape."

There was a bright lightning. They looked up, frightened. Above them black furious clouds started to gather. They began to run. Then the thunder roared, and the rain came down in torrents.

---

7. **saturated** (sach′ə rā′tid), *adj.* soaked thoroughly.
8. **retaliation** (ri tal′ē ā′shən), *n.* paying back wrong.

After Reading

Making Connections

Shaping Your
Response

1. Were you satisfied with the ending of the story? Why or why not?

2. What would you do if you learned that you had been selected as the person your community would sacrifice during a crisis?

3. Draw a thought bubble and inside it write what you think are Oganda's feelings when she learns she is to be sacrificed.

Analyzing the
Story

4. Why did the people think Oganda was lucky to be chosen?

5. Describe the **character** of Oganda, using details from the story.

6. What external and internal **conflict** does Labong'o undergo when he returns to the village at the beginning of the story?

7. How does this story reflect the **theme** "Trying to Beat the Odds"?

Extending the
Ideas

8. 🐾 Do you think that Oganda was justified in putting her personal interests above those of the **group**?

9. 🐾 What other groups, cultures, and stories can you think of that include the tradition of sacrifice of one for the salvation of many?

Literary Focus: Setting

The **setting** is the time and place in which the action in a story occurs. The setting can also make the action and characters more believable.

- Given the setting and circumstances of the story, do you think Labong'o acted as a responsible father? Did Oganda act responsibly? Explain.

- 🐾 Why is it important that this story is set in a tribal, agricultural society?

Vocabulary Study

Decide whether the italicized words are used correctly in the sentences below. Write *Correct* or *Incorrect*.

bereaved
calabash
denizen
rebuke
retaliation

1. Grace Ogot describes the reactions of a *bereaved* father who is expected to sacrifice his only daughter.

2. Any parent who loves his daughter as Labong'o does will *rebuke* her to show his affection.

3. All the co-wives of Labong'o live in the same *calabash*.

4. Each *denizen* of the village stands at the gate to say goodbye to Oganda.

5. Oganda fears the *retaliation* of the angry rain monster.

Expressing Your Ideas

Writing Choices

Writer's Notebook Update Glance at the notes you made before reading "The Rain Came." Compare your ideas on personal and social sacrifice to Oganda's. Write a paragraph that begins, "If I had been Oganda, I would have. . . ."

They Lived Happily Ever After Or did they? Extend the **ending** of the story to tell what happens to Oganda and Osinda after they escape the lake monster. You may want to describe the new setting where the couple lives.

Chant The sad song that Oganda sings as she walks the lonely path in the wilderness summarizes the story up to that point. With a partner, write new **lyrics** to describe the story events after she crosses the barrier to the sacred land. You might want to set your words to an existing melody or write your own music and perform your song for the class.

Other Options

Draw One for the Kids Rewrite and illustrate "The Rain Came" as a **picture book** for nursery school children. Pick out the main idea and details of the story. Sketch pictures to show each event. Summarize the text, writing no more than two simple sentences under each illustration. Work in a medium of your choice.

Raise Your Banner You are a member of the women's liberation movement in Kenya, marching in a parade to promote feminist literature. Do you think "The Rain Came" promotes feminism? Consider the following: Oganda's actions, her obedience to her father, her escape, her ideas of marriage, and her rescuer. Now make a **banner** either promoting this story or condemning it.

Marketing Gimmicks Imagine you work in the marketing department that is promoting the movie version of "The Rain Came." What products—games, drinking glasses, clothing, accessories, music—will you develop to promote the movie? Sketch out your ideas in a **portfolio** and present it to the class.

Trying to Beat the Odds

Random, Rigged, or Rational?

Media Connection

You might attribute the odd twists and outcomes of stories in this group to fortune, luck, or strange coincidence. This Interdisciplinary Study explores the sometimes fine line between things that are random, rigged, or rational.

On Display

The Quiz Show That Was Rigged

Is it cheating or is it just good fun when a television game show is rigged? That was one of the questions raised by the quiz show scandal of 1959 and the movie, *Quiz Show*, released in 1994.

Quiz shows were popular during the 1950s. Audiences like the family pictured on page 115 loved cheering their favorite contestants, shouting answers at the television set, and being amazed at what people knew. Charles Van Doren, who became reigning champion of the weekly quiz show, *Twenty-One*, was adopted as a hero by the American public. He was smart, handsome, and polite, and he came from a literary family. When Van Doren admitted to cheating on the show, many people felt betrayed. The fact that the producers had asked him to cheat only made the scandal worse.

Some people, especially the game show producers, claimed that rigging the game shows made them more exciting. Van Doren, who won more than $100,000.00, always claimed that he wanted only to promote knowledge and make learning popular. Others, however, were quick to point out that the audience expected—and identified with— real people solving real problems. They were cheated out of the real-life experience they expected. In short, they were handed a lie.

Would the game shows really have lacked drama and popular appeal if producers hadn't rigged them? No one knows for sure. We do know, however, that by "fixing" the games, the producers lost the trust and respect of their audience.

Ralph Fiennes plays a conflicted Charles Van Doren in the 1994 movie, Quiz Show.

With his rise to fame as a human encyclopedia, Charles Van Doren became an American culture hero.

MR. VAN DOREN
ON THE AIR

MR. VAN DOREN
ON THE AIR

Responding

1. Do you think modern viewers would rather know the truth or merely be entertained? Explain.

2. Explain whether you think people should regard docudramas or reenactments on TV as fact or fiction.

Math Connection

Try your luck answering these questions based on odds and statistics. Odds are that some of your guesses will be correct.

Playing the

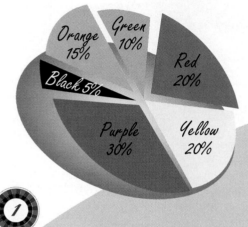

Orange 15%
Green 10%
Red 20%
Black 5%
Purple 30%
Yellow 20%

Use this pie chart to determine approximately how many purple spice drops you could expect to get in a handful of fifty.

   a. 5
   b. 10
   c. 15

2

In being dealt five cards from a shuffled deck of 52 cards, what are your chances of getting two pair?

   a. 1 in 21
   b. 1 in 35
   c. 1 in 50

According to *Harper's Index*, what is the average number of sesame seeds on a Big Mac bun?

   a. 30
   b. 60
   c. 178

If you double a penny each day, how much will you get on the 30th day?

   a. $63,591.04
   b. $126,875.32
   c. $5,368,709.12

Numbers

5 Former Shenandoah Park Ranger Roy C. Sullivan had phenomenally bad luck with lightning. Guess how many times he was hit over a 24-year period.
- a. 3
- b. 7
- c. 21

6 Are the odds of having a summer day with at least 0.01 inch of rain greater in Juneau, Alaska, or in Los Angeles, California?

7 A man named Marty Timmons had a lucky ticket that won two prizes in the New Jersey lottery: first $10,000 and then, an hour later, a million. What are the odds of anyone hitting both the jackpot and a consolation prize with one ticket in such a state lottery?
- a. 334 million to 1
- b. 334 billion to 1
- c. 334 trillion to 1

8 Although the odds are unlikely, one assassinated U.S. President had a grandfather of the same name who also was assassinated. (The two also had sons with the same name and wives with the same name.) Who was he?
- a. John F. Kennedy
- b. Abraham Lincoln
- c. James Garfield

9 You have tossed a coin 10 times and it has landed on heads every time. What are your chances of getting tails on the eleventh try?
- a. 1 in 2
- b. 1 in 10
- c. 1 in 27

Answers 1. c; 2. a; 3. c; 4. c; 5. b; 6. Juneau (13 to 10 in favor vs. Los Angeles 40 to 1 against); 7. c (as calculated by statisticians); 8. b; 9. a

Hedging Your Bets

> "It is no great wonder if, in the long process of time, while fortune takes her course hither and thither, numerous coincidences should spontaneously occur."
>
> — *Plutarch*

One forenoon a freeborn nobleman arrived and ran into Solomon's hall of justice, his countenance pale with anguish and both lips blue. Then Solomon said, "Good sir, what is the matter?"

He replied, "Azrael [the Angel of Death] cast on me such a look, so full of wrath and hate."

"Come," said the king, "what boon do you desire now? Ask!"

"O protector of my life," said he, "command the wind to bear me from here to India. Maybe, when thy slave is come thither he will save his life."

Solomon commanded the wind to bear him quickly over the water to the uttermost part of India. Next day, at the time of conference and meeting, Solomon said to Azrael: "Didst thou look with anger on that Moslem in order that he might wander as an exile far from his home?"

Azrael said, "When did I look on him angrily? I saw him as I passed by, and looked at him in astonishment, for God had commanded me, saying, 'Hark, today do thou take his spirit in India.' From wonder I said to myself, 'Even if he has a hundred wings, 'tis a far journey for him to be in India today.'"

— *The Man Who Fled from Azrael*
Rumi from *the Mathnavi*

A man who travels a lot was concerned about the possibility of a bomb on board his plane. He determined the probability of this, found it to be low but not low enough for him, so now he always travels with a bomb in his suitcase. He reasons that the probability of two bombs being on board would be infinitessimal.

—from *Innumeracy* by *John Allen Paulos*

During individual sessions astrologers pick up on clues about clients' personalities from their facial expressions, mannerisms, body language, etc. Consider the famous case of Clever Hans, the horse who seemed to be able to count. His trainer would roll a die and ask him what number appeared on the die's face. Hans would slowly paw the ground the appropriate number of times and then stop, much to the amazement of onlookers. What was not so noticeable, however, was that the trainer stood stone-still until the horse pawed the correct number of times, and then, consciously or not, stirred slightly, which caused Hans to stop. The horse was not the source of the answers but merely a reflection of the trainer's knowledge of the answer. People often unwittingly play the role of trainer to astrologers who, like Hans, reflect their clients' needs.

—from *Innumeracy* by *John Allen Paulos*

Responding

1. What is the fallacy of the reasoning of the man with the bomb?

2. Relate the story of Clever Hans to the astrologer in "An Astrologer's Day." How do both the astrologer and the horse "reflect their clients' needs"?

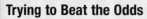

Writing Workshop

Selling an Idea

Assignment Imagine that a producer of a TV suspense series called *Beating the Odds* has asked you to submit a proposal for a show. Working in teams of three to five, create a proposal for a half-hour TV show based on one of the stories you read in this part of the unit.

WRITER'S BLUEPRINT

Product   A group proposal for a TV show
Purpose   To sell an idea
Audience   A TV producer
Specs   As the creators of an effective proposal, your group should:

❏ Agree on a story from this part as the basis for your proposal. Make a cover page naming the story and its author and listing team members.

❏ Describe the main characters and settings and summarize the plot. Suggest who ought to play each part and why. Explain how the settings and plot will be suspenseful. Use a no-nonsense, businesslike tone throughout.

❏ Present one crucial scene from the plot in script or storyboard form.

❏ Close by urging the producer to accept your proposal.

❏ Follow the rules of grammar, usage, spelling, and mechanics, including using commas correctly.

Brainstorm ideas. In your group, review the stories from this part. Jot down ideas about how you might adapt each story into a half-hour TV suspense show. Discuss which one would make the best TV show and make your choice.

Describe the main characters for your proposed show. Work with your group and use a chart like the one that follows to organize your ideas.

Main Characters	Actors to Play Them	Appearance	Personality	Motivations (wishes, dreams, needs)	Goals
Prince Prospero in "The Masque of the Red Death"	Sean Connery	"Had a fine eye for colors and effects . . . there are some who would have thought him mad."	—ignorantly, stubbornly fearless —knowing —eccentric	—to ward off death —to be happy —to indulge himself	escaping the Red Death

OR . . .
Make drawings or build a model of the settings. Consider backgrounds, furniture, colors, and light.

Set the stage. The setting—landscape, weather, light, architecture, furnishings, colors—should reflect the mood of the story. With your group, look back at the story and describe the suspenseful settings for your show.

Chart the plot. Fill in this chart of plot elements for your TV show by answering the questions.

Conflict	Key Scenes	Climax	Resolution
What problems do the characters face?	What events or complications move the plot along?	What is the most exciting part of the story?	How does the climax tie together the loose ends of the story?

Choose a crucial scene, perhaps the climax. Sketch key moments from this scene on pieces of paper or poster board. On the back of each sketch make notes about the suspenseful settings and action and some lines of dialogue you might want to use.

Brainstorm reasons for accepting your proposal. Look back at your notes on character, setting, and plot. How are they suspenseful? Why will a TV audience want to watch your show? Choose the five best reasons from your list and arrange them in the order you plan to present them.

OR . . .
Quickwrite for ten minutes or so about why the producer should accept your proposal. Have everyone in the group contribute, with one person doing the actual writing.

Plan the proposal. Look over the information your group has gathered as you make your writing plan. Use these categories to organize your ideas:

- Cover page
- Characters and actors to play them
- Settings and how they create suspense
- Key scenes in plot and how they create suspense
- Key moments from crucial scene
- Five persuasive reasons why producer should accept proposal

Do a live presentation of your plan. Assemble your materials on a table and go over them with another group. Try to make your plan sound as attractive as possible. When you finish, have the other group comment, and revise your plan in line with their comments.

STEP 2 DRAFTING

Before you draft, review the Writer's Blueprint, your writing plan, and your prewriting notes. Assign each group member a section of the proposal to draft.

As you draft, remember:

- You're writing this proposal as a group, so ask the other group members when you need advice or ideas.

- You're writing a business proposal, so use a businesslike tone when you address the producer. See the Revising Strategy in Step 3 of this lesson.

Ask another group for comments on the draft before you revise it. Ask questions such as these.

✔ Have we explained how the settings and plots are suspenseful?

✔ Have we used a businesslike tone in making our proposal?

Revising Strategy

Creating a Businesslike Tone

Tone reflects the writer's attitude toward the audience. A textbook, like this one, has a somewhat formal tone, but friendly too, since the writers want you, the student, to enjoy learning.

In writing a business proposal like this one, in which you want to persuade your audience to buy your idea, you should:

• Come straight to the point—your audience does not have time to waste.

• Let the facts speak for themselves—don't tell people what to think.

• Keep a respectful distance—don't gush or use slang.

The writer of this student model used a partner's comment to help make the tone more businesslike.

The tension in "An Astrologer's Day" results from the imposing figure
~~The plot of this story is so tense. You'll be on the edge of your~~
of the customer and the sudden new-found "abilities" of the astrologer
~~seat as the astrologer reveals all these really weird things he can do to~~
                    At first   who is
the customer. ~~Before that~~ it's the customer, ~~who's really~~ mysterious.
The audience   who he is and what he wants   Isn't this a
~~Everyone will~~ wonder who this guy is and what he's after.
                                                       little casual?

EDITING

Ask another group to review your revised draft before you edit. When you edit, look for errors in grammar, usage, spelling, and mechanics. Pay special attention to errors in comma usage.

Editing Strategy

Using Commas Correctly

When you edit, be sure you use commas correctly. Here are some basic rules to guide you.

- In a series of three or more words, phrases, or clauses, use a comma to separate the items, and use a comma before the conjunction (*and, but, or, nor*).

  Edgar Allan Poe uses *somber, morbid, and grotesque* images to set the moods of his stories.

- When a descriptive phrase renames or explains the noun or pronoun it follows by adding extra information, set it off with commas.

  Prince Prospero, *a character in "The Masque of the Red Death,"* tries to avoid the plague by sealing himself in his castle.

- When the explanation in a descriptive phrase is vital to the meaning of the sentence, no comma is used.

  I meant the prince *in the story* instead of the real prince.

FOR REFERENCE
For more information on correct comma usage, see the Language and Grammar Handbook at the back of this text.

STEP **5** PRESENTING

Here are two ideas for presenting your proposal.

- Stage your scripted scene for the class with costumes and scenery. If you have access to a video recorder, you might videotape your production.

- Record your show as a radio play, with suspenseful sound effects and music.

6 LOOKING BACK

Self-evaluate. Work with your group to decide on a grade for the proposal. Look back at the Writer's Blueprint and give your group's product a score on each point, from 6 (superior) down to 1 (inadequate). Discuss the results and try to agree on one grade for the whole group.

Reflect. Individually, think about what you have learned from this group writing process and write answers to these questions.

- What aspect of collaborating on this project was most interesting to you? Is working with a group ultimately more or less satisfying than working alone?

- What would you change or add to your proposal if you could revise it again? Explain.

For Your Working Portfolio Add a copy of the finished proposal and your reflection responses to your working portfolio.

Beyond Print

Computer Talk

If you think a server is a waitress and a hard drive is a traffic jam, read on and learn a few of the important terms in a new language.

Application A particular computer program or piece of software.

CD-ROM Compact Disc Read Only Memory. A CD-ROM is used to store information such as text, sound, pictures, and movies. While CD-ROMs look like audio CDs, they are readable only with a computer.

Database An organized collection of information.

Desktop The area on a computer screen that contains icons, menus, and windows.

Download To copy a file from a server or network.

Electronic Mail Messages sent over the Internet from one user to another.

Hard Drive A storage device usually found inside your computer.

Internet A series of servers connected across the country and world.

Log On The procedure for gaining access to a computer or network.

Menu A pull-down list of items at the top of the computer screen.

Modem A device that uses a phone line to connect your computer with a variety of online services or other computers.

Network Two or more computers connected together by cables, allowing them to communicate with each other.

Online Information available to a user through a network or telephone connection.

RAM Random Access Memory.

Server A computer that operates a network.

Activity Options

1. Create a dialogue between two people in "computerspeak." How many of these terms can you use and still make sense?

2. Create a glossary of your own with other technology terms, and add new terms as you come across them.

Part Three

Dealing with Consequences

A hunting adventure in the jungles of Peru, a confrontation in China, a post-typhoon discovery in Japan—incidents in the selections you are about to read illustrate that people worldwide often act without considering the consequences.

 Multicultural Connection **Choice** may be influenced by cultural situations and settings. In the following selections, do individuals choose to respect or reject such settings, and what are the results of their decisions?

Literature

Interdisciplinary Study Lessons Through the Ages

Writing Workshop Expository Writing

Beyond Print Critical Thinking

The Interlopers

by Saki   Great Britain

Saki
1870–1916

H. H. Munro, who adopted the pen name Saki, is best known for stories that blend humor and horror. Munro was born in Akyab, Burma, where his father was a colonel in the Bengal Staff Corps. After the death of his mother when he was two, he was sent home to relatives in England. There he eventually wrote political sketches for the *Westminster Gazette*, as well as short stories that displayed his satirical humor and his fascination with the unusual. When World War I broke out, Munro enlisted at age 43 as a private in the British army. In 1915, he went to France and was killed by a German sniper within a year.

Building Background

Feuding Friends Conduct a quick survey of classmates to determine what kinds of things usually cause quarrels between friends. List on the board things most frequently mentioned, and write the top five in chart form. Then brainstorm ways in which such disagreements can be resolved, writing the best suggestions in the chart.

Things That Cause Quarrels	Ways to Resolve Them

Literary Focus

Irony The word **irony** refers to a contrast between what is expected, or what appears to be, and what really is. You may have noticed irony when someone used a tone of voice to indicate the opposite of what was said. Or maybe you expected one event to occur but something quite surprising happened instead. You even may have noticed irony while watching a sitcom in which you knew more about what was going to happen than the characters did. As you read "The Interlopers," list examples of irony. Don't forget to expect the unexpected!

Writer's Notebook

Here Come the Interlopers Did you know that an *interloper* is someone who intrudes or interferes? Make a web around the word *interloper* listing at least six different people or things that could fit this description. Now preview the art and the first paragraph of this story and predict who the interlopers of the title might be.

THE
INTERLOPERS

SAKI

In a forest of mixed growth somewhere on the eastern spurs[1] of the Carpathians,[2] a man stood one winter night watching and listening, as though he waited for some beast of the woods to come within the range of his vision, and, later, of his rifle. But the game for whose presence he kept so keen an outlook was none that figured in the sportsman's calendar as lawful and proper for the chase; Ulrich von Gradwitz[3] patrolled the dark forest in quest of a human enemy.

The forest lands of Gradwitz were of wide extent and well stocked with game; the narrow strip of precipitous woodland that lay on its outskirts was not remarkable for the game it harbored or the shooting it afforded, but it was the most jealously guarded of all its owner's territorial possessions. A famous lawsuit, in the days of his grandfather, had wrested it from the illegal possession of a neighboring family of petty landowners; the dispossessed party had never acquiesced in the judgment of the Courts, and a long series of poaching affrays and similar scandals had embittered the relationships between the fam-

ilies for three generations. The neighbors' feud had grown into a personal one since Ulrich had come to be head of his family; if there was a man in the world whom he detested and wished ill to it was Georg Znaeym,[4] the inheritor of the quarrel and the tireless game snatcher and raider of the disputed border forest.

The feud might, perhaps, have died down or been compromised if the personal ill will of the two men had not stood in the way; as boys they had thirsted for one another's blood, as men each prayed that misfortune might fall on the other, and this wind-scourged winter night Ulrich had banded together his foresters to watch the dark forest, not in quest of four-footed quarry,[5] but to keep a look-

---

1. **spur** (spėr), *n.* ridge sticking out from or smaller than the main body of a mountain or mountain range.
2. **Carpathians** (kär pā′thē ənz), mountain chain located in southeast Europe.
3. **Ulrich von Gradwitz** (ül′rik fən gräd′vits)
4. **Georg Znaeym** (gā′ôrg znä′im)
5. **quarry** (kwôr′ē), *n.* animal chased in a hunt; prey.

▲ *Huntsmen on the Edge of Night,* an oil by René Magritte, presents the groping, animallike hunters as if they are themselves hunted by some dark force. What details in the painting offer parallels to Georg and Ulrich?

out for the prowling thieves whom he suspected of being afoot from across the land boundary. The roebuck, which usually kept in the sheltered hollows during a storm-wind, were running like driven things tonight, and there was movement and unrest among the creatures that were wont[6] to sleep through the dark hours. Assuredly there was a disturbing element in the forest, and Ulrich could guess the quarter from whence it came.

He strayed away by himself from the watchers whom he had placed in ambush on the crest of the hill, and wandered far down the steep slopes amid the wild tangle of undergrowth, peering through the tree trunks and listening through the whistling and skirling of the wind and the restless beating of the branches for sight or sound of the marauders. If only on this wild night, in this dark, lone spot, he might come across Georg Znaeym, man to man, with none to witness—that was the wish that was uppermost in his thoughts. And as he stepped

------

6. **wont** (wunt), *adj.* accustomed.

round the trunk of a huge beech he came face to face with the man he sought.

The two enemies stood glaring at one another for a long silent moment. Each had a rifle in his hand, each had hate in his heart and murder uppermost in his mind. The chance had come to give full play to the passions of a lifetime. But a man who has been brought up under the code of a restraining civilization cannot easily nerve himself to shoot down his neighbor in cold blood and without a word spoken, except for an offense against his hearth and honor. And before the moment of hesitation had given way to action, a deed of Nature's own violence overwhelmed them both. A fierce shriek of the storm had been answered by a splitting crash over their heads, and ere they could leap aside a mass of falling beech tree had thundered down on them. Ulrich von Gradwitz found himself stretched on the ground, one arm numb beneath him and the other held almost as helpless in a tight tangle of forked branches, while both legs were pinned beneath the fallen mass. His heavy shooting boots had saved his feet from being crushed to pieces, but if his fractures were not so serious as they might have been, at least it was evident that he could not move from his present position till someone came to release him. The descending twigs had slashed the skin of his face, and he had to wink away some drops of blood from his eyelashes before he could take in a general view of the disaster. At his side, so near that under ordinary circumstances he could almost have touched him, lay Georg Znaeym, alive and struggling, but obviously as helplessly pinioned down as himself. All round them lay a thick-strewn wreckage of splintered branches and broken twigs.

Relief at being alive and exasperation at his captive plight[7] brought a strange medley of pious thank offerings and sharp curses to Ulrich's lips. Georg, who was nearly blinded with the blood which trickled across his eyes, stopped his struggling for a moment to listen, and then gave a short, snarling laugh.

"So you're not killed, as you ought to be, but you're caught, anyway," he cried; "caught fast. Ho, what a jest,[8] Ulrich von Gradwitz snared in his stolen forest. There's real justice for you!"

And he laughed again, mockingly and savagely.

"I'm caught in my own forest land," retorted Ulrich. "When my men come to release us, you will wish, perhaps, that you were in a better plight than caught poaching on a neighbor's land. Shame on you!"

Georg was silent for a moment; then he answered quietly:

"Are you sure that your men will find much to release? I have men, too, in the forest tonight, close behind me, and *they* will be here first and do the releasing. When they drag me out from under these damned branches, it won't need much clumsiness on their part to roll this mass of trunk right over on the top of you. Your men will find you dead under a fallen beech tree. For form's sake I shall send my condolences to your family."

"It is a useful hint," said Ulrich fiercely. "My men had orders to follow in ten minutes' time, seven of which must have gone by already, and when they get me out—I will remember the hint. Only as you will have met your death poaching on my lands, I don't think I can decently send any message of condolence to your family."

"Good," snarled Georg, "good. We'll fight this quarrel out to the death, you and I and our foresters, with no cursed interlopers to come between us. Death and damnation to you, Ulrich von Gradwitz!"

"The same to you, Georg Znaeym, forest thief, game snatcher."

Both men spoke with the bitterness of possible defeat before them, for each knew that it might be long before his men would seek him

---

7. **plight** (plīt), *n.* condition or situation, usually bad.
8. **jest** (jest), *n.* something said to cause laughter; joke.

out or find him; it was a bare matter of chance which party would arrive first on the scene.

Both had now given up the useless struggle to free themselves from the mass of wood that held them down; Ulrich limited his endeavors to an effort to bring his one partially free arm near enough to his outer coat pocket to draw out his wine flask. Even when he had accomplished that operation, it was long before he could manage the unscrewing of the stopper or get any of the liquid down his throat. But what a Heaven-sent draft it seemed! It was an open winter, and little snow had fallen as yet, hence the captives suffered less from the cold than might have been the case at that season of the year; nevertheless, the wine was warming and reviving to the wounded man, and he looked across with something like a throb of pity to where his enemy lay, just keeping the groans of pain and weariness from crossing his lips.

"Could you reach this flask if I threw it over to you?" asked Ulrich suddenly; "there is good wine in it, and one may as well be as comfortable as one can. Let us drink, even if tonight one of us dies."

"No, I can scarcely see anything; there is so much blood caked round my eyes," said Georg, "and in any case I don't drink wine with an enemy."

Ulrich was silent for a few minutes, and lay listening to the weary screeching of the wind. An idea was slowly forming and growing in his brain, an idea that gained strength every time that he looked across at the man who was fighting so grimly against pain and exhaustion. In the pain and languor that Ulrich himself was feeling, the old fierce hatred seemed to be dying down.

"Neighbor," he said presently, "do as you please if your men come first. It was a fair compact.[9] But as for me, I've changed my mind. If my men are the first to come, you shall be the first to be helped, as though you were my guest. We have quarreled like devils all our lives over this stupid strip of forest, where the trees can't even stand upright in a breath of wind. Lying here tonight, thinking, I've come to think that we've been rather fools; there are better things in life than getting the better of a boundary dispute. Neighbor, if you will help me to bury the old quarrel I—I will ask you to be my friend."

Georg Znaeym was silent for so long that Ulrich thought, perhaps, he had fainted with the pain of his injuries. Then he spoke slowly and in jerks.

"How the whole region would stare and gabble if we rode into the market-square together. No one living can remember seeing a Znaeym and a von Gradwitz talking to one another in friendship. And what peace there would be among the forester folk if we ended our feud tonight. And if we choose to make peace among our people there is none other to interfere, no

...THERE ARE BETTER THINGS IN LIFE THAN GETTING THE BETTER OF A BOUNDARY DISPUTE.

interlopers from outside.... You would come and keep the Sylvester night[10] beneath my roof, and I would come and feast on some high day[11] at your castle.... I would never fire a shot on your land, save when you invited me as a guest; and you should come and shoot with me down in the marshes where the wildfowl are. In all the countryside there are none that could hinder if we willed to make peace. I never thought to have wanted to do other than hate you all my life, but I think I have changed my mind about things too, this last half-hour. And you offered

---

9. compact (kom′pakt), n. agreement or contract.
10. **Sylvester night,** New Year's Eve. Festivities honor St. Sylvester.
11. **high day,** any holy day in the Church calendar.

me your wine flask. . . . Ulrich von Gradwitz, I will be your friend."

For a space both men were silent, turning over in their minds the wonderful changes that this dramatic reconciliation would bring about. In the cold, gloomy forest, with the wind tearing in fitful gusts through the naked branches and whistling around the tree trunks, they lay and waited for the help that would now bring release and succor to both parties. And each prayed a private prayer that his men might be the first to arrive, so that he might be the first to show honorable attention to the enemy that had become a friend.

Presently, as the wind dropped for a moment, Ulrich broke silence.

"Let's shout for help," he said; "in this lull[12] our voices may carry a little way."

"They won't carry far through the trees and undergrowth," said Georg, "but we can try. Together, then."

The two raised their voices in a prolonged hunting call.

"Together again," said Ulrich a few minutes later, after listening in vain for an answering halloo.

"I heard something that time, I think," said Ulrich.

"I heard nothing but the pestilential wind," said Georg hoarsely.

There was silence again for some minutes, and then Georg gave a joyful cry.

"I can see figures coming through the wood. They are following in the way I came down the hillside."

Both men raised their voices in as loud a shout as they could muster.[13]

"They hear us! They've stopped. Now they see us. They're running down the hill toward us," cried Ulrich.

"How many of them are there?" asked Georg.

"I can't see distinctly," said Ulrich; "nine or ten."

"Then they are yours," said Georg; "I had only seven out with me."

"They are making all the speed they can, brave lads," said Ulrich gladly.

"Are they your men?" asked Georg. "Are they your men?" he repeated impatiently as Ulrich did not answer.

"No," said Ulrich with a laugh, the idiotic chattering laugh of a man unstrung with hideous fear.

"Who are they?" asked Georg quickly, straining his eyes to see what the other would gladly not have seen.

"*Wolves!*"

---

12. **lull** (lul), *n.* period of less noise or violence; brief calm.
13. **muster** (mus′tər), *v.* gather together.

After Reading

Making Connections

Shaping Your Response

1. Describe your feelings at the end of the story.

2. In your notebook, list three words you would use to describe this story to a friend.

3. Do you think this would have been a better story if the men had been rescued? Why or why not?

Analyzing the Story

4. What information is provided in the **flashback** appearing in the second paragraph of the story?

5. Cite words or phrases from the story that describe the **setting** and convey a **mood** of menace and wildness.

6. Find wording early in the story that **foreshadows** the ending.

7. Identify three different **conflicts** in the story. Which one do you think ultimately proves to be the most important? Explain.

Extending the Ideas

8. 🐾 Mention some recent international feuds over group boundaries. Find out who the "interlopers" are thought to be in one or two of these disputes.

9. In "The Interlopers," the author exposes petty behavior that causes an enduring feud. What **moral** can you draw from the story that might help people around the world get along better?

Literary Focus: Irony

Irony is a contrast between what appears to be and what actually is. In *verbal irony* the actual meaning of a statement is different from what the statement literally says. *Irony of situation* refers to an occurrence that is contrary to what is expected or intended. *Dramatic irony* refers to a situation in which events or facts not known to a character on stage or in a fictional work are known to the audience.

• What is ironic about the story's title? about the men's encounter of each other in the forest? about the end of the story?

Vocabulary Study

compact
jest
lull
muster
plight
quarry
spur
wont

Solve the riddles by writing a vocabulary word for each numbered item. If necessary, consult the Glossary at the back of this book.

1. Both cowboys and mountains might have more than one.
2. You might find this in a purse or at a meeting of diplomats.
3. This can refer to prey or to a place where stone is blasted or cut.
4. If you add an apostrophe, this becomes a contraction.
5. This can be a condition or a solemn promise.

Expressing Your Ideas

Writing Choices

Writer's Notebook Update Did you guess that the interlopers would not be human? Did any of the words in your cluster come close to describing the interlopers in the story? Use your web to describe an incident in your life in which an interloper intruded.

In Lieu of Flowers Use your imagination to write an **obituary** for Ulrich von Gradwitz or Georg Znaeym for the local newspaper. Include a nickname, if you think he had one; age; place of residence; date of death; circumstances of the death; list of survivors; and information about the funeral services.

Surprise! It Wasn't Wolves! Some readers would prefer a less violent outcome for the story. Write a **new ending** to the story that maintains the element of surprise but is less violent than the original. Make sure that your ending does not contradict the details provided throughout the story.

Other Options

Tonight's Episode Work with a group to plan a **radio play** of "The Interlopers." Think about how you can best relate the information given in the flashback at the beginning of the story. What music will add to the mood of the story? What sound effects will you use? Present your radio play to the class.

At a Theater Near You Movie posters are advertisements that give the viewer a "sneak preview" of the action and stars of a film. Create a **movie poster** for the film version of "The Interlopers," keeping the tone of the story and giving the viewers just enough information about the story and actors to make them want to buy a ticket.

The Boar Hunt

by José Vasconcelos   Mexico

José Vasconcelos
1882–1959

Educator, writer, politician, and historian, José Vasconcelos (hō zā′ väs cōn sā′lōs) did much to improve the standard of living in his native land of Mexico. In the decade prior to the revolution of 1910, he graduated from law school and co-founded a group dedicated to the revival of Mexican culture. As Minister of Public Education from 1920 to 1924, he instituted important reforms by opening rural schools, commissioning mural painting, assisting musicians, and inviting other Latin American intellectual leaders to Mexico. His autobiography, *The Mexican Ulysses*, is an excellent study of culture and life in twentieth-century Mexico.

Building Background

To Hunt or Not to Hunt As a class project, conduct a survey to find out how students feel about hunting animals. Use items such as the following, or think of your own. Write each item on the board and tally students' answers. Then make up five rules for hunting.

1. Hunting animals is permissible ____.

    a. always   **b.** never   **c.** sometimes

2. People can kill animals ____.

    a. for food   **b.** for clothing   **c.** for sport   **d.** for any reason

3. It is ____ that killing certain animals can restore an ecological balance.

    a. true   **b.** false   **c.** unprovable

Literary Focus

Moral Do you recall childhood fables, such as "The Hare and the Tortoise" or "The Boy Who Cried Wolf"? These stories teach a **moral**, or lesson. For example, the moral of "The Boy Who Cried Wolf" can be stated something like this: "If you try to deceive people, they eventually won't believe you even when you're telling the truth." When you have finished reading "The Boar Hunt," think about the lesson, or moral, it teaches. At what cost does the main character learn this lesson?

Writer's Notebook

Truth or Consequences The theme of this group of stories is "Dealing with Consequences." As you read "The Boar Hunt," jot down words and phrases that seem to suggest what will happen, along with your predictions about these consequences. You might also use the artwork to help make your predictions.

THE BOAR HUNT

JOSÉ VASCONCELOS

We were four companions, and we went by the names of our respective nationalities: the Colombian, the Peruvian, the Mexican; the fourth, a native of Ecuador, was called Quito[1] for short. Unforeseen chance had joined us together a few years ago on a large sugar plantation on the Peruvian coast. We worked at different occupations during the day and met during the evening in our off time. Not being Englishmen, we did not play cards. Instead, our constant discussions led to disputes. These didn't stop us from wanting to see each other the next night, however, to continue the interrupted debates and support them with new arguments. Nor did the rough sentences of the preceding wrangles indicate a lessening of our affection, of which we assured ourselves reciprocally with the clasping of hands and a look. On Sundays we used to go on hunting parties. We roamed the fertile glens, stalking, generally with poor results, the game of the warm region around the coast, or we entertained ourselves killing birds that flew in the sunlight during the siesta hour.

We came to be tireless wanderers and excellent marksmen. Whenever we climbed a hill and gazed at the imposing range of mountains in the interior, its attractiveness stirred us and we wanted to climb it. What attracted us more was the trans-Andean region:[2] fertile plateaus extending on the other side of the range in the direction of the Atlantic toward the immense land of Brazil. It was as if primitive

---

1. **Ecuador** (ek′wə dôr) **. . . Quito** (kē′tō). Ecuador is located in northwestern South America. Quito is its capital.
2. **trans-Andean region,** the area across—that is, to the east of—the Andes Mountains. The Andes run in a generally north-south direction through the length of South America.

nature called us to her breast. The vigor of the fertile, untouched jungles promised to rejuvenate[3] our minds, the same vigor which rejuvenates the strength and the thickness of the trees each year. At times we devised crazy plans. As with all things that are given a lot of thought, these schemes generally materialized. Ultimately nature and events are largely what our imaginations make them out to be. And so we went ahead planning and acting. At the end of the year, with arranged vacations, accumulated money, good rifles, abundant munitions, stone- and mud-proof boots, four hammocks, and a half dozen faithful Indians, our caravan descended the Andean slopes, leading to the endless green ocean.

At last we came upon a village at the edge of the Marañón River.[4] Here we changed our safari. The region we were going to penetrate had no roads. It was unexplored underbrush into which we could enter only by going down the river in a canoe. In time we came to the area where we proposed to carry out the purpose of our journey, the hunting of wild boars.

We had been informed that boars travel in herds of several thousands, occupying a region, eating grass and staying together, exploiting the grazing areas, organized just like an army. They are very easy to kill if one attacks them when they are scattered out satisfying their appetites—an army given over to the delights of victory. When they march about hungry, on the other hand, they are usually vicious. In our search we glided down river between imposing jungles with our provisions and the company of three faithful Indian oarsmen.

One morning we stopped at some huts near the river. Thanks to the information gathered there, we decided to disembark a little farther on in order to spend the night on land and continue the hunt for the boars in the thicket the following day.

Sheltered in a backwater, we came ashore, and after a short exploration found a clearing in which to make camp. We unloaded the provisions and the rifles, tied the boat securely, then with the help of the Indians set up our camp one-half kilometer from the riverbank. In marking the path to the landing, we were careful not to lose ourselves in the thicket. The Indians withdrew toward their huts, promising to return two days later. At dawn we would set out in search of the prey.

Though night had scarcely come and the heat was great, we gathered at the fire to see each other's faces, to look instinctively for protection. We talked a little, confessed to being tired, and decided to go to bed. Each hammock had been tied by one end to a single tree, firm though not very thick in the trunk. Stretching out from this axis in different directions, the hammocks were supported by the other end on other trunks. Each of us carried his rifle, cartridges, and some provisions which couldn't remain exposed on the ground. The sight of the weapons made us consider the place where we were, surrounded by the unknown. A slight feeling of terror made us laugh, cough, and talk. But fatigue overcame us, that heavy fatigue which compels the soldier to scorn danger, to put down his rifle, and to fall asleep though the most persistent enemy pursues him. We scarcely noticed the supreme grandeur of that remote tropical night.

I don't know whether it was the light of the magnificent dawn or the strange noises which awakened me and made me sit up in my hammock and look carefully at my surroundings. I saw nothing but the awakening of that life which at night falls into the lethargy[5] of the jungle. I called my sleeping companions and, alert and seated in our hanging beds, we dressed ourselves. We were preparing to jump to the ground when we clearly heard a somewhat distant, sudden sound of rustling branches. Since

---

3. **rejuvenate** (ri jü′və nāt), *v.* make young or vigorous again; renew.
4. **Marañón** (mä′rä nyôn′) **River,** a river in Peru, flowing north and then east into the Amazon.
5. **lethargy** (leth′ər jē), *n.* lack of energy; inactivity.

▲ This detail from George Catlin's painting, *A Fight with Peccaries, Rio Trombutas, Brazil*, uses vertical and horizontal lines to contrast the weapons and active thought of human beings with the natural instinct of wild animals. Which details in the painting fit your impressions of the story? Which details seem to depart from the story?

it did not continue, however, we descended confidently, washed our faces with water from our canteens, and slowly prepared and enjoyed breakfast. By about 11:00 in the morning we were armed and bold and preparing to make our way through the jungle.

But then the sound again. Its persistence and proximity in the thicket made us change our minds. An instinct made us take refuge in our hammocks. We cautiously moved our cartridges and rifles into them again, and without consulting each other we agreed on the idea of putting our provisions safely away. We passed them up into the hammocks, and we ourselves finally climbed in. Stretched out face down, comfortably suspended with rifles in hand, we did not have to wait long. Black, agile boars quickly appeared from all directions. We wel-

comed them with shouts of joy and well-aimed shots. Some fell immediately, giving comical snorts, but many more came out of the jungle. We shot again, spending all the cartridges in the magazine. Then we stopped to reload. Finding ourselves safe in the height of our hammocks, we continued after a pause.

We counted dozens of them. At a glance we made rapid calculations of the magnitude of the destruction, while the boars continued to come out of the jungle in uncountable numbers. Instead of going on their way or fleeing, they seemed confused. All of them emerged from the jungle where it was easy for us to shoot them. Occasionally we had to stop firing because the frequent shooting heated the barrels of our rifles. While they were cooling we were able to joke, celebrating our good fortune. The impotent[6] anger of the boars amazed us. They raised their tusks in our direction, uselessly threatening us. We laughed at their snorts, quietly aimed at those who were near, and Bang! a dead boar. We carefully studied the angle of the shoulder blade so that the bullet would cross the heart. The slaughter lasted for hours.

At 4:00 P.M. we noticed an alarming shortage of our ammunition. We had been well supplied and had shot at will. Though the slaughter was gratifying,[7] the boars must have numbered, as we had been informed previously, several thousands, because their hordes didn't diminish. On the contrary, they gathered directly beneath our hammocks in increasing groups. They slashed furiously at the trunk of the tree which held the four points of the hammocks. The marks of the tusks remained on the hard bark. Not without a certain fear we watched them gather compactly, tenaciously,[8] in tight masses against the resisting trunk. We wondered what would happen to a man who fell within their reach. Our shots were now sporadic,[9] well aimed, carefully husbanded.[10] They did not drive away the aggressive beasts, but only redoubled their fury. One of us ironically noted that from being the attackers we had gone on the defensive. We did not laugh very long at the joke. Now we hardly shot at all. We needed to save our cartridges.

The afternoon waned and evening came upon us. After consulting each other, we decided to eat in our hammocks. We applauded ourselves for taking the food up—meat, bread, and bottles of water. Stretching ourselves on our hammocks, we passed things to each other, sharing what we needed. The boars deafened us with their angry snorts.

After eating, we began to feel calm. We lit cigars. Surely the boars would go. Their numbers were great, but they would finally leave peacefully. As we said so, however, we looked with greedy eyes at the few unused cartridges that remained. Our enemies, like enormous angry ants, stirred beneath us, encouraged by the ceasing of our fire. From time to time we carefully aimed and killed one or two of them, driving off the huge group of uselessly enraged boars at the base of the trunk which served as a prop for our hammocks.

Night enveloped us almost without our noticing the change from twilight. Anxiety also overtook us. When would the cursed boars leave? Already there were enough dead to serve as trophies to several dozen hunters. Our feat would be talked about; we had to show ourselves worthy of such fame. Since there was nothing else to do, it was necessary to sleep. Even if we had had enough bullets it would have been impossible to continue the fight in the darkness. It occurred to us to start a fire to drive the herd off with flames, but apart from the fact that we couldn't leave the place in which we were suspended, there were no dry branches in the lush forest. Finally, we slept.

We woke up a little after midnight. The darkness was profound, but the well-known noise made us aware that our enemies were still there. We imagined they must be the last ones which were leaving, however. If a good army needs several hours to break camp and march off, what can be expected of a vile army of boars but disorder and delay? The following morning we would fire upon the stragglers, but this painful thought bothered us: they were in large and apparently active numbers. What were they up to? Why didn't they leave? We thus spent long hours of worry. Dawn finally came, splendid in the sky but noisy in the jungle still enveloped inwardly in shadows. We eagerly waited for the sun to penetrate the foliage in order to survey the appearance of the field of battle of the day before.

What we finally saw made us gasp. It terrified

---

6. **impotent** (im′pə tənt), *adj.* powerless; helpless.
7. **gratifying** (grat′ə fī ing), *adj.* satisfying; pleasing.
8. **tenaciously** (ti nā′shəs lē), *adv.* stubbornly.
9. **sporadic** (spə rad′ik), *adj.* appearing or happening at intervals in time; occasional.
10. **husbanded** (huz′bənd əd), *adj.* managed carefully.

us. The boars were painstakingly continuing the work which they had engaged in throughout the entire night. Guided by some extraordinary instinct, with their tusks they were digging out the ground underneath the tree from which our hammocks hung; they gnawed the roots and continued to undermine them like large, industrious rats. Presently the tree was bound to fall and we with it, among the beasts. From that moment we neither thought nor talked. In desperation we used up our last shots, killing more ferocious beasts. Still, the rest renewed their activity. They seemed to be endowed with intelligence. However much we concentrated our fire against them, they did not stop their attack against the tree.

Soon our shots stopped. We emptied our pistols, and then silently listened to the tusks gnawing beneath the soft, wet, pleasant-smelling earth. From time to time the boars pressed against the tree, pushing it and making it creak, eager to smash it quickly. We looked on, hypnotized by their devilish activity. It was impossible to flee because the black monsters covered every inch in sight. It seemed to us that, by a sudden inspiration, they were preparing to take revenge on us for the ruthless nature of man, the unpunished destroyer of animals since the beginning of time. Our imagination, distorted by fear, showed us our fate as an atonement for the unpardonable crimes implicit[11] in the struggle of biological selection. Before my eyes passed the vision of sacred India, where the believer refuses to eat meat in order to prevent the methodical killing of beasts and in order to atone for man's evil, bloody, treacherous slaughter, such as ours, for mere vicious pleasure. I felt that the multitude of boars was raising its accusing voice against me. I now understood the infamy[12] of the hunter, but what was repentance worth if I was going to die with my companions, hopelessly devoured by that horde of brutes with demonlike eyes?

Stirred by terror and without realizing what I was doing, I hung from the upper end of my hammock, I balanced myself in the air, I swung in a long leap, I grasped a branch of a tree facing the one on which the boars were digging. From there I leaped to other branches and to others, reviving in myself habits which the species had forgotten.

The next moment a terrifying sound and unforgettable cries told me of the fall of the tree and the end of my companions. I clung to a trunk, trembling and listening to the chattering of my jaws. Later, the desire to flee gave me back my strength. Leaning out over the foliage, I looked for a path, and I saw the boars in the distance, marching in compressed ranks and holding their insolent snouts in the air. I knew that they were now withdrawing, and I got down from the tree. Horror overwhelmed me as I approached the site of our encampment, but some idea of duty made me return there. Perhaps one of my friends had managed to save himself. I approached hesitantly. Each dead boar made me tremble with fear.

But what I saw next was so frightful that I could not fix it clearly in my mind: remains of clothing—and footwear. There was no doubt; the boars had devoured them. Then I ran toward the river, following the tracks we had made two days before. I fled with great haste, limbs stiff from panic.

Running with long strides, I came upon the boat. With a great effort, I managed to row to the huts. There I went to bed with a high fever which lasted many days.

I will participate in no more hunts. I will contribute, if I have to, to the extermination of harmful beasts. But I will not kill for pleasure. I will not amuse myself with the ignoble[13] pleasure of the hunt.

---

11. **implicit** (im plis′it), *adj.* meant, but not clearly expressed or distinctly stated; implied.
12. **infamy** (in′fə mē), *n.* a very bad reputation; public disgrace.
13. **ignoble** (ig nō′bəl), *adj.* without honor; disgraceful.

After Reading

Making Connections

Shaping Your Response

1. By the end of the story, for whom do you feel more compassion—the hunters or the boars? Why?

2. If you were filming this story, what sounds, images, or camera tricks would you use to create a mood of increasing tension?

3. Do you think the outcome of the story is appropriate, or could the author have made his point more effectively another way? Explain.

Analyzing the Story

4. **Personification** is the attributing of human characteristics to nonhuman creatures or objects. Find two instances in which boars are personified; explain what human qualities they seem to have.

5. In what way is the hunters' decision to tie all four hammocks to the same tree significant to the **plot**?

6. Trace the narrator's attitude toward killing animals from the beginning of the story through the very end.

7. This story is set east of the Andes Mountains in Peru. Explain why this **setting** is important to the story.

Extending the Ideas

8. 🐾 Do you think that cultural settings and conditions such as food supply should determine our **choices** about how we use (and use up) natural resources? Or are there universal rules about conservation that all people should obey? Explain.

9. If you have read "The Interlopers," draw a Venn diagram showing similarities and differences between the men in both stories.

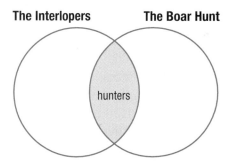

The Interlopers   The Boar Hunt

hunters

Literary Focus: Moral

A **moral** is a lesson conveyed in a work. In "The Boar Hunt," the narrator learns a lesson after he and his companions become the hunted.

- Explain the moral of "The Boar Hunt."

- Do you think the message of this story would have been conveyed as effectively in a nonfiction article? Explain.

Vocabulary Study

Number your paper from 1 to 10. Then match each numbered word with the letter of its synonym.

gratifying
husbanded
ignoble
implicit
impotent
infamy
lethargy
rejuvenate
sporadic
tenaciously

1. *impotent*   a. powerful b. helpless c. severe d. loud
2. *lethargy*   a. inactivity b. denseness c. energy d. injury
3. *rejuvenate*   a. renew b. impoverish c. enlighten d. repeat
4. *tenaciously*   a. flexibly b. stubbornly c. willfully d. reluctantly
5. *husbanded*   a. wasted b. married c. cut d. managed carefully
6. *implicit*   a. specific b. expressed c. implied d. obvious
7. *infamy*   a. sorrow b. esteem c. fame d. disgrace
8. *ignoble*   a. honorable b. fortunate c. ignorant d. disgraceful
9. *sporadic*   a. occasional b. subsequent c. frequent d. steady
10. *gratifying*   a. opposing b. envying c. satisfying d. surprising

Expressing Your Ideas

Writing Choices

Writer's Notebook Update How accurate were your predictions? Go back and see if you can list more clues that point to the outcome. Then write several sentences that complete the following observation: *The fact that the narrator survives makes the ending more (less) effective than if everyone had perished.*

Attack of the Killer Broccoli Imagine that you are a creature or an item in the environment that has been misused by humans. Think of a way to seek revenge. What kind of science fiction movie would this revenge story be? Think of a title for such a movie and write an **advertisement** for it.

What I Think of Your Mink Someone whom you admire is planning to buy a mink coat. This person asks you what you think of the decision. Write a brief **dialogue** in which you express your ideas, including those relating to ecology and to animal rights.

Other Options

You're on the Air Plan a **radio talk program** in your classroom to discuss your class's views of whether animals should be killed for human purposes such as medicine, clothing, and food. One or two students will "host" the program, accept "calls" from listeners, and keep the discussion on track. Other students will "call in" to the program with statements of opinion on the subject. Callers must listen carefully to preceding callers in order to build on previous discussions. Only a host can interrupt a caller.

Drawing a Moral Many cartoons promote greater awareness of ecological problems. Work with a partner to plan and draw a **cartoon** about an ecological issue or moral dilemma presented in "The Boar Hunt."

Before Reading

from Red Azalea

by Anchee Min   China

Anchee Min
born 1957

Anchee Min (än′shē min) was born in Shanghai, China, during the communist rule of Mao Tse-tung (mä′ō dzu′dùng). During the Cultural Revolution, she become a leader of the Little Red Guards, and was later chosen to star in one of Madame Mao's movies. But her fortunes changed with the death of Chairman Mao, the execution of Madame Mao, and the ensuing political turmoil. In 1983 Min fled to the United States, where she published *Red Azalea* and a novel, *Katherine,* both about the horrors of the revolution. When Min toured China to promote *Red Azalea,* the government ironically touted her as an example of what Chinese women could accomplish.

Building Background

The time line below shows some of the events that preceded and followed the **Cultural Revolution.** Additional information is provided on page 145.

China

Mao Tse-tung

Events Surrounding the Cultural Revolution 1966–1970

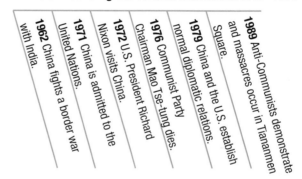

1962 China fights a border war with India.

1971 China is admitted to the United Nations.

1972 U.S. President Richard Nixon visits China.

1976 Communist Party Chairman Mao Tse-tung dies.

1979 China and the U.S. establish normal diplomatic relations.

1989 Anti-Communists demonstrate and massacres occur in Tiananmen Square.

Literary Focus

Conflict The struggle between a character and an opposing force in a story is called **conflict.** A story may have more than one kind of conflict, as you will see in the selection you are about to read.

Writer's Notebook

Pressure Points Growing up is never easy, but growing up in China during the Cultural Revolution presented special challenges. List some of the conflicts and challenges you recall having at age thirteen. Then as you read Anchee Min's autobiography, list the conflicts and challenges she faced as a member of the Little Red Guards.

RED AZALEA

ANCHEE MIN

During the Cultural Revolution, which began in 1966, Mao Tse-tung, the Chinese Communist leader from 1945 to 1976, authorized radicals in the Communist Party to remove from power any people they believed failed to follow Communist principles. The accused were dismissed from their positions, and the different factions of radicals who replaced them fought for power. Violence often resulted in cities and provinces as a result of these power struggles. Militant student groups called Red Guards were formed, demonstrations that were sometimes violent were held, and universities were closed from 1966 to 1970. At the time this excerpt from Red Azalea *takes place, China was undergoing the turmoil of the Cultural Revolution.*

◄ The 1967 propaganda poster entitled *Hail the Defeat of Revisionism in Our China* uses Western perceptions and scale (note the gregarious expressions and muscular proportions) and advertising techniques to sell communism to the Chinese public. Using details from this poster, cite at least five things Maoist China considers important.

In school Mao's books were our texts. I was the head of the class on the history of the Communist Party of China. To me, history meant how proletarians[1] won over the reactionaries. Western history was a history of capitalist exploitation.[2] We hung portraits of Marx, Engels, Lenin and Stalin[3] next to Mao in our classrooms. Each morning we bowed to them as well as bowing to Mao, praying for a long, long life for him. My sisters copied my compositions. My compositions were collected slogans. I always began with this: "The East wind is blowing, the fighting drum is beating. Who is afraid in the world today? It is not the people who are afraid of American imperialists.[4] It is the American imperialists who are afraid of the people." Those phrases won me prizes. Space Conqueror[5] looked up to me as if I were a magician. For me, compositions were nothing; it was abacus competitions that were difficult. I wrote compositions for my brother and sisters, but I felt I had not much in common with the children. I felt like an adult. I longed for challenges. I was at the school day and night promoting Communism, making revolution by painting slogans on walls and boards. I led my schoolmates in collecting pennies. We wanted to donate the pennies to the starving children in America. We were proud of what we did. We were sure that we were making red dots on the world's map. We were fighting for the final peace of the planet. Not for a day did I not feel heroic. I was the opera.

I was asked to attend the school's Revolutionary Committee meeting. It was 1970 and I was thirteen years old. I discussed how to carry on the Cultural Revolution at our Long Happiness Elementary School with the committee people, the true revolutionaries. When I raised my hand and said I would like to speak, my face would no longer flush. I knew what I was talking about. Phrases from *People's Daily* and *Red Flag* magazine poured out of my mouth. My speeches were filled with an impassioned and noble spirit. I was honored. In the early seventies my being a head of the Little Red Guards[6] at school brought our family honor. My award certificates were my mother's pride, although she never hung them on the wall. My name was constantly mentioned by the school authority and praised as "Study Mao Thoughts Activist," "Mao's Good Child" and "Student of Excellences." Whenever I would speak through a microphone in the school's broadcasting station, my sisters and brother would be listening in their classrooms and their classmates would look at them with admiration and envy.

The school's new Party secretary, a man named Chain, was a workers' representative from the Shanghai[7] Shipping Factory. He was about fifty years old, extremely thin, like a bamboo stick. He taught me how to hold political meetings. He liked to say, We have to let our little general play a full role in the Cultural Revolution and give full scope to the initiative[8] of the Little Red Guards. He told me not to be afraid of things that I did not understand. You must learn to think like this, he said. If the earth stops spinning, I'll continue to spin.

---

1. proletarian (prō′lə ter′ē ən), *n.* someone belonging to the proletariat, the lowest class in economic and social status, including all unskilled laborers.
2. exploitation (ek′sploi tā′shən), *n.* selfish or unfair use.
3. **Marx . . . Stalin.** Karl Marx, 1818–1883, was a German political philosopher, writer on economics, and advocate of socialism. Friedrich Engels, 1820–1895, was a German socialist writer. Vladimir Ilyich Lenin, 1870–1924, was a Russian Communist leader, the founder of the Soviet government and its first premier from 1918 to 1924. Joseph Stalin, 1879–1953, was a Soviet political leader and dictator of the Soviet Union from 1929 to 1953.
4. **imperialist,** *n.* someone who favors imperialism, or the policy of extending the rule or authority of one country over other countries and colonies.
5. **Space Conqueror,** one of Anchee Min's siblings.
6. **Little Red Guards,** children in elementary school who formed a younger group of Red Guards.
7. **Shanghai** (shang′hī′), seaport in E. China.
8. initiative (i nish′ē ə tiv), *n.* active part in taking the first steps in any undertaking; lead.

QUESTION: Jot down in your notebook any questions you have about the Cultural Revolution.

It was the first week of November when Secretary Chain called me in. He told me excitedly that the committee had finally dug out a hidden class enemy, an American spy. He said, We are going to have a meeting against her, a rally which two thousand people will be attending. You will be the student representative to speak against her. I asked who it was. Wrinkling his eyebrows, the secretary pronounced a shocking name. It was Autumn Leaves, my teacher. I thought I heard Secretary Chain wrong. But he nodded at me slowly, confirming that I heard him exactly right.

I sat down. I actually dropped down on the chair. My legs all of a sudden lost their strength.

Autumn Leaves was a thin, middle-aged lady and was seriously nearsighted. She wore a dark pair of glasses and had a hoarse voice and a short temper. She loved Chinese, mathematics and music. The first day she stepped into the classroom, she asked all the students if any of us could tell what her name Autumn Leaves meant. No one was able to figure it out. Then she explained it. She said that there was a famous poem written in the Tang Dynasty[9] about autumn leaves. It praised the beauty and significance of the falling leaves. It said that when a leaf fell naturally, it symbolized a full life. The touch of the ground meant the transformation of a ripe leaf to fresh mud. It fertilized the seeds through the winter. Its pregnancy came to term with the next spring. She said that we were her spring.

She was an energetic teacher who never seemed to be tired of teaching. Her methods were unique. One moment she raised her arms to shoulder level and stretched them out to the sides, making herself look like a cross when explaining infinity; the next moment she spoke with a strong Hunan[10] accent when explaining where a poet was from. Once she completely lost her voice while trying to explain geometric progression[11] to me. When she finally made me understand, she laughed silently like a mute with her arms dancing in the air. When I thanked her, she said that she was glad that I was serious about learning. She set me up as the example for our class and then the entire grade. When she knew that I wanted to improve my Chinese, she brought me her own books to read. She was this way with all her students. One day when it was raining hard after class, she gave students her raincoat, rain shoes and her umbrella as they went home. She herself went home wet. The next day she had a fever, but she came to class and struggled on, despite her fever. By the time she finished her lecture, she had lost her voice again. There was no way I could picture Autumn Leaves as an American spy.

As if reading my mind, Secretary Chain smiled and asked me if I had ever heard the phrase "Raging flames refine the real gold." I

THERE WAS NO WAY I COULD PICTURE AUTUMN LEAVES AS AN AMERICAN SPY.

shook my head. He said, It is time for you to test yourself out to see whether you are a real revolutionary or an armchair revolutionary. He recited a Mao quotation: "To have a revolution is not like having a dinner party, not like painting a pretty picture or making embroidery. It is not that easy and relaxing. Revolution is an

---

9. **Tang** (täng) **Dynasty,** a Chinese dynasty from A.D. 618 to 907, under which China expanded toward central Asia, Buddhism gained its political influence, printing was invented, and Chinese poetry reached its finest development.
10. **Hunan** (hü nän′), a province in SE central China.
11. **geometric progression,** sequence of numbers in which each number is multiplied by the same factor in order to obtain the following number. 2, 4, 8, 16, and 32 form a geometric progression.

Red Azalea   **147**

insurrection[12] in which one class overthrows the other with violent force."

I found my words were blocked by my stiff tongue. I kept saying, Autumn Leaves is my teacher. Secretary Chain suggested that we work on my problem. He lit a cigarette and told me the fable of "A Wolf in Sheep's Skin." He said Autumn Leaves was the wolf. He told me that Autumn Leaves' father was a Chinese American who was still living in America. Autumn Leaves was born and educated in America. Secretary Chain said, The capitalist sent his daughter back to China to educate our children. Don't you see this as problematic?

For the next two hours Secretary Chain convinced me that Autumn Leaves was a secret agent of the imperialists and was using teaching as a weapon to destroy our minds. Secretary Chain asked whether I would tolerate that. Of course not, I said. No one can pull our proletarians back to the old society. Good, said Secretary Chain, tapping my shoulders. He said he knew I would be a sharp spear for the Party. I raised my head and said, Secretary, please tell me what to do. He said, Write a speech. I asked what I should write. He said, Tell the masses how you were mentally poisoned. I said that I did not quite understand the words "mentally poisoned." Secretary Chain said, You are not mature enough to understand that yet. He then asked me to give an opinion on what kind of person I thought Autumn Leaves was. I told him the truth.

Secretary Chain laughed loudly at me. He said that I had already become a victim of the spy who had almost killed me with the skill of the wolf who killed the sheep, leaving no trace of blood. He punched his fist on the table and said loudly, That in itself is wonderful material to be discussed! I felt awkward. He stopped laughing and said, You shouldn't be discouraged by your immaturity.

He made me feel disappointed in myself. Let me help you, he suggested. He asked me

the name of the books she loaned me. *An Old Man of Invention,* I began to recall, *The Little Mermaid,* and *Snow White.* He asked for the author's name. I said it was something like Andersen.

Secretary Chain suddenly raised his hand in the air and furrowed his brow. He said, Stop, this is it. Who is Andersen? An old foreign man, I guess, I replied. What were his fairy tales about? About lives of princes, princesses and little people. What does Andersen do now? he asked. I do not know, I replied.

Look how careless you are! Secretary Chain almost yelled at me. He could be a foreign spy! Taking out a little glass vial, Secretary Chain put a few pills into his mouth. He explained that it was the medicine for his liver pain. He said his liver was hurting badly, but he could not tell his doctor about this because he would be hospitalized immediately. He said his pain was getting worse, but he could not afford to waste a second in the hospital. How can I disappoint Chairman Mao, who put his trust in people like us, the working class, the class that was once even lower than the pigs and dogs before Liberation?

His face was turning purple. I suggested that he take a rest. He waved me to go on as he pressed his liver with his hands to endure the pain. He told me that he did not have much schooling. His parents died of hunger when he was five. His brother and little sister were thrown into the sea after they died of cholera. He was sold to a child dealer for fifteen pounds of rice. He became a child worker in a shipping factory in Shanghai and was beaten often by the owner. After the Liberation he joined the Party and was sent to a workers' night school. He said, I owe our Party a great deal and I haven't worked hard enough to show my appreciation.

I looked at him and was touched. His pain seemed to be increasing. His fingers pressed

---

12. **insurrection** (in′sə rek′shən), *n.* a rising against established authority; revolt.

against his liver harder, but he refused to rest. You know, we found Autumn Leaves' diary and it had a paragraph about you, he said. What . . . what did she say about me? I became nervous. She said that you were one of the very few children who were educable. She put quotation marks around "educable." Can you think of what that means? Without waiting for my reply, Secretary Chain concluded, It was obvious that Autumn Leaves thought that you could be educated into her type, her father's type, the imperialists' type. He pointed out that the purpose of writing this diary was to present it to her American boss as proof of her success as a spy.

My world turned upside down. I felt deeply hurt and used. Secretary Chain asked me whether I was aware of the fact that I was set up as a model by Autumn Leaves to influence the others. Her goal is to make you all *betray* Communism! I felt the guilt and anger. I said to Secretary Chain that I would speak tomorrow. He nodded at me. He said, Our Party trusts you and Mao would be very proud of you.

Pull out the hidden class enemy, the American spy Autumn Leaves! Expose her under the bare sun! the crowd shouted as soon as the meeting started. I was sitting on the stage on one of the risers. Two strong men escorted Autumn Leaves onto the stage facing the crowd of two thousand people, including her students and colleagues. Her arms were twisted behind her. She was almost unrecognizable. Only a few days had passed since I had seen her, but it seemed as though she had aged ten years. Her hair had suddenly turned gray. Her face was colorless. A rectangular board reading "Down with American Spy" hung from her neck. Two men forced her to bow to Mao's portrait three times. One of the men bent her left arm very hard and said, Beg Chairman Mao for forgiveness now! Autumn Leaves refused to say the words. The two men bent her arms up backward. They bent her harder. Autumn Leaves' face contorted[13] in pain

and then her mouth moved. She said the words and the men let her loose.

PREDICT: Do you think the narrator will betray Autumn Leaves? Explain.

My mouth was terribly dry. It was hard to bear what I saw. The string of the heavy board seemed to cut into Autumn Leaves' skin. I forgot what I was supposed to do—to lead the crowd to shout the slogans—until Secretary Chain came to remind me of my duty.

Long live the great proletarian dictatorship! I shouted, following the slogan menu. I was getting more and more scared when I saw Autumn Leaves struggling with the two men who had been trying to press her head toward the floor while she tried to face the sky. When her eyeglasses fell off, I saw her eyes close tightly.

Secretary Chain shouted at her. The crowd shouted, Confess! Confess! Secretary Chain took the microphone and said that the masses would not have much patience. By acting this way Autumn Leaves was digging her own grave.

Autumn Leaves kept silent. When kicked hard, she said that she had nothing to confess. She said she was innocent. Our Party never accuses anyone who is innocent, said Secretary Chain, and yet the Party would never allow a class enemy to slip away from the net of the proletarian dictatorship. He said now it was time to demonstrate that Autumn Leaves was a criminal. He nodded at me and turned to the crowd. He said, Let's have the victim speak out!

I stood up and felt dizzy. The crowd began clapping their hands. The sunlight was dazzlingly bright and was hurting my eyes. My vision became blurred and I saw a million bees wheeling in front of me sounding like helicopters. As the crowd kept clapping, I moved to the front of the stage. I stopped in front of the

---

13. **contort** (kən tôrt′), *v.* twist or bend out of shape.

Red Azalea   **149**

microphone. Taking out the speech I had written last night, I suddenly felt a need to speak with my parents. I had not gone home but slept in the classroom on the table with other Little Red Guards. Five of us wrote the speech. I regretted not having my parents go over the speech with me. I took a deep breath. My fingers were shaking and would not obey in turning the pages.

Don't be afraid, we are all with you, Secretary Chain said in my ear as he came to adjust the height of the microphone. He placed a cup of water in front of me. I took the water and drank it down in one breath. I felt a little better. I began to read.

I read to the crowd that Autumn Leaves was the wolf in sheep's skin. I took out the books she loaned me and showed them to the crowd. As I was delivering my speech, I saw from the corner of my eye that Autumn Leaves had turned her head in my direction. She was murmuring. I became nervous but managed to continue. Comrades,[14] I said, now I understand why Autumn Leaves was so kind to me. She was trying to turn me into an enemy of our country, and a running dog of the imperialists! I read on.

There was some slogan-shouting, during which I glanced secretly at Autumn Leaves. She was breathing hard and was about to fall. I stood, my limbs turning cold. I tried to remove my eyes from Autumn Leaves, but she caught them. I was terrified when I saw her staring at me without her eyeglasses. Her eyes looked like two Ping-Pong balls that almost popped out of her eye sockets.

The crowd shouted, Confess! Confess! Autumn Leaves began to speak slowly to the crowd with her hoarse voice. She said that she would never want to turn any of her students into the country's enemy. She broke into tears. Why would I? she repeated again and again. She was losing her voice. She began to swing her head trying to project her words, but no sound came out. She swung her head again making an effort to let her words out. She said that her father loved this country and that was the reason she came back to teach. Both her father and she believed in education. Spy? What are you talking about? Where did you get this idea? She looked at me.

If the enemy doesn't surrender, let's boil her, fry her and burn her to death! Secretary Chain shouted. The crowd followed, shouting and waving their fists. Secretary Chain signaled for me to go on. But I was trembling too hard to continue. Secretary Chain walked to the microphone from the back of the stage. He took over the microphone. He told the crowd that this was a class enemy's live performance. It had given us an opportunity to learn how deceitful an enemy could be. Can we allow her to go on like this? No! the crowd shouted.

Secretary Chain was ordering Autumn Leaves to shut up and accept the criticism of the revolutionary masses with a correct attitude. Autumn Leaves said that she could not accept any untrue facts. Autumn Leaves said that a young girl such as I should not be used by someone with an evil intention.

You underestimated our Little Red Guard's political awareness, Secretary Chain said with a scornful laugh. Autumn Leaves demanded to speak to me. Secretary Chain told her to go ahead. He said that as a thorough-going dialectical materialist[15] he never underestimated the role of teachers by negative example.

As the crowd quieted down, Autumn Leaves squatted on her heels to seek her glasses on the floor. When she put her glasses back on, she started to question me. I was scared. I did not expect that she would talk to me so seriously. My terror turned into fury. I wanted to get away. I

---

14. **comrade** (kom′rad), *n.* member of the Communist party.
15. **dialectical** (dī′ə lek′tə kəl) **materialist** (mə tir′ē ə list) a follower of the socialist doctrine that advocates a classless society emerging as the result of a long struggle between economic classes.

▲ Tsao Yu-tung's painting, *Night Battle,* shows happy and energetic workers laboring into the night to repair a dam. How does this painting, along with the poster on page 144, reinforce the philosophy of Secretary Chain in this story?

said, How dare you put me in such a spot to be questioned like a reactionary? You had used me in the past to serve the imperialists; now you want to use me to get away from the criticism? It would be a shame if I lost to you!

Autumn Leaves called my name and asked if I really believed that she was an enemy of the country. If I did not think so, could I tell her who assigned me to do the speech. She said she wanted the truth. She said Chairman Mao always liked to have children show their honesty. She asked me with the exact same tone she used when she helped me with my homework. Her eyes were demanding me to focus on them. I could not bear looking at her eyes. They had looked at me when the magic of mathematics

was explained; they had looked at me when the beautiful Little Mermaid story was told. When I won the first place in the Calculation-with-Abacus Competition, they had looked at me with joy; when I was ill, they had looked at me with sympathy and love. I had not realized the true value of what all this meant to me until I lost it forever that day at the meeting.

I heard people shouting at me. My head felt like a boiling teapot. Autumn Leaves' eyes behind the thick glasses now were like gun barrels shooting at me with fire. Just be honest! her hoarse voice raised to its extreme. I turned to Secretary Chain. He nodded at me as if to say, Are you going to lose to an enemy? He was smiling scornfully. Think about the snake, he said.

Yes, the snake, I remembered. It was a story Mao told in his book. It was about a peasant who found a frozen snake lying in his path on a snowy day. The snake had the most beautiful skin the peasant had ever seen. He felt sorry for her and decided to save her life. He picked up the snake and put her into his jacket to warm her with the heat of his body. Soon the snake woke up and felt hungry. She bit her savior. The peasant died. Our Chairman's point is, Secretary Chain said as he ended the story, to our enemy, we must be absolutely cruel and merciless.

I turned to look at the wall-size portrait of Mao. It was mounted on the back of the stage. The Chairman's eyes looked like two swinging lanterns. I was reminded of my duty. I must fight against anyone who dared to oppose Mao's teaching. The shouting of the slogans encouraged me.

Show us your standpoint—Secretary Chain passed me the microphone. I did not know why I was crying. I heard myself calling for my parents as I took the microphone. I said Mama, Papa, where are you? The crowd waved their angry fists at me and shouted, Down! Down! Down! I was so scared, scared of losing Secretary Chain's trust, and scared of not being able to denounce[16] Autumn Leaves. Finally, I gathered all my strength and yelled hysterically at Autumn Leaves with tears in my throat: Yes, yes, yes, I do believe that you poisoned me; and I do believe that you are a true enemy! Your dirty tricks will have no more effect on me! If you dare to try them on me again, I'll shut you up! I'll use a needle to stitch your lips together!

I was never forgiven. Even after twenty-some years. After the Revolution was over. It was after my begging for forgiveness, I heard the familiar hoarse voice say, I am very sorry, I don't remember you. I don't think I ever had you as my student.

It was at that meeting I learned the meaning of the word "betrayal" as well as "punishment."

I MUST FIGHT AGAINST ANYONE WHO DARED TO OPPOSE MAO'S TEACHING.

Indeed, I was too young then, yet one is never too young to have vanity. When my parents learned about the meeting from Blooming, Coral and Space Conqueror, they were terrified. They talked about disowning me. My mother said, I am a teacher too. How would you like to have my student do the same to me? She shut me out of the house for six hours. She said being my mother made her ashamed.

I wrote what my mother asked of me a thousand times. It was an old teaching passed down since Confucius.[17] It said, Do not treat others how you yourself would not like to be treated. My mother demanded I copy it on rice paper using ink and a brush pen. She said, I want to carve this phrase in your mind. You are not my child if you ever disobey this teaching.

---

16. **denounce** (di nouns′), *v.* condemn publicly.
17. **Confucius** (kən fyü′shəs), 551?–479 B.C., Chinese philosopher and moral teacher.

After Reading

Making Connections

Shaping Your Response

1. Would you recommend that this selection be included in a world literature book? Why or why not?

2. How do you think you would have responded if you had been in Anchee Min's place?

3. Draw a chart like the one below and rate Autumn Leaves as a teacher in each category. Be prepared to explain your ratings.

Quality	Excellent	Average	Poor
dedicated			
energetic			
unselfish			
creative			
inspirational			

Analyzing the Autobiography

4. What do you **infer** are Autumn Leaves's reasons for refusing to beg Chairman Mao for forgiveness?

5. Explain how the **fable** about the peasant and the snake states a **theme** of the story.

6. What **character** traits does Autumn Leaves reveal as she faces her accusers and Anchee Min?

7. 🐾 Given this **setting**—China during the Cultural Revolution—do you think Anchee Min had a **choice** about whether or not to betray Autumn Leaves? Explain.

Extending the Ideas

8. 🐾 Although the Cultural Revolution is long over, human rights continues to be an issue in China and in virtually every other country in the world. Cite contemporary examples of people who **choose** to fight for their rights and speak out against human injustice.

9. How does Autumn Leaves compare to your favorite teacher?

Literary Focus: Conflict

Conflict, the struggle between a character and an opposing force, can be *external* (character against character, nature, or society) or *internal* (character torn between opposing emotions involving conscience, duty, desire, etc.).

• What internal and external conflicts are in *Red Azalea?*

Vocabulary Study

Use your knowledge of the italicized words to answer *Yes* or *No* to the following questions. Be prepared to explain your answers.

contort
exploitation
initiative
insurrection
proletarian

1. Are people with *initiative* likely to be good leaders?
2. If you *contort* your body, would you be standing straight?
3. Is *insurrection* a synonym for "rebellion"?
4. Does *exploitation* refer to unfair use?
5. Does a *proletarian* belong to the upper classes?

Expressing Your Ideas

Writing Choices

Writer's Notebook Update Now that you have read *Red Azalea*, compare Anchee Min's conflicts and challenges with the ones you described before reading. Make a Venn diagram indicating both common experiences and those unique to you and to Anchee Min.

Compare Notes Develop ideas from your notebook into a **comparison** describing what it was like to be thirteen in the 1990s in the U.S. and in 1970 in China.

Ask the Author Imagine that Anchee Min will be reading this excerpt aloud at your school. In preparation for her presentation, reread the excerpt and write down at least eight **questions** you want to ask the author to clarify the story or to find out more about her family and life in China or her life since she came to the United States.

Autumn Leaves Autumn Leaves explains that her name refers to a poem praising the beauty, significance, and transformation of leaves in the cycle of life. Write your own **poem** that expresses this subject.

Other Options

It's Your Time With a partner, make a **time line**, like that the one on page 143, that lists at least ten important events from the past thirty years in *your* country. Draw your time line on wide butcher paper, illustrate it, and present it to the class.

News Around the World Choose a partner with whom to "co-anchor" a special **news report** on human rights around the world. Gather recent news clips and pictures about human rights demonstrations and violence. Briefly describe each incident, show the location on a map, and display accompanying pictures.

Before Reading

He-y, Come on Ou-t!

by Shinichi Hoshi   Japan

Shinichi Hoshi
born 1926

Many people associate Japanese science fiction exclusively with images of the monster Godzilla or giant attacking ants. But during the 1950s and 1960s, while the Godzilla movies were appearing, talented and serious Japanese science fiction writers were producing stories, and the genre was becoming so popular that there were fan magazines—"fanzines"—and SF clubs. One such writer, Shinichi Hoshi (sin ə shē ô shē), has written over one thousand short stories and uses the genre to explore social and economic issues. In a simple and often humorous style, he portrays the environmental effects resulting from rapid growth and change.

Building Background

It's a Waste *Environmental pollution*, human destruction of the natural environment, is one of the most serious problems facing the world today. Both solid waste (garbage) and hazardous waste (poisonous or polluting substances) threaten health and contaminate the environment. In an effort to enforce conservation, many countries have pollution controls. For example, the U.S. bans DDT and leaded gasoline and stipulates that landfills must be lined with substances that prevent the escape of toxic chemicals into the water supply.

The story you are about to read, although fantasy, presents a very real problem and a dramatic warning about the consequences of irresponsible use of the environment.

Literary Focus

Inference What is the cartoon poking fun at? How can you tell? When you used clues in the cartoon to draw a conclusion, you were making an **inference**. As you read "He-y, Come on Ou-t!" look for clues to help you infer the author's main point.

"There was a whole bunch of people here protesting about something . . . pollution, probably."

Writer's Notebook

What's It All About? Science fiction is set wholly or partly in an unreal world with farfetched events that cannot be explained by current science.

Sometimes one or more characters are nonhuman. Judging from the title and the fact that this is a science fiction story, quickwrite your ideas about what "He-y, Come on Ou-t!" might be about.

HE—Y, COME ON OU—T!

Shinichi Hoshi

Computer-generated art by David Em titled *Where 3* harnesses the power of technology to create futuristic special effects. What does the passageway in this image have in common with the hole in the village? ➤

The typhoon had passed and the sky was a gorgeous blue. Even a certain village not far from the city had suffered damage. A little distance from the village and near the mountains, a small shrine[1] had been swept away by a landslide.

"I wonder how long that shrine's been here."

"Well, in any case, it must have been here since an awfully long time ago."

"We've got to rebuild it right away."

While the villagers exchanged views, several more of their number came over.

"It sure was wrecked."

"I think it used to be right here."

"No, looks like it was a little more over there."

Just then one of them raised his voice. "Hey what in the world is this hole?"

---

1. **shrine** (shrīn), *n.* place of worship.

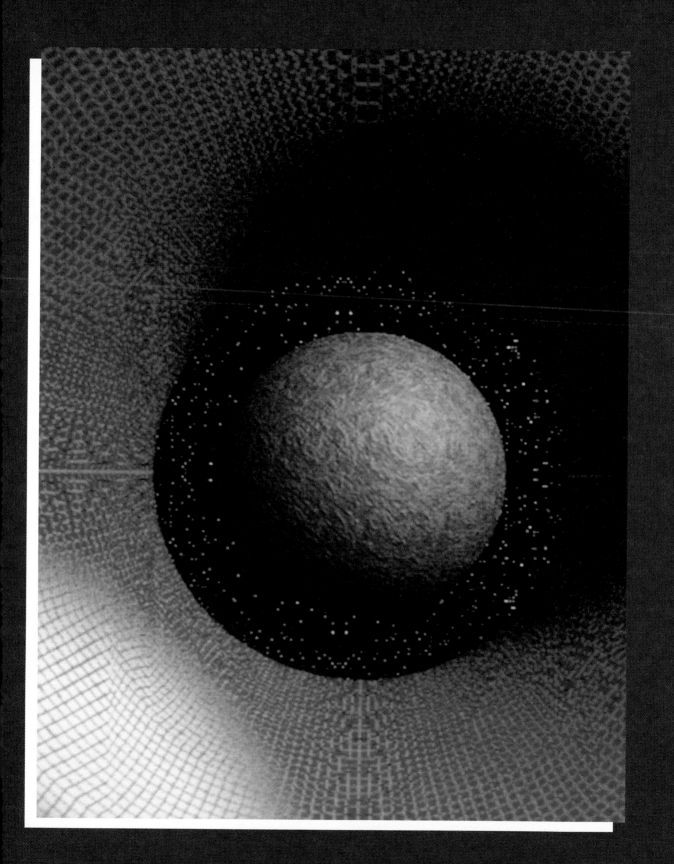

Where they had all gathered there was a hole about a meter in diameter. They peered in, but it was so dark nothing could be seen. However, it gave one the feeling that it was so deep it went clear through to the center of the earth.

There was even one person who said, "I wonder if it's a fox's hole."

"He—y, come on ou—t!" shouted a young man into the hole. There was no echo from the bottom. Next he picked up a pebble and was about to throw it in.

"You might bring down a curse on us. Lay off," warned an old man, but the younger one energetically threw the pebble in. As before, however, there was no answering response from the bottom. The villagers cut down some trees, tied them with rope and made a fence which they put around the hole. Then they repaired to the village.

"What do you suppose we ought to do?"

"Shouldn't we build the shrine up just as it was over the hole?"

A day passed with no agreement. The news traveled fast, and a car from the newspaper company rushed over. In no time a scientist came out, and with an all-knowing expression on his face he went over to the hole. Next, a bunch of gawking curiosity seekers showed up; one could also pick out here and there men of shifty glances who appeared to be concessionaires. Concerned that someone might fall into the hole, a policeman from the local substation kept a careful watch.

One newspaper reporter tied a weight to the end of a long cord and lowered it into the hole. A long way down it went. The cord ran out, however, and he tried to pull it out, but it would not come back up. Two or three people helped out, but when they all pulled too hard, the cord parted at the edge of the hole. Another reporter, a camera in hand, who had been watching all of this, quietly untied a stout rope that had been wound around his waist.

The scientist contacted people at his laboratory and had them bring out a high-powered bull horn, with which he was going to check out the echo from the hole's bottom. He tried switching through various sounds, but there was no echo. The scientist was puzzled, but he could not very well give up with everyone watching him so intently. He put the bull horn right up to the hole, turned it to its highest volume, and let it sound continuously for a long time. It was a noise that would have carried several dozen kilometers above ground. But the hole just calmly swallowed up the sound.

In his own mind the scientist was at a loss, but with a look of apparent <u>composure</u>[2] he cut off the sound and, in a manner suggesting that the whole thing had a perfectly <u>plausible</u>[3] explanation, said simply, "Fill it in."

Safer to get rid of something one didn't understand.

The onlookers, disappointed that this was all that was going to happen, prepared to disperse.[4] Just then one of the concessionaires, having broken through the <u>throng</u>[5] and come forward, made a proposal.

"Let me have that hole. I'll fill it in for you."

"We'd be grateful to you for filling it in," replied the mayor of the village, "but we can't very well give you the hole. We have to build a shrine there."

"If it's a shrine you want, I'll build you a fine one later. Shall I make it with an attached meeting hall?"

Before the mayor could answer, the people of the village all shouted out.

"Really? Well, in that case, we ought to have it closer to the village."

"It's just an old hole. We'll give it to you!"

---

2. composure (kəm pō′zhər), *n.* calmness; quietness.
3. plausible (plô′zə bəl), *adj.* appearing true, reasonable, or fair.
4. **disperse** (dis pėrs′), *v.* spread in different directions; scatter.
5. throng (thrông), *n.* a crowd; multitude.

So it was settled. And the mayor, of course, had no objection.

The concessionaire was true to his promise. It was small, but closer to the village he did build for them a shrine and an attached meeting hall.

About the time the autumn festival was held at the new shrine, the hole-filling company established by the concessionaire hung out its small shingle at a shack near the hole.

The concessionaire had his cohorts[6] mount a loud campaign in the city. "We've got a fabulously deep hole! Scientists say it's at least five thousand meters deep! Perfect for the disposal of such things as waste from nuclear reactors."

Government authorities granted permission. Nuclear power plants fought for contracts. The people of the village were a bit worried about this, but they consented when it was explained that there would be absolutely no above-ground contamination for several thousand years and that they would share in the profits. Into the bargain, very shortly a magnificent road was built from the city to the village.

Trucks rolled in over the road, transporting lead boxes. Above the hole the lids were opened, and the wastes from nuclear reactors tumbled away into the hole.

From the Foreign Ministry and the Defense Agency boxes of unnecessary classified documents were brought for disposal. Officials who came to supervise the disposal held discussions on golf. The lesser functionaries, as they threw in the papers, chatted about pinball.

The hole showed no signs of filling up. It was awfully deep, thought some; or else it might be very spacious at the bottom. Little by little the hole-filling company expanded its business.

Bodies of animals used in contagious[7] disease experiments at the universities were brought out, and to these were added the unclaimed corpses of vagrants.[8] Better than dumping all of its garbage in the ocean, went the thinking in the city, and plans were made for a long pipe to carry it to the hole.

The hole gave peace of mind to the dwellers of the city. They concentrated solely on producing one thing after another. Everyone disliked thinking about the eventual consequences. People wanted only to work for production companies and sales corporations; they had no interest in becoming junk dealers. But, it was thought, these problems too would gradually be resolved by the hole.

Young girls whose betrothals had been arranged discarded old diaries in the hole. There were also those who were inaugurating new love affairs and threw into the hole old photographs of themselves taken with former sweethearts. The police felt comforted as they used the hole to get rid of accumulations of expertly done counterfeit bills. Criminals breathed easier after throwing material evidence into the hole.

Whatever one wished to discard, the hole accepted it all. The hole cleansed the city of its filth; the sea and sky seemed to have become a bit clearer than before.

Aiming at the heavens, new buildings went on being constructed one after the other.

One day, atop the high steel frame of a new building under construction, a workman was taking a break. Above his head he heard a voice shout:

"He—y, come on ou—t!"

But, in the sky to which he lifted his gaze there was nothing at all. A clear blue sky merely spread over all. He thought it must be his imagination. Then, as he resumed his former position, from the direction where the voice had come, a small pebble skimmed by him and fell on past.

The man, however, was gazing in idle reverie at the city's skyline growing ever more beautiful, and he failed to notice.

---

6. **cohort** (kō′hôrt), *n.* associate or follower.
7. contagious (kən tā′jəs), *adj.* spreading by direct or indirect contact; catching.
8. **vagrant** (vā′grənt), *n.* idle wanderer; tramp.

After Reading

Making Connections

Shaping Your Response

1. Do you think this a realistic story, or is it mostly fantasy? Explain where you would place this story on the spectrum below.

    real ←————————→ fantasy

2. Describe a picture and slogan that you would use to make an ecological poster based on this story.

3. What new meaning does this story give to the word *recycle*?

Analyzing the Story

4. What do you think the hole **symbolizes**, or represents?

5. Explain the **irony** in this statement from the story: "The hole cleansed the city of its filth."

6. In your opinion, what is a **theme** of this story.

Extending the Ideas

7. What other stories from books, movies, or TV present similar ecological warnings?

Literary Focus: Inference

When you read stories like "He–y, Come on Ou–t!" you must examine clues, suggestions, or hints, to **infer** the author's meaning. What can you infer about the following people from their actions?

- The scientist cannot explain the hole, yet he says, "Fill it in."

- The concessionaire offers to fill up the hole and build a new shrine.

- The villagers trade the concessionaire the hole for a new shrine.

Vocabulary Study

Word analogy tests require you to understand the relationship between a pair of words and choose another pair of words with the same relationship. Analogies reflect relationships such as these:

- antonyms *(impotent : powerful)*

- synonyms *(beg : implore)*

- part-to-whole *(finger : hand)*

- place-activity *(pool : swim)*

An analogy can be expressed this way: "*Spoke* is to *wheel* as ___ is to ___." To complete this analogy, you would first determine that a spoke is part of a wheel and then decide what other word pair expresses a similar relationship. Study the relationship of each of the following pairs of words in capital letters; then choose another pair that has the same relationship.

composure
contagious
plausible
shrine
throng

1. COMPOSURE : CALMNESS :: **a.** anger : shout **b.** think : succeed
   c. graduate : study **d.** gratitude : thankfulness
2. PLAUSIBLE : UNBELIEVABLE :: **a.** impossible : doubtful
   b. solemn : serious **c.** lively : dull **d.** agree : wonder
3. INDIVIDUAL : THRONG :: **a.** bird : flock **b.** tree : bush
   c. melody : rhythm **d.** hand : foot
4. SHRINE : PRAY :: **a.** mall : clothes **b.** school : teacher
   c. restaurant : eat **d.** swim : athlete
5. CONTAGIOUS : CATCHING :: **a.** flu : cold **b.** remember : recall
   c. gather : scatter **d.** fish : trout

Expressing Your Ideas

Writing Choices

Writer's Notebook Update Look back at your quickwrite about "He–y, Come on Ou–t!" Did you come close to guessing what the story is about? Now skim the story again, and list five phrases or sentences that would alert a reader to the story plot.

Cutbacks Many people in the wealthier nations choose comfortable lifestyles that consume large amounts of raw materials and energy and produce many wastes. Write a **newspaper editorial** attempting to convince these people that they must choose a lifestyle that is less destructive to the environment.

Front-Page Scandal The construction worker mentioned at the end of the story goes to *The Blab*, which prints the sensationalized story. Write the **story** and **headline** that expose officials who agreed to fill the hole and their attempts to cover up their decision.

Five Years Later In a science fiction **fantasy** of your own, imagine it is five years after the story ends. Describe what the village is like now.

Other Options

Sales Pitch With the help of your classmates, plan an **infomercial** to get viewers to read this story or another story in this book. Remember that your job is to persuade other students to read this story. Present your infomercial to another class.

Comics and Culture With your team rework "He–y, Come on Ou-t!" as a **comic book**, using some of the dialogue from the story. Try to capture the setting and mood in vivid drawings.

Sci-Fi Infomercial With one or two classmates, plan an **infomercial** to tell viewers about the best of science fiction. Explain what makes a work science fiction. Provide examples of outstanding sci-fi television shows, movies, stories, books, and cartoons. Present your infomercial to the class.

Before Reading

Flash Cards by Rita Dove   USA

In Memory of Richi by Carmen Tafolla   USA

The Rabbit by Edna St. Vincent Millay   USA

Building Background

What Is It? Read what three poets have to say about poetry.

"If I feel physically as if the top of my head were taken off, I know that is poetry." *Emily Dickinson*

"Poetry is the art of understanding what it is to be alive." *Archibald MacLeish*

"Poetry is the opening and closing of a door, leaving those who look through to guess about what was seen during a moment." *Carl Sandburg*

What do you think each poet is saying about poetry? Which statement comes closest to *your* view of poetry? Now make up your own statement about poetry.

Literary Focus

Sound Devices Poets use words for their sound effects to convey mood, establish meaning, create music, and unify a work. Even poems with no regular rhyme have **sound devices** such as repeated words and sounds. As you read the following poems aloud, listen for word melodies. Let words and phrases such as *sputtering, hissed, embroidered, tulip trees,* and *high sky* work their magic on you.

Writer's Notebook

Poetry Web Brainstorm with a partner all the things you associate with poetry. Then make a web to show ideas you connect with this word.

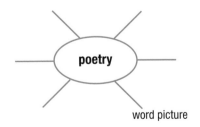

word picture

Rita Dove
born 1952

As a child, Rita Dove loved math—"the neatness of fractions, all those pies sliced into ever-diminishing wedges." But drilling with flash cards reminded her of dull routines such as washing dishes and taking out garbage. After mulling over the subject, Dove, who is a self-acknowledged daydreamer, wrote "Flash Cards." Among Dove's many honors are a Pulitzer Prize for poetry and the title of Poet Laureate of the United States, awarded in 1993.

Carmen Tafolla
born 1951

When she was in junior high school, a principal told Carmen Tafolla (tä foi′yä) that she had the "potential to make it all the way to high school" if she'd just quit speaking Spanish. Instead, she kept speaking Spanish and learned English, going on to earn a doctorate degree in bilingual education and gaining a national reputation as a story writer, a memoirist, and a poet. She lives in Texas with her family, three cats, a computer, a houseful of books, and the voices of all the people of her barrio, past and present.

Edna St. Vincent Millay
1892–1950

In November 1920, a slim volume of poems appeared whose bright green cover carried the title *A Few Figs from Thistles.* The author was a young woman named Edna St. Vincent Millay. Young people in the years after World War I, who had lost their idealism, immediately identified with the cynical, defiant spirit of Millay's verse. Millay, who also wrote short stories under the pen name Nancy Boyd, used her poetry to freely express her views of the modern woman, democracy, humanism, and individualism.

Flash Cards Rita Dove

In math I was the whiz kid, keeper
of oranges and apples. *What you don't understand,
master,* my father said; the faster
I answered, the faster they came.

5 I could see one bud on the teacher's geranium,
one clear bee sputtering at the wet pane.
The tulip trees always dragged after heavy rain
so I tucked my head as my boots slapped home.

My father put up his feet after work
10 and relaxed with a highball and *The Life of Lincoln.*
After supper we drilled and I climbed the dark

before sleep, before a thin voice hissed
numbers as I spun on a wheel. I had to guess.
Ten, I kept saying, *I'm only ten.*

This panel is from the series *Migration of the Negro,* painted in 1940–41 by Jacob Lawrence. The series of paintings chronicles the movement of Southern African Americans to the urban North to search for greater opportunities, including education. What about "Flash Cards" suggests that the speaker comes from a different social class than the migrants that Lawrence pictures?

In Memory of Richi

Carmen Tafolla

First day
of school
for both of you
—one of you six and glowing copper, running
    with eagerness and proud
5 the other 22, young teacher, eager for this
    school.
Your blue eyes warm to his brown coals
as you both chat
and share your missions,
as you ask his name.
10 He rolls it like a round of wealth
and, deep in Spanish tones, responds
    "Richi."
You try to imitate, say
    "Ritchie."
"No!" he teases, confident,
"It's Ri-chi—just like this."
15 You notice that each syllable
could rhyme with *see*
and try again.
He pats you on the back.
You go on to your separate tasks—
20 he to his room, and you to yours.
One day, six hours,
really not a speck of sand
in all this shore of time, and yet,
so crucial,[1]
25 as you gather papers,
turn to flee the cell
and gain some comfort
in some other place.
Your ray of hope
30 comes filtering down the hall.
In eagerness for someone's warmth,
you shout and wave,
    "Hey, Richi!"
He corrects,
the light and wealth all gone
35 from his new eyes,
    "No.
    Ritchie."

---

1. **crucial** (krü′shəl), *adj.* very important or decisive; critical.

The Rabbit   Edna St. Vincent Millay

Hearing the hawk squeal in the high sky
I and the rabbit trembled.
Only the dark small rabbits newly kittled[1] in their neatly dissembled[2]
Hollowed nest in the thicket[3] thatched with straw
5   Did not respect his cry.
At least, not that I saw.

But I have said to the rabbit with rage and a hundred times, "Hop!
Streak it for the bushes! Why do you sit so still?
You are bigger than a house, I tell you, you are bigger than a hill, you are
      a beacon for air-planes!

10   O indiscreet![4]
And the hawk and all my friends are out to kill!
Get under cover!" But the rabbit never stirred; she never will.

And I shall see again and again the large eye blaze
With death, and gently glaze;[5]
15   The leap into the air I shall see again and again, and the kicking feet;
And the sudden quiet everlasting, and the blade of grass green in the
      strange mouth of the interrupted grazer.[6]

---

1. **kittled** (kit′ ld), *adj.* born.
2. **dissembled** (di sem′bəld), *adj.* hidden; disguised.
3. **thicket** (thik′ət), *n.* shrubs, bushes, or small trees growing close together.
4. **indiscreet** (in′dis krēt′), *adj.* not wise; foolish.
5. **glaze** (glāz), *v.* become smooth, glassy, or glossy.
6. **grazer** (grā′zər), *n.* feeder on growing grass.

5 Horned Agama.
Tapayaxin of Hernandis.

1, Common Buzzard, Female.
Buteo vulgaris.

2, Slate-coloured Hawk, Male.
3 Female.
Falco velox, Wils.

4 Marsh Hare, Female.
Lepus palustris, Bachman.

After Reading

Making Connections

Shaping Your
Response

1. Work with a partner to present a still picture, or tableau, that captures a scene or a mood from one of these poems. You might invite classmates to guess what your tableau represents.

2. Which character from the poems do you relate to most? Why?

3. In your notebook, write three words that these poems make you think of.

Analyzing the
Poems

4. What **inferences** can you make about the speaker and her father in "Flash Cards"?

5. What **rhymes** or words that sound alike do you find in "Flash Cards"? Before answering, look for words that are repeated or rhymed within lines as well as at the ends of lines.

6. In "In Memory of Richi," how do you think both the teacher and Richi have changed from the beginning of the day to the end?

7. What **image**, or word picture, do you have of the rabbit at the end of Millay's poem?

8. State what you consider the **theme** of two of these poems.

Extending the
Ideas

9. In Tafolla's poem, Richi views his name with "new eyes." What advice do you have for students who **choose** to maintain their culture and traditions in American schools?

Literary Focus: Sound Devices

Poets choose and arrange words so that their sounds are pleasing to the ear and appropriate to the meaning. **Sound devices** are elements such as **rhyme, alliteration,** and **onomatopoeia**. As you read poetry, be aware of rhyme (similar word endings such as *right/light* and *rumble/grumble*), alliteration (the repetition of consonant sounds such as *lovely liquid lullaby*), and onomatopoeia (words such as *crack* and *wobble* that suggest the sounds or movements made by objects or activities).

- As someone from the class slowly reads each poem aloud, jot down examples of rhyme, alliteration, and onomatopoeia. Compare your findings to those of your classmates.

Vocabulary Study

Choose the letter of the word that is most nearly *opposite* the numbered word.

crucial
dissembled
glaze
indiscreet
kittled

1. *dissembled* **a.** revealed **b.** forgotten **c.** broken **d.** collected

2. *indiscreet* **a.** foolish **b.** quiet **c.** wise **d.** happy

3. *crucial* **a.** necessary **b.** unimportant **c.** lucky **d.** unknown

4. *kittled* **a.** died **b.** born **c.** damaged **d.** remembered

5. *glaze* **a.** become silent **b.** become angry **c.** become bumpy **d.** become angry

Expressing Your Ideas

Writing Choices

Writer's Notebook Compare your poetry web with that of other classmates. Would you add other words and phrases or change the ones you wrote, after reading these poems? Have any of your previous ideas about poetry changed? Use your web to write about your impressions of poetry. You might try to cast your ideas into a poem.

Give Poetry a Good Rap School, parental pressure, violence in nature? The subjects of these poems have found their way into contemporary songs. Working in a small group, recast one of these poems as a **rap**. Feel free to add or change things. Perform your rap for the class.

Start with Art Look at the piece of art at the right. What feelings, event, person, or memory does it bring to mind? Quickly write down your first impressions, while they're still fresh. Let your ideas serve as the beginning of a **poem**. Add some sound devices such as rhyme, alliteration, or onomatopoeia and shape your ideas into a poem.

Other Options

Reader's Theater In a small group, research other poems by Rita Dove, Carmen Tafolla, or Edna St. Vincent Millay. Select several poems to **read aloud** that you think classmates will enjoy. After rehearsing, present your reading to the class.

Show Them a Poem Give a **chalk talk** to the class about poetry—how it differs from prose, how sound devices and images contribute to its effects, and how poets manage to say a lot in a few words. To illustrate your points, write words from the poems in this group or draw pictures to show images.

Dealing with Consequences

Lessons Through the Ages

Multicultural Connection
Like the selections you have just read, the fable, proverbs, and other works in this Interdisciplinary Study provide truths about people and lessons about life.

The Elephant in the Dark House
by Rumi

The elephant was in a dark house: some Hindus had brought it for exhibition.

In order to see it, many people were going, every one, into that darkness.

As seeing it with the eye was impossible, each one was feeling it in the dark with the palm of his hand.

The hand of one fell on its trunk: he said, "This creature is like a waterpipe."

The hand of another touched its ear: to him it appeared to be like a fan.

Since another handled its leg, he said, "I found the elephant's shape to be like a pillar."

Another laid his hand on its back: he said, "Truly, this elephant was like a throne."

Similarly, when any one heard a description of the elephant, he understood it only in respect of the part that he had touched. If there had been a candle in each one's hand, the difference would have gone out of their words.

TRADITIONAL WISDOM

THE QUACK FROG
BY AESOP

Once upon a time a Frog came forth from his home in the marshes and proclaimed to all the world that he was a learned physician, skilled in drugs and able to cure all diseases. Among the crowd was a Fox, who called out, "You a doctor! Why, how can you set up to heal others when you cannot even cure your own lame legs and blotched and wrinkled skin?" Physician heal thyself.

THE MOST VALUABLE THING IN THE WORLD
ZEN STORY

Sozan, a Chinese Zen master, was asked by a student: "What is the most valuable thing in the world?"

The master replied: "The head of a dead cat."

"Why is the head of a dead cat the most valuable thing in the world?" inquired the student.

Sozan replied: "Because no one can name its price."

from
Pride and Prejudice
by Jane Austen

It is a truth universally acknowledged, that a single man in possession of a good fortune must be in want of a wife.

Thought for a Sunshiny Morning
by Dorothy Parker

It costs me never a stab nor squirm
To tread by chance upon a worm.
"Aha, my little dear," I say,
"Your clan will pay me back one day."

IF THE PATIENT DIES, THE DOCTOR HAS KILLED HIM. BUT IF HE GETS WELL, THE SAINTS HAVE SAVED HIM.
Italy

The Country School ➤ by Winslow Homer

NOT EVERYTHING THAT SHINES IS GOLD.
Spain

THE FOOL SPEAKS, THE WISE MAN LISTENS.
Ethiopia

IF YOU LIVE IN MY HEART, YOU LIVE RENT-FREE.
Ireland

THY FRIEND HAS A FRIEND, AND THY FRIEND'S FRIEND HAS A FRIEND, SO BE DISCREET.
Talmud

PROVERBS

HE WHO CANNOT DANCE WILL SAY: "THE DRUM IS BAD."
Ashanti

EXPERIENCE IS A COMB WHICH NATURE GIVES US WHEN WE ARE BALD.
China

I WAS ANGERED, FOR I HAD NO SHOES. THEN I MET A MAN WHO HAD NO FEET.
China

HE THAT RISETH LATE MUST TROT ALL DAY.
Benjamin Franklin, United States

Responding

1. What do you think is the most valuable thing in the world? Write a brief "lesson" about it.

2. Do you consider Jane Austen's observations on marriage out of date? Write your own truism about life or love.

Writing Workshop

Presenting Alternatives

Assignment The main characters in "Red Azalea," "The Boar Hunt," and "The Interlopers" and the villagers in "He—y, Come on Ou—t!" all have something in common. They are faced with dilemmas—difficult choices— that lead to ironic consequences—outcomes that are different from what is expected. Explore these ironic consequences in writing.

WRITER'S BLUEPRINT

Product	An interpretive essay
Purpose	To analyze characters' decisions
Audience	People who have read the stories
Specs	As the writer of a successful essay, you should:

❑ Focus on one of the stories listed in "Assignment" above. Begin by explaining the dilemma of the main character (or characters). What difficult choices does he or she face?

❑ Go on to explain the decision the character makes and the ironic consequences of that decision. What went wrong with the original plans?

❑ Speculate on other alternatives the character could have chosen instead. What other actions might have led to different consequences?

❑ Conclude by giving your view of why things went wrong. Consider (1) elements in the character's personality that prevented him or her from making a better choice and (2) circumstances beyond the character's control.

❑ Offer evidence from the story to support your analysis, including quotations where appropriate. State cause-effect relationships clearly.

❑ Follow the rules of grammar, usage, spelling, and mechanics, including correct pronoun reference.

Chart ironic consequences. Look back at the material on irony on pages 127 and 133. Then in a small group, look at the dilemmas faced by the main characters in "Red Azalea," "The Boar Hunt," "The Interlopers," and "He—y, Come on Ou—t!" Use a chart like the one shown. Then choose the story that you want to interpret in your essay.

The Character's Dilemma	The Ironic Consequences	Supporting Evidence from Story
List the choices facing the character and the decision he or she made.	List the things that went wrong with the character's plans.	List events and quotations that illustrate the dilemma and consequences.

> **OR . . .**
> Have each group member take a different story and explain the dilemma and ironic consequences to the rest of the group.

Identify alternatives. On your own, list several instances in the story where the character could have made a different decision and avoided the dilemma. For each instance, complete an If-Then sentence:

If (character) had _____ instead of _____, then _____.

Analyze the reasons why the character did not take these alternatives. List (1) elements of the character's personality and (2) circumstances beyond the character's control that contributed to his or her not taking each alternative. List pieces of evidence—events or quotations from the story—to support your reasons.

Plan your essay. Review your prewriting activities as you make your writing plan. Organize your notes into an outline like the one shown here. Add supporting evidence—events and quotations from the story—for your conclusions.

Introduction	Body	Conclusion
Character's dilemma— difficult choices (+ supporting evidence)	Character's decision Ironic consequences (what went wrong) Alternative choices (+ supporting evidence)	Reasons things went wrong —Character's personality —Circumstances beyond character's control (+ supporting evidence)

As you draft, follow your writing plan. The following tips may help:

- Begin with a question that asks "What would you expect to happen if . . . ?" and go on to explain the character's dilemma.

- Begin with a quotation from the story and follow with an explanation of how this quotation illustrates the character's dilemma.

Ask a partner to comment on your draft before you revise it.

✔ Did I illustrate my explanations with quotations from the literature?

✔ Did I state cause-effect relationships clearly? (See the Beyond Print article on page 179 and the "Revising Strategy" below.)

OR . . .
Go through the outline orally first, using a tape recorder. Cover each point in the outline. Then listen to the tape and make notes for your writing plan.

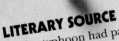
LITERARY SOURCE
"The typhoon had passed and the sky was a gorgeous blue. Even a certain village not far from the city had suffered damage. A little distance from the village and near the mountains, a small shrine had been swept away by a landslide."
from "He—y, Come on Ou—t!" by Shinichi Hoshi

Revising Strategy

Clarifying Cause-Effect Relationships

Think about cause as *why* something happens and effect as *what* happens. For example, in "He—y, Come on Ou—t!" the typhoon (cause) brings about a landslide (effect). The landslide (cause) sweeps away the shrine (effect).

Look back at your essay to make sure that your cause-effect relationships are clearly expressed. Notice how this student model has been changed, in response to a partner's comment, to clarify why something happened.

Anchee must choose between a teacher whom she truly admires

or stay loyal to Chain and the political party. This teacher was always *, who think the teacher is a spy*

helpful to all her students and encouraged them to do their very best.

Once she worked with Anchee on her geometric progression till she no

longer had a voice.

STUDENT MODEL

Ask a partner to review your revised draft before you edit. When you edit, look for errors in grammar, usage, spelling, and mechanics. Look over each sentence to make sure your pronouns all have clear antecedents.

Editing Strategy

Clarifying Pronoun References

A pronoun usually takes the place of a noun used earlier—the antecedent of the pronoun. A pronoun must have a clear antecedent.

> *Autumn Leaves* brought *her* books to share with Anchee Min.

The possessive pronoun *her* refers to *Autumn Leaves*, that's clear. But what about this example?

> Anchee Min's parents learned of the betrayal of Autumn Leaves from Blooming, Coral, and Space Conqueror. *They* were terrified.

Who are *They*—Anchee Min's parents or her three siblings? We could clear up this confusion by replacing the pronoun *They* with *Anchee Min's parents*, but that would sound awkward. A better solution would be to move the pronoun closer to its antecedent, as in the example below:

> Anchee Min's parents were terrified when *they* learned of the betrayal of Autumn Leaves from Blooming, Coral, and Space Conqueror.

When you revise, make sure each pronoun has a clear antecedent.

FOR REFERENCE
See the Language and Grammar Handbook at the back of this text for more information on pronoun reference.

STEP 5 PRESENTING

Consider these ideas for presenting your essay.

- Get together in a small group and read each other's papers. Then role-play the characters having a discussion about the alternatives that were proposed. You might want to do this in the format of a TV talk show.

- Make a sketch of the character or characters you dealt with and include it with your essay.

STEP 6 LOOKING BACK

Self-Evaluate. What grade would you give your paper? Look back at the Writer's Blueprint and give your paper a score on each point, from 6 (superior) to 1 (inadequate).

Reflect. Think about what you've learned from writing this essay as you write answers to these questions.

✔ Now that you've explored irony, think of ironic situations you've encountered in your own life. What happened? What made the situations ironic?

✔ Time can make a difference in how you see things that are close to you. Put your final draft away for a few days and read it again, when you're not so close to it. What do you see about it now that you didn't see then?

For Your Working Portfolio Add your essay and reflection responses to your working portfolio.

Beyond Print

Analyzing Cause and Effect

A *cause* is any person, thing, or event that produces an effect. It is the reason something happens. An *effect* is the result of an event, idea, or action. It is whatever is produced or made to happen by a cause. The simplest cause-effect relationships are those where one cause has one effect: for example, you turn the ignition key and the car's engine starts.

Cause-effect relationships, however, are usually more complex than those in which a single cause produces a single effect. One type of complex cause-effect relationship occurs when a single cause produces a chain of effects. For example, in Saki's story, "The Interlopers," an old feud leads two men to stalk each other in a forest. They are both injured by a falling tree, leaving them defenseless when attacked by a band of wolves.

Drawing a diagram can help you understand this kind of chain of causation:

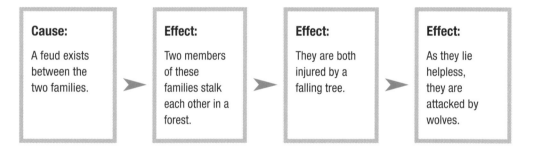

Cause:	**Effect:**	**Effect:**	**Effect:**
A feud exists between the two families.	Two members of these families stalk each other in a forest.	They are both injured by a falling tree.	As they lie helpless, they are attacked by wolves.

Activity Options

1. Diagram the cause-effect relationship that exists in "He—y, Come on Ou—t!"

2. Create a cause-effect diagram in the form of a storyboard illustrating key events in one of the stories in this unit.

3. With a group of students, select a movie that exhibits complex cause-effect relationships, such as *Jurassic Park*, and discuss how they contribute to the film's theme.

Multicultural Connections

Individuality

Part One: Pushing Toward the Top Rufus in "The Voter" walks a thin line between pursuing individual goals and achieving the broader goals of his political machine. Jing-mei in "Two Kinds" rebels against her mother's attempts to impose culturally influenced standards.

■ Compare the ways that Rufus and Jing-mei seek to preserve their individuality while responding to group pressures.

Group

Part Two: Trying to Beat the Odds A character who abandons group interests in favor of personal goals is Oganda in "The Rain Came." Unlike her father, who puts the interests of the larger group over his family bonds, Oganda eventually chooses to escape with her lover, thus forsaking the larger group.

■ Do you think that Oganda has done a good job of balancing individual needs with group obligations? Why or why not?

Choice

Part Three: Dealing with Consequences These selections highlight the need for responsible choices. The price of irresponsible choices can be betrayal, death, or the destruction of the environment.

■ What advice could you give Anchee Min in "Red Azalea" or the village people in "He—y, Come on Ou—t!" that would have led to more informed decisions on their parts?

Activities

1. In a group, brainstorm examples of people in history who managed to maintain their individuality despite strong group pressure.

2. Explain how you would handle this situation: Although you are an honor student, most of your friends get C's. What are some things you could do when they constantly mock you for being a "brain"?

3. Think of situations you have experienced or heard about in which group pressure caused you or someone else to do (or not do) something. (Remember group pressure can be a positive influence.) Then select one of these situations to re-enact.

Independent and Group Projects

Research

Armchair Travelers Form a group and tell your classmates to pack their bags and prepare for adventure in the jungles of Peru, politics in Nigeria, education in China during the Cultural Revolution, or fine dining in France. Review the settings of selections in this unit and have each group member research a different country. Then, with the help of your notes and a world map, take classmates on a culture tour.

Media

Tune In With a small group, choose one of the selections in this unit that would make a good television movie. Create a sixty-second TV commercial that highlights the actors and some dialogue and provides a glimpse of a major scene from the story to pique audience interest. Add sound effects and appropriate music. Now have your classmates tune in as you present your commercial.

Art

In the Mood Work in a group to identify the mood in ten of the selections from this unit. Then research different forms of art—collages, drawings, paintings, sculptures, photographs—to find a piece that captures the mood of each work. To make a mood book, photocopy pictures of the art you find, or create your own artwork, and provide a caption with the title and artist's name. On separate sheets of paper, write a brief explanation of how an artwork captures the mood of each selection. Compile the mood descriptions and art into a book and put it on display for the class or for other grades.

Oral Presentation

Critic's Corner You and your partner are to the world of literary critics what Siskel and Ebert are to the world of movie critics. You voice your opinions of literary works in a weekly thirty-minute television program titled *Meeting the Challenge*. This week's show consists of your critiques of five selections from this unit. Prepare your individual critique for each work and then surprise your partner (and the audience) with your views.

MAKING JUDGMENTS

On Trial
Part One, pages 186–267

Beneath the Surface
Part Two, pages 268–333

READING

Y ou are about to read two very different plays—one an ancient Greek drama, the other, a television play. Despite their differences, however, you can use some common reading techniques that will add to your enjoyment and understanding.

REMEMBER THAT A PLAY IS WRITTEN TO BE ACTED.

When you read any play, consider it a performance waiting to happen. "Staging the play" in your imagination as you read will allow you to visualize events beyond the printed page, speculating on how characters will deliver their lines and react in a specific setting.

Also keep in mind that while *Antigone* was written to be staged in a large arena, *Twelve Angry Men* is a television play with the advantage of an agile camera that can supply techniques such as quick cuts and close-ups. Consequently, gestures and tones may be more subtle in the television play, while the gestures and delivery of lines in *Antigone* must be conveyed dramatically to an audience at a distance.

LOOK AT THE PICTURES AND MARGINAL NOTES.

Artwork can provide clues to the plot and mood of the play, as well as to the characters' feelings. Both Antigone's distress and the juror's weary irritability are conveyed through the photographs.

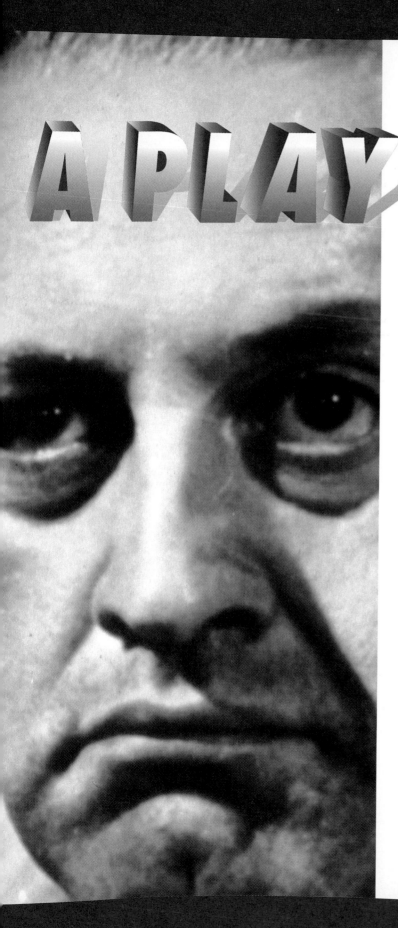

A PLAY

Likewise, notes can provide help on background information and vocabulary. By all means use the notes in a close reading of the text, but don't get bogged down or distracted from understanding the basic story line.

STUDY THE CAST OF CHARACTERS. Examine the cast of characters and refer to it as you read for clarification. This will be particularly important in establishing the family relationships in *Antigone* and in keeping the jurors straight in *Twelve Angry Men.* You might keep track of characters and critical events with a quick notation. For example, you might note each juror's number, along with words such as *loud, flashy, naïve* and *bigot* that the playwright provides to characterize each personality.

PAY ATTENTION TO STAGE DIRECTIONS. These directions indicate how lines are to be delivered (*briskly, flustered, annoyed, amazed*) and provide insights into setting and characters. (Antigone is described in the initial directions as *anxious* and *urgent.*) Note that the hot jury room is "unpleasant-looking" with walls that are "bare, drab, and badly in need of a fresh coat of paint."

Now plunge in and take the play beyond the printed page, visualizing the action, reading aloud and acting out scenes if possible. Move to center stage and enjoy the spirit of drama!

Part One

On Trial

In *Antigone* and *Twelve Angry Men,* the lives of a young woman in ancient Greece and a contemporary murder suspect are both at the mercy of those who judge them.

👣 Multicultural Connection **Interactions** can become tense when people that have diverse cultural backgrounds or different goals try to arrive at a consensus about important decisions. As you read the following plays, decide in what respects ethnicity, social class, family allegiances, and age influence decision making.

About Greek Drama

Greek drama grew out of the religious festivals held in Athens each spring to honor Dionysus (dī′ə nī′səs), god of wine. The earliest festivals consisted of dancing, games, and choral songs led by a conductor. During the sixth century B.C., a poet/leader named Thespis (*thespian* is still a synonym for actor) began to insert spoken lines into the songs, thus introducing the idea of dialogue. As you prepare to read *Antigone*, the following information will help you visualize how Greek drama was originally performed.

The Theater

Performances were held from dawn to dusk in enormous, open-air arenas. A typical arena, such as the theater of Dionysus southwest of the Acropolis, was built into a hillside. This gave the seating area, or *theatron* ("seeing place"), a natural rise so that thousands of spectators had a clear view of the action. At the foot of the seating area was a large circular *orchestra* ("dancing place") where the chorus, in unison or in small groups, sang or chanted and danced—in slow, stately movements.

One or two steps above the orchestra was the platform where the actors performed. Beyond it and facing the audience stood the *skene* (skē′nē), a painted, wooden building behind which the actors could change costumes, and from which they could enter through one of three doors. Our word *scenery* comes from *skene*.

The Actors

Because of the immensity of Greek theaters, the actors—exclusively men—increased their height and impressiveness artificially. Each actor wore a linen, cork, or wood mask painted with a single, exaggerated expression: a sad face for a troubled king, a haggard, worn face for a weary soldier. Each mask had a funnel-shaped mouth opening, like a megaphone, to help project the voice. Elevated boots, padded clothing, and a high headdress could make a six-foot actor appear over seven feet tall. Such items also allowed actors to play more than one role.

The acting style for Greek drama differed from the realistic style of modern drama. The Greek actor could not change facial expressions while on stage, and any gestures or changes in voice had to be noticeable half a hill away. As a result, the Greek acting style was broader and more formal and ceremonial than contemporary acting.

The Conventions of Greek Drama

Greek drama differs from modern drama in several other significant ways.

■ Unlike most modern audiences, who put a premium on originality, Greek audiences were familiar with the plots and characters of the dramas presented since most plots were derived from myths, legends, or other traditional stories. This familiarity enabled them to focus on the irony of the situations and the poetry of the words.

■ The *chorus*, typically a group of twelve to fifteen men, represented either the ideas and feelings of the townspeople or of one of the major characters. The chorus or its leader could have any of the following functions: to recall and interpret past events, to initiate and to comment on the action, or to foretell the future. The role and importance of the chorus varied from play to play; in *Antigone* the chorus represents the elders of the city of Thebes.

■ Partly because of the heavy costumes, acts of violence occur offstage and are reported in long, descriptive narratives by a messenger.

■ As they were originally written, these ancient plays had no stage directions; those you see in the textbook are supplied by the translator so that you can visualize the action or better understand the motives and emotions of the characters.

The Greek Concept of Tragedy

It is ironic that the joyful Dionysian festivals were the source of the dramatic form we know as tragedy. Borrowing from a story or legend that the Greek audiences knew well, a tragedy shows how a character's proud or willful choices lead to inescapable disaster. Though deeply moralistic, tragedies are more than solemn stories of wrongs being punished. These dramas are complex studies of human beings in conflict with themselves, with society, and with the gods. As an audience, we can appreciate the rightness of the punishment, the sadness of the fall, yet also the nobility of the struggle.

Before Reading

Antigone

by Sophocles   Greece

Sophocles
496-406 B.C.

The son of a wealthy armor manufacturer, Sophocles (sof′ə klēz′) studied under the great dramatist Aeschylus (es′kə ləs). His training included play writing, musical composition, and choreography—elements central to Greek drama. His reputedly weak voice led him to abandon acting for writing. In 468 B.C., at the annual Dionysian festival, one of his plays won the play competition. Over his ninety-year life, Sophocles wrote more than 120 tragedies, twenty-four of them winning first prize. He served in the military and is said to have been appointed an official ambassador to several foreign states. Only seven of his plays survive.

Building Background

Imagine the Scene The city Dionysia had begun its festival with an elaborate procession of citizens escorting an image of Dionysus, the "godfather" of theater, to its place of honor in the orchestra. Athenians eagerly await Sophocles' newest tragedy. Will he go home with the skin of the *tragos* (goat), the coveted prize awarded the winner of first place? Eager citizens rise early, for the first tragedy will begin at dawn, followed in the afternoon by a comedy. Some walk to the great amphitheater on the side of the Acropolis; others are carried on the shoulders of slaves. Many carry provisions to throw at an actor whose performance offends. Some remember the time when a dissatisfied audience threw stones, and an actor almost died. But the actors today are Athens's best, and the word in the *agora* (marketplace) is that *Antigone* might win Sophocles another first prize.

Literary Focus

Protagonist/Antagonist The word **protagonist** comes from two Greek words, *protos* and *agoniste*, and means "first actor." Today it refers to the main or chief character in a work of fiction. The protagonist's adversary, or opponent—person, society, or force of nature—is called the **antagonist**. As you read *Antigone*, ask yourself: Who or what is the title character's adversary?

Writer's Notebook

Who's Your Hero? Heroes come in many sizes and guises. Who are some heroes—from literature, movies, and real life? List qualities that make them heroic. Check those qualities that Antigone possesses. You might keep track of your ideas in a chart like this one.

Heroic Qualities	Antigone Possesses

Two Women Talking, an example of painted Greek sculpture from the third century B.C., reveals a delicate style and a pyramid structure. Speculate on why a serene picture like this might appear at the beginning of a tragedy. ➤

ANTIGONE

SOPHOCLES

Although Antigone *is a complete play, it is closely associated with two other plays by Sophocles:* Oedipus the King *and* Oedipus at Colonus. *Oedipus, separated from his royal parents at birth, fulfills a dreadful prophecy. When he becomes an adult, he unknowingly kills his father and marries his mother, Jocasta. As king of Thebes, Oedipus blinds and banishes himself when he learns what he has done, leaving his brother-in-law Creon to rule. With his daughters Antigone and Ismene, Oedipus wanders in torment for years, finally dying in Colonus. Antigone and Ismene return to Thebes to find their brothers, Eteocles and Polynices, arguing about who should rule the kingdom. After Creon sides with Eteocles, Polynices raises an army and attacks Thebes. The brothers kill one another in battle. When Creon orders full burial honors for Eteocles but commands that Polynices remain unburied, he condemns the soul to eternal unrest. At this point the play* Antigone *begins.*

CHARACTERS

ISMENE (is mē′nē)
ANTIGONE (an tig′ə nē) } *daughters of Oedipus*

CREON (krē′on), *King of Thebes*

HAEMON (hē′mən), *son of Creon*

TEIRESIAS (tī rē′sē əs), *a blind prophet*

A SENTRY

A MESSENGER

EURYDICE (yù rid′ə sē′), *wife of Creon*

CHORUS OF THEBAN ELDERS

KING'S ATTENDANTS

QUEEN'S ATTENDANTS

A BOY LEADING TEIRESIAS

SOLDIERS

Scene: Before the Palace at Thebes.

Enter ISMENE *from the central door of the Palace.* ANTIGONE *follows, anxious and urgent; she closes the door carefully, and comes to join her sister.*

ANTIGONE. O sister! Ismene dear, dear sister Ismene!
　　You know how heavy the hand of God is upon us;
　　How we who are left must suffer for our father, Oedipus.
　　There is no pain, no sorrow, no suffering, no dishonor
5　　We have not shared together, you and I.
　　And now there is something more. Have you heard this order,
　　This latest order that the King has proclaimed to the city?
　　Have you heard how our dearest are being treated like enemies?

ISMENE. I have heard nothing about any of those we love,
10　　Neither good nor evil—not, I mean, since the death
　　Of our two brothers, both fallen in a day.
　　The Argive army, I hear, was withdrawn last night.
　　I know no more to make me sad or glad.

ANTIGONE. I thought you did not. That's why I brought you out
　　　　here,
15　　Where we shan't be heard, to tell you something alone.

ISMENE. What is it, Antigone? Black news, I can see already.

ANTIGONE. O Ismene, what do you think? Our two dear brothers . . .
　　Creon has given funeral honors to one,
　　And not to the other; nothing but shame and ignominy.
20　　Eteocles has been buried, they tell me, in state,
　　With all honorable observances due to the dead.
　　But Polynices, just as unhappily fallen—the order
　　Says he is not to be buried, not to be mourned;
　　To be left unburied, unwept, a feast of flesh
25　　For keen-eyed carrion birds. The noble Creon!
　　It is against you and me he has made this order.
　　Yes, against me. And soon he will be here himself
　　To make it plain to those that have not heard it,
　　And to enforce it. This is no idle threat;
30　　The punishment for disobedience is death by stoning.
　　So now you know. And now is the time to show
　　Whether or not you are worthy of your high blood.

ISMENE. My poor Antigone, if this is really true,
　　What more can I do, or undo, to help you?

35 **ANTIGONE.** *Will* you help me? Will you do something with me? Will
　　　　you?

ISMENE. Help you do what, Antigone? What do you mean?

ANTIGONE. Would you help me lift the body . . . you and me?

ISMENE. You cannot mean . . . to bury him? Against the order?

ANTIGONE. Is he not my brother, and yours, whether you like it
40　　Or not? *I* shall never desert him, never.

12 Argive army (är′jīv *or* är′gīv). Polynices's army came from **Argos** (är′gos), a city in southern Greece.

18 funeral honors. In Greek mythology, the souls of unburied human beings could not cross the River Styx to the realm of the dead but were compelled to wander forever with no permanent resting place. Burying the dead was a sacred duty for surviving friends and relatives.

19 ignominy (ig′nə min′ē), *n.* public shame and disgrace; dishonor.

20 Eteocles (i tē′ə klēz).

22 Polynices (pol′ə nī′sēz′).

■ What do you think that Antigone expects from someone who is "worthy of your high blood"?

ISMENE. How could you dare, when Creon has expressly forbidden it?

ANTIGONE. He has no right to keep me from my own.

ISMENE. O sister, sister, do you forget how our father
Perished in shame and misery, his awful sin
45 Self-proved, blinded by his own self-mutilation?
And then his mother, his wife—for she was both—
Destroyed herself in a noose of her own making.
And now our brothers, both in a single day
Fallen in an awful exaction of death for death.
50 Blood for blood, each slain by the other's hand.
Now we two left; and what will be the end of us,
If we transgress the law and defy our king?
O think, Antigone; we are women; it is not for us
To fight against men; our rulers are stronger than we,
55 And we must obey in this, or in worse than this.
May the dead forgive me, I can do no other
But as I am commanded; to do more is madness.

ANTIGONE. No; then I will not ask you for your help.
Nor would I thank you for it, if you gave it.
60 Go your own way; I will bury my brother;
And if I die for it, what happiness!
Convicted of reverence—I shall be content
To lie beside a brother whom I love.
We have only a little time to please the living.
65 But all eternity to love the dead.
There I shall lie for ever. Live, if you will;
Live, and defy the holiest laws of heaven.

ISMENE. I do not defy them; but I cannot act
Against the State. I am not strong enough.

70 **ANTIGONE.** Let that be your excuse, then. I will go
And heap a mound of earth over my brother.

ISMENE. I fear for you, Antigone; I fear—

ANTIGONE. You need not fear for me. Fear for yourself.

ISMENE. At least be secret. Do not breathe a word.
75 I'll not betray your secret.

ANTIGONE.   Publish it
To all the world! Else I shall hate you more.

ISMENE. Your heart burns! Mine is frozen at the thought.

ANTIGONE. I know my duty, where true duty lies.

ISMENE. If you can do it; but you're bound to fail.

80 **ANTIGONE.** When I have *tried* and failed, I shall have failed.

ISMENE. No sense in starting on a hopeless task.

ANTIGONE. Oh, I shall hate you if you talk like that!
And *he* will hate you, rightly. Leave me alone
With my own madness. There is no punishment

---

45 **self-mutilation**
(self′myü′tl ā′shən), *n.*
When he realized that he
had killed his father and
married his mother, Oedipus
blinded himself by piercing
his eyes with a brooch worn
by his wife/mother.
46–7 **his mother . . . own
making.** Jocasta (jō kas′tə),
realizing that she was both
wife and mother to Oedipus,
hanged herself.
52 **transgress** (trans gres′),
v. go contrary to; sin against.

■ Which sister do you think
makes the wiser decision
about burying Polynices?

83 **he,** Polynices.

Antigone   **193**

85   Can rob me of my honorable death.

ISMENE. Go then, if you are determined, to your folly.

        But remember that those who love you . . . love you still.

(ISMENE *goes into the Palace.* ANTIGONE *leaves the stage by a side exit.*)

■ What does the main conflict in the play appear to be?

(Enter the CHORUS *of Theban elders.)*

CHORUS. Hail the sun! the brightest of all that ever

        Dawned on the City of Seven Gates, City of Thebes!

90   Hail the golden dawn over Dirce's river

        Rising to speed the flight of the white invaders

        Homeward in full retreat!

        The army of Polynices was gathered against us,

        In angry dispute his voice was lifted against us,

95   Like a ravening bird of prey he swooped around us

        With white wings flashing, with flying plumes,

        With armed hosts ranked in thousands.

        At the threshold of seven gates in a circle of blood

        His swords stood round us, his jaws were opened against us;

100   But before he could taste our blood, or consume us with fire,

        He fled, fled with the roar of the dragon behind him

        And thunder of war in his ears.

        The Father of Heaven abhors the proud tongue's boasting;

        He marked the oncoming torrent, the flashing stream

105   Of their golden harness, the clash of their battle gear;

        He heard the invader cry Victory over our ramparts,

        And smote him with fire to the ground.

        Down to the ground from the crest of his hurricane onslaught

        He swung, with the fiery brands of his hate brought low;

110   Each and all to their doom of destruction appointed

        By the god that fighteth for us.

        Seven invaders at seven gates seven defenders

        Spoiled of their bronze for a tribute to Zeus; save two

        Luckless brothers in one fight matched together

115   And in one death laid low.

        Great is the victory, great be the joy

        In the city of Thebes, the city of chariots.

        Now is the time to fill the temples

        With glad thanksgiving for warfare ended;

120   Shake the ground with the night-long dances,

        Bacchus afoot and delight abounding.

90 Dirce's river. Dirce (dèr′sē), the wife of a previous ruler of Thebes, was brutally murdered and her corpse thrown into a stream, thereafter called by her name.

101 the dragon, a metaphor for the army of Thebes. According to legend, Thebes was founded by Cadmus (kad′məs) whose first followers were killed by a dragon. Cadmus slew the dragon and planted its teeth; from the teeth came a race of giants who submitted to Cadmus and re-founded the city.

103–107 The Father of Heaven . . . to the ground. Zeus, who favored the Thebans in the battle, struck down the invading Argive army with thunderbolts.

108 onslaught (ôn′slôt′), *n.* a vigorous attack.

112–113 Seven invaders . . . tribute to Zeus. Polynices and six Argive generals each attacked one of Thebes's seven gates, which were successfully defended by seven Theban heroes. Instead of keeping the armor of the slain Argives, the defenders offered it as a tribute to Zeus.

114–115 Luckless brothers . . . laid low. Antigone's brothers, Eteocles and Polynices, killed each other in single combat, ending the war.

But see, the King comes here,
Creon, the son of Menoeceus,
Whom the gods have appointed for us
125 In our recent change of fortune,
What matter is it, I wonder,
That has led him to call us together
By his special proclamation?

(The central door is opened, and CREON *enters.)*

CREON. My councillors: now that the gods have brought our city
130 Safe through a storm of trouble to tranquillity,
I have called you especially out of all my people
To conference together, knowing that you
Were loyal subjects when King Laius reigned,
And when King Oedipus so wisely ruled us,
135 And again, upon his death, faithfully served
His sons, till they in turn fell—both slayers, both slain,
Both stained with brother-blood, dead in a day—
And I, their next of kin, inherited
The throne and kingdom which I now possess.
140 No other touchstone can test the heart of a man,
The temper of his mind and spirit, till he be tried
In the practice of authority and rule.
For my part, I have always held the view,
And hold it still, that a king whose lips are sealed
145 By fear, unwilling to seek advice, is damned.
And no less damned is he who puts a friend
Above his country; I have no good word for him.
As God above is my witness, who sees all,
When I see any danger threatening my people,
150 Whatever it may be, I shall declare it.
No man who is his country's enemy
Shall call himself my friend. Of this I am sure—
Our country is our life; only when she
Rides safely, have we any friends at all.
155 Such is my policy for our common weal.

In pursuance of this, I have made a proclamation
Concerning the sons of Oedipus, as follows:
Eteocles, who fell fighting in defense of the city,
Fighting gallantly, is to be honored with burial
160 And with all the rites due to the noble dead.
The other—you know whom I mean—his brother Polynices,
Who came back from exile intending to burn and destroy
His fatherland and the gods of his fatherland,
To drink the blood of his kin, to make them slaves—

123 Menoeceus
(mə nē′sē əs).

■ What background infor-
mation does the Chorus
provide in this speech?

130 tranquillity (trang-
kwil′ə tē), *n.* calmness;
quiet.

133 King Laius (lā′əs), a former king of Thebes and
father of Oedipus.

140 touchstone
(tuch′stōn′), *n.* a black
stone used to test the purity
of gold or silver; hence, any
test.

153 she, Thebes.

155 weal (wēl), *n.* well-
being; prosperity.

■ Why is Creon willing
to bury Eteocles but not
Polynices?

165 He is to have no grave, no burial,
No mourning from anyone; it is forbidden.
He is to be left unburied, left to be eaten
By dogs and vultures, a horror for all to see.
I am determined that never, if I can help it,
170 Shall evil triumph over good. Alive
Or dead, the faithful servant of his country
Shall be rewarded.

CHORUS. Creon, son of Menoeceus,
You have given your judgment for the friend and for the enemy.
As for those that are dead, so for us who remain,
175 Your will is law.

CREON. See then that it be kept.

CHORUS. My lord, some younger would be fitter for that task.

CREON. Watchers are already set over the corpse.

CHORUS. What other duty then remains for us?

CREON. Not to connive at any disobedience.

180 **CHORUS.** If there were any so mad as to ask for death ——

CREON. Ay, that is the penalty. There is always someone
Ready to be lured to ruin by hope of gain.

(He turns to go. A SENTRY *enters from the side of the stage.* CREON *pauses at the Palace door.)*

SENTRY. My lord: if I am out of breath, it is not from haste.
I have not been running. On the contrary, many a time
185 I stopped to think and loitered on the way,
Saying to myself "Why hurry to your doom,
Poor fool?" and then I said "Hurry, you fool.
If Creon hears this from another man,
Your head's as good as off." So here I am,
190 As quick as my unwilling haste could bring me;
In no great hurry, in fact. So now I am here . . .
But I'll tell my story . . . though it may be nothing after all.
And whatever I have to suffer, it can't be more
Than what God wills, so I cling to that for my comfort.

195 **CREON.** Good heavens, man, whatever is the matter?

SENTRY. To speak of myself first—I never did it, sir;
Nor saw who did; no one can punish me for that.

CREON. You tell your story with a deal of artful precaution.
It's evidently something strange.

SENTRY. It is.
200 So strange, it's very difficult to tell.

CREON. Well, out with it, and let's be done with you.

SENTRY. It's this, sir. The corpse . . . someone has just
Buried it and gone. Dry dust over the body
They scattered, in the manner of holy burial.

179 connive (kə nīv′), *v.*
cooperate secretly.

**186–187 Why hurry . . .
poor fool?** The sentry
worries that what he has to
tell Creon will result in his
death; killing the messenger
who brought bad news was
presumably a common
practice.

205 **CREON.** What! Who dared to do it?

SENTRY.   I don't know, sir.

There was no sign of a pick, no scratch of a shovel;
The ground was hard and dry—no trace of a wheel;
Whoever it was has left no clues behind him.
When the sentry on the first watch showed it us,

210 We were amazed. The corpse was covered from sight—
Not with a proper grave—just a layer of earth—
As it might be, the act of some pious passer-by.
There were no tracks of an animal either, a dog
Or anything that might have come and mauled the body.

215 Of course we all started pitching in to each other,
Accusing each other, and might have come to blows,
With no one to stop us; for anyone might have done it,
But it couldn't be proved against him, and all denied it.
We were all ready to take hot iron in hand

220 And go through fire and swear by God and heaven
We hadn't done it, nor knew of anyone
That could have thought of doing it, much less done it.
Well, we could make nothing of it. Then one of our men
Said something that made all our blood run cold—

225 Something we could neither refuse to do, nor do,
But at our own risk. What he said was "This
Must be reported to the King; we can't conceal it."
So it was agreed. We drew lots for it, and I,
Such is my luck, was chosen. So here I am,

230 As much against my will as yours, I'm sure;
A bringer of bad news expects no welcome.

CHORUS. My lord, I fear—I feared it from the first—
That this may prove to be an act of the gods.

CREON. Enough of that! Or I shall lose my patience.

235 Don't talk like an old fool, old though you be.
Blasphemy, to say the gods could give a thought
To carrion flesh! Held him in high esteem,
I suppose, and buried him like a benefactor—
A man who came to burn their temples down,

240 Ransack their holy shrines, their land, their laws?
Is that the sort of man you think gods love?
Not they. No. There's a party of malcontents
In the city, rebels against my word and law,
Shakers of heads in secret, impatient of rule;

245 *They* are the people, I see it well enough,
Who have bribed their instruments to do this thing.
Money! Money's the curse of man, none greater.
That's what wrecks cities, banishes men from home,

212 pious (pī′əs), *adj.* having or showing reverence for God; righteous.

214 maul (môl), *v.* treat roughly; physically harm.

236 blasphemy (blas′fə mē), *n.* abuse or contempt for God or sacred things.

■ Whom does Creon first suspect has buried Polynices? Whom do you suspect?

246 instrument (in′strə mənt), *n.* thing with or by which something is done; person made use of by another.

Tempts and deludes the most well-meaning soul,
250   Pointing out the way to infamy and shame.
      Well, they shall pay for their success. (*To the* SENTRY.) See to it!
      See to it, you! Upon my oath, I swear,
      As Zeus is my god above: either you find
      The perpetrator of this burial
255   And bring him here into my sight, or death—
      No, not your mere death shall pay the reckoning,
      But, for a living lesson against such infamy,
      You shall be racked and tortured till you tell
      The whole truth of this outrage; so you may learn
260   To seek your gain where gain is yours to get,
      Not try to grasp it everywhere. In wickedness
      You'll find more loss than profit.

SENTRY.   May I say more?
CREON. No more; each word you say but stings me more.
SENTRY. Stings in your ears, sir, or in your deeper feelings?
265 **CREON.** Don't bandy words, fellow, about my feelings.
SENTRY. Though I offend your ears, sir, it is not I
      But he that's guilty that offends your soul.
CREON. Oh, born to argue, were you?
SENTRY.   Maybe so;
      But still not guilty in this business.
270 **CREON.** Doubly so, if you have sold your soul for money.
SENTRY. To think that thinking men should think so wrongly!
CREON. Think what you will. But if you fail to find
      The doer of this deed, you'll learn one thing:
      Ill-gotten gain brings no one any good.   (*He goes into the Palace.*)
275 **SENTRY.** Well, heaven send they find him. But whether or no,
      They'll not find me again, that's sure. Once free,
      Who never thought to see another day,
      I'll thank my lucky stars, and keep away.   (*Exit.*)
CHORUS. Wonders are many on earth, and the greatest of these
280   Is man, who rides the ocean and takes his way
      Through the deeps, through wide-swept valleys of perilous seas
      That surge and sway.

      He is master of ageless Earth, to his own will bending
      The immortal mother of gods by the sweat of his brow,
285   As year succeeds to year, with toil unending
      Of mule and plough.

      He is lord of all things living; birds of the air,
      Beasts of the field, all creatures of sea and land.
      He taketh, cunning to capture and ensnare

254 perpetrator (pėr′pə-trā′tər), *n.* one who commits anything bad or foolish.

265 bandy (ban′dē), *v.* exchange.

290 With sleight of hand;

Hunting the savage beast from the upland rocks,
Taming the mountain monarch in his lair,
Teaching the wild horse and the roaming ox
His yoke to bear.

295 The use of language, the wind-swift motion of brain
He learnt; found out the laws of living together
In cities, building him shelter against the rain
And wintry weather.

There is nothing beyond his power. His subtlety
300 Meeteth all chance, all danger conquereth.
For every ill he hath found its remedy,
Save only death.

O wondrous subtlety of man, that draws
To good or evil ways! Great honor is given
305 And power to him who upholdeth his country's laws
And the justice of heaven.

But he that, too rashly daring, walks in sin
In solitary pride to his life's end
At door of mine shall never enter in
310 To call me friend.

(Severally, seeing some persons approach from a distance.)
O gods! A wonder to see!
Surely it cannot be——
It is no other——
Antigone!
315 Unhappy maid——
Unhappy Oedipus's daughter; it is she they bring.
Can she have rashly disobeyed
The order of our King?

(Enter the SENTRY, *bringing* ANTIGONE *guarded by two more soldiers.)*
SENTRY. We've got her. Here's the woman that did the deed.
320 We found her in the act of burying him. Where's the King?
CHORUS. He is just coming out of the palace now. (*Enter* CREON.)
CREON. What's this? What am I just in time to see?
SENTRY. My lord, an oath's a very dangerous thing.
Second thoughts may prove us liars. Not long since
325 I swore I wouldn't trust myself again

290 **sleight of hand,** skill and quickness in moving the hands; tricks of a modern magician.

after 310 **severally**. Each of the following lines is spoken by a different member of the Chorus.

■ What question would you ask the Chorus about this speech?

To face your threats; you gave me a drubbing the first time.
But there's no pleasure like an unexpected pleasure,
Not by a long way. And so I've come again,
Though against my solemn oath. And I've brought this lady,

330 Who's been caught in the act of setting that grave in order.
And no casting lots for it this time—the prize is mine
And no one else's. So take her; judge and convict her.
I'm free, I hope, and quit of the horrible business.

CREON. How did you find her? Where have you brought her from?

335 **SENTRY.** She was burying the man with her own hands, and that's
    the truth.

CREON. Are you in your senses? Do you know what you are saying?

SENTRY. I saw her myself, burying the body of the man
    Whom you said not to bury. Don't I speak plain?

CREON. How did she come to be seen and taken in the act?

340 **SENTRY.** It was this way. After I got back to the place,
With all your threats and curses ringing in my ears,
We swept off all the earth that covered the body,
And left it a sodden naked corpse again;
Then sat up on the hill, on the windward side,

345 Keeping clear of the stench of him, as far as we could;
All of us keeping each other up to the mark,
With pretty sharp speaking, not to be caught napping this time.
So this went on some hours, till the flaming sun
Was high in the top of the sky, and the heat was blazing.

350 Suddenly a storm of dust, like a plague from heaven,
Swept over the ground, stripping the trees stark bare,
Filling the sky; you had to shut your eyes
To stand against it. When at last it stopped,
There was the girl, screaming like an angry bird,

355 When it finds its nest empty and little ones gone.
Just like that she screamed, seeing the body
Naked, crying and cursing the ones that had done it.
Then she picks up the dry earth in her hands,
And pouring out of a fine bronze urn she's brought

360 She makes her offering three times to the dead.
Soon as we saw it, down we came and caught her.
She wasn't at all frightened. And so we charged her
With what she'd done before, and this. She admitted it,
I'm glad to say—though sorry too, in a way.

365 It's good to save your own skin, but a pity
To have to see another get into trouble,
Whom you've no grudge against. However, I can't say
I've ever valued anyone else's life
More than my own, and that's the honest truth.

▲ This is an ivory statuette
of a tragic actor.

**359–360 And pouring . . . to
the dead,** pouring wine,
water, or oil as an offering to
the gods.

370 **CREON** (*to* ANTIGONE). Well, what do you say—you, hiding your head
        there:
    Do you admit, or do you deny the deed?
ANTIGONE. I do admit it. I do not deny it.
CREON (*to the* SENTRY). You—you may go. You are discharged from
        blame.
(*Exit* SENTRY.)
    Now tell me, in as few words as you can,
375   Did you know the order forbidding such an act?
ANTIGONE. I knew it, naturally. It was plain enough.
CREON. And yet you dared to contravene it?
ANTIGONE.   Yes.
    That order did not come from God. Justice,
    That dwells with the gods below, knows no such law.
380   I did not think your <u>edicts</u> strong enough
    To overrule the unwritten unalterable laws
    Of God and heaven, you being only a man.
    They are not of yesterday or today, but everlasting
    Though where they came from, none of us can tell.
385   Guilty of their transgression before God
    I cannot be, for any man on earth.
    I knew that I should have to die, of course,
    With or without your order. If it be soon,
    So much the better. Living in daily torment
390   As I do, who would not be glad to die?
    This punishment will not be any pain.
    Only if I had let my mother's son
    Lie there unburied, then I could not have borne it.
    This I can bear. Does that seem foolish to you?
395   Or is it you that are foolish to judge me so?
CHORUS. She shows her father's stubborn spirit: foolish
    Not to give way when everything's against her.
CREON. Ah, but you'll see. The over-obstinate spirit
    Is soonest broken; as the strongest iron will snap
400   If over-tempered in the fire to brittleness.
    A little halter is enough to break
    The wildest horse. Proud thoughts do not sit well
    Upon subordinates. This girl's proud spirit
    Was first in evidence when she broke the law;
405   And now, to add insult to her injury,
    She gloats over her deed. But, as I live,
    She shall not <u>flout</u> my orders with <u>impunity</u>.
    My sister's child—ay, were she even nearer,
    Nearest and dearest, she should not escape
410   Full punishment—she, and her sister too,

■ What is Antigone's philosophy in lines 377–395?

380 edict (ē′dikt), *n.* decree or law proclaimed by a king or other ruler on his sole authority.

400 over-tempered. The tempering of steel or any other metal involves bringing it to a proper or desired condition of hardness, elasticity, etc., by heating and cooling it.

407 flout (flout), *v.* treat with contempt or scorn.
407 impunity (im pyü′nə-tē), *n.* freedom from injury, punishment, or other bad consequences.

Her partner, doubtless, in this burying.
Let her be fetched! She was in the house just now;
I saw her, hardly in her right mind either.
Often the thoughts of those who plan dark deeds
415 Betray themselves before the deed is done.
The criminal who being caught still tries
To make a fair excuse, is damned indeed.

ANTIGONE. Now you have caught, will you do more than kill me?

CREON. No, nothing more; that is all I could wish.

420 **ANTIGONE.** Why then delay? There is nothing that you can say
That I should wish to hear, as nothing I say
Can weigh with you. I have given my brother burial.
What greater honor could I wish? All these
Would say that what I did was honorable,
425 But fear locks up their lips. To speak and act
Just as he likes is a king's prerogative.

CREON. You are wrong. None of my subjects thinks as you do.

ANTIGONE. Yes, sir, they do; but dare not tell you so.

CREON. And you are not only alone, but unashamed.

430 **ANTIGONE.** There is no shame in honoring my brother.

426 prerogative (pri rog′ə-
tiv), *n.* right or privilege that
nobody else has.

CREON. Was not his enemy, who died with him, your brother?

ANTIGONE. Yes, both were brothers, both of the same parents.

CREON. You honor one, and so insult the other.

ANTIGONE. He that is dead will not accuse me of that.

435 **CREON.** He will, if you honor him no more than the traitor.

ANTIGONE. It was not a slave, but his brother that died with him.

CREON. Attacking his country, while the other defended it.

ANTIGONE. Even so, we have a duty to the dead.

CREON. Not to give equal honour to good and bad.

440 **ANTIGONE.** Who knows? In the country of the dead that may be the
law.

CREON. An enemy can't be a friend, even when dead.

ANTIGONE. My way is to share my love, not share my hate.

CREON. Go then, and share your love among the dead.
We'll have no woman's law here, while I live.

(Enter ISMENE *from the Palace.)*

445 **CHORUS.** Here comes Ismene, weeping
In sisterly sorrow; a darkened brow,
Flushed face, and the fair cheek marred
With flooding rain.

CREON. You crawling viper! Lurking in my house

450 To suck my blood! Two traitors unbeknown
Plotting against my throne. Do you admit
To share in this burying, or deny all knowledge?

ISMENE. I did it—yes—if she will let me say so.
I am as much to blame as she is.

ANTIGONE.   No.

455 That is not just. You would not lend a hand
And I refused your help in what I did.

ISMENE. But I am not ashamed to stand beside you
Now in your hour of trial, Antigone.

ANTIGONE. Whose was the deed, Death and the dead are witness.

460 I love no friend whose love is only words.

ISMENE. O sister, sister, let me share your death,
Share in the tribute of honor to him that is dead.

ANTIGONE. You shall not die with me. You shall not claim
That which you would not touch. One death is enough.

465 **ISMENE.** How can I bear to live, if you must die?

ANTIGONE. Ask Creon. Is not he the one you care for?

ISMENE. You do yourself no good to taunt me so.

ANTIGONE. Indeed no: even my jests are bitter pains.

ISMENE. But how, O tell me, how can I still help you?

470 **ANTIGONE.** Help yourself. I shall not stand in your way.

ISMENE. For pity, Antigone—can I not die with you?

■ Do you think that Creon
will eventually reverse his
decision to put Antigone to
death? Why or why not?

**447-448 fair cheek . . . flood-
ing rain.** Ismene's face is
spoiled by tears.

ANTIGONE. You chose; life was your choice, when mine was death.

ISMENE. Although I warned you that it would be so.

ANTIGONE. Your way seemed right to some, to others mine.

475 **ISMENE.** But now both in the wrong, and both condemned.

ANTIGONE. No, no. You live. My heart was long since dead,
So it was right for me to help the dead.

CREON. I do believe the creatures both are mad;
One lately crazed, the other from her birth.

480 **ISMENE.** Is it not likely, sir? The strongest mind
Cannot but break under misfortune's blows.

CREON. Yours did, when you threw in your lot with hers.

ISMENE. How could I wish to live without my sister?

CREON. You have no sister. Count her dead already.

485 **ISMENE.** You could not take her—kill your own son's bride?

CREON. Oh, there are other fields for him to plough.

ISMENE. No truer troth was ever made than theirs.

CREON. No son of mine shall wed so vile a creature.

ANTIGONE. O Haemon, can your father spite you so?

490 **CREON.** You and your paramour, I hate you both.

CHORUS. Sir, would you take her from your own son's arms?

CREON. Not I, but death shall take her.

CHORUS.   Be it so.
Her death, it seems, is certain.

CREON.   Certain it is.
No more delay. Take them, and keep them within—

495 The proper place for women. None so brave
As not to look for some way to escape
When they see life stand face to face with death.

(The women are taken away.)

CHORUS. Happy are they who know not the taste of evil.
From a house that heaven hath shaken

500 The curse departs not
But falls upon all of the blood,
Like the restless surge of the sea when the dark storm drives
The black sand hurled from the deeps
And the Thracian gales boom down

505 On the echoing shore.

In life and in death is the house of Labdacus stricken.
Generation to generation,
With no atonement,
It is scourged by the wrath of a god.

510 And now for the dead dust's sake is the light of promise,
The tree's last root, crushed out

■ What other literary couples do you know whose parents oppose their union?

490 paramour (par′ə mu̇r), *n.* lover.

500–501 The curse . . . upon all of the blood. The curse on Oedipus has passed on to his descendants.
506 the house of Labdacus (lab′də kəs), the ruling family of Thebes. Labdacus, a former king, was the grandfather of Oedipus.
508 atonement (ə tōn′mənt), *n.* a giving of satisfaction for a wrong, loss, or injury.
509 scourge (skėrj), *v.* punish severely.

■ What does the Chorus mean by "the tree's last root" in line 511? You may want to refer to the headnote on page 191.

By pride of heart and the sin
Of presumptuous tongue.

For what presumption of man can match thy power,
515   O Zeus, that art not subject to sleep or time
Or age, living for ever in bright Olympus?
Tomorrow and for all time to come,
As in the past,
This law is immutable:
520   For mortals greatly to live is greatly to suffer.

Roving ambition helps many a man to good,
And many it falsely lures to light desires,
Till failure trips them unawares, and they fall
On the fire that consumes them. Well was it said,
525   Evil seems good
To him who is doomed to suffer;

And short is the time before that suffering comes.
But here comes Haemon,
Your youngest son.
530   Does he come to speak his sorrow
For the doom of his promised bride,
The loss of his marriage hopes?

CREON. We shall know it soon, and need no prophet to tell us.

(*Enter* HAEMON.)
Son, you have heard, I think, our final judgment
535   On your late betrothed. No angry words, I hope?
Still friends, in spite of everything, my son?
HAEMON. I am your son, sir; by your wise decisions
My life is ruled, and them I shall always obey.
I cannot value any marriage tie
540   Above your own good guidance.
CREON.   Rightly said.
Your father's will should have your heart's first place.
Only for this do fathers pray for sons
Obedient, loyal, ready to strike down
Their fathers' foes, and love their fathers' friends.
545   To be the father of unprofitable sons
Is to be the father of sorrows, a laughingstock
To all one's enemies. Do not be fooled, my son,
By lust and the wiles of a woman. You'll have bought
Cold comfort if your wife's a worthless one.
550   No wound strikes deeper than love that is turned to hate.

---

513 presumptuous (pri-zump′chü əs), *adj.* bold.

519 immutable (i myü′tə-bəl), *adj.* never changing.

525–527 Evil seems good . . . suffering comes. People who convince themselves that the evil they do is good must eventually suffer punishment.

This girl's an enemy; away with her,
And let her go and find a mate in Hades.
Once having caught her in a flagrant act—
The one and only traitor in our State—
555 I cannot make myself a traitor too;
So she must die. Well may she pray to Zeus,
The god of family love. How, if I tolerate
A traitor at home, shall I rule those abroad?
He that is a righteous master of his house
560 Will be a righteous statesman. To transgress
Or twist the law to one's own pleasure, presume
To order where one should obey, is sinful,
And I will have none of it.
He whom the State appoints must be obeyed
565 To the smallest matter, be it right—or wrong.
And he that rules his household, without a doubt,
Will make the wisest king, or, for that matter,
The staunchest subject. He will be the man
You can depend on in the storm of war,
570 The faithfulest comrade in the day of battle.
There is no more deadly peril than disobedience;
States are devoured by it, homes laid in ruins,
Armies defeated, victory turned to rout.
While simple obedience saves the lives of hundreds
575 Of honest folk. Therefore, I hold to the law,
And will never betray it—least of all for a woman.
Better be beaten, if need be, by a man,
Than let a woman get the better of us.
CHORUS. To me, as far as an old man can tell,
580 It seems your Majesty has spoken well.
HAEMON. Father, man's wisdom is the gift of heaven,
The greatest gift of all. I neither am
Nor wish to be clever enough to prove you wrong,
Though all men might not think the same as you do.
585 Nevertheless, I have to be your watchdog,
To know what others say and what they do,
And what they find to praise and what to blame.
Your frown is a sufficient silencer
Of any word that is not for your ears.
590 But *I* hear whispers spoken in the dark;
On every side I hear voices of pity
For this poor girl, doomed to the cruelest death,
And most unjust, that ever woman suffered
For an honourable action—burying a brother
595 Who was killed in battle, rather than leave him naked

553 flagrant (flā′grənt), *adj.* glaringly offensive; outrageous.

■ Do you think that Creon's appraisal of Antigone as one who "twist[s] the law to one's own pleasure" is a fair one? Explain.

573 rout (rout), *n.* a complete defeat.

For dogs to maul and carrion birds to peck at.
Has she not rather earned a crown of gold?—
Such is the secret talk about the town.
Father, there is nothing I can prize above
600 Your happiness and well-being. What greater good
Can any son desire? Can any father
Desire more from his son? Therefore I say,
Let not your first thought be your only thought.
Think if there cannot be some other way.
605 Surely, to think your own the only wisdom,
And yours the only word, the only will,
Betrays a shallow spirit, an empty heart.
It is no weakness for the wisest man
To learn when he is wrong, know when to yield.
610 So, on the margin of a flooded river
Trees bending to the torrent live unbroken,
While those that strain against it arc snapped off.
A sailor has to tack and slacken sheets
Before the gale, or find himself capsized.
615 So, father, pause, and put aside your anger.
I think, for what my young opinion's worth,
That, good as it is to have infallible wisdom,
Since this is rarely found, the next best thing
Is to be willing to listen to wise advice.
620 **CHORUS.** There is something to be said, my lord, for this point of
        view,
        And for yours as well; there is much to be said on both sides.
CREON. Indeed! Am I to take lessons at my time of life
        From a fellow of his age?
HAEMON. No lesson you need be ashamed of.
625 It isn't a question of age, but of right and wrong.
CREON. Would you call it right to admire an act of disobedience?
HAEMON. Not if the act were also dishonorable.
CREON. And was not this woman's action dishonorable?
HAEMON. The people of Thebes think not.
CREON.   The people of Thebes!
630 Since when do I take my orders from the people of Thebes?
HAEMON. Isn't that rather a childish thing to say?
CREON. No, I am king, and responsible only to myself.
HAEMON. A one-man state? What sort of a state is that?
CREON. Why, does not every state belong to its ruler?
635 **HAEMON.** You'd be an excellent king—on a desert island.
CREON. Of course, if you're on the woman's side—
HAEMON.   No, no—
        Unless you're the woman. It's you I'm fighting for.

■ What questions do you still have about what's happening? Jot them down in your notebook.

617 infallible (in fal′ə bəl), *adj.* free from error.

CREON. What, villain, when every word you speak is against me?

HAEMON. Only because I know you are wrong, wrong.

640 **CREON.** Wrong? To respect my own authority?

HAEMON. What sort of respect tramples on all that is holy?

CREON. Despicable coward! No more will than a woman!

HAEMON. I have nothing to be ashamed of.

CREON.   Yet you plead her cause.

HAEMON. No, *yours,* and mine, and that of the gods of the dead.

645 **CREON.** You'll never marry her this side of death.

HAEMON. Then, if she dies, she does not die alone.

CREON. Is that a threat, you impudent—

HAEMON.   Is it a threat
To try to argue against wrong-headedness?

CREON. You'll learn what wrong-headedness is, my friend, to your
cost.

650 **HAEMON.** O father, I could call you mad, were you not my father.

CREON. Don't toady me, boy; keep that for your lady-love.

HAEMON. You mean to have the last word, then?

CREON.   I do.
And what is more, by all the gods in heaven,
I'll make you sorry for your impudence.
(Calling to those within.)

655   Bring out that she-devil, and let her die
Now, with her bridegroom by to see it done!

HAEMON. That sight I'll never see. Nor from this hour
Shall you see me again. Let those that will
Be witness of your wickedness and folly.   *(Exit.)*

660 **CHORUS.** He is gone, my lord, in very passionate haste.
And who shall say what a young man's wrath may do?

CREON. Let him go! Let him do! Let him rage as never man raged,
He shall not save those women from their doom.

CHORUS. You mean, then, sire, to put them both to death?

665 **CREON.** No, not the one whose hand was innocent.

CHORUS. And to what death do you condemn the other?

CREON. I'll have her taken to a desert place
Where no man ever walked, and there walled up
Inside a cave, alive, with food enough

670   To acquit ourselves of the blood-guiltiness
That else would lie upon our commonwealth.
There she may pray to Death, the god she loves,
And ask release from death; or learn at last
What hope there is for those who worship death.   *(Exit.)*

▲ This marble relief from the first or second century A.D., is a theater mask that added height to the actor's stature.

667–674 I'll have her taken . . . worship death. If Antigone is provided with enough food to enable her to pray for her life, then whether or not she dies is up to the gods, and Creon and the state are thus blameless.

■ Do you think that Antigone is one of "those who worship death"? Explain.

After Reading

Making Connections

1. If you could put a piece of advice or encouragement into a fortune cookie for Antigone, what would you say?

2. If Antigone were alive today, what career do you think she would choose? Why?

3. For whom do you have the most sympathy: Antigone, Ismene, Creon, or Haemon? Explain your reasons.

4. What noble qualities does Antigone reveal? Does she reveal any faults?

5. How would you describe Ismene's **character**?

6. Why does Antigone reject Ismene's offer to share the blame for defying Creon and burying their brother?

7. ☙ What opposing ideals do Haemon and Creon reveal through their **interactions**?

8. Do you find the **mood** of the scenes featuring the Sentry humorous? Why or why not?

9. Do you think that Creon exhibits both positive and negative traits? Explain.

10. Why would Antigone's decision to bury Polynices isolate her from both her sister and her city?

11. What modern instances of people who break laws for reasons of personal conscience can you think of? Explain which, if any, of these you think are justified.

Vocabulary Study

On a piece of paper, number from 1-5. Write the word that best completes each sentence. You will not use all the words.

**blasphemy
edict
flagrant
flout
impunity
onslaught
rout**

1. Antigone is foolish to think she can bury Polynices with ____.

2. Ismene is grieved to think that Antigone would ____ her good advice.

3. The guards catch Antigone in her ____ act of disobedience.

4. After the Argive army flees, Creon claims that the battle ended in a ____.

5. Creon is too proud to tolerate a(n) ____ of curses from Antigone.

675 **CHORUS.** Where is the equal of Love?
Where is the battle he cannot win,
The power he cannot outmatch?
In the farthest corners of earth, in the midst of the sea,
He is there; he is here
680 In the bloom of a fair face
Lying in wait;
And the grip of his madness
Spares not god or man,
Marring the righteous man,
685 Driving his soul into mazes of sin
And strife, dividing a house.
For the light that burns in the eyes of a bride of desire
Is a fire that consumes.
At the side of the great gods
690 Aphrodite immortal
Works her will upon all.

(The doors are opened and ANTIGONE *enters, guarded.)*
But here is a sight beyond all bearing,
At which my eyes cannot but weep;
Antigone forth faring
695 To her bridal bower of endless sleep.
ANTIGONE. You see me, countrymen, on my last journey,
Taking my last leave of the light of day;
Going to my rest, where death shall take me
Alive across the silent river.
700 No wedding day; no marriage music;
Death will be all my bridal dower.
CHORUS. But glory and praise go with you, lady,
To your resting place. You go with your beauty
Unmarred by the hand of consuming sickness,
705 Untouched by the sword, living and free,
As none other that ever died before you.
ANTIGONE. The daughter of Tantalus, a Phrygian maid,
Was doomed to a piteous death on the rock
Of Sipylus, which embraced and imprisoned her,
710 Merciless as the ivy; rain and snow
Beat down upon her, mingled with her tears,
As she wasted and died. Such was her story,
And such is the sleep that I shall go to.
CHORUS. She was a goddess of immortal birth,
715 And we are mortals; the greater the glory,
To share the fate of a god-born maiden,
A living death, but a name undying.

690 Aphrodite (af′rə dī′tē),
goddess of love and beauty.

694 faring (fer′ing),
ARCHAIC. traveling.

699 silent river, in Greek
mythology, one of the rivers
that separated the land of
the dead from the land of
the living.
701 dower (dour), *n.* dowry.

**707 the daughter of
Tantalus,** Niobe (nī′ō bē′),
whose children were slain by
the gods to punish her for
her excessive pride.
Overcome with grief, she
turned into a stone from
which tears continued to
flow. The stone was carried
by a whirlwind to Mount
Sipylus (sip′i ləs) in Phrygia
(frij′ē ə), the kingdom of
Niobe's father.

ANTIGONE. Mockery, mockery! By the gods of our fathers,
Must you make me a laughingstock while I yet live?

720 O lordly sons of my city! O Thebes!
Your valleys of rivers, your chariots and horses!
No friend to weep at my banishment
To a rock-hewn chamber of endless durance,
In a strange cold tomb alone to linger

725 Lost between life and death for ever.

CHORUS. My child, you have gone your way
To the outermost limit of daring
And have stumbled against Law enthroned.
This is the expiation

730 You must make for the sin of your father.

ANTIGONE. My father—the thought that sears my soul—
The unending burden of the house of Labdacus.
Monstrous marriage of mother and son . . .
My father . . . my parents . . . O hideous shame!

735 Whom now I follow, unwed, curse-ridden,
Doomed to this death by the ill-starred marriage
That marred my brother's life.

CHORUS. An act of homage is good in itself, my daughter;
But authority cannot afford to connive at disobedience.

740 You are the victim of your own self-will.

ANTIGONE. And must go the way that lies before me.
No funeral hymn; no marriage music;
No sun from this day forth, no light,
No friend to weep at my departing.   (*Enter* CREON.)

745 **CREON.** Weeping and wailing at the door of death!
There'd be no end of it, if it had force
To buy death off. Away with her at once.
And close her up in her rock-vaulted tomb.
Leave her and let her die, if die she must,

750 Or live within her dungeon. Though on earth
Her life is ended from this day, her blood
Will not be on our hands.

ANTIGONE.   So to my grave,
My bridal bower, my everlasting prison,
I go, to join those many of my kinsmen

755 Who dwell in the mansions of Persephone,
Last and unhappiest, before my time.
Yet I believe my father will be there
To welcome me, my mother greet me gladly,
And you, my brother, gladly see me come.

760 Each one of you my hands have laid to rest,
Pouring the due libations on your graves.

718 mockery. Antigone mistakenly thinks that the Chorus, in comparing her to the gods, is making fun of her.

729 expiation (ek′spē-ā′shən), *n.* atonement.

■ Describe the role of the Chorus in this scene.

755 Persephone (pėr sef′ə-nē), daughter of Zeus and Demeter (di mē′tər); made queen of the lower world (Hades).
761 libation (lī bā′shən), *n.* the wine, water, etc. offered to a god.

It was by this service to your dear body, Polynices,
I earned the punishment which now I suffer,
Though all good people know it was for your honor.
765   O but I would not have done the forbidden thing
For any husband or for any son.
For why? I could have had another husband
And by him other sons, if one were lost;
But, father and mother lost, where would I get
770   Another brother? For thus preferring you,
My brother, Creon condemns me and hales me away,
Never a bride, never a mother, unfriended,
Condemned alive to solitary death.
What law of heaven have I transgressed? What god
775   Can save me now? What help or hope have I,
In whom devotion is deemed sacrilege?
If this is God's will, I shall learn my lesson
In death; but if my enemies are wrong,
I wish them no worse punishment than mine.
780   **CHORUS.** Still the same tempest in the heart
Torments her soul with angry gusts.
CREON. The more cause then have they that guard her
To hasten their work; or they too suffer.
CHORUS. Alas, that word had the sound of death.
785   **CREON.** Indeed there is no more to hope for.
ANTIGONE. Gods of our fathers, my city, my home,
Rulers of Thebes! Time stays no longer.
Last daughter of your royal house
Go I, *his* prisoner, because I honored
790   Those things to which honor truly belongs.
(ANTIGONE *is led away.*)

CHORUS. So, long ago, lay Danae
Entombed within her brazen bower;
Noble and beautiful was she,
On whom there fell the golden shower
795   Of life from Zeus. There is no tower
So high, no armory so great,
No ship so swift, as is the power
Of man's inexorable fate.

There was the proud Edonian king,
800   Lycurgus, in rock-prison pent
For arrogantly challenging
God's laws: it was his punishment
Of that swift passion to repent

■ Explain Antigone's argument for defending her brother over a husband or a son.

776 sacrilege (sak′rə lij), *n.* an intentional injury or disrespectful treatment of anyone or anything sacred.

791 Danae (dan′ā ē), a maiden imprisoned in a bronze (brazen) chamber by her father, who feared a prophecy that a child born to Danae would someday kill him. Zeus entered her bronze chamber as a golden rain, and from their union Perseus, who eventually did kill his grandfather, was born.

791–814 So, long ago . . . as upon thee, my child. In these lines, the Chorus compares Antigone's fate to that of three other mortals who had been imprisoned.

798 inexorable (in ek′sər ə-bəl), *adj.* relentless, unyielding.

800 Lycurgus (lī kėr′gəs), a Greek king who opposed the worship of Dionysus (dī′ə-nī′səs) and was punished by being imprisoned in a cave and driven insane.

In slow perception, for that he
805   Had braved the rule omnipotent
Of Dionysus' <u>sovereignty</u>.

On Phineus' wife the hand of fate
Was heavy, when her children fell
Victims to a stepmother's hate,
810   And she endured a prison-cell
Where the North Wind stood sentinel
In caverns amid mountains wild.
Thus the grey spinners wove their spell
On her, as upon thee, my child.

(Enter TEIRESIAS, *the blind prophet, led by a boy.)*
815 **TEIRESIAS.** Gentlemen of Thebes, we greet you, my companion and I,
     Who share one pair of eyes on our journeys together—
     For the blind man goes where his leader tells him to.
CREON. You are welcome, father Teiresias. What's your news?
TEIRESIAS. Ay, news you shall have; and advice, if you can heed it.
820 **CREON.** There was never a time when I failed to heed it, father.
TEIRESIAS. And thereby have so far steered a steady course.
CREON. And gladly acknowledge the debt we owe to you.
TEIRESIAS. Then mark me now; for you stand on a razor's edge.
CREON. Indeed? Grave words from your lips, good priest. Say on.
825 **TEIRESIAS.** I will; and show you all that my skill reveals.
     At my seat of divination, where I sit
     These many years to read the signs of heaven,
     An unfamiliar sound came to my ears
     Of birds in vicious combat, savage cries
830   In strange outlandish language, and the whirr
     Of flapping wings; from which I well could picture
     The gruesome warfare of their deadly talons.
     Full of foreboding then I made the test
     Of sacrifice upon the altar fire.
835   There was no answering flame; only rank juice
     Oozed from the flesh and dripped among the ashes,
     Smoldering and sputtering; the gall vanished in a puff,
     And the fat ran down and left the haunches bare.
     Thus (through the eyes of my young acolyte,
840   Who sees for me, that I may see for others)
     I read the signs of failure in my quest.
        And why? The <u>blight</u> upon us is *your* doing.
     The blood that stains our altars and our shrines,
     The blood that dogs and vultures have licked up,
845   It is none other than the blood of Oedipus

806 sovereignty (sov′rən-tē), *n.* supreme power or authority.
807 Phineus' wife. King Phineus (fin′ē əs) imprisoned his former wife and their two sons when he believed false accusations about them made by their stepmother, Idaea (i dē′ə).
813 grey spinners, the three Fates who control the length and nature of human lives.

826 seat of divination, the place where Teiresias sat to listen to the birds, which were believed to foretell (divine) the future.

842 blight (blīt), *n.* disease, or anything that causes destruction or ruin.

Spilled from the veins of his ill-fated son.
Our fires, our sacrifices, and our prayers
The gods abominate. How should the birds
Give any other than ill-omened voices,
850 Gorged with the dregs of blood that man has shed?
Mark this, my son: all men fall into sin.
But sinning, he is not forever lost
Hapless and helpless, who can make amends
And has not set his face against repentance.
855 Only a fool is governed by self-will.
　　　Pay to the dead his due. Wound not the fallen.
It is no glory to kill and kill again.
My words are for your good, as is my will,
And should be acceptable, being for your good.
860 **CREON.** You take me for your target, reverend sir,
Like all the rest. I know your art of old,
And how you make me your commodity
To trade and traffic in for your advancement.
Trade as you will; but all the silver of Sardis
865 And all the gold of India will not buy
A tomb for yonder traitor. No. Let the eagles
Carry his carcass up to the throne of Zeus;
Even that would not be sacrilege enough
To frighten me from my determination
870 Not to allow this burial. No man's act

853 hapless (hap′lis), *adj.*
unlucky; unfortunate.

■ How do you think Creon
will respond to Teiresias's
plea to forgive Antigone?

864 Sardis (sar′dis), capital
of ancient Lydia (present-day
Turkey), famous for its
wealth and luxury.

Antigone   **217**

Has power enough to pollute the goodness of God.
But great and terrible is the fall, Teiresias,
Of mortal men who seek their own advantage
By uttering evil in the guise of good.

875 **TEIRESIAS.** Ah, is there any wisdom in the world?

CREON. Why, what is the meaning of that wide-flung taunt?

TEIRESIAS. What prize outweighs the priceless worth of prudence?

CREON. Ay, what indeed? What mischief matches the lack of it?

TEIRESIAS. And there you speak of your own symptom, sir.

880 **CREON.** I am loth to pick a quarrel with you, priest.

TEIRESIAS. You do so, calling my divination false.

CREON. I say all prophets seek their own advantage.

TEIRESIAS. All kings, say I, seek gain unrighteously.

CREON. Do you forget to whom you say it?

TEIRESIAS. No.

885 Our king and benefactor, by my guidance.

CREON. Clever you may be, but not therefore honest.

TEIRESIAS. Must I reveal my yet unspoken mind?

CREON. Reveal all; but expect no gain from it.

TEIRESIAS. Does that still seem to you my motive, then?

890 **CREON.** Nor is my will for sale, sir, in your market.

TEIRESIAS. Then hear this. Ere the chariot of the sun
Has rounded once or twice his wheeling way,
You shall have given a son of your own loins
To death, in payment for death—two debts to pay:

895 One for the life that you have sent to death,
The life you have abominably entombed;
One for the dead still lying above ground
Unburied, unhonoured, unblest by the gods below.
You cannot alter this. The gods themselves

900 Cannot undo it. It follows of necessity
From what you have done. Even now the avenging Furies,
The hunters of Hell that follow and destroy,
Are lying in wait for you, and will have their prey,
When the evil you have worked for others falls on you.

905 Do I speak this for my gain? The time shall come,
And soon, when your house will be filled with the lamentation
Of men and of women; and every neighbouring city
Will be goaded to fury against you, for upon them
Too the pollution falls when the dogs and vultures

910 Bring the defilement of blood to their hearths and altars.
I have done. You pricked me, and these shafts of wrath
Will find their mark in your heart. You cannot escape
The sting of their sharpness. Lead me home, my boy.
Let us leave him to vent his anger on younger ears,

880 loth (lōth), *adj.* loath, unwilling.

905–910 The time shall come . . . and altars. This prophecy by Teiresias later comes true when the families of the slain Argive chiefs enlist the aid of the Athenian king, Theseus, to obtain burial rites for their dead. The Athenian army marches against Thebes and conquers it.

910 defilement (di fil′mənt), *n.* destruction of the purity or cleanness of (anything sacred); desecration.

915   Or school his mind and tongue to a milder mood
        Than that which now possesses him. Lead on.   *(Exit.)*

CHORUS. He has gone, my lord. He has prophesied terrible things.
        And for my part, I that was young and now am old
        Have never known his prophecies proved false.
920 **CREON.** It is true enough; and my heart is torn in two.
        It is hard to give way, and hard to stand and abide
        The coming of the curse. Both ways are hard.
CHORUS. If you would be advised, my good lord Creon——
CREON. What must I do? Tell me, and I will do it.
925 **CHORUS.** Release the woman from her rocky prison.
        Set up a tomb for him that lies unburied.
CREON. Is it your wish that I consent to this?
CHORUS. It is, and quickly. The gods do not delay
        The stroke of their swift vengeance on the sinner.
930 **CREON.** It is hard, but I must do it. Well I know
        There is no armor against necessity.
CHORUS. Go. Let your own hand do it, and no other.
CREON. I will go this instant. Slaves there! One and all.
        Bring spades and mattocks out on the hill!
935   My mind is made; 'twas I imprisoned her,
        And I will set her free. Now I believe
        It is by the laws of heaven that man must live.   *(Exit.)*
CHORUS. O Thou whose name is many,
        Son of the Thunderer, dear child of his Cadmean bride,
940   Whose hand is mighty
        In Italia,
        In the hospitable valley
        Of Eleusis,
        And in Thebes,
945   The mother-city of thy worshippers,
        Where sweet Ismenus gently watereth
        The soil whence sprang the harvest of the dragon's teeth,

        Where torches on the crested mountains gleam,
        And by the Castalia's stream
950   The nymph-train in thy dance rejoices,
        When from the ivy-tangled glens
        Of Nysa and from vine-clad plains
        Thou comest to Thebes where the immortal voices
        Sing thy glad strains.

955   Thebes, where thou lovest most to be,
        With her, thy mother, the fire-stricken one,

■ If you could ask Tieresias one question on behalf of Antigone, what would it be?

938 Thou whose name is many. The Chorus invokes the god Dionysus, whose native city of Thebes was under his special protection. Bacchus, Iacchus, and God of Wine are three of his many names.

946–947 Ismenus . . . dragon's teeth. The city that Cadmus and the giants founded is near the river Ismenus.

950–952 nymph-train . . . Nysa. When Semele (sem′ə lē), the mother of Dionysus, died, Zeus took his infant son to the nymphs of Nysa (nī′sə), who cared for him during his childhood.

956 thy mother, the fire-stricken one. Zeus had promised Semele that he would grant her one wish. Her wish was to see him in his full splendor as the king of gods and men. Being mortal, she could not endure the sight and was consumed to ashes.

Sickens for need of thee.
Healer of all her ills;
Come swiftly o'er the high Parnassian hills,
960   Come o'er the sighing sea.

    The stars, whose breath is fire, delight
    To dance for thee; the echoing night
    Shall with thy praises ring.
    Zeus-born, appear! With Thyiads revelling
965   Come, bountiful
    Iacchus, King!

(Enter a MESSENGER, *from the side of the stage.)*

MESSENGER. Hear, men of Cadmus's city, hear and attend,
    Men of the house of Amphion, people of Thebes!
    What is the life of man? A thing not fixed
970   For good or evil, fashioned for praise or blame.
    Chance raises a man to the heights, chance casts him down,
    And none can foretell what will be from what is.
    Creon was once an enviable man;
    He saved his country from her enemies,
975   Assumed the sovereign power, and bore it well,
    The honoured father of a royal house.
    Now all is lost; for life without life's joys
    Is living death; and such a life is his.
    Riches and rank and show of majesty
980   And state, where no joy is, are empty, vain
    And unsubstantial shadows, of no weight
    To be compared with happiness of heart.

CHORUS. What is your news? Disaster in the royal house?

MESSENGER. Death; and the guilt of it on living heads.

985 **CHORUS.** Who dead? And by what hand?

MESSENGER.   Haemon is dead,
    Slain by his own——

CHORUS.   His father?

MESSENGER.   His own hand.
    His father's act it was that drove him to it.

CHORUS. Then all has happened as the prophet said.

MESSENGER. What's next to do, your worships will decide.

(The Palace door opens.)

990 **CHORUS.** Here comes the Queen, Eurydice. Poor soul,
    It may be she has heard about her son.

(Enter EURYDICE, *attended by women.)*

959 Parnassian hills.
Parnassus (pär nas′əs), a
mountain in southern
Greece, was sacred to Apollo
and the nine Muses.

964 Thyiads (thī′yadz),
women driven mad by wine
and the power of Dionysus.
Also called Maenads
(mē′nadz).

■ What does Antigone have
in common with these gods
and goddesses mentioned by
the Chorus in lines 938–966?

968 Amphion (am fī′ən), a
former king of Thebes.

EURYDICE. My friends, I heard something of what you were saying
    As I came to the door. I was on my way to prayer
    At the temple of Pallas, and had barely turned the latch
995   When I caught your talk of some near calamity.
    I was sick with fear and reeled in the arms of my women.
    But tell me what is the matter; what have you heard?
    I am not unacquainted with grief, and I can bear it.
MESSENGER. Madam, it was I that saw it, and will tell you all.
1000   To try to make it any lighter now
    Would be to prove myself a liar. Truth
    Is always best.

              It was thus. I attended your husband,
    The King, to the edge of the field where lay the body
    Of Polynices, in pitiable state, mauled by the dogs.
1005   We prayed for him to the Goddess of the Roads, and to Pluto,
    That they might have mercy upon him. We washed the remains
    In holy water, and on a fire of fresh-cut branches
    We burned all that was left of him, and raised
    Over his ashes a mound of his native earth.
1010   That done, we turned toward the deep rock-chamber
    Of the maid that was married with death.

                      Before we reached it,
    One that stood near the accursed place had heard
    Loud cries of anguish, and came to tell King Creon.
    As he approached, came strange uncertain sounds
1015   Of lamentation, and he cried aloud:
    "Unhappy wretch! Is my foreboding true?
    Is this the most sorrowful journey that ever I went?
    My son's voice greets me. Go, some of you, quickly
    Through the passage where the stones are thrown apart,
1020   Into the mouth of the cave, and see if it be
    My son, my own son Haemon that I hear.
    If not, I am the sport of gods."

                    We went
    And looked, as bidden by our anxious master.
    There in the furthest corner of the cave
1025   We saw her hanging by the neck. The rope
    Was of the woven linen of her dress.
    And, with his arms about her, there stood he
    Lamenting his lost bride, his luckless love,
    His father's cruelty.

              When Creon saw them,
1030   Into the cave he went, moaning piteously.
    "O my unhappy boy," he cried again,

998 I am not unacquainted with grief. Menoeceus, a son of Creon and Eurydice, had sacrificed himself at the beginning of the war because of a prophecy that Thebes would be saved only if he were killed.

1005 Goddess of the Roads, Hecate (hek′ə tē), a goddess of the underworld who sent apparitions to frighten travelers at night.

▲ This terra cotta statuette of Melpomene (mel pom′ə-nē), the Muse of Tragedy, holding a tragic mask, dates from around 300 B.C.

"What have you done? What madness brings you here
To your destruction? Come away, my son,
My son, I do beseech you, come away!"
1035 His son looked at him with one angry stare,
Spat in his face, and then without a word
Drew sword and struck out. But his father fled
Unscathed. Whereon the poor demented boy
Leaned on his sword and thrust it deeply home
1040 In his own side, and while his life ebbed out
Embraced the maid in loose-enfolding arms,
His spurting blood staining her pale cheeks red.
(EURYDICE *goes quickly back into the Palace.*)
Two bodies lie together, wedded in death,
Their bridal sleep a witness to the world
1045 How great calamity can come to man
Through man's perversity.

CHORUS.   But what is this?
The Queen has turned and gone without a word.

MESSENGER. Yes. It is strange. The best that I can hope
Is that she would not sorrow for her son
1050 Before us all, but vents her grief in private
Among her women. She is too wise, I think,
To take a false step rashly.

CHORUS.   It may be.
Yet there is danger in unnatural silence
No less than in excess of lamentation.
1055 **MESSENGER.** I will go in and see, whether in truth
There is some fatal purpose in her grief.
Such silence, as you say, may well be dangerous.
(*He goes in.*)

(*Enter* ATTENDANTS *preceding the King.*)
CHORUS. The King comes here.
What the tongue scarce dares to tell
1060 Must now be known
By the burden that proves too well
The guilt, no other man's
But his alone.

(*Enter* CREON *with the body of* HAEMON.)
CREON. The sin, the sin of the erring soul
1065 Drives hard unto death.
Behold the slayer, the slain,
The father, the son.
O the curse of my stubborn will!

1038 unscathed
(un skātнd′), *adj.* not
harmed.

■ What events does the
Messenger recount in lines
999 to 1042?

1046 perversity (pər vėr′sə-
tē), *n.* quality of being contrary and willful.

Son, newly cut off in the newness of youth,
1070   Dead for my fault, not yours.

CHORUS. Alas, too late you have seen the truth.

CREON. I learn in sorrow. Upon my head
      God has delivered this heavy punishment,
      Has struck me down in the ways of wickedness,
1075   And trod my gladness under foot.
      Such is the bitter affliction of mortal man.

(Enter the MESSENGER *from the Palace.)*

MESSENGER. Sir, you have this and more than this to bear.
      Within there's more to know, more to your pain.

CREON. What more? What pain can overtop this pain?

1080 **MESSENGER.** She is dead—your wife, the mother of him that is
        dead—
      The death wound fresh in her heart. Alas, poor lady!

CREON. Insatiable Death, wilt thou destroy me yet?
      What say you, teller of evil?
      I am already dead,
1085   And is there more?
      Blood upon blood?
      More death? My wife?

(The central doors open, revealing the body of EURYDICE.)

CHORUS. Look then, and see; nothing is hidden now.

CREON. O second horror!
1090   What fate awaits me now?
      My child here in my arms . . . and there, the other . . .
      The son . . . the mother . . .

MESSENGER. There at the altar with the whetted knife
      She stood, and as the darkness dimmed her eyes
1095   Called on the dead, her elder son and this,
      And with her dying breath cursed you, their slayer.

CREON. O horrible . . .
      Is there no sword for me
      To end this misery?

1100 **MESSENGER.** Indeed you bear the burden of two deaths.
      It was her dying word.

CREON. And her last act?

MESSENGER. Hearing her son was dead, with her own hand
      She drove the sharp sword home into her heart.

1105 **CREON.** There is no man can bear this guilt but I.
      It is true, I killed him.
      Lead me away, away. I live no longer.

CHORUS. 'Twere best, if anything is best in evil times.
      What's soonest done, is best, when all is ill.

■ Do you think that Creon has gained wisdom through this tragedy? Explain.

1082 insatiable (in sā′shə-bəl), *adj.* that cannot be satisfied; greedy.

1110 **CREON.** Come, my last hour and fairest,
　　　My only happiness . . . come soon.
　　　Let me not see another day.
　　　Away . . . away . . .
　　CHORUS. The future is not to be known; our present care
1115　　Is with the present; the rest is in other hands.
　　CREON. I ask no more than I have asked.
　　CHORUS. Ask nothing.
　　　What is to be, no mortal can escape.
　　CREON. I am nothing. I have no life.
1120　　Lead me away . . .
　　　That have killed unwittingly
　　　My son, my wife.
　　　I know not where I should turn,
　　　Where look for help.
1125　　My hands have done amiss, my head is bowed
　　　With fate too heavy for me.　　*(Exit.)*

　　CHORUS. Of happiness the crown
　　　And chiefest part
　　　Is wisdom, and to hold
1130　　The gods in awe.
　　　This is the law
　　　That, seeing the stricken heart
　　　Of pride brought down,
　　　We learn when we are old.　　*(Exit.)*

After Reading

Making Connections

1. If a person like Antigone were in your class, what description might appear beneath her picture in the yearbook?

2. If Antigone and Haemon had married, what kind of marriage do you think they would have had?

3. Use a Venn diagram like the one below to show how the characters of Antigone and Creon are both alike and different.

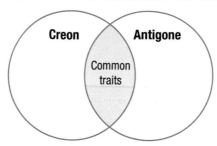

Creon   Antigone

Common traits

4. In her final appearance, why do you think Antigone makes an **allusion** to the "daughter of Tantalus" (lines 707-713)?

5. How would you describe the **tone** of Creon's remarks during his scene with Antigone?

6. How does the Chorus **personify** Love in its opening ode on page 212?

7. In what way does his accusation of Teiresias serve to **characterize** Creon?

8. At the end of the play, the Chorus states a **theme** of "pride brought down." Explain to which character(s) you think this theme applies.

9. How is Creon's decision to stop and bury Polynices on the way to free Antigone an example of **irony**?

10. Why do you think Eurydice is introduced so late in the play?

11. In *Antigone*, the Chorus is the voice of public opinion, while leaders in today's world rely on polls. Do you think that polls are reliable indicators of public opinion? Why or why not?

Literary Focus: Protagonist/Antagonist

In Greek tragedy, the **protagonist** is the character whose flaws or poor judgment brings about his or her downfall.

- According to this definition, who is the protagonist in this play?

- Do you think that Antigone could have avoided her fate? Why or why not?

Vocabulary Study

Number a sheet of paper from 1–10. Using the words listed below, write the word that best completes each sentence.

blight
defilement
expiation
hapless
inexorable
insatiable
perversity
sacrilege
sovereignty
unscathed

1. The gods, with their ____ appetite for revenge, demand that those who disobey them be punished.

2. Creon condemns the ____ of his contrary, willful niece.

3. Although Antigone is punished, Ismene survives the events ____.

4. Creon needs to make ____ for his many sins.

5. The ____ Eurydice is an unfortunate victim of circumstances.

6. Antigone considers it an intentional injury, or ____, for Polynices to remain unburied.

7. The ____ of a body is a crime the Greeks found hateful.

8. In a Greek tragedy, relentless fate moves in a(n) ____ manner.

9. Teiresias accuses Creon of causing the ____ that is spreading.

10. Creon reigns supreme, with absolute ____ over his people.

Expressing Your Ideas

Writing Choices

Writer's Notebook Update Now that you have finished reading the play, examine your chart of heroic traits. Does Antigone have others that you could add to your chart? Explain whether or not you think Antigone is heroic.

Imagine This! Moments before Antigone hangs herself, the god Dionysus saves her. Report this event as a Greek dramatist would: in a **monologue** by a messenger. Be prepared to deliver your monologue in class.

Interactions Working with a partner, find instances in the play that illustrate one of these conflicts: youth vs. age; human law vs. divine law; personal conscience vs. social laws; loyalty to family vs. loyalty to country. Then collaborate on a **persuasive paper** that explores this theme in the play.

Other Options

Characterization in Color Explain whether or not you would use this picture as an **illustration** of Creon at the end of the play.

Twelve Angry Men

by Reginald Rose   USA

Reginald Rose
born 1920

Reginald Rose got the idea for *Twelve Angry Men* while serving on the jury of a manslaughter case in New York. The experience left him struck by "the absolute finality of the decision" the jurors had to make. Rose wrote *Twelve Angry Men* in 1954 for television; later he wrote the scripts for both a film and a stage version. He was awarded three Emmys, one for *Twelve Angry Men* and two for the television series *The Defenders,* another work that deals with the American legal system. Rose has said, ". . . my main purpose has always been to project my own view of good and evil—and this is the essence of controversy."

Building Background

Ladies and Gentlemen of the Jury

> *"Murder in the first degree . . . is the most serious charge tried in our criminal courts. . . . One man is dead. The life of another is at stake. If there is a reasonable doubt in your minds as to the guilt of the accused . . . then you must declare him not guilty. If, however, there is no reasonable doubt, then he must be found guilty. Whichever way you decide, the verdict must be unanimous. I urge you to deliberate honestly and thoughtfully."*

If you were a juror listening to these instructions, would you understand your duties? In a small group discuss the meaning of the underlined words. Rewrite the judge's instructions using simpler language. Then present your version of the instructions to the class.

Literary Focus

Stage Directions The written instructions in the script of a play are called **stage directions**. These directions help the reader imagine how the characters look and move as they speak, how the setting looks, and what props appear. In *Twelve Angry Men,* notice the italic typeface used for stage directions and the information these directions convey.

Writer's Notebook

A Change of Heart At different stages, the jurors in *Twelve Angry Men* change their votes in order to reach a unanimous verdict. As you read the play, keep track of the number of jurors voting *guilty* and the number voting *not guilty* as well as the details that cause the jurors to change their votes during their deliberations.

TWELVE ANGRY MEN

REGINALD ROSE

▲ *Twelve Angry Men* was produced in 1957 by Henry Fonda and Reginald Rose and
directed by Sidney Lumet. The cast includes the following: *Juror 1* (Martin Balsam), *Juror 2*
(John Fielder), *Juror 3* (Lee J. Cobb), *Juror 4* (E. G. Marshall), *Juror 5* (Jack Klugman), *Juror
6* (Edward Binns), *Juror 7* (Jack Warden), *Juror 8* (Henry Fonda), *Juror 9* (Joseph Sweeney),
Juror 10 (Ed Begley), *Juror 11* (George Voskovec), *Juror 12* (Robert Webber).

DESCRIPTIONS OF JURORS

FOREMAN (JUROR NUMBER ONE). A small, petty man who is impressed with the authority he has and handles himself quite formally. Not overly bright, but dogged.

JUROR NUMBER TWO A meek, hesitant man who finds it difficult to maintain any opinions of his own. Easily swayed and usually adopts the opinion of the last person to whom he has spoken.

JUROR NUMBER THREE A very strong, very forceful, extremely opinionated man within whom can be detected a streak of sadism. A humorless man who is intolerant[1] of opinions other than his own and accustomed to forcing his wishes and views upon others.

JUROR NUMBER FOUR Seems to be a man of wealth and position. A practiced speaker who presents himself well at all times. Seems to feel a little bit above the rest of the jurors. His only concern is with the facts in this case, and he is appalled[2] at the behavior of the others.

JUROR NUMBER FIVE A naïve,[3] very frightened young man who takes his obligations in this case very seriously, but who finds it difficult to speak up when his elders have the floor.

JUROR NUMBER SIX An honest but dull-witted man who comes upon his decisions slowly and carefully. A man who finds it difficult to create positive opinions, but who must listen to and digest and accept those opinions offered by others which appeal to him most.

JUROR NUMBER SEVEN A loud, flashy, glad-handed salesman type who has more important things to do than to sit on a jury. He is quick to show temper, quick to form opinions on things about which he knows nothing. Is a bully and, of course, a coward.

JUROR NUMBER EIGHT A quiet, thoughtful, gentle man. A man who sees all sides of every question and constantly seeks the truth. A man of strength tempered[4] with compassion. Above all, a man who wants justice to be done and will fight to see that it is.

JUROR NUMBER NINE A mild, gentle old man, long since defeated by life and now merely waiting to die. A man who recognizes himself for what he is and mourns the days when it would have been possible to be courageous without shielding himself behind his many years.

JUROR NUMBER TEN An angry, bitter man. A man who antagonizes almost at sight. A bigot[5] who places no values on any human life save his own. A man who has been nowhere and is going nowhere and knows it deep within him.

JUROR NUMBER ELEVEN A refugee from Europe who had come to this country in 1941. A man who speaks with an accent and who is ashamed, humble, almost subservient to the people around him, but who will honestly seek justice because he has suffered through so much injustice.

JUROR NUMBER TWELVE A slick, bright advertising man who thinks of human beings in terms of percentages, graphs, and polls and has no real understanding of people. A superficial[6] snob, but trying to be a good fellow.

ACT ONE

Fade in[7] on a jury box. Twelve men are seated in it, listening intently to the voice of the JUDGE *as he charges them.[8] We do not see the* JUDGE. *He speaks in slow, measured tones and his voice is grave. The camera*

---

1. **intolerant** (in tol′ər ənt), *adj.* unwilling to let others do or believe as they want.
2. **appalled** (ə pôld′), *adj.* shocked; dismayed.
3. **naïve** (nä ēv′), *adj.* simple in nature; like a child.
4. **tempered** (tem′pərd), *adj.* softened or moderated.
5. **bigot** (big′ət), *n.* intolerant person.
6. **superficial** (sü′pər fish′əl), *adj.* concerned with or understanding only what is on the surface; shallow.
7. **fade in,** term used in television to indicate that the picture or scene is slowly brought into focus. When the camera "fades out," the picture gradually disappears.
8. **he charges them,** he tells them what their duties are as jurors.

drifts over the faces of the JURYMEN *as the* JUDGE *speaks and we see that most of their heads are turned to camera's left.* SEVEN *looks down at his hands.* THREE *looks off in another direction, the direction in which the defendant would be sitting.* TEN *keeps moving his head back and forth nervously. The* JUDGE *drones on.*

JUDGE. Murder in the first degree—premeditated homicide—is the most serious charge tried in our criminal courts. You've heard a long and complex case, gentlemen, and it is now your duty to sit down to try and separate the facts from the fancy. One man is dead. The life of another is at stake. If there is a reasonable doubt in your minds as to the guilt of the accused . . . then you must declare him not guilty. If, however, there is no reasonable doubt, then he must be found guilty. Whichever way you decide, the verdict must be unanimous. I urge you to deliberate honestly and thoughtfully. You are faced with a grave responsibility. Thank you, gentlemen.

(There is a long pause.)

CLERK *(droning).* The jury will retire.

(And now, slowly, almost hesitantly, the members of the jury begin to rise. Awkwardly, they file out of the jury box and off camera to the left. Camera holds on jury box, then fades out.

Fade in on a large, bare unpleasant-looking room. This is the jury room in the county criminal court of a large Eastern city. It is about 4:00 P.M. The room is furnished with a long conference table and a dozen chairs. The walls are bare, drab, and badly in need of a fresh coat of paint. Along one wall is a row of windows which look out on the skyline of the city's financial district. High on another wall is an electric clock. A washroom opens off the jury room. In one corner of the room is a water fountain. On the table are pads, pencils, ashtrays. One of the windows is open. Papers blow across the table and onto the floor as the door opens. Lettered on the outside of the door are the words "Jury Room." A uniformed GUARD *holds the door open. Slowly, almost self-consciously, the twelve* JURORS *file in. The* GUARD *counts them as they enter the door, his lips moving, but no sound coming forth. Four or five of the* JURORS *light cigarettes as they enter the room.* FIVE *lights his pipe, which he smokes constantly throughout the play.* TWO *and* TWELVE *go to the water fountain,* NINE *goes into the washroom, the door of which is lettered "Men." Several of the* JURORS *take seats at the table. Others stand awkwardly around the room. Several look out the windows. These are men who are ill at ease, who do not really know each other to talk to, and who wish they were anywhere but here.* SEVEN, *standing at window, takes out a pack of gum, takes a piece, and offers it around. There are no takers. He mops his brow.)*

SEVEN *(to* SIX*).* Y'know something? It's hot. *(*SIX *nods.)* You'd think they'd at least air-condition the place. I almost dropped dead in court.

*(*SEVEN *opens the window a bit wider. The* GUARD *looks them over and checks his count. Then, satisfied, he makes ready to leave.)*

GUARD. Okay, gentlemen. Everybody's here. If there's anything you want, I'm right outside. Just knock.

(He exits, closing the door. Silently they all look at the door. We hear the lock clicking.)

FIVE. I never knew they locked the door.

TEN *(blowing nose).* Sure, they lock the door. What did you think?

FIVE. I don't know. It just never occurred to me.

(Some of the JURORS *are taking off their jackets. Others are sitting down at the table. They still are reluctant to talk to each other.* FOREMAN *is at head of table, tearing slips of paper for ballots. Now we get a close shot of* EIGHT. *He looks out the window. We hear* THREE *talking to* TWO.*)*

THREE. Six days. They should have finished it in two. Talk, talk, talk. Did you ever hear so much talk about nothing?

TWO *(nervously laughing).* Well . . . I guess . . . they're entitled.

THREE. Everybody gets a fair trial. *(He shakes his head.)* That's the system. Well, I suppose you can't say anything against it.

*(*TWO *looks at him nervously, nods, and goes over to water cooler. Cut[9] to shot of* EIGHT *staring out win-*

---

9. **cut,** switch from one camera to another to show what is happening on another part of the stage.

dow. Cut to table. SEVEN *stands at the table, putting out a cigarette.*)

SEVEN (*to* TEN). How did you like that business about the knife? Did you ever hear a phonier story?

TEN (*wisely*). Well, look, you gotta expect that. You know what you're dealing with.

SEVEN. Yeah, I suppose. What's the matter, you got a cold?

TEN (*blowing*). A lulu. These hot-weather colds can kill you.

(SEVEN *nods sympathetically.*)

FOREMAN (*briskly*). All right, gentlemen. Let's take seats.

SEVEN. Right. This better be fast, I've got tickets to *The Seven Year Itch*[10] tonight. I must be the only guy in the whole world who hasn't seen it yet. (*He laughs and sits down.*) Okay, your honor, start the show.

(*They all begin to sit down. The* FOREMAN *is seated at the head of the table.* EIGHT *continues to look out the window.*)

FOREMAN (*to* EIGHT). How about sitting down? (EIGHT *doesn't hear him.*) The gentleman at the window.

(EIGHT *turns, startled.*)

FOREMAN. How about sitting down?

EIGHT. Oh, I'm sorry. (*He heads for a seat.*)

TEN (*to* SIX). It's tough to figure, isn't it? A kid kills his father. Bing! Just like that. Well, it's the element. They let the kids run wild. Maybe it serves 'em right.

FOREMAN. Is everybody here?

TWELVE. The old man's inside.

(*The* FOREMAN *turns to the washroom just as the door opens.* NINE *comes out, embarrassed.*)

FOREMAN. We'd like to get started.

NINE. Forgive me, gentlemen. I didn't mean to keep you waiting.

FOREMAN. It's all right. Find a seat.

(NINE *heads for a seat and sits down. They look at the* FOREMAN *expectantly.*)

FOREMAN. All right. Now, you gentlemen can handle this any way you want to. I mean, I'm not going to make any rules. If we want to

discuss it first and then vote, that's one way. Or we can vote right now to see how we stand.

SEVEN. Let's vote now. Who knows, maybe we can all go home.

TEN. Yeah. Let's see who's where.

THREE. Right. Let's vote now.

FOREMAN. Anybody doesn't want to vote? (*He looks around the table. There is no answer.*) Okay, all those voting guilty raise your hands. (*Seven or eight hands go up immediately. Several others go up more slowly. Everyone looks around the table. There are two hands not raised,* NINE's *hand goes up slowly now as the* FOREMAN *counts.*)

FOREMAN. . . . Nine . . . ten . . . eleven . . . That's eleven for guilty. Okay. Not guilty? (EIGHT's *hand is raised.*) One. Right. Okay. Eleven to one, guilty. Now we know where we are.

THREE. Somebody's in left field.[11] (*To* EIGHT.) You think he's not guilty?

EIGHT (*quietly*). I don't know.

THREE. I never saw a guiltier man in my life. You sat right in court and heard the same thing I did. The man's a dangerous killer. You could see it.

EIGHT. He's nineteen years old.

THREE. That's old enough. He knifed his own father. Four inches into the chest. An innocent little nineteen-year-old kid. They proved it a dozen different ways. Do you want me to list them?

EIGHT. No.

TEN (*to* EIGHT). Well, do you believe his story?

EIGHT. I don't know whether I believe it or not. Maybe I don't.

SEVEN. So what'd you vote not guilty for?

EIGHT. There were eleven votes for guilty. It's not so easy for me to raise my hand and send a boy off to die without talking about it first.

SEVEN. Who says it's easy for me?

---

10. ***The Seven Year Itch,*** a comedy that opened on Broadway in 1952.

11. **in left field,** SLANG. out of contact with reality; unreasonable or improbable.

EIGHT. No one.

SEVEN. What, just because I voted fast? I think the guy's guilty. You couldn't change my mind if you talked for a hundred years.

EIGHT. I don't want to change your mind. I just want to talk for a while. Look, this boy's been kicked around all his life. You know, living in a slum, his mother dead since he was nine. That's not a very good head start. He's a tough, angry kid. You know why slum kids get that way? Because we knock 'em on the head once a day, every day. I think maybe we owe him a few words. That's all.

(He looks around the table. Some of them look back coldly. Some cannot look at him. Only NINE *nods slowly.* TWELVE *doodles steadily.* FOUR *begins to comb his hair.)*

TEN. I don't mind telling you this, mister. We don't owe him a thing. He got a fair trial, didn't he? You know what that trial cost? He's lucky he got it. Look, we're all grownups here. You're not going to tell us that we're supposed to believe him, knowing what he is. I've lived among 'em all my life. You can't believe a word they say. You know that.

NINE *(to* TEN *very slowly)*. I don't know that. What a terrible thing for a man to believe! Since when is dishonesty a group characteristic? You have no monopoly[12] on the truth—

THREE (*interrupting*). All right. It's not Sunday. We don't need a sermon.

NINE. What this man says is very dangerous— (EIGHT *puts his hand on* NINE's *arm and stops him. Somehow his touch and his gentle expression calm the old man. He draws a deep breath and relaxes.*)

FOUR. I don't see any need for arguing like this. I think we ought to be able to behave like gentlemen.

SEVEN. Right!

FOUR. If we're going to discuss this case, let's discuss the facts.

FOREMAN. I think that's a good point. We have a job to do. Let's do it.

ELEVEN (*with accent*). If you gentlemen don't mind, I'm going to close the window. (*He gets up and does so.*) (*Apologetically.*) It was blowing on my neck. (TEN *blows his nose fiercely.*)

TWELVE. I may have an idea here. I'm just thinking out loud now, but it seems to me that it's up to us to convince this gentleman— (*Indicating* EIGHT.)—that we're right and he's wrong. Maybe if we each took a minute or two, you know, if we sort of try it on for size—

FOREMAN. That sounds fair enough. Supposing we go once around the table.

SEVEN. Okay, let's start off.

FOREMAN. Right. (*To* TWO.) I guess you're first.

TWO (*timidly*). Oh. Well . . . (*Long pause.*) I just think he's guilty. I thought it was obvious. I mean nobody proved otherwise.

EIGHT (*quietly*). Nobody has to prove otherwise. The burden of proof is on the prosecution. The defendant doesn't have to open his mouth. That's in the Constitution. The Fifth Amendment.[13] You've heard of it.

TWO (*flustered*). Well sure, I've heard of it. I know what it is. I . . . what I meant . . . well, anyway, I think he was guilty.

THREE. Okay, let's get to the facts. Number one, let's take the old man who lived on the second floor right underneath the room where the murder took place. At ten minutes after twelve on the night of the killing he heard loud noises in the upstairs apartment. He said it sounded like a fight. Then he heard the kid say to his father, "I'm gonna kill you." A second later he heard a body falling, and he ran to the door of his apartment, looked out, and saw the kid running down the stairs and out of the house. Then he called the police. They found the father with a knife in his chest.

FOREMAN. And the coroner fixed the time of death at around midnight.

THREE. Right. Now what else do you want?

FOUR. The boy's entire story is flimsy. He claimed he was at the movies. That's a little ridiculous, isn't it? He couldn't even remember what pictures he saw.

THREE. That's right. Did you hear that? (*To* FOUR.) You're absolutely right.

TEN. Look, what about the woman across the street? If her testimony don't prove it, then nothing does.

TWELVE. That's right. She saw the killing, didn't she?

FOREMAN. Let's go in order.

TEN (*loud*). Just a minute. Here's a woman who's lying in bed and can't sleep. It's hot, you know. (*He gets up and begins to walk around, blowing his nose and talking.*) Anyway, she looks out the window, and right across the street she sees the kid stick the knife into his father. She's known the kid all his life. His window is right opposite hers, across the el tracks, and she swore she saw him do it.

EIGHT. Through the windows of a passing elevated train.

TEN. Okay. And they proved in court that you can look through the windows of a passing el

---

12. **monopoly** (mə nop′ə lē), *n*. the exclusive possession or control of something.

13. **The Fifth Amendment,** the amendment to the United States Constitution that guarantees a person on trial for a criminal offense cannot be forced to testify against himself or herself.

train at night and see what's happening on the other side. They proved it.

EIGHT. I'd like to ask you something. How come you believed her? She's one of "them," too, isn't she?

(TEN *walks over to* EIGHT.)

TEN. You're a pretty smart fellow, aren't you?

FOREMAN *(rising).* Now take it easy.

(THREE *gets up and goes to* TEN.)

THREE. Come on. Sit down. *(He leads* TEN *back to his seat.)* What're you letting him get you all upset for? Relax.

(TEN *and* THREE *sit down.)*

FOREMAN. Let's calm down now. (*To* FIVE.) It's your turn.

FIVE. I'll pass it.

FOREMAN. That's your privilege. (*To* SIX.) How about you?

SIX *(slowly).* I don't know. I started to be convinced, you know, with the testimony from those people across the hall. Didn't they say something about an argument between the father and the boy around seven o'clock that night? I mean, I can be wrong.

ELEVEN. I think it was eight o'clock. Not seven.

EIGHT. That's right. Eight o'clock. They heard the father hit the boy twice and then saw the boy walk angrily out of the house. What does that prove?

SIX. Well, it doesn't exactly prove anything. It's just part of the picture. I didn't say it proved anything.

FOREMAN. Anything else?

SIX. No.

(SIX *goes to the water fountain.)*

FOREMAN (*to* SEVEN). All right. How about you?

SEVEN. I don't know, most of it's been said already. We can talk all day about this thing, but I think we're wasting our time. Look at the kid's record. At fifteen he was in reform school. He stole a car. He's been arrested for mugging. He was picked up for knife-fighting. I think they said he stabbed somebody in the arm. This is a very fine boy.

EIGHT. Ever since he was five years old his father beat him up regularly. He used his fists.

SEVEN. So would I! A kid like that.

THREE. You're right. It's the kids. The way they are—you know? They don't listen. *(Bitter.)* I've got a kid. When he was eight years old he ran away from a fight. I saw him. I was so ashamed, I told him right out, "I'm gonna make a man out of you or I'm gonna bust you up into little pieces trying." When he was fifteen he hit me in the face. He's big, you know. I haven't seen him in three years. Rotten kid! You work your heart out. . . . *(Pause.)* All right. Let's get on with it. *(Looks away embarrassed.)*

FOUR. We're missing the point here. This boy—let's say he's a product of a filthy neighborhood and a broken home. We can't help that. We're not here to go into reasons why slums are breeding grounds for criminals. They are. I know it. So do you. The children who come out of slum backgrounds are potential menaces[14] to society.

TEN. You said it there. I don't want any part of them, believe me.

(*There is a dead silence for a moment, and then* FIVE *speaks haltingly.*)

FIVE. I've lived in a slum all my life—

TEN. Oh, now wait a second!

FIVE. I used to play in a backyard that was filled with garbage. Maybe it still smells on me.

FOREMAN. Now let's be reasonable. There's nothing personal—(FIVE *stands up.*)

FIVE. There is something personal!

(*Then he catches himself and, seeing everyone looking at him, sits down, fists clenched.*)

THREE *(persuasively).* Come on, now. He didn't mean you, feller. Let's not be so sensitive. . . .

(*There is a long pause.*)

ELEVEN. I can understand this sensitivity.

FOREMAN. Now let's stop the bickering.[15] We're wasting time. (*To* EIGHT.) It's your turn.

EIGHT. All right. I had a peculiar feeling about

---

14. **menace** (men′is), *n.* threat.
15. **bickering** (bik′ər ing), *n.* petty, noisy quarreling.

this trial. Somehow I felt that the defense counsel never really conducted a thorough cross-examination.[16] I mean, he was appointed by the court to defend the boy. He hardly seemed interested. Too many questions were left unasked.

THREE *(annoyed)*. What about the ones that were asked? For instance, let's talk about that cute little switch-knife.[17] You know, the one that fine upright kid admitted buying.

EIGHT. All right. Let's talk about it. Let's get it in here and look at it. I'd like to see it again, Mr. Foreman.

(The FOREMAN *looks at him questioningly and then* *gets up and goes to the door. During the following dialogue the* FOREMAN *knocks, the* GUARD *comes in, the* FOREMAN *whispers to him, the* GUARD *nods and leaves, locking the door.)*

THREE. We all know what it looks like. I don't see why we have to look at it again. (*To* FOUR.) What do you think?

FOUR. The gentleman has a right to see exhibits in evidence.

---

16. **cross-examination,** examination to check a previous examination, especially the questioning of a witness by the lawyer for the opposing side to test the truth of the witness's testimony.
17. **switch-knife,** switchblade knife.

THREE (*shrugging*). Okay with me.

FOUR (*to* EIGHT). This knife is a pretty strong piece of evidence, don't you agree?

EIGHT. I do.

FOUR. The boy admits going out of his house at eight o'clock after being slapped by his father.

EIGHT. Or punched.

FOUR. Or punched. He went to a neighborhood store and bought a switch-knife. The storekeeper was arrested the following day when he admitted selling it to the boy. It's a very unusual knife. The storekeeper identified it and said it was the only one of its kind he had in stock. Why did the boy get it? (*Sarcastically.*) As a present for a friend of his, he says. Am I right so far?

EIGHT. Right.

THREE. You bet he's right. (*To all.*) Now listen to this man. He knows what he's talking about.

FOUR. Next, the boy claims that on the way home the knife must have fallen through a hole in his coat pocket, that he never saw it again. Now there's a story, gentlemen. You know what actually happened. The boy took the knife home and a few hours later stabbed his father with it and even remembered to wipe off the fingerprints.

(*The door opens and the* GUARD *walks in with an oddly designed knife with a tag on it.* FOUR *gets up and takes it from him. The* GUARD *exits.*)

FOUR. Everyone connected with the case identified this knife. Now are you trying to tell me that someone picked it up off the street and went up to the boy's house and stabbed his father with it just to be amusing?

EIGHT. No, I'm saying that it's possible that the boy lost the knife and that someone else stabbed his father with a similar knife. It's possible.

(FOUR *flips open the knife and jams it into the table.*)

FOUR. Take a look at that knife. It's a very strange knife. I've never seen one like it before in my life. Neither had the storekeeper who sold it to him.

(EIGHT *reaches casually into his pocket and withdraws an object. No one notices this. He stands up quietly.*)

FOUR. Aren't you trying to make us accept a pretty incredible coincidence?

EIGHT. I'm not trying to make anyone accept it. I'm just saying it's possible.

THREE (*shouting*). And I'm saying it's not possible.

(EIGHT *swiftly flicks open the blade of a switch-knife and jams it into the table next to the first one. They are exactly alike. There are several gasps and everyone stares at the knife. There is a long silence.*)

THREE (*slowly, amazed*). What are you trying to do?

TEN (*loud*). Yeah, what is this? Who do you think you are?

FIVE. Look at it! It's the same knife!

FOREMAN. Quiet! Let's be quiet.

(*They quiet down.*)

FOUR. Where did you get it?

EIGHT. I got it last night in a little junk shop around the corner from the boy's house. It cost two dollars.

THREE. Now listen to me! You pulled a real smart trick here, but you proved absolutely zero. Maybe there are ten knives like that, so what?

EIGHT. Maybe there are.

THREE. The boy lied and you know it.

EIGHT. He may have lied. (*To* TEN.) Do you think he lied?

TEN (*violently*). Now that's a stupid question. Sure he lied!

EIGHT (*to* FOUR). Do you?

FOUR. You don't have to ask me that. You know my answer. He lied.

EIGHT (*to* FIVE). Do you think he lied?

(FIVE *can't answer immediately. He looks around nervously.*)

FIVE. I . . . I don't know.

SEVEN. Now wait a second. What are you, the guy's lawyer? Listen, there are still eleven of us who think he's guilty. You're alone. What do you think you're gonna accomplish? If you want to be stubborn and hang this jury,[18] he'll be tried again and found guilty, sure as he's born.

EIGHT. You're probably right.

SEVEN. So what are you gonna do about it? We can be here all night.

NINE. It's only one night. A man may die.

(SEVEN *glares at* NINE *for a long while, but has no answer.* EIGHT *looks closely at* NINE *and we can begin to sense a* rapport[19] *between them. There is a long silence. Then suddenly everyone begins to talk at once.*)

THREE. Well, whose fault is that?

SIX. Do you think maybe if we went over it again? What I mean is—

TEN. Did anyone force him to kill his father? (*To* THREE.) How do you like him? Like someone forced him!

ELEVEN. Perhaps this is not the point.

FIVE. No one forced anyone. But listen—

TWELVE. Look, gentlemen, we can spitball all night here.

TWO. Well, I was going to say—

SEVEN. Just a minute. Some of us've got better things to do than sit around a jury room.

FOUR. I can't understand a word in here. Why do we all have to talk at once?

FOREMAN. He's right. I think we ought to get on with it.

(EIGHT *has been listening to this exchange closely.*)

THREE (*to* EIGHT). Well, what do you say? You're the one holding up the show.

EIGHT (*standing*). I've got a proposition to make.

(*We catch a close shot of* FIVE *looking steadily at him as he talks.* FIVE, *seemingly puzzled, listens closely.*)

EIGHT. I want to call for a vote. I want you eleven men to vote by secret ballot. I'll abstain. If there are still eleven votes for guilty, I won't stand alone. We'll take in a guilty verdict right now.

SEVEN. Okay. Let's do it.

FOREMAN. That sounds fair. Is everyone agreed?

(*They all nod their heads.* EIGHT *walks over to the window, looks out for a moment, and then faces them.*)

FOREMAN. Pass these along.

(*The* FOREMAN *passes ballot slips to all of them, and now* EIGHT *watches them tensely as they begin to write. Fade out.*)

---

18. **hang this jury,** keep this jury from reaching a verdict. A jury that fails to reach a verdict is called a "hung" jury.

19. **rapport** (ra pôr′, ra pôrt′), *n.* agreement; connection.

After Reading

Making Connections

1. Conduct a class poll on which juror students would prefer to have as a boss and which they think would be the most difficult boss. Cite character qualities on which you base your decisions.

2. Do you think it's realistic to expect twelve people to agree on any verdict? Why or why not?

3. Based on what you know so far about the trial, would you vote *guilty* or *not guilty*? Why?

4. How does the **setting**—the time of day, the weather, and the room—affect the general atmosphere and the behavior of the jurors?

5. Identify the **protagonist(s)** and the **antagonist(s)** in act 1.

6. How has testimony about the murder weapon figured in the trial, both for the prosecution and the defense?

7. Why might some of the jurors begin to have doubts after Eight takes an identical switchblade knife from his pocket and jams it into the table?

8. If you were a juror, would you assume a defendant was guilty because he or she pleaded the Fifth Amendment on the basis of self-incrimination? Why or why not?

9. Knowing what you know now, would you like to serve on a jury? Why or why not?

Vocabulary Study

Replace each italicized item with a synonym from the list.

appalled
bickering
bigot
intolerant
menace
monopoly
naïve
rapport
superficial
tempered

1. Juror Twelve is a *shallow* snob who is concerned with appearances.

2. Juror Eight is a man of strength *softened* with compassion.

3. The Foreman reminds his fellow jurors to avoid *arguing.*

4. The *simple* young man thinks his elders will laugh at his comments.

5. Since he is a *narrow-minded, intolerant person,* Juror Three is unable to see the good side of people.

6. The audience senses a natural *agreement* between Eight and Nine.

7. Juror Three believes the accused boy is a *threat* to his neighbors.

8. Juror Three has *shocked* the others with his prejudiced comments.

9. Juror Nine tells Ten he has no *total control* of the truth about people in the slums.

10. Some of the jurors grow *impatient* with Three and his strong opinions.

ACT TWO

Fade in on same scene, no time lapse. EIGHT *stands tensely watching as the* JURORS *write on their ballots. He stays perfectly still as one by one they fold the ballots and pass them along to the* FOREMAN. *The* FORE- MAN *takes them, riffles through the folded ballots, counts eleven, and now begins to open them. He reads each one out loud and lays it aside. They watch him quietly, and all we hear is his voice and the sound of* TWO *sucking on a cough drop.*

FOREMAN. Guilty. Guilty. Guilty. Guilty. Guilty. Guilty. Guilty. Guilty. Guilty. *(He pauses at the tenth ballot and then reads it.)* Not Guilty.

*(*THREE *slams down hard on the table. The* FOREMAN *opens the last ballot.)* Guilty.

TEN *(angry).* How do you like that!

SEVEN. Who was it? I think we have a right to know.

ELEVEN. Excuse me. This was a secret ballot. We agreed on this point, no? If the gentleman wants it to remain secret—

THREE *(standing up angrily).* What do you mean? There are no secrets in here! I know who it was. *(He turns to* FIVE.*)* What's the matter with you? You come in here and you vote guilty and then this slick preacher starts to tear your heart out with stories about a poor little kid who just couldn't help becoming a murderer. So you change your vote. If that isn't the most sickening—

(FIVE *stares at* THREE, *frightened at this outburst.*)

FOREMAN. Now hold it.

THREE. Hold it? We're trying to put a guilty man into the chair where he belongs—and all of a sudden we're paying attention to fairy tales.

FIVE. Now just a minute—

ELEVEN. Please. I would like to say something here. I have always thought that a man was entitled to have unpopular opinions in this country. This is the reason I came here. I wanted to have the right to disagree. In my own country, I am ashamed to say—

TEN. What do we have to listen to now—the whole history of your country?

SEVEN. Yeah, let's stick to the subject. (*To* FIVE.) I want to ask you what made you change your vote.

(*There is a long pause as* SEVEN *and* FIVE *eye each other angrily.*)

NINE (*quietly*). There's nothing for him to tell you. He didn't change his vote. I did. (*There is a pause.*) Maybe you'd like to know why.

THREE. No, we wouldn't like to know why.

FOREMAN. The man wants to talk.

NINE. Thank you. (*Pointing at* EIGHT.) This gentleman chose to stand alone against us. That's his right. It takes a great deal of courage to stand alone even if you believe in something very strongly. He left the verdict up to us. He gambled for support and I gave it to him. I want to hear more. The vote is ten to two.

TEN. That's fine. If the speech is over, let's go on.

(FOREMAN *gets up, goes to door, knocks, hands* GUARD *the tagged switch-knife and sits down again.*)

THREE (*to* FIVE). Look buddy, I was a little excited. Well, you know how it is. I . . . I didn't mean to get nasty. Nothing personal.

(FIVE *looks at him.*)

SEVEN (*to* EIGHT). Look, supposing you answer me this. If the kid didn't kill him, who did?

EIGHT. As far as I know, we're supposed to decide whether or not the boy on trial is guilty. We're not concerned with anyone else's motives here.

NINE. Guilty beyond a reasonable doubt. This is an important thing to remember.

THREE (*to* TEN). Everyone's a lawyer. (*To* NINE.) Supposing you explain what your reasonable doubts are.

NINE. This is not easy. So far, it's only a feeling I have. A feeling. Perhaps you don't understand.

TEN. A feeling! What are we gonna do, spend the night talking about your feelings? What about the facts?

THREE. You said a mouthful. (*To* NINE.) Look, the old man heard the kid yell, "I'm gonna kill you." A second later he heard the father's body falling, and he saw the boy running out of the house fifteen seconds after that.

TWELVE. That's right. And let's not forget the woman across the street. She looked into the open window and saw the boy stab his father. She saw it. Now if that's not enough for you . . .

EIGHT. It's not enough for me.

SEVEN. How do you like him? It's like talking into a dead phone.

FOUR. The woman saw the killing through the windows of a moving elevated train. The train had five cars, and she saw it through the windows of the last two. She remembers the most insignificant[1] details.

(*Cut to close shot of* TWELVE, *who doodles a picture of an el train on a scrap of paper.*)

THREE. Well, what have you got to say about that?

EIGHT. I don't know. It doesn't sound right to me.

THREE. Well, supposing you think about it. (*To* TWELVE.) Lend me your pencil.

(TWELVE *gives it to him. He draws a tick-tack-toe*

---

1. **insignificant** (in′sig nif′ə kənt), *adj.* unimportant; trivial.

square on the same sheet of paper on which TWELVE *has drawn the train. He fills in an X, hands the pencil to* TWELVE.)

THREE. Your turn. We might as well pass the time. (TWELVE *takes the pencil.* EIGHT *stands up and snatches the paper away.* THREE *leaps up.*)

THREE. Wait a minute!

EIGHT *(hard).* This isn't a game.

THREE *(angry).* Who do you think you are?

SEVEN *(rising).* All right, let's take it easy.

THREE. I've got a good mind to walk around this table and belt him one!

FOREMAN. Now, please. I don't want any fights in here.

THREE. Did ya see him? The nerve! The absolute nerve!

TEN. All right. Forget it. It don't mean anything.

SIX. How about sitting down.

THREE. This isn't a game. Who does he think he is?

(He lets them sit him down. EIGHT *remains standing, holding the scrap of paper. He looks at it closely now and seems to be suddenly interested in it. Then he throws it back toward* THREE. *It lands in center of table.* THREE *is angered again at this, but* FOUR *puts his hand on his arm.* EIGHT *speaks now and his voice is more intense.*)

EIGHT *(to* FOUR). Take a look at that sketch. How long does it take an elevated train going at top speed to pass a given point?

FOUR. What has that got to do with anything?

EIGHT. How long? Guess.

FOUR. I wouldn't have the slightest idea.

EIGHT *(to* FIVE). What do you think?

FIVE. About ten or twelve seconds, maybe.

EIGHT. I'd say that was a fair guess. Anyone else?

ELEVEN. I would think about ten seconds, perhaps.

TWO. About ten seconds.

FOUR. All right. Say ten seconds. What are you getting at?

EIGHT. This. An el train passes a given point in ten seconds. That given point is the window of the room in which the killing took place. You can almost reach out of the window of

that room and touch the el. Right? *(Several of them nod.)* All right. Now let me ask you this. Did anyone here ever live right next to the el tracks? I have. When your window is open and the train goes by, the noise is almost unbearable. You can't hear yourself think.

TEN. Okay. You can't hear yourself think. Will you get to the point?

EIGHT. The old man heard the boy say, "I'm going to kill you," and one second later he heard a body fall. One second. That's the testimony, right?

TWO. Right.

EIGHT. The woman across the street looked through the windows of the last two cars of the el and saw the body fall. Right? The *last two* cars.

TEN. What are you giving us here?

EIGHT. An el takes ten seconds to pass a given point or two seconds per car. That el had been going by the old man's window for at least six seconds, and maybe more, before the body fell, according to the woman. The old man would have had to hear the boy say, "I'm going to kill you," while the front of the el was roaring past his nose. It's not possible that he could have heard it.

THREE. What d'ya mean! Sure he could have heard it.

EIGHT. Could he?

THREE. He said the boy yelled it out. That's enough for me.

NINE. I don't think he could have heard it.

TWO. Maybe he didn't hear it. I mean with the el noise—

THREE. What are you people talking about? Are you calling the old man a liar?

FIVE. Well, it stands to reason.

THREE. You're crazy? Why would he lie? What's he got to gain?

NINE. Attention, maybe.

THREE. You keep coming up with these bright sayings. Why don't you send one in to a newspaper? They pay two dollars.

*(EIGHT *looks hard at* THREE *and then turns to* NINE.*)

EIGHT (*softly*). Why might the old man have lied? You have a right to be heard.

NINE. It's just that I looked at him for a very long time. The seam of his jacket was split under the arm. Did you notice that? He was a very old man with a torn jacket, and he carried two canes. I think I know him better than anyone here. This is a quiet, frightened, insignificant man who has been nothing all his life, who has never had recognition—his name in the newspapers. Nobody knows him after seventy-five years. That's a very sad thing. A man like this needs to be recognized. To be questioned, and listened to, and quoted just once. This is very important.

TWELVE. And you're trying to tell us he lied about a thing like this just so that he could be important?

NINE. No, he wouldn't really lie. But perhaps he'd make himself believe that he heard those words and recognized the boy's face.

THREE (*loud*). Well, that's the most fantastic story I've every heard. How can you make up a thing like that? What do you know about it?

NINE (*low*). I speak from experience.

(*There is a long pause. Then the* FOREMAN *clears his throat.*)

FOREMAN (*to* EIGHT). All right. Is there anything else?

(EIGHT *is looking at* NINE. TWO *offers the* FOREMAN *a box of cough drops. The* FOREMAN *pushes it away.*)

TWO (*hesitantly*). Anybody . . . want a cough . . . drop?

FOREMAN (*sharply*). Come on. Let's get on with it.

EIGHT. I'll take one. (TWO almost *gratefully slides him one along the table.*) Thanks. (TWO *nods and* EIGHT *puts the cough drop into his mouth.*) Now. There's something else I'd like to point out here. I think we proved that the old man couldn't have heard the boy say, "I'm going to kill you," but supposing he really did hear it? This phrase. How many times has each of you used it? Probably hundreds. "If you do that once more, Junior, I'm going to murder you." "Come on, Rocky, kill him!" We say it every day. This doesn't mean that we're going to kill someone.

THREE. Wait a minute. The phrase was "I'm going to kill you," and the kid screamed it out at the top of his lungs. Don't try and tell me he didn't mean it. Anybody says a thing like that the way he said it—they mean it.

TEN. And how they mean it!

EIGHT. Well, let me ask you this. Do you really think the boy would shout out a thing like that so the whole neighborhood would hear it? I don't think so. He's much too bright for that.

TEN (*exploding*). Bright! He's a common, ignorant slob. He don't even speak good English!

ELEVEN (*slowly*). He *doesn't* even speak good English.

(TEN *stares angrily at* ELEVEN, *and there is silence for a moment. Then* FIVE *looks around the table nervously.*)

FIVE. I'd like to change my vote to not guilty.

(THREE *gets up and walks to the window, furious, but trying to control himself.*)

FOREMAN. Are you sure?

FIVE. Yes. I'm sure.

FOREMAN. The vote is nine to three in favor of guilty.

SEVEN. Well, if that isn't the end. (*To* FIVE.) What are you basing it on? Stories this guy—(*indicating* EIGHT)—made up! He oughta write for *Amazing Detective Monthly*. He'd make a fortune. Listen, the kid had a lawyer, didn't he? Why didn't his lawyer bring up all these points?

FIVE. Lawyers can't think of everything.

SEVEN. Oh, brother! (*To* EIGHT.) You sit in here and pull stories out of thin air. Now we're supposed to believe that the old man didn't get up out of bed, run to the door, and see the kid beat it downstairs fifteen seconds after the killing. He's only saying he did to be important.

FIVE. Did the old man say he ran to the door?

SEVEN. Ran. Walked. What's the difference? He got there.

FIVE. I don't remember what he said. But I don't see how he could run.

FOUR. He said he went from his bedroom to the front door. That's enough, isn't it?

EIGHT. Where was his bedroom again?

TEN. Down the hall somewhere. I thought you remembered everything. Don't you remember that?

EIGHT. No. Mr. Foreman, I'd like to take a look at the diagram of the apartment.

SEVEN. Why don't we have them run the trial over just so you can get everything straight?

EIGHT. Mr. Foreman—

FOREMAN (*rising*). I heard you.

(*The* FOREMAN *gets up, goes to door during following dialogue. He knocks on door,* GUARD *opens it, he whispers to* GUARD, GUARD *nods and closes door.*)

THREE (*to* EIGHT). All right. What's this for? How come you're the only one in the room who wants to see exhibits all the time?

FIVE. I want to see this one, too.

THREE. And I want to stop wasting time.

FOUR. If we're going to start wading through all that nonsense about where the body was found . . .

EIGHT. We're not. We're going to find out how a man who's had two strokes in the past three years, and who walks with a pair of canes, could get to his front door in fifteen seconds.

THREE. He said twenty seconds.

TWO. He said fifteen.

THREE. How does he know how long fifteen seconds is? You can't judge that kind of a thing.

NINE. He said fifteen. He was positive about it.

THREE (*angry*). He's an old man. You saw him. Half the time he was confused. How could he be positive about . . . anything?

(THREE *looks around sheepishly,[2] unable to cover up his blunder. The door opens and the* GUARD *walks in, carrying a large pen-and-ink diagram of the apartment. It is a railroad flat.[3] A bedroom faces the el tracks. Behind it is a series of rooms off a long hall. In the front bedroom is a diagram of the spot where the body was found. At the back of the apartment we see the entrance into the apartment hall from the building hall. We see a flight of stairs in the building hall. The diagram is clearly labeled and included in the information on it are the dimensions of the various rooms. The* GUARD *gives the diagram to the* FOREMAN.)

GUARD. This what you wanted?

FOREMAN. That's right. Thank you.

(*The* GUARD *nods and exits.* EIGHT *goes to* FOREMAN *and reaches for it.*)

EIGHT. May I?

(*The* FOREMAN *nods.* EIGHT *takes the diagram and sets it up on a chair so that all can see it.* EIGHT *looks it over. Several of the* JURORS *get up to see it better.* THREE, TEN, *and* SEVEN, *however, barely bother to look at it.*)

SEVEN (*to* TEN). Do me a favor. Wake me up when this is over.

EIGHT (*ignoring him*). All right. This is the apartment in which the killing took place. The old man's apartment is directly beneath it and exactly the same. (*Pointing.*) Here are the el tracks. The bedroom. Another bedroom. Living room. Bathroom. Kitchen. And this is the hall. Here's the front door to the apartment. And here are the steps. (*Pointing to front bedroom and then front door.*) Now the old man was in bed in this room. He says he got up, went out into the hall, down the hall to the front door, opened it, and looked out just in time to see the boy racing down the stairs. Am I right?

THREE. That's the story.

EIGHT. Fifteen seconds after he heard the body fall.

ELEVEN. Correct.

EIGHT. His bed was at the window. It's—(*looking closer*)—twelve feet from his bed to the bedroom door. The length of the hall is forty-three feet, six inches. He had to get up out of bed, get his canes, walk twelve feet, open

---

2. **sheepishly** (shē′pish lē), *adv.* awkwardly bashful or embarrassed.
3. **railroad flat,** long, narrow apartment with rooms joined in a line.

ELEVEN. Perhaps if we could see it . . . this is an important point.

THREE *(mad)*. It's a ridiculous waste of time.

SIX. Let him do it.

EIGHT. Hand me a chair. *(Someone pushes a chair to him.)* All right. This is the bedroom door. Now how far would you say it is from here to the door of this room?

SIX. I'd say it was twenty feet.

TWO. Just about.

EIGHT. Twenty feet is close enough. All right, from here to the door and back is about forty feet. It's shorter than the length of the hall, wouldn't you say that?

NINE. A few feet maybe.

TEN. Look, this is absolutely insane. What makes you think you can—

EIGHT. Do you mind if I try it? According to you, it'll only take fifteen seconds. We can spare that. *(He walks over to the two chairs now and lies down on them.)* Who's got a watch with a second hand?

TWO. I have.

EIGHT. When you want me to start, stamp your foot. That'll be the body falling. Time me from there. *(He lies down on the chairs.)* Let's say he keeps his canes right at his bedside. Right?

TWO. Right!

EIGHT. Okay. I'm ready.

(They all watch carefully. TWO *stares at his watch, waiting for the second hand to reach sixty. Then, as it does, he stamps his foot loudly.* EIGHT *begins to get up. Slowly he swings his legs over the edges of the chairs, reaches for imaginary canes, and struggles to his feet.* TWO *stares at the watch.* EIGHT *walks as a crippled old man would walk, toward the chair which is serving as the bedroom door. He gets to it and pretends to open it.)*

TEN *(shouting)*. Speed it up. He walked twice as fast as that.

*(*EIGHT, *not having stopped for this outburst, begins to walk the <u>simulated</u>[4] forty-foot hallway.)*

the bedroom door, walk forty-three feet, and open the front door—all in fifteen seconds. Do you think this possible?

TEN. You know it's possible.

ELEVEN. He can only walk very slowly. They had to help him into the witness chair.

THREE. You make it sound like a long walk. It's not.

*(*EIGHT *gets up, goes to the end of the room, and takes two chairs. He puts them together to indicate a bed.)*

NINE. For an old man who uses canes, it's a long walk.

THREE *(to* EIGHT*)*. What are you doing?

EIGHT. I want to try this thing. Let's see how long it took him. I'm going to pace off twelve feet— the length of the bedroom. *(He begins to do so.)*

THREE. You're crazy. You can't re-create a thing like that.

---

4. **simulated** (sim′yə lāt əd), *adj.* fake; pretend.

ELEVEN. This is, I think, even more quickly than the old man walked in the courtroom.

EIGHT. If you think I should go faster, I will. *(He speeds up his pace slightly. He reaches the door and turns now, heading back, hobbling as an old man would hobble, bent over his imaginary canes. They watch him tensely. He hobbles back to the chair, which also serves as the front door. He stops there and pretends to unlock the door. Then he pretends to push it open.)*

EIGHT *(loud)*. Stop.

TWO. Right.

EIGHT. What's the time?

TWO. Fifteen . . . twenty . . . thirty . . . thirty-one seconds exactly.

ELEVEN. Thirty-one seconds.

(Some of the JURORS *adlib[5] their surprise to each other.)*

EIGHT. It's my guess that the old man was trying to get to the door, heard someone racing down the stairs, and assumed that it was the boy.

SIX. I think that's possible.

THREE *(infuriated)*. Assumed? Now, listen to me, you people. I've seen all kinds of dishonesty in my day . . . but this little display takes the cake. (*To* FOUR.) Tell him, will you?

*(*FOUR *sits silently.* THREE *looks at him and then he strides over to* EIGHT.)*

THREE. You come in here with your heart bleeding all over the floor about slum kids and injustice and you make up these wild stories, and you've got some soft-hearted old ladies listening to you. Well I'm not. I'm getting real sick of it. *(To all)*. What's the matter with you people? This kid is guilty! He's got to burn! We're letting him slip through our fingers here.

EIGHT *(calmly)*. Our fingers. Are you his executioner?

THREE *(raging)*. I'm one of 'em.

EIGHT. Perhaps you'd like to pull the switch.

THREE *(shouting)*. For this kid? You bet I'd like to pull the switch!

EIGHT. I'm sorry for you.

THREE *(shouting)*. Don't start with me.

EIGHT. What it must feel like to want to pull the switch!

THREE. Shut up!

EIGHT. You're a sadist.[6]

THREE *(louder)*. Shut up!

EIGHT *(strong)*. You want to see this boy die because you personally want it—not because of the facts.

THREE *(shouting)*. Shut up!

(He lunges at EIGHT, *but is caught by two of the* JURORS *and held. He struggles as* EIGHT *watches calmly.)*

THREE *(screaming)*. Let me go! I'll kill him. I'll kill him!

EIGHT *(softly)*. You don't really mean you'll kill me, do you?

*(*THREE *stops struggling now and stares at* EIGHT. *All the* JURORS *watch in silence as we fade out.)*

---

5. **adlib** (ad lib′), *v.* make up words or music as one goes along; improvise.

6. **sadist** (sā′dist, sad′ist), *n.* person displaying cruel tendencies.

After Reading

Making Connections

1. If you were one of the jurors, what would your vote be at the end of this act? Cast your vote with your classmates, showing thumbs up for *guilty* or thumbs down for *not guilty.*

2. Predict who the next juror will be to change his vote. Be prepared to give reasons for this prediction.

3. What do you think are the most important scenes in act 2? Why?

4. How does the playwright create **suspense** as the foreman reads the count at the beginning of act 2?

5. Reread Nine's comments about why the old man may have lied. Are the comments based on fact or on Nine's feelings? Explain.

6. What is **ironic** about Eleven correcting Ten's grammar when he says, "He don't even speak good English!"?

7. What effect does Eight's timed experiment have on the other jurors?

8. Explain whether or not you think that the death penalty should be a sentencing option in a civilized society.

Vocabulary Study

Use your Glossary, if necessary, to answer the following items.

1. Three looks around *sheepishly,* which indicates he is ____.
   a. angry   **b.** thrifty   **c.** embarrassed **d.** energetic

2. *Simulated* means ____.
   a. encouraged **b.** pretend   **c.** transmitted   **d.** activated

3. Actors who *adlib* lines ____ the words.
   a. make up   **b.** enunciate   **c.** rehearse   **d.** sing

4. Three is called a *sadist* because he is ____.
   a. unhappy   **b.** grumpy   **c.** vocal   **d.** cruel

5. The woman remembers the most *insignificant,* or ____, details.
   a. visual   **b.** unimportant **c.** memorable   **d.** symbolic

Expressing Your Ideas

Writer's Notebook Update In your notebook, explain whether you think it's good or bad that jurors sometimes change their minds after deliberating.

ACT THREE

Fade in on same scene. No time lapse. THREE *glares angrily at* EIGHT. *He is still held by two* JURORS. *After a long pause, he shakes himself loose and turns away. He walks to the windows. The other* JURORS *stand around the room now, shocked by this display of anger. There is silence. Then the door opens and the* GUARD *enters. He looks around the room.*

GUARD. Is there anything wrong, gentlemen? I heard some noise.

FOREMAN. No. There's nothing wrong. *(He points to the large diagram[1] of the apartment.)* You can take that back. We're finished with it.

(The GUARD *nods and takes the diagram. He looks curiously at some of the* JURORS *and exits. The* JURORS *still are silent. Some of them slowly begin to sit down.* THREE *still stands at the window. He turns around now. The* JURORS *look at him.)*

THREE *(loud).* Well, what are you looking at?

(They turn away. He goes back to his seat now. Silently the rest of the JURORS *take their seats.* TWELVE

---

1. **diagram** (dī′ə gram), *n.* sketch showing an outline or general scheme of something with its various parts.

begins to doodle. TEN *blows his nose, but no one speaks. Then, finally—)*

FOUR. I don't see why we have to behave like children here.

ELEVEN. Nor do I. We have a responsibility. This is a remarkable thing about democracy. That we are . . . what is the word? . . . Ah, notified! That we are notified by mail to come down to this place and decide on the guilt or innocence of a man we have not known before. We have nothing to gain or lose by our verdict. This is one of the reasons why we are strong. We should not make it a personal thing.

(There is a long, awkward pause.)

TWELVE. Well—we're still nowhere. Who's got an idea?

SIX. I think maybe we should try another vote. Mr. Foreman?

FOREMAN. It's all right with me. Anybody doesn't want to vote? *(He looks around the table.)*

SEVEN. All right, let's do it.

THREE. I want an open ballot. Let's call out our votes. I want to know who stands where.

FOREMAN. That sounds fair. Anyone object? *(No one does.)* All right. I'll call off your jury numbers.

(He takes a pencil and paper and makes marks now in one of two columns after each vote.)

FOREMAN. I vote guilty. Number Two?

TWO. Not guilty.

FOREMAN. Number Three?

THREE. Guilty.

FOREMAN. Number Four?

FOUR. Guilty.

FOREMAN. Number Five?

FIVE. Not guilty.

FOREMAN. Number Six?

SIX. Not guilty.

FOREMAN. Number Seven?

SEVEN. Guilty.

FOREMAN. Number Eight?

EIGHT. Not guilty.

FOREMAN. Number Nine?

NINE. Not guilty.

FOREMAN. Number Ten?

TEN. Guilty.

FOREMAN. Number Eleven?

ELEVEN. Not guilty.

FOREMAN. Number Twelve?

TWELVE. Guilty.

FOUR. Six to six.

TEN *(mad).* I'll tell you something. The crime is being committed right in this room.

FOREMAN. The vote is six to six.

THREE. I'm ready to walk into court right now and declare a hung jury. There's no point in this going on anymore.

SEVEN. I go for that, too. Let's take it in to the judge and let the kid take his chances with twelve other guys.

FIVE *(to* SEVEN*).* You mean you still don't think there's room for reasonable doubt?

SEVEN. No, I don't.

ELEVEN. I beg your pardon. Maybe you don't understand the term "reasonable doubt."

SEVEN *(angry).* What do you mean I don't understand it? Who do you think you are to talk to me like that? *(To all.)* How do you like this guy? He comes over here running for his life, and before he can even take a big breath he's telling us how to run the show. The arrogance of him!

FIVE *(to* SEVEN*).* Wait a second. Nobody around here's asking where you came from.

SEVEN. I was born right here.

FIVE. Or where your father came from. . . . *(He looks at* SEVEN, *who doesn't answer but looks away.)* Maybe it wouldn't hurt us to take a few tips from people who come running here! Maybe they learned something we don't know. We're not so perfect!

ELEVEN. Please—I am used to this. It's all right. Thank you.

FIVE. It's not all right!

SEVEN. Okay, okay, I apologize. Is that what you want?

FIVE. That's what I want.

FOREMAN. All right. Let's stop the arguing. Who's got something constructive to say?

TWO (*hesitantly*). Well, something's been bothering me a little . . . this whole business about the stab wound and how it was made, the downward angle of it, you know?

THREE. Don't tell me we're gonna start that. They went over it and over it in court.

TWO. I know they did—but I don't go along with it. The boy is five feet eight inches tall. His father was six two. That's a difference of six inches. It's a very awkward thing to stab *down* into the chest of someone who's half a foot taller than you are.

(THREE *jumps up, holding the knife.*)

THREE. Look, you're not going to be satisfied till you see it again. I'm going to give you a demonstration. Somebody get up.

(*He looks around the table.* EIGHT *stands up and walks toward him.* THREE *closes the knife and puts it in his pocket. They stand face to face and look at each other for a moment.*)

THREE. Okay. (*To* TWO.) Now watch this. I don't want to have to do it again. (*He crouches down now until he is quite a bit shorter than* EIGHT.) Is that six inches?

TWELVE. That's more than six inches.

THREE. Okay, let it be more.

(*He reaches into his pocket and takes out the knife. He flicks it open, changes its position in his hand, and holds the knife aloft,*[2] *ready to stab. He and* EIGHT *look steadily into each other's eyes. Then he stabs downward, hard.*)

TWO (*shouting*). Look out!

(*He stops short just as the blade reaches* EIGHT*'s chest.* THREE *laughs.*)

SIX. That's not funny.

FIVE. What's the matter with you?

THREE. Now just calm down. Nobody's hurt, are they?

EIGHT (*low*). No. Nobody's hurt.

THREE. All right. There's your angle. Take a look at it. Down and in. That's how I'd stab a taller man in the chest, and that's how it was done. Take a look at it and tell me I'm wrong.

(TWO *doesn't answer.* THREE *looks at him for a*

moment, then jams the knife into the table, and sits down. They all look at the knife.*)

SIX. Down and in. I guess there's no argument.

(EIGHT *picks the knife out of the table and closes it. He flicks it open and, changing its position in his hand, stabs downward with it.*)

EIGHT (*to* SIX). Did you ever stab a man?

SIX. Of course not.

EIGHT (*to* THREE). Did you?

THREE. All right, let's not be silly.

EIGHT. Did you?

THREE (*loud*). No, I didn't!

EIGHT. Where do you get all your information about how it's done?

THREE. What do you mean? It's just common sense.

EIGHT. Have you ever seen a man stabbed?

THREE (*pauses and looks around the room nervously*). No.

EIGHT. All right. I want to ask you something. The boy was an experienced knife fighter. He was even sent to reform school for knifing someone, isn't that so?

TWELVE. That's right.

EIGHT. Look at this. (EIGHT *closes the knife, flicks it open, and changes the position of the knife so that he can stab overhanded.*) Doesn't it seem like an awkward way to handle a knife?

THREE. What are you asking me for?

(EIGHT *closes the blade and flicks it open, holds it ready to slash underhanded.*)

FIVE. Wait a minute! What's the matter with me? Give me that. (*He reaches out for the knife.*)

EIGHT. Have you ever seen a knife fight?

FIVE. Yes, I have.

EIGHT. In the movies?

FIVE. In my backyard. On my stoop. In the vacant lot across the street. Too many of them. Switch-knives came with the neighborhood where I lived. Funny I didn't think of it before. I guess you try to forget those things. (*Flicking the knife open.*) Anyone who's ever used a switch-knife would never have

---

2. **aloft** (ə lôft′), *adj.* in the air.

stabbed downward. You don't handle a switch-knife that way. You use it under-handed.

EIGHT. Then he couldn't have made the kind of wound which killed his father.

FIVE. No. He couldn't have. Not if he'd ever had any experience with switch-knives.

THREE. I don't believe it.

TEN. Neither do I. You're giving us a lot of mumbo jumbo.

EIGHT (*to* TWELVE). What do you think?

TWELVE (*hesitantly*). Well . . . I don't know.

EIGHT (*to* SEVEN). What about you?

SEVEN. Listen, I'll tell you something. I'm a lit-tle sick of this whole thing already. We're get-ting nowhere fast. Let's break it up and go home. I'm changing my vote to not guilty.

THREE. You're what?

SEVEN. You heard me. I've had enough.

THREE. What do you mean, you've had enough? That's no answer.

ELEVEN (*angry*). I think perhaps you're right. This is not an answer. (*To* SEVEN.) What kind of a man are you? You have sat here and voted guilty with everyone else because there are some theater tickets burning a hole in your pocket. Now you have changed your vote for the same reason. I do not think you have the right to play like this with a man's life. This is an ugly and terrible thing to do.

SEVEN. Now wait a minute . . . you can't talk like that to me.

ELEVEN (*strong*). I can talk like that to you! If you want to vote not guilty, then do it because you are convinced the man is not guilty. If you believe he is guilty, then vote that way. Or don't you have the . . . the . . . guts—the guts to do what you think is right?

SEVEN. Now listen . . .

ELEVEN. Is it guilty or not guilty?

SEVEN (*hesitantly*). I told you. Not . . . guilty.

ELEVEN (*hard*). Why?

SEVEN. I don't have to—

ELEVEN. You have to! Say it! Why?

(*They stare at each other for a long while.*)

SEVEN (*low*). I . . . don't think . . . he's guilty.

EIGHT (*fast*). I want another vote.

FOREMAN. Okay, there's another vote called for. I guess the quickest way is a show of hands. Anybody object? (*No one does.*) All right. All those voting not guilty, raise your hands.

(TWO, FIVE, SIX, SEVEN, EIGHT, NINE, *and* ELEVEN *raise their hands immediately. Then, slowly,* TWELVE *raises his hand. The* FOREMAN *looks around the table carefully and then he too raises his hand. He looks around the table, counting silently.*)

FOREMAN. Nine. (*The hands go down.*) All those voting guilty.

(THREE, FOUR, *and* TEN *raise their hands.*)

FOREMAN. Three. (*They lower their hands.*) The vote is nine to three in favor of acquittal.[3]

TEN. I don't understand you people. How can you believe this kid is innocent? Look, you know how those people lie. I don't have to tell you. They don't know what the truth is. And lemme tell you, they—(FIVE *gets up from table, turns his back to it, and goes to window.*)—don't need any real big reason to kill some-one either. You know, they get drunk, and *bang*, someone's lying in the gutter. Nobody's blaming them. That's how they are. You know what I mean? Violent! (NINE *gets up and does the same. He is followed by* ELEVEN.)

TEN. Human life don't mean as much to them as it does to us. Hey, where are you going? Look, these people are drinking and fight-ing all the time, and if somebody gets killed, so somebody gets killed. They don't care. Oh, sure, there are some good things about them, too. Look, I'm the first to say that. (EIGHT *gets up, and then* TWO *and* SIX *follow him to the window.*)

TEN. I've known a few who were pretty decent, but that's the exception. Most of them, it's like they have no feelings. They can do any-thing. What's going on here?

(*The* FOREMAN *gets up and goes to the window, fol-lowed by* SEVEN *and* TWELVE.)

---

3. **acquittal** (ə kwitʹl), *n.* discharge; release.

TEN. I'm speaking my piece, and you—Listen to me! They're no good. There's not a one of 'em who's any good. We better watch out. Take it from me. This kid on trial . . .

(THREE *sits at table toying with the knife and* FOUR *gets up and starts for the window. All have their backs to* TEN.)

TEN. Well, don't you know about them? Listen to me! What are you doing? I'm trying to tell you something . . . .

(FOUR *stands over him as he trails off. There is a dead silence. Then* FOUR *speaks softly.*)

FOUR. I've had enough. If you open your mouth again, I'm going to split your skull. (FOUR *stands there and looks at him. No one moves or speaks.* TEN *looks at him, then looks down at the table.*)

TEN *(softly).* I'm only trying to tell you. . . .

(*There is a long pause as* FOUR *stares down at* TEN.)

FOUR *(to all).* All right. Sit down, everybody.

(*They all move back to their seats. When they are all seated,* FOUR *then sits down.*)

FOUR *(quietly).* I still believe the boy is guilty of murder. I'll tell you why. To me, the most damning evidence was given by the woman across the street who claimed she actually saw the murder committed.

THREE. That's right. As far as I'm concerned, that's the most important testimony.

EIGHT. All right. Let's go over her testimony. What exactly did she say?

FOUR. I believe I can recount[4] it accurately. She said that she went to bed at about eleven o'clock that night. Her bed was next to the open window, and she could look out of the window while lying down and see directly into the window across the street. She tossed and turned for over an hour, unable to fall asleep. Finally she turned toward the window at about twelve-ten and, as she looked out, she saw the boy stab his father. As far as I can see, this is unshakable[5] testimony.

THREE. That's what I mean. That's the whole case.

(FOUR *takes off his eyeglasses and begins to polish them, as they all sit silently watching him.*)

FOUR (*to the* JURY). Frankly, I don't see how you can vote for acquittal. (*To* TWELVE.) What do you think about it?

TWELVE. Well . . . maybe . . . there's so much evidence to sift.

THREE. What do you mean, maybe? He's absolutely right. You can throw out all the other evidence.

FOUR. That was my feeling. (TWO, *polishing his glasses, squints at clock, can't see it.* SIX *watches him closely.*)

TWO. What time is it?

ELEVEN. Ten minutes of six.

TWO. It's late. You don't suppose they'd let us go home and finish it in the morning. I've got a kid with mumps.

FIVE. Not a chance.

SIX (*to* TWO). Pardon me. Can't you see the clock without your glasses?

TWO. Not clearly. Why?

SIX. Oh, I don't know. Look, this may be a dumb thought, but what do you do when you wake up at night and want to know what time it is?

TWO. What do you mean? I put on my glasses and look at the clock.

SIX. You don't wear them to bed.

TWO. Of course not. No one wears eyeglasses to bed.

TWELVE. What's all this for?

SIX. Well, I was thinking. You know the woman who testified that she saw the killing wears glasses.

THREE. So does my grandmother. So what?

EIGHT. Your grandmother isn't a murder witness.

SIX. Look, stop me if I'm wrong. This woman wouldn't wear her eyeglasses to bed, would she?

FOREMAN. Wait a minute! Did she wear glasses at all? I don't remember.

ELEVEN (*excited*). Of course she did. The woman wore bifocals.[6] I remember this very clearly. They looked quite strong.

NINE. That's right. Bifocals. She never took them off.

FOUR. She did wear glasses. Funny. I never thought of it.

EIGHT. Listen, she wasn't wearing them in bed. That's for sure. She testified that in the midst of her tossing and turning she rolled over and looked casually out the window. The murder was taking place as she looked out, and the lights went out a split second later. She couldn't have had time to put on her glasses. Now maybe she honestly thought she saw the boy kill his father. I say that she saw only a blur.

THREE. How do you know what she saw? Maybe she's farsighted. (*He looks around. No one answers.*)

THREE (*loud*). How does he know all these things? (*There is silence.*)

EIGHT. Does anyone think there still is not a reasonable doubt?

---

4. **recount** (ri kount′), *v.* tell in detail.
5. **unshakable** (un shā′kə bl), *adj.* undisturbed; not able to be upset.
6. **bifocals** (bī fō′kəlz), *n.* pair of glasses having two focuses.

(He looks around the room, then squarely at TEN. TEN *looks down and shakes his head no.)*

THREE *(loud).* I think he's guilty.

EIGHT *(calmly).* Does anyone else?

FOUR *(quietly).* No. I'm convinced.

EIGHT *(to* THREE*).* You're alone.

THREE. I don't care whether I'm alone or not! I have a right.

EIGHT. You have a right.

(There is a pause. They all look at THREE.*)*

THREE. Well, I told you I think the kid's guilty. What else do you want?

EIGHT. Your arguments. *(They all look at* THREE.*)*

THREE. I gave you my arguments.

EIGHT. We're not convinced. We're waiting to hear them again. We have time.

*(THREE *runs to* FOUR *and grabs his arm.)*

THREE *(pleading).* Listen. What's the matter with you? You're the guy. You made all the arguments. You can't turn now. A guilty man's gonna be walking the streets. A murderer. He's got to die! Stay with me.

FOUR. I'm sorry. There's a reasonable doubt in my mind.

EIGHT. We're waiting.

*(THREE *turns violently on him.)*

THREE *(shouting).* Well, you're not going to intimidate⁷ me! *(They all look at* THREE.*)* I'm entitled to my opinion! *(No one answers him.)* It's gonna be a hung jury! That's it!

EIGHT. There's nothing we can do about that, except hope that some night, maybe in a few months, you'll get some sleep.

FIVE. You're all alone.

NINE. It takes a great deal of courage to stand alone.

*(THREE *looks around at all of them for a long time. They sit silently, waiting for him to speak, and all of them despise⁸ him for his stubbornness. Then, suddenly, his face contorts⁹ as if he is about to cry, and he slams his fist down on the table.)*

THREE *(thundering).* All right!

*(THREE *turns his back on them. There is silence for a moment and then the* FOREMAN *goes to the door and knocks on it. It opens. The* GUARD *looks in and sees them all standing. The* GUARD *holds the door for them as they begin slowly to file out.* EIGHT *waits at the door as the others file past him. Finally he and* THREE *are the only ones left.* THREE *turns around and sees that they are alone. Slowly he moves toward the door. Then he stops at the table. He pulls the switch-knife out of the table and walks over to* EIGHT *with it. He holds it in the approved knife-fighter fashion and looks long and hard at* EIGHT, *pointing the knife at his belly.* EIGHT *stares back. Then* THREE *turns the knife around.* EIGHT *takes it by the handle.* THREE *exits.* EIGHT *closes the knife, puts it away, and, taking a last look around the room, exits, closing the door. The camera moves in close on the littered table in the empty room, and we clearly see a slip of crumpled paper on which are scribbled the words "Not guilty."*)*

(Fade out.)

---

7. **intimidate** (in tim′ə dāt), *v.* influence or force by fear.
8. **despise** (di spīz′) *v.*, feel hatred or scorn for.
9. **contort** (kən tôrt′), *v.* twist or bend out of shape.

After Reading

Act 3

Making Connections

Shaping Your Response

1. If you were casting a remake of the movie version of this play, who would play the jurors? Be prepared to explain your casting choices.

2. In your notebook, write three questions you still have about the facts of the case.

3. If you were a member of the jury, how would you vote at the end of the play? Why?

Analyzing the Play

4. Why do you think Eleven questions Seven so closely after he changes his vote?

5. Explain the behavior of the other jurors when Ten begins to rant and rave about the way "those people" (meaning people like the accused) behave.

6. How is the evidence provided by the woman from beyond the el tracks cast into doubt?

7. What is the main **conflict** of the play?

8. At the end of the play, Five tells Three that he's all alone. Do you consider this the **climax** of the play? Explain.

9. Why do you think these men are referred to as *angry* in the **title**? Can you suggest a better title for the play?

Extending the Ideas

10. ☝ Do you think the jurors have difficulty arriving at a consensus because of their differing cultural backgrounds or because of other factors? Explain.

11. If the murder described in *Twelve Angry Men* occurred today, what modern ways of detecting and examining the evidence might be used to prove the guilt or innocence of the boy?

12. ☝ Do you think "those people," a label used to describe the accused and people like him, refers to an ethnic, social, or economic group? Why? Explain how labels like this can affect **interactions**.

Literary Focus: Stage Directions

Through his **stage directions** Reginald Rose provides information about the characters and their surroundings. Reread the stage directions on page 230, that begin "And now, slowly, almost hesitantly, . . ."

- What do you learn about the setting?
- What mood do the stage directions relay?
- What can you infer about the characters at this point?

Vocabulary Study

acquittal
aloft
bifocals
contort
despise
diagram
intimidate
recount
unshakable

Use the table of prefixes below to make a word association cluster for two of the vocabulary words in the list. An example cluster for *bifocals* is shown.

Prefix	Meaning	Prefix	Meaning
a-	in, on, to	dia-	through
ac-	to, toward	un-	not
bi-	having two	in-	in, into
con-	with	re-	back
de-	from		

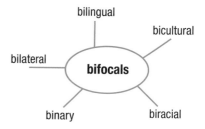

Expressing Your Ideas

Writing Choices

Writer's Notebook Update By the end of the play, all jurors have voted *not guilty* because they have reasonable doubts about facts in the case. Look at the reasons for changing their votes that you listed in your notebook. Describe the evidence and arguments you think were most influential in swaying the jury.

Protect Your Client's Rights The jurors point out that the boy's defense attorney failed to raise pertinent questions during cross-examination of the witnesses. If you were the defense attorney, what would you have asked the old man and the woman based on their testimonies and on what you now know from the jury deliberations? Draw up at least eight **defense questions**.

Two Trials, Two Verdicts Consider who is on trial in *Antigone* and *Twelve Angry Men*. Do you think justice has been served in either play? Using these plays as examples, write an **opinion paper** discussing whether or not you think the jury system is the most effective way to determine guilt or innocence.

Other Options

Sounding Off Critics of the jury system have argued that the number of jurors should be fewer, that jurors should be required to have a certain level of education, or that all cases should be decided by judges alone. Prepare a **debate** on one of the issues raised above, with one group in favor and the other opposed. Gather evidence, present the debate to the class, and let classmates take sides with a show of hands after the debate is presented.

Your Fingerprints Are Showing Jury trials that take place today often present evidence such as DNA patterns and medical reports that rely on the latest technology. Do some **research** on modern methods of analyzing evidence. As a start, you might want to expand the information provided in the interview on page 260. Present your findings to the class.

On Trial

Guilty or Innocent?

History Connection
Though it may be flawed, today's jury system is far superior to former methods used to determine guilt or innocence—trial by combat, and ordeal by fire, water, or poison.

W
T H E

by Barbara Holland

. . . The laws are established, facts discovered, witnesses heard and judgment made. These functions have been separated in our fancier world, but in the early tribunals they were all one. The group called in to consider the matter was made up of witnesses; if no law already applied to the case, they made one that would; they talked it over and decided.

ROMAN GLADIATORS

They were all amateurs. Laws were so simple that ordinary folk could understand them. Now professionals have taken over the courts and, I hear, get well paid for it, but juries are still amateurs called in for the occasion, unattached to the system. The good thing about juries is that they're amateurs. The bad thing about juries is that they're amateurs.

Rome refined the system and separated the law from the facts. A magistrate defined the dispute, cited the law and referred the problem to a citizen judex—a fellow of some standing—who called in a few associates to help. They listened to the speeches, weighed the evidence and pronounced sentence. (Nobody was supervising them, so it helped if one of them was a lawyer, to explain.) This was more orderly than a tribunal. The Romans were passionately fond of order and wrote down all their laws in books.

They were also fond of a good public spectacle, and a convicted criminal could always opt for the arena and entertain the citizens by duking it out with other criminals or prisoners of war. A talented gladiator not only got to live, but he could wind up as a popular sports hero, surrounded by pretty ladies. The Romans loved a winner, regardless of his criminal record.

Meanwhile, the Scandinavians were gathering regularly in tribunals, called Things, dating back further than anyone remembered. Groups of delegates met to represent their districts, and committees of 12 or of multiples of 12 were picked to administer or invent the laws.

In 1976, Cecilia M. Pizzo filed suit in New Orleans to nullify the Louisiana Purchase, claiming that neither Napoleon nor Thomas Jefferson had the authority to make the deal.

In 1972, a Los Angeles judge sentenced a pickpocket to a jail term and ordered that he wear thick woolen mittens in public after he was released.

A Florida law banned unmarried women from parachuting on the Sabbath.

E

JURORS

Twelve is the solemn number. When Morgan of Glamorgan, Prince of Wales, established trial by jury in A.D. 725, he wrote, "For as Christ and his Twelve Apostles were finally to judge the world, so human tribunals should be composed of the king and twelve wise men." Maybe, though apparently Christ was following an older tradition. The number 12 crops up all over. The zodiac has 12 signs, based on 12 constellations; we divide our days into twice-12 hours, 12 midnight rings in the witching hour. . . .

After Rome fell apart, its former empire went all to sixes and sevens, and its orderly laws decayed into gibberish. In Britain, King Arthur had to set his possibly legendary knights out to ride around righting wrongs and rescuing maidens from sexual harassment, a far from comprehensive judicial system. There were still trials, though, with an ordeal serving as jury.

Great faith has been placed in trial by ordeal, all the way from the Old Testament to the Australian outback. The idea is that something out there "knows" who's guilty and will point to him if given a chance. The chance usually involves fire or water or poison.

Poison was recommended in the Bible and was popular in Africa and Brahmanic India for trials by ordeal. Those who survived at all, though likely to be ill, were considered inno-

cent. The Saxons developed a variation called "corsnaed," a morsel of something that would choke the guilty (perhaps their throats were dry with apprehension). Godwin, Earl of Kent, is said to have choked on his.

Under Saxon law, if you could carry several pounds of glowing red-hot iron in your bare hands for nine steps or walk barefoot over nine red-hot plowshares without getting any blisters, you were not guilty. Similar proof was accepted in Hindu and Scandinavian law. In Britain, Africa and parts of Asia, plunging your arm into boiling water, oil or lead without the usual results proved your innocence.

Water was also knowledgeable stuff. The innocent sank; the guilty floated and could be fished out and dealt with. This was the customary method of identifying witches, who were cross-tied thumb-to-toe before being thrown in. True witches refused to drown and were dried off and burned at the stake. . . .

A WITCH-DUNKING

Folks back then were so primitive that they thought the victim, rather than the law, had been damaged, and bodily harm was redeemed at so much for a finger, so much for an ear, all the way up to murder, which, around the 800s, cost 200 shillings, payable to the deceased's family. (Among the Germans it was payable in sheep.) Thieves paid the value of the stolen object plus a fine; repeat offenders and those who stole from the church paid with a hand or a foot as well.

This would mean that if someone broke your arm while stealing your car, he paid for your arm and your car, and you got to keep

The city fathers of Barre, Vermont, once made it obligatory for everyone to take at least one bath a week—on Saturday night.

In 1978, an accountant named Tom Horsley sued a woman who failed to show up for a date for "breach of oral contract."

In Fairbanks, Alaska, it is illegal to feed alcohol to a moose.

Cats are banned from howling after 9:00 P.M. in Columbus, Georgia.

the fine and possibly his foot too. Now he just goes to jail, and you get to pay for his room and board with taxes. Progress has been made.

When William the Conqueror took over England in 1066, he left the Saxon system in place and added some Norman flourishes, like trial by combat. Combat was a judicial entertainment similar to the gladiatorial, in which right was thought to make might—whoever was right would win. The accuser had to do battle with the accused, causing the small and frail to think twice before complaining, but if you were not good at fighting you could hire someone to fight for you. The man with the fiercest hired help won—rather like hiring the most expensive lawyer today.

(Ordeals fell into disuse in the 13th century, but the right to trial by combat stayed on

THE BENCH BY WILLIAM HOGARTH

the books until Ashford v. Thornton in 1819.) By Norman times, laws were more complicated, so professionals, called justiciars, were sent around to keep an eye on the courts and the rules of evidence, rather like judges. They knew more about the law and less about what had happened than the jurors did.

We were told in school that jury trials sprang newborn from the Magna Carta, but juries were around before 1215. The Magna Carta just guaranteed them as a right not to be ignored by capricious powers like bad King John, but some kings went right on being capricious anyway. In these enlightened times, we merely torch the neighborhood if we don't like a verdict, but back then, juries got punished if the authorities didn't like it. Since juries were still considered witnesses, a wrong vote was considered perjury. Acquitting unpopular or possibly treasonous people got jurors hauled into the star chamber, where a group of the king's dear friends dealt severely with them. They lost their goods and chattels and went to jail for at least a year; sometimes their wives and children were thrown out of their houses, the houses demolished, the meadows destroyed and even the trees chopped down. . . .

In 1650, under Cromwell, a newly reinstated law called for hanging adulteresses—and scarcely an adulteress was found in the land. In 1670 William Penn was tried for preaching Quaker doctrine, and he couldn't have been guiltier, caught red-handed and far from a first offense. The jurors stubbornly found in his favor and were fined 40 marks apiece for wrongness. Four of them refused to pay and spent a year in prison, until one was brought before the court on habeas corpus, and lo, it was decided that the law couldn't jail jurors for their decisions. We can't put them in jail anymore, but we can select them half to death.

As we limp toward the 21st century, the rural community of nosy neighbors has faded into history, and the problem now is, Who are these jurors? Prince Morgan called them "wise men." Under Edward I, they were to be 12 of the "better and lawful men." (Except for adulteresses, witches and common scolds, legal history doesn't mention women; perhaps they're a recent invention.) It seems to have been so simple then, naming our good, wise, lawful peers. But how do we choose among strangers not necessarily wise but merely registered to vote?

Once the blatantly prejudiced have been sent packing, both sides take up the peremp-

Only two incumbent U.S. Presidents have ever been arrested. None has been tried, convicted, or jailed.

In ancient Persia, judges at trials often sat on cushions upholstered with the skins of their dishonest predecessors in office.

In Minnesota, it was illegal for a woman to dress up and try to impersonate Santa on any city street.

JUDGE LANCE ITO AT THE O.J. SIMPSON TRIAL

tory challenge of turning down jurors for the way they look, dress or comb their hair. A new professional has sprung up among us, the jury-selection consultant. For the O. J. Simpson trial, consultants submitted an 80-page list of 294 questions for prospective jurors, including essay questions like "What do you think is the main cause of domestic violence?" The theory is that we ordinary citizens are such a bunch of sheep that we'll always vote according to our kind, regardless of the evidence. The more narrowly the consultants can identify our kind, the easier it is to predict the vote.

The differing agendas of the prosecution and the defense complicate matters. Prosecution lawyer Jeffrey Toobin says that when he first came to the bar, he was always told to avoid men with beards (too independent) and teachers and social workers (too sympathetic), and aim for "the little old Lutheran lady in pearls, quick to judge and slow to forgive."

For the defense, Clarence Darrow advised not to "take a German; they are bull-headed. Rarely take a Swede; they are stubborn. Always take an Irishman or a Jew; they are the easiest to move to emotional sympathy." . . .

Whatever it may read or watch, the modern jury doesn't know what it was designed to know—its neighbors—and a clever lawyer can sometimes play on it as upon a harp. Such was William Howe of Howe and Hummel, defender of the underworld in rowdy post-Civil War New York. Howe was an enormous, lion-headed man with a wardrobe of costumes for his courtroom performances and a talent for crying copiously over any case, however dull. Once he delivered an hourlong summation, kneeling before the jury. Another time he convinced a jury that his client's trigger finger had accidentally slipped, not once but six times. So many of his clients were forgers that his office accepted only cash, so many were thieves that his office safe contained nothing but a coal scuttle—but murderers were his meat and drink. He personally appeared for more than 650 of them. He virtually invented "temporary insanity." He wept; the jury wept. According to a newspaper account, during his defense of Annie Walden, the "Man-Killing Race-Track Girl," the "sobs of juror nine could have been heard in the corridors, and there was moisture in the eyes of all but one or two of the other jurors."

Howe kept a stable of white-haired mothers, distraught wives and cherubic children available to represent the family of the accused. He once pointed out his own wife and child, who happened to be in the courtroom, as his client's prospective widow and orphan. How would a New York jury know? And how the hometown juries of old would have laughed.

Here and there a voice suggests returning at least minor offenses to neighborhood judicial counsels, as in the old courts of the hundreds, taking the law into our own hands where it began. This may be utopian. We don't want to know our 99 nearest neighbors, let alone be accountable for their behavior. Some of us don't even want to read the papers. We gripe about the results, but we leave civil order to the professionals. It wasn't designed to work that way. . . .

According to an old New Jersey law, anyone slurping soup in a public restaurant was subject to arrest, a fine, and a possible term in jail.

According to an Arkansas law, pay raises were not given to teachers who bobbed their hair.

Responding

1. Conduct a panel discussion on the strengths and weaknesses of the present-day jury system.

2. What do you think of the proposal that neighborhood councils try minor offenses?

Career Connection

Recent scientific advances provide jurors with new forms of evidence to help them make informed decisions.

TAMARA CAMP
FORENSIC SCIENTIST

We've come a long way from witch-dunking to DNA! Recent scientific advances provide jurors and others required to determine guilt and innocence with new forms of evidence to help them make informed decisions. Forensic scientist Tamara Camp from the Northern Illinois Police Crime Laboratory describes some of the techniques she uses as a molecular biologist to analyze evidence.

My section of the lab is called forensic biology. We identify stains from body fluids. For example, a specimen of a blood stain found at a crime scene is brought to the lab. This is our unknown, which we call a sample. Since ours is a comparative science, we also collect blood specimens from the victim and from the suspect, and these specimens are called the standards. We compare the sample to the standards and make a probability statement from one of the known persons.

"When we examine blood, we use various methods and look at genetic markers like blood type, DNA, or proteins. To look at proteins, we first take a slab of agar, a jelly-like substance, and embed our blood specimen in it. Then we apply an electric current across the gel, and the protein molecules in the blood will migrate across the agar, with the smaller ones moving faster. We look at the bands of migrated protein to determine whether these patterns match the suspect's specimen. Although the protein type is not as definite for identification as a fingerprint, it is extremely valuable in establishing innocence: if the sample and the suspect's specimen don't match at all, there is no possibility that the suspect could have left the stain.

"DNA (deoxyribonucleic acid) typing, the newest crime lab technique, has been widely used only since the 1980s. DNA, called the 'master molecule of life,' can be extracted from body fluids or tissues. One method of typing DNA is to break it into smaller pieces using chemicals. Then it is tagged with a radioactive probe to expose a piece of X-ray film. We study the resulting patterns that resemble a bar code and use them for identification. This is a DNA 'fingerprint.' Another means of DNA identification, called PCR analysis, requires only tiny amounts of a specimen and is quicker, though less definitive."

DNA evidence has been accepted in most courts across the country, although lawyers have argued that the varying probability factors (which can range from 1 in many billion to 1 in 100), are sometimes insufficient to establish guilt. Nonetheless, it is commonly used to settle paternity suits, to protect endangered species of animals, and to identify remains of war veterans. One of DNA's most stunning successes was the identification of a 1994 World Trade Center bomber through his saliva used to lick an envelope.

Responding

1. Research recent uses of technology involving DNA, fingerprinting, polygraph testing, and other methods of detection.

2. Prepare an explanation of DNA testing, complete with graphic aids, that would clarify this process for the average person.

Reading Mini-Lesson

Chronology and Time Lines

Authors often organize a narrative into chronological, or time, order. In "We the Jurors" (page 256), Barbara Holland tracks the history of the jury system from its earliest times to the present. Introductory phrases such as "After Rome fell apart" and "As we limp toward the 21st century" are one way Holland cues readers to time periods. She indicates when two or more events take place simultaneously with words such as *meanwhile* and *during*. Actual dates within the text also inform readers of time frames and shifts.

Some articles you read may jump around in time or use a literary device known as a flashback to recall events from the past. Sometimes you can make a time line to help clarify the selection's sequence of events.

The Rosemont High School homecoming game was October 15. Our team won, but that's not the whole story. Three days before the big game, the star quarterback, Jamal Rodgers, came down with the flu. By October 13, he was no better. Meanwhile, the rest of the team started practicing with Andy Hicks, the substitute quarterback. The day before the game, Jamal began to feel better. By game day, he was ready to play.

Read the passage to the left. Notice that the first event mentioned in the paragraph is actually the last event in the chronology. The third sentence begins a flashback sequence involving the three days before the game. What introductory words indicate time clues? An abbreviated time line for this passage might look like this:

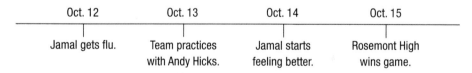

Oct. 12	Oct. 13	Oct. 14	Oct. 15
Jamal gets flu.	Team practices with Andy Hicks.	Jamal starts feeling better.	Rosemont High wins game.

As you read, pay close attention to the sequence of events. When necessary, fill in time gaps or mentally rearrange events into chronological order in order to understand difficult material.

Activity Options

1. Work with a partner to create a poster-size time line for the events detailed in Barbara Holland's article, "We the Jurors" (page 256).

2. Think of a TV show or movie that uses flashbacks. Discuss with someone who has seen the same feature why you think there were time shifts. Consider also how time shifts were indicated—for example signs of age on a character's face, shifts in the season or setting, camera fadeouts, voice-overs, and so forth.

Writing Workshop

Antigone Updated

Assignment What would the characters from *Antigone* be like if they lived today? How would they react to modern-day problems? Write a scene for a play, set in the present, featuring updated versions of the major characters from *Antigone*. See the Writer's Blueprint for details.

WRITER'S BLUEPRINT

Product   A scene for a play
Purpose   To update *Antigone*
Audience   People who have read or seen a production of *Antigone*
Specs   To write a successful scene, you should:

❑ Choose two characters from *Antigone* and update them—turn them into people who have the same personalities but who live now, in the present day. Then choose a modern-day conflict to serve as the basis for your scene.

❑ Begin by writing personality profiles of the characters and a description of the setting.

❑ Then write the scene itself. Use dialogue that sounds natural—not too formal, but not too informal either. See that your characters behave in ways that are true to the personalities of the original *Antigone* characters.

❑ Follow the applicable rules of grammar, usage, spelling, and mechanics. Use the proper form for a play script.

The instructions that follow are designed to lead you to a successful scene.

Revisit *Antigone*. Your scene will focus on a **protagonist**, a central character who is in conflict with an **antagonist**, a character who opposes the protagonist. With a group, revisit *Antigone* to find pairs of antagonists and protagonists and conflicts in the play. Make notes on what you find and put them into a chart like the one below.

Protagonist–Antagonist	Their Conflict
• Antigone/Ismene	• whether to obey the king's demand to leave their brother unburied

List modern-day conflicts. With your group, list examples of conflicts people might have over issues such as ownership of property, money, legal rights, and family matters.

Choose your characters and conflict. On your own, review your notes and choose the character pair and modern-day conflict you'll use for the focus of your scene.

Visualize the characters. Make notes on the personalities of your protagonist and antagonist. How do they typically behave? See the Literary Source for ideas.

Visualize the setting. Where will your scene take place? Think of the characters and the conflict. Do you see things happening indoors or outdoors? Visualize the setting and make notes on what you see.

Plan your character profiles, setting description, and scene. Follow these steps.

1. Gather together your character notes. These will serve as the basis for the personality profiles you will write for your protagonist and antagonist. See the Literary Source at the right for a good example of a character profile.

2. Gather together your setting notes. These will serve as the basis for the description you will write of your setting. See the Literary Source on page 264 for a good example of the kind of description you should write.

3. Summarize the action. List the key events in your scene and some key lines of dialogue you plan to include when you write your scene.

LITERARY SOURCE

Juror number two. A meek, hesitant man who finds it difficult to maintain any opinions of his own. Easily swayed and usually adopts the opinion of the last person to whom he has spoken.

from *Twelve Angry Men* by Reginald Rose

2 DRAFTING

Before you write, reread the Writer's Blueprint and review your notes and writing plan.

As you draft, concentrate on the action rather than matters of correctness, such as spelling and grammar. These ideas might help you as you draft.

- As you profile your protagonist and antagonist, keep in mind that they must behave in ways that are true to the original *Antigone* characters.

- As you describe your setting, be sure to supply enough details for your audience to be able to visualize the scene. See the Literary Source below for an example.

LITERARY SOURCE

The room is furnished with a long conference table and a dozen chairs. The walls are bare, drab, and badly in need of a fresh coat of paint. Along one wall is a row of windows which look out on the skyline of the city's financial district. High on another wall is an electric clock. . . .
from *Twelve Angry Men* by Reginald Rose

- As you write the scene, stand up and act out what a character is saying or doing, and then capture what you did in writing.

- As you write dialogue, try to make it as realistic as possible. (See the Revising Strategy in Step 3 of this lesson.)

- Use the standard form for a play script. (See the Editing Strategy in Step 4 of this lesson.)

3 REVISING

Ask a partner to read your scene and make suggestions before you revise it. Use these questions as a guide.

✔ Have I focused on the conflict between an antagonist and a protagonist?

✔ Are my characters true to the personalities in *Antigone*?

✔ Does my dialogue seem realistic?

OR . . .
As you draft, narrate portions of your script into a tape recorder. Play the tape back to see if the dialogue flows smoothly and sounds realistic.

Revising Strategy

COMPUTER TIP
When revising, you can define various paragraph styles in the word-processing program to help you indent the dialogue and italicize the directions.

Writing Realistic Dialogue

Realistic dialogue sounds natural when you read it aloud. For example, when real people talk to each other they usually use informal language. Take care, though, that you don't make your dialogue too informal by throwing in too much slang. Notice how the writer of the student model revised dialogue, with the help of a partner's comment.

> ANNIE. Can ~~ya~~ *you* believe all that ~~yellin~~ *yelling* last night? That landlord's been on Peter's back ever since he moved in, ~~ya know? Gimme a break.~~
>
> It's the long hair and the ragged clothes, ~~ya know?~~ *I know it* That landlord is such a bigot, ~~ya know?~~ Know what he did?
>
> *Too many "ya know"s. Is that how Annie really talks?*

STUDENT MODEL

STEP 4 EDITING

Ask a partner to review your revised draft before you edit. Look especially for errors related to script format.

Editing Strategy

FOR REFERENCE
Look back at *Antigone* if you have any questions about play-script format.

Writing in Script Format

When you write in a script format, follow these rules.

- Write the speaker's name in all capitals followed by a period and then the first line of the speech. Indent the remaining lines of the speech by two spaces.

- Always enclose stage directions in parentheses. If you're using a computer, write the stage directions in italics. If you're writing by hand, underline them.

5 PRESENTING

Here are two ideas for presenting your scene.

- In a group, read your scenes to each other with different group members taking the different parts. Choose one scene you all especially liked, rehearse it, and present it to the class.

- Make a videotape or audiotape of your scene, adding the visual or sound effects called for in the script.

6 LOOKING BACK

Self-evaluate. What grade would *you* give your paper? Look back at the Writer's Blueprint and give yourself a score for each point, from 6 (superior) down to 1 (inadequate).

Reflect. Think about what you learned from writing your scene as you write in response to these questions.

✔ If you were to write the entire play, how would it end?

✔ How was writing the script for a scene different from other writing assignments you have done? What made it easier or more difficult than writing an essay?

For Your Working Portfolio Add your scene and your reflection responses to your working portfolio.

Beyond Print

Weighing the Evidence

Creon is charged with the death of Antigone. If you, the jury, finds him guilty, he will be put to death.

- Divide your class into groups of from six to twelve students.

- Find a space in your classroom or in another area where each group can weigh the evidence, discuss, and try to reach a consensus.

- Jot down ideas about the role that Creon plays in Antigone's death.

Deliberation Tips

Agree on responsibilities. Decide who will serve as a recorder and a spokesperson, and fill other roles as the need arises.

Brainstorm. Collaborate to find as many reasons as possible for Creon's guilt, as well as reasons for his innocence. Work together to put these reasons in order from most persuasive to least persuasive.

Invite discussion. Each group member should express his or her opinions. Group members should encourage everyone to speak, as well as keep discussion going and on track.

Listen carefully and ask questions. Ask for clarification if necessary. Stay with the facts and avoid personal attacks.

Ask for a summary. Have your spokesperson summarize the basic arguments for and against Creon.

Vote. After considering the strongest evidence, cast a secret ballot.

If you have a hung jury, have group members discuss why they voted as they did. Vote again to see if anyone feels differently after deliberation.

Activity Options

1. Discuss how effectively group members worked together. What things did you do well? What things could be improved?

2. Based on your collaboration as a group, discuss what things could be done to make a real jury work together effectively.

Part Two

Beneath the Surface

Do you rely on first impressions, or do you base judgments on second thoughts? The selections you are about to read provide reminders that it's wise to look beneath the surface.

 **Multicultural Connection** **Perspective** involves seeing and interpreting a situation from different cultural viewpoints. As you read the following selections, decide how group values contribute to both the understanding and misunderstanding of what's beneath the surface.

The Flying Doctor

by Molière   France

Molière
1622–1673

From an early age, John Baptiste Poquelin, who adopted the pen name Molière (mō lyer′), enjoyed attending the theater and watching broad comedies known as farces. He became director of an acting troupe, performed throughout France, and eventually began writing his own satiric comedies. He gained favor at the court of Louis XIV, called the Sun King, and frequently performed his elaborate spectaculars at the king's splendid castle at Versailles. Ironically, Molière suffered a fatal hemorrhage while performing the title role of the hypochondriac in his play, *The Imaginary Invalid;* he finished the performance and died shortly thereafter.

Building Background

Type Casting The rollicking Italian plays popular around the 1500s in Italy and later throughout Europe were known as ***commedia dell'arte*** (kə mā′dē ə del är′tā). Actors (all male) loosely followed a basic script, making up dialogue as they went along. The lively plots often involved love affairs and intrigue and always involved deception. But it was the broadly comic characters that stole the show. These characters included such basic types as Harlequin the clown and Pantaloon the wise old man. The wily servant, whom you are about to encounter in *The Flying Doctor,* was also a popular character type.

Literary Focus

Farce Comedy that involves improbable situations, exaggerated characters, and slapstick action is called **farce**. You can watch this type of comedy in old Marx Brothers or Three Stooges movies. As you read the following play by Molière, look for ways that the writer achieves this broad comedy.

Writer's Notebook

Where's the Plot?

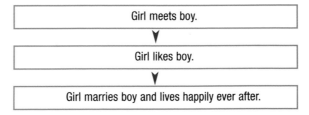

A story with this kind of plot wouldn't have much appeal. Audiences cheer love fulfilled, but only after a hard-won battle. Now if the boy's father objected to this match, or if the girl were already engaged, or if there were a serious misunderstanding between them, or an earthquake. . . . In your notebook, suggest a few plot twists to this basic pattern that would make this story outline more exciting.

The Flying

These models created by Franz Anton Bustelli around 1760 represent the classic *commedia dell'arte* figures of Harlequin and Columbine. What do their costumes, expressions, and poses suggest about the characters they represent? ➤

Molière

CHARACTERS

GORGIBUS (gôr′jə bəs), *a respectable but simple-minded citizen*
LUCILE *daughter of Gorgibus*
SABINE (sä bēn′), *niece of Gorgibus*
VALÈRE (vä lär′), *young man in love with Lucile*
SGANARELLE (sga′nə rel′), *servant to Valère*
GROS-RENÉ (grō′rə nā), *servant to Gorgibus*
A LAWYER

Scene. *A street in a small French town.*

VALÈRE, *a young man, is talking to* SABINE, *a young woman, in front of the house of* GORGIBUS, *her uncle.*

VALÈRE. Sabine, what do you advise me to do?

SABINE. We'll have to work fast. My uncle is determined to make Lucile marry this rich man, Villebrequin, and he's pushed the preparations so far that the marriage would have taken place today if my cousin were not in love with you. But she is—she has told me so—and since my greedy uncle is forcing our hand, we've come up with a device[1] for putting off the wedding. Lucile is pretending to be ill, and the old man, who'll believe almost anything, has sent me for a doctor. If you have a friend we can trust, I'll take him to my uncle and he can suggest that Lucile is not getting nearly enough fresh air. The old boy will then let her live in the pavilion[2] at the end of our garden, and you can meet her secretly, marry her, and leave my uncle to take out his anger on Villebrequin.

VALÈRE. But where can I find a doctor who will be sympathetic to me and risk his reputation? Frankly, I can't think of a single one.

---

1. **device** (di vīs′), *n.* plan, scheme, or trick.
2. **pavilion** (pə vil′yən), *n.* summer house.

SABINE. I was wondering if you could disguise your valet? It'll be easy for him to fool the old man.

VALÈRE. If you knew my valet as I do—He's so dense he'll ruin everything. Still, I can't think of anybody else. I'll try to find him. (SABINE *leaves*.) Where can I start to look for the halfwit? (SGANARELLE *comes in, playing intently with a yo-yo*.) Sganarelle, my dear boy, I'm delighted to see you. I need you for an important assignment. But I don't know what you can do—

SGANARELLE. Don't worry, Master, I can do anything. I can handle any assignment, especially important ones. Give me a difficult job. Ask me to find out what time it is. Or to check on the price of butter at the market. Or to water your horse. You'll soon see what I can do.

VALÈRE. This is more complicated. I want you to impersonate[3] a doctor.

SGANARELLE. A doctor! You know I'll do anything you want, Master, but when it comes to impersonating a doctor, I couldn't do it if I tried—wouldn't know how to start. I think you're making fun of me.

VALÈRE. If you care to try, I'll give you one hundred francs.[4]

SGANARELLE. One hundred whole francs, just for pretending to be a doctor? No, Master, it's impossible. You see I don't have the brains for it. I'm not subtle enough; I'm not even bright. So that's settled. I impersonate a doctor. Where?

VALÈRE. You know Gorgibus? His daughter is lying in there ill—No, it's no use; you'll only confuse matters.

SGANARELLE. I bet I can confuse matters as well as all the doctors in this town put together. Or kill patients as easily. You know the old saying, "After you're dead, the doctor comes." When I take a hand there'll be a new saying: "After the doctor comes, you're dead." Now I think it over, though, it's not that easy to play a doctor. What if something goes wrong?

VALÈRE. What can go wrong? Gorgibus is a simple man, not to say stupid, and you can dazzle him by talking about Hippocrates and Galen.[5] Put on a bold front.

SGANARELLE. In other words, talk about philosophy and mathematics and the like. Leave it to me, Master; if he's a fool, as you say, I think I can swing it. All I need is a doctor's cloak and a few instructions. And also my license to practice, or to put it another way, those hundred francs. (*They go out together.*)

(GORGIBUS *enters with his fat valet,* GROS-RENÉ.)

GORGIBUS. Hurry away and find a doctor. My daughter's sick. Hurry.

GROS-RENÉ. Hell's bells, the trouble is you're trying to marry her off to an old man when she wants a young man; that's the only thing making her sick. Don't you see any connection between the appetite and the illness?

GORGIBUS. I can see that the illness will delay the wedding. Get a move on.

GROS-RENÉ. All this running about and my stomach's crying out for a new inner lining of food and now I have to wait for it. I need the doctor for myself as much as for your daughter. I'm in a desperate state. (*He lumbers off.*)

(SABINE *comes in with* SGANARELLE *behind her.*)

SABINE. Uncle, I have good news. I've brought a remarkably skilled doctor with me, a man who has traveled across the world and knows the medical secrets of Asia and Africa. He'll certainly be able to cure Lucile. As luck would have it, somebody pointed him out to me and I knew you'd want to meet him. He's

---

3. impersonate (im pėr′sə nāt), *v.* pretend to be.
4. **one hundred francs** presently worth about $20.
5. **Hippocrates** (hi pok′rə tēz′, 460?-370 B.C.?) . . . **Galen** (gā′lən; A.D. 138-201?), Ancient Greek physicians.

Created in the late 1600s, this painting portrays various actors who appeared at the Théatre Royal in Paris. Molière is at the far left. Judging from the painting, what inferences can you make about the entertainment and characters popular at the time? ➤

so clever that I wish I were ill myself so that he could cure me.

GORGIBUS. Where is he?

SABINE. Standing right behind me. *(She moves away.)* There he is.

GORGIBUS. Thank you so much for coming, Doctor. I'll take you straight to my daughter, who is unwell. I'm putting all my trust in you.

SGANARELLE. Hippocrates has said—and Galen has confirmed it with many persuasive arguments—that when a girl is not in good health she must be sick. You are right to put your trust in me, for I am the greatest, the most brilliant, the most doctoral physician in the vegetable, mineral, and animal kingdoms.

GORGIBUS. I'm overjoyed to hear it.

SGANARELLE. No ordinary physician am I, no common medico. In my opinion, all others are quacks. I have peculiar talents. I have secrets. *Salamalec* and *shalom aleichem. Nil nisi bonum? Si, Signor. Nein, mein Herr. Para siempre.*[6] But let us begin. *(He takes GORGIBUS's pulse.)*

SABINE. He's not the patient. His daughter is. . . . She may be up by now. I'll bring her out. *(She goes into the house and brings LUCILE back with her.)*

SGANARELLE. How do you do, Mademoiselle?

---

6. *Salamalec . . . siempre*, words in several languages jumbled together with no meaning.

So you are sick?

LUCILE. Yes, Doctor.

SGANARELLE. That is a striking sign that you are not well. Do you feel pains in your head, in your kidneys?

LUCILE. Yes, Doctor.

SGANARELLE. Very good. As one great physician has said in regard to the nature of animal life—well—he said many things. We must attribute[7] this to the interconnections between the humors and the vapors.[8] For example, since melancholy is the natural enemy of joy, and since the bile that spreads through the body makes us turn yellow, and since there is nothing more inimical[9] to good health than sickness, we may conclude with that great man that your daughter is indisposed. Let me write you a prescription.

GORGIBUS. Quick! A table, paper, some ink—

SGANARELLE. Is there anybody here who knows how to write?

GORGIBUS. Don't you?

SGANARELLE. I have so many things to think of I forget half of them. Now it's obvious to me that your daughter needs fresh air and open prospects.

GORGIBUS. We have a very beautiful garden and a pavilion with some rooms that look out on it. If you agree, I can have her stay there.

SGANARELLE. Let us examine this dwelling. *(They start to go out. The* LAWYER *appears.)*

LAWYER. Monsieur Gorgibus—

GORGIBUS. Your servant, Monsieur.

LAWYER. I hear that your daughter is sick. May I offer my services, as a friend of the family?

GORGIBUS. I have the most scholarly doctor you ever met looking into this.

LAWYER. Really? I wonder if I might be able to meet him, however briefly?

*(*GORGIBUS *beckons to* SGANARELLE. LUCILE *and* SABINE *have moved offstage.)*

GORGIBUS. Doctor, I would like you to meet one of my dear friends, who is a lawyer and would like the privilege of conversing with you.

SGANARELLE. I wish I could spare the time, Monsieur, but I dare not neglect my patients. Please forgive me. *(He tries to go. The lawyer holds his sleeve.)*

LAWYER. My friend Gorgibus has intimated,[10] Monsieur, that your learning and abilities are formidable, and I am honored to make your acquaintance. I therefore take the liberty of saluting you in your noble work, and trust that it may resolve itself well. Those who excel in any branch of knowledge are worthy of all praise, but particularly those who practice medicine, not only because of its utility, but because it contains within itself other branches of knowledge, all of which render a perfect familiarity with it almost impossible to achieve. As Hippocrates so well observes in his first aphorism,[11] "Life is short, art is long, opportunity fleeting, experiment perilous, judgment difficult: *Vita brevis, ars vero longa, occasio autem praeceps, experimentum periculosum, judicium difficile.*"[12]

SGANARELLE *(confidentially to* GORGIBUS*).* Ficile, bicile, uptus, downtus, inandaboutus, wrigglo, gigolo.[13]

LAWYER. You are not one of those doctors who apply themselves to so-called rational or dogmatic medicine, and I am sure that you conduct your work with unusual success. Experience is the great teacher: *experientia magistra rerum.* The first men who practiced medicine were so esteemed that their daily cures earned them the status of gods on earth. One must not condemn a doctor who does not restore his patients to health, for healing

---

7. **attribute** (ə trib′yŭt), *v.* think of as caused by.
8. **the humors and the vapors**, body fluids and gases once considered responsible for health and mood.
9. **inimical** (in im′ə kəl), *adj.* unfavorable.
10. **intimate** (in′tə māt), *v.* hint.
11. **aphorism** (af′ə riz′əm), *n.* brief statement expressing a truth.
12. *Vita brevis . . . difficile*, Latin translation of the lawyer's observation, "Life is short . . . judgment difficult."
13. **Ficile . . . gigolo**, nonsense words made to sound like Latin.

may not be effected by his remedies and wisdom alone. Ovid[14] remarks, "Sometimes the ill is stronger than art and learning combined." Monsieur, I will not detain you longer. I have enjoyed this dialogue and am more impressed than before with your percipience[15] and breadth of knowledge. I take my leave, hoping that I may have the pleasure of conversing with you further at your leisure. I am sure that your time is precious, and . . .

(He goes off, walking backwards, still talking, waving good-bye.)

GORGIBUS. How did he strike you?

SGANARELLE. He's moderately well informed. If I had more time I could engage him in a spirited discussion on some sublime and elevated topic. However, I must go. What is this?

*(*GORGIBUS* is tucking some money into his hand.)*

GORGIBUS. Believe me, Doctor, I know how much I owe you.

SGANARELLE. You must be joking, Monsieur Gorgibus. I am no mercenary. *(He takes the money.)* Thank you very much.

*(*GORGIBUS* goes off, and *SGANARELLE* drops his doctor's cloak and hat at the edge of the stage, just as *VALÈRE* reappears.)*

VALÈRE. Sganarelle, how did it go? I've been worried. I was looking for you. Did you ruin the plan?

SGANARELLE. Marvel of marvels. I played the part so well that Gorgibus thought I knew what I was talking about—and paid me. I looked at his home and told him that his daughter needed air, and he's moved her into the little house at the far end of his garden. You can visit her at your pleasure.

VALÈRE. You've made me very happy, Sganarelle. I'm going to her now. *(He rushes away.)*

SGANARELLE. That Gorgibus is a bigger dimwit than I am to let me get away with a trick like that. Save me—here he comes again. I'll have to talk fast. *(*GORGIBUS* returns.)*

GORGIBUS. Good morning, Monsieur.

SGANARELLE. Monsieur, you see before you a poor lad in despair. Have you come across a doctor who arrived in town a short while ago and cures people miraculously?

GORGIBUS. Yes, I've met him. He just left my house.

SGANARELLE. I am his brother. We are identical twins and people sometimes take one of us for the other.

GORGIBUS. Heaven help me if I didn't nearly make the same mistake. What is your name?

SGANARELLE. Narcissus, Monsieur, at your service. I should explain that once, when I was in his study, I accidentally knocked over two containers perched on the edge of his table. He flew into such a rage that he threw me out and swore he never wanted to see me again. So here I am now, a poor boy without means or connections.

GORGIBUS. Don't worry; I'll put in a good word for you. I'm a friend of his; I promise to bring you together again. As soon as I see him, I'll speak to him about it.

SGANARELLE. I am very much obliged to you, Monsieur.

(He goes out and reappears in the cloak and hat, playing the doctor again and talking to himself.)

When patients refuse to follow their doctor's advice and abandon themselves to debauchery[16] and—

GORGIBUS. Doctor, your humble servant. May I ask a favor of you?

SGANARELLE. What can I do for you, Monsieur Gorgibus?

GORGIBUS. I just happened to meet your brother, who is quite distressed—

SGANARELLE. He's a rascal, Monsieur Gorgibus.

GORGIBUS. But he truly regrets that he made you so angry, and—

SGANARELLE. He's a drunkard, Monsieur Gorgibus.

---

14. **Ovid** (43 B.C.-A.D.17), Roman poet.
15. **percipience** (pər sip′ē əns), *n.* shrewdness; ability to perceive.
16. **debauchery** (di bô′chər ē), *n.* corruption.

GORGIBUS. But surely, Doctor, you're not going to give the poor boy up?

SGANARELLE. Not another word about him. The impudence of the rogue, seeking you out to intercede for him! I implore you not to mention him to me.

GORGIBUS. In God's name, Doctor, and out of respect for me, too, have pity on him. I'll do anything for you in return. I promised—

SGANARELLE. You plead so insistently that, even though I swore a violent oath never to forgive him—well, I'll shake your hand on it; I forgive him. You can be assured that I am doing myself a great injury and that I would not have consented to this for any other man. Good-bye, Monsieur Gorgibus.

GORGIBUS. Thank you, Doctor, thank you. I'll go off and look for the boy to tell him the glad news.

(*He walks off.* SGANARELLE *takes off the doctor's cloak and hat.* VALÈRE *appears.*)

VALÈRE. I never thought Sganarelle would do his duty so magnificently. Ah, my dear boy, I don't know how to repay you. I'm so happy I—

SGANARELLE. It's easy for you to talk. Gorgibus just ran into me without my doctor's outfit, and if I hadn't come up with a quick story we'd have been sunk. Here he comes again. Disappear.

(VALÈRE *runs away.* GORGIBUS *returns.*)

GORGIBUS. Narcissus, I've been looking everywhere for you. I spoke to your brother and he forgives you. But to be safe, I want to see the two of you patch up your quarrel in front of me. Wait here in my house, and I'll find him.

SGANARELLE. I don't think you'll find him, Monsieur. Anyhow, I wouldn't dare to wait; I'm terrified of him.

GORGIBUS (*pushing* SGANARELLE *inside*). Yes, you will stay. I'm locking you in. Don't be afraid of your brother. I promise you that he's not angry now.

(*He slams the door and locks it, then goes off to look for the doctor.*)

SGANARELLE (*at the upstairs window*). Serves me right; I trapped myself and there's no way out. The weather in my future looks threatening, and if there's a storm I'm afraid I'll feel a rain of blows on my back. Or else they'll brand me across the shoulders with a whip—not exactly the brand of medicine any doctor ever prescribed. Yes, I'm in trouble. But why give up when we've come this far? Let's go the limit. I can still make a bid for freedom and prove that Sganarelle is the king of swindlers.

(*He holds his nose, closes his eyes, and jumps to the ground, just as* GROS-RENÉ *comes back. Then he darts away, picking up the cloak and hat.* GROS-RENÉ *stands staring.*)

GROS-RENÉ. A flying man! What a laugh! I'll wait around and see if there's another one.

(GORGIBUS *reenters with* SGANARELLE *following him in the doctor's outfit.*)

GORGIBUS. Can't find that doctor. Where the devil has he hidden himself?

(*He turns and* SGANARELLE *walks into him.*)

There you are. Now, Doctor, I know you said you forgive your brother, but that's not enough. I won't be satisfied until I see you embrace him. He's waiting here in my house.

SGANARELLE. You are joking. Monsieur Gorgibus. Have I not extended myself enough already? I wish never to see him again.

GORGIBUS. Please, Doctor, for me.

SGANARELLE. I cannot refuse when you ask me like that. Tell him to come down.

(*As* GORGIBUS *goes into the house,* SGANARELLE *drops the clothes, clambers swiftly up to the window again, and scrambles inside.*)

GORGIBUS (*at the window*). Your brother is waiting for you downstairs, Narcissus. He said he'd do what I asked.

SGANARELLE (*at the window*). Couldn't you please make him come up here? I beg of you—let me see him in private to ask his forgiveness, because if I go down there he'll show me up and say nasty things to me in front of everybody.

GORGIBUS. All right. Let me tell him. *(He leaves the window, and* SGANARELLE *leaps out, swiftly puts on his outfit again, and stands waiting for* GORGIBUS *outside the door.)* Doctor, he's so ashamed of himself he wants to beg your forgiveness in private, upstairs. Here's the key. Please don't refuse me.

SGANARELLE. There is nothing I would not do for you, Monsieur Gorgibus. You will hear how I deal with him.

(He walks into the house and soon appears at the window. GORGIBUS *has his ear cocked at the door below.* SGANARELLE *alternates his voice, playing the characters one at a time.)*

SGANARELLE. So there you are, you scoundrel!
—Brother, listen to me, please. I'm sorry I knocked those containers over—
—You clumsy ox
—It wasn't my fault, I swear it.
—Not your fault, you bumpkin? I'll teach you to destroy my work.
—Brother, no, please—
—I'll teach you to trade on Monsieur Gorgibus's good nature. How dare you ask him to ask me to forgive you!
—Brother, I'm sorry, but—
—Silence, you dog!
—I never wanted to hurt you or—
—Silence, I say—

GROS-RENÉ. What exactly do you think is going on up there?

GORGIBUS. It's the doctor and his brother, Narcissus. They had a little disagreement, but now they're making it up.

GROS-RENÉ. Doctor and his brother? But there's only one man.

SGANARELLE *(at the window).* Yes, you drunkard. I'll thump some good behavior into you. *(Pretends to strike a blow.)* Ah, he's lowering his eyes; he knows what he's done wrong, the jailbird. And now this hypocrite wants to play the good apostle—

GROS-RENÉ. Just for fun, tell him to let his brother appear at the window.

GORGIBUS. I will. (*To* SGANARELLE.) Doctor, let me see your brother for a moment.

SGANARELLE. He is not fit to be seen by an honest gentleman like yourself. Besides, I cannot bear to have him next to me.

GORGIBUS. Please don't say no, after all you've done for me.

SGANARELLE. Monsieur Gorgibus, you have such power over me that I must grant whatever you wish. Show yourself, beast!

(He appears at the window as Narcissus.) Monsieur Gorgibus, I thank you for your kindness.

(He reappears as the doctor.) Well, Monsieur, did you take a good look at that image of impurity?

GROS-RENÉ. There's only one man there, Monsieur. We can prove it. Tell them to stand by the window together.

GORGIBUS. Doctor, I want to see you at the window embracing your brother, and then I'll be satisfied.

SGANARELLE. To any other man in the world I would return a swift and negative answer, but to you, Monsieur Gorgibus, I will yield, although not without much pain to myself. But first I want this knave to beg your pardon for all the trouble he has caused you.

(He comes back as Narcissus.) Yes, Monsieur Gorgibus, I beg your pardon for having bothered you, and I promise you, brother, in front of Monsieur Gorgibus there, that I'll be so good from now on that you'll never be angry with me again. Please let bygones be bygones.

(He embraces the cloak and hat.)

GORGIBUS. There they are, the two of them together.

GROS-RENÉ. The man's a magician.

(He hides; SGANARELLE *comes out of the house, dressed as the doctor.)*

SGANARELLE. Here is your key, Monsieur. I have left my brother inside because I am ashamed of him. One does not wish to be seen in his company now that one has some reputation in this town. You may release him whenever you think fit. Good-bye, Monsieur.

(He strides off; then as GORGIBUS *goes into the house he wheels, dropping the cloak and hat, and climbs back through the window.)*

GORGIBUS *(upstairs).* There you are, my boy, you're free. I am pleased that your brother forgave you, although I think he was rather hard on you.

SGANARELLE. Monsieur, I cannot thank you enough. A brother's blessing on you. I will remember you all my life.

(While they are upstairs, GROS-RENÉ *has picked up the cloak and hat, and stands waiting for them. They come out of the door.)*

GROS-RENÉ. Well, where do you think your doctor is now?

GORGIBUS. Gone, of course.

GROS-RENÉ. He's right here, under my arm. And by the way, while this fellow was getting in and out of the cloak, the hat, and the window, Valère ran off with your daughter and married her.

GORGIBUS. I'm ruined!

Harlequin and Columbine are stock characters who represent, respectively, the amusing, goodnatured servant and the saucy, clever young woman. From a modern **perspective**, what character types can you identify from comics, TV, or movies? ➤

I'll have you strung up, you dog, you knave! Yes, you deserve every name your brother called you— What am I saying?

SGANARELLE. You don't really want to string me up, do you, Monsieur? Please listen for one second. It's true that I was having a game with you while my master was with Mademoiselle Lucile. But in serving him I haven't done you any harm. He's a most suitable partner for her, by rank and by income, by God. Believe me, if you make a row about this you'll only bring more confusion on your head. As for that porker there, let him get lost and take Villebrequin with him. Here come our loving couple.

*(*VALÈRE *enters contritely with* LUCILE. *They kneel to* GORGIBUS.)*

VALÈRE. We apologize to you.

GORGIBUS. Well, perhaps it's lucky that I was tricked by Sganarelle; he's brought me a fine son-in-law. Let's go out to celebrate the marriage and drink a toast to the health of all the company.

(They dance off in couples: VALÈRE *with* LUCILE, GORGIBUS *with* GROS-RENÉ, *and* SGANARELLE *with* SABINE.)

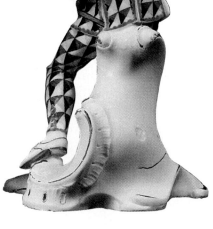

After Reading

Making Connections

Shaping Your Response

1. Do you think modern audiences are too sophisticated to enjoy Molière's slapstick humor? Why or why not?

2. In your notebook, write three words that describe Sganarelle.

3. Do you consider this a play about love or about something else? Explain.

Analyzing the Play

4. When asked to impersonate a doctor, Sganarelle says, ". . . I don't have the brains for it. I'm not subtle enough; I'm not even bright." Do you agree with his self-appraisal? Explain.

5. How would you **characterize** Gorgibus?

6. What do the following **stage directions** indicate about the Lawyer: *"He goes off, walking backwards, still talking, waving good-bye"*?

7. How does this play illustrate the **theme** "Beneath the Surface"?

8. What aspects of the medical and legal professions does Molière **satirize** in this play?

9. Which characters do you think represent **stereotypes**?

Extending the Ideas

10. Compare *The Flying Doctor* to other works of literature (perhaps ones appearing in this book), movies, or TV programs that satirize human qualities such as greed, hypocrisy, or vanity.

Literary Focus: Farce

A type of comedy that involves broad characters, unlikely situations, and slapstick action is called **farce.** Farce relies heavily on fast pacing, exaggeration, and physical action and often includes mistaken identity and deception. In the hands of Molière, farce is a vehicle for exposing human faults and absurd social customs. Find examples of each of the following in *The Flying Doctor.*

- mistaken identity
- deception
- slapstick action
- broad characters

Vocabulary Study

Use context clues to complete each sentence with one of the listed words. Not all the words will be used.

aphorism
attribute
debauchery
device
impersonate
inimical

1. In the farces of Molière, there is often a scheme, or ____, by which to trick a foolish person.

2. Lovers usually overcome ____ circumstances and are eventually united despite unfavorable odds.

3. Molière satirizes ____ in corrupt individuals.

4. Although people often ____ the kind of comedy we call farce to Molière, it existed many centuries before he lived.

5. Do you find it humorous that a lowly servant could ____ a doctor so well?

Expressing Your Ideas

Writing Choices

Writer's Notebook Update Look at the plot twists you suggested. Do you have material for an interesting love story? Maybe, maybe not. Try writing an opening paragraph that would make a reader want to continue. You may have the beginnings of a farce!

Be a Critic Work with a partner, with each of you writing a **review** of the play: one designed to attract an audience, the other designed to keep people away. You might get some ideas of how to sway an audience by reading current film or drama reviews.

Comic Twist In a group, take any story from this book that you think lends itself to comedy and **rewrite** the first page or two as a dramatic farce, complete with stage directions.

Other Choices

Broad Strokes The broadly drawn characters in *The Flying Doctor* lend themselves to artistic expressions. Choose a character to represent in a **caricature,** or exaggerated sketch.

Walk This Way, Sir Review some movies of the Marx brothers, the Three Stooges, or other comedians who are noted for their broad comedy. Make a list of gags that recur throughout such works, such as puns and slapstick like slipping on a banana peel. Work with a small group to put on a **comedy skit** using visual and verbal tricks of comedy.

Before Reading

The Chameleon by Anton Chekhov   Russia
The Fox and the Woodcutter by Aesop   Greece
A Poison Tree by William Blake   Great Britain

Building Background

Nothing But the Truth Do you associate truthfulness more with certain professions than with others? Conduct a quick survey to determine which professions classmates associate with truthfulness. How did politicians fare? Are some of the class's opinions based on stereotypical assumptions? Are professionals who are in the public eye more likely to appear dishonest? Are elected officials under more pressure than other professionals to please people? After a discussion, prepare to read about a political figure who acts in his own best interests.

Literary Focus

Tone The **tone** of a selection is the attitude of the writer toward his or her subject. An author communicates a tone, such as awe, anger, fear, humor, and cynicism, through word choice and in the arrangement of ideas, events, and descriptions. As you read "The Chameleon," "The Fox and the Woodcutter," and "A Poison Tree," try to determine each author's attitude toward his subject.

Writer's Notebook

False Fronts Everyone has at some time presented a false front, appearing to be or to feel something that is not authentic. It may have been to save face, to avoid hurting someone's feelings, or to avoid consequences. Think of one such incident and write about the circumstances and your feelings at the time.

Anton Chekhov
1860–1904

Anton Chekhov grew up in Taganrog, Russia, in the era when czars still ruled the Russian empire. He enrolled in medical school in 1879 and supported his family by writing for magazines and newspapers. Friends and relatives, he observed, "were always condescending toward my writing and constantly advised me in a friendly way not to give up real work [medicine] for scribbling." Nevertheless, he began earning a literary reputation, writing stories and plays about characters caught up in poverty, love, family struggles, and old-world class distinctions. Many of his stories and plays such as *The Cherry Orchard, Uncle Vanya,* and *Three Sisters* have become modern classics.

Aesop
620?–560? B.C.

Although it is not known for certain whether the man Aesop (ē′səp) ever really lived, the most prevalent theory is that he was a slave whose witty stories and tales about animals eventually earned him his freedom. Traveling throughout Greece and Egypt during times of political tyranny, Aesop told fables that barely disguised his political views. His wit and ingenuity usually got him out of tricky situations, but his luck ran out at Delphi when someone planted a gold cup in his bag. After being condemned to death and thrown off a cliff, numerous disasters occurred in Delphi until the citizens made public reparation to Aesop's memory.

William Blake
1757–1827

William Blake received no formal schooling, but "picked up his education as well as he could" by studying Shakespeare, Milton, and the Bible. At fourteen he was apprenticed as an engraver in London and also began writing verse, printing it by himself from engraved copper plates with hand-colored illustrations. Judged by some of his contemporaries to be insane, Blake was recognized as a poetic genius by later generations. His friends, however, appreciated his gifts. As his friend Edward Calvert said, "He was not mad, but perverse and willful; he reasoned correctly from arbitrary, and often false premises."

The Chameleon

Anton Chekhov

Across the market square comes Police Inspector Moronoff. He is wearing a new greatcoat and carrying a small package. Behind him strides a ginger-headed constable bearing a sieve filled to the brim with confiscated[1] gooseberries. There is silence all around . . . Not a soul in the square . . . The wide-open doors of the shops and taverns look out dolefully[2] on the world, like hungry jaws; even their beggars have vanished.

"Bite me, would you, you little devil?" Moronoff suddenly hears. "Catch him, lads, catch him! Biting's against the law now! Grab him! Ouch!"

A dog squeals. Moronoff looks round—and sees a dog run out of merchant Spatchkin's woodyard, hopping along on three legs and glancing backwards. A man in a starched calico shirt and unbuttoned waistcoat comes chasing out after it. He runs behind, bends down right over it, and tumbles to the ground catching the dog by the hind legs. There is another squeal and a shout: "Hold him, lads!" Sleepy countenances[3] thrust themselves out of the shop windows and soon a crowd has sprung up from nowhere by the woodyard.

"Looks like trouble, your honor!" says the constable.

Moronoff executes a half-turn to his left and marches towards the throng. He sees the aforementioned man in the unbuttoned shirt is standing at the yard gates and with his right hand raised high in the air is showing the crowd a blood-stained finger. His half-sozzled face seems to be saying "You'll pay for this, you scoundrel!" and his very finger has the air of a victory banner. Moronoff recognizes the man as Grunkin the goldsmith. On the ground in the midst of the crowd, its front legs splayed out and its whole body trembling, sits the actual cause of the commotion; a white borzoi[4] puppy with a pointed muzzle and a yellow patch on its back. The expression in its watering eyes is one of terror and despair.

"What's all this about?" asks Moronoff, cut-

---

1. **confiscated** (kon′fə skāt ed), *adj.* seized; taken.
2. **dolefully** (dōl′fəl lē), *adv.* mournfully.
3. **countenance** (koun′tə nəns), *n.* expression of the face.
4. **borzoi** (bôr′zoi), *n.* any of a breed of tall, slender, swift dogs with silky hair, developed in Russia; Russian wolfhound.

ting through the crowd. "Why are you lot here? What's your finger—? Who shouted just now?"

"I was walking along, your honor, minding me own business . . ." Grunkin begins, giving a slight cough, "on my way to see Mitry Mitrich about some firewood—when all of a sudden, for no reason, this little tyke goes for my finger . . . Beg pardon, sir, but I'm a man what's working . . . My work's delicate work. I want compensation[5] for this—after all, I may not be able to lift this finger for a week now . . . There's nothing in the law even that says we have to put up with that from beasts, is there your honor? If we all went round biting, we might as well be dead . . ."

"Hm! All right . . ." says Moronoff sternly, clearing his throat and knitting his brows, "Right . . . Who owns this dog? I shall not let this matter rest. I'll teach you to let dogs run loose! It's time we took a closer look at these people who won't obey regulations! A good fat fine'll teach the blighter[6] what I think of dogs and suchlike vagrant cattle! I'll take him down a peg! Dildin," says the inspector, turning to the constable, "find out who owns this dog, and take a statement! And the dog must be put down. Forthwith! It's probably mad anyway . . . Come on then, who's the owner?"

"Looks like General Tartaroff's!" says a voice from the crowd.

"General Tartaroff's? Hm . . . Dildin, remove my coat for me, will you? . . . Phew it's hot! We must be in for rain . . . What I don't understand, though, is this: how did it manage to bite you?" says Moronoff, turning to Grunkin. "How could it reach up to your finger? A little dog like that, and a hulking great bloke like you! I expect what happened was, you skinned your finger on a nail, then had the bright idea of making some money out of it. I know your lot! You devils don't fool me!"

CLARIFY: What do you think causes Moronoff's change in tone?

"He shoved a fag in its mug for a lark, your honor, but she weren't having any and went for him . . . He's always stirring up trouble, your honor!"

"Don't lie, Boss-Eye! You couldn't see, so why tell lies? His honor here's a clever gent, he knows who's lying and who's telling the gospel truth . . . And if he thinks I'm lying, then let the justice decide. He's got it all written down there in the law . . . We're all equal now . . . I've got a brother myself who's in the police . . . you may like to know—"

"Stop arguing!"

"No, it's not the General's . . ." the constable observes profoundly.[7] "The General ain't got any like this. His are more setters . . ."

"Are you sure of that?"

"Quite sure, your honor—"

"Well of course I know that, too. The General has dogs that are worth something, thoroughbreds, but this is goodness knows what! It's got no coat, it's nothing to look at—just a load of rubbish . . . Do you seriously think he'd keep a dog like that? Use your brains. You know what'd happen if a dog like that turned up in Petersburg or Moscow? They wouldn't bother looking in the law books, they'd dispatch him— double quick! You've got a grievance,[8] Grunkin, and you mustn't let the matter rest . . . Teach 'em a lesson! It's high time . . ."

"Could be the General's, though . . ." muses[9] the constable aloud. "It ain't written on its snout . . . I did see one like that in his yard the

---

5. compensation (kom′pən sā′shən), *n.* something given to make up for a loss or injury.
6. **blighter** (blīt′er), *n.* rascal.
7. profoundly (prə found′lē), *adv.* going more deeply than what is easily understood.
8. grievance (grē′vəns), *n.* a cause for complaint.
9. muse (myüz), *v.* say thoughtfully.

Boris Kustodiev's political caricature, produced in 1906, satirizes a Russian government official. Find a contemporary political cartoon that uses similar broad strokes to poke fun at a public figure. ➤

№ 3

1906
Годъ 1

АДСКАЯ ПОЧТА

ЦѢНА
15к

ОЛИМПЪ

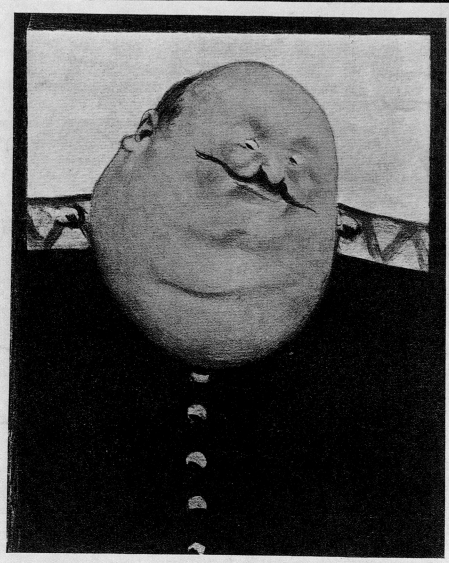

ГРАФЪ ИГНАТЬЕВЪ

snout . . . I did see one like that in his yard the other day."

"Course it's the General's!" says a voice from the crowd.

"Hm . . . Help me on with my coat, Dildin old chap . . . There's a bit of a breeze got up . . . It's quite chilly . . . Right, take this dog to the General's and ask them there. Say I found it and am sending it back. And tell them not to let it out on the street in future. It may be worth a lot, and if every swine is going to poke cigarettes up its nose, it won't be for much longer. A dog's a delicate creature . . . And you put your hand down, you oaf! Stop showing your stupid finger off! It was all your own fault!"

"Here comes the General's cook, let's ask him . . . Hey, Prokhor! Come over here a moment, will you? Take a look at this dog . . . One of yours, is it?"

"You must be joking! We've never had none like that!"

"Right, we can stop making enquiries," says Moronoff. "It's a stray! We can cut the chat . . . If everyone says it's a stray, it is a stray . . . So that's that, it must be put down."

"No, it's not one of ours," Prokhor continues. "It belongs to the General's brother what come down the other day. Our General don't go much on borzois. His brother does, though—"

"You mean to say his Excellency's brother's arrived? Vladimir Ivanych?"[10] asks Moronoff, his

---

A dog's a delicate creature . . .

---

face breaking into an ecstatic[11] smile. "Well blow me down! And I didn't know! Come for a little stay, has he?"

"He's on a visit . . ."

"Well I never . . . So he felt like seeing his dear old brother again . . . And fancy me not knowing! So it's his little dog, is it? Jolly good . . . Take him away with you, then . . . He's a good little doggie . . . Pretty quick off the mark, too . . . Took a bite out of this bloke's finger—ha, ha, ha! No need to shiver, little chap! 'Grr-rrr'. . . He's angry, the rascal . . . the little scamp . . .'"

EVALUATE: Do you think Moronoff displays the qualities of an effective politician? Explain.

Prokhor calls the dog over and it follows him out of the woodyard . . .The crowd roars with laughter at Grunkin.

"I'll deal with you later!" Moronoff threatens him, and wrapping his greatcoat tightly round him, resumes his progress across the market square.

---

10. **Vladimir Ivanych** (vlad′ə mir ē von′ich), a Russian name meaning "Vladimir, son of Ivan."
11. ecstatic (ek stat′ik), *adj.* feeling great joy.

The Fox and the Woodcutter

Aesop

A fox was fleeing. As she fled
A hunter fast behind her sped.
But being wearied, when she spied
An old man cutting wood, she cried,
5 "By all the gods that keep you well,
Hide me among these trees you fell,
And don't reveal the place, I pray."
He swore that he would not betray
The wily[1] vixen;[2] so she hid,
10 And then the hunter came to bid
The old man tell him if she'd fled,
Or if she'd hidden there. He said,
"I did not see her," but he showed
The place the cunning beast was stowed
15 By pointing at it with his finger.
But still the hunter did not linger.
He put no faith in leering eye,
But trusting in the words, went by.
Escaped from danger for a while
20 The fox peeked out with coaxing smile.
The old man said to her, "You owe
Me thanks for saving you, you know."
"Most certainly; for I was there
As witness of your expert care.
25 But now farewell. And don't forget,
The god of oaths will catch you yet
For saving with your voice and lips
While slaying with your finger tips."

---

1. wily (wī′lē), *adj.* crafty; sly.
2. vixen (vik′sən), *n.* a female fox.

A Poison Tree

William Blake

▲ This contemporary illustration by Guy Billout hints at death lurking in the shadows of life. How does he highlight these contrasts?

I was angry with my friend:
I told my wrath,[1] my wrath did end.
I was angry with my foe:
I told it not, my wrath did grow.

5 And I water'd it in fears,
Night & morning with my tears;
And I sunnèd it with smiles,
And with soft deceitful wiles.

And it grew both day and night,
10 Till it bore an apple bright.
And my foe beheld it shine,
And he knew that it was mine,

And into my garden stole,
When the night had veil'd the pole;[2]
15 In the morning glad I see
My foe outstretch'd beneath the tree.

---

1. wrath (rath), *n.* very great anger; rage.
2. **night had veil'd the pole**, night had covered one half of the earth, including the North Pole.

After Reading

Making Connections

Shaping Your Response

1. Copy the spectrum below into your notebook and mark where you think Inspector Moronoff falls. Be prepared to explain your response.

   trustworthy ⟵⟶ undependable

2. Do you think that Moronoff's name and the picture of him on page 285 provide a good portrayal of his character? Why or why not?

3. In your opinion, which character commits the worst offense — Inspector Moronoff in "The Chameleon," the old man in "The Fox and the Woodcutter," or the speaker in "A Poison Tree"? Explain your thinking.

Analyzing the Selections

4. How do Moronoff's activities with his coat comically reflect his **character?**

5. "The Chameleon" uses **satire**, a way of poking fun at individuals or society to expose weaknesses or evils, to comment on a type of public official. What kind of person do you think the author is satirizing?

6. Why do you think Chekhov chose "The Chameleon" as the **title** of this story?

7. Do you think "The Chameleon," "The Fox and the Woodcutter," and "A Poison Tree" have different **themes** or a common one? Explain.

Extending the Ideas

8. Explain how you can apply themes in "The Fox and the Woodcutter" and "A Poison Tree" to situations in your own life.

Literary Focus: Tone

A selection's **tone** is the author's attitude toward a subject, as revealed through the language of the selection.

- In which of these three selections is the tone humorous? How can you tell?

- In which selection(s) is the tone instructive or moralistic?

- Choose another literary selection in this book and explain whether its tone is humorous, peaceful, angry, or something else.

compensation
confiscated
countenance
dolefully
ecstatic
grievance
muse
profoundly
vixen
wily
wrath

Vocabulary Study

Use eight of the vocabulary words to write about one of the following topics. When you have finished, underline the vocabulary words you have used.

- an account of "The Chameleon" from the dog's point of view
- an opinion article criticizing the special treatment of powerful people
- a brief fable exposing a human weakness

Expressing Your Ideas

Writing Choices

Writer's Notebook Update Reread the notes you wrote about a time when you put on a false front. How does your experience compare with the descriptions mentioned in these three works? Write a paragraph in your notebook explaining the similarities and the differences.

Beneath the Surface Products, like the characters in these selections, can appear to be something they are not. Think about advertisements that suggest unrealistic results—shampoo to make your hair look like a movie star's, gym shoes to improve your basketball game, a diet drink to make you slim and popular. Write a **consumer complaint** letter expressing your dissatisfaction with a product that has not measured up to its promise.

Modernize the Story Work with a partner to modernize "The Chameleon." What type of person, group, or activity in society do you think could be deservedly criticized by using humor? How could you use exaggeration and sarcasm to poke fun at your target? Change or elaborate on the original story to write a **satire** using a modern setting, characters, plot, and language.

Other Options

TV Satire Many television programs are based on satiric skits about political or other newsworthy events. Work with a group to present a satiric **skit** about a political or media figure or event. You might take some cues from the changeable Inspector Moronoff.

Pop-Up Publication Work with a partner to design and illustrate "The Fox and the Woodcutter" or another fable about deceptive appearances as a **pop-up storybook** for children. You may want to review several children's pop-up books to identify an appropriate design for your book. Which character(s) and/or elements of the setting would create the best effect for "popping" off the pages? How can you use the pop-up design to maintain the tone of the fable?

Dip in the Pool

by Roald Dahl   Great Britain

Roald Dahl
1916–1990

Roald Dahl (rü äl däl), noted for stories that blend the horrible and the humorous, said that when an idea for a plot came along, he would "grab it with both hands and hang on to it tight." He scribbled his thoughts with a crayon, a lipstick, whatever was at hand. After serving as a fighter pilot for the Royal Air Force in World War II, Dahl returned to England and started writing short stories in a brick hut in his apple orchard. His stories for children, such as *James and the Giant Peach,* began as bedtime entertainment, and he claimed his ability to "tickle" and "jolt" audiences resulted from his own children's demands to be entertained and shocked.

Building Background

Lively Labels Many of Dahl's titles—*The Magic Finger, The Great Switcheroo,* and *Twenty-nine Kisses from Roald Dahl*—are as lively as his writing itself. You can analyze the title, "Dip in the Pool," to make some predictions about the story you are about to read. Copy the web below into your notebook. Then with a partner, complete the web by analyzing the words in the title and jotting down associated words, multiple meanings, and story predictions that come to mind.

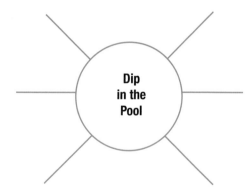

Literary Focus

Plot is a series of related events that present and resolve a conflict. Sometimes a plot is fairly predictable; that is, the author provides clues that a careful reader can use to guess the outcome. An author like Roald Dahl, however, may devise plot twists that catch a reader offguard. Be forewarned!

Writer's Notebook

Creative Solutions Are you a creative problem solver? Can you respond quickly in times of crises? Are you willing to take risks? Have your solutions ever backfired? Think of a time when you were required to think quickly and creatively. In your notebook, write three words that describe how you reacted. Now match wits with Mr. Botibol, a character whose quick thinking may (or may not) earn him a small fortune.

DIP IN THE POOL

Roald Dahl

This illustration by Bob Scott shows the huge scale of a luxury liner as it threatens the tiny sails in its path. How do shapes and perspective help establish a mood? ➤

On the morning of the third day, the sea calmed. Even the most delicate passengers—those who had not been seen around the ship since sailing time—emerged from their cabins and crept up onto the sun deck where the deck steward gave them chairs and tucked rugs around their legs and left them lying in rows, their faces upturned to the pale, almost heatless January sun.

It had been moderately rough the first two days, and this sudden calm and the sense of comfort that it brought created a more genial atmosphere over the whole ship. By the time evening came, the passengers, with twelve hours of good weather behind them, were beginning to feel confident, and at eight o'clock that night the main dining room was filled with people eating and drinking with the assured, complacent[1] air of seasoned sailors.

The meal was not half over when the passengers became aware, by a slight friction[2] between their bodies and the seats of their chairs, that the big ship had actually started rolling again. It was very gentle at first, just a slow, lazy leaning to one side, then to the other, but it was enough to cause a subtle, immediate change of mood over the whole room. A few of

---

1. **complacent** (kəm plā′snt), *adj.* self-satisfied.
2. **friction** (frik′shən), *n.* a rubbing of one object against another; a clash.

the passengers glanced up from their food, hesitating, waiting, almost listening for the next roll, smiling nervously, little secret glimmers of apprehension in their eyes. Some were completely unruffled, some were openly smug, a number of the smug ones making jokes about food and weather in order to torture the few who were beginning to suffer. The movement of the ship then became rapidly more and more violent, and only five or six minutes after the first roll had been noticed, she was swinging heavily from side to side, the passengers bracing themselves in their chairs, leaning against the pull as in a car cornering.

At last the really bad roll came, and Mr. William Botibol, sitting at the purser's[3] table, saw his plate of poached[4] turbot[5] with hollandaise sauce sliding suddenly away from under his fork. There was a flutter of excitement, everybody reaching for plates and wineglasses. Mrs. Renshaw, seated at the purser's right, gave a little scream and clutched that gentleman's arm.

"Going to be a dirty night," the purser said, looking at Mrs. Renshaw. "I think it's blowing up for a very dirty night." There was just the faintest suggestion of relish in the way he said it.

A steward[6] came hurrying up and sprinkled water on the tablecloth between the plates. The excitement subsided.[7] Most of the passengers continued with their meal. A small number, including Mrs. Renshaw, got carefully to their feet and threaded their ways with a kind of concealed haste between the tables and through the doorway.

"Well," the purser said, "there she goes." He glanced around with approval at the remainder of his flock who were sitting quiet, looking complacent, their faces reflecting openly that extraordinary pride that travelers seem to take in being recognized as "good sailors."

When the eating was finished and the coffee had been served, Mr. Botibol, who had been unusually grave and thoughtful since the rolling

started, suddenly stood up and carried his cup of coffee around to Mrs. Renshaw's vacant place, next to the purser. He seated himself in her chair, then immediately leaned over and began to whisper urgently in the purser's ear. "Excuse me," he said, "but could you tell me something please?"

The purser, small and fat and red, bent forward to listen. "What's the trouble, Mr. Botibol?"

"What I want to know is this." The man's face was anxious and the purser was watching it. "What I want to know is will the captain already have made his estimate on the day's run—you know, for the auction pool? I mean before it began to get rough like this?"

The purser, who had prepared himself to receive a personal confidence, smiled and leaned back in his seat to relax his full belly. "I should say so—yes," he answered. He didn't bother to whisper his reply, although automatically he lowered his voice, as one does when answering a whisperer.

"About how long ago do you think he did it?"

"Some time this afternoon. He usually does it in the afternoon."

"About what time?"

"Oh, I don't know. Around four o'clock I should guess.

"Now tell me another thing. How does the captain decide which number it shall be? Does he take a lot of trouble over that?"

The purser looked at the anxious frowning face of Mr. Botibol and he smiled, knowing quite well what the man was driving at. "Well, you see, the captain has a little conference with

---

3. **purser** (pėr′sər), *n.* a ship's officer who attends to business matters and is responsible for the welfare of passengers.
4 poached (pōchd), *adj.* cooked by simmering in a liquid.
5. turbot (tėr′bət, tėr′bō), *n.* a European fish, much valued as food.
6. steward (stü′ərd), *n.* a person employed on a ship to look after passengers.
7. subside (səb sīd′), *v.* die down.

the navigating officer, and they study the weather and a lot of other things, and then they make their estimate."

Mr. Botibol nodded, pondering this answer for a moment. Then he said, "Do you think the captain knew there was bad weather coming today?"

"I couldn't tell you," the purser replied. He was looking into the small black eyes of the other man, seeing the two single little sparks of excitement dancing in their centers. "I really couldn't tell you, Mr. Botibol. I wouldn't know."

"If this gets any worse it might be worth buying some of the low numbers. What do you think?" The whispering was more urgent, more anxious now.

"Perhaps it will," the purser said. "I doubt the old man allowed for a really rough night. It was pretty calm this afternoon when he made his estimate."

The others at the table had become silent and were trying to hear, watching the purser with that intent, half-cocked, listening look that you can see also at the race track when they are trying to overhear a trainer talking about his chance: the slightly open lips, the upstretched eyebrows, the head forward and cocked a little to one side—that desperately straining, half-hypnotized, listening look that comes to all of them when they are hearing something straight from the horse's mouth.

"Now suppose *you* were allowed to buy a number, which one would *you* choose today?" Mr. Botibol whispered.

"I don't know what the range is yet," the purser patiently answered. "They don't announce the range till the auction starts after dinner. And I'm really not very good at it anyway. I'm only the purser, you know."

At that point Mr. Botibol stood up. "Excuse me, all," he said, and he walked carefully away over the swaying floor between the other tables, and twice he had to catch hold of the back of a chair to steady himself against the ship's roll.

"The sun deck, please," he said to the elevator man.

The wind caught him full in the face as he stepped out onto the open deck. He staggered and grabbed hold of the rail and held on tight with both hands, and he stood there looking out over the darkening sea where the great waves were welling up high and white horses were riding against the wind with plumes of spray behind them as they went.

"Pretty bad out there, wasn't it, sir?" the elevator man said on the way down.

Mr. Botibol was combing his hair back into place with a small red comb. "Do you think we've slackened speed at all on account of the weather?" he asked.

"Oh my word yes, sir. We slacked off considerable since this started. You got to slacken off speed in weather like this or you'll be throwing the passengers all over the ship."

Down in the smoking room people were already gathering for the auction. They were grouping themselves politely around the various tables, the men a little stiff in their dinner jackets, a little pink and overshaved and stiff beside their cool, white-armed women. Mr. Botibol took a chair close to the auctioneer's table. He crossed his legs, folded his arms, and settled himself in his seat with the rather desperate air of a man who has made a tremendous decision and refuses to be frightened.

The pool, he was telling himself, would probably be around seven thousand dollars. That was almost exactly what it had been the last two days with the numbers selling for between three and four hundred apiece. Being a British ship they did it in pounds, but he liked to do his thinking in his own currency. Seven thousand dollars was plenty of money. My goodness yes! And what he would do he would get them to pay him in hundred-dollar bills and he would take it ashore in the inside pocket of his jacket. No problem there. And right away, yes right away, he would buy a Lincoln convertible. He would pick it up on the way from the ship and drive it home just for the pleasure of seeing Ethel's face when she came out the front door and looked at it. Wouldn't that be something, to see Ethel's face when he glided up to the door in a brand-new pale-green Lincoln convertible! Hello Ethel honey, he would say, speaking very casual. I just thought I'd get you a little present. I saw it in the window as I went by, so I thought of you and how you were always wanting one. You like it, honey? he would say. You like the colour? And then he would watch her face.

The auctioneer was standing up behind his table now. "Ladies and gentlemen!" he shouted. "The captain has estimated the day's run, ending midday tomorrow, at five hundred and fifteen miles. As usual we will take the ten numbers on either side of it to make up the range. That makes it five hundred and five to

> ## Sit absolutely still and don't look up. It's unlucky to look up.

five hundred and twenty-five. And of course for those who think the true figure will be still farther away, there'll be 'low field' and 'high field' sold separately as well. Now, we'll draw the first number out of the hat . . . here we are . . . five hundred and twelve?"

The room became quiet. The people sat still in their chairs, all eyes watching the auctioneer. There was a certain tension in the air, and as the bids got higher, the tension grew. This wasn't a game or a joke; you could be sure of that by the way one man would look across at another who had raised his bid—smiling perhaps, but only the lips smiling, the eyes bright and absolutely cold.

Number five hundred and twelve was knocked down for one hundred and ten

pounds. The next three or four numbers fetched roughly the same amount.

The ship was rolling heavily, and each time she went over, the wooden paneling on the walls creaked as if it were going to split. The passengers held on to the arms of their chairs, concentrating upon the auction.

"Low field!" the auctioneer called out. "The next number is low field."

Mr. Botibol sat up very straight and tense. He would wait, he had decided, until the others had finished bidding, then he would jump in and make the last bid. He had figured that there must be at least five hundred dollars in his account at the bank at home, probably nearer six. That was about two hundred pounds—over two hundred. This ticket wouldn't fetch more than that.

"As you all know," the auctioneer was saying, "low field covers every number *below* the smallest number in the range, in this case every number below five hundred and five. So, if you think this ship is going to cover less than five hundred and five miles in the twenty-four hours ending at noon tomorrow, you better get in and buy this number. So what am I bid?"

It went clear up to one hundred and thirty pounds. Others besides Mr. Botibol seemed to have noticed that the weather was rough. One hundred and forty . . . fifty . . . There it stopped. The auctioneer raised his hammer.

"Going at one hundred and fifty . . ."

"Sixty!" Mr. Botibol called, and every face in the room turned and looked at him.

"Seventy!"

"Eighty!" Mr. Botibol called.

"Ninety!"

"Two hundred!" Mr. Botibol called. He wasn't stopping now—not for anyone.

There was a pause.

"Any advance on two hundred pounds?"

Sit still, he told himself. Sit absolutely still

and don't look up. It's unlucky to look up. Hold your breath. No one's going to bid you up so long as you hold your breath.

"Going for two hundred pounds . . ." The auctioneer had a pink bald head and there were little beads of sweat sparkling on top of it. "Going . . ." Mr. Botibol held his breath. "Going . . . Gone!" The man banged the hammer on the table. Mr. Botibol wrote out a check and handed it to the auctioneer's assistant, then he settled back in his chair to wait for the finish. He did not want to go to bed before he knew how much there was in the pool.

They added it up after the last number had been sold and it came to twenty-one hundred-odd pounds. That was around six thousand dollars. Ninety per cent to go to the winner, ten per cent to seamen's charities. Ninety per cent of six thousand was five thousand four hundred. Well—that was enough. He could buy the Lincoln convertible and there would be something left over, too. With this gratifying thought he went off, happy and excited, to his cabin.

When Mr. Botibol awoke the next morning he lay quite still for several minutes with his eyes shut, listening for the sound of the gale, waiting for the roll of the ship. There was no sound of any gale and the ship was not rolling. He jumped up and peered out of the porthole. The sea . . . was smooth as glass, the great ship was moving through it fast, obviously making up for time lost during the night. Mr. Botibol turned away and sat slowly down on the edge of his bunk. A fine electricity of fear was beginning to prickle under the skin of his stomach. He hadn't a hope now. One of the higher numbers was certain to win it after this.

"Oh my God," he said aloud. "What shall I do?"

What, for example, would Ethel say? It was simply not possible to tell her that he had spent almost all of their two years' savings on a ticket in the ship's pool. Nor was it possible to keep the matter secret. To do that he would have to tell her to stop drawing checks. And what about the monthly installments on the television set and the Encyclopaedia Britannica? Already he could see the anger and contempt in the woman's eyes, the blue becoming gray and the eyes themselves narrowing as they always did when there was anger in them.

"Oh my God. What *shall* I do?"

There was no point in pretending that he had the slightest chance now—not unless the . . . ship started to go backward. They'd have to put her in reverse and go full speed astern and keep right on going if he was to have any chance of winning it now. Well, maybe he should ask the captain to do just that. Offer him ten per cent of the profits. Offer him more if he wanted it. Mr. Botibol started to giggle. Then very suddenly he stopped, his eyes and mouth both opening wide in a kind of shocked surprise. For it was at this moment that the idea came. It hit him hard and quick, and he jumped up from his bed, terribly excited, ran over to the porthole and looked out again. Well, he thought, why not? Why ever not? The sea was calm and he wouldn't have any trouble keeping afloat until they picked him up. He had a vague feeling that someone had done this thing before, but that didn't prevent him from doing it again. The ship would have to stop and lower a boat, and the boat would have to go back maybe half a mile to get him, and then it would have to return to the ship and be hoisted back on board. It would take at least an hour, the whole thing. An hour was about thirty miles. It would knock thirty miles off the day's run. That would do it. "Low field" would be sure to win it then. Just so long as he made certain someone saw him falling over; but that would be simple to arrange. And he'd better wear light clothes, something easy to swim in. Sports clothes, that was it. He would dress as though he were going up to play some deck tennis—just a shirt and a pair of shorts and tennis shoes. And leave his watch behind. What was the time? Nine-fifteen.

The sooner the better, then. Do it now and get it over with. Have to do it soon, because the time limit was midday.

Mr. Botibol was both frightened and excited when he stepped out onto the sundeck in his sports clothes. His small body was wide at the hips, tapering upward to extremely narrow sloping shoulders, so that it resembled, in shape at any rate, a bollard.[8] His white skinny legs were covered with black hairs, and he came cautiously out on deck, treading softly in his tennis shoes. Nervously he looked around him. There was only one other person in sight, an elderly woman with very thick ankles and immense buttocks who was leaning over the rail staring at the sea. She was wearing a coat of Persian lamb and the collar was turned up so Mr. Botibol couldn't see her face.

He stood still, examining her carefully from a distance. Yes, he told himself, she would probably do. She would probably give the alarm just as quickly as anyone else. But wait one minute, take your time, William Botibol, take your time. Remember what you told yourself a few minutes ago in the cabin when you were changing? You remember that?

The thought of leaping off a ship into the ocean a thousand miles from the nearest land had made Mr. Botibol—a cautious man at the best of times—unusually advertent.[9] He was by no means satisfied yet that this woman he saw before him was *absolutely certain* to give the alarm when he made his jump. In his opinion there were two possible reasons why she might fail him. Firstly, she might be deaf and blind. It was not very probable, but on the other hand it *might* be so, and why take a chance? All he had to do was check it by talking to her for a moment beforehand. Secondly—and this will demonstrate how suspicious the mind of a man can become when it is working through self-preservation and fear—secondly, it had occurred to him that the woman might herself be the owner of one of the high numbers in the pool and as such would have a sound financial

reason for not wishing to stop the ship. Mr. Botibol recalled that people had killed their fellows for far less than six thousand dollars. It was happening every day in the newspapers. So why take a chance on that either? Check on it first. Be sure of your facts. Find out about it by a little polite conversation. Then, provided that the woman appeared also to be a pleasant, kindly human being, the thing was a cinch and he could leap overboard with a light heart.

Mr. Botibol advanced casually toward the woman and took up a position beside her, leaning on the rail. "Hullo," he said pleasantly.

She turned and smiled at him, a surprisingly lovely, almost a beautiful smile, although the face itself was very plain. "Hullo," she answered him.

Check, Mr. Botibol told himself, on the first question. She is neither blind nor deaf. "Tell me," he said, coming straight to the point, "what did you think of the auction last night?"

"Auction?" she asked, frowning. "Auction? What auction?"

"You know, that silly old thing they have in the lounge after dinner, selling numbers on the ship's daily run. I just wondered what you thought about it."

She shook her head, and again she smiled, a sweet and pleasant smile that had in it perhaps the trace of an apology. "I'm very lazy," she said. "I always go to bed early. I have my dinner in bed. It's so restful to have dinner in bed."

Mr. Botibol smiled back at her and began to edge away. "Got to go and get my exercise now," he said. "Never miss my exercise in the morning. It was nice seeing you. Very nice seeing you . . ." He retreated about ten paces, and the woman let him go without looking around.

Everything was now in order. The sea was

8. **bollard** (bol′ərd), *n.* an upright wooden or metal post.
9. advertent (əd vėrt′nt), *adj.* alert.

calm, he was lightly dressed for swimming, there were almost certainly no man-eating sharks in this part of the Atlantic, and there was this pleasant kindly old woman to give the alarm. It was a question now only of whether the ship would be delayed long enough to swing the balance in his favor. Almost certainly it would. In any event, he could do a little to help in that direction himself. He could make a few difficulties about getting hauled up into the lifeboat. Swim around a bit, back away from them surreptitiously[10] as they tried to come up close to fish him out. Every minute, every second gained would help him win. He began to move forward again to the rail, but now a new fear assailed[11] him. Would he get caught in the propeller? He had heard about that happening to persons falling off the sides of big ships. But then, he wasn't going to fall, he was going to jump, and that was a very different thing. Provided he jumped out far enough he would be sure to clear the propeller.

Mr. Botibol advanced slowly to a position at the rail about twenty yards away from the woman. She wasn't looking at him now. So much the better. He didn't want her watching him as he jumped off. So long as no one was watching he would be able to say afterward that he had slipped and fallen by accident. He peered over the side of the ship. It was a long, long drop. Come to think of it now, he might easily hurt himself badly if he hit the water flat. Wasn't there someone who once split his stomach open that way, doing a belly flop from the high dive? He must jump straight and land feet first. Go in like a knife. Yes sir. The water seemed cold and deep and gray and it made him shiver to look at it. But it was now or

never. Be a man, William Botibol, be a man. All right then . . . now . . . here goes . . .

He climbed up onto the wide wooden toprail, stood there poised, balancing for three terrifying seconds, then he leaped—he leaped up and out as far as he could go and at the same time he shouted *"Help!"*

"Help! Help!" he shouted as he fell. Then he hit the water and went under.

> ## She looked around quickly and saw sailing past her through the air this small man . . .

When the first shout for help sounded, the woman who was leaning on the rail started up and gave a little jump of surprise. She looked around quickly and saw sailing past her through the air this small man dressed in white shorts and tennis shoes, spread-eagled and shouting as he went. For a moment she looked as though she weren't quite sure what she ought to do: throw a life belt, run away and give the alarm, or simply turn and yell. She drew back a pace from the rail and swung half around facing up to the bridge, and for this brief moment she remained motionless, tense, undecided. Then almost at once she seemed to relax, and she leaned forward far over the rail, staring at the water where it was turbulent[12] in the ship's wake. Soon a tiny round black head appeared in the foam, an arm was raised about it, once, twice, vigorously waving, and a small faraway voice was heard calling something that was difficult to understand. The woman leaned still farther over the rail, trying to keep the little bobbing black speck in sight, but

---

10. **surreptitiously** (sėr′əp tish′əs lē), *adv.* secretly.
11. **assail** (ə sāl′), *v.* bother; trouble.
12. **turbulent** (tėr′byə lənt), *adj.* filled with commotion; violent.

Dip in the Pool   **299**

soon, so very soon, it was such a long way away that she couldn't even be sure it was there at all.

After a while another woman came out on deck. This one was bony and angular, and she wore horn-rimmed spectacles. She spotted the first woman and walked over to her, treading the deck in the deliberate, military fashion of all spinsters.

"So *there* you are," she said. The woman with the fat ankles turned and looked at her, but said nothing.

"I've been searching for you," the bony one continued. "Searching all over."

"It's very odd," the woman with the fat ankles said. "A man dived overboard just now, with his clothes on."

"Nonsense!"

A man dived overboard just now, with his clothes on.

"Oh yes. He said he wanted to get some exercise and he dived in and didn't even bother to take his clothes off."

"You better come down now," the bony woman said. Her mouth had suddenly become firm, her whole face sharp and alert, and she spoke less kindly than before. "And don't you ever go wandering about on deck alone like this again. You know quite well you're meant to wait for me."

"Yes, Maggie," the woman with the fat ankles answered, and again she smiled, a tender, trusting smile, and she took the hand of the other one and allowed herself to be led away across the deck.

"Such a nice man," she said. "He waved to me."

After Reading

Making Connections

Shaping Your Response

1. What do you think is going on in Mr. Botibol's mind at the end of the story? Portray his thoughts and emotions in a cartoonlike drawing.

2. Do you think Mr. Botibol deserves to be rescued? Why or why not?

3. What music or style of music would you choose as the theme song to be played at the end of the story?

Analyzing the Story

4. What contrasting **moods** are in the first three paragraphs? What words establish these moods?

5. Can you find anything in the woman's behavior or appearance before Mr. Botibol jumps that would suggest she will not be a reliable witness? Explain.

6. Choose three words to describe Mr. Botibol's **character** and explain your choices.

7. Explain the **pun(s),** or play on words, in the title.

Extending the Ideas

8. How does this story compare with other stories you have read by Roald Dahl or with other stories having surprise endings?

9. Who do you consider the quicker thinker—Mr. Botibol in "Dip in the Pool" or Inspector Moronoff in "The Chameleon"? You may want to show the characters' similarities and differences in a Venn diagram.

Literary Focus: Plot

The usual pattern of related events in a **plot** is *conflict, climax,* and *resolution,* or *conclusion.*

- Use a chart like the one below to record in your notebook the conflict, climax, and resolution of "Dip in the Pool".

Conflict	
Climax	
Resolution	

- Are you satisfied with the resolution of the story, or can you suggest a more satisfactory conclusion? Explain.

Vocabulary Study

Write the word that best completes each numbered item in the following paragraph.

advertent
assail
complacent
friction
poached
steward
subside
surreptitiously
turbot
turbulent

Come Aboard!

Like Mr. Botibol, you can take the fantasy trip that you have __(1)__ longed for! Welcome aboard the Luxury Liner Tour, where you will get the special attention of a __(2)__ , who will take care of your every request. Eat luxury meals, which may include a tasty __(3)__ that has been __(4)__ in a broth. If a __(5)__ storm should arise, be assured that rough waters will soon __(6)__ under the skillful navigation of our captain. All our crew will be __(7)__ to your needs. No troubles will __(8)__ you on this trip. So if you want to escape the irritations and __(9)__ of everyday life, come aboard. You can feel __(10)__ about your choice of LLT for your dream vacation.

Expressing Your Ideas

Writing Choices

Writer's Notebook Update While preparing to read "Dip in the Pool," you assessed yourself as a problem solver. How do you stack up with Mr. Botibol as a quick and creative thinker? Make up a list of six words that you think name qualities a good problem solver should have. Circle qualities that you possess. Underline qualities you think Mr. Botibol possesses.

The Next Chapter Continue the story to show what happens next. Is Mr. Botibol rescued? Does he live on to write a bestseller about winning bets? Is his widow Ethel able to buy the pale-green Lincoln convertible? Use your imagination to write a **new ending** for the story.

Submerged Thoughts Write a brief **explanation** of how this story fits the theme "Beneath the Surface." You may want to pun on the word *surface* as Dahl does on the word *pool* in the story's title.

Other Options

Missing Person Create a news bulletin describing Mr. Botibol and the circumstances surrounding his disappearance. Use details from the story to construct an **artist's sketch** of him to accompany the bulletin.

Talk Your Way Out of This One! Mr. Botibol arrives home, damp and penniless. His wife is waiting at the door for an explanation. Remember that he prides himself on his ability to think quickly and to devise creative solutions to problems. Now work with a partner to write a **dialogue** to deliver to the class.

Stories on Stage Form a group to read other stories by Roald Dahl. Choose one of these stories to perform as a **dramatic reading** for the rest of the class, complete with music, props, and sound effects.

Before Reading

The Need to Say It

By Patricia Hampl   USA

Patricia Hampl
born 1946

Of her writing, Patricia Hampl says, "I suppose I write about all the things I intended to leave behind, to grow out of, or deny: being a Midwesterner, a Catholic, a woman." Accordingly her writing expresses a nostalgic and melancholy reflection of events from her youth in Minnesota. Hampl currently is an associate professor of English at the University of Minnesota and a founding member of Loft (for literature and the arts). She gives lectures, presents workshops, and performs readings of her poetry.

Building Background

Things Have Changed in Czechoslovakia The Czech grandmother in "The Need to Say It" would find the country she left 100 years ago vastly changed today. At the end of World War I, Austria-Hungary collapsed, and Czechoslovakia, which was carved from part of it, became a democratic republic. Just before World War II broke out, Germany, Hungary, and Poland claimed various parts of the country. It was freed by Soviet troops by 1945. In 1989, following mass protests, non-Communists took over the government and elected Václav Havel president. On December 31, 1992, Czechoslovakia ceased to exist, and the Czech Republic and Slovakia were formed in its place.

Literary Focus

Narrator An author choose s a **narrator** when telling a story—whether it's fictional or real. In this autobiographical essay, the narrator is a character (Hempl herself) who speaks in the first person. The reader learns about the characters and events from her viewpoint only. A third-person narrator stands anonymously outside the events and may reveal the thoughts, feelings and behavior of all characters. As you read "The Need to Say It," notice how details are presented and shaped by the narrator.

Writer's Notebook

Joint Efforts Before you read "The Need to Say It," think about a time when you shared your expertise with a family member who needed your help. How did you work together? What task did you accomplish? Would you have been as successful if either of you had tackled the task alone? Would you do things differently now? Note brief answers to these questions in your notebook.

The Need to Say It

PATRICIA HAMPL

My Czech[1] grandmother hated to see me with a book. She snatched it away if I sat still too long (dead to her), absorbed in my reading. "Bad for you," she would say, holding the loathsome[2] thing behind her back, furious at my enchantment.

She kept her distance from the printed word of English, but she lavished attention on her lodge newspaper which came once a month, written in the quaint nineteenth-century Czech she and her generation had brought to America before the turn of the century. Like wedding cake saved from the feast, this language, over the years, had become a fossil, still recognizable but no longer something to be put in the mouth.

Did she read English? I'm not sure. I do know that she couldn't—or didn't—write it. That's where I came in.

My first commissioned work was to write letters for her. "You write for me, honey?" she would say, holding out a ballpoint she had been given at a grocery store promotion, clicking it like a castanet. My fee was cookies and milk, payable before, during, and after completion of the project.

I settled down at her kitchen table while she rooted around the drawer where she kept coupons and playing cards and bank calendars. Eventually she located a piece of stationery and a mismatched envelope. She laid the small, pastel sheet before me, smoothing it out; a floral motif[3] was clotted across the top of the page and bled down one side. The paper was so insubstantial even ballpoint ink seeped through to the other side. "That's okay," she would say. "We only need one side."

True. In life she was a gifted gossip, unfurling an extended riff of chatter from a bare motif of rumor. But her writing style displayed a brevity[4] that made Hemingway's prose[5] look like nattering garrulity.[6] She dictated her letters as if she were paying by the word.

"Dear Sister," she began, followed by a little time-buying cough and throat-clearing. "We are all well here." Pause. "And hope you are well too." Longer pause, the steamy broth of inspiration heating up on her side of the table. Then, in a lurch, "Winter is hard so I don't get out much."

---

1. **Czech** (chek), *adj.* of or having to do with what was formerly Czechoslovakia, its people, or language.
2. **loathsome** (lōᴛH′səm), *adj.* disgusting.
3. **motif** (mō tēf′), *n.* a distinctive figure or pattern in a design, painting, etc.
4. **brevity** (brev′ə tē), *n.* shortness in speech or writing; conciseness.
5. **Hemingway's prose.** Ernest Hemingway (1899–1961) was a novelist and short story writer noted for his lean, condensed style.
6. **garrulity** (gə rü′lə tē), *n.* wordiness.

◄ In Milton Avery's 1941 oil titled *Girl Writing*, the writing paper seems like an extension of the girl herself. What does the writer in the painting have in common with the girl in the story?

This was followed instantly by an unconquerable fit of envy: "Not like you in California." Then she came to a complete halt, perhaps demoralized by this evidence that you can't put much on paper before you betray your secret self, try as you will to keep things civil.

She sat, she brooded, she stared out the window. She was locked in the perverse reticence[7] of composition. She gazed at me, but I understood she did not see me. She was looking for her next thought. "Read what I wrote," she would finally say, having lost not only what she was looking for but what she already had pinned down. I went over the little trail of sentences that led to her dead end.

More silence, then a sigh. She gave up the ghost. "Put 'God bless you,'" she said. She reached across to see the lean rectangle of words on the paper. "Now leave some space," she said, "and put 'Love.'" I handed over the paper for her to sign.

She always asked if her signature looked nice. She wrote her one word—Teresa—with a flourish. For her, writing was painting, a visual art, not declarative but sensuous.

She sent her lean documents regularly to her only remaining sister who lived in Los Angeles, a place she had not visited. They had last seen each other as children in their village in Bohemia.[8] But she never mentioned that or anything from that world. There was no taint[9] of reminiscence in her prose.

Even at ten I was appalled by the minimalism of these letters. They enraged me. "Is that all you have to say?" I would ask her, a nasty edge to my voice.

It wasn't long before I began padding the text. Without telling her, I added an anecdote[10] my father had told at dinner the night before, or I conducted this unknown reader through the heavy plot of my brother's attempt to make first string on the St. Thomas hockey team. I allowed myself a descriptive aria on the beauty of Minnesota winters (for the benefit of my California reader who might need some background material on the subject of ice hockey). A little of this, a little of that—there was always something I could toss into my grandmother's meager soup to thicken it up.

Of course the protagonist of the hockey tale was not "my brother." He was "my grandson." I departed from my own life without a regret and breezily inhabited my grandmother's.

I complained about my hip joint, I bemoaned the rising cost of hamburger, I even touched on the loneliness of old age, and hinted at the inattention of my son's wife (that is, my own mother, who was next door, oblivious to treachery).[11]

In time, my grandmother gave in to the inevitable. Without ever discussing it, we understood that when she came looking for me, clicking her ballpoint, I was to write the letter, and her job was to keep the cookies coming. I abandoned her skimpy floral stationery, which badly cramped my style, and thumped down on the table a stack of ruled 8 ½ by 11.

"Just say something interesting," she would say. And I was off to the races.

I took over her life in prose. Somewhere along the line, though, she decided to take full possession of her sign-off. She asked me to show her how to write "Love" so she could add it to "Teresa" in her own hand. She practiced the new word many times on scratch paper before she allowed herself to commit it to the bottom of a letter.

But when she finally took the leap, I realized I had forgotten to tell her about the comma. On a single slanting line she had written: *Love Teresa*. The words didn't look like a closure, but a command.

---

7. reticence (ret′ə sens), *n.* tendency to be silent or say little.
8. **Bohemia** (bō hē′mē ə), *n.* former country in central Europe, now a region of the Czech Republic.
9. taint (tānt), *n.* a stain or spot.
10. **anecdote** (an′ik dōt), *n.* a short account of some interesting incident or single event.
11. **treachery** (trech′ər ē), *n.* deceit.

After Reading

Making Connections

Shaping Your Response

1. Would you like to have this grandmother or the narrator in your family circle? Explain.

2. In your opinion, was the narrator lying by writing her grandmother's letters? Why or why not?

3. Who do you think benefited most from these letter-writing sessions, grandmother or granddaughter? Explain.

Analyzing the Essay

4. To whom do you think the **title** "The Need to Say It" refers? Why?

5. What might the author have meant by saying "you can't put much on paper before you betray your secret self"?

6. Do you think the grandmother and granddaughter have any **character traits** in common? Explain.

Extending the Ideas

7. Think of people you know or have read about who have left their native countries for various reasons. Why might they not talk about their homelands?

8. The narrator says, "I departed from my own life without regret and breezily inhabited my grandmother's." What professions might enable someone to "inhabit" another person's life? Explain.

Literary Focus: Narrator

By choosing to write an autobiographical essay with herself as **narrator,** the author directly communicates her own experiences, ideas, and attitudes to the reader.

- Think about how the narrator describes her experiences with her grandmother. In your opinion, what are the author's attitudes toward Teresa?

- How might the grandmother describe herself and her granddaughter if the older woman were the narrator?

Vocabulary Study

On your paper, write the letter of the best definition for each word.

garrulity
loathsome
motif
reticence
taint

1. *loathsome*
  a. harmless   b. favorite
  c. frightening   d. disgusting

2. *motif*
  a. cause   b. design
  c. memory   d. book

3. *garrulity*
  a. shyness   b. shortness
  c. wordiness   d. vulgarity

4. *taint*
  a. memory   b. belief
  c. lie   d. stain

5. *reticence*
  a. silence   b. gleam
  c. rumor   d. laughter

Expressing Your Ideas

Writing Choices

Writer's Notebook Update Now that you've read "The Need to Say It," reread your notes about a time when you teamed up with someone to accomplish a task. Write a brief comparison of your situation and the one described in the essay. How are the two situations alike? How are they different?

Thinking of You Imagine you are the granddaughter in "The Need to Say It." You've done such a good job "padding the text" in your grandmother's letters that now she wants you to write a **greeting card** sentiment to her sister. Write a "Thinking of You" poem for the grandmother to send.

Other Options

Family History Some letters, like the ones the author wrote for her grandmother, are a chronicle of a family's history. Expand your knowledge of your personal history by locating letters from your relatives. Look for details about historic events, prices of goods, and so on. You may also look in your local library for letters that describe life in your community in other eras. Tell anecdotes about your family history or the community to the class, using quotes from the letters.

The Art of Lettering The narrator of "The Need to Say It" describes her grandmother's handwriting as "painting, a visual art, not declarative but sensuous." Use the grandmother's name—Teresa, your own name, or a name of your choice to create a piece of **art**. You might consider using calligraphy or a computer program.

Before Reading

Crossroads by Carlos Solórzano   Mexico
Two Bodies by Octavio Paz   Mexico

Carlos Solórzano
born 1922

Carlos Solórzano (sō lôr zä′nō) describes the characters in his drama as people locked in a struggle to attain liberty. After receiving degrees in architecture and literature, he studied drama in Paris. A professor at the National University of Mexico, he also directed its theater.

Octavio Paz
born 1914

Octavio Paz (ok tä′vē ō pāz) has observed that "a poem is a shell that echoes the music of the world." At nineteen, he published his first book of poetry, earning a reputation as one of Mexico's most gifted writers. As a young man, he served in the diplomatic corps in France and Japan. Later, he was appointed Mexico's ambassador in India. He won the Nobel Prize in 1990 "for impassioned writings with wide horizons."

Building Background

Imagine the Scene On the first day back to school, you discover that your high school is really wired—computer network wired, that is. From the English writing lab, you can log on to the great communications highway and chat with people across the country. Soon you're discussing politics with someone in Washington, D. C., basketball with a fellow fan in Phoenix, and personal problems with juliet75@aol.com, who lives in Denver and whose online warmth and sympathetic understanding make her your favorite correspondent. When your parents announce that the family is going to Colorado, you alert juliet75@aol.com and arrange to meet her in the lobby of your hotel. You arrive early, looking eagerly for a girl with a white flower on her dress. When juliet75@aol.com finally shows up, you are amazed.

Brainstorm with classmates possible outcomes of this scenario. Then prepare to read about a similar experience.

Literary Focus

Foreshadowing Just as a teacher might alert you to what to expect on a test, an author may provide hints of what will eventually happen in a story. Such clues are called **foreshadowing**. You may find examples of foreshadowing in movies as well: a significant cough may foreshadow a character's death; a special glance between characters may clue viewers into their later collaboration or romance. As you read *Crossroads*, be alert to examples of foreshadowing.

Writer's Notebook

Common Ground Consider how differing **perspectives** due to heritage, culture, age, experience, religion, values, or social class might affect a romantic relationship. Which of these factors do you think is most important for a couple to have in common? Rank them in order of importance.

Crossroads
A Sad Vaudeville[1]   CARLOS SOLÓRZANO

CHARACTERS

FLAGMAN

TRAIN

MAN

WOMAN

Setting. Stage empty, dark. At one end, a semaphore[2] that alternately flashes a green light and a red one. In the center, hanging from the ceiling, a big clock whose hands show five o'clock sharp.

The characters will move mechanically, like characters in the silent movies. The MAN *in fast motion; the* WOMAN, *in slow motion. As the curtain rises, the* FLAGMAN *is at the end of the stage, opposite the semaphore, with a lighted lantern in his hand. He is standing very stiffly and* <u>indifferently</u>.[3]

FLAGMAN (*staring into space, in an impersonal voice*). The trains from the North travel toward the South, the trains from the North travel toward the South, the trains from the North travel toward the South. (*He repeats the refrain[4] several times while the* TRAIN *crosses the back of the stage. The* TRAIN *will be formed by three men dressed in gray. As they pass by, they each mechanically perform a pantomime with one arm extended,*

---

1. **vaudeville** (vôd′vil), *n.* a theatrical entertainment featuring a variety of acts, such as songs, dances, acrobatic feats, and trained animals.
2. **semaphore** (sem′ə fôr), *n.* an upright structure with movable arms or an arrangement of colored lights, lanterns, flags, etc., used in railroad signaling.
3. **indifferently,** (in dif′ər ənt lē) *adv.* in a manner that shows little interest.
4. **refrain** (ri frān′), *n.* phrase or verse recurring regularly.

the hand on the shoulder of the man in front, and the other arm making a circular motion, synchronized with the rhythm of the FLAGMAN's *words.)* The trains from the North travel toward the South *(etc.).*

(Loud train whistle. The MAN *who comes at the end of the* TRAIN *breaks free of it by making a movement as though he were jumping off. The* TRAIN *disappears on the right.)*

MAN *(carrying a small valise. He glances around the place, then looks at the clock, which he compares with his watch. He is young, serene of face, approximately twenty-five years old. He addresses the* FLAGMAN*).* Good afternoon. *(As a reply, he receives the latter's refrain.)* Is this the place this ticket indicates? *(He places it in front of the* FLAGMAN's *eyes. The* FLAGMAN *nods.)* A train stops here, just about now, doesn't it?

FLAGMAN *(without looking at him).* Trains never stop here.

MAN. Are you the flagman?

FLAGMAN. They call me by many names.

MAN. Then, perhaps you've seen a woman around here.

FLAGMAN. I've seen no one.

MAN *(approaching him).* Do you know? The woman I'm looking for is . . .

FLAGMAN *(interrupting).* They all look alike.

MAN. Oh, no! She's different. She's the woman that I've been waiting for for many years. She'll be wearing a white flower on her dress. Or is it yellow? *(He searches nervously in his pockets and takes out a paper that he reads.)* No, it's white . . . that's what she says in her letter. *(The* FLAGMAN *takes a few steps, feeling ill at ease.)* Pardon me for telling you all this, but now you'll be able to understand how important it is for me to find this woman, because . . .

FLAGMAN *(interrupting again).* What woman?

MAN. The one that I'm looking for.

FLAGMAN. I don't know what woman you're looking for.

MAN. The one that I've just told you about.

FLAGMAN. Ah. . . .

MAN. Perhaps she has passed by and you didn't see her. *(The* FLAGMAN *shrugs his shoulders.)* Well, I guess that I have to tell you everything to see if you can remember. She's tall, slender, with black hair and big blue eyes. She's wearing a white flower on her dress. . . . *(Anxiously.)* Hasn't she been around here?

FLAGMAN. I can't know if someone I don't know has been around.

MAN. Excuse me. I know that I'm nervous but I have the impression that we aren't speaking the same language, that is, that you aren't answering my questions. . . .

FLAGMAN. That's not my job.

MAN. Nevertheless, I believe that a flagman ought to know how to answer questions. *(Transition.)* She wrote to me that she'd be here at five, at the railroad crossing of . . . *(He reads the ticket.)* I'll never know how to pronounce this name, but I know that it's here. We chose this point because it's halfway between our homes. Even for this kind of date, a romantic one, one must be fair. *(The* FLAGMAN *looks at him without understanding.)* Yes, romantic. *(With ingenuous[5] pride.)* Maybe I'll bore you, but I must tell you that one day I saw an ad in a magazine. It was hers. How well written that ad was! She said that she needed a young man like me, to establish relations with so as not to live so alone. *(Pause.)* I wrote to her and she answered me. Then I sent her my photo and she sent me hers. You can't imagine what a beauty!

FLAGMAN *(who has not heard most of the account).* Is she selling something?

---

5. **ingenuous** (in jen′yŭ əs), *adj.* simple and natural.

MAN (*surprised*). Who?

FLAGMAN. The woman who placed the ad.

MAN. No, for heaven's sake! She placed that ad because she said that she was shy, and she thought it might help and . . .

FLAGMAN. Everyone sells something.

MAN (*impatiently*). You just don't understand me.

FLAGMAN. It's possible. . . .

MAN. Well, I mean . . . understand how excited I am on coming to meet someone whom I don't know but who . . .

FLAGMAN. How's that?

MAN (*upset*). That is, I know her well, but I haven't seen her.

FLAGMAN. That's very common.

MAN. Do you think so?

FLAGMAN. The contrary's also common.

MAN. I don't understand.

FLAGMAN. It isn't necessary.

MAN. But you only speak nonsense! I should warn you that although I've an inclination toward romantic things, I'm a man who isn't pleased by jokes in bad taste. (*The* FLAGMAN *shrugs his shoulders again.*) Besides, this delay upsets me as does this dark place with that clock that doesn't run. It seems like a timeless place.

(*Suddenly a loud train whistle is heard. The semaphore comes to life flashing the green light. The flagman again adopts his rigid posture, staring into space, he repeats his refrain.*)

FLAGMAN (*loudly*). The trains from the South travel toward the North. The trains from the South travel toward the North. The trains from the South travel toward the North (*etc.*).

(*The* TRAIN *passes across the back of the stage, from right to left.*)

MAN (*shouting*). There, on that train! . . . She should be on it. (*He rushes to meet the* TRAIN *which passes by without stopping, almost knocking him down. The* MAN *remains at stage center, his arms at his sides. Disillusioned.*) She wasn't on it.

FLAGMAN. It's only natural.

MAN. What do you mean?

FLAGMAN. He's never coming. . . .

MAN. Who?

FLAGMAN. The man we're waiting for.

MAN. But it's a question of a woman.

FLAGMAN. It's the same.

MAN. How is a man going to be the same as a woman?

FLAGMAN. He isn't the same, but in a certain way he is.

MAN. You change your mind quickly.

FLAGMAN. I don't know.

MAN (*furiously*). Then, what is it that you do know?

FLAGMAN (*indifferently*). Where they're going.

MAN. The trains?

FLAGMAN. They all go to the same place.

MAN. What do you mean?

FLAGMAN. They come and go, but they end by meeting one another. . . .

MAN. That would be impossible.

FLAGMAN. But it's true. The impossible is always true.

MAN (*as if these last words brought him back to reality, he abandons his furious attitude and calms down*). You're right in what you say. (*Hesitating.*) For example, my meeting with that woman seems impossible and it's the only certain thing of my whole existence. (*Suddenly, with an unexpected tone of anguish.*) But it's five ten. (*He looks at his watch.*) And she isn't coming. (*He takes the arm of the* FLAGMAN *who remains indifferent.*) Help me, do all that is possible to remember! I'm sure that if you want to, you can tell me if you saw her or not. . . .

FLAGMAN. One can't know by just seeing a person whether it was the one who placed an ad in the newspaper.

MAN (*once again containing his ill humor*). But I already described what she's like to you! . . .

FLAGMAN (*imperturbably*).[6] I'm sorry. I forgot. . . .

(*Meanwhile a* WOMAN *dressed in black has come in behind the* MAN. *She is tall and slim. Her face is cov-*

---

6. **imperturbably** (im′pər tėr′bə blē), *adv.* calmly.

▲ Georgia O'Keeffe's 1932 oil painting, *White Trumpet Flower*, reveals rich textures and delicate details embedded in a plain flower. Do you consider this an appropriate flower to represent the woman in *Crossroads* or would you suggest another kind of flower?

ered by a heavy veil. She walks softly with a pantomime motion. On her dress she wears a very large white flower. On seeing her the FLAGMAN *raises his lantern and examines her. The* MAN, *blinded by the light, covers his eyes. On seeing herself discovered, the* WOMAN *tears the white flower violently from her dress. She puts it in her purse and turns her back, remaining motionless.*)

MAN (*still covering his eyes*). Ooh! You're going to blind me with that lantern.

FLAGMAN (*returning to his habitual stiffness*). I beg your pardon. . . .

MAN (*to the* FLAGMAN). Someone has come in, right?

FLAGMAN. It's not important.

MAN (*recovering from the glare, he notices the presence of the* WOMAN *and runs toward her. He stops suddenly*). Ah . . . (*Timidly.*) I beg you to. . . .

WOMAN (*her back turned*). Yes?

MAN (*embarrassed*). I thought that you . . . were someone . . .

WOMAN. Yes . . .

MAN (*with determination*). Someone I'm looking for. (*She does not move. Pause.*) Will you permit me to see you from the front?

WOMAN. From the front?

MAN (*upset*). Yes . . . it's absolutely necessary that I see you . . .

WOMAN (*without turning*). But . . . why? (*She begins to turn slowly.*)

MAN. Well . . . in order to . . . *(On seeing that her face is covered, he backs away.)* You aren't wearing anything on your dress . . . and nevertheless . . .

WOMAN *(trembling).* And nevertheless?

MAN. You have the same stature and build. . . .

WOMAN *(with a jesting[7] tone).* Really?

MAN *(with distrust).* Could you tell me how you got here? I didn't see a train.

WOMAN *(interrupting, stammering).* I arrived . . . ahead of time . . . and I waited.

MAN. Ahead of what time?

WOMAN. We all wait for a time. Aren't you waiting for it?

MAN *(sadly).* Yes.

WOMAN. I believe that there is but one moment to recognize one another, to extend our hands. One mustn't let it pass by.

MAN. What do you mean by that? Who are you?

WOMAN. Now I'm the woman I've always wanted to be.

MAN *(timidly).* Will you let me see your face?

WOMAN *(frightened).* Why?

MAN. I need to find that one face, the special one, the different one.

WOMAN *(moving away).* I am sorry. I can't.

MAN *(following her with a tortured motion).* Excuse me. I'm stupid, I know. For a moment I thought that you could be she. But it's absurd. If it were so, you'd come straight to me, for we have called one another from afar.

WOMAN *(trembling).* Perhaps she's more afraid of finding the one she seeks than of letting him pass by without stopping.

MAN. No, that would also be absurd. *(Transition.)* In any case, I beg your pardon. *(He moves away and sits down on his small suitcase, his back to the* WOMAN.*)* I'll wait here.

(In the meantime, while the MAN *is not looking at her, the* WOMAN *has raised her veil with long slow movements. When she uncovers her face, it is obvious that she is old. Her forehead is furrowed by deep wrinkles. She is like the mask of old age. This face contrasts obviously with her body, still slender, ageless.)*

WOMAN *(to the* FLAGMAN *who stares at her).* You saw me from the beginning, didn't you? Why didn't you tell him?

FLAGMAN *(indifferently).* Whom?

WOMAN *(pointing to the* MAN*).* Him, the only one.

FLAGMAN. I'd forgotten him.

WOMAN *(in a surge of anguish).* Shall I tell him that I'm that woman he's waiting for? Will he recognize in this old face the unsatisfied longing still in this body of mine? How can I tell him that I need him even more than when I was young, as young as I am in that touched-up photo that he's looking at?

(In the meantime, the MAN *studies the photograph with fascination. The* WOMAN *covers her face again with the veil and goes up to the* MAN.*)*

WOMAN. Is she very late?

MAN *(his back turned).* Of course. . . .

WOMAN. It would hurt you a great deal if she wouldn't come!

MAN *(turning forcefully).*[8] She has to come.

WOMAN. Nevertheless, you must realize that perhaps she's afraid to reveal herself, that maybe she's waiting for you to discover her.

MAN. I don't understand.

WOMAN *(very close to the* MAN*).* I have a friend . . . who always lived alone, thinking nevertheless that the best thing for her was to get together with someone. *(She pauses. The* MAN *listens to her, interested.)* She was ugly, very ugly, perhaps that was why she dreamed of a man instead of looking for him. She liked to have her pictures taken. She had the photographs touched up, so that the picture turned out to be hers, but at the same time it was someone else's. She used to write to young men, sending them her photograph. She called them close to her house, with loving words. . . . When they arrived, she'd wait behind the windows; she wouldn't let herself be seen . . . .

MAN. Why are you telling me all this?

WOMAN *(without hearing).* She'd see them. She knew that they were there on account of her.

---

7. **jesting** (jest′ing), *adj.* joking; making fun of.
8. **forcefully** (fôrs′fəl lē), *adv.* powerfully.

Each day, a different one. She accumulated many memories, the faces, the bodies of those strong men who had waited for her.

MAN. How absurd! I think. . . .

WOMAN. You're also strong and young.

MAN *(confused)*. Yes, but . . .

WOMAN. And today she's one day older than yesterday.

MAN *(after allowing a pause)*. Really I don't see what relation all this can have to . . .

WOMAN *(drawing near and placing her hand on the* MAN*'s head)*. Perhaps you'll understand now. Close your eyes. *(She passes her hand over the eyes of the* MAN *in a loving manner.)* Have you never felt fear?

MAN. Fear? Of what?

WOMAN. Of living, of being . . . as if all your life you'd been waiting for something that never comes?

MAN. No. . . . *(He opens his eyes.)*

WOMAN. Tell me the truth. Close your eyes, those eyes that are separating us now. Have you been afraid?

(The MAN *closes his eyes.)*

MAN *(hesitatingly)*. Well, a little. . . .

WOMAN *(with an absent voice)*. A suffering . . . in solitude . . .

MAN. Yes, at times. . . . *(He takes the* WOMAN*'s hand.)*

WOMAN. Above all when you begin to fall asleep. The solitude of your body, a body alone, that inevitably ages.

MAN. Yes, but . . .

WOMAN. The solitude of the heart that tries hard every night to prolong its cry against silence.

MAN. I've felt something like that . . . but . . . not so clearly . . . not so pointedly.

WOMAN. It's that . . . perhaps you were waiting for that voice, the one of someone invented by you, to your measure. . . .

MAN. Yes . . . I think that's it.

WOMAN. Would you be able to recognize that voice with your eyes open?

MAN. I'm sure that I could. . . .

WOMAN. Even if it were a voice invented many years before, in the dark inmost recesses of time?

MAN. It wouldn't matter. I'd know how to recognize it.

WOMAN. Then, is that what you're waiting for?

MAN. Yes, I'm here for her sake, looking for her.

WOMAN. She's waiting for you also. *(The* WOMAN *raises the veil little by little until she leaves her withered face in the open.)* She'll be only a memory for you, if you don't allow yourself to be overcome by time. Time is her worst enemy. Will you fight it?

(They are seated very close to one another.)

MAN. Yes.

WOMAN. All right. . . . Open your eyes.

(The MAN *opens his eyes slowly and is surprised to find himself held by the* WOMAN*'s two hands. He stands up with a brusque⁹ movement.)*

MAN *(bewildered)*. Excuse me, I'm confused . . .

WOMAN *(entreatingly)*.¹⁰ Oh, no! . . . Don't tell me that . . .

MAN. It was a stupidity of mine . . .

WOMAN *(imploringly)*. But you said . . .

MAN. It's ridiculous! For a moment I thought that you were she. Understand me. It was a wild dream . . .

WOMAN *(grieved)*. Yes, yes . . .

MAN. I don't know how I could . . .

WOMAN *(calming herself)*. I understand you. A wild dream and nothing more . . .

MAN. You're really very kind to pardon me. . . . *(Looking at his watch, astonished.)* It's five thirty! . . . *(Pause.)*

WOMAN *(sadly)*. Yes. . . . Now I believe that she won't come.

MAN. How would that be possible?

WOMAN. It's better that way.

MAN. Who are you to tell me that?

WOMAN. No one. *(She opens her purse.)* Do you want this white flower?

---

9. **brusque** (brusk), *adj.* abrupt in manner or speech.

10. entreatingly (en trēt′ing lē), *adv.* in a begging or praying manner.

MAN (*snatching it from her*). Where did you get it? Why are you giving it to me?

WOMAN. I picked it up . . . in passing . . .

MAN (*with great excitement*). But then, she has been here. Perhaps she has gotten lost or mistaken the place. Or perhaps, while I was here talking with you, she has passed by without stopping.

WOMAN (*covering her face*). I already told you that there is but a moment to recognize oneself, to close one's eyes . . .

MAN. But now . . . what can I do in order to . . . find her?

WOMAN. Wait . . . as everyone does . . . Wait . . . (*She takes the flower again.*)

MAN. But, what about you?

WOMAN. I'll continue searching, calling them, seeing them pass by. When you're old, you'll understand. (*The train whistle is heard. The* WOMAN *moves away from the* MAN, *with sorrowful movements.*) Good-bye, good-bye . . .

MAN (*to himself*). Who can this woman be who speaks to me as if she knew me? (*He runs toward her. He checks himself.*) Good-bye . . .

(*The semaphore flashes the green light. The* FLAGMAN *becomes stiff in order to repeat his refrain.*)

FLAGMAN. The trains from the North travel toward the South, the trains from the North travel toward the South, the trains from the North travel toward the South, the trains from the North travel toward the South (*etc.*).

(*The* TRAIN *crosses the back of the stage. The* WOMAN *waves the flower sadly and with long movements approaches the* TRAIN. *She gets on it. The* FLAGMAN *repeats his refrain while the* TRAIN *leaves dragging the* WOMAN, *who goes off with writhing and anguished pantomime movements.*)

MAN (*with a certain sadness, to the* FLAGMAN *who remains indifferent*). There was something in her that . . . anyhow, I believe it's better that that woman has left.

FLAGMAN. Which one, sir?

MAN. That one, the one who had picked up a white flower . . .

FLAGMAN. I didn't notice that. . . .

MAN. No? (*He looks at the* FLAGMAN *dejectedly.*)[11] But, really, haven't you seen the other one?

FLAGMAN. What other one?

MAN. The one that I'm looking for.

FLAGMAN. I don't know who it can be. . . .

MAN. One who is wearing a white flower, but who isn't the one that you saw a moment ago.

FLAGMAN (*harshly*). I saw the one that you aren't looking for, and the one you're looking for I didn't see!

MAN (*irritated*). Can't you be useful for anything? What the devil are you good for?

(*Loud train whistle.*)

FLAGMAN. What did you say?

MAN (*shouting*). What the devil are you good for!

(*Green light of the semaphore. The* TRAIN *crosses the back of the stage very slowly.*)

FLAGMAN (*in a distant voice*). The trains from the North travel toward the South, the trains from the North travel toward the South, the trains from the North travel toward the South, the trains from the North travel toward the South (*etc.*).

(*The* MAN *covers his head with his hands, desperate. The* FLAGMAN *repeats his refrain while the* TRAIN *passes by slowly. Before it leaves the stage, the curtain falls gently.*)

CURTAIN

---

11. **dejectedly** (di jek′tid lē), *adv.* sadly.

Two Bodies

OCTAVIO PAZ

Two bodies face to face
are at times two waves
and night is an ocean.

Two bodies face to face
5 are at times two stones
and night a desert.

Two bodies face to face
are at times two roots
laced into night.

10 Two bodies face to face
are at times two knives
and night strikes sparks.

Two bodies face to face
are two stars falling
15 in an empty sky.

Starry Night by Vincent Van Gogh conveys an agitated quality through writhing lines and bold brushwork. Do you think this painting echoes the emotional state of the two bodies in the poem, or would you suggest a different piece of art? ▼

After Reading

Making Connections

Shaping Your
Response

1. What advice would you give the Man and the Woman about seeking future relationships?

2. The Woman says, "I believe that there is but one moment to recognize one another, to extend our hands. One mustn't let it pass by." Do you agree? Explain.

3. Do you think that this couple could be happy together? Why or why not?

Analyzing the
Selections

4. Why might Solórzano have chosen a train station for the **setting** of the play?

5. Who or what might the Flagman **symbolize,** or represent?

6. Why do you think the characters are identified only as the Man, the Woman, and the Flagman?

7. How and why does the playwright emphasize the idea of time?

8. What similarities in **theme** can you find between *Crossroads* and "Two Bodies"?

Extending the
Ideas

9. What other stories, movies, or TV episodes can you think of in which two people of widely differing ages teamed up? Were these successful partnerships? Explain.

Literary Focus: Foreshadowing

Foreshadowing is a literary technique by which authors hint or imply what will happen. Foreshadowing can appear in dialogue, in gestures, and in a setting or a situation. For example, the train that goes nowhere might foreshadow the futile relationship between the Man and the Woman. How does each of the following foreshadow the conclusion of *Crossroads*?

- "One can't know by just seeing a person whether it was the one who placed an ad in the newspaper."

- The Woman's act of tearing off the flower

- The observation: "Perhaps she's more afraid of finding the one she seeks than of letting him pass by without stopping."

Vocabulary Study

Stage directions often contain adverbs that indicate how the actors should deliver their lines. Match each word with the letter of its meaning. Then deliver the following sentence in five different ways, using each of the numbered adverbs as your cue: "May I help you?"

dejectedly
entreatingly
forcefully
imperturbably
indifferently

1. indifferently
2. imperturbably
3. entreatingly
4. dejectedly
5. forcefully

a. powerfully
b. neutrally
c. calmly
d. in a begging manner
e. sadly

Expressing Your Ideas

Writing Choices

Writer's Notebook Update Which of these factors do you feel contributed to the miscommunication between the Man and the Woman in *Crossroads*: heritage, culture, age, experience, religion, values, social class. Write a paragraph expressing your opinions on the subject.

It Might Have Been Both the title *Crossroads* and the title of Robert Frost's poem "The Road Not Taken" suggest that the choices we make affect our lives forever. Write a **capsule** summary of what might have happened had the Woman revealed her identity.

Looking for Love

Tall, red-haired computer programmer, extremely funny, attractive, fit.
Looking for energetic, nonsmoking female athlete to share life's adventures.

P.O. Box 3359

Write an ad for the Personal column of your local newspaper, itemizing what you're like and what you're looking for in an ideal mate.

Other Options

Look Again Examine the picture. What do you see? Look again. Now prepare a brief **art talk** explaining how this picture relates to the theme, "Beneath the Surface." Invite classmates to write captions for the picture.

Stage It! This brief play can be staged in your classroom. Props such as the flower and the semaphore can be easily made, or, like the 3-person train, enacted. Decide whether or not music would enhance your **presentation**, rehearse your parts, and entertain your classmates.

Beneath the Surface

Skin Deep

History Connection

Do you make judgments about people based on their appearance or do you look beneath the surface? The next few pages should help put beauty and fashion into perspective.

1 *This limestone sculpture depicts a stately Egyptian princess during the XVIIIth Dynasty, which began in 1554 B.C.*

2 *In this fifteenth century portrait of Margherita Gonzaga, the severe hair style depicts the classical manner of the times.*

3 *Corkscrew curls make up the fashionable coiffure of the woman in this Roman sculpture from around A.D. 90.*

4 *This Masai warrior wears braids and beads.*

CROWNING GLORY

5 *Fashionable men of the eighteenth century, like German composer Johann Sebastian Bach (1685-1750), wore powdered wigs.*

6 *Contemporary experiments with hair styles achieve a spiked effect.*

7 *"No hair" is the style popularized by celebrities like Michael Jordan.*

Responding

1. Write a caption for your own hair style.

2. Look through old magazines or yearbooks. Report to the class about hair styles of these different periods.

3. With a partner, debate the pros and cons of having rules about hair styles in schools or places of work.

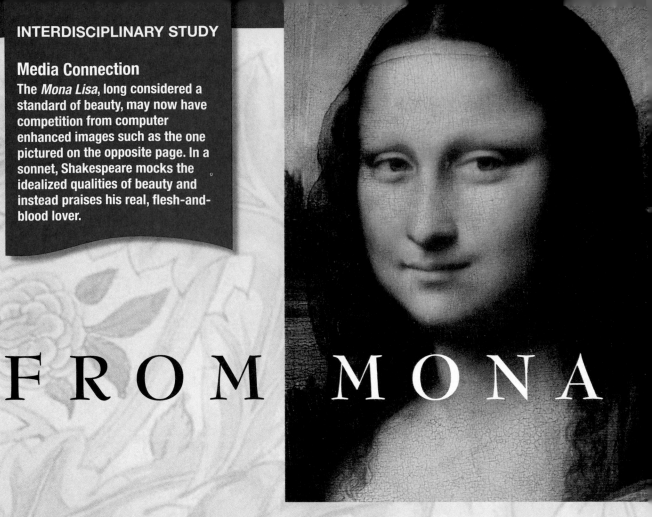

Media Connection

The *Mona Lisa*, long considered a standard of beauty, may now have competition from computer enhanced images such as the one pictured on the opposite page. In a sonnet, Shakespeare mocks the idealized qualities of beauty and instead praises his real, flesh-and-blood lover.

FROM MONA

SONNET 130

BY WILLIAM SHAKESPEARE

My mistress' eyes are nothing like the sun;

Coral is far more red than her lips' red;

If snow be white, why then her breasts are dun;

If hairs be wires, black wires grow on her head.

I have seen roses damasked, red and white,

But no such roses see I in her cheeks;

And in some perfumes is there more delight

Than in the breath that from my mistress reeks.

I love to hear her speak, yet well I know

That music hath a far more pleasing sound;

I grant I never saw a goddess go;

My mistress, when she walks, treads on the ground.

And yet, by heaven, I think my love as rare

As any she belied with false compare.

AMERICA'S CHANGING FACE

It began as an experiment. *Time* magazine's design staff combined computerized images of fourteen models from seven different ethnic groups. They played with percentages, mixed, matched, and morphed until they created the face of a woman whose features were 35% Southern European, 17.5% Middle Eastern, 17.5% African, 15% Anglo-Saxon, 7.5% Asian, and 7.5% Hispanic. The resulting multiethnic image was so beautiful that several staff members claimed to have fallen in love on sight.

Have the norms for beauty changed? In past centuries beautiful woman were often portrayed as pale and sedentary. Today, they often appear in art and the media as active people with a wide range of skin tones.

The woman in the magazine picture is fictional, it's true. But so are many models we see in magazines. They start out as real people, of course. Yet after imaging specialists finish slimming their hips, filling in wrinkles and pores, lightening shadows, and erasing blemishes, the models attain a state of impossible perfection. They are no longer people, but idealized images that reflect our values and dreams.

So next time you see an image of your ideal, ask yourself what qualities he or she embodies. And remember, if someone looks too good to be true—he or she probably is.

TO MORPHING

SPECIAL ISSUE

TIME

Take a good look at this woman. She was created by a computer from a mix of several races. What you see is a remarkable preview of . . .

THE NEW FACE OF AMERICA
How Immigrants Are Shaping the World's First Multicultural Society

Responding
1. Explain how the *Mona Lisa* fits—or does not fit—your concept of beauty.

2. Does the computer-enhanced woman on the cover of *Time* (special issue, Fall 1993) meet your standards of beauty? Do you think standards of beauty have changed in the past generation to fit our changing society? Why or why not?

3. Do you think the lover addressed in Shakespeare's sonnet should be flattered or insulted? Explain.

Writing Workshop

Exploring Stereotypes

Assignment The crooked politician, the lonely spinster, the scheming servant—these stereotypical characters show up in the selections in this part of the unit. These and other stereotypical characters also show up in scores of other stories in literature and the mass media. Now explore stereotypical characters in pictures and words.

WRITER'S BLUEPRINT

Product   A gallery of stereotypical characters

Purpose   To explore stereotypes from literature and the mass media

Audience   People who want to become more knowledgeable about what they read and watch

Specs   As the creator of a successful gallery of characters, you should:

❑ Make notes on stereotypical characters—the oversimplified, conventional types of characters who seem to show up again and again in literature and the mass media.

❑ Choose four distinctly different stereotypical characters for your gallery and make visuals—drawings or collages—to represent them.

❑ Write a description to accompany each of your four visuals. What does this character typically look like? How does this character typically feel and behave? Include likes and dislikes, how this character relates to others, and examples of this character from literature and the mass media.

❑ Use parallel structure to help knit each description together.

❑ Follow the rules of grammar, usage, spelling, and mechanics. Avoid confusing adjectives with adverbs.

---

1 PREWRITING

Review the literature. Create a chart listing stereotypical characters from the selections in this part of the unit. State the stereotype each character represents in the center column. In the last column, note descriptive details from the literature that help define each stereotype.

Character	Stereotype Character Represents	Descriptive Details
the woman in *Crossroads*	the lonely spinster	hides her age; afraid of finding the right man; fearful of revealing herself; lives alone

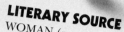

LITERARY SOURCE

WOMAN (*very close to the MAN*): I have a friend . . . who always lived alone, thinking nevertheless that the best thing for her was to get together with someone. (*She pauses. The* MAN *listens to her, interested.*) She was ugly, very ugly, perhaps that was why she dreamed of a man instead of looking for him.

from *Crossroads* by Carlos Solórzano

Brainstorm a list of stereotypical characters. In a group or with a partner, brainstorm a list of stereotypical characters from literature and the mass media and add them to your chart.

Remember, you're not looking for one particular character, like, say, Batman. You're looking for a character type, such as The Superhero. Other examples: the prim librarian, the sensitive poet, the alienated adolescent, the perky cheerleader.

Compile a nice long list to give yourself plenty of options to choose from.

Make webs for the four character types you choose. List descriptive details radiating out from the center.

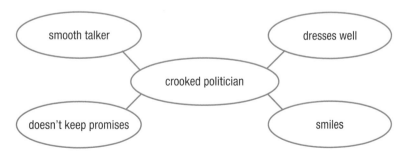

OR . . .
Working in a group, have each group member portray a character type, using typical words, gestures, and expressions, while other group members try to guess which character type is being portrayed.

Try a quickwrite. Write for two minutes or so about each of the character types you've chosen. Include details about the character's appearance and behavior. Use your webs for inspiration. If you find that you don't have enough to write about, do some more thinking or select other character types.

Create your visuals. Make one to illustrate each of your four character types. You might draw a picture that includes descriptive details from your web, or make a collage from newspaper and magazine clippings consisting of words and images that all in some way suggest the appearance or personality of your character type.

Plan your descriptions. First, read the character descriptions from *Twelve Angry Men* on page 229. They're good models. Your descriptions should be as specific as those. Then look back at your prewriting activities as you make your writing plan. You might organize your notes for each character type into categories like these:

Character type

- How character typically looks—clothes, facial features, gestures

- How character typically behaves—temperament, mannerisms

- How character typically feels

- Character's likes and dislikes

- How character relates to other people

- Examples of this character type from literature and the mass media (Batman and Wonder Woman as examples of The Superhero, etc.)

Ask a partner to review your plan.

✔ Have I chosen four distinctly different stereotypical characters to write about?

✔ Have I followed the Specs in the Writer's Blueprint?

Use any helpful comments from your partner to revise your plan.

2 DRAFTING

Before you write, look back at your prewriting materials and writing plan and reread the last three points in the Writer's Blueprint.

As you draft, concentrate on getting the ideas from your writing plan on paper. Try these drafting tips to help you get started.

- Keep your sketches or collages in front of you as you write.

- When describing how characters look, start at the toes and work up or vice-versa.

- Mention specific examples from literature and the mass media to help define each character type.

- Use parallel structure to help knit each description together. See the Revising Strategy in Step 3 of this lesson.

Notice how this writer used a famous pair of characters to help define one of his character types. (He'll correct technical mistakes later on, at the editing stage.)

> The sidekick is almost always shorter than the hero. This is to emphasize his inferioruty to the hero. A typical example is Robin and Batman. The sidekick must be good humored and never resent being continusly upstaged by the hero.

STUDENT MODEL

3 REVISING

Ask a partner to comment on your draft before you revise it. Use this checklist as a guide.

✔ Have I followed the Specs in the Writer's Blueprint?

✔ Does each written description belong with the corresponding sketch or collage?

✔ Did I use parallel structure to help knit each description together?

Revising Strategy

Using Parallel Structure

Parallel structure is the use of phrases or sentences that are similar, or parallel, in meaning and structure in order to knit together coordinate ideas.

Not parallel The crooked politician is always *smiling, shaking* hands, and *asked* everyone for large contributions. (The sentence suddenly switches from *-ing* words to an *-ed* word. The sentence sounds rough and clumsy.)

Revised to be parallel The crooked politician is always smiling, shaking hands, and asking everyone for large contributions. (Now, with everything in the *-ing* form, the sentence sounds smooth and graceful.)

The revised student model below shows another kind of parallel structure. Here, the writer has knitted the two parts of a sentence more firmly together by beginning each one with the same word.

○   She is the definition of wild. If you see her in the halls at school
                                                                  if
and all of her clothes match you KNOW there is a problem, and ~~when~~ her
                                                                  ^
○   hair is the same color for more than 3 months, there must be something

wrong (or a small money shortage).

Reread your descriptions to see if you can help knit ideas together with parallel structure.

STEP 4 EDITING

Ask a partner to review your revised draft before you edit. When you edit, look for errors in grammar, usage, spelling, and mechanics. Look over each sentence to make sure you avoid confusing adjectives with adverbs.

Editing Strategy

Using Adjectives and Adverbs Correctly

Don't confuse adjectives and adverbs in your writing. Words like *good*, *bad*, *real*, and *strong* are adjectives that modify nouns or pronouns, not verbs. Words like *well*, *badly,* and *really* are adverbs. Use them to modify verbs, adjectives, or other adverbs.

FOR REFERENCE
See the Language and Grammar Handbook at the back of this text for more information on using adjectives and adverbs correctly.

Don't write:	She drives *real* good.
Write:	She drives *really* well.
Don't write:	Her car is rusting *bad*.
Write:	Her car is rusting *badly*.

Take care to avoid confusing adjectives and adverbs in your writing.

STEP 5 PRESENTING

Consider these ideas for presenting your work.

- Read your descriptions aloud in a small group, but don't tell which description goes with which visual. Let the group try to match the two.

- Display a class gallery of stereotypical characters. Give guided tours to students and teachers.

STEP 6 LOOKING BACK

Self-Evaluate. What grade would *you* give your paper? Look back at the Writer's Blueprint and give your paper a score on each item, from 6 (superior) to 1 (inadequate).

Reflect. Think about what you've learned from this assignment as you write answers to these questions.

✔ Why do you think the mass media rely so heavily on stereotypes?

✔ Which part of this assignment did you find most enjoyable, the visual part or the writing part? Why?

For Your Working Portfolio Add your gallery and reflection responses to your working portfolio.

Beyond Print

Looking at Images

What do the varied artworks represented in this book—paintings, sculpture, collages, photographs, signs, film stills, and posters—have in common? They are all forms of communication. What can you do to understand what these artists are trying to say? Try these approaches.

1. **Determine the artist's purpose.** As you look at works of art, try to figure out what the artist was trying to convey or accomplish. Some works are created for everyday use—pottery or quilts, for example. Others serve as tributes, such as stamps or commemorative coins. Many are purely decorative, such as figurines. Art can be promotional or commercial, such as ads, posters, or shop signs. Photographs may create a mood, state an opinion, or capture a special effect.

2. **Remember that every artist has a point of view.** In analyzing a piece of art, consider the artist who produced it and the times in which the artist lived. How might culture shape the artist's attitudes? Is the artist depicting a culture or a social class to which he or she does not belong? Does the artist espouse a special idea or philosophy? From whose vantage point are subjects seen? Is there a *we-they* attitude? Are details such as clothing, facial features, and lifestyles portrayed accurately? Is the tone respectful? cynical? humorous?

3. **Note details that lead to the big picture.** Try to detect patterns in shapes, colors, lines, and textures. Is there a focal point that draws your attention? Do things such as facial expressions, shadows, surroundings, and print provide clues to what's going on? If you're still stumped about a work of art, put it aside for a while; then look at it "fresh" and try to get an overall impression. Ask yourself if it reminds you of anything that you've experienced, seen, or felt.

4. **Be an active viewer.** Not everybody loves the *Mona Lisa!* Viewing art is a personal experience, and individuals will react differently to a piece of art, depending on personal tastes, experiences, and familiarity with various types of artwork. In fact, the feelings you had about a work of art last year may be very different from those you have today about the same work. If you view art actively, knowledgeably, and with an open mind, you can enjoy a most enriching experience.

Activity Options

1. The picture on this page is of Pocahontas, daughter of an Indian chief of Virginia, who aided the Jamestown colonists on several occasions.

   - What do you think the artist is trying to communicate?

   - Explain whether or not this seems to be an authentic portrayal of a Native American woman. On what do you base your opinion?

   - What can you infer about the artist's cultural background and perspective?

2. With a small group, view a work of art in this book, applying the four approaches mentioned on the opposite page. Don't be afraid to have different opinions. Then present your analyses to the class in the form of an Art Critic's Choice panel.

Multicultural Connections

Interaction

Part One: On Trial A lack of communication and common goals affects the interactions between group members in *Antigone.* A jury in a criminal trial allows petty differences and cultural biases to impede their efforts to form a consensus in *Twelve Angry Men.* Both plays illustrate how conflict may result when people with diverse goals or backgrounds fail to work out their differences.

■ If Antigone were on the jury of *Twelve Angry Men,* with which jury member do you think she would interact most effectively? Why?

■ Prospective jury members are screened in an attempt to ensure that people with cultural biases do not serve. Do you think it is possible to find twelve jury members who will be fair and unbiased in reaching a verdict? Why or why not?

Perspective

Part Two: Beneath the Surface Perspective is the vantage point from which you view and react to the world. Your culture has a profound influence on how you view others and life in general.

■ Doctors, lawyers, and politicians are objects of satire in some of these works. Why do you think that particular professions are accorded more respect in some cultures than in others? Do you think it's fair that a professional athlete earns a considerably higher salary in the U.S. than, say, a professional poet? Explain.

Activities

Work in small groups on the following activities.

1. Interview people who have recently immigrated to the U.S. Ask them what things they consider important in life, what they would do if they won the lottery, what their favorite food is, who their favorite celebrity is, and what they found hardest to adjust to in this new country. Then present the cultural insights you gain in a TV-type documentary titled *Perspective.*

2. Plan a skit that shows how several people with different cultural values might react differently to a musical work, an article of clothing, or a TV program.

Independent and Group Projects

Writing

Evaluating a Character The selections in this unit include characters who have one thing in common—they each make judgments about a situation and react to the best of their ability under the circumstances. Write a character study of one of the characters in this unit. Evaluate that character's personality, actions, and ability to make valid judgments.

Mass Media

On the Air You and two classmates—taking the roles of interviewer, interviewee, and commentator—are presenting a segment of a weekly news program titled *Making Judgments.* Prepare a report to be performed live for the class or videotaped. This report will consist of (1) an introduction of the interviewee; (2) an interview with one of the following: Antigone, the young man acquitted in *Twelve Angry Men,* or the Man or Woman in *Crossroads;* (3) a wrap-up after the interview in which the commentator makes his or her own personal judgments about the character.

Research

Famous Trials Find out about a noted trial in history—for example, that of Socrates, Joan of Arc, Catherine of Aragon, Galileo, Alfred Dreyfus, Lizzie Borden, John Scopes, the Chicago Seven, or O. J. Simpson. Prepare a legal lesson for classmates, complete with pictures, facts, and an analysis of evidence. Or, if you prefer, work with a group to perform a reenactment of high points of the trial.

Art

Eye Foolers The selections in the second half of this unit examine deceptive appearances. Find or draw a picture that conveys an idea of deception. You might consider art dealing with optical illusions, such as the works of M. C. Escher, computer art, or photographs that portray false or misleading impressions.

Answering
the Call

Arthurian Legends
Part One, pages 338–393

Many Kinds of Heroes
Part Two, pages 394–449

Morgan le Fay
by Frederick Sandys

Reading Arthurian Legends

When you read a legendary tale, remember that you are reading neither pure history nor pure fiction, but a narrative that includes elements of both. Legends are told not only to entertain, but to celebrate folk or national heroes, and to pass on the cultural values of a people. Here are some points to keep in mind as you read.

Different versions of the tale exist. Seldom is there one "correct" version of a legend. Usually legends are told orally for generations before being written down, a process that assures variety and, sometimes, contradictions. Sir Thomas Malory based his stories of King Arthur on sources such as Welsh tales and French romances. Arthur's story continues to be told today in a variety of ways, including novels, films, video games, and medieval reenactments.

Extraordinary events are commonplace. A hand holding the sword Excalibur appears in the middle of a lake. Spells and enchantments are routine. Arthur's adviser is a magician who sees into the future. Knights duel for hours with superhuman energy. Instead of dismissing these unrealistic elements, set aside your skepticism and enjoy the wonder and mystery they add to the story.

Heroes and villains are clearly defined. King Arthur is presented as the hero of all heroes, a model of character and fighting skill for all knights to follow.

By contrast, the wicked Sir Modred, Arthur's illegitimate son, displays the dark side of human nature, as does Morgan le Fay, Arthur's half-sister, a villainous sorceress. The clear difference between good and evil helps Malory teach virtue and honor. Good does not mean perfect, however; the best of knights—even Arthur—display human weaknesses.

The action is episodic. The legend of King Arthur is made up of many stories that focus not only on Arthur, but also on the actions of his knights of the Round Table. When a knight sets out looking for adventure, his story soon breaks up into a series of independent episodes, each with its own setting, characters, and conflict. You might use your notebook to keep track of various plots.

Part One

Arthurian Legends

The stories of chivalry that originated during the twelfth century featured noble knight-heroes and tales of high adventure, excitement, and triumph of good over evil.

🐾 **Multicultural Connection** The concept of **Group** for medieval knights involved the collective development of codes, rules for behavior that they were expected to follow. In Arthurian legends, these group codes uphold loyalty, bravery, honesty, and courtesy. As you read, decide how the characters in these selections follow or depart from these codes of honor.

Genre Overview

Literature

Interdisciplinary Study   Knights in Many Guises

Writing Workshop   Persuasive Writing

Beyond Print   Visual Literacy

The Coronation of Arthur by Sir Thomas Malory   Great Britain

from The Hollow Hills by Mary Stewart   Great Britain

Sir Thomas Malory
1408–1471

The charges that led to Sir Thomas Malory's imprisonment may have been trumped up by political enemies. During this long imprisonment, Malory wrote *Le Morte d'Arthur*, a reworking of the Arthurian legend. After his death, this work was published by William Caxton on the newly invented printing press.

Mary Stewart
born 1916

For most of her career, Florence Elinor, whose pen name is Mary Stewart, specialized in romantic thrillers. But in 1970, Stewart published *The Crystal Cave,* her first work of historical fiction. Giving a new twist to Arthurian material, Stewart placed her story in fifth-century Britain and told events from Merlin's viewpoint.

Building Background

Larger Than Life! Almost every nation has a legendary hero—brave, noble, larger than life! (You will become acquainted with some of these heroes in the Interdisciplinary Study that begins on page 382.) Great Britain had Arthur, whose exploits continue to fascinate people today. Working in small groups, list on the blackboard things that you associate with Arthur and his times. You might use a chart such as the one below, or make up your own categories.

Medieval Life	The Round Table	Ideals of Chivalry	Weapons and Armor	Knights

Literary Focus

Style includes choices such as the following:

- *Types of words* (Are they plain or fancy?)
- *Purpose of the work* (Is it to inform, amuse, argue, describe?)
- *Tone* (Is it humorous, serious, angry, and so forth?)
- *Mood* (Is it mysterious, peaceful, nostalgic, and so forth?)
- *Use of figurative language* (Is the work purely literal? somewhat figurative? highly figurative?)
- *Sound devices* (Are the sounds and rhythms of words important?)

You will notice that the two selections you are about to read treat the same subject matter in very different styles.

Writer's Notebook

That's Great! William Shakespeare observed: "Some are born great, some achieve greatness, and some have greatness thrust upon them." Do you agree with this observation? By which of these ways would *you* rather gain greatness? Jot down your thoughts before you read. Then, as you read, decide how Arthur achieves greatness.

·THE· CORONATION ·OF· ARTHUR

SIR THOMAS MALORY

The marriage of King Uther and Igraine was celebrated joyously, and then, at the king's request, Igraine's sisters were also married: Margawse, who later bore Sir Gawain, to King Lot of Lowthean and Orkney; Elayne, to King Nentres of Garlot. Igraine's daughter Morgan le Fay, was put to school in a nunnery; in after years she was to become a witch, and to be married to King Uryens of Gore,

In this 1903 painting titled *King Arthur,* Charles Ernest Butler captures the drama and solemnity of Arthur's crowning. Speculate on why Arthur is pictured in armor rather than regal robes and why the setting is dark and ominous. ➤

and give birth to Sir Uwayne of the Fair Hands.[1]

A few months later it was seen that Igraine was with child. . . .

Sometime later Merlin appeared before the king. "Sire," he said, "you know that you must provide for the upbringing of your child?"

"I will do as you advise," the king replied.

"That is good," said Merlin. . . . "Your child is destined for glory, and I want him brought to me for his baptism. I shall then give him into the care of foster parents who can be trusted not to reveal his identity before the proper time. Sir Ector would be suitable: he is extremely loyal, owns good estates, and his wife has just borne him a child. She could give her child into the care of another woman, and herself look after yours."

Sir Ector was summoned, and gladly agreed to the king's request, who then rewarded him handsomely. When the child was born he was at once wrapped in a gold cloth and taken by two knights and two ladies to Merlin, who stood waiting at the rear entrance to the castle in his beggar's disguise. Merlin took the child to a priest, who baptized him with the name of Arthur, and thence to Sir Ector, whose wife fed him at her breast.

Two years later King Uther fell sick, and his enemies once more overran his kingdom, inflicting heavy losses on

---

1. **Margawse . . . Sir Uwayne of the Fair Hands.** The royal relatives and descendants are named here because they figure later in the tales of King Arthur. Sir Gawain, for example, becomes one of the most celebrated knights at the Round Table.

NOTABLE NAMES IN THE ARTHURIAN WORLD

UTHER PENDRAGON King of Britain and father of Arthur. He gives his son to Merlin for secret upbringing and dies two years later.

IGRAINE wife of Uther Pendragon; mother of Arthur.

MERLIN prophet and magician. He arranges for Arthur to be raised by Sir Ector and serves as Arthur's adviser during childhood and the early years of Arthur's reign.

GWYNEVERE Arthur's queen. The Round Table is her dowry. She later falls in love with Sir Launcelot. Many writers spell her name Guinevere.

CAMELOT where Arthur holds his court.

EXCALIBUR Arthur's magical sword.

LADY OF THE LAKE a supernatural being who gives Excalibur to Arthur. She is one of the queens who carry the mortally wounded Arthur to Avalon where he may be healed.

MORGAN LE FAY a sorceress who often plots against Arthur. She is Arthur's half-sister.

SIR LAUNCELOT the bravest of Arthur's knights. His love for Queen Gwynevere eventually destroys the fellowship of the Round Table. His name is often rendered as Sir Launcelot du Lake or Sir Lancelot.

SIR KAY the son of Sir Ector. He and Arthur are reared as brothers. When Arthur becomes king, the churlish Kay is appointed Royal Seneschal and becomes a knight.

SIR GAWAIN nephew of Arthur and knight of the Round Table. His strength—like that of the sun—grows each morning and then wanes during the afternoon.

SIR MODRED a knight of the Round Table, often identified as Arthur's nephew or illegitimate son. He tries to usurp the throne during Arthur's absence abroad. Arthur slays Modred but receives a fatal wound. Some writers spell the name Mordred.

SIR BEDIVERE surviving companion of Arthur who returns Excalibur to the Lady of the Lake at the dying king's request.

him as they advanced. Merlin prophesied that they could be checked only by the presence of the king himself on the battlefield, and suggested that he should be conveyed there on a horse litter. King Uther's army met the invader on the plain at St. Albans, and the king duly[2] appeared on the horse litter. Inspired by his presence, and by the lively leadership of Sir Brastius and Sir Jordanus, his army quickly defeated the enemy and the battle finished in a rout. The king returned to London to celebrate the victory.

But his sickness grew worse, and after he had lain speechless for three days and three nights Merlin summoned the nobles to attend the king in his chamber on the following morning. "By the grace of God," he said, "I hope to make him speak."

In the morning, when all the nobles were assembled, Merlin addressed the king: "Sire, is it your will that Arthur shall succeed to the throne, together with all its prerogatives?"[3]

The king stirred in his bed, and then spoke so that all could hear: "I bestow[4] on Arthur God's blessing and my own, and Arthur shall succeed to the throne on pain of forfeiting my blessing." Then King Uther gave up the ghost. He was buried and mourned the next day, as befitted his rank, by Igraine and the nobility of Britain.

During the years that followed the death of King Uther, while Arthur was still a child, the ambitious barons fought one another for the throne, and the whole of Britain stood in jeopardy.[5] Finally the day came when the Archbishop of Canterbury,[6] on the advice of Merlin, summoned the nobility to London for Christmas morning. In his message the Archbishop promised that the true succession to the British throne would be miraculously revealed. Many of the nobles purified themselves during their journey, in the hope that it would be to them that the succession would fall.

The Archbishop held his service in the city's greatest church (St. Paul's), and when matins[7]

were done the congregation filed out to the yard. They were confronted by a marble block into which had been thrust a beautiful sword. The block was four feet square, and the sword passed through a steel anvil which had been struck in the stone, and which projected a foot from it. The anvil had been inscribed with letters of gold:

WHOSO PULLETH OUTE THIS SWERD OF THIS STONE AND ANVYLD IS RIGHTWYS KYNGE BORNE OF ALL BRYTAYGNE.[8]

The congregation was awed by this miraculous sight, but the Archbishop forbade anyone to touch the sword before mass had been heard. After mass, many of the nobles tried to pull the sword out of the stone, but none was able to, so a watch of ten knights was set over the sword, and a tournament proclaimed for New Year's Day, to provide men of noble blood with the opportunity of proving their right to the succession.

Sir Ector, who had been living on an estate near London, rode to the tournament with Arthur and his own son Sir Kay, who had been recently knighted. When they arrived at the tournament, Sir Kay found to his annoyance that his sword was missing from its sheath, so he begged Arthur to ride back and fetch it from their lodging.

Arthur found the door of the lodging locked and bolted, the landlord and his wife having left for the tournament. In order not to disappoint his brother, he rode on to St. Paul's, determined to get for him the sword which was lodged in the stone. The yard was empty, the guard also having

---

2. **duly** (dü′lē), *adv.* rightly; suitably.
3. **prerogative** (pri rog′ə tiv), *n.* right or privilege that nobody else has.
4. **bestow** (bi stō′), *v.* give (something) as a gift.
5. **jeopardy** (jep′ər dē), *n.* risk; danger.
6. **Archbishop of Canterbury**, an official who now serves as head of the Church of England at Canterbury Cathedral.
7. **matins** (mat′nz), *n.* morning prayers.
8. **WHOSO . . . BRYTAYGNE.** "Whoever pulls this sword out of this stone and anvil is rightwise king born of all Britain."

slipped off to see the tournament, so Arthur strode up to the sword, and, without troubling to read the inscription, tugged it free. He then rode straight back to Sir Kay and presented him with it.

Sir Kay recognized the sword, and taking it to Sir Ector, said, "Father, the succession falls to me, for I have here the sword that was lodged in the stone." But Sir Ector insisted that they should all ride to the churchyard, and once there bound Sir Kay by oath to tell how he had come by the sword. Sir Kay then admitted that Arthur had given it to him. Sir Ector

...THERE IS ONLY ONE MAN LIVING WHO CAN DRAW THE SWORD FROM THE STONE ...

turned to Arthur and said, "Was the sword not guarded?"

"It was not," Arthur replied.

"Would you please thrust it into the stone again?" said Sir Ector. Arthur did so, and first Sir Ector and then Sir Kay tried to remove it, but both were unable to. Then Arthur, for the second time, pulled it out. Sir Ector and Sir Kay both knelt before him.

"Why," said Arthur, "do you both kneel before me?"

"My lord," Sir Ector replied, "there is only one man living who can draw the sword from the stone, and he is the true-born King of Britain." Sir Ector then told Arthur the story of his birth and upbringing.

"My dear father," said Arthur, "for so I shall always think of you—if, as you say, I am to be king, please know that any request you have to make is already granted.

Sir Ector asked that Sir Kay should be made Royal Seneschal,[9] and Arthur declared that while they both lived it should be so. Then the three of them visited the Archbishop and told him what had taken place.

All those dukes and barons with ambitions to rule were present at the tournament on New Year's Day. But when all of them had failed, and Arthur alone had succeeded in drawing the sword from the stone, they protested against one so young, and of ignoble[10] blood, succeeding to the throne.

The secret of Arthur's birth was known only to a few of the nobles surviving from the days of King Uther. The Archbishop urged them to make Arthur's cause their own; but their support proved ineffective. The tournament was repeated at Candlemas and at Easter, and with the same outcome as before.

Finally at Pentecost,[11] when once more Arthur alone had been able to remove the sword, the commoners arose with a tumultuous[12] cry and demanded that Arthur should at once be made king. The nobles, knowing in their hearts that the commoners were right, all knelt before Arthur and begged forgiveness for having delayed his succession for so long. Arthur forgave them, and then, offering his sword at the high altar, was dubbed first knight of the realm. The coronation took place a few days later, when Arthur swore to rule justly, and the nobles swore him their allegiance.

King Arthur's first task was to re-establish those nobles who had been robbed of their lands during the troubled years since the reign of King Uther. Next, to establish peace and order in the counties near London. . . .

---

9. **Royal Seneschal**, the steward (or manager) in charge of the royal household.
10. ignoble (ig nō′bəl), *adj.* not of noble birth or position; humble.
11. **Candlemas . . . Pentecost,** two church festivals.
12. tumultuous (tū mul′chü əs), *adj.* very noisy or disorderly.

THE
HOLLOW HILLS

MARY STEWART

As you read, keep in mind that Merlin is the narrator.

The place was small, the throng of men great. But the awe of the occasion prevailed; orders were given, but subdued; soft commands which might have come from priests in ritual rather than warriors recently in battle. There were no rites[1] to follow, but somehow men kept their places; kings and nobles and kings' guards within the chapel, the press of lesser men outside in the silent clearing and overflowing into the gloom of the forest itself. There, they still had lights; the clearing was ringed with light and sound where the horses waited and men stood with torches ready; but forward under the open sky men came lightless and weaponless, as beseemed them in the presence of God and their King. And still, this one night of all the great nights, there was no priest present; the only intermediary was myself, who had been used by the driving god for thirty years, and brought at last to this place.

At length all were assembled, according to order and precedence.[2] It was as if they had divided by arrangement, or more likely by instinct. Outside, crowding the steps, waited the little men from the hills; they do not willingly come under a roof. Inside the chapel, to my right, stood Lot, King of Lothian, with his group of friends and followers; to the left Cador, and those who went with him. There were a hundred others, perhaps more, crowded into that small and echoing space, but these two, the white Boar of Cornwall, and the red Leopard of Lothian,[3] seemed to face one another balefully[4] from either side of the altar, with Ector four-square and watchful at the door between them. Then Ector, with Cei[5] behind him, brought Arthur forward, and after that I saw no one but the boy.

The chapel swam with color and the glint of

---

1. **rite** (rīt), *n.* solemn ceremony.
2. **precedence** (pres′ə dəns), *n.* higher position or rank; great importance.
3. **white Boar . . . Lothian.** Two kings, Cador of Cornwall and Lot of Lothian, use the symbols of a white boar and a red leopard, respectively, on their flags or emblems.
4. **balefully** (bāl′fə lē), *adv.* destructively or threateningly.
5. **Cei** (kā), variant spelling of *Kay,* Ector's son.

◄ *May,* from *Les très riches heures* (c. 1416), is a calendar picture of a seasonal landscape. What inferences can you draw about nobility, architecture, courtship, and entertainment of the time from this picture?

jewels and gold. The air smelled cold and fragrant, of pines and water and scented smoke. The rustle and murmuring of the throng filled the air and sounded like the rustle of flames licking through a pile of fuel, taking hold. . . .

Flames from the nine lamps, flaring and then dying; flames licking up the stone of the altar; flames running along the blade of the sword until it glowed white hot. I stretched my hands out over it, palms flat. The fire licked my robe, blazing white from sleeve and finger, but where it touched, it did not even singe. It was the ice-cold fire, the fire called by a word out of the dark, with the searing heat at its heart, where the sword lay. The sword lay in its flames as a jewel lies embedded in white wool. *Whoso taketh this sword. . . .*[6] The runes[7] danced along the metal: the emeralds burned. The chapel was a dark globe with a center of fire. The blaze from the altar threw my shadow upwards, gigantic, into the vaulted roof. I heard my own voice, ringing hollow from the vault like a voice in a dream.

"Take up the sword, he who dares."

Movement, and men's voices, full of dread. Then Cador: "That is the sword. I would know it anywhere. I saw it in his hand, full of light.[8] It is his, God witness it. I would not touch it if Merlin himself bade me."

There were cries of, "Nor I, nor I," and then, "Let the King take it up, let the High King show us Macsen's[9] sword."

Then finally, alone, Lot's voice, gruffly: "Yes. Let him take it. I have seen, by God's death, I have seen. If it is his indeed, then God is with him, and it is not for me."

Arthur came slowly forward. Behind him the place was dim, the crowd shrunk back into darkness, the shuffle and murmur of their presence no more than the breeze in the forest trees outside. Here between us, the white light blazed and the blade shivered. The darkness flashed and sparkled, a crystal cave of vision, crowded and whirling with bright images.[10] A white stag, collared with gold. A shooting star, dragon-shaped, and trailing fire. A king, restless and desirous, with a dragon of red gold shimmering on the wall behind him. A woman, white-robed and queenly, and behind her in the shadows a sword standing in an altar like a cross. A circle of vast linked stones standing on a windy plain with a king's grave at its center. A child, handed into my arms on a winter night. A grail, shrouded in mouldering cloth, hidden in a dark vault. A young king, crowned.

He looked at me through the pulse and flash of vision. For him, they were flames only, flames which might burn, or not; that was for me. He waited, not doubtful, nor blindly trusting; waiting only.

"Come," I said gently. "It is yours."

He put his hand through the white blaze of fire and the hilt slid cool into the grip for which, a hundred and a hundred years before, it had been made.

---

6. **Whoso . . . sword.** The words "Whoso taketh [takes] this sword from under this stone is rightwise King born of all Britain" appear in their entirety earlier in Stewart's novel.
7. **rune** (rün), *n.* inscription or letter.
8. **I saw . . . light.** Cador had seen Arthur with the same sword earlier, when it was found in a cavern.
9. **Macsen's.** *Macsen* is the British name for the Roman ruler Magnus Maximus, who lived in the fourth century in Britain. Mary Stewart has introduced the idea that the sword once belonged to another ruler of Great Britain, a new twist on the Arthurian legend.
10. **bright images.** Merlin proceeds to identify images of a stag, a shooting star, and other omens and scenes from Arthur's life up to this point.

After Reading

Making Connections

Shaping Your
Response

1. What were your feelings toward Arthur as you read these selections?

2. Do you think Arthur is fortunate to have such an acquaintance as Merlin? Why or why not?

3. Which of these narratives would you prefer portraying in art? Why?

Analyzing the
Legends

4. What does Malory imply is the cause of unrest in Britain during Arthur's childhood?

5. What details **foreshadow** that Arthur may encounter opposition during his rule?

6. List three personal qualities that you think **characterize** Arthur.

7. What differences do you find in **setting** and **tone** in Stewart's and Malory's accounts?

8. What details in Malory's account does Stewart change or add to in order to heighten dramatic effect?

Extending the Ideas

9. 👣 Compare Arthur to other heroes that you know of, such as Odysseus, Hercules, and other legendary figures. Do these heroes seem more concerned with individual goals or with the welfare of the **groups** they lead?

10. What public "tests" do politicians undergo today to prove their ability to lead?

Literary Focus: Style

Reread the description of **style** that appears before the Malory selection, as well as the two passages below. Then comment on the difference in styles, referring to things such as imagery, mood, and repetition.

- "The yard was empty, the guard also having slipped off to see the tournament, so Arthur strode up to the sword and, without troubling to read the inscription, tugged it free." *Malory*

- "He put his hand through the white blaze of fire and the hilt slid cool into the grip for which, a hundred and a hundred years before, it had been made." *Stewart*

Vocabulary Study

Match the numbered word with the letter of its correct synonym.

balefully
bestow
duly
ignoble
jeopardy
precedence
prerogative
rite
rune
tumultuous

1. balefully   a. noisy or disorderly
2. bestow   b. rightly
3. ignoble   c. humble
4. jeopardy   d. give
5. precedence   e. unique privilege
6. duly   f. higher rank
7. rite   g. danger
8. prerogative   h. destructively
9. tumultuous   i. solemn ceremony
10. rune   j. inscription

Expressing Your Ideas

Writing Choices

Writer's Notebook Update Review the quotation by Shakespeare about greatness. Then write a paragraph applying this quotation to Arthur.

Second Best What do you think were Sir Kay's thoughts and feelings at discovering Arthur's true identity? Write Sir Kay's reactions in the form of an **interior monologue**—one of those uncensored dialogues people have with themselves.

Extra! Extra! As editor of the *Camelot Chronicle*, you and your staff are to publish a **special issue** about the new king. It might include items such as the following: a news story on Arthur's early life and how he became king, comic strips, an interview with Arthur focusing on his plans for the future, political cartoons, an editorial about the future of Britain under King Arthur, advertisements for products of the time.

Other Options

Name of the Game Working in a group of three or four, create a **board game** based on the legends of King Arthur's time. The game should have a definite goal (attaining the crown, perhaps), penalties, and rewards.

Draw Your Sword Do some research on ancient weapons to discover what a medieval sword looked like. Combine these details with your imagination to create a **drawing** or a **model** of the sword in the stone. Alternatively, you might research weaponry of war or honor in different cultures and create artwork based on your findings.

A Dramatic Moment Mary Stewart's account lends itself to a **dramatic reading**. A narrator can prepare a reading of the account, up to the paragraph beginning, "Arthur came slowly forward." The remainder can be acted, with music. Special effects can be achieved by lighting, colored cloth, and simple props.

Before Reading

Youth and Chivalry from A Distant Mirror

by Barbara Tuchman   USA

Barbara Tuchman
1912–1989

Best-selling historian Barbara Tuchman found stories worth telling, researched available information, visited the sites, and then wove historical accounts into exciting narratives. For *A Distant Mirror: The Calamitous Fourteenth Century,* from which the following excerpt is taken, she crossed the same mountains traveled by Crusaders more than six centuries earlier. Her lively narration, thorough research, ability to tie the past to the present, and keen eye for details earned her two Pulitzer prizes.

Building Background

How Does a Culture Sound? What are the sounds of your typical day? alarm clocks buzzing? water running? trains rumbling? car radio playing? locker doors slamming? How do these compare with the sounds heard in the 1300s? According to historian Johan Huizinga: "One sound rose ceaselessly above the noises of busy life and lifted all things unto a sphere of order and serenity: the sound of bells. . . . They were known by their names: big Jacqueline, or the bell Roland. Every one knew the difference in meaning of the various ways of ringing." Why might bells have been important to the people of the Middle Ages? How would bells have suggested order and serenity?

Literary Focus

Sensory Details Writers use **sensory details,** or words that appeal to the senses, to create images and feelings in their readers. Such words help readers see, hear, feel, smell, and taste the world the writer portrays. For example, Barbara Tuchman describes a mother "delousing her child's hair with his head in her lap" and a book of advice on "not spitting or picking teeth with a knife." Make a chart like the one below, and list examples of appropriate details that you find in this historical account.

Sight	Sound	Touch	Smell	Taste

Writer's Notebook

Were They Really Like That? In the following excerpt from *A Distant Mirror,* Tuchman presents a picture of everyday life over six centuries ago. Imagine that a team of archaeologists unearths your house six hundred years from now. Make a list of five items they might find that would give them a clue to life today. List five other items that might confuse or puzzle them.

Youth and Chivalry

Barbara Tuchman

Of all the characteristics in which the medieval age differs from the modern, none is so striking as the comparative absence of interest in children. Emotion in relation to them rarely appears in art or literature or documentary evidence. The Christ child is of course repeatedly pictured, usually in his mother's arms, but prior to the mid-14th century he is generally held stiffly, away from her body, by a mother who is aloof[1] even when nursing. Or else the holy infant lies alone on the ground, swaddled or sometimes quite naked and uncovered, while an unsmiling mother gazes at him abstractedly. Her separateness from the child was meant to indicate his divinity. If the ordinary mother felt a warmer, more intimate emotion, it found small expression in medieval art because the attitudes of motherhood were preempted[2] by the Virgin Mary.

In literature the chief role of children was to die, usually drowned, smothered, or abandoned in a forest on the orders of some king fearing prophecy or mad husband testing a wife's endurance. Women appear rarely as mothers. They are flirts, bawds, and deceiving wives in the popular tales, saints and martyrs in the drama, unattainable objects of passionate and illicit love in the romances. Occasionally motherhood may break through, as when an English preacher, to point a moral in a sermon, tells how a mother "that hath a childe in wynter when the childes hondes ben cold, the modur taketh hym a stree

---

1. **aloof** (ə lüf′), *adj.* unsympathetic; reserved.
2. **preempt** (prē empt′), *v.* take over beforehand.

Il ceste partie
nous dist this
toire que apres
ce que la nuit
du tournoiemt
fu passee et que ce vint a len
demain matin le roy artus se
leua chaussa et vestir et lors quil

fu appareillie il oy la messe pre
mier oeuure car il en estoit
coustumier/ et pour ce le tenoi
ent tous ceuls qui le congnois
soient a moult preudomme tan
tost que la messe fu ditte et que
tous ses barons furet assemble
ou en partie il leur commenca

[straw] or a rusche and byddeth him warme itt, not for love of the stree to hete it . . . but for to hete the childes honds."[3] An occasional illustration or carving in stone shows parents teaching a child to walk, a peasant mother combing or delousing her child's hair with his head in her lap, a more elegant mother of the 14th century knitting a child's garment on four needles, an acknowledgment from a saint's life of the "beauty of infancy," and from the 12th century *Ancren Riwle*[4] a description of a peasant mother playing hide-and-seek with her child and who, when he cries for her, "leapeth forth lightly with outspread arms and embraceth and kisseth him and wipeth his eyes." These are isolated mentions which leave the empty spaces between more noticeable.

Medieval illustrations show people in every other human activity—making love and dying, sleeping and eating, in bed and in the bath, praying, hunting, dancing, plowing, in games and in combat, trading, traveling, reading and writing—yet so rarely with children as to raise the question: Why not?

Maternal love, like sex, is generally considered too innate[5] to be eradicable,[6] but perhaps under certain unfavorable conditions it may atrophy.[7] Owing to the high infant mortality of the times, estimated at one or two in three, the investment of love in a young child may have been so unrewarding that by some ruse[8] of nature, as when overcrowded rodents in captivity will not breed, it was suppressed. Perhaps also the frequent childbearing put less value on the product. A child was born and died and another took its place.

CLARIFY: What point is the author making with the comparison to rodents?

Well-off noble and bourgeois families bore more children than the poor because they married young and because, as a result of employing wet-nurses, the period of infertility was short. They also raised more, often as many as six to ten reaching adulthood. Guillaume de Coucy,[9] grandfather of Enguerrand VII, raised five sons and five daughters; his son Raoul raised four of each. Nine out of the twelve children of Edward III[10] and Queen Philippa of England reached maturity. The average woman of twenty, it has been estimated, could expect about twelve years of childbearing, with live births spaced out—owing to stillbirths, abortions, and nursing—at fairly long intervals of about thirty months. At this rate, the average of births per family was about five, of whom half survived.

Like everything else, childhood escapes a flat generalization. Love and lullabies and cradle-rocking did exist. God in his grace, wrote Philip of Novara in the 13th century, gave children three gifts: to love and recognize the person who nurses him at her breast; to show "joy and love" to those who play with him; to inspire love and tenderness in those who rear him, of which the last is the most important, for "without this, they will be so dirty and annoying in infancy and so naughty and

---

3. **"that hath a childe . . . the childes honds,"** that has a child in winter when the child's hands be cold, the mother takes him a straw or a rush [grasslike plant] and bids him warm it, not for love of the straw to heat it . . . but to heat the child's hands.

4. *Ancren Riwle,* a book of devotional advice, probably written for nuns.

5. **innate** (i nāt′), *adj.* natural, inborn.

6. **eradicable** (i rad′ə kə bəl), *adj.* that can be gotten rid of or destroyed.

7. **atrophy** (at′rə fē), *v.* waste away.

8. **ruse** (rüz), *n.* scheme or device to mislead others; trick.

9. **Guillaume de Coucy** (gē yōm′ də kü sē′) . . . **Enguerrand** (eng′yə rän) **VII.** In her narrative, *A Distant Mirror,* Tuchman details the life of de Coucy, "the most skilled and experienced of all the knights of France."

10. **Edward III**, king of England who lived from 1312–1377 and reigned for fifty years.

capricious[11] that it is hardly worth nurturing them through childhood." Philip advocated,[12] however, a strict upbringing, for "few children perish from excess of severity but many from being permitted too much."

Books of advice on child-rearing were rare. There were books—that is, bound manuscripts—of etiquette, housewifery, deportment, home remedies, even phrase books of foreign vocabularies. A reader could find advice on washing hands and cleaning nails before a banquet, on eating fennel and anise in case of bad breath, on not spitting or picking teeth with a knife, not wiping hands on sleeves, or nose and eyes on the tablecloth. A woman could learn how to make ink, poison for rats, sand for hourglasses; how to make hippocras or spiced wine, the favorite medieval drink; how to care for pet birds in cages and get them to breed: how to obtain character references for servants and make sure they extinguished their bed candles with fingers or breath, "not with their shirts"; how to grow peas and graft roses; how to rid the house of flies; how to remove grease stains with chicken feathers steeped in hot water; how to keep a husband happy by ensuring him a smokeless fire in winter and a bed free of fleas in summer. A young married woman would be advised on fasting and alms-giving and saying prayers at the sound of the matins bell "before going to sleep again," and on walking with dignity and modesty in public, not "in ribald[13] wise with roving eyes and neck stretched forth like a stag in flight, looking this way and that like unto a runaway horse." She could find books on estate management for times when her husband was away at war, with advice on making budgets and withstanding sieges and on tenure and feudal law so that her husband's rights would not be invaded.

EVALUATE: Do you think that a medieval housewife had more or less power than her modern counterpart?

But she would find few books for mothers with advice on breast-feeding, swaddling, bathing, weaning, solid-feeding, and other complexities of infant care, although these might seem to have been of more moment for survival of the race than breeding birds in cages or even keeping husbands comfortable. When breast-feeding was mentioned, it was generally advocated—by one 13th century encyclopedist, Bartholomew of England in his *Book on the Nature of Things*—for its emotional value. In the process the mother "loves her own child most tenderly, embraces and kisses it, nurses and cares for it most solicitously." A physician of the same period, Aldobrandino of Siena, who practiced in France, advised frequent cleaning and changing and two baths a day, weaning on porridge made of bread with honey and milk, ample playtime and unforced teaching at school, with time for sleep and diversion. But how widely his humane teaching was known or followed it is impossible to say.

On the whole, babies and young children appear to have been left to survive or die without great concern in the first five or six years. What psychological effect this may have had on character, and possibly on history, can only be conjectured.[14] Possibly the relative emotional blankness of a medieval infancy may account for the casual attitude toward life and suffering of the medieval man.

Children did, however, have toys: dolls and doll carriages harnessed to mice, wooden knights and weapons, little animals of baked clay, windmills, balls, battledores and shuttlecocks,[15] stilts and seesaws and merry-go-rounds. Little boys were like little boys of any time, "living without thought or care," according to

---

11. **capricious** (kə prish′əs), *adj.* changeable.
12. **advocate** (ad′və kāt), *v.* support.
13. **ribald** (rib′əld), *adj.* offensive in speech; obscene.
14. **conjecture** (kən jek′chər), *v.* guess; admit without sufficient evidence.
15. **battledores and shuttlecocks.** A battledore is a small racquet used to hit a shuttlecock (a cork with feathers) back and forth in badminton or similar games.

Bartholomew of England, "loving only to play, fearing no danger more than being beaten with a rod, always hungry and hence disposed to infirmities from being overfed, wanting everything they see, quick to laughter and as quick to tears, resisting their mothers' efforts to wash and comb them, and no sooner clean but dirty again." Girls were better behaved, according to Bartholomew, and dearer to their mothers. If children survived to age seven, their recognized life began, more or less as miniature adults. Childhood was already over. The childishness noticeable in medieval behavior, with its marked inability to restrain any kind of impulse, may have been simply due to the fact that so large a proportion of active society was actually very young in years. About half the population, it has been estimated, was under twenty-one, and about one third under fourteen.

A boy of noble family was left for his first seven years in the charge of women, who schooled him in manners and to some extent in letters. Significantly, St. Anne, the patron saint of mothers, is usually portrayed teaching her child, the Virgin Mary, how to read from a book. From age eight to fourteen the noble's son was sent as a page to the castle of a neighboring lord, in the same way that boys of lower orders went at seven or eight to another family as apprentices or servants. Personal service was not considered degrading:[16] a page or even a squire as a grown man assisted his lord to bathe and dress, took care of his clothes, waited on him at table while sharing noble status. In return for free labor, the lord provided a free school for the sons of his peers. The boy would learn to ride, to fight, and to hawk, the three chief physical elements of noble life, to play chess and backgammon, to sing and dance, play an instrument, and compose, and other romantic skills. The castle's private chaplain or a local abbey would supply his religious education, and teach him the rudiments[17] of reading and writing and possibly some elements of the grammar-school curriculum that non-noble boys studied.

At fourteen or fifteen, when he became a squire, the training for combat intensified. He learned to pierce the swinging dummy of the quintain with a lance, wield the sword and a variety of other murderous weapons, and know the rules of heraldry and jousting. As squire he led his lord's war-horse to battle and held it when the fighting was on foot. He assisted the seneschal in the business of the castle, kept the keys, acted as confidential courier, carried the purse and valuables on a journey. Book learning had little place in this program, although a young noble, depending on his bent, could make some acquaintance of geometry, law, elocution, and, in a few cases, Latin.

Women of noble estate were frequently more accomplished in Latin and other school learning than the men, for though girls did not leave home at seven like boys, their education was encouraged by the Church so that they might be better instructed in the faith and more fitted for the religious life in a nunnery, should their parents wish to dedicate them, with suitable endowment, to the Church. Besides reading and writing in French and Latin, they were taught music, astronomy, and some medicine and first aid. . . .

CONNECT: How does your education compare with that of a young male or female noble?

16. **degrading** (di grā′ding), *adj.* dishonorable.
17. **rudiment** (rü′də mənt), *n.* part to be learned first; beginning.

After Reading

Making Connections

Shaping Your Response

1. What are the advantages and disadvantages you can see in growing up in the 1300s?

2. Do you think the term *chivalry* had more meaning for males than for females? Why or why not?

3. What words would you use to describe a medieval boy's education? a medieval girl's?

Analyzing the Selection

4. What **allusions** does Tuchman make to other historical people or documents to support her observations?

5. What examples can you find of male-female **stereotypes** in this account?

6. What **images** of medieval life in this account do you find memorable?

Extending the Ideas

7. Study the description of a medieval wife's duties in the seventh paragraph that begins, "Books of advice. . . ." Do you think it was harder to be a housewife then or now? Explain.

8. Do you agree with Philip of Novara that "few children perish from excess of severity but many from being permitted too much"? Why or why not?

9. Describe how your education differs from that of your fourteenth-century male or female counterpart. Explain which kind of education you consider more practical.

Literary Focus: Sensory Details

Tuchman's use of **sensory details** makes her historical account lively and memorable. Look at the chart you filled out as you read. In a paragraph, explain what these details reveal about life in the Middle Ages.

Vocabulary Study

Number a paper from 1 to 10. Then complete each sentence with one of the listed words.

advocate
aloof
atrophy
capricious
conjecture
degrading
eradicable
ribald
rudiment
ruse

1. Even pure knights enjoyed offensive, ____ tales.

2. Since divorce was forbidden, medieval marriages were not ____.

3. Did the church ____ chastity until marriage?

4. Youths learned each basic ____ of reading and writing.

5. Mothers were reserved and ____ toward children because many died before their teens.

6. A knight's skill might ____ from lack of use in peace time.

7. One ____ knights might employ to enter an enemy castle was dressing as a monk.

8. Knights considered association with lowly peasants ____.

9. Children were as mischievous and ____ then as they are today.

10. What would you ____ about the status of women from this account?

Expressing Your Ideas

Writing Choices

Writer's Notebook Update Look again at the first list of five items archaeologists might find in your house. Write conclusions they could draw from them about life around the year 2000. Then write about the second list of items and the erroneous (and perhaps humorous) conclusions that might result. Use sensory details and some vocabulary words to enliven your writing.

Survival Skills What skills do you consider essential for a person your age in today's society? For example, do you consider changing a tire important? changing a baby? fixing a meal? fixing a VCR? speaking a second language? **List** ten skills, present them to classmates, and be prepared to defend your choices.

Home Improvement How-to books are just as popular today as during the medieval period. Think of a problem that might occur in any modern household—a clogged sink, a broken window—and write a list of **how-to steps** explaining how to fix it. Since your reader will be totally dependent on your directions, choose precise words for each of the steps in the process.

Other Options

A Little Knight Music In the Middle Ages, troubadours composed songs about knights' heroic adventures. Compose your own **song** about medieval life or knighthood. Present your song, accompanied by a guitar or recorder if possible, to classmates.

Castles in the Air Working in small groups, research a medieval castle—its architectural features, maintenance, inhabitants, and any other areas of interest. Make a model, draw, or use photographs of the castle to take the class on a **castle tour**. Show how the castle reflects medieval life.

Before Reading

The Tale of Sir Launcelot du Lake by Sir Thomas Malory   Great Britain
from The Once and Future King by T. H. White   Great Britain

T. H. White
1906–1964

Perhaps his career as a teacher gave Terence Hanbury White his rare gift for writing books that appeal to both adults and children. Born in Bombay, India, White grew up in England. At thirty, he resigned his teaching position to research filmmaking, falconry, and Arthurian lore. His most celebrated work, *The Once and Future King,* became the basis for the musical *Camelot,* which has enjoyed tremendous success since it first appeared in 1960. The excerpt from his book that appears here shows how White plays on Malory's original, viewing things from a twentieth-century perspective.

Building Background

A Very Good Knight When things were a bit slow in the castle, a knight who began "feeling weary of his life at the court," set out for adventure, as Launcelot does in the account you are about to read. Such quests gave knights an opportunity to practice the chivalric code, which was based on certain rules and customs. In compliance with this code, knights pledged:

- supreme allegiance to God;
- loyalty to a liege lord;
- to act honorably and bravely;
- to protect the weak and helpless.

Note how this code values **group welfare** over personal goals. Although knights generally upheld this code, they sometimes abandoned fair play and loyalty in pursuit of their own interests. Sir Launcelot (whose pursuit of Queen Gwynevere is a betrayal of King Arthur) is a fascinating and complex character because he displays both idealized qualities and human weaknesses.

Literary Focus

Allusion An **allusion** is a reference to a real, mythical, or literary event, thing, person, or place. An allusion to "thirty pieces of silver" brings to mind both the biblical character Judas and his act of betrayal. Authors employ allusions because they are economical ways to reinforce meaning or emotion. T. H. White's use of contemporary allusions to describe medieval life helps enliven his writing and establish a playful tone.

Writer's Notebook

A Man of Honor For many readers, Launcelot represents the ideal knight. Make a web of characteristics you associate with a "knight in shining armor" and be prepared to explain each trait. As you read the following excerpts, add other qualities that Launcelot exhibits.

THE TALE OF SIR LAUNCELOT DU LAKE

SIR THOMAS MALORY

When King Arthur returned from Rome he settled his court at Camelot, and there gathered about him his knights of the Round Table, who diverted[1] themselves with jousting and tournaments. Of all his knights one was supreme, both in prowess[2] at arms and in nobility of bearing, and this was Sir Launcelot, who was also the favorite of Queen Gwynevere, to whom he had sworn oaths of fidelity.

One day Sir Launcelot, feeling weary of his life at the court, and of only playing at arms, decided to set forth in search of adventure. He asked his nephew Sir Lyonel to accompany him, and when both were suitably armed and mounted, they rode off together through the forest.

At noon they started across a plain, but the intensity of the sun made Sir Launcelot feel sleepy, so Sir Lyonel suggested that they should rest beneath the shade of an apple tree that grew by a hedge not far from the road. They dismounted, tethered their horses, and settled down.

"Not for seven years have I felt so sleepy," said Sir Launcelot, and with that fell fast asleep, while Sir Lyonel watched over him.

Soon three knights came galloping past, and Sir Lyonel noticed that they were being pursued by a fourth knight, who was one of the most powerful he had yet seen. The pursuing knight overtook each of the others in turn, and as he did so, knocked each off his horse with a thrust of his spear. When all three lay stunned he dismounted, bound them securely to their horses with the reins, and led them away.

Without waking Sir Launcelot, Sir Lyonel mounted his horse and rode after the knight, and as soon as he had drawn close enough, shouted his challenge. The knight turned about and they charged at each other, with the result that Sir Lyonel was likewise flung from his horse, bound, and led away a prisoner.

The victorious knight, whose name was Sir Tarquine, led his prisoners to his castle, and there threw them on the ground, stripped them naked, and beat them with thorn twigs. After that he locked them in the dungeon where many other prisoners, who had received like treatment, were complaining dismally.

Meanwhile, Sir Ector de Marys,[3] who liked to accompany Sir Launcelot on his adventures, and finding him gone, decided to ride after him. Before long he came upon a forester.

"My good fellow, if you know the forest hereabouts, could you tell me in which direction I am most likely to meet with adventure?"

---

1. **divert** (də vėrt′), *v.* amuse; entertain.
2. prowess (prou′is), *n.* bravery; skill.
3. **Sir Ector de Marys,** Sir Launcelot's half-brother.

"Sir, I can tell you: Less than a mile from here stands a well-moated castle. On the left of the entrance you will find a ford where you can water your horse, and across from the ford a large tree from which hang shields of many famous knights. Below the shields hangs a caldron, of copper and brass: strike it three times with your spear, and then surely you will meet with adventure—such, indeed, that if you survive it, you will prove yourself the foremost knight in these parts for many years."

"May God reward you!" Sir Ector replied.

The castle was exactly as the forester had described it, and among the shields Sir Ector recognized several as belonging to knights of the Round Table. After watering his horse, he knocked on the caldron and Sir Tarquine, whose castle it was, appeared.

They jousted, and at the first encounter Sir Ector sent his opponent's horse spinning twice about before he could recover.

"That was a fine stroke; now let us try again," said Sir Tarquine.

This time Sir Tarquine caught Sir Ector just below the right arm and, having impaled[4] him on his spear, lifted him clean out of the saddle, and rode with him into the castle, where he threw him on the ground.

"Sir," said Sir Tarquine, "you have fought better than any knight I have encountered in the last twelve years; therefore, if you wish, I will demand no more of you than your parole[5] as my prisoner."

"Sir, that I will never give."

"Then I am sorry for you," said Sir Tarquine, and with that he stripped and beat him and locked him in the dungeon with the other prisoners. There Sir Ector saw Sir Lyonel.

"Alas, Sir Lyonel, we are in a sorry plight. But tell me, what has happened to Sir Launcelot? For he surely is the one knight who could save us."

"I left him sleeping beneath an apple tree, and what has befallen him since I do not know," Sir Lyonel replied; and then all the unhappy prisoners once more bewailed their lot.

While Sir Launcelot still slept beneath the apple tree, four queens started across the plain. They were riding white mules and accompanied by four knights who held above them, at the tips of their spears, a green silk canopy, to protect them from the sun. The party was startled by the neighing of Sir Launcelot's horse and, changing direction, rode up to the apple tree, where they discovered the sleeping knight. And as each of the queens gazed at the handsome Sir Launcelot, so each wanted him for her own.

"Let us not quarrel," said Morgan le Fay.[6] "Instead, I will cast a spell over him so that he remains asleep while we take him to my castle and make him our prisoner. We can then oblige him to choose one of us for his paramour."[7]

Sir Launcelot was laid on his shield and borne by two of the knights to the Castle Charyot, which was Morgan le Fay's stronghold. He awoke to find himself in a cold cell, where a young noblewoman was serving him supper.

"What cheer?" she asked.

"My lady, I hardly know, except that I must have been brought here by means of an enchantment."

"Sir, if you are the knight you appear to be, you will learn your fate at dawn tomorrow." And with that the young noblewoman left him. Sir Launcelot spent an uncomfortable night but at dawn the four queens presented themselves and Morgan le Fay spoke to him:

"Sir Launcelot, I know that Queen Gwynevere loves you, and you her. But now you are my prisoner, and you will have to choose: either to take one of us for your paramour, or to die miserably in this cell—just as you please.

---

4. impale (im pāl′), v. pierce through with something pointed.
5. parole (pǝ rōl′), n. word [French]; here, word of honor not to escape.
6. Morgan le Fay, a sorceress, half-sister of King Arthur.
7. paramour (par′ǝ mür), n. lover.

Now I will tell you who we are: I am Morgan le Fay, Queen of Gore; my companions are the Queens of North Galys, of Estelonde, and of the Outer Isles. So make your choice."

"A hard choice! Understand that I choose none of you, lewd sorceresses that you are; rather will I die in this cell. But were I free, I would take pleasure in proving it against any who would champion you that Queen Gwynevere is the finest lady of this land."

"So, you refuse us?" asked Morgan le Fay.

"On my life, I do," Sir Launcelot said finally, and so the queens departed.

Sometime later, the young noblewoman who had served Sir Launcelot's supper reappeared.

"What news?" she asked.

"It is the end," Sir Launcelot replied.

"Sir Launcelot, I know that you have refused the four queens, and that they wish to kill you out of spite. But if you will be ruled by me, I can save you. I ask that you will champion my father at a tournament next Tuesday, when he has to combat the King of North Galys, and three knights of the Round Table, who last Tuesday defeated him ignominiously."[8]

"My lady, pray tell me, what is your father's name?"

"King Bagdemagus."

"Excellent, my lady, I know him for a good king and a true knight, so I shall be happy to serve him."

"May God reward you! And tomorrow at dawn I will release you, and direct you to an abbey which is ten miles from here, and where the good monks will care for you while I fetch my father."

"I am at your service, my lady."

As promised, the young noblewoman released Sir Launcelot at dawn. When she had led him through the twelve doors to the castle entrance, she gave him his horse and armor, and directions for finding the abbey.

"God bless you, my lady; and when the time comes I promise I shall not fail you."

Sir Launcelot rode through the forest in search of the abbey, but at dusk had still failed to find it, and coming upon a red silk pavilion, apparently unoccupied, decided to rest there overnight, and continue his search in the morning. . . .

As soon as it was daylight, Sir Launcelot armed, mounted, and rode away in search of the abbey, which he found in less than two hours. King Bagdemagus' daughter was waiting for him, and as soon as she heard his horse's footsteps in the yard, ran to the window, and, seeing that it was Sir Launcelot, herself ordered the servants to stable his horse. She then led him to her chamber, disarmed him, and gave him a long gown to wear, welcoming him warmly as she did so.

King Bagdemagus' castle was twelve miles away, and his daughter sent for him as soon as she had settled Sir Launcelot. The king arrived with his retinue[9] and embraced Sir Launcelot, who then described his recent enchantment, and the great obligation he was under to his daughter for releasing him.

"Sir, you will fight for me on Tuesday next?"

"Sire, I shall not fail you; but please tell me the names of the three Round Table knights whom I shall be fighting."

"Sir Modred, Sir Madore de la Porte, and Sir Gahalantyne. I must admit that last Tuesday they defeated me and my knights completely."

"Sire, I hear that the tournament is to be fought within three miles of the abbey. Could you send me three of your most trustworthy knights, clad in plain armor, and with no device,[10] and a fourth suit of armor which I myself shall wear? We will take up our position just outside the tournament field and watch while you and the King of North Galys enter into combat with your followers; and then, as soon as you are in difficulties, we will come to

---

8. **ignominiously** (ig′nə min′ē əs lē), v. shamefully.
9. **retinue** (ret′n ū), n. followers, including friends, companions, and servants.
10. **device** (di vīs′), n. heraldic emblem of identification.

▲ This was a popular railway poster in 1924 by Maurice Greiffenhagen. Note how the curves of the horse's neck, the knight's helmet, and the archway unify the images of travel and adventure. Do you think the commercial purpose of this poster makes it any less effective as a work of art? Why or why not?

your rescue, and show your opponents what kind of knights you command."

This was arranged on Sunday, and on the following Tuesday Sir Launcelot and the three knights of King Bagdemagus waited in a copse,[11] not far from the pavilion which had been erected for the lords and ladies who were to judge the tournament and award the prizes.

The King of North Galys was the first on the field, with a company of ninescore[12] knights; he was followed by King Bagdemagus with fourscore[13] knights, and then by the three

knights of the Round Table, who remained apart from both companies. At the first encounter King Bagdemagus lost twelve knights, all killed, and the King of North Galys six.

With that, Sir Launcelot galloped onto the field, and with his first spear unhorsed five of the King of North Galys' knights, breaking the backs of four of them. With his next spear he

---

11. **copse** (kops), *n.* clump of trees.
12. **ninescore** (nīn′skôr′), *n.* nine times twenty, or 180.
13. **fourscore** (fôr′skôr′), *n.* four times twenty, or 80.

charged the king, and wounded him deeply in the thigh.

"That was a shrewd blow," commented Sir Madore, and galloped onto the field to challenge Sir Launcelot. But he too was tumbled from his horse, and with such violence that his shoulder was broken.

Sir Modred was the next to challenge Sir Launcelot, and he was sent spinning over his horse's tail. He landed head first, his helmet became buried in the soil, and he nearly broke his neck, and for a long time lay stunned.

Finally Sir Gahalantyne tried; at the first encounter both he and Sir Launcelot broke their spears, so both drew their swords and hacked vehemently at each other. But Sir Launcelot, with mounting wrath, soon struck his opponent a blow on the helmet which brought the blood streaming from eyes, ears, and mouth. Sir Gahalantyne slumped forward in the saddle, his horse panicked, and he was thrown to the ground, useless for further combat.

Sir Launcelot took another spear, and unhorsed sixteen more of the King of North Galys' knights, and with his next, unhorsed another twelve; and in each case with such violence that none of the knights ever fully recovered. The King of North Galys was forced to admit defeat, and the prize was awarded to King Bagdemagus.

That night Sir Launcelot was entertained as the guest of honor by King Bagdemagus and his daughter at their castle, and before leaving was loaded with gifts.

"My lady, please, if ever again you should need my services, remember that I shall not fail you."

The next day Sir Launcelot rode once more

My lady, I am riding in search of adventure...

through the forest, and by chance came to the apple tree where he had previously slept. This time he met a young noblewoman riding a white palfrey.

"My lady, I am riding in search of adventure; pray tell me if you know of any I might find hereabouts."

"Sir, there are adventures hereabouts if you believe that you are equal to them; but please tell me, what is your name?"

"Sir Launcelot du Lake."

"Very well, Sir Launcelot, you appear to be a sturdy enough knight, so I will tell you. Not far away stands the castle of Sir Tarquine, a knight who in fair combat has overcome more than sixty opponents whom he now holds prisoner. Many are from the court of King Arthur, and if you can rescue them, I will then ask you to deliver me and my companions from a knight who distresses us daily, either by robbery or by other kinds of outrage."

"My lady, please first lead me to Sir Tarquine, then I will most happily challenge this miscreant knight of yours."

When they arrived at the castle, Sir Launcelot watered his horse at the ford, and then beat the caldron until the bottom fell out. However, none came to answer the challenge, so they waited by the castle gate for half an hour or so. Then Sir Tarquine appeared, riding toward the castle with a wounded prisoner slung over his horse, whom Sir Launcelot recognized as Sir Gaheris, Sir Gawain's brother and a knight of the Round Table.

"Good knight," said Sir Launcelot, "it is known to me that you have put to shame many of the knights of the Round Table. Pray allow your prisoner, who I see is wounded, to recover, while I vindicate the honor of the knights whom you have defeated."

"I defy you, and all your fellowship of the Round Table," Sir Tarquine replied.

"You boast!" said Sir Launcelot.

At the first charge the backs of the horses were broken and both knights stunned. But they soon recovered and set to with their swords, and both struck so lustily[14] that neither shield nor armor could resist, and within two hours they were cutting each other's flesh, from which the blood flowed liberally. Finally they paused for a moment, resting on their shields.

"Worthy knight," said Sir Tarquine, "pray hold your hand for a while, and if you will, answer my question."

"Sir, speak on."

"You are the most powerful knight I have fought yet, but I fear you may be the one whom in the whole world I most hate. If you are not, for the love of you I will release all my prisoners and swear eternal friendship."

"What is the name of the knight you hate above all others?"

"Sir Launcelot du Lake; for it was he who slew my brother, Sir Carados of the Dolorous Tower, and it is because of him that I have killed a hundred knights, and maimed as many more, apart from the sixty-four I still hold prisoner. And so, if you are Sir Launcelot, speak up, for we must then fight to the death."

"Sir, I see now that I might go in peace and good fellowship, or otherwise fight to the death; but being the knight I am, I must tell you: I am Sir Launcelot du Lake, son of King Ban of Benwick, of Arthur's court, and a knight of the Round Table. So defend yourself!"

"Ah! this is most welcome."

Now the two knights hurled themselves at each other like two wild bulls; swords and shields clashed together, and often their swords drove into the flesh. Then sometimes one, sometimes the other, would stagger and fall, only to recover immediately and resume the contest. At last, however, Sir Tarquine grew faint, and unwittingly lowered his shield, Sir Launcelot was swift to follow up his advantage, and dragging the other down to his knees, unlaced his helmet and beheaded him.

Sir Launcelot then strode over to the young noblewoman: "My lady, now I am at your service, but first I must find a horse."

Then the wounded Sir Gaheris spoke up: "Sir, please take my horse. Today you have overcome the most formidable knight, excepting only yourself, and by so doing have saved us all. But before leaving, please tell me your name."

"Sir Launcelot du Lake. Today I have fought to vindicate the honor of the knights of the Round Table, and I know that among Sir Tarquine's prisoners are two of my brethren, Sir Lyonel and Sir Ector, also your own brother, Sir Gawain. According to the shields there are also: Sir Brandiles, Sir Galyhuddis, Sir Kay, Sir Alydukis, Sir Marhaus, and many others. Please release the prisoners and ask them to help themselves to the castle treasure. Give them all my greetings and say I will see them at the next Pentecost. And please request Sir Ector and Sir Lyonel to go straight to the court and await me there."

When Sir Launcelot had ridden away with the young noblewoman, Sir Gaheris entered the castle, and finding the porter[15] in the hall, threw him on the ground and took the castle keys. He then released the prisoners, who, seeing his wounds, thanked him for their deliverance.

"Do not thank me for this work, but Sir Launcelot. He sends his greetings to you all, and asks you to help yourselves to the castle treasure. He has ridden away on another quest, but said that he will see you at the next Pentecost." . . .

Sir Launcelot returned to Camelot two days before the feast of Pentecost, and at the court was acclaimed by many of the knights he had met on his adventures.

---

14. **lustily** (lust′ə lē), *v.* vigorously.
15. **porter** (pôr′tər), *n.* gatekeeper.

Sir Gaheris described to the court the terrible battle Sir Launcelot had fought with Sir Tarquine, and how sixty-four prisoners had been freed as a result of his victory.

Sir Kay related how Sir Launcelot had twice saved his life, and then exchanged armor with him, so that he should ride unchallenged.

Sir Gawtere, Sir Gylmere, and Sir Raynolde described how he had defeated them at the bridge, and forced them to yield as prisoners of Sir Kay; and they were overjoyed to discover that it had been Sir Launcelot nevertheless.

...Sir Launcelot became the most famous knight at King Arthur's court.

Sir Modred, Sir Mador, and Sir Gahalantyne described his tremendous feats in the battle against the King of North Galys; and Sir Launcelot himself described his enchantment by the four queens, and his rescue at the hands of the daughter of King Bagdemagus. . . .

And thus it was, at this time that Sir Launcelot became the most famous knight at King Arthur's court.

THE ONCE AND FUTURE KING

T. H. WHITE

When the fair damsel came in with the next meal, she showed signs of wanting to talk to him. Lancelot[1] noticed that she was a bold creature, who was probably fond of getting her own way.

"You said you might be able to help me?"

The girl looked suspiciously at him and said: "I can help you if you are who you are supposed to be. Are you really Sir Lancelot?"

"I am afraid I am."

"I will help you," she said, "if you will help me."

Then she burst into tears.

While the damsel is weeping, which she did in a charming and determined way, we had better explain about the tournaments which used to take place in Gramarye[2] in the early days. A real tournament was distinct from a joust. In a joust the knights tilted or fenced with each other singly, for a prize. But a tournament was more like a free fight. A body of knights would pick sides, so that there were twenty or thirty on either side, and then they would rush together harum-scarum. These mass battles were considered to be important—for instance, once you had paid your green fee for the tournament, you were admitted on the same ticket to fight in the jousts—but if you had only paid the jousting fee, you were not allowed to fight in the tourney. People were liable to be dangerously injured in the mêlées.[3] They were not bad things altogether, provided they were properly controlled. Unfortunately, in the early days, they were seldom controlled at all.

Merry England in Pendragon's time was a little like Poor Ould Ireland in O'Connell's.[4] There were factions. The knights of one county, or the inhabitants of one district, or the retainers[5] of one nobleman, might get themselves into a state in which they felt a hatred for the faction which lived next door. This hatred would become a feud, and then the king or leader of the one place would challenge the leader of the other one to a tourney—and both factions would go to the meeting with full intent to do each other mischief. It was the same in the days of Papist and Protestant, or Stuart and

---

1. **Lancelot**, modern spelling of Launcelot.
2. **Gramarye** (gram′ər ē), a term White uses for the geographical area of England in which the events take place.
3. **mêlée** (mā′lā), *n*. confused fight.
4. **Pendragon's time . . . O'Connell's.** Pendragon is Uther Pendragon, Arthur's father. "Poor, Ould Ireland" in the time of Daniel O'Connell (1775-1847), Irish leader known as the "Liberator," was wracked by battles for the freedom of Ireland from Great Britain.
5. **retainer** (ri tā′nər), *n*. attendant who serves a person of rank.

This battle scene from *Le Roman de Lancelot du Lac*, completed in the early 1300s, depicts Lancelot fighting for King Bagdemagus, as the queen and her ladies look on. After defeating all challengers, Lancelot allegedly faints when he sees the queen. What does his behavior indicate about chivalry in general and Lancelot in particular? ➤

Orangeman,[6] who would meet together with shillelaghs[7] in their hands and murder in their hearts.

"Why are you crying?" asked Sir Lancelot.

"Oh dear," sobbed the damsel. "That horrid King of Northgalis has challenged my father to a tournament next Tuesday, and he has got three knights of King Arthur's on his side, and my poor father is bound to lose. I am afraid he will get hurt."

"I see. And what is your father's name?"

"He is King Bagdemagus."

Sir Lancelot got up and kissed her politely on the forehead. He saw at once what he was expected to do.

"Very well," he said. "If you can rescue me out of this prison, I will fight in the faction of King Bagdemagus next Tuesday."

"Oh, thank you," said the maiden, wringing out her handkerchief. "Now I must go, I am afraid, or they will miss me downstairs."

Naturally she was not going to help the magic Queen of Northgalis to keep Lancelot in prison—when it was the King of

---

6. **Papist . . . Orangemen,** references to religious disputes and wars in British history between Roman Catholics (sometimes called Papists) and Protestants. The royal Stuart family included James II, who reigned 1685-1688 and had Catholic sympathies. He was forcibly replaced by the Dutch Protestant, William of Orange, whose reign lasted 1689-1702.

7. shillelagh (shə lā′lē), *n*. a club used in fights.

Northgalis himself who was going to fight her father. . . .

There is no need to give a long description of the tourney. Malory gives it. Lancelot picked three knights who were recommended by the young damsel to go with him, and he arranged that all four of them should bear the vergescu. This was the white shield carried by <u>unfledged</u>[8] knights, and Lancelot insisted on this arrangement because he knew that three of his own brethren of the Round Table were going to fight on the other side. He did not want them to recognize him, because it might cause ill-feeling at court. On the other hand, he felt that it was his duty to fight against them because of the promise which he had given to the damsel. The King of Northgalis, who was

the leader of the opposite side, had one hundred and sixty knights in his faction, and King Bagdemagus only had eighty. Lancelot went for the first knight of the Round Table, and put his shoulder out of joint. He went for the second one so hard that the unlucky fellow was carried over his horse's tail and buried his helm[9] several inches in the ground. He hit the third knight on the head so hard that his nose bled, and his horse ran away with him. By the time he had broken the thigh of the King of Northgalis, everybody could see that to all intents and purposes[10] the tournament was over.

---

8. **unfledged** (un flejd′), *adj.* inexperienced.
9. **helm** (helm), *n.* helmet. [*Old English*]
10. **to all intents and purposes,** in almost every way.

The Once and Future King   **367**

After Reading

Making Connections

Shaping Your
Response

1. If you were a Hollywood director, what actor would you cast as Launcelot? Why?

2. Do you think that some aspects of chivalry displayed by Launcelot are still alive today? Explain.

Analyzing the
Legends

3. In Malory's account, how does Launcelot display the codes of chivalry?

4. What evidence do you find to indicate that chivalry is both romantic and barbaric?

5. What is **ironic** about White's description of the damsel weeping in a "determined way"?

6. In what way is White's **image** of the damsel "wringing out her hand-kerchief" an example of **hyperbole,** or exaggeration?

7. What is the difference in **tone** between these two selections? Find passages that indicate each tone.

8. The daughter of King Bagdemagus is referred to as "my lady" in Malory's account, while White refers to her as a "damsel." What different associations do these terms have for you?

Extending the Ideas

9. What kinds of contests today are similar to the jousts and tournaments both authors describe? Why do you think such contests still exist?

10. 👆 Based on what you have learned about Launcelot, would you say that he pursued individual glory or the welfare of the **group**? Explain.

Literary Focus: Allusion

White uses the term "green fee," an **allusion** to a fee paid in order to play golf.

- What similarities do you think he is implying exist between a golf game and a medieval tournament?

- If someone called you a Launcelot, what do you think he or she would mean by this allusion?

- Why do you think White compares feuding medieval knights to battling factions from later centuries?

Vocabulary Study

Write the letter of the most appropriate answer for each numbered item.

impale
mêlée
prowess
shillelagh
unfledged

1. When Launcelot was an *unfledged* knight, he had _____.
   a. fought many battles   **b.** fought few battles
   c. just become married   **d.** become injured

2. What could one use to *impale* a knight?
   a. a horse   **b.** a coin   **c.** a chess game   **d.** a pointed object

3. A *mêlée* is a _____.
   a. small weapon   **b.** sweet dessert   **c.** confused fight   **d.** sword

4. A knight who displayed his *prowess* would show his _____.
   a. beloved   **b.** shield   **c.** horse   **d.** skill

5. Bagdemagus's *shillelagh* probably resembled a _____.
   a. baseball bat   **b.** gremlin   **c.** violin   **d.** small animal

Expressing Your Ideas

Writing Choices

Writer's Notebook Update Now that you have read the selections, review your web about a knight. Would you add any other words? Which qualities do you consider important today? Write several sentences illustrating the observation: "Chivalry exists (does not exist) today."

Fair Maidens and Feminists Consider how women are portrayed in the selections about the Middle Ages that you have read so far. Do you think the status of females has changed in the past six centuries? Write an **opinion essay** that explains the steps women have taken forward or backward.

My Excellent Adventure Although you may not have encountered dragons or dungeons, you too have had adventures worthy of a knight. Write a brief **narrative** about a quest or battle in your life and your noble efforts to emerge victorious. Include an allusion to Arthur's time. Adopt a humorous tone if you wish.

Other Options

Lance and the Lakers Choose one episode from Launcelot's story and retell it in a modern setting. Suppose, for example, that King Bagdemagus were the owner of a professional basketball team. How would Lance Lott be able to assist (or foil) him? Write a brief **screenplay** to videotape and present in class.

Looking for Something? Think about the Quest theme in movies, books, TV programs, and video games. Work with a group to present a **media resource list** of titles illustrating this theme. Accompany your list with a brief description of what each title is about.

Multicultural Quest Quiz What was the object of the quest in *Indiana Jones and the Last Crusade?* Who were the samurai? What was the Sumerian hero Gilgamesh seeking? Work with a group to make up a **trivia quiz** of quests and pursuits from around the world, both factual and fictional. Challenge your classmates to answer the quiz.

The Once and Future King   **369**

Before Reading

The Death of King Arthur by Sir Thomas Malory   Great Britain

from Idylls of the King by Alfred, Lord Tennyson   Great Britain

Alfred, Lord Tennyson
1809–1893

Just as another boy might train to be an athlete or singer, the young Tennyson focused on becoming a poet, writing an epic poem of six thousand lines by the age of twelve. More than any other poet of the nineteenth century, he became the voice of the Victorian Age, representing its hopes as well as its concerns about the conflict between emerging scientific principles and religion. In 1850 he became England's poet laureate. A man of dignity, courage, and devotion to duty, it seems appropriate that Tennyson chose to explore Arthurian tales in his own poetic narrative, *Idylls of the King.*

Building Background

Malory and Middle English Sir Thomas Malory wrote *Le Morte d'Arthur* in Middle English. The following passage describes — in Malory's original language — a scene you will encounter in the next selection. Try reading this passage aloud and translating it. Then compare it to the translation that appears at the bottom of column 1 on page 376.

> THAN SIR BEDWERE . . . BOUNDE THE GYRDYLL ABOUTE THE HYLTIS, AND THREW THE SWERDE AS FARRE INTO THE WATIR AS HE MYGHT. AND THERE CAM AN ARME AND AN HONDE ABOVE THE WATIR, AND TOKE HIT AND CLEYGHT HIT, AND SHOKE HIT THRYSE AND BRAUNDYSSHED, AND THAN VANYSSHED WITH THE SWERDE INTO THE WATIR.

Literary Focus

Denotation and Connotation If you look up the word *car* in a dictionary, you will find it described something like this: "a four-wheeled passenger vehicle driven by an internal combustion engine." Yet this word may suggest other things to you: *freedom, expense, independence, power, speed, being sixteen.* The dictionary definition of a word is its **denotation.** The associations and added meanings are its **connotations.** Be on the lookout in the following selections for words such as *chains, dawn, king, flag,* and *sword,* which are rich in connotations.

Writer's Notebook

Batman Needs the Joker In the selection by Malory that you are about to read, you will meet a classic villain, Sir Modred, King Arthur's illegitimate son and rival. Before starting to read, jot down the names of hero/villain pairs from literature, TV, video games, and movies. Think about why so many stories have such pairs.

The Death of King Arthur

Sir Thomas Malory

The beginning of the end of Arthur's reign comes with the discovery by knights of the Round Table of the love between Launcelot and Gwynevere. Arthur feels forced by law to burn his wife at the stake. Launcelot saves Gwynevere at the last moment, but in the process kills two brothers of Gawain, Arthur's favorite nephew. Arthur leads an attack on Launcelot in France, but Launcelot seriously wounds Gawain. While Arthur is away in France, Modred, Arthur's mean-spirited illegitimate son, seizes the throne. Arthur hastens back to England.

During the absence of King Arthur from Britain, Sir Modred, already vested with sovereign powers, had decided to usurp[1] the throne. Accordingly, he had false letters written—announcing the death of King Arthur in battle—and delivered to himself. Then, calling a parliament, he ordered the letters to be read and persuaded the nobility to elect him king. The coronation took place at Canterbury and was celebrated with a fifteen-day feast.

Sir Modred then settled in Camelot and made overtures to Queen Gwynevere to marry him. The queen seemingly acquiesced, but as soon as she had won his confidence, begged leave to make a journey to London in order to prepare her trousseau. Sir Modred consented, and the queen rode straight to the Tower[2] which, with the aid of her loyal nobles, she manned and provisioned for her defense.

Sir Modred, outraged, at once marched against her, and laid siege to the Tower, but despite his large army, siege engines,[3] and guns, was unable to effect a breach. He then tried to entice[4] the queen from the Tower, first by guile[5] and then by threats, but she would listen to neither. Finally the Archbishop of Canterbury came forward to protest:

"Sir Modred, do you not fear God's displeasure?. . . If you do not

---

1. **usurp** (yū zėrp′), *v.* seize by force.
2. **Tower**, Tower of London, a stronghold of several buildings located on the banks of the Thames River.
3. **siege engines**, mechanical equipment such as catapults.
4. **entice** (en tīs′), *v.* tempt; lure.
5. **guile** (gīl), *n.* sly trick; cunning.

revoke your evil deeds I shall curse you with bell, book, and candle."[6]

"Fie on you! Do your worst!" Sir Modred replied.

"Sir Modred, I warn you take heed! Or the wrath of the Lord will descend upon you."

"Away, false priest, or I shall behead you!"

The Archbishop withdrew, and after excommunicating[7] Sir Modred, abandoned his office and fled to Glastonbury.[8] There he took up his abode as a simple hermit, and by fasting and prayer sought divine intercession in the troubled affairs of his country.

Sir Modred tried to assassinate the Archbishop, but was too late. He continued to assail[9] the queen with entreaties and threats, both of which failed, and then the news reached him that King Arthur was returning with his army from France in order to seek revenge.

Sir Modred now appealed to the barony to support him, and it has to be told that they came forward in large numbers to do so. Why? it will be asked. Was not King Arthur, the noblest sovereign Christendom had seen, now leading his armies in a righteous cause? The answer lies in the people of Britain, who, then as now, were fickle. Those who so readily transferred their allegiance to Sir Modred did so with the excuse that whereas King Arthur's reign had led them into war and strife, Sir Modred promised them peace and festivity.

Hence it was with an army of a hundred thousand that Sir Modred marched to Dover[10] to battle against his own father, and to withhold from him his rightful crown.

As King Arthur with his fleet drew into the harbor, Sir Modred and his army launched forth in every available craft, and a bloody battle ensued[11] in the ships and on the beach. If King Arthur's army were the smaller, their courage was the higher, confident as they were of the righteousness of their cause. Without stint they battled through the burning ships, the screaming wounded, and the corpses floating on the blood-stained waters. Once ashore they put Sir Modred's entire army to flight.

The battle over, King Arthur began a search for his casualties, and on peering into one of the ships found Sir Gawain, mortally wounded. Sir Gawain fainted when King Arthur lifted him in his arms; and when he came to, the king spoke:

"Alas! dear nephew, that you lie here thus, mortally wounded! What joy is now left to me on this earth? You must know it was you and Sir Launcelot I loved above all others, and it seems that I have lost you both."

"My good uncle, it was my pride and my stubbornness that brought all this about, for had I not urged you to war with Sir Launcelot your subjects would not now be in revolt. Alas, that Sir Launcelot is not here, for he would soon drive them out! And it is at Sir Launcelot's hands that I suffer my own death: the wound which he dealt me has reopened. I would not wish it otherwise, because is he not the greatest and gentlest of knights?

"I know that by noon I shall be dead, and I repent bitterly that I may not be reconciled to Sir Launcelot; therefore I pray you, good uncle, give me pen, paper, and ink so that I may write to him."

A priest was summoned and Sir Gawain confessed;[12] then a clerk brought ink, pen, and

---

6. **curse you with bell, book and candle,** expulsion from the Catholic Church. After pronouncing sentence, the officiating cleric closes his book, quenches the candle by throwing it to the ground, and tolls the bell as for one who has died.

7. **excommunicating** (ek′skə myü′nə kā′ting), *n.* severing from membership in the church.

8. **Glastonbury,** a town in present-day Somerset and the site of an ancient abbey thought in legends to be the burial place of King Arthur.

9. **assail** (ə sāl′), *v.* attack with hostile words, arguments, or abuse.

10. **Dover,** port city on the south coast of England, across from France.

11. **ensue** (en sü′), *v.* follow.

12. **confess** (kən fes′), *v.* make a confession to a priest.

▲ What details in *Le Morte D'Arthur*, painted in 1861 by James Archer, suggest hope? Who do you think the figures in the background might be?

paper, and Sir Gawain wrote to Sir Launcelot as follows:

"Sir Launcelot, flower of the knighthood: I, Sir Gawain, son of King Lot of Orkney and of King Arthur's sister, send you my greetings!

"I am about to die; the cause of my death is the wound I received from you outside the city of Benwick; and I would make it known that my death was of my own seeking, that I was moved by the spirit of revenge and spite to provoke you to battle.

"Therefore, Sir Launcelot, I beseech you to visit my tomb and offer what prayers you will on my behalf; and for myself, I am content to die at the hands of the noblest knight living.

"One more request: that you hasten with your armies across the sea and give succor[13] to our noble king. Sir Modred, his bastard son, has usurped the throne and now holds against him with an army of a hundred thousand. He would have won the queen, too, but she fled to the Tower of London and there charged her loyal supporters with her defense.

"Today is the tenth of May, and at noon I shall give up the ghost; this letter is written partly with my blood. This morning we fought our way ashore, against the armies of Sir Modred, and that is how my wound came to be

---

13. **succor** (suk′ər), *n.* assistance.

The Death of King Arthur   **373**

reopened. We won the day, but my lord King Arthur needs you, and I too, that on my tomb you may bestow your blessing."

Sir Gawain fainted when he had finished, and the king wept. When he came to he was given extreme unction, and died, as he had anticipated, at the hour of noon. The king buried him in the chapel at Dover Castle, and there many came to see him, and all noticed the wound on his head which he had received from Sir Launcelot.

Then the news reached Arthur that Sir Modred offered him battle on the field at Baron Down.[14] Arthur hastened there with his army, they fought, and Sir Modred fled once more, this time to Canterbury.

When King Arthur had begun the search for his wounded and dead, many volunteers from all parts of the country came to fight under his flag, convinced now of the rightness of his cause. Arthur marched westward, and Sir Modred once more offered him battle. It was assigned for the Monday following Trinity Sunday,[15] on Salisbury Down.

Sir Modred levied fresh troops from East Anglia and the places about London, and fresh volunteers came forward to help Arthur. Then, on the night of Trinity Sunday, Arthur was vouchsafed[16] a strange dream:

He was appareled in gold cloth and seated in a chair which stood on a pivoted scaffold. Below him, many fathoms deep, was a dark well, and in the water swam serpents, dragons, and wild beasts. Suddenly the scaffold tilted and Arthur was flung into the water, where all the creatures struggled toward him and began tearing him limb from limb.

Arthur cried out in his sleep and his squires hastened to waken him. Later, as he lay between waking and sleeping, he thought he saw Sir Gawain, and with him a host of beautiful noblewomen. Arthur spoke:

Alas for this fateful day!

"My sister's son! I thought you had died; but now I see you live, and I thank the lord Jesu! I pray you, tell me, who are these ladies?"

"My lord, these are the ladies I championed in righteous quarrels when I was on earth. Our lord God has vouchsafed that we visit you and plead with you not to give battle to Sir Modred tomorrow, for if you do, not only will you yourself be killed, but all your noble followers too. We beg you to be warned, and to make a treaty with Sir Modred, calling a truce for a month, and granting him whatever terms he may demand. In a month Sir Launcelot will be here, and he will defeat Sir Modred."

Thereupon Sir Gawain and the ladies vanished, and King Arthur once more summoned his squires and his counselors and told them his vision. Sir Lucas and Sir Bedivere were commissioned to make a treaty with Sir Modred. They were to be accompanied by two bishops and to grant, within reason, whatever terms he demanded.

The ambassadors found Sir Modred in command of an army of a hundred thousand and unwilling to listen to overtures of peace. However, the ambassadors eventually prevailed on him, and in return for the truce granted him suzerainty of Cornwall and Kent,[17] and succession to the British throne when King Arthur died. The treaty was to be signed by King Arthur and Sir Modred the next day. They were to meet

---

14. **Down,** an expanse of rolling, grassy land. Though Baron Down no longer appears on maps, Salisbury Down, or Plain, is famous as the site of Stonehenge.
15. **Trinity Sunday,** feast day honoring the Holy Trinity, observed the eighth Sunday after Easter.
16. **vouchsafe** (vouch sāf′), *v.* grant.
17. **suzerainty** (sü zə ran′tē) **of Cornwall and Kent,** dominion or power over two southern counties of England.

between the two armies, and each was to be accompanied by no more than fourteen knights.

Both King Arthur and Sir Modred suspected the other of treachery, and gave orders for their armies to attack at the sight of a naked sword. When they met at the appointed place the treaty was signed and both drank a glass of wine.

Then, by chance, one of the soldiers was bitten in the foot by an adder which had lain concealed in the brush. The soldier unthinkingly drew his sword to kill it, and at once, as the sword flashed in the light, the alarums were given, trumpets sounded, and both armies galloped into the attack.

"Alas for this fateful day!" exclaimed King Arthur, as both he and Sir Modred hastily mounted and galloped back to their armies. There followed one of those rare and heartless battles in which both armies fought until they were destroyed. King Arthur, with his customary valor, led squadron after squadron of cavalry into the attack, and Sir Modred encountered him unflinchingly. As the number of dead and wounded mounted on both sides, the active combatants continued dauntless[18] until nightfall, when four men alone survived.

King Arthur wept with dismay to see his beloved followers fallen; then, struggling toward him, unhorsed and badly wounded, he saw Sir Lucas the Butler and his brother, Sir Bedivere.

"Alas!" said the king, "that the day should come when I see all my noble knights destroyed! I would prefer that I myself had fallen. But what has become of the traitor Sir Modred, whose evil ambition was responsible for this carnage?"[19]

Looking about him King Arthur then noticed Sir Modred leaning with his sword on a heap of the dead.

"Sir Lucas, I pray you give me my spear, for I have seen Sir Modred."

"Sire, I entreat you, remember your vision— how Sir Gawain appeared with a heaven-sent message to dissuade you from fighting Sir Modred. Allow this fateful day to pass; it is ours, for we three hold the field, while the enemy is broken."

"My lords, I care nothing for my life now! And while Sir Modred is at large I must kill him: there may not be another chance."

"God speed you, then!" said Sir Bedivere.

When Sir Modred saw King Arthur advance with his spear, he rushed to meet him with drawn sword. Arthur caught Sir Modred below the shield and drove his spear through his body; Sir Modred, knowing that the wound was mortal, thrust himself up to the handle of the spear, and then, brandishing his sword in both hands, struck Arthur on the side of the helmet, cutting through it and into the skull beneath; then he crashed to the ground, gruesome and dead.

King Arthur fainted many times as Sir Lucas and Sir Bedivere struggled with him to a small chapel nearby, where they managed to ease his wounds a little. When Arthur came to, he thought he heard cries coming from the battlefield.

"Sir Lucas, I pray you, find out who cries on the battlefield," he said.

Wounded as he was, Sir Lucas hobbled painfully to the field, and there in the moonlight saw the camp followers stealing gold and jewels from the dead, and murdering the wounded. He returned to the king and reported to him what he had seen, and then added:

"My lord, it surely would be better to move you to the nearest town?"

"My wounds forbid it. But alas for the good Sir Launcelot! How sadly I have missed him today! And now I must die—as Sir Gawain warned me I would—repenting our quarrel with my last breath."

---

18. **dauntless** (dônt′lis), *adj.* brave.
19. **carnage** (kär′nij), *n.* slaughter of a great number of people.

Sir Lucas and Sir Bedivere made one further attempt to lift the king. He fainted as they did so.

Then Sir Lucas fainted as part of his intestines broke through a wound in the stomach. When the king came to, he saw Sir Lucas lying dead with foam at his mouth.

"Sweet Jesu, give him succor!" he said. "This noble knight has died trying to save my life—alas that this was so!"

Sir Bedivere wept for his brother.

"Sir Bedivere, weep no more," said King Arthur, "for you can save neither your brother nor me; and I would ask you to take my sword Excalibur to the shore of the lake and throw it in the water. Then return to me and tell me what you have seen."

"My lord, as you command, it shall be done."

Sir Bedivere took the sword, but when he came to the water's edge, it appeared so beautiful that he could not bring himself to throw it in, so instead he hid it by a tree, and then returned to the king.

"Sir Bedivere, what did you see?"

"My lord, I saw nothing but the wind upon the waves."

"Then you did not obey me; I pray you, go swiftly again, and this time fulfill my command."

Sir Bedivere went and returned again, but this time too he had failed to fulfill the king's command.

"Sir Bedivere, what did you see?"

"My lord, nothing but the lapping of the waves."

"Sir Bedivere, twice you have betrayed me! And for the sake only of my sword: it is unworthy of you! Now I pray you, do as I command, for I have not long to live."

This time Sir Bedivere wrapped the girdle[20] around the sheath and hurled it as far as he could into the water. A hand appeared from below the surface, took the sword, waved it thrice, and disappeared again. Sir Bedivere

returned to the king and told him what he had seen.

"Sir Bedivere, I pray you now help me hence, or I fear it will be too late."

Sir Bedivere carried the king to the water's edge, and there found a barge in which sat many beautiful ladies with their queen. All were wearing black hoods, and when they saw the king, they raised their voices in a piteous lament.

"I pray you, set me in the barge," said the king.

Sir Bedivere did so, and one of the ladies laid the king's head in her lap; then the queen spoke to him:

"My dear brother, you have stayed too long: I fear that the wound on your head is already cold."

Thereupon they rowed away from the land and Sir Bedivere wept to see them go.

"My lord King Arthur, you have deserted me! I am alone now, and among enemies."

"Sir Bedivere, take what comfort you may, for my time is passed, and now I must be taken to Avalon for my wound to be healed. If you hear of me no more, I beg you pray for my soul."

The barge slowly crossed the water and out of sight while the ladies wept. Sir Bedivere walked alone into the forest and there remained for the night.

In the morning he saw beyond the trees of a copse a small hermitage. He entered and found a hermit kneeling down by a fresh tomb. The hermit was weeping as he prayed, and then Sir Bedivere recognized him as the Archbishop of Canterbury, who had been banished by Sir Modred.

"Father, I pray you, tell me, whose tomb is this?"

"My son, I do not know. At midnight the body was brought here by a company of ladies. We buried it, they lit a hundred candles for the

---

20. **girdle** (gėr′dl), *n.* a band encircling the waist.

service, and rewarded me with a thousand bezants."[21]

"Father, King Arthur lies buried in this tomb."

Sir Bedivere fainted when he had spoken, and when he came to he begged the Archbishop to allow him to remain at the hermitage and end his days in fasting and prayer.

"Father, I wish only to be near to my true liege."

"My son, you are welcome; and do I not recognize you as Sir Bedivere the Bold, brother to Sir Lucas the Butler?"

Thus the Archbishop and Sir Bedivere remained at the hermitage, wearing the habits of hermits and devoting themselves to the tomb with fasting and prayers of contrition.

Such was the death of King Arthur as written down by Sir Bedivere. By some it is told that there were three queens on the barge: Queen Morgan le Fay, the Queen of North Galys, and the Queen of the Waste Lands; and others

A hand appeared from below the surface, took the sword, waved it thrice, and disappeared again.

include the name of Nyneve, the Lady of the Lake who had served King Arthur well in the past, and had married the good knight Sir Pelleas.

In many parts of Britain it is believed that King Arthur did not die and that he will return to us and win fresh glory and the Holy Cross of our Lord Jesu Christ; but for myself I do not believe this, and would leave him buried peacefully in his tomb at Glastonbury, where the Archbishop of Canterbury and Sir Bedivere humbled themselves, and with prayers and fasting honored his memory. And inscribed on his tomb, men say, is this legend:

HIC IACET ARTHURUS, REX QUONDAM REXQUE FUTURUS.[22]

---

21. **bezant** (bez′ənt), *n*. gold coin.
22. **HIC . . . FUTURUS**, "Here lies Arthur, the once and future king." [*Latin*]

Idylls of the King

Alfred, Lord Tennyson

Then loudly cried the bold Sir Bedivere:
"Ah! my Lord Arthur, whither shall I go?
Where shall I hide my forehead and my eyes?
For now I see the true old times are dead,
5 When every morning brought a noble chance,
And every chance brought out a noble knight.
Such times have been not since the light that led
The holy Elders with the gift of myrrh.[1]
But now the whole Round Table is dissolved
10 Which was an image of the mighty world,
And I, the last, go forth companionless,
And the days darken round me, and the years,
Among new men, strange faces, other minds."
And slowly answer'd Arthur from the barge:
15 "The old order changeth, yielding place to new,
And God fulfills himself in many ways,
Lest one good custom should corrupt the world.
Comfort thyself: what comfort is in me?
I have lived my life, and that which I have done
20 May He within himself make pure! but thou,
If thou shouldst never see my face again,
Pray for my soul. More things are wrought by prayer
Than this world dreams of. Wherefore, let thy voice
Rise like a fountain for me night and day.
25 For what are men better than sheep or goats
That nourish a blind life within the brain,
If, knowing God, they lift not hands of prayer
Both for themselves and those who call them friend?
For so the whole round earth is every way
30 Bound by gold chains about the feet of God.
But now farewell. I am going a long way
With these thou seest—if indeed I go—
For all my mind is clouded with a doubt—
To the island-valley of Avilion;
35 Where falls not hail, or rain, or any snow,
Nor ever wind blows loudly; but it lies
Deep-meadow'd, happy, fair with orchard lawns
And bowery hollows crown'd with summer sea,
Where I will heal me of my grievous wound."
40 So said he, and the barge with oar and sail
Moved from the brink, like some full-breasted swan
That, fluting a wild carol ere her death,
Ruffles her pure cold plume, and takes the flood

With swarthy webs. Long stood Sir Bedivere
45 Revolving many memories, till the hull
Look'd one black dot against the verge of dawn,
And on the mere[2] the wailing died away.

---

1. **holy Elders with the gift of myrrh**, the wise men in
   the Gospel of Matthew who follow the star to
   Bethlehem to offer the infant Jesus gifts of gold,
   frankincense, and myrrh (a fragrant gum resin from
   the myrrh shrub used for making incense, perfume,
   and medicine).
2. **mere** (mir), *n.* lake or pond.

◄ Note the geometric
patterns and lines in
this detail by Aubrey
Beardsley from a 1909
edition of *Le Morte
d'Arthur*. Where do
the dominant lines
direct your eyes?
What does this direc-
tion suggest?

After Reading

Making Connections

Shaping Your Response

1. Do you think Arthur's life was a triumph or a tragedy? Why?

2. Who do you think will be Arthur's successor as king? Why?

3. In your notebook, write down at least three words that describe your impressions of Arthurian times.

Analyzing the Selections

4. In Malory's account, how do Arthur's two dreams **foreshadow** the future?

5. Why do you think Arthur chooses to engage in personal combat with Modred?

6. What **images** in Malory's account emphasize the grimness and savagery of the last battle?

7. Explain how the label, "the once and future king," which seems to be a contradiction, or **paradox,** can be true.

8. What is the purpose of the **allusion** Bedivere makes in Tennyson's poem?

Extending the Ideas

9. Arthur observes, "The old order changeth, yielding place to new." Do you think these words apply as much today as they did in Arthur's era? Why or why not?

10. What modern celebrities can you think of whose character or actions have brought about their own downfalls?

Literary Focus: Connotation and Denotation

> **chains**
> **dawn**
> **king**
> **flag**
> **sword**

Write two of these words in separate circles, leaving room to write the dictionary definition, or **denotation,** of each word. After writing the definition, draw spokes radiating from each circle. On the spokes, write the **connotations,** or associations, that you have for each word. You may want to read the article on Connotation and Denotation on page 492 before you do this activity.

Vocabulary Study

Write a synonym from the list to replace each italicized word in the sentences below. You will not use all the words.

carnage
dauntless
ensue
entice
guile
usurp

1. A true knight remained *brave* in the face of extraordinary obstacles.
2. No one could *lure* a knight away from his noble mission.
3. After a glorious victory, a celebration would *follow*.
4. Even victorious knights would regret the *slaughter* caused by battles.
5. Sir Modred did not observe the code of chivalry when he tried to *seize* the crown.

Expressing Your Ideas

Writing Choices

Writer's Notebook Update Write a comparison between Arthur and Modred and one of the hero/villain pairs you noted in your notebook. Explain what you think would be lost if the heroes had no foils, or opposites. You might use some of the vocabulary words in your comparison.

The Once and Future King Write an **obituary** for King Arthur that contains descriptions, quotations, or testimonials to him from the selections you have read. You might accompany the obituary with a sketch.

Last Letter Imagine that Arthur, like Gawain, had time to write one letter before he died. To whom do you think he would write? Gwynevere? Launcelot? his subjects? Would he be forgiving? accusing? consoling? encouraging? Choose a recipient; then write Arthur's last **letter.**

Other Options

Put on a Coat The medieval knight, along with warriors of other cultures, represented his skills, heritage, and allegiance on his personal heraldic shield, or **coat of arms**. Design a coat of arms for one of the characters you have just read about, or for yourself, which reflects family background, interests, culture, personality traits, and accomplishments. Accompany your coat of arms with a motto.

Knightworthy Create a **new knight** for King Arthur's Round Table. This could be someone noteworthy, real or fictional, from any era. Describe in words or draw that person's physical characteristics, clothing, and armor, as well as character traits that make him or her "knightworthy."

Arthurian Legends

Knights in Many Guises

Knights

Multicultural Connection

Knighthood has existed in many ages and cultures. The code of chivalry—with some adaptations—still exists today. Look for traces of Arthur in the world around you.

Contemporary Hausa riders take part in a state celebration in Nigeria.

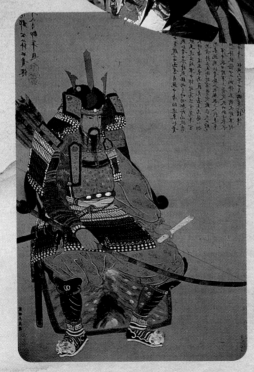

This painted scroll features a samurai warrior in feudal Japan.

This photograph shows a participant in a contemporary jousting tournament in England.

in many Guises

Darth Vader in *The Empire Strikes Back* was formerly a Jedi knight.

Joan of Arc (1412–1431) led French armies against the invading English and saved the city of Orléans.

Honoré Daumier's *Don Quixote* depicts the comic knight who mistakes windmills for giants.

chivalry

Lady Pulchritude, a modern woman of the 21st century, has decided to choose her own "knight" in marriage. Imagine that 24 suitors sat in numbered chairs at the Round Table. One of them is to win her hand in marriage. She points to the suitor in chair 1, saying, "You stay." To the second suitor in chair 2, she says, "You forfeit your life." To the third, she says, "You stay," to the fourth, she says, "You forfeit your life," continuing around the table, with every other suitor forfeiting his life until only one remains. In what chair does the lucky knight sit?

Dear Miss Manners:

A young woman from my office who lives near me takes the same bus to work every day that I do. We have even occasionally paid each other's fares when one or the other of us doesn't have the exact change. Since we work at the same place, naturally we get off at the same stop. I want to be correct with her, but always letting her go first has been awkward. When we get on, does it depend on who pays the fares? How about getting off? She seems to stand there, and one of these days we're going to miss our stop.

The dragon, jester, and this young man on stilts are all part of a Renaissance Festival in Minnesota.

Updated

Gentle Reader:

A lady gets off a bus after the gentleman with her, although she boards the bus before. That way, if she can't make the steps in either direction, he will be there to catch her. (Don't blame Miss Manners for these rules; she doesn't make them up.) This order need not be violated if she pays both fares. She merely fixes the bus driver's attention with a half smile and nods toward the accompanying gentleman to indicate the financial relationship.

THE KNIGHT
by Adrienne Rich

A knight rides into the noon,
and his helmet points to the sun,
and a thousand splintered suns
and the gaiety of his mail.
The soles of his feet glitter
and his palms flash in reply,
and under his crackling banner
he rides like a ship in sail.

A knight rides into the noon,
and only his eye is living,
a lump of bitter jelly
set in a metal mask,
betraying rags and tatters
that cling to the flesh beneath
and wear his nerves to ribbons
under the radiant casque.

Who will unhorse this rider
and free him from between
the walls of iron, the emblems
crushing his chest with their weight?
Will they defeat him gently,
or leave him hurled on the green,
his rags and wounds still hidden
under the great breastplate?

Responding

1. Think of an outmoded "courtly" custom, such as a male walking on the outside of the street to protect a female. In a brief speech, explain why this custom should or should not be abandoned.

2. The quest is a common motif throughout literature and media. Brainstorm with a partner a list of movies and stories that involve a search.

3. In what respect is this poem a departure from the traditional view of knighthood?

Answer to Round Table problem: Chair number 17.

Writing Workshop

A Quest Game

Assignment In this part of the unit you read tales of a far-off time when people set out in quest of freedom, kingship, and victory in battle. Now collaborate with a partner or group to design a quest of your own. Together, design, describe, and explain an original board game or video game based on a quest.

WRITER'S BLUEPRINT

Product	A proposal for a quest game
Audience	Game makers
Purpose	As a group, to (1) propose an idea for a board or video game based on a quest and (2) persuade a game maker to buy it
Specs	To create a successful proposal, your group should:

❑ Make a cover sheet listing the title of your quest game and names of team members. Begin by giving an overview of the world in which your game unfolds—the time period and place, real or imagined.

❑ Go on to explain the other key elements:

—the goal of the quest on which your game is based

—the characters, good and evil

—the obstacles characters face and the tools to help overcome them

Use colorful language with rich connotations.

❑ Include strategic illustrations such as drawings, diagrams, and maps to help explain the game.

❑ Conclude by giving your audience five convincing reasons why they should buy your idea and market your game. What makes it unique and appealing? Be specific.

❑ Follow the rules of grammar, usage, spelling, and mechanics. Take care to correctly capitalize proper nouns and proper adjectives.

Brainstorm key elements of the world in which your game takes place. You'll want the names of people, places, and things to be vivid, so try to think of words and phrases that have strong **connotations** of dread, help, wealth, and power, as in the Literary Source below at the right. Categorize your ideas under headings like those in the Key Elements chart.

Key Elements

Time and Place	Goals of a Quest	Forces for Good	Forces for Evil	Perilous Obstacles	Helps
Medieval England	justice, gold, kingship	Lancelot, Arthur, Lady of the Lake	Sir Modred, Morgan Le Fay	dragons, serpents, deep wells	swords, armor, horses, boats

Discuss key elements. By now your game should be taking shape in your mind. Get together and discuss your key elements. As you discuss, make preliminary sketches of the game board or, if it's a video game, sketches of some of the screens.

Brainstorm persuasive reasons for why a game maker should buy your idea. Have each group member list as many reasons as possible. Then share your lists and rate each reason on a scale of 10 (highly persuasive) down to 1 (not persuasive at all). Choose your top five reasons and arrange them in order of importance.

LITERARY SOURCE
"He was appareled in *gold cloth* and seated in a chair which stood on a *pivoted scaffold.* Below him, *many fathoms deep,* was a *dark well,* and in the water swam *serpents, dragons,* and *wild beasts.*"
from *The Death of King Arthur* by Sir Thomas Malory

Make a game plan. Organize your notes and sketches based on the Specs in the Writer's Blueprint. Make notes on these categories:

- Title
- Team members
- Overview of world —time —place
- Goal
- Characters
- Obstacles
- Five good reasons the game maker should buy your idea (from least to most important)
- Illustrations (maps, sketches of characters, drawings of video game screens, diagrams of rooms, etc.)

Ask another group to examine your game plan and comment on it.

✔ Are we on the right track? Does our plan look like it could be turned into a game that would be fun to play?

✔ Are we following the Specs in the Writer's Blueprint?

Consider their comments as you finalize your game plan, but if they suggest going off in a direction that doesn't work for you, stick with your own ideas. Remember, this is *your* game.

STEP 2 DRAFTING

Before you write, divide up the work among the members of the group. Be sure someone's in charge of each part of your game plan.

As you write, use your game plan and the Writer's Blueprint as guides. As you work, remember, this is just a draft. Things are bound to change, so don't try to get everything perfect the first time through. Here are some drafting ideas.

• Keep it simple. Since this is a proposal that involves a good deal of explanation, break up your copy into separate pieces. Don't produce long paragraphs. That way you're more likely to keep things clear and concise.

• Cooperate. Communicate. Make sure everyone knows what everyone else is doing. If you make a major change, such as adding a new character or changing one of the rules, make sure your other group members know about it—and approve.

• When you write up your reasons for why game makers should buy your ideas, present them in order of importance.

STEP 3 REVISING

COMPUTER TIP
If your word processing program has a built-in thesaurus, use it as you revise to help make your language richer and more precise.

Ask another group to look over your game and comment before you revise it.

✔ Are we explaining a game, as we should be? Or are we just telling a story instead?

✔ Are our reasons persuasive? Could we find better reasons?

✔ Are our explanations clear and concise?

Revising Strategy

Being Clear and Concise

When explaining a concept as complex as a game, do your readers a favor and make your explanations as brief and uncomplicated as you can.

○ **complicated** First, at the bottom of the mountain, there's a warrior that Ipi meets named Morg. He has a red spear. Another warrior

○ is halfway up. He has a spear too. He has to face Amba at the top, who carries a yellow spear. He is also a warrior.

○ **concise** Moving up the mountain, Ipi must confront three different spear-carrying warriors.

Notice how the lengthy, choppy first passage has been pared down to one simple sentence that still contains the important information and clears up the confusion about whom the pronoun "he" refers to. When you revise:

- Simplify the complicated.

- Clarify the confusing.

- Compress the lengthy.

Work with another group to review and comment on your revised draft before you edit. Pay special attention to errors with capitalizing proper nouns and proper adjectives.

Editing Strategy

FOR REFERENCE
For more rules on capitalization, see the Language and Grammar Handbook at the back of this text.

Capitalizing Proper Nouns and Proper Adjectives

Your game probably will have lots of names for particular people, places, and things. Follow these rules for capitalizing proper nouns and proper adjectives:

- Capitalize words that name a particular person, place, or thing. Capitalize only the important words in a noun of two or more words:

  the Lady of the Lake   Excalibur   the Isle of Avalon

- Capitalize proper adjectives—but not the nouns they modify:

  the English king   Arthurian legends   a Christian church

  Notice how this writer fixed mistakes with proper nouns and proper adjectives.

STUDENT MODEL

This quest takes place in the 1990s, but it has medieval characters in it. Somehow King Arthur's Sword, Excalibur, has been hidden (i.e., lost) in a modern shopping mall. Your job is to find the sword and get it back safely to King Arthur's Court. You will have some assistance from Sir Lancelot, King Arthur's most trusted and courageous knight.

5 PRESENTING

Here are some ideas for presenting your finished proposal.

- Assemble your proposal and present it to another group. Rehearse your presentation first. Remember, your goal is to be persuasive. Ask your audience how well you did.

- Create an advertisement for your game.

- Design a box for your game.

- Try it out. If you've made a board game, try playing it with friends.

- Do you really think you have a good idea for your game? Do you think you've created a truly effective proposal? Then find the address of a company that makes games and submit your proposal.

6 LOOKING BACK

Self-evaluate. How well do you think your finished product meets the Specs in the Writer's Blueprint? Rate yourself on each item in the blueprint, from 6 (superior) to 1 (inadequate).

Reflect. What was it like working on a project where success depends on how well you work as a group? Write your reactions to these questions:

✔ What were some of the advantages of working in a group?

✔ What were some of the problems that cropped up?

✔ How did you go about trying to solve them and how successful were you?

✔ What advice would you have for other groups who collaborate on other projects?

For Your Working Portfolio Add your finished product and reflection responses to your working portfolio. If you created a board game, you could take photos of the board and any game pieces you created and put them in your portfolio along with your drawings and writing.

Beyond Print

Looking at Paintings

St. George and the Dragon by Paolo Uccello depicts a legendary knight, St. George, in the process of rescuing a lady in distress from a horrible monster. At first glance, the painting appears to be a traditional portrayal of a knight in combat: the white steed; the armored hero; the helpless lady; the ferocious enemy. But look more closely. Is the damsel in serious distress? What is she holding? Does the knight look like a muscular champion of good? Does the dragon seem at all frightening? When analyzing this or any piece of art, keep three C's in mind.

Context

Determine the meaning. What is the subject? Does the picture tell a story? Is the artist painting a contemporary scene, or going back or ahead in time to find a subject? What details help establish meaning? How does the artist feel about this subject? In this painting, for example, the leashed dragon and the unnaturally elongated lance suggest the painter's ironic intent.

Composition

Look at the focal point, colors, and shapes. How and where does the artist attract your attention? How do colors and shapes affect the meaning and mood of the work? Note how Uccello draws your eyes to the dragon by using the long shaft of the lance and the downward spiral of the leash. How do the colors Uccello selects influence your feelings about this painting? Shapes add interest and balance to this work. Note, for example, that the outline of the cave almost swallows the dragon. If the cave were turned upside-down, it would be the same shape as the sky.

Critical View

Decide whether the artist achieved his or her objective and whether or not you like the painting. After analyzing a painting and deciding that an artist has accomplished his or her objective, you still may not like the work. Or you might enjoy viewing a piece of art that you think is not very successful. The important thing is that you have analyzed its context and composition and made an informed judgment. No fair saying, I like (don't like) it, but I don't know why!

Activity Options

1. Paint the same story from another viewpoint—for example, the dragon's, the woman's, the horse's, or an aerial view. Use shapes, colors, and details to let a reader know your tone and meaning.

2. Analyze another work of art in this book, using the three C's.

Part Two

Many Kinds of Heroes

What's happened to our heroes? you might ask. Gone are the noble knights of old. In their place, are the little heroes, the antiheroes, the people who cope rather than conquer. As you read the following selections, decide where each character falls on a broad hero spectrum.

🐾 **Multicultural Connection Individuality** allows us to redefine heroism in specific cultural settings. As you read the following selections, determine how individuals respond heroically to their circumstances and their surroundings. Have these characters accepted or rejected group standards in their heroic efforts?

Before Reading

And of Clay Are We Created

by Isabel Allende   Chile

Isabel Allende
born 1942

A major Chilean writer now living in the United States, Isabel Allende (ä yen′dā) says that many factors helped her become a writer: "The storytelling of my mother, the books I read, the love of words, this desire that I've always had to communicate." Allende, formerly a journalist, combines these influences with personal experiences—such as the assassination in 1973 of her uncle, Chilean President Salvador Allende—to realistically portray violence, inequality, poverty, and illiteracy. "Those things appear constantly. . . . We cannot control everything in our reality." Allende's words proved prophetic with the death in 1992 of her daughter Paula, a victim of a hospital mishap.

Building Background

Fiction Based on Fact In November 1985, a volcanic flow of mud and lava buried the town of Armero, Colombia, killing more than 20,000. National attention was focused on attempts to rescue thirteen-year-old Omairo Sánchez, who was mired neck-deep in mud. Rescuers unsuccessfully tried to free the girl's legs, which were caught way below the surface in the death grip of her aunt. After sixty hours, the girl died of heart failure. The story you are about to read is based on this incident.

Literary Focus

Point of View Just as a photographer directs a camera to capture selected images and impressions, a writer of fiction chooses a narrator who determines what the reader will learn. The relationship between the narrator of a story and the story he or she relates is called the **point of view**.

Writer's Notebook

Who Are the Heroes? Many people who *make* the news are considered heroes—firefighters, athletes, the person-on-the-street who responds in times of crisis. But how about those who *record* news— photographers and reporters, who sometimes endanger their lives in order to bring news to the public? Before you read, jot down a definition of heroism that could apply to many kinds of people.

AND OF CLAY ARE WE CREATED

ISABEL ALLENDE

They discovered the girl's head protruding from the mudpit, eyes wide open, calling soundlessly. She had a First Communion name, Azucena. Lily. In that vast cemetery where the odor of death was already attracting vultures from far away, and where the weeping of orphans and wails of the injured filled the air, the little girl obstinately clinging to life became the symbol of the tragedy. The television cameras transmitted so often the unbearable image of the head budding like a black squash from the clay that there was no one who did not recognize her and know her name. And every time we saw her on the screen, right behind her was Rolf Carlé, who had gone there on assignment, never suspecting that he would find a fragment of his past, lost thirty years before.

First a subterranean sob rocked the cotton fields, curling them like waves of foam. Geologists had set up their seismographs weeks before and knew that the mountain had awakened again. For some time they had predicted that the heat of the eruption could detach the eternal ice from the slopes of the volcano, but no one heeded their warnings; they sounded like the tales of frightened old women. The towns in the valley went about their daily life, deaf to the moaning of the earth, until that fateful Wednesday night in November when a prolonged roar announced the end of the world, and walls of snow broke loose, rolling in an avalanche of clay, stones, and water that descended on the villages and buried them beneath unfathomable meters of telluric vomit. As soon as the survivors emerged from the paralysis of that first awful terror, they could see that houses, plazas, churches, white cotton plantations, dark coffee forests, cattle pastures—all had disappeared. Much later, after soldiers and volunteers had arrived to rescue the living and try to assess the magnitude of the cataclysm,[1] it was calculated that beneath the mud lay more

---

1. **cataclysm** (kat′ə kliz′əm), *n.* any violent change or upheaval.

◄ Max Ernst used vivid oil paints to create *Two Cardinal Points* in 1950. What qualities of nature are suggested in the deep layers of earth and the brilliant colors? Explain whether or not you associate these qualities with a volcano.

And of Clay Are We Created   **397**

than twenty thousand human beings and an indefinite number of animals putrefying in a viscous[2] soup. Forests and rivers had also been swept away, and there was nothing to be seen but an immense desert of mire.

When the station called before dawn, Rolf Carlé and I were together. I crawled out of bed, dazed with sleep, and went to prepare coffee while he hurriedly dressed. He stuffed his gear in the green canvas backpack he always carried, and we said goodbye, as we had so many times before. I had no presentiments. I sat in the kitchen, sipping my coffee and planning the long hours without him, sure that he would be back the next day.

He was one of the first to reach the scene, because while other reporters were fighting their way to the edges of that morass in jeeps, bicycles, or on foot, each getting there however he could, Rolf Carlé had the advantage of the television helicopter, which flew him over the avalanche. We watched on our screens the footage captured by his assistant's camera, in which he was up to his knees in muck, a microphone in his hand, in the midst of a bedlam of lost children, wounded survivors, corpses, and devastation.[3] The story came to us in his calm voice. For years he had been a familiar figure in newscasts, reporting live at the scene of battles and catastrophes with awesome tenacity. Nothing could stop him, and I was always amazed at his equanimity in the face of danger and suffering; it seemed as if nothing could shake his fortitude or deter his curiosity. Fear seemed never to touch him, although he had confessed to me that he was not a courageous man, far from it. I believe that the lens of the camera had a strange effect on him; it was as if it transported him to a different time from which he could watch events without actually participating in them. When I knew him better, I came to realize that this fictive distance seemed to protect him from his own emotions.

CLARIFY: How does the camera serve to protect Rolf Carlé?

Rolf Carlé was in on the story of Azucena from the beginning. He filmed the volunteers who discovered her, and the first persons who tried to reach her; his camera zoomed in on the girl, her dark face, her large desolate eyes, the plastered-down tangle of her hair. The mud was like quicksand around her, and anyone attempting to reach her was in danger of sinking. They threw a rope to her that she made no effort to grasp until they shouted to her to catch it; then she pulled a hand from the mire and tried to move, but immediately sank a little deeper. Rolf threw down his knapsack and the rest of his equipment and waded into the quagmire,[4] commenting for his assistant's microphone that it was cold and that one could begin to smell the stench of corpses.

"What's your name?" he asked the girl, and she told him her flower name. "Don't move, Azucena," Rolf Carlé directed, and kept talking to her, without a thought for what he was saying, just to distract her, while slowly he worked his way forward in mud up to his waist. The air around him seemed as murky as the mud.

It was impossible to reach her from the approach he was attempting, so he retreated and circled around where there seemed to be firmer footing. When finally he was close enough, he took the rope and tied it beneath her arms, so they could pull her out. He smiled at her with that smile that crinkles his eyes and makes him look like a little boy; he told her that everything was fine, that he was here with her now, that soon they would have her out. He signaled the others to pull, but as soon as the cord tensed, the girl screamed. They tried again, and her shoulders and arms appeared, but they

---

2. **viscous** (vis′kəs), *adj.* thick, like heavy syrup; sticky.
3. **devastation** (dev′ə stā′shən), *n.* waste; destruction.
4. **quagmire** (kwag′mīr′), *n.* soft, muddy ground.

could move her no farther; she was trapped. Someone suggested that her legs might be caught in the collapsed walls of her house, but she said it was not just rubble, that she was also held by the bodies of her brothers and sisters clinging to her legs.

"Don't worry, we'll get you out of here," Rolf promised. Despite the quality of the transmission, I could hear his voice break, and I loved him more than ever. Azucena looked at him, but said nothing.

During those first hours Rolf Carlé exhausted all the resources of his ingenuity to rescue her. He struggled with poles and ropes, but every tug was an intolerable torture for the imprisoned girl. It occurred to him to use one of the poles as a lever but got no result and had to abandon the idea. He talked a couple of soldiers into working with him for a while, but they had to leave because so many other victims were calling for help. The girl could not move, she barely could breathe, but she did not seem desperate, as if an ancestral resignation allowed her to accept her fate. The reporter, on the other hand, was determined to snatch her from death. Someone brought him a tire, which he placed beneath her arms like a life buoy, and then laid a plank near the hole to hold his weight and allow him to stay closer to her. As it was impossible to remove the rubble blindly, he tried once or twice to dive toward her feet, but emerged frustrated, covered with mud, and spitting gravel. He concluded that he would have to have a pump to drain the water, and radioed a request for one, but received in return a message that there was no available transport and it could not be sent until the next morning.

"We can't wait that long!" Rolf Carlé shouted, but in the pandemonium[5] no one stopped to commiserate. Many more hours would go by before he accepted that time had stagnated and reality had been irreparably distorted. A military doctor came to examine the girl, and observed that her heart was functioning well and that if she did not get too cold she could survive the night.

"Hang on, Azucena, we'll have the pump tomorrow," Rolf Carlé tried to console her.

"Don't leave me alone," she begged.

"No, of course I won't leave you."

Someone brought him coffee, and he helped the girl drink it, sip by sip. The warm liquid revived her and she began telling him about her small life, about her family and her school, about how things were in that little bit of world before the volcano had erupted. She was thirteen, and she had never been outside her village. Rolf Carlé, buoyed by a premature optimism, was convinced that everything would end well: the pump would arrive, they would drain the water, move the rubble, and Azucena would be transported by helicopter to a hospital where she would recover rapidly and where he could visit her and bring her gifts. He thought, She's already too old for dolls, and I don't know what would please her; maybe a dress. I don't know much about women, he concluded, amused, reflecting that although he had known many women in his lifetime, none had taught him these details. To pass the hours he began to tell Azucena about his travels and adventures as a newshound, and when he exhausted his memory, he called upon imagination, inventing things he thought might entertain her. From time to time she dozed, but he kept talking in the darkness, to assure her that he was still there and to overcome the menace of uncertainty.

EVALUATE: Do you think that Rolf Carlé's optimism is justified? Why or why not?

That was a long night.

Many miles away, I watched Rolf Carlé and the girl on a television screen. I could not bear

---

5. **pandemonium** (pan′də mō′nē əm), *n.* wild disorder.

the wait at home, so I went to National Television, where I often spent entire nights with Rolf editing programs. There, I was near his world, and I could at least get a feeling of what he lived through during those three decisive days. I called all the important people in the city, senators, commanders of the armed forces, the North American ambassador, and the president of National Petroleum, begging them for a pump to remove the silt, but obtained only vague promises. I began to ask for urgent help on radio and television, to see if there wasn't *someone* who could help us. Between calls I would run to the newsroom to monitor the satellite transmissions that periodically brought new details of the catastrophe. While reporters selected scenes with most impact for the news report, I searched for footage that featured Azucena's mudpit. The screen reduced the disaster to a single plane and accentuated the tremendous distance that separated me from Rolf Carlé; nonetheless, I was there with him. The child's every suffering hurt me as it did him; I felt his frustration, his impotence.[6] Faced with the impossibility of communicating with him, the fantastic idea came to me that if I tried, I could reach him by force of mind and in that way give him encouragement. I concentrated until I was dizzy—a frenzied[7] and futile[8] activity. At times I would be overcome with compassion and burst out crying; at other times, I was so drained I felt as if I were staring through a telescope at the light of a star dead for a million years.

I watched that hell on the first morning broadcast, cadavers of people and animals awash in the current of new rivers formed overnight from the melted snow. Above the mud rose the tops of trees and the bell towers of a church where several people had taken refuge and were patiently awaiting rescue teams. Hundreds of soldiers and volunteers from the Civil Defense were clawing through rubble searching for survivors, while long rows of ragged specters awaited their turn for a cup of hot broth. Radio networks announced that their phones were jammed with calls from families offering shelter to orphaned children. Drinking water was in scarce supply, along with gasoline and food. Doctors, resigned to amputating arms and legs without anesthesia, pled that at least they be sent serum and painkillers and antibiotics; most of the roads, however, were impassable, and worse were the bureaucratic[9] obstacles that stood in the way. To top it all, the clay contaminated by decomposing bodies threatened the living with an outbreak of epidemics.

Azucena was shivering inside the tire that held her above the surface. Immobility and tension had greatly weakened her, but she was con-

He had completely forgotten the camera; he could not look at the girl through a lens any longer.

scious and could still be heard when a microphone was held out to her. Her tone was humble, as if apologizing for all the fuss. Rolf Carlé had a growth of beard, and dark circles beneath his eyes; he looked near exhaustion. Even from that enormous distance I could sense the quality of his weariness, so different from the fatigue of other adventures. He had completely forgotten the camera; he could not look at the girl through a lens any longer. The pictures we were receiving were not his assistant's

---

6. **impotence** (im′pə təns), *n.* helplessness.
7. **frenzied** (fren′zēd), *adj.* greatly excited; frantic.
8. **futile** (fyü′tl), *adj.* not successful; useless.
9. **bureaucratic** (byūr′ə krat′ik), *adj.* marked by an excessive insistence on rigid routine that causes delays in getting things done.

but those of other reporters who had appropriated Azucena, bestowing on her the pathetic responsibility of embodying the horror of what had happened in that place. With the first light Rolf tried again to dislodge the obstacles that held the girl in her tomb, but he had only his hands to work with; he did not dare use a tool for fear of injuring her. He fed Azucena a cup of the cornmeal mush and bananas the Army was distributing, but she immediately vomited it up. A doctor stated that she had a fever, but added that there was little he could do: antibiotics were being reserved for cases of gangrene. A priest also passed by and blessed her, hanging a medal of the Virgin around her neck. By evening a gentle, persistent drizzle began to fall.

"The sky is weeping," Azucena murmured, and she, too, began to cry.

"Don't be afraid," Rolf begged. "You have to keep your strength up and be calm. Everything will be fine. I'm with you, and I'll get you out somehow."

Reporters returned to photograph Azucena and ask her the same questions, which she no longer tried to answer. In the meanwhile, more television and movie teams arrived with spools of cable, tapes, film, videos, precision lenses, recorders, sound consoles, lights, reflecting screens, auxiliary motors, cartons of supplies, electricians, sound technicians, and cameramen: Azucena's face was beamed to millions of screens around the world. And all the while Rolf Carlé kept pleading for a pump. The improved technical facilities bore results, and National Television began receiving sharper pictures and clearer sound; the distance seemed suddenly compressed, and I had the horrible sensation that Azucena and Rolf were by my side, separated from me by impenetrable glass. I was able to follow events hour by hour; I knew everything my love did to wrest the girl from her prison and help her endure her suffering; I overheard fragments of what they said to one another and could guess the rest; I was present when she taught Rolf to pray,

and when he distracted her with the stories I had told him in a thousand and one nights beneath the white mosquito netting of our bed.

CONNECT: Do you think the public is entitled to watch personal suffering such as Azucena's? Why or why not?

When darkness came on the second day, Rolf tried to sing Azucena to sleep with old Austrian folk songs he had learned from his mother, but she was far beyond sleep. They spent most of the night talking, each in a stupor of exhaustion and hunger, and shaking with cold. That night, imperceptibly, the unyielding floodgates that had contained Rolf Carlé's past for so many years began to open, and the torrent of all that had lain hidden in the deepest and most secret layers of memory poured out, leveling before it the obstacles that had blocked his consciousness for so long. He could not tell it all to Azucena; she perhaps did not know there was a world beyond the sea or time previous to her own; she was not capable of imagining Europe in the years of the war. So he could not tell her of defeat, nor of the afternoon the Russians had led them to the concentration camp to bury prisoners dead from starvation. Why should he describe to her how the naked bodies piled like a mountain of firewood resembled fragile china? How could he tell this dying child about ovens and gallows? Nor did he mention the night that he had seen his mother naked, shod in stiletto-heeled red boots, sobbing with humiliation. There was much he did not tell, but in those hours he relived for the first time all the things his mind had tried to erase. Azucena had surrendered her fear to him and so, without wishing it, had obliged Rolf to confront his own. There, beside that hellhole of mud, it was impossible for Rolf to flee from himself any longer, and the visceral[10] terror he had

_____

10. **visceral** (vis′ər əl), *adj.* arising from instinct or strong feelings; not intellectual or rational.

lived as a boy suddenly invaded him. He reverted to the years when he was the age of Azucena, and younger, and, like her, found himself trapped in a pit without escape, buried in life, his head barely above ground; he saw before his eyes the boots and legs of his father, who had removed his belt and was whipping it in the air with the never-forgotten hiss of a viper coiled to strike. Sorrow flooded through him, intact and precise, as if it had lain always in his mind, waiting. He was once again in the armoire where his father locked him to punish him for imagined misbehavior, there where for eternal hours he had crouched with his eyes closed, not to see the darkness, with his hands over his ears, to shut out the beating of his heart, trembling, huddled like a cornered animal. Wandering in the mist of his memories he found his sister Katharina, a sweet, retarded child who spent her life hiding, with the hope that her father would forget the disgrace of her having been born. With Katharina, Rolf crawled beneath the dining room table, and with her hid there under the long white tablecloth, two children forever embraced, alert to footsteps and voices. Katharina's scent melded with his own sweat, with aromas of cooking, garlic, soup, freshly baked bread, and the unexpected odor of putrescent clay. His sister's hand in his, her frightened breathing, her silk hair against his cheek, the candid[11] gaze of her eyes. Katharina . . . Katharina materialized before him, floating on the air like a flag, clothed in the white tablecloth, now a winding sheet, and at last he could weep for her death and for the guilt of having abandoned her. He understood then that all his exploits as a reporter, the feats that had won him such recognition and fame, were merely an attempt to keep his most ancient fears at bay, a stratagem for taking refuge behind a lens to test whether reality was more tolerable from that perspective. He took excessive risks as an exercise of courage, training by day to conquer the monsters that tormented him by night. But he had come face to face with the moment of truth; he could not continue to escape his past. He *was* Azucena; he was buried in the clayey mud; his terror was not the distant emotion of an almost forgotten childhood, it was a claw sunk in his throat. In the flush of his tears he saw his mother, dressed in black and clutching her imitation-crocodile pocketbook to her bosom, just as he had last seen her on the dock when she had come to put him on the boat to South America. She had not come to dry his tears, but to tell him to pick up a shovel: the war was over and now they must bury the dead.

CLARIFY: Why do you think Rolf Carlé finally felt that "he *was* Azucena"?

"Don't cry. I don't hurt anymore. I'm fine," Azucena said when dawn came.

"I'm not crying for you," Rolf Carlé smiled. "I'm crying for myself. I hurt all over."

The third day in the valley of the cataclysm began with a pale light filtering through storm clouds. The President of the Republic visited the area in his tailored safari jacket to confirm that this was the worst catastrophe of the century; the country was in mourning; sister nations had offered aid; he had ordered a state of siege; the Armed Forces would be merciless, anyone caught stealing or committing other offenses would be shot on sight. He added that it was impossible to remove all the corpses or count the thousands who had disappeared; the entire valley would be declared holy ground, and bishops would come to celebrate a solemn mass for the souls of the victims. He went to the Army field tents to offer relief in the form of vague promises to crowds of the rescued, then to the improvised hospital to offer a word of encouragement to doctors and

---

11. **candid** (kan′did), *adj.* frank and sincere.

▲ This 1990 print done with pen, brush, and ink by Rocío Maldonado is titled *La Mano*, or *The Hand*. What is your immediate response to this image? Explain whether or not you think it would be effective as a poster publicizing a national disaster.

nurses worn down from so many hours of tribulations.[12] Then he asked to be taken to see Azucena, the little girl the whole world had seen. He waved to her with a limp statesman's hand, and microphones recorded his emotional voice and paternal tone as he told her that her courage had served as an example to the nation. Rolf Carlé interrupted to ask for a pump, and the President assured him that he personally would attend to the matter. I caught a glimpse of Rolf for a few seconds kneeling beside the mudpit. On the evening news broadcast, he was still in the same position; and I, glued to the screen like a fortune-teller to her crystal ball, could tell that something fundamental had changed in him. I knew somehow that during the night his defenses had crumbled and he had given in to grief; finally he was vulnerable. The girl had touched a part of him that he him-

_____

12. **tribulation** (trib′yə lā′shən), *n.* great trouble; severe trial.

And of Clay Are We Created   **403**

self had no access to, a part he had never shared with me. Rolf had wanted to console her, but it was Azucena who had given him consolation.

I recognized the precise moment at which Rolf gave up the fight and surrendered to the torture of watching the girl die. I was with them, three days and two nights, spying on them from the other side of life. I was there when she told him that in all her thirteen years no boy had ever loved her and that it was a pity to leave this world without knowing love. Rolf assured her that he loved her more than he could ever love anyone, more than he loved his mother, more than his sister, more than all the women who had slept in his arms, more than he loved me, his life companion, who would have given anything to be trapped in that well in her place, who would have exchanged her life for Azucena's, and I watched as he leaned down to kiss her poor forehead, consumed by a sweet, sad emotion he could not name. I felt how in that instant both were saved from despair, how they were freed from the clay, how they rose above the vultures and helicopters, how together they flew above the vast swamp of corruption and laments. How, finally, they were able to accept death. Rolf Carlé prayed in silence that she would die quickly, because such pain cannot be borne.

By then I had obtained a pump and was in touch with a general who had agreed to ship it the next morning on a military cargo plane. But on the night of that third day, beneath the unblinking focus of quartz lamps and the lens of a hundred cameras, Azucena gave up, her eyes locked with those of the friend who had sustained her to the end. Rolf Carlé removed the life buoy, closed her eyelids, held her to his chest for a few moments, and then let her go. She sank slowly, a flower in the mud.

The girl had touched a part of him that he himself had no access to. . .

You are back with me, but you are not the same man. I often accompany you to the station and we watch the videos of Azucena again; you study them intently, looking for something you could have done to save her, something you did not think of in time. Or maybe you study them to see yourself as if in a mirror, naked. Your cameras lie forgotten in a closet; you do not write or sing; you sit long hours before the window, staring at the mountains. Beside you, I wait for you to complete the voyage into yourself, for the old wounds to heal. I know that when you return from your nightmares, we shall again walk hand in hand, as before.

After Reading

Making Connections

Shaping Your Response

1. In your opinion, does this story, based on an actual incident, seem stranger than fiction? Explain.

2. Do you think that this story should be included in a world literature anthology? Why or why not?

3. 👣 Do you think that all heroes, like Rolf Carlé, must forget their **individual** needs in trying to help someone else? Why or why not?

Analyzing the Story

4. Explain the **irony** in the narrator's observations of the "improved technical facilities" that ensure worldwide coverage of Azucena's tragedy.

5. Find five memorable **images** in this story and explain why they appeal to you.

6. How do you think this story reflects the **theme** "Many Kinds of Heroes"?

7. What is the significance of the fact that Rolf "could not look at the girl through a lens any longer"?

8. Explain this **paradox:** Rolf Carlé and Azucena "were freed from the clay" only after they were able to accept death.

9. What do you think the **title** means?

Extending the Ideas

10. With a group, brainstorm stories, movies, or news accounts in which a disaster provides an opportunity for greater self-awareness. Why do you think a disaster might lead to self-knowledge?

Literary Focus: Point of View

This story is told by a *first-person* narrator—a character who presents events from a personal **point of view**, drawing readers directly into the action.

- Who is the narrator of this story?

- Speculate on why this narrator is able to supply more information about Rolf than he himself can.

- How does the narrator's focus shift in the final paragraph?

Vocabulary Study

candid
cataclysm
devastation
futile
impotence
pandemonium
quagmire
tribulation
visceral
viscous

Replace each italicized word in the sentences below with a synonym from the list.

1. The terrible *destruction* from the *upheaval* was clear to rescuers.

2. Wild *disorder* broke out when people followed their *instinctive* tendencies toward self-preservation.

3. The girl could not be removed from the *swamp* of *sticky* clay.

4. Rolf's *helplessness* in rescuing the girl was a terrible *trial* in his life.

5. Knowing that her dream of being rescued was *useless*, Azucena was *frank* about facing death.

Expressing Your Ideas

Writing Choices

Writer's Notebook Update Which characters in the story fit the definition of *hero* that you wrote in your notebook? If necessary, change or adjust your definition of heroism based on this story. Then make a web of heroic qualities.

Hero of the Year Imagine that *Time* magazine is accepting nominations for an annual Hero of the Year award. Write a **letter** to the nominating committee, identifying someone you think should be honored as Hero of the Year. Refer to the web of heroic qualities that you made in your notebook.

The Write to Know There's a fine line between the individual's right to privacy and the public's right to know. Do you think that in its effort to report the news, the media sometimes crosses the boundaries of good taste into sensationalism? Express your ideas on the subject in an **editorial.**

Other Options

Disaster Team Natural disasters, such as hurricanes, tornadoes, and earthquakes, occur every year. If a community near you were struck by such a catastrophe, would you be able to offer rescue or relief services to the survivors? With your group, develop a **teen rescue/relief plan** to help a community whose citizens are displaced, injured, or emotionally upset from the disastrous events.

Private Eye Using a camera or a video-camera, focus on details from a scene that you want the viewer to see, and capture the mood, impression, and feelings of the moment. Share your **photographs** or **video** with the class.

Political Fallout As president of the Republic, your administration is being criticized for not heeding the geologists' warnings and thus preventing the death of 20,000 citizens. Hold a **press conference** in which you answer reporters' questions and explain your plans for a new law that will ensure timely evacuations of areas threatened by future natural disasters.

Before Reading

A Soldier of Urbina by Jorge Luis Borges   Argentina   **The Gift** by Li-Young Lee   USA

Lineage by Margaret Walker   USA   **Turning Pro** by Ishmael Reed   USA

Building Background

Echoes of Admiration

> By law of Nature, no man can admire, for no man can understand, that of which he has no echo in himself.

> *Francis Thompson*

What do you think Thompson means? To prove or disprove his observation, think of the characteristics of someone you admire. Then compare those characteristics to those you possess.

Literary Focus

Metaphor

Reprinted with special permission of North America Syndicate.

- What two things are being compared in this cartoon?

- What do these two things have in common?

An implied comparison between two essentially unlike things is called a **metaphor.** A comparison between life and an elevator (or a roller coaster) implies that both have their ups and downs, highs and lows.

Writer's Notebook

A Hero Is a Tower The poems you are about to read capture special qualities of unsung heroes through metaphors. For example, there is a father whose hands are "two measures of tenderness." Think of someone you consider heroic and describe a quality of that person (gentleness, wisdom, stubbornness, strength, etc.) in terms of a metaphor.

Jorge Luis Borges
1899–1986

Born in Buenos Aires, Argentina, Jorge Luis Borges (hôr′hä lwēs bôr′hās) had written a short story in Spanish by the time he was six and at nine had read the works of authors such as Dickens, Twain, Poe, and Cervantes. From 1919 to 1921, Borges was in Spain, where his first poems were published. Borges also wrote short stories, essays, and movie scenarios. By the time he was thirty, his eyesight was seriously impaired, a degenerative condition he referred to as a "slow, summer twilight."

Margaret Walker
born 1915

As a child, Margaret Walker listened to her grandmother's bedtime stories about slavery, vowing to preserve those tales in writing. She kept her promise by writing poetry and novels that have validated the folk roots of African American life. Walker believes, however, that "writers should not write exclusively for black or white audiences, but most inclusively." She adds, "All humanity must be involved in both the writing and in the reading" of the human condition.

Li-Young Lee
born 1957

Much of Li-Young Lee's poetry describes his father, who had been Chairman Mao's personal physician until the senior Lee and his wife fled China's political turmoil. Li-Young Lee was born in Indonesia shortly before his father's two-year imprisonment during a period of anti-Chinese sentiment. The family escaped to Hong Kong, where Lee's father became a distinguished evangelical preacher, and later fled to the United States. Lee's relaxed style of writing blends images pertaining to cultural politics and personal longings.

Ishmael Reed
born 1938

Novelist, poet, essayist, and critic, Ishmael Reed uses the language and beliefs of folk culture in unusual ways to satirize America's cultural arrogance and racism. Reed's poetic techniques include striking images as well as phonetic spellings and unconventional capitalization. In the introduction to his book, *Writin' Is Fightin',* Reed compares the life of a boxer who spars with opponents to that of a black male who is confronted by a hostile society.

A Soldier of Urbina

Jorge Luis Borges

Feeling himself unfitted for the strain
Of battles like the last he fought at sea,
This soldier, doomed to sordid[1] usury,[2]
Wandered unknown throughout his own harsh Spain.

5 To blot out or to mitigate[3] the pain
Of all reality, he hid in dream;
A magic past was opened up to him
Through Roland and the tales of Ancient Britain.

At sunset he would contemplate[4] the vast
10 Plain with its copper light lingering on;
He felt himself defeated, poor, alone,

Ignorant of what music he was master;
Already, in the still depths of some dream,
Don Quixote and Sancho were alive in him.

A Soldier of Urbina refers to the Spanish writer
Miguel de Cervantes (ser vän′tēz), the author of the
novel, *Don Quixote.* Cervantes, who was wounded in
battle, sold into slavery, and jailed for debt, finally
took up a literary career. The adventures of Don
Quixote and his sidekick, Sancho Panza, satirize
medieval romances of chivalry such as the story of
Roland.

1. **sordid** (sôr′did), *adj.* filthy, contemptible.
2. **usury** (yü′zhər ē), *n.* the lending of money at an
   unusually high or unlawful rate of interest.
3. **mitigate** (mit′ə gāt), *v.* make less harsh.
4. **contemplate** (kon′təm plāt). *v.* gaze at; think about.

Lineage

Margaret Walker

My grandmothers were strong.
They followed plows and bent to toil.
They moved through fields sowing seed.
They touched earth and grain grew.
5 They were full of sturdiness and singing.
My grandmothers were strong.

My grandmothers are full of memories
Smelling of soap and onions and wet clay
With veins rolling roughly over quick hands
10 They have many clean words to say.
My grandmothers were strong.
Why am I not as they?

---

lineage (lin′ē ij), *n.* descent in a direct line from a
common ancestor.

In her woodcut, Elizabeth Catlett uses
lines and planes to create an extraordinary
image of dignity, pain, and endurance. Why
might the artist have chosen to title this
work, so obviously a portrait of an
individual, simply *Sharecropper?* What title
might you have given it?

The Gift

Li-Young Lee

To pull the metal splinter from my palm
my father recited a story in a low voice.
I watched his lovely face and not the blade.
Before the story ended, he'd removed
5 the iron sliver I thought I'd die from.

I can't remember the tale,
but hear his voice still, a well
of dark water, a prayer.
And I recall his hands,
10 two measures of tenderness
he laid against my face,
the flames of discipline
he raised above my head.

Had you entered that afternoon
15 you would have thought you saw a man
planting something in a boy's palm,
a silver tear, a tiny flame.
Had you followed that boy
you would have arrived here,
20 where I bend over my wife's right hand.

Look how I shave her thumbnail down
so carefully she feels no pain.
Watch as I lift the splinter out.
I was seven when my father
25 took my hand like this,

and I did not hold that shard[1]
between my fingers and think,
Metal that will bury me,
christen it Little Assassin,
30 Ore Going Deep for My Heart.
And I did not lift up my wound and cry,
Death visited here!
I did what a child does
when he's given something to keep.
35 I kissed my father.

---

1. **shard** (shärd), *n.* broken piece.

Turning Pro

Ishmael Reed

There are just so many years
you can play amateur baseball
without turning pro
All of a sudden you realize
5   you're ten years older than
everybody in the dugout
and that the shortstop could
be your son

The front office complains
10 about your slowness in making
the line-up
They send down memos about
your faulty bunts and point out
how the runners are always faking
15 you out
"His ability to steal bases
has faded" they say
They say they can't convince
the accountant that there's such
20 a thing as "old Time's Sake"
But just as the scribes[1] were
beginning to write you
off
as a has-been on his last leg
25 You pulled out that fateful
shut-out
and the whistles went off
and the fireworks scorched a
747
30 And your name lit up the scoreboard
and the fans carried you on their
shoulders right out of the stadium
and into the majors

---

1. **scribe** (skrīb), *n.* writer; author.

Baseball Machine, a painted polychrome wood sculpture by Leo Jensen, is a construction that can be played as a game by laying it flat, spinning the bats, and making the ball bounce. Do you think that the playful purpose of this work makes it any less effective as a work of art? Why or why not? ➤

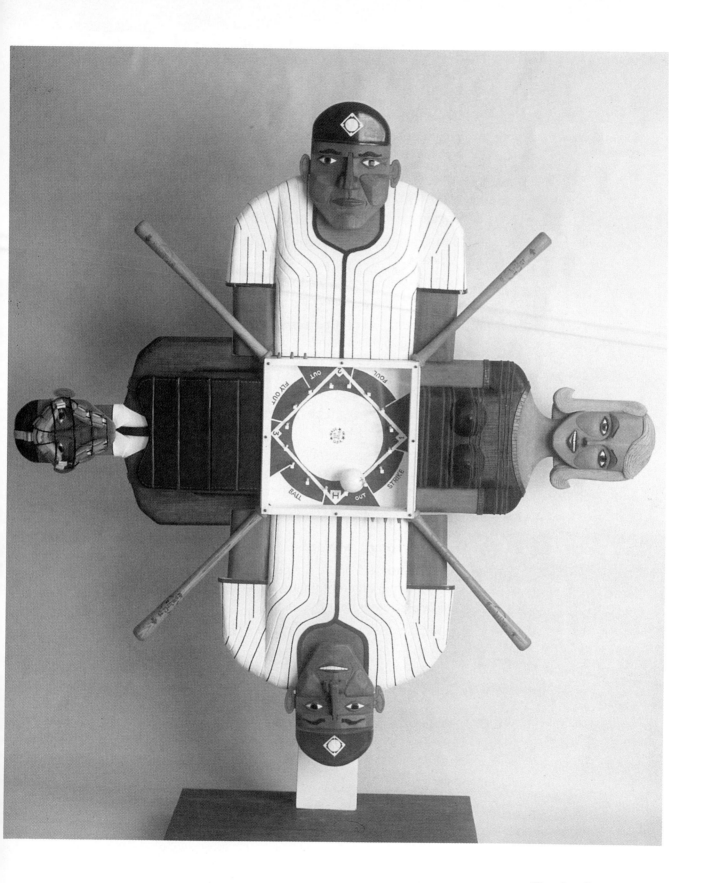

After Reading

Making Connections

Shaping Your Response

1. Which poem most closely reflects your idea of a person to be admired? Why?

2. Work with a partner or group to capture a moment from one of these poems in a "freeze frame" tableau for classmates to identify.

3. Design a symbol for one of the poems. Explain your choice.

Analyzing the Poems

4. Cite examples of **alliteration,** repeated consonant sounds, in "Lineage."

5. Explain what each of the following indicates about the grandmothers in "Lineage": soap, onions, wet clay, veins.

6. How would you **characterize** Cervantes, the Soldier of Urbina, as described in this poem?

7. State a **moral** that you think is illustrated in "Turning Pro."

8. Describe how the **mood** shifts in the final stanza of "The Gift."

Extending the Ideas

9. What response might be given to the question in line 12 of "Lineage"?

10. 👣 Make a mental list of Americans who have achieved heroic status throughout history, such as media celebrities, cowboys, legendary figures, sports "greats," and news headliners. Then try to arrive at some generalizations about what heroism means in American culture.

Literary Focus: Metaphor

A **metaphor** is a figure of speech involving an implied comparison between two different things. Refer to "The Gift" to answer the following questions:

- What is the "silver tear" in line 17?

- In what way is the metal sliver comparable to a "Little Assassin"?

Vocabulary Study

contemplate
lineage
scribe
shard
sordid
usury

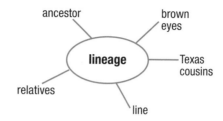

Study the web for *lineage,* thinking about the relationship of the words on the branches to *lineage.* Then make a web to illustrate the meanings and associations you have for one of the listed words.

Expressing Your Ideas ____

Writing Choices

Writer's Notebook Update Look again at the metaphor you created. Exchange metaphors with a classmate and try to explain what character trait you think is being emphasized in his or her work. Discuss anything that doesn't seem clear and revise accordingly.

Celebratory Poetry Write a **poem** to celebrate the life of someone special—a family member, acquaintance, or public figure. You might get ideas from your notebook or from the word web that you made in the Vocabulary Study.

One More Question As Margaret Walker grew up, she asked her grandmother many questions about the bedtime stories she told. The information Walker gathered during these discussions helped her write "Lineage." **Interview** someone who can shed light on you and your culture. Write down your questions beforehand. Then summarize the information you gather in an oral report to the class.

Other Options

Lyrics Heroic In a small group, analyze a song or rap about a hero (or an antihero). Or you may write **lyrics** describing a hero and create your own song or rap. In either case, be prepared to explain or perform your song for the class with your teacher's approval.

Hallmark Heroes Had enough of this hero business? Create a **greeting card** honoring someone for being just plain ordinary, for doing everyday things. Your card might be humorous, or a sincere tribute to the "common person." You might deliver the card in person to give that nonhero a lift.

Speaking Up To enjoy poetry, try reading it aloud. Choose one of the poems in this group to **read aloud** to the class. You might use special effects or have a classmate pantomime as you read the words.

The Secret Room

by Corrie ten Boom   The Netherlands

Corrie ten Boom
1892–1983

When German armies occupied Holland and started exterminating Jews, "my own family and my friends and I did all that we could do to save Jewish lives until we were betrayed and arrested. . . . From that moment forward, everything in our lives was changed." Thus spoke Corrie ten Boom, whose father died in prison and whose sister Betsie died in a German concentration camp. After a clerical error caused Corrie ten Boom to be released from the same concentration camp, she returned to her home, regained her health, and after the war established a home for victims of Nazi purges. Ten Boom's autobiography, *The Hiding Place*, records her experiences.

Building Background

The Horror of the Holocaust During the **Third Reich** (Germany from 1933 to 1945), the Nazi dictator Adolf Hitler took away the citizenship of Jewish people. The Nazis burned Jewish books, destroyed their synagogues, and looted and burned their stores. Jews were methodically persecuted, enslaved, and exterminated. By the end of World War II, an estimated six million European Jews had died.

1936	Germany reoccupies the Rhineland.
1938	Germany invades Austria and Czechoslovakia.
1939	Germany invades Poland. World War II begins.
1940	Germany invades Denmark, Norway, Belgium, the Netherlands, Luxembourg, and France. Italy invades Greece and British Somaliland.
1941	Germany invades Yugoslavia, Greece.
1942	Germany beseiges Stalingrad.
1943	Italy surrenders to the Allies.
1945	Germany surrenders to the Allies.

Literary Focus

Idioms "Hold your tongue!" "Hit the hay." These are **idioms** whose meanings cannot be understood from the ordinary meaning of the words in them. Idioms can often "throw dust in a person's eyes," or mislead someone who is unfamiliar with them. "Take the bull by the horns"—that is, attack the problem fearlessly—as you read "The Secret Room" by watching for idioms and using context to determine their meanings.

Writer's Notebook

What Else Do You Know? Brainstorm with a small group other information you know about the Holocaust and conditions in Nazi Germany. Then quickwrite several sentences to summarize this information.

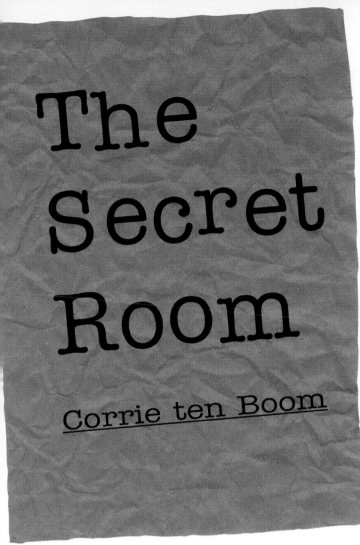

The Secret Room

Corrie ten Boom

When Nazi armies invaded Corrie ten Boom's home-land in 1940, she and her fellow citizens observed many dreadful changes. Living in the Dutch city of Haarlem (här′ləm) *with her sister, Betsie, and elderly father, she tried to maintain the appearance of an ordinary life, working as a watchmaker at the Beje* (bā′yā), *their combined home and shop. But as the following excerpt makes clear, there was also an unseen side to her life.*

Other family members introduced in ten Boom's story are Peter, her nephew; Willem (vil′əm), *her minister brother (who ran a home for the aged at Hilversum that he used as an escape route for fleeing Jews); Tine and Kik, Willem's wife and son; and Nollie, Peter's mother and another sister of Corrie's.*

It was Sunday, May 10, 1942, exactly two years after the fall of Holland. The sunny spring skies, the flowers in the lamppost boxes, did not at all reflect the city's mood. German soldiers wandered aimlessly through the streets, some looking as if they had not yet recovered from a hard Saturday night.

Each month the occupation seemed to grow harsher, restrictions more numerous. The latest heartache for Dutchmen was an edict[1] making it a crime to sing the "Wilhelmus,"[2] our national anthem.

Father, Betsie, and I were on our way to the Dutch Reformed church in Velsen,[3] a small town not far from Haarlem, where Peter had won the post of organist in competition against forty older and more experienced musicians. The organ at Velsen was one of the finest in the country; though the train seemed slower each time, we went frequently.

Peter was already playing, invisible in the tall organ loft, when we squeezed into the crowded pew. That was one thing the occupation had done for Holland: churches were packed.

After hymns and prayers came the sermon, a good one today, I thought. The closing prayers were said. And then, electrically, the whole church sat at attention. Without preamble,

---

1. **edict** (ē′dikt), *n.* decree or law.
2. **"Wilhelmus"** (vil′helm əs).
3. **Velsen** (vel′zən). Other Netherlands locations mentioned in the selection are Rotterdam, Amsterdam, Utrecht (yü′trəkt), and Aerdenhout (er′dən hout′).

every stop pulled out to full volume, Peter was playing the "Wilhelmus"!

Father, at eighty-two, was the first one on his feet. Now everyone was standing. From somewhere in back of us a voice sang out the words. Another joined in, and another. Then we were all singing together, the full voice of Holland singing her forbidden anthem. We sang at the top of our lungs, sang our oneness, our hope, our love for Queen and country. On this anniversary of defeat it seemed almost for a moment that we were victors.

Afterward we waited for Peter at the small side door of the church. It was a long time before he was free to come away with us, so many people wanted to embrace him, to shake his hand and thump his back. Clearly he was enormously pleased with himself.

But now that the moment had passed I was, as usual, angry with him. The Gestapo[4] was certain to hear about it, perhaps already had: their eyes and ears were everywhere. For what had Peter risked so much? Not for people's lives but for a gesture. For a moment's meaningless defiance.

At Bos en Hoven Straat,[5] however, Peter was a hero as one by one his family made us describe again what had happened. The only members of the household who felt as I did were the two Jewish women staying at Nollie's. One of these was an elderly Austrian lady whom Willem had sent into hiding here.

The other woman was a young, blonde, blue-eyed Dutch Jew with flawless false identity papers supplied by the Dutch national underground itself. The papers were so good and Annaliese looked so unlike the Nazi stereotype of a Jew that she went freely in and out of the house, shopping and helping out at the school, giving herself out to be a friend of the family whose husband had died in the bombing of Rotterdam.

I spent an anxious afternoon, tensing at the sound of every motor, for only the police, Germans, and NSBers[6] had automobiles nowa-days. But the time came to go home to the Beje and still nothing had happened.

I worried two more days, then decided either Peter had not been reported or that the Gestapo had more important things to occupy them. It was Wednesday morning just as Father and I were unlocking our workbenches that Peter's little sister Cocky burst into the shop.

"Opa! Tante Corrie![7] They came for Peter! They took him away!"

"Who? Where?"

But she didn't know and it was three days before the family learned that he had been taken to the federal prison in Amsterdam.

It was 7:55 in the evening, just a few minutes before the new curfew hour of 8:00. Peter had been in prison for two weeks. Father and Betsie and I were seated around the dining-room table, Father replacing watches in their pockets and Betsie doing needlework, our big, black, slightly Persian cat curled contentedly in her lap. A knock on the alley door made me glance in the window mirror. There in the bright spring twilight stood a woman. She carried a small suitcase and—odd for the time of year—wore a fur coat, gloves, and a heavy veil.

I ran down and opened the door. "Can I come in?" she asked. Her voice was high-pitched in fear.

"Of course." I stepped back. The woman looked over her shoulder before moving into the little hallway.

> We sang at the top of our lungs, sang our oneness, our hope, our love. . .

---

4. **Gestapo** (gə stä′pō), an official organization of secret police in Nazi Germany, known for its brutality.
5. **Straat** (strät), street.
6. **NSBers**. The letters stand for the Dutch name of the National Socialist Movement. The members of this Dutch political party collaborated with the Nazis.
7. **Opa!** (ō′pä), **Tante** (tän′tə) **Corrie!** Grandfather, Auntie Corrie.

"My name is Kleermaker. I'm a Jew."

"How do you do?" I reached out to take her bag, but she held on to it. "Won't you come upstairs?"

Father and Betsie stood up as we entered the dining room. "Mrs. Kleermaker, my father and my sister."

"I was about to make some tea!" cried Betsie. "You're just in time to join us!"

Father drew out a chair from the table and Mrs. Kleermaker sat down, still gripping the suitcase. The "tea" consisted of old leaves which had been crushed and reused so often they did little more than color the water. But Mrs. Kleermaker accepted it gratefully, plunging into the story of how her husband had been arrested some months before, her son gone into hiding. Yesterday the S.D.—the political police who worked under the Gestapo—had ordered her to close the family clothing store. She was afraid now to go back to the apartment above it. She had heard that we had befriended a man on this street. . . .

"In this household," Father said, "God's people are always welcome."

"We have four empty beds upstairs," said Betsie. "Your problem will be choosing which one to sleep in!"

J ust two nights later the same scene was repeated. The time was again just before 8:00 on another bright May evening. Again there was a furtive[8] knock at the side door. This time an elderly couple was standing outside.

"Come in!"

It was the same story: the same tight-clutched possessions, the same fearful glance and tentative[9] tread. The story of neighbors arrested, the fear that tomorrow their turn would come.

That night after prayer time the six of us faced our dilemma.[10] "This location is too dangerous," I told our three guests. "We're half a block from the main police headquarters. And yet I don't know where else to suggest."

Clearly it was time to visit Willem again. So the next day I repeated the difficult trip to Hilversum. "Willem," I said, "we have three Jews staying right at the Beje. Can you get places for them in the country?"

Willem pressed his fingers to his eyes and I noticed suddenly how much white was in his beard. "It's getting harder," he said. "Harder

---

8. **furtive** (fėr′tiv), *adj.* done quickly and with stealth; secret.

9. **tentative** (ten′tə tiv), *adj.* hesitating.

10. **dilemma** (də lem′ə), *n.* difficult choice.

◄ This building, called the Beje, contained the ten Boom family home, the watch shop, and eventually the secret room.

every month. They're feeling the food shortage now even on the farms. I still have addresses, yes, a few. But they won't take anyone without a ration card."

"Without a ration card! But Jews aren't issued ration cards!"

"I know." Willem turned to stare out the window. For the first time I wondered how he and Tine were feeding the elderly men and women in their care.

"I know," he repeated. "And ration cards can't be counterfeited. They're changed too often and they're too easy to spot. Identity cards are different. I know several printers who do them. Of course you need a photographer."

A photographer? Printers? What was Willem talking about? "Willem, if people need ration cards and there aren't any counterfeit ones, what do they do?"

Willem turned slowly from the window. He seemed to have forgotten me and my particular problem. "Ration cards?" He gestured vaguely. "You steal them."

I stared at this Dutch Reformed clergyman. "Then, Willem, could you steal . . . I mean . . . could you get three stolen cards?"

"No, Corrie! I'm watched! Don't you understand that? Every move I make is watched!"

He put an arm around my shoulder and went on more kindly. "Even if I can continue working for a while, it will be far better for you to develop your own sources. The less connection with me—the less connection with anyone else—the better."

Joggling home on the crowded train, I turned Willem's words over and over in my mind. "Your own sources." That sounded so— so professional. How was I going to find a source of stolen ration cards? Who in the world did I know? . . .

And at that moment a name appeared in my mind.

Fred Koornstra.

Fred was the man who used to read the electric meter at the Beje. The Koornstras had a retarded daughter, now a grown woman, who attended the "church" I had been conducting for the feebleminded for some twenty years. And now Fred had a new job working for the Food Office. Wasn't it in the department where ration books were issued?

That evening after supper I bumped over the brick streets to the Koornstra house. The tires on my faithful old bicycle had finally given out and I joined the hundreds clattering about town on metal wheel rims. Each bump reminded me jarringly of my fifty years.

Fred, a bald man with a military bearing, came to the door and stared at me blankly when I said I wanted to talk to him about the Sunday service. He invited me in, closed the door, and said, "Now Corrie, what is it you really came to see me about?"

("Lord," I prayed silently, "if it is not safe to confide in Fred, stop this conversation now before it is too late.") "I must first tell you that we've had some unexpected company at the Beje. First it was a single woman, then a couple, when I got back this afternoon, another couple." I paused for just an instant. "They are Jews."

Fred's expression did not change.

"We can provide safe places for these people but they must provide something too. Ration cards."

Fred's eyes smiled. "So. Now I know why you came here."

"Fred, is there any way you can give out extra cards? More than you report?"

"None at all, Corrie. Those cards have to be accounted for a dozen ways. They're checked and double-checked."

The hope that had begun to mount in me tumbled. But Fred was frowning.

"Unless—" he began.

"Unless?"

"Unless there should be a holdup. The Food Office in Utrecht was robbed last month—but the men were caught."

He was silent a while. "If it happened at noon," he said slowly, "when just the record clerk and I are there . . . and if they found us tied and gagged . . ." He snapped his fingers. "And I know just the man who might do it! Do you remember the—"

"Don't!" I said, remembering Willem's warning. "Don't tell me who. And don't tell me how. Just get the cards if you possibly can."

Fred stared at me a moment. "How many do you need?"

I opened my mouth to say, "Five." But the number that unexpectedly and astonishingly came out instead was, "One hundred."

When Fred opened the door to me just a week later, I gasped at the sight of him. Both eyes were a greenish purple, his lower lip cut and swollen.

"My friend took very naturally to the part," was all he would say.

But he had the cards. On the table in a brown envelope were one hundred passports to safety. Fred had already torn the "continuing coupon" from each one. This final coupon was presented at the Food Office the last day of each month in exchange for the next month's card. With these coupons Fred could "legally" continue to issue us one hundred cards.

We agreed that it would be risky for me to keep coming to his house each month. What if he were to come to the Beje instead, dressed in his old meterman uniform?

The meter in the Beje was in the back hall at the foot of the stairs. When I got home that afternoon I pried up the tread of the bottom step, as Peter had done higher to hide a radio, and found a hollow space inside. Peter would be proud of me, I thought as I worked—and was flooded by a wave of lonesomeness for that brave and cocksure boy. The hinge was hidden deep in the wood, the ancient riser undisturbed. I was ridiculously pleased with it.

We had our first test of the system on July 1. Fred was to come in through the shop as he always had, carrying the cards beneath his shirt.

He would come at 5:30, when Betsie would have the back hall free of callers. To my horror at 5:25 the shop door opened and in stepped a policeman.

He was a tall man with close-cropped orange-red hair whom I knew by name—Rolf van Vliet—but little else. Rolf had brought in a watch that needed cleaning, and he seemed in a mood to talk. My throat had gone dry, but Father chatted cheerfully as he took off the back of Rolf's watch and examined it. What were we going to do? There was no way to warn Fred Koornstra. Promptly at 5:30 the door of the shop opened and in he walked, dressed in his blue workclothes. It seemed to me that his chest was too thick by a foot at least.

With magnificent aplomb[11] Fred nodded to Father, the policeman, and me. "Good evening." Courteous but a little bored.

He strode through the door at the rear of the shop and shut it behind him. My ears strained to hear him lift the secret lid. There! Surely Rolf must have heard it too.

The door behind us opened again. So great was Fred's control that he had not ducked out the alleyway exit, but came strolling back through the shop.

"Good evening," he said again.

"Evening."

He reached the street door and was gone. We had got away with it this time, but somehow, some way, we were going to have to work out a warning system.

For meanwhile, in the weeks since Mrs. Kleermaker's unexpected visit, a great deal had happened at the Beje. Supplied with ration cards, Mrs. Kleermaker and the elderly couple and the next arrivals and the next had found homes in safer locations. But still the hunted people kept coming, and the needs were often more complicated than ration cards and addresses. If a Jewish woman became pregnant,

---

11. **aplomb** (ə plom'), *n.* assurance; poise.

where could she go to have her baby? If a Jew in hiding died, how could he be buried?

"Develop your own sources," Willem had said. And from the moment Fred Koornstra's name had popped into my mind, an uncanny[12] realization had been growing in me. We were friends with half of Haarlem! We knew nurses in the maternity hospital. We knew clerks in the Records Office. We knew someone in every business and service in the city.

We didn't know, of course, the political views of all these people. But—and here I felt a strange leaping of my heart—God did! I knew I was not clever or subtle or sophisticated; if the Beje was becoming a meeting place for need and supply, it was through some strategy far higher than mine.

A few nights after Fred's first "meterman" visit the alley bell rang long after curfew. I sped downstairs, expecting another sad and stammering refugee. Betsie and I had already made up beds for four new overnight guests that evening: a Jewish woman and her three small children.

But to my surprise, close against the wall of the dark alley, stood Kik. "Get your bicycle," he ordered with his usual young abruptness. "And put on a sweater. I have some people I want you to meet."

"Now? After curfew?" But I knew it was useless to ask questions. Kik's bicycle was tireless too, the wheel rims swathed in cloth. He

---

12. **uncanny** (un kan′ē), *adj.* strange and mysterious.

The rooms of the building offered many odd spaces, and there was a great distance between the street and the hiding place. ▼

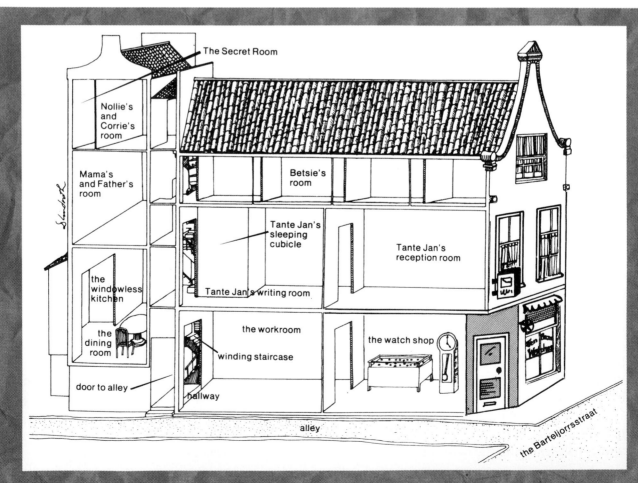

wrapped mine also to keep down the clatter, and soon we were pedaling through the blacked-out streets of Haarlem at a speed that would have scared me even in daylight.

"Put a hand on my shoulder," Kik whispered. "I know the way."

We crossed dark side streets, crested bridges, wheeled round invisible corners. At last we crossed a broad canal and I knew we had reached the fashionable suburb of Aerdenhout.

We turned into a driveway beneath shadowy trees. To my astonishment Kik picked up my bicycle and carried both his and mine up the front steps. A serving girl with starched white apron and ruffled cap opened the door. The entrance hall was jammed with bicycles.

Then I saw him. One eye smiling at me, the other at the door, his vast stomach hastening ahead of him. Pickwick![13]

He led Kik and me into the drawing room where, sipping coffee and chatting in small groups, was the most distinguished-looking group of men and women I had ever seen. But all my attention, that first moment, was on the inexpressibly fragrant aroma in that room. Surely, was it possible, they were drinking real coffee?

Pickwick drew me a cup from the silver urn on the sideboard. It was coffee. After two years, rich, black, pungent[14] Dutch coffee. He poured himself a cup too, dropping in his usual five lumps of sugar as though rationing had never been invented. Another starched and ruffled maid was passing a tray heaped high with cakes.

Gobbling and gulping I trailed about the room after Pickwick, shaking the hands of the people he singled out. They were strange introductions for no names were mentioned, only, occasionally, an address, and "Ask for Mrs. Smit." When I had met my fourth Smit, Kik explained with a grin, "It's the only last name in the underground."

So this was really and truly the underground! But—where were these people from? I had never laid eyes on any of them. A second later I realized with a shiver down my spine that I was meeting the national group.

Their chief work, I gleaned from bits of conversation, was liaison[15] with England and the Free Dutch forces fighting elsewhere on the continent. They also maintained the underground route through which downed Allied plane crews reached the North Sea coast.

But they were instantly sympathetic with my efforts to help Haarlem's Jews. I blushed to my hair roots to hear Pickwick describe me as "the head of an operation here in this city." A hollow space under the stairs and some haphazard[16] friendships were not an operation. The others here were obviously competent, disciplined, and professional.

But they greeted me with grave courtesy, murmuring what they had to offer as we shook hands. False identity papers. The use of a car with official government plates. Signature forgery.

In a far corner of the room Pickwick introduced me to a frail-appearing little man with a wispy goatee. "Our host informs me," the little man began formally, "that your headquarters building lacks a secret room. This is a danger for all, those you are helping as well as yourselves and those who work with you. With your permission I will pay you a visit in the coming week. . . ."

Years later I learned that he was one of the most famous architects in Europe. I knew him only as Mr. Smit.

Just before Kik and I started our dash back to the Beje, Pickwick slipped an arm through mine. "My dear, I have good news. I

---

13. **Pickwick** (pik′wik). The author recognizes one of her wealthy Dutch customers who looks like Pickwick, the title character in a novel by Charles Dickens.

14. pungent (pun′jənt), *adj.* sharply affecting the organs of taste and smell.

15. liaison (lē′ā zon′), *n.* connection between military units, branches of a service, etc., to secure proper cooperation.

16. haphazard (hap′haz′ərd), *adj.* not planned; random.

understand that Peter is about to be released." . . .

So he was, three days later, thinner, paler, and not a whit daunted[17] by his two months in a concrete cell. Nollie, Tine, and Betsie used up a month's sugar ration baking cakes for his welcome-home party.

And one morning soon afterward the first customer in the shop was a small thin-bearded man named Smit. Father took his jeweler's glass from his eye. If there was one thing he loved better than making a new acquaintance, it was discovering a link with an old one.

"Smit," he said eagerly. "I know several Smits in Amsterdam. Are you by any chance related to the family who—"

"Father," I interrupted, "this is the man I told you about. He's come to, ah, inspect the house."

"A building inspector? Then you must be the Smit with offices in the Grote Hout Straat. I wonder that I haven't—"

"Father!" I pleaded, "he's not a building inspector, and his name is not Smit."

"Not Smit?"

Together Mr. Smit and I attempted to explain, but Father simply could not understand a person's being called by a name not his own. As I led Mr. Smit into the back hall we heard him musing to himself, "I once knew a Smit on Koning Straat. . . ."

Mr. Smit examined and approved the hiding place for ration cards beneath the bottom step. He also pronounced acceptable the warning system we had worked out. This was a triangle-shaped wooden sign advertising "Alpina Watches" which I had placed in the dining-room window. As long as the sign was in place, it was safe to enter.

But when I showed him a cubbyhole behind the corner cupboard in the dining room, he shook his head. Some ancient redesigning of the house had left a crawl space in that corner and we'd been secreting jewelry, silver coins,

> As long as
> the sign
> was in place,
> it was safe
> to enter.

and other valuables there since the start of the occupation. Not only the rabbi had brought us his library but other Jewish families had brought their treasures to the Beje for safekeeping. The space was large enough that we had believed a person could crawl in there if necessary, but Mr. Smit dismissed it without a second glance.

"First place they'd look. Don't bother to change it though. It's only silver. We're interested in saving people, not things."

He started up the narrow corkscrew stairs, and as he mounted so did his spirits. He paused in delight at the odd-placed landings, pounded on the crooked walls, and laughed aloud as the floor levels of the two old houses continued out of phase.

"What an impossibility!" he said in an awestruck voice. "What an improbable, unbelievable, unpredictable impossibility! Miss ten Boom, if all houses were constructed like this one, you would see before you a less worried man."

At last, at the very top of the stairs, he entered my room and gave a little cry of delight. "This is it!" he exclaimed.

"You want your hiding place as high as possible," he went on eagerly. "Gives you the best chance to reach it while the search is on below." He leaned out the window, craning his thin neck, the little faun's beard pointing this way and that.

"But . . . this is my bedroom. . . ."

Mr. Smit paid no attention. He was already measuring. He moved the heavy, wobbly old wardrobe away from the wall with surprising ease and pulled my bed into the center of the room. "This is where the false wall will go!" Excitedly he drew out a pencil and drew a line

---

17. **daunt** (dônt), *v.* overcome with fear; frighten.

along the floor thirty inches from the back wall. He stood up and gazed at it moodily.

"That's as big as I dare," he said. "It will take a cot mattress, though. Oh, yes. Easily!"

I tried again to protest, but Mr. Smit had forgotten I existed. Over the next few days he and his workmen were in and out of our house constantly. They never knocked. At each visit each man carried in something. Tools in a folded newspaper. A few bricks in a briefcase. "Wood!" he exclaimed when I ventured to wonder if a wooden wall would not be easier to build. "Wood sounds hollow. Hear it in a minute. No, no. Brick's the only thing for false walls."

After the wall was up, the plasterer came, then the carpenter, finally the painter. Six days after he had begun, Mr. Smit called Father, Betsie, and me to see.

We stood in the doorway and gaped. The smell of fresh paint was everywhere. But surely nothing in this room was newly painted! All four walls had that streaked and grimy look that old rooms got in coal-burning Haarlem. The ancient molding ran unbroken around the ceiling, chipped and peeling here and there, obviously undisturbed for a hundred and fifty years. Old water stains streaked the back wall, a wall that even I, who had lived half a century in this room, could scarcely believe was not the original, but set back a precious two-and-a-half feet from the true wall of the building.

Built-in bookshelves ran along this false wall, old, sagging shelves whose blistered wood bore the same water stains as the wall behind them. Down in the far lefthand corner, beneath the bottom shelf, a sliding panel, two feet high and two wide, opened into the secret room.

Mr. Smit stooped and silently pulled this panel up. On hands and knees Betsie and I crawled into the narrow room behind it. Once inside we could stand up, sit or even stretch out one at a time on the single mattress. A concealed vent, cunningly let into the real wall, allowed air to enter from outside.

"Keep a water jug there," said Mr. Smit, crawling in behind us. "Change the water once a week. Hardtack and vitamins keep indefinitely. Anytime there is anyone in the house whose presence is unofficial, all possessions except the clothes actually on his back must be stored in here."

Dropping to our knees again, we crawled single file out into my bedroom. "Move back into this room," he told me. "Everything exactly as before."

With his fist he struck the wall above the bookshelves.

"The Gestapo could search for a year," he said. "They'll never find this one."

After Reading

Making Connections

Shaping Your Response

1. In your notebook, write three questions you would like to ask Corrie ten Boom.

2. What do you think are the most important moments in the selection? Why?

3. Does Corrie ten Boom measure up to your idea of a hero? Why or why not?

Analyzing the Autobiography

4. Why do you think Peter's playing the "Wilhelmus" arouses such intense feelings in the audience?

5. How does this episode in the church help set the **mood** for what follows in this narrative?

6. What **character** traits does ten Boom have that make her valuable in the underground movement?

7. Make two **inferences** about wartime living conditions based on ten Boom's autobiographical account.

Extending the Ideas

8. After the war, Corrie ten Boom set up a home in the Netherlands for other victims of Nazi atrocities. How do her efforts compare with current efforts to protect victims of war around the world?

9. In a Venn diagram, compare ten Boom with Arthur or Launcelot as heroes, noting common and differing heroic qualities.

Literary Focus: Idiom

An **idiom** is a phrase or an expression whose meaning cannot be understood from the ordinary meaning of the words in it. For example, when Corrie ten Boom says of the Gestapo, "their eyes and ears were everywhere," she is speaking figuratively, not literally. What does she mean? Use a chart like the one below to record two other idioms and their meanings. Then illustrate the literal meaning of one of the idioms.

Idiom	Meaning

Vocabulary Study

Tell whether the following word pairs are synonyms, antonyms, or neither by writing *S, A,* or *N* on your paper.

aplomb
daunt
dilemma
edict
furtive
haphazard
liaison
pungent
tentative
uncanny

1. furtive: secret
2. aplomb: vegetable
3. uncanny: ordinary
4. pungent: sharp
5. liaison: connection to secure cooperation
6. haphazard: planned
7. daunt: frighten
8. tentative: confident
9. edict: memory
10. dilemma: difficult choice

Expressing Your Ideas

Writing Choices

Writer's Notebook Update Use the quickwrite you did before reading "The Secret Room," along with ideas in ten Boom's account, as the basis for a paragraph that might launch an encyclopedia article.

Underground Tipster Your name is "Smit," and you have been asked to write a **news clip** for all of the other Smits in the underground to help them provide a haven for Jews. Write down concise tips that you think would be helpful, and provide a title for the news clip.

An Inspiring Flap "The Secret Room" is an excerpt from Corrie ten Boom's autobiography, *The Hiding Place*. If you were publishing the book, what would you want readers to know at a glance about ten Boom and her experiences during the German occupation? Write a paragraph for the inside flap of the **book jacket**.

Other Options

Preservation Society The Haarlem preservation society is concerned with the preservation of historical landmarks and memorials. Prepare a **proposal**, supported with historical facts, asking the Haarlem city council to designate buildings and sites as either landmarks or memorials to those who risked their lives to aid Jews during the German occupation.

The Architect in You Working with a partner, take a critical look at the buildings in which you both live. Which building do you think is more conducive to containing a secret room? Where would be the best location for a secret room in that building? Using the diagram of the Beje (page 422) as a model, draw a **diagram**.

Making Referrals Compile a list of resources about the Holocaust—books, movies, magazines, and personal interviews. Prepare an **annotated bibliography** of eight sources.

Before Reading

The Street of the Cañon

by Josefina Niggli   Mexico

Josefina Niggli
born 1910

Born in Monterrey, Mexico, in the year of the great Mexican revolution, Josefina Niggli (nig′lē) moved to Texas in order to escape political turmoil. There, as a teenager, she began to write. Her spirited characters lead lives complicated by conflicts involving love, pride, deceit, and tradition. In addition to stories, poems, and plays, Niggli has written scripts for radio and film. Probably best known for her novel, *Mexican Village,* a classic portrait of small-town life and customs, Niggli explores the human comedy against a tapestry of rural Mexican life.

Building Background

Niggli Country The area south of Laredo, Texas, during the 1920s was composed of small Mexican villages located in valleys separated by low mountains. Petty feuds could isolate one village from another.

The town of Hidalgo, named after a rebel priest who helped bring about Mexico's War of Independence against Spain, undoubtedly fought feuds, held festivals, and cherished traditions similar to those represented in "The Street of the Cañon."

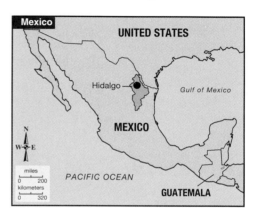

Literary Focus

Imagery The use of concrete details that appeal to the five senses is called **imagery.** In "The Street of the Cañon," you are invited to share a banquet, to enjoy the scent of spring breezes, and to spy on young lovers who dance to violins. Let imagery work its magic on you as you step into the story.

Writer's Notebook

Romancing the Cheese We generally think of flowers, candy, or jewelry as romantic expressions. In this story, however, a young man courts a girl with an unlikely item. Before reading this story, write down an unusual but romantic gift you have received or have heard about and the circumstances that made it romantic.

The Street of the Cañon

Josefina Niggli

It was May, the flowering thorn was sweet in the air, and the village of San Juan Iglesias[1] in the Valley of the Three Marys was celebrating. The long, dark streets were empty because all of the people, from the lowest-paid cowboy to the mayor, were helping Don Roméo Calderón[2] celebrate his daughter's eighteenth birthday.

On the other side of the town, where the Cañon Road led across the mountains to the Sabinas Valley, a tall, slender man, a package clutched tightly against his side, slipped from shadow to shadow. Once a dog barked, and the man's black suit merged into the blackness of a wall. But no voice called out, and after a moment he slid into the narrow, dirt-packed street again.

The moonlight touched his shoulder and spilled across his narrow hips. He was young, no more than twenty-five, and his black curly head was bare. He walked swiftly along, heading always for the distant sound of guitar and flute. If he met anyone now, who could say from which direction he had come? He might be a trader from Monterrey or a buyer of cow's milk from farther north in the Valley of the Three Marys. Who would guess that an Hidalgo[3] man dared to walk alone in the moonlit streets of San Juan Iglesias?

Carefully adjusting his flat package so that it was not too prominent, he squared his shoulders and walked jauntily[4] across the street to the laughter-filled house. Little boys packed in the doorway made way for him, smiling and nodding to him. The long, narrow room with the orchestra at one end was filled with whirling dancers. Rigid-backed chaperones were gossiping together, seated in their straight chairs against the plaster walls. Over the scene was the yellow glow of kerosene lanterns, and the air was hot with the too sweet perfume of gardenias, tuberoses, and the pungent scent of close-packed humanity.

The man in the doorway, while trying to appear at ease, was carefully examining every smiling face. If just one person recognized him, the room would turn on him like a den of

---

1. **San Juan Iglesias,** (sän hwän ē gle′sē äs).
2. **Don Roméo Calderón,** (dōn rō me′ō käl də rōn′).
3. **Hidalgo,** (ē däl′gō).
4. jauntily (jôn′tə lē), *adv.* in an easy and lively way.

snarling mountain cats, but so far all the laughter-dancing eyes were friendly.

Suddenly a plump, officious[5] little man, his round cheeks glistening with perspiration, pushed his way through the crowd. His voice, many times too large for his small body, boomed at the man in the doorway, "Welcome, stranger, welcome to our house." Thrusting his arm through the stranger's, and almost dislodging the package, he started to lead the way through the maze of dancers. "Come and drink a toast to my daughter—to my beautiful Sarita.[6] She is eighteen this night."

In the square patio the gentle breeze ruffled the pink and white oleander bushes. A long table set up on sawhorses held loaves of flaky-crusted French bread, stacks of thin, delicate tortillas,[7] plates of barbecued beef, and long red rolls of spicy sausages. But most of all there were cheeses, for the Three Marys was a cheese-eating valley. There were yellow cheese and white cheese and curded cheese from cow's milk. There was even a flat white cake of goat cheese from distant Linares,[8] a delicacy too expensive for any but feast days.

To set off this feast were bottles of beer floating in ice-filled tin tubs, and another table was covered with bottles of mescal, of tequila, of maguey wine.

Don Roméo Calderón thrust a glass of tequila into the stranger's hand. "Drink, friend, to the prettiest girl in San Juan. As pretty as my fine fighting cocks, she is. On her wedding day she takes to her man, and by the Blessed Ribs may she find him soon, the best fighter in my flock. Drink deep, friend. Even the rivers flow with wine."

The Hidalgo man laughed and raised his glass high. "May the earth be always fertile beneath her feet."

Someone called to Don Roméo that more guests were arriving, and with a final delighted pat on the stranger's shoulder, the little man

scurried away. As the young fellow smiled after his retreating host, his eyes caught and held another pair of eyes—laughing black eyes set in a young girl's face. The last time he had seen that face it had been white and tense with rage, and the lips clenched tight to prevent an outgushing stream of angry words. That had been in February, and she had worn a white lace shawl over her hair. Now it was May, and a gardenia was a splash of white in the glossy, dark braids. The moonlight had mottled his face that February night, and he knew that she did not recognize him. He grinned impudently[9] back at her, and her eyes widened, then slid sideways to one of the chaperones. The fan in her small hand snapped shut. She tapped its parchment tip against her mouth and slipped away to join the dancing couples in the front room. The gestures of a fan translate into a coded language on the frontier. The stranger raised one eyebrow as he interpreted the signal.

But he did not move toward her at once. Instead, he inched slowly back against the table. No one was behind him, and his hands quickly unfastened the package he had been guarding so long. Then he nonchalantly walked into the front room.

The girl was sitting close to a chaperone. As he came up to her, he swerved slightly toward the bushy-browed old lady.

"Your servant, señora. I kiss your hands and feet."

The chaperone stared at him in astonishment. Such fine manners were not common to the town of San Juan Iglesias.

"Eh, you're a stranger," she said. "I thought so."

"But a stranger no longer, señora, now that I have met you." He bent over her, so close she

---

5. **officious** (ə fish′əs), *adj.* too ready to offer services.
6. **Sarita,** (sä rē′tä).
7. **tortilla** (tôr tē′yə), *n.* thin, flat, round cake made of corn meal.
8. **Linares,** (lē nä′res).
9. **impudently** (im′pyə dənt lē), *adv.* rudely.

This oil painting titled *Fiesta Tehuanas*, or *Dance in Tehuantepec*, illustrates some of Diego Rivera's trademarks— bold color, simple forms, and architectural harmony. Mention several things in this story that the painting captures and several other things it does not portray.

could smell the faint fragrance of talcum on his freshly shaven cheek. "Will you dance the *parada* with me?"

This request startled her eyes into popping open beneath the heavy brows. "So, my young rooster, would you flirt with me, and I old enough to be your grandmother?"

"Can you show me a prettier woman to flirt with in the Valley of the Three Marys?" he asked audaciously.[10]

She grinned at him and turned toward the girl at her side. "This young fool wants to meet you, my child."

The girl blushed to the roots of her hair and shyly lowered her white lids. The old woman laughed aloud.

"Go out and dance, the two of you. A man clever enough to pat the sheep has a right to play with the lamb."

The next moment they had joined the circle of dancers, and Sarita was trying to control her laughter.

---

10. **audaciously** (ô dā′shəs lē), *adv.* courageously taking risks; daringly.

The Street of the Cañon   **431**

"She is the worst dragon in San Juan. And how easily you won her!"

"What is a dragon," he asked imperiously,[11] "when I longed to dance with you?"

"Ay," she retorted, "you have a quick tongue. I think you are a dangerous man."

In answer he drew her closer to him and turned her toward the orchestra. As he reached the chief violinist, he called out, "Play the *Virgencita*,[12] 'The Shy Young Maiden.'"

The violinist's mouth opened in soundless surprise. The girl in his arms said sharply, "You heard him, the *Borachita*,[13] 'The Little Drunken Girl.'"

With a relieved grin the violinist tapped his music stand with his bow, and the music swung into the sad farewell of a man to his sweetheart:

Farewell, my little drunken one.
I must go to the capital
To serve the master
Who makes me weep for my return.

The stranger frowned down at her. "Is this a joke, señorita?" he asked coldly.

"No," she whispered, looking about her quickly to see if the incident had been observed. "But the *Virgencita* is the favorite song of Hidalgo, a village on the other side of the mountains in the next valley. The people of Hidalgo and San Juan Iglesias do not speak."

"That is a stupid thing," said the man from Hidalgo as he swung her around in a large turn. "Is not music free as air? Why should one town own the rights to a song?"

The girl shuddered slightly. "Those people from Hidalgo—they are wicked monsters. Can you guess what they did not six months since?"

The man started to point out that the space of time from February to May was three months, but he thought it better not to appear too wise. "Did these Hidalgo monsters frighten you, señorita? If they did, I personally will kill them all."

She moved closer against him and tilted her face until her mouth was close to his ear. "They attempted to steal the bones of Don Rómolo Balderas."[14]

"Is it possible?" He made his eyes grow round and his lips purse up in disdain.[15] "Surely not that! Why, all the world knows that Don Rómolo Balderas was the greatest historian in the entire republic.[16] Every school child reads his books. Wise men from Quintana Roo to the Río Bravo[17] bow their heads in admiration to his name. What a wicked thing to do!" He hoped his virtuous tone was not too virtuous for plausibility, but she did not seem to notice.

"It is true! In the night they came. Three devils!"

"Young devils, I hope."

"Young or old, who cares? They were devils. The blacksmith surprised them even as they were opening the grave. He raised such a shout that all of San Juan rushed to his aid, for they were fighting, I can tell you. Especially one of them—their leader."

"And who was he?"

"You have heard of him doubtless. A proper wild one named Pepe Gonzalez."[18]

"And what happened to them?"

"They had horses and got away, but one, I think, was hurt."

The Hidalgo man twisted his mouth, remembering how Rubén the candymaker had ridden across the whitewashed line high on the cañon trail that marked the division between the Three Marys' and the Sabinas' sides of the mountains and then had fallen in a faint from

---

11. **imperiously** (im pir′ē əs lē), *adv.* in a haughty or arrogant manner.
12. *Virgencita*, (vēr hen sē′tä).
13. *Borachita*, (bō rä chē′tä).
14. **Don Rómolo Balderas,** (dōn rō′mō lō bäl de′ras).
15. **disdain** (dis dān′), *n.* scorn.
16. **the entire republic,** Mexico.
17. **Quintana Roo to the Río Bravo,** from the Yucatan peninsula in southeast Mexico north to the Rio Grande.
18. **Pepe Gonzalez,** (pe′pā gōn sä′les).

his saddle because his left arm was broken. There was no candy in Hidalgo for six weeks, and the entire Sabinas Valley resented that broken arm as fiercely as did Rubén.

The stranger tightened his arm in reflexed anger about Sarita's waist as she said, "All the world knows that the men of Hidalgo are sons of the mountain witches."

"But even devils are shy of disturbing the honored dead," he said gravely.

"'Don Rómolo was born in our village,' Hidalgo says. 'His bones belong to us.' Well, anyone in the valley can tell you he died in San Juan Iglesias, and here his bones will stay! Is that not proper? Is that not right?"

To keep from answering, he guided her through an intricate dance pattern that led them past the patio door. Over her head he could see two men and a woman staring with amazement at the open package on the table.

His eyes on the patio, he asked blandly,[19] "You say the leader was one Pepe Gonzalez? The name seems to have a familiar sound."

"But naturally. He has a talent." She tossed her head and stepped away from him as the music stopped. It was a dance of two *paradas*. He slipped his hand through her arm and guided her into place in the large oval of parading couples. Twice around the room and the orchestra would play again.

"A talent?" he prompted.

"For doing the impossible. When all the world says a thing cannot be done, he does it to prove the world wrong. Why, he climbed to the top of the Prow, and not even the long-vanished Joaquín Castillo had ever climbed that mountain before. And this same Pepe caught a mountain lion with nothing to aid him but a rope and his two bare hands."

"He doesn't sound such a bad friend," protested the stranger, slipping his arm around her waist as the music began to play the merry song of the soap bubbles:

Pretty bubbles of a thousand colors
That ride on the wind
And break as swiftly
As a lover's heart.

The events in the patio were claiming his attention. Little by little he edged her closer to the door. The group at the table had considerably enlarged. There was a low murmur of excitement from the crowd.

"What happened?" asked Sarita, attracted by the noise.

"There seems to be something wrong at the table," he answered, while trying to peer over the heads of the people in front of him. Realizing that this might be the last moment of peace he would have that evening, he bent toward her.

"If I come back on Sunday, will you walk around the plaza with me?"

She was startled into exclaiming, "Ay, no!"

"Please. Just once around."

"And you think I'd walk more than once with you, señor, even if you were no stranger? In San Juan Iglesias, to walk around the plaza with a girl means a wedding."

"Ha, and you think that is common to San Juan alone? Even the devils of Hidalgo respect that law." He added hastily at her puzzled upward glance. "And so they do in all the villages." To cover his lapse he said softly, "I don't even know your name."

A mischievous grin crinkled the corners of her eyes. "Nor do I know yours, señor. Strangers do not often walk the streets of San Juan."

Before he could answer, the chattering in the patio swelled to louder proportions. Don Roméo's voice lay on top, like thick cream on milk. "I tell you it is a jewel of a cheese. Such flavor, such texture, such whiteness. It is a jewel of a cheese."

---

19. **blandly** (bland′lē), *adv.* in a smoothly agreeable, polite manner.

"What has happened?" Sarita asked of a woman at her elbow.

"A fine goat's cheese appeared as if by magic on the table. No one knows where it came from."

"Probably an extra one from Linares," snorted a fat, bald man on the right.

"Linares never made such a cheese as this," said the woman decisively.

"Silence!" roared Don Roméo. "Old Tío[20] Daniel would speak a word to us."

A great hand of silence closed down over the mouths of the people. The girl was standing on tiptoe trying vainly to see what was happening. She was hardly aware of the stranger's whispering voice, although she remembered the words that he said. "Sunday night—once around the plaza."

She did not realize that he had moved away, leaving a gap that was quickly filled by the blacksmith.

Old Tío Daniel's voice was a shrill squeak, and his thin, stringy neck jutted forth from his body like a turtle's from its shell. "This is no cheese from Linares," he said with authority, his mouth sucking in over his toothless gums between his sentences. "Years ago, when the great Don Rómolo Balderas was still alive, we had such cheese as this—ay, in those days we had it. But after he died and was buried in our own sainted ground, as was right and proper. . . ."

"Yes, yes," murmured voices in the crowd. He glared at the interruption. As soon as there was silence again, he continued:

"After he died, we had it no more. Shall I tell you why?"

"Tell us, Tío Daniel," said the voices humbly.

"Because it is made in Hidalgo!"

The sound of a waterfall, the sound of a wind in a narrow cañon, and the sound of an angry crowd are much the same. There were no distinct words, but the sound was enough.

"Are you certain, Tío?" boomed Don Roméo.

"As certain as I am that a donkey has long ears. The people of Hidalgo have been famous for generations for making cheese like this— especially that wicked one, that owner of a cheese factory, Timotéo Gonzalez, father to Pepe, the wild one, whom we have good cause to remember."

"We do, we do," came the sigh of assurance.

"But on the whole northern frontier there are no vats like his to produce so fine a product. Ask the people of Chihuahua, of Sonora. Ask the man on the bridge at Laredo, or the man in his boat at Tampico, '*Hola*, friend, who makes the finest goat cheese?'

"And the answer will always be the same, 'Don Timotéo of Hidalgo.'"

It was the blacksmith who asked the great question. "Then where did that cheese come from, and we haters of Hidalgo these ten long years?"

No voice said, "The stranger," but with one fluid movement every head in the patio turned toward the girl in the doorway. She also turned, her eyes wide with something that she realized to her own amazement was more apprehension[21] than anger.

But the stranger was not in the room. When the angry, muttering men pushed through to the street, the stranger was not on the plaza. He was not anywhere in sight. A few of the more religious crossed themselves for fear that the Devil had walked in their midst. "Who was he?" one voice asked another. But Sarita, who was meekly listening to a lecture from Don Roméo on the propriety[22] of dancing with strangers, did not have to ask. She had a strong suspicion that she had danced that night within the circling arm of Pepe Gonzalez.

---

20. **Tío** (tē′ō), Spanish for uncle.
21. **apprehension** (ap′ri hen′shən), *n.* fear.
22. **propriety** (prə prī′ə tē), *n.* proper behavior.

After Reading

Making Connections

Shaping Your
Response

1. What do you think are the chances of survival for this budding romance? Why?

2. If you could give some advice to Sarita, what would you say?

3. Do you agree that love can make people do bold and crazy things? Explain.

Analyzing the Story

4. 🐾 How do Sarita's **individual** goals conflict with the expectations of her family and community? Do you think that there is a way to reconcile the two sets of goals? Why or why not?

5. Sarita's chaperone says, "A man clever enough to pat the sheep has a right to play with the lamb." What does she mean by this **proverb?**

6. Sarita observes that Pepe Gonzalez has "a talent for the impossible." How does this detail help **characterize** him?

Extending the Ideas

7. 🐾 What in the story supports the following critical evaluation of one of Niggli's **themes**: "Tradition is seen as an immensely important aspect of . . . life, and social customs are emphasized as key elements in day-to-day activities"?

8. Would the fathers you know welcome a total stranger into their houses on such an occasion? Why or why not?

9. What modern conflicts can you think of within or between groups, schools, towns, states, or countries? Do you think the reasons for these conflicts are legitimate or silly? Explain.

Literary Focus: Imagery

In "The Street of the Cañon," Niggli uses **images** that appeal to the five senses. Find an image that appeals to each sense and write it beside the appropriate label in a chart such as the one below.

Sense	Example
Sight	
Smell	
Hearing	
Taste	
Touch	

Vocabulary Study

apprehension
audaciously
blandly
disdain
imperiously
jauntily
officious
propriety

Use at least four vocabulary words to describe one of the following scenes.

- You encounter a large, fierce-looking, unleashed dog on the sidewalk.

- You are chaperoning ten fifth-graders, who refuse to go to sleep, at a slumber party.

- You and a parent are expressing different opinions on whether or not you should go to a particular event.

Expressing Your Ideas

Writing Choices

Writer's Notebook Update In a paragraph, compare your idea of a romantic gift to Pepe's choice in "The Street of the Cañon." Speculate on what in general makes a "romantic" gift romantic.

Dear Miss Manners Write a **letter** to Miss Manners, the etiquette expert, in which you defend or criticize the concept of chaperones in today's society. You might want to use humor to describe a specific incident that happened to you or to someone you know.

Eavesdropping At the end of the story, Sarita is "meekly listening" to a lecture from her father "on the propriety of dancing with strangers." You are close enough to hear what Don Roméo is saying. Report the conversation in a **gossip column**.

Other Options

Wall Art and Life In the twentieth century, several Mexican artists became world famous for their murals—pictures painted on walls. With a group, research one of the following artists: Diego Rivera, José Clemente Orozco, or David Alfaro Siqueiros. Present information and examples of the artist's work to the class in an **art talk.** You might refer to the Beyond Print article titled "Looking at Paintings," page 392, for tips in discussing art.

Dress Rehearsal As a group, do some **research** on the kinds of clothes dancers at a party in a Mexican village in the early 1900s might have worn, the music that could have been played, and the dance steps that might have been performed. Demonstrate your findings for classmates.

Multicultural Connection
Compare the real-life heroes that Michael Dorris mentions with the larger-than-life fictional heroes on pages 438-439. Who would you say are legendary heroes in your country?

MODERN HEROES

by Michael Dorris

In the following interview, Michael Dorris, a writer of French, Modoc Indian, and Irish ancestry, discusses contemporary heroes. One such hero is Rosa Parks, an activist who triggered the civil rights movement in the U.S. when she refused to give up her bus seat to a white passenger in 1955. Another personal hero was Dorris's adopted son Adam who was born with fetal alcohol syndrome, an affliction passed to a newborn by a drinking mother.

Q. IS THERE NO LONGER A PLACE FOR HEROES IN CONTEMPORARY AMERICA?

A. It's not that we have no heroes anymore. The problem is that we just don't recognize the heroes we have. We make the Terminator a hero or Barney a hero, and we barely react when Rosa Parks gets beaten up in her own home. What a horrible thing, what a truly horrible thing!

Q. WHO WOULD BE SOME OF YOUR OTHER CANDIDATES FOR HEROES IN AMERICA TODAY?

A. Well, I think Jimmy Carter is a real hero in this society. I happened to be on the podium with him at the American Booksellers Association convention in California a couple of years ago, and he was introduced as the only person who has ever used the American presidency as a steppingstone to greatness. He came across as genuinely wise and articulate and positive.

Being positive, I think is part of being a hero—maybe the hardest part, because if you're a hero you're smart enough to know all the reasons why you *should* be discouraged. Social life, after all, is simply a collective illusion, a shared set of boundaries and possibilities. If we all believe something to be true, in an odd way it is true. Maybe a hero is the person who inspires a collective belief in our best dream of ourselves as a people.

Our late son was such a hero. Without ever being aware of it or knowing what it meant, the example of his life and his inherent charisma forced those who encountered him to ask questions. His small, brave story, told in *The Broken Cord,* changed a lot of lives and saved a lot of lives.

He evoked a heartbreaking sense of what he might have been but for the insult he suffered before birth. Even when he was unconscious in the hospital before he died, he made a profound impact on the doctors. There was something about his very presence that reminded them of why they were in medicine.

I think there are a whole lot of heroes, and most of them are people that we know personally. They're our parents or our children or our brothers and sisters who are going through adversity. We don't have to reach out to Abraham Lincoln to be inspired; we can find heroism in ordinary people and in the daily, undramatic crises of faith and hope that we encounter and struggle through against the odds.

MAPPING

MEXICO
Quetzalcoatl vanishes east over the sea. When the Spaniard Cortés arrived in Mexico, the Aztecs believed him to be Quetzalcoatl returning to them.

POLYNESIA
The name Maui and the tales of some of his thousand tricks have spread throughout the people of the Pacific.

MESOPOTAMIA
After his friend dies, Gilgamesh makes a long and finally unsuccessful journey to find the secret of immortality.

OUT HEROES

Brynhild is chief of the Valkyries, "the choosers of the slain," who guide dead warriors to the afterworld.

Sita and her husband Rama represent the ideals of married life in Indian tradition.

Rustem mistakenly kills his son, Sohrab, in combat.

Responding

1. What does Dorris mean when he says: "Maybe a hero is the person who inspires a collective belief in our best dream of ourselves as a people?" Do you agree with his statement? Explain.

2. Make up your own definition of heroism.

3. With a partner, research in greater depth a hero who appears on this map.

Career Connection
A journalist reminds us of the power of the media to create or destroy heroes.

Currently living in the Detroit area and writing freelance on environmental issues, Emilia Askari has covered a variety of beats for newspapers in Miami, Los Angeles, and Detroit. Her work has made her aware of the power of the press to create heroes, as she explains in the following interview.

P R E S S

P O W E R

Emilia Askari, journalist

Journalists create heroes—and antiheroes. They don't sit around scratching their heads and wondering, 'Who are we going to make a hero today?' But simply because we do our jobs—and ask questions and tell the stories—heroes are created in the process. Some people who achieve heroic status are common folks who have heroism thrust upon them; others work hard to acquire a heroic image—or have a public relations image maker to help things along.

"There is an element of luck as to who is made a hero. In the cycle of news, Monday is a slow day, since most of the news involves government, which is closed over the weekend. Someone who saves a child from a burning building has greater chances of making the news on Monday than on Thursday.

"Usually a single newspaper article doesn't create a hero, but it can happen. In fact, it once happened because of an article that I wrote in Los Angeles. One day an elderly woman barged into the newsroom and said, 'I have an important story that I must tell!' I took her aside and listened to her fantastic tale: her tawdry life as a young beauty, and the

description of her daughter, who decided to turn her own life around and escape the crime-ridden neighborhood. The girl earned a GED (General Educational Development) and was now about to graduate from medical school and become a surgeon. After verifying the woman's story, I wrote an article about her that appeared on the front page.

The daughter received offers to make a TV movie of her life. The article probably had a greater impact in Los Angeles, being so close to Hollywood, than it would have had in Detroit.

"Hero-making can happen in reverse, sometimes to a whole class of people—especially when people of color or the poor are stereotyped. This happened with the 1995 Oklahoma City bombing in which a federal office was bombed and many people were killed. Police and the media originally described the incident as a Middle East-type terrorist attack. On the basis of that label, anyone from an Arab country became suspect. One man was even detained at the airport simply because of his nationality. Upon investigation, however, Middle Easterners were cleared from any involvement in the crime."

Ms. Askari concludes, "I really enjoy my job and I'm proud of my work. I try to do a public service—gathering, sorting, and conveying information—and try to provide a balance to public officials who have power and might run amuck if the media did not keep the public informed."

Responding
With a group, brainstorm examples of hero-making or hero-bashing in the media. Do you feel that advertising helps shape our concepts of heroism? Explain.

Reading Mini-Lesson

Classifying

Whenever you create files on a computer, arrange your CDs in some order, use subject dividers in a notebook, or put your socks into a special drawer, you are using classification to make your personal life a bit more orderly. Libraries, supermarkets, and the Yellow Pages of the phone directory use methods of classifying for easy public access.

In addition, classifying is a basic thinking skill that good readers use to group new ideas into more familiar categories or to break large categories into smaller groups. Likewise, classification is a tool for mentally storing knowledge (for example, famous Texans, mystery writers, state capitals).

Much of the information on heroes in the Interdisciplinary Study on pages 437–440 lends itself to classification. The map displays heroes according to different geographic areas. In his interview, Michael Dorris mentions personal heroes, historical heroes, and media heroes.

Use the following headings, along with headings of your own, to make a chart in which you classify the heroes listed at the left. (You may need to review information in the Interdisciplinary Study.) Note that one hero may fit into several categories. Think of other heroes to add to the chart.

Terminator

Rosa Parks

Abraham Lincoln

Quetzalcoatl

Brynhild

Sita

a favorite teacher

Jimmy Carter

King Arthur

Indiana Jones

Michael Dorris's son Adam

Geographical	Historical	Media	Personal	Legendary

Activity Options

1. Using categories such as Adventure, Comedy, Romance, Drama, Fantasy, Westerns, and Sports, work with a group to classify your favorite films, TV shows, video games, or books. List the results on a chart and present it to the class.

2. Create a list of survey questions to classify the people in your class. For example, you could create categories and subcategories such as pet owners (owners of cats, dogs, or unusual pets), musicians, team members, or movie buffs.

Writing Workshop

What Makes a Hero?

Assignment You have read about many kinds of heroes. Now write an essay in which you express your own thoughts about heroism.

WRITER'S BLUEPRINT

Product   An interpretive essay
Purpose   To explore the concept of heroism
Audience   Your teacher, classmates, and friends
Specs   As the writer of a successful essay, you should:

❑ Decide on your own definition of a hero, including the four traits that you feel are most important to a hero. Then choose the two characters from the selections who come closest to living up to your definition.

❑ Begin your paper by giving your own definition of a hero, keeping in mind that readers may not see a hero in the same way that you do.

❑ Go on to analyze how well your two characters live up to your definition of a hero, citing specific details from the stories in support of your analysis.

❑ Structure your paper in one of two ways:
—deal with each trait from your definition, one at a time, and measure the characters against it, or
—deal with each character, one at a time, and measure her or him against the traits in your definition.

❑ Conclude by telling which character comes closer to being your idea of a hero and why.

❑ Make smooth transitions between thoughts.

❑ Follow the rules of grammar, usage, spelling, and mechanics. Avoid stringy sentences.

Discuss heroic traits. With a partner, discuss real or fictional people you think of as heroic. What do they do and think, outwardly and inwardly, that makes them heroic? List character traits that come to mind as you discuss what makes someone heroic.

Then, on your own, decide on four traits that you feel are most important for a true hero to possess. Here are some suggestions for heroic traits:

> courageous, remains calm in the face of danger, determined, has great patience, helpful, honest, slow to anger, respects the law, has great physical strength, does not wish to harm others, merciful, speedy, athletic, decisive, loving, quick-witted, clever, shy and quiet, friendly, never gives up, aggressive, generous, impulsive, respects the rights of others, is a loner, is a leader, feels superior and shows it, unconventional, charismatic, secretive

OR . . .
Try a quickwrite before you discuss. Write for five minutes or so about what comes to mind when you think of heroes. Use your quickwrite when you discuss heroic traits with a partner.

Rate the characters in the stories in this part of the unit on a scale of 1–10, with 10 being most heroic and 1 least heroic. Then choose the two characters who received your highest rating.

Chart heroic traits. Measure each character against your four traits, using a chart like the one that follows. Find specific examples of things the characters say and do that demonstrate these traits.

LITERARY SOURCE
" . . . Peter was playing the 'Wilhelmus'! . . . Then we were all singing together, the full voice of Holland singing her forbidden anthem. We sang at the top of our lungs, sang our oneness, our hope. . . ."
from "The Secret Room" by Corrie ten Boom

Character	#1 Courageous	#2_____	#3_____	#4_____
Peter from "The Secret Room"	Peter plays "Wilhelmus" in church, knowing the anthem is forbidden and he could be imprisoned. This is inner courage— inner strength, not physical.			

Plan your essay. Create a plan like the one shown, pulling together the information you've gathered up to now.

Introduction
- Your definition of a hero
- Transition to Body (See the Revising Strategy in Step 3 of this lesson.)

Body
- Character #1
  - Trait one and detail from the story
  - Trait two and detail from the story
  and so on
- Transition to Character #2
- Character #2 (same as above)
- Transition to Conclusion

Conclusion
- Which character is more of a hero
- Reasons why

OR . . .
Organize the body of your essay around the four traits and discuss them one at a time. Show how your two characters exemplify each trait.

STEP 2 DRAFTING

Before you write, review your discussion notes, chart, and writing plan. Then reread the Writer's Blueprint.

As you draft, concentrate on getting the ideas from your writing plan down on paper. Here are some drafting tips.

- As you move from idea to idea, knit them together with smooth transitions. See the Revising Strategy in Step 3 of this lesson.

- Be sure that your examples are specific and true to what happens in the story.

STEP 3 REVISING

COMPUTER TIP
Use the Cut and Paste functions of your word processor to rearrange the paragraphs in your essay to find the best order.

Ask a partner for comments on your draft before you revise it.

✔ Have I explained my definition of a hero in detail?

✔ Have I used specific details from the literature to show how well my two characters live up to my definition of a hero?

✔ Have I made smooth transitions between paragraphs?

Revising Strategy

Making Smooth Transitions

Use transitional sentences to connect the paragraphs within an essay. In the same way, use transitional phrases, like those below, to connect sentences within a paragraph.

To signal a new idea:	first, next
To compare (show similarities):	in the same way, similarly
To contrast (show differences):	on the other hand, in spite of
To conclude or summarize:	as a result, in conclusion
To add information:	furthermore, for instance
To clarify:	in other words, put another way

Notice how a transitional sentence has been added in the student model to connect the paragraphs.

Carlé is an extremely strong character. He is always able to get the best scoops on the news. Furthermore, he is courageous, risking his life to get the story in even very dangerous places. His bravery and skill as a journalist have made him famous.

In spite of his fame as a reporter, Rolf Carlé is still very level-headed. He didn't mind being in the public eye and being disheveled in front of the world as he tried to save a 13-year-old girl. He was willing to put his personal comfort aside to help her any way he could.

 **EDITING**

Ask a partner to review your revised draft before you edit. When you edit, look for errors in grammar, usage, spelling, and mechanics. Be on the lookout for stringy sentences.

Editing Strategy

Correcting Stringy Sentences

FOR REFERENCE
You'll find more tips on revising stringy sentences in the Language and Grammar Handbook at the back of this text.

In a stringy sentence, several independent clauses are strung together with one *and* after another. Correct stringy sentences by breaking them into individual sentences or turning independent clauses into subordinate clauses or phrases.

Stringy Sentence: Corrie ten Boom wanted to help Jews but she knew it was dangerous *and* she planned to have a secret room to hide them *and* she went looking for an architect in the underground to design and build the hiding place.

Corrected: Even though she knew it was dangerous, Corrie ten Boom wanted to help Jews. She planned to have a secret room to hide them. To find someone to build her hiding place, she went looking for an architect in the underground.

STEP 5 PRESENTING

- Use your essays as the basis for a class debate on the question: What makes a true hero?

- Get together with a partner or a small group and design a poster that illustrates the traits that a true hero should have.

STEP 6 LOOKING BACK

Self-evaluate. Look back at the Writer's Blueprint and give yourself a score for each item, from 6 (superior) to 1 (inadequate).

Reflect. Reflect on the following questions in writing:

✔ Who would be a real-life person who lives up to my definition of a hero? Why?

✔ How am I doing as a writer in terms of being technically correct? How would I rate my spelling, grammar, usage, and mechanics skills?

For Your Working Portfolio Add your finished paper and your reflection responses to your working portfolio.

Beyond Print

Multimedia Presentations

Welcome to the Information Age! Among the many wonders of modern technology—computers, VCRs, CD-ROMs, and programs such as HyperCard—is the power to transform traditional speeches into exciting media events. Any time you use a combination of media to communicate to an audience, you are making a multimedia presentation. This includes speech, posters, slides, video, projected images, graphs, computers, recordings, or even skits.

A great tool in producing any multimedia presentation is the computer. Hooking the computer to a projection unit allows you to use the program during an oral presentation, much like a slide projector but with animation, special effects, sound, and video. You can even create an interactive program in which viewers manipulate the type and order of information they receive by merely clicking a button.

The key to successful multimedia presentations is organization. Each piece of media you add makes the presentation more complex, so spend time thinking and practicing. Don't create posters or computer screens that are "busy" or unclear.

Here are some hints for using multimedia in oral presentations.

- Use pictures and music that will supplement the information, not distract the audience.

- Use large type (for readability) and important heads (for emphasis) in projections. Present additional details orally.

- Apply writing skills to ensure concise, clear, and correctly spelled text.

- Plan, organize, and practice presenting your material.

- Project your voice so that everyone can hear.

Activity Option

Prepare a multimedia presentation based on a selection, an author, or a theme related to the selections in the group titled Many Kinds of Heroes. Start by preparing a speech and adding a simple graphic, such as a poster, graph, transparency, or computer image, and music.

Multicultural Connections

Group

Part One: Arthurian Legends For medieval knights, the concept of *group* was determined by the codes and rules for behavior embodied in chivalry. Although the ideal knight was to act on behalf of his king, his country, and his lady, knights sometimes pursued their own interests rather than those of the group.

■ In what respects is it necessary for any group engaged in battle, including modern-day military bodies, to pursue group interests rather than individual goals?

■ To what degree was the end of the Arthurian era caused by group differences and dissent?

Individuality

Part Two: Many Kinds of Heroes All heroes—not just knights— must subordinate individual goals in pursuing the common good. Ironically, however, characters like Rolf Carlé and Corrie ten Boom arrive at individual self-knowledge in their efforts to meet the needs of others.

■ How can people learn to know themselves through their helping of others?

■ Compare the ways that Corrie ten Boom and Rolf Carlé emerge as stronger individuals through their acts of unselfishness.

Activities

1. Stage a debate on the following topic: "Modern heroes are (are not) individuals. Instead, they are generic types created by the media."

2. With a group, brainstorm what qualities seem to characterize the modern hero. Explain whether or not the modern hero seems more independent than his or her Arthurian counterparts.

Independent and Group Projects

Writing

The Making of a Legend This unit includes legendary Arthurian heroes and heroes who aren't legends—that is, not until now! Rewrite as a legend a scene from one of the selections, adding a few extraordinary events, a touch of magic, and a villain. Make your hero a superhero in the Arthurian tradition!

Comics

Heroes in the Comics Your first encounter with fictitious heroes may have been with the superheroes portrayed in the comics and cartoons, such as Superman, Wonder Woman, and the Ninja Turtles. Using ideas from these sources and your imagination, make up a comic strip about an episode in the life of your own hero.

Film

Batman and Beyond As well-known movie critics, you and a partner have been selected to compile the prestigious catalog of *Famous Folks in Flicks.* Scan your memory banks, enlist the help of a movie buff, and look up titles in a reference book such as *Halliwell's Film Guide* to find movies that focus on heroes past or present. Select ten movies to endorse in a movie guide. Write a brief review of each.

Research

Big Shots Who are the people who have gained fame over the past fifty years? Choose an area and a focus (for example, Top Female Athletes of the 1970s, Leading Actors in Recent Soaps). With a group, research back issues of magazines for photographs and descriptions of people that fit your category. Then present your information in a slide show, video, or scrapbook.

Entertainment

Heroes You Should Know Create a trivia game of past and present heroes, including some from this unit. Begin by making lists of names. Then categorize them into different groups, such as Politics, Sports, Media, Explorers, Inventors, and so forth. Create trivia cards on which you summarize information that identifies each hero. You can play this as a card game or a board game with markers.

What Really Matters?

Worth Fighting For?

Something of Value

Reading

Nonfiction is prose literature that deals with real people and events rather than imaginary ones. A broad literary genre, nonfiction includes almost any kind of literature that does not involve fictional characters and events. Types of nonfiction you will encounter in Unit Four are autobiographies, essays, and speeches. Other forms of nonfiction include biographies, letters, and diaries.

Biography and Autobiography

A biography, an account of a person's life written by someone else, presents a third-person point of view. Biographers should give a complete picture without unfairly eliminating or slanting important information to suit their own purposes. Readers must be willing to question and, if necessary, investigate the author's use of facts.

The group of selections that follow are autobiographies, the story of a writer's own life. As you read these selections, you will enter into each person's special world and meet the people who have shared that world. By the time you have finished the autobiography, you may feel that there is a bit of your own story in this writer's life. If you have ever thrown a snowball at a car, disagreed with a parent, had a bad day at school, or fondly recalled a relative, you will find something of yourself in the selections that follow.

The most authentic autobiographies and biographies are truthful, presenting the world and the featured subject honestly without trying to glamorize or distort things. Yet even the most truthful nonfiction works resort to imagination and memory, taking license in portraying details and capturing the spirit of things rather than presenting absolute fact. For example, the dialogue in *Kaffir Boy* is recollected rather than quoted exactly. Likewise, autobiographers shape and focus their materials, highlighting interesting parts and omitting dull or unimportant details.

As you read the nonfiction selections that follow, look for the same things you find in fiction—characterization, theme, plot, and setting. It would be hard to find more memorable characters than Maya Angelou's Aunt Tee or Mark Mathabane's granny. The importance of using education as a tool in combating prejudice is a dominant theme in *Kaffir Boy*, while *An American Childhood* emphasizes the value of pursuing a goal wholeheartedly. Even though these are excerpts, they contain plot elements, including a climax and some kind of resolution. Setting is a crucial factor in all these excerpts; just try to trade the settings of Mathabane's and Dillard's stories to see how these works would fall apart without their respective settings. Especially noteworthy in this type of nonfiction is point of view. Although

Nonfiction

autobiography and biography are based on fact, the writer seldom presents these facts in a completely objective manner. So as you read, keep in mind that these writers necessarily emphasize things that they consider important and color events and people according to their own perspectives.

Watch also for tone—the writer's attitude toward a subject. Annie Dillard's light attitude—"I got in trouble throwing snowballs, and have seldom been happier since"—which is perfect for her selection, would be inappropriate in Santha Rama Rau's account.

Tips for Reading Biography and Autobiography
- Look for the same things you find in fiction—characterization, theme, plot, setting, tone, and point of view.
- Consider how the writer's personal feelings may affect his or her treatment of people and interpretation of events.
- Ask yourself why the author has focused on particular incidents. What do these incidents reveal?

Essays and Speeches
Writers of essays and speeches explore topics and express their opinions. They may be less concerned with telling a story than with presenting their ideas. Both essays and speeches are usually brief, reflecting the writers' attitudes and knowledge. You can usually find a main idea in these works. Subject matter is virtually unlimited, and tone can range from humorous and light to serious. Both Wiesel and Camus adopt a serious tone in their Nobel speeches.

Tips for Reading Essays and Speeches
- Locate and identify the main idea.
- Find details that support the main idea—facts, arguments, and examples.
- Try to differentiate between fact and opinion.
- Draw upon your own knowledge and experience in evaluating the writer's ideas and conclusion.

Part One

Worth Fighting For?

What would you stand up for, speak out for, or physically protect? In defending rights and redressing wrongs, you have to determine what is worth fighting for. Pick your battles and hope for the kind of successes that some of the characters in these selections achieve.

🐾 **Multicultural Connection** **Communication** may be complicated when diverse factors such as age, language, culture, and social class present obstacles. In the following selections, what challenges and misunderstandings are a result of miscommunication? How do characters meet such challenges?

Before Reading

from **Kaffir Boy**

by Mark Mathabane   South Africa

Mark Mathabane
born 1960

The grandmother of Mark Mathabane (ma′thä bän) gardened for the Smiths, a white family. When Mark was eleven, Clyde, the Smith's son, said to him, "My teachers tell us that Kaffirs can't read, speak, or write English like white people because they have smaller brains, which are already full of tribal things." An angry Mathabane resolved to excel in school and to teach himself English—a language blacks were not then allowed to learn—from comic books. Mathabane became a top tennis player and earned an athletic scholarship to an American college. He now lives in the United States where he is a noted writer and lecturer.

Building Background

Separate and Unequal As a young boy, Mark Mathabane encountered the word *Kaffir,* an Arabic word meaning "infidel" and used in South Africa as a derogatory term to refer to blacks. Its use was symbolic of the many indignities of *apartheid* (ə part′hāt), an Afrikaans word for "separateness" that refers to the government policy of legalized racism. Blacks were restricted to tribal reserves and allowed to work in cities only if they had identification

▲ Nelson Mandela and F. W. de Klerk

cards. Since Mathabane's parents had emigrated illegally, they were ready prey for police raids, jail, or deportation. His father, Jackson, in fact, was imprisoned repeatedly. Through the efforts of Nelson Mandela, then head of the African National Congress, and F. W. de Klerk, then South Africa's president, apartheid was abolished in the 1990s. In 1994, Nelson Mandela succeeded de Klerk in the first multiracial election in South Africa's history.

Literary Focus

Characterization As you read this excerpt from the autobiography, *Kaffir Boy,* note Mathabane's **characterization** of his mother and father. What techniques does he use to bring these two people to life? Note other memorable characters in this selection.

Writer's Notebook

School Choice Recall an early experience in school—perhaps your first day. Write several words that describe someone who made this day memorable for you.

Kaffir Boy

Mark Mathabane

Education will

open doors

where none seem

to exist.

When my mother began dropping hints that I would soon be going to school, I vowed never to go because school was a waste of time. She laughed and said, "We'll see. You don't know what you're talking about." My philosophy on school was that of a gang of ten-, eleven- and twelve-year-olds whom I so revered that their every word seemed that of an oracle.

These boys had long left their homes and were now living in various neighborhood junkyards, making it on their own. They slept in

◄ An apprehensive boy looks out from a backdrop of graffiti in this photograph of a Soweto ghetto by David C. Turnley. *Cry, the Beloved Country* is the title of a well-known novel about South Africa by Alan Paton. What do you think a boy like the one pictured might hope for in a "beloved country"?

abandoned cars, smoked glue and benzene, ate pilchards[1] and brown bread, sneaked into the white world to caddy and, if unsuccessful, came back to the township to steal beer and soda bottles from shebeens,[2] or goods from the Indian traders on First Avenue. Their lifestyle was exciting, adventurous and full of surprises; and I was attracted to it. My mother told me that they were no-gooders, that they would amount to nothing, that I should not associate with them, but I paid no heed. What does she know? I used to tell myself. One thing she did not know was that the gang's way of life had captivated me wholly, particularly their philosophy on school: they hated it and considered an education a waste of time.

They, like myself, had grown up in an environment where the value of an education was never emphasized, where the first thing a child learned was not how to read and write and spell, but how to fight and steal and rebel; where the money to send children to school was grossly lacking, for survival was first priority. I kept my membership in the gang, knowing that for as long as I was under its influence, I would never go to school.

One day my mother woke me up at four in the morning.

"Are they here? I didn't hear any noises," I asked in the usual way.

"No," my mother said. "I want you to get into that washtub over there."

"What!" I balked, upon hearing the word *washtub*. I feared taking baths like one feared the plague. Throughout seven years of hectic living the number of baths I had taken could be counted on one hand with several fingers missing. I simply had no natural inclination for water; cleanliness was a trait I still had to acquire. Besides, we had only one bathtub in the house, and it constantly sprung a leak.

"I said get into that tub!" My mother shook a finger in my face.

Reluctantly, I obeyed, yet wondered why all of a sudden I had to take a bath. My mother, armed with a scrobrush and a piece of Lifebuoy soap, purged[3] me of years and years of grime till I ached and bled. As I howled, feeling pain shoot through my limbs as the thistles

---

1. **pilchard** (pil′chərd), *n.* small oily fish, such as a sardine.
2. **shebeen** (shi bēn′), *n.* an unlicensed establishment selling beer and soda.
3. **purge** (pėrj), *v.* make clean.

of the brush encountered stubborn callouses, there was a loud knock at the door.

Instantly my mother leaped away from the tub and headed, on tiptoe, toward the bedroom. Fear seized me as I, too, thought of the police. I sat frozen in the bathtub, not knowing what to do.

"Open up, Mujaji [my mother's maiden name]," Granny's voice came shrilling through the door. "It's me."

My mother heaved a sigh of relief; her tense limbs relaxed. She turned and headed to the kitchen door, unlatched it and in came Granny and Aunt Bushy.

"You scared me half to death," my mother said to Granny. "I had forgotten all about your coming."

"Are you ready?" Granny asked my mother.

"Yes—just about," my mother said, beckoning me to get out of the washtub.

She handed me a piece of cloth to dry myself. As I dried myself, questions raced through my mind: What's going on? What's Granny doing at our house this ungodly hour of the morning? And why did she ask my mother, "Are you ready?" While I stood debating, my mother went into the bedroom and came out with a stained white shirt and a pair of faded black shorts.

"Here," she said, handing me the togs, "put these on."

"Why?" I asked.

"Put them on I said!"

I put the shirt on; it was grossly loose-fitting. It reached all the way down to my ankles. Then I saw the reason why: it was my father's shirt!

"But this is Papa's shirt," I complained. "It don't fit me."

"Put it on," my mother insisted. "I'll make it fit."

"The pants don't fit me either," I said. "Whose are they anyway?"

"Put them on," my mother said. "I'll make them fit."

Moments later I had the garments on; I looked ridiculous. My mother started working on the pants and shirt to make them fit. She folded the shirt in so many intricate ways and stashed it inside the pants, they too having been folded several times at the waist. She then choked the pants at the waist with a piece of sisal rope to hold them up. She then lavishly smeared my face, arms and legs with a mixture of pig's fat and vaseline. "This will insulate you from the cold," she said. My skin gleamed like the morning star and I felt as hot as the center of the sun and I smelled God knows like what. After embalming me, she headed to the bedroom.

"Where are we going, Gran'ma?" I said, hoping that she would tell me what my mother refused to tell me. I still had no idea I was about to be taken to school.

"Didn't your mother tell you?" Granny said with a smile. "You're going to start school."

"What!" I gasped, leaping from the chair where I was sitting as if it were made of hot lead. "I am not going to school!" I blurted out and raced toward the kitchen door.

My mother had just reappeared from the bedroom and guessing what I was up to, she yelled, "Someone get the door!"

Aunt Bushy immediately barred the door. I turned and headed for the window. As I leaped for the windowsill, my mother lunged at me and brought me down. I tussled, "Let go of me! I don't want to go to school! Let me go!" but my mother held fast onto me.

"It's no use now," she said, grinning triumphantly as she pinned me down. Turning her head in Granny's direction, she shouted, "Granny! Get a rope quickly!"

Granny grabbed a piece of rope nearby and came to my mother's aid. I bit and clawed every hand that grabbed me, and howled protestations against going to school; however, I was no match for the two determined matriarchs. In a jiffy they had me bound, hands and feet.

"What's the matter with him?" Granny, bewildered, asked my mother. "Why did he suddenly turn into an imp when I told him you're taking him to school?"

"You shouldn't have told him that he's being taken to school," my mother said. "He doesn't want to go there. That's why I requested you come today, to help me take him there. Those boys in the streets have been a bad influence on him."

As the two matriarchs hauled me through the door, they told Aunt Bushy not to go to school but stay behind and mind the house and the children.

The sun was beginning to rise from beyond the veld when Granny and my mother dragged me to school. The streets were beginning to fill with their everyday traffic: old men and women, wizened, bent and ragged, were beginning their rambling; workless men and women were beginning to assemble in their usual coteries and head for shebeens in the backyards where they discussed how they escaped the morning pass raids[4] and contemplated the conditions of life amidst intense beer drinking and vacant, uneasy laughter; young boys and girls, some as young as myself, were beginning their aimless wanderings along the narrow, dusty streets in search of food, carrying bawling infants piggyback.

> **CONNECT: How is life among the city poor in South Africa both alike and different from that in the United States?**

As we went along some of the streets, boys and girls who shared the same fears about school as I were making their feelings known in a variety of ways. They were howling their protests and trying to escape. A few managed to break loose and make a mad dash for freedom, only to be recaptured in no time, admonished[5] or whipped, or both, and ordered to march again.

As we made a turn into Sixteenth Avenue, the street leading to the tribal school I was being taken to, a short, chubby black woman came along from the opposite direction. She had a scuttle overflowing with coal on her *doek*-covered (cloth-covered) head. An infant, bawling deafeningly, was loosely swathed[6] with a piece of sheepskin onto her back. Following closely behind the woman, and picking up pieces of coal as they fell from the scuttle and placing them in a small plastic bag, was a half-naked, pot-bellied and thumb-sucking boy of about four. The woman stopped abreast. For some reason we stopped too.

"I wish I had done the same to my oldest son," the strange woman said in a regretful voice, gazing at me. I was confounded by her stopping and offering her unsolicited opinion.

"I wish I had done that to my oldest son," she repeated, and suddenly burst into tears; amidst sobs, she continued, "before . . . the street claimed him . . . and . . . turned him into a *tsotsi*."[7]

Granny and my mother offered consolatory remarks to the strange woman.

"But it's too late now," the strange woman continued, tears now streaming freely down her puffy cheeks. She made no attempt to dry them. "It's too late now," she said for the second time, "he's beyond any help. I can't help him even if I want to. *Uswile* [He is dead]."

"How did he die?" my mother asked in a sympathetic voice.

"He shunned school and, instead, grew up to live by the knife. And the same knife he lived by ended his life. That's why whenever I see a boy-child refuse to go to school, I stop and tell the story of my dear little *mbitsini* [heartbreak]."

Having said that, the strange woman left as mysteriously as she had arrived.

"Did you hear what that woman said!" my

---

4. **pass raid,** a raid, often pre-dawn, by South African police or soldiers checking whether the inhabitants of a house have an official government pass allowing them to be there.
5. **admonish** (ad mon′ish), *v.* scold gently.
6. **swathe** (swoᴛʜ), *v.* wrap up closely or fully.
7. **tsotsi** (tsō′tsē), *n.* thug, mugger, or gangster, usually armed with a weapon such as a knife.

mother screamed into my ears. "Do you want the same to happen to you?"

I dropped my eyes. I was confused.

"Poor woman," Granny said ruefully.[8] "She must have truly loved her son."

Finally, we reached the school and I was ushered into the principal's office, a tiny cubicle[9] facing a row of privies and a patch of yellowed grass.

"So this is the rascal we'd been talking about," the principal, a tall, wiry man, foppishly dressed in a black pinstriped suit, said to my mother as we entered. His austere,[10] shiny face, inscrutable and imposing, reminded me of my father. He was sitting behind a brown table upon which stood piles

Once they get out into the streets, they become wild.

of dust and cobweb-covered books and papers. In one upper pocket of his jacket was arrayed a variety of pens and pencils; in the other nestled a lily-white handkerchief whose presence was more decorative than utilitarian. Alongside him stood a disproportionately portly black woman, fashionably dressed in a black skirt and a white blouse. She had but one pen, and this she held in her hand. The room was hot and stuffy and buzzing with flies.

"Yes, Principal," my mother answered, "this is he."

"I see he's living up to his notoriety," remarked the principal, noticing that I had been bound. "Did he give you too much trouble?"

"Trouble, Principal," my mother sighed. "He was like an imp."

"He's just like the rest of them, Principal," Granny sighed. "Once they get out into the streets, they become wild. They take to the many vices of the streets like an infant takes to its mother's milk. They begin to think that there's no other life but the one shown them by the *tsotsis*. They come to hate school and forget about the future."

"Well," the principal said. "We'll soon remedy all that. Untie him."

"He'll run away," my mother cried.

"I don't think he's that foolish to attempt that with all of us here."

"He *is* that foolish, Principal," my mother said as she and Granny began untying me. "He's tried it before. Getting him here was an ordeal in itself."

The principal rose from his seat, took two steps to the door and closed it. As the door swung closed, I spotted a row of canes of different lengths and thicknesses hanging behind it. The principal, seeing me staring at the canes, grinned and said, in a manner suggesting that he had wanted me to see them, "As long as you behave, I won't have to use any of those on you."

Use those canes on me? I gasped. I stared at my mother—she smiled; at Granny—she smiled too. That made me abandon any inkling of escaping.

"So they finally gave you the birth certificate and the papers," the principal addressed my mother as he returned to his chair.

"Yes, Principal," my mother said, "they finally did. But what a battle it was. It took me nearly a year to get all them papers together." She took out of her handbag a neatly wrapped package and handed it to the principal. "They've been running us around for so long that there were times when I thought he would never attend school, Principal," she said.

"That's pretty much standard procedure, Mrs. Mathabane," the principal said, unwrapping the package. "But you now have the papers and that's what's important."

"As long as we have the papers," he continued, minutely perusing[11] the contents of the

---

8. **ruefully** (rū′fə lē), *adv.* sorrowfully.
9. **cubicle** (kyü′bə kəl), *n.* a very small room or compartment.
10. **austere** (ô stir′), *adj.* stern in manner or appearance.
11. **peruse** (pə rüz′), *v.* read, especially thoroughly and carefully.

package, "we won't be breaking the law in admitting your son to this school, for we'll be in full compliance with the requirements set by the authorities in Pretoria."[12]

"Sometimes I don't understand the laws from Pitori," Granny said. "They did the same to me with my Piet and Bushy. Why, Principal, should our children not be allowed to learn because of some piece of paper?"

"The piece of paper you're referring to, Mrs. Mabaso [Granny's maiden name]," the principal said to Granny, "is as important to our children as a pass is to us adults. We all hate passes; therefore, it's only natural we should hate the regulations our children are subjected to. But as we have to live with passes, so our children have to live with the regulations, Mrs. Mabaso. I hope you understand, that is the law of the country. We would have admitted your grandson a long time ago, as you well know, had it not been for the papers. I hope you understand."

"I understand, Principal," Granny said, "but I don't understand," she added paradoxically.

One of the papers caught the principal's eye and he turned to my mother and asked, "Is your husband a Shangaan, Mrs. Mathabane?"

"No, he's not, Principal," my mother said. "Is there anything wrong? He's Venda and I'm Shangaan."

The principal reflected for a moment or so and then said, concernedly, "No, there's nothing seriously wrong. Nothing that we can't take care of. You see, Mrs. Mathabane, technically, the fact that your child's father is a Venda makes him ineligible to attend this tribal school because it is only for children whose parents are of the Shangaan tribe. May I ask what language the children speak at home?"

"Both languages," my mother said worriedly, "Venda and Shangaan. Is there anything wrong?"

The principal coughed, clearing his throat, then said, "I mean which language do they speak more?"

"It depends, Principal," my mother said, swallowing hard. "When their father is around, he wants them to speak only Venda. And when he's not, they speak Shangaan. And when they are out at play, they speak Zulu and Sisotho."

"Well," the principal said, heaving a sigh of relief. "In that case, I think an exception can be made. The reason for such an exception is that there's currently no school for Vendas in Alexandra. And should the authorities come asking why we took in your son, we can tell them that. Anyway, your child is half-half."

Everyone broke into a nervous laugh, except me. I was bewildered by the whole thing. I looked at my mother, and she seemed greatly relieved as she watched the principal register me; a broad smile broke across her face. It was as if some enormously heavy burden had finally been lifted from her shoulders and her conscience.

"Bring him back two weeks from today," the principal said as he saw us to the door. "There're so many children registering today that classes won't begin until two weeks hence. Also, the school needs repair and cleaning up after the holidays. If he refuses to come, simply notify us, and we'll send a couple of big boys to come fetch him, and he'll be very sorry if it ever comes to that."

As we left the principal's office and headed home, my mind was still against going to school. I was thinking of running away from home and joining my friends in the junkyard.

I didn't want to go to school for three reasons: I was reluctant to surrender my freedom and independence over to what I heard every school-going child call "tyrannous discipline." I had heard many bad things about life in tribal school—from daily beatings by teachers and mistresses who worked you like a mule to long school hours—and the sight of those canes in the prin-

---

12. **Pretoria** (pri tôr′ē ə), *n.* capital of South Africa; also called Pitori.

cipal's office gave ample credence[13] to rumors that school was nothing but a torture chamber. And there was my allegiance to the gang.

But the thought of the strange woman's lamentations over her dead son presented a somewhat strong case for going to school: I didn't want to end up dead in the streets. A more compelling argument for going to school, however, was the vivid recollection of all that humiliation and pain my mother had gone through to get me the papers and the birth certificate so I could enroll in school. What should I do? I was torn between two worlds.

But later that evening something happened to force me to go to school.

I was returning home from playing soccer when a neighbor accosted[14] me by the gate and told me that there had been a bloody fight at my home.

"Your mother and father have been at it again," the neighbor, a woman, said.

"And your mother left."

I was stunned.

"Was she hurt badly?"

"A little bit," the woman said. "But she'll be all right. We took her to your grandma's place."

I became hot with anger.

"Is anyone in the house?" I stammered, trying to control my rage.

"Yes, your father is. But I don't think you should go near the house. He's raving mad. He's armed with a meat cleaver. He's chased out your brother and sisters, also. And some of the neighbors who tried to intervene he's threatened to carve them to pieces. I have never seen him this mad before."

I brushed aside the woman's warnings and went. Shattered windows convinced me that there had indeed been a skirmish of some sort. Several pieces of broken bricks, evidently broken after being thrown at the door, were lying about the door. I tried opening the door; it was locked from the inside. I knocked. No one answered. I knocked again. Still no one answered, until, as I turned to leave:

"Who's out there?" my father's voice came growling from inside.

"It's me, Johannes," I said.

"Go away . . . !" he bellowed. "I don't want you or that . . . mother of yours setting foot in this house. Go away before I come out there and kill you!"

"Let me in!" I cried. "Dammit, let me in! I want my things!"

"What things? Go away, you black swine!"

I went to the broken window and screamed obscenities at my father, daring him to come out, hoping that if he as much as ever stuck his black face out, I would pelt him with the half-a-loaf brick in my hand. He didn't come out. He continued launching a tirade of obscenities at my mother and her mother. . . . He was drunk, but I wondered where he had gotten the money to buy beer because it was still the middle of the week and he was dead broke. He had lost his entire wage for the past week in dice and had had to borrow bus fare.

"I'll kill you someday for all you're doing to my mother," I threatened him, overwhelmed with rage. Several nosey neighbors were beginning to congregate by open windows and doors. Not wanting to make a spectacle of myself, which was something many of our neighbors seemed to always expect from our family, I backtracked away from the door and vanished into the dark street. I ran, without stopping, all the way to the other end of the township where Granny lived. There I found my mother, her face swollen and bruised and her eyes puffed up to the point where she could scarcely see.

"What happened, Mama?" I asked, fighting to hold back the tears at the sight of her disfigured face.

"Nothing, child, nothing," she mumbled

---

13. **credence** (krēd′ns), *n.* belief.
14. **accost** (ə kôst′), *v.* approach and speak to first; address.

▲ This woman's tribal homeland has become "independent," depriving its residents of South African citizenship. What advice might she give the boy photographed on page 456?

almost apologetically, between swollen lips. "Your papa simply lost his temper, that's all."

"But why did he beat you up like this, Mama?" Tears came down my face. "He's never beaten you like this before."

My mother appeared reluctant to answer me. She looked searchingly at Granny, who was pounding millet with pestle and mortar[15] and mixing it with sorghum and nuts for an African delicacy. Granny said, "Tell him, child, tell him. He's got a right to know. Anyway, he's the cause of it all."

"Your father and I fought because I took you to school this morning," my mother began. "He had told me not to, and when I told him that I had, he became very upset. He was drunk. We started arguing, and one thing led to another."

"Why doesn't he want me to go to school?"

"He says he doesn't have money to waste paying for you to get what he calls a useless white man's education," my mother replied. "But I told him that if he won't pay for your schooling, I

_____

15. **millet . . . mortar.** A mortar is a bowl in which substances such as the cereal grain millet can be pounded or crushed by a pestle, a small, clublike tool.

would try and look for a job and pay, but he didn't want to hear that, also. 'There are better things for you to work for,' he said. 'Besides, I don't want you to work. How would I look to other men if you, a woman I owned, were to start working?' When I asked him why shouldn't I take you to school, seeing that you were now of age, he replied that he doesn't believe in schools. I told him that school would keep you off the streets and out of trouble, but still he was belligerent."[16]

"Is that why he beat you up?"

"Yes, he said I disobeyed his orders."

"He's right, child," Granny interjected. "He paid *lobola* [bride price] for you. And your father ate it all up before he left me."

To which my mother replied, "But I desperately want to leave this beast of a man. But with his *lobola* gone I can't do it. That worthless thing you call your husband shouldn't have sold Jackson's scrawny cattle and left you penniless."

"Don't talk like that about your father, child," Granny said. "Despite all, he's still your father, you know. Anyway, he asked for *lobola* only because he had to get back what he spent raising you. And you know it would have been taboo for him to let you or any of your sisters go without asking for *lobola.*"

"You and Papa seemed to forget that my sisters and I have minds of our own," my mother said. "We didn't need you to tell us whom to marry, and why, and how. If it hadn't been for your interference, I could have married that schoolteacher."

Granny did not reply; she knew well not to. When it came to the act of "selling" women as marriage partners, my mother was vehemently opposed to it. Not only was she opposed to this one aspect of tribal culture, but to others as well, particularly those involving relations between men and women and the upbringing of children. But my mother's sharply differing opinion was an exception rather than the rule among tribal women. Most times, many tribal women questioned her sanity in daring to question well-established mores. But my mother did not seem to care; she would always scoff at her opponents and call them fools in letting their husbands enslave them completely.

CLARIFY: What aspects of tribal culture does Johannes's mother oppose? Why?

Though I disliked school, largely because I knew nothing about what actually went on there, and the little I knew had painted a dreadful picture, the fact that a father would not want his son to go to school, especially a father who didn't go to school, seemed hard to understand.

"Why do you want me to go to school, Mama?" I asked, hoping that she might, somehow, clear up some of the confusion that was building in my mind.

"I want you to have a future, child," my mother said. "And, contrary to what your father says, school is the only means to a future. I don't want you growing up to be like your father."

The latter statement hit me like a bolt of lightning. It just about shattered every defense mechanism and every pretext[17] I had against going to school.

"Your father didn't go to school," she continued, dabbing her puffed eyes to reduce the swelling with a piece of cloth dipped in warm water, "that's why he's doing some of the bad things he's doing. Things like drinking, gambling and neglecting his family. He didn't learn how to read and write; therefore, he can't find a decent job. Lack of any education has narrowly focused his life. He sees nothing beyond himself. He still thinks in the old, tribal way, and still believes that things should be as they were back in the old days when he was growing up as a tribal boy in Louis Trichardt. Though he's my husband, and your father, he doesn't see any of that."

"Why didn't he go to school, Mama?"

"He refused to go to school because his

---

16. **belligerent** (bə lij′ər ənt), *adj.* fond of fights.
17. **pretext** (prē′tekst), *n.* a false reason concealing the real reason; misleading excuse.

father led him to believe that an education was a tool through which white people were going to take things away from him, like they did black people in the old days. And that a white man's education was worthless insofar as black people were concerned because it prepared them for jobs they can't have. But I know it isn't totally so, child, because times have changed somewhat. Though our lot isn't any better today, an education will get you a decent job. If you can read or write you'll be better off than those of us who can't. Take my situation: I can't find a job because I don't have papers, and I can't get papers because white people mainly want to register people who can read and write. But I want things to be different for you, child. For you and your brother and sisters. I want you to go to school, because I believe that an education is the key you need to open up a new world and a new life for yourself, a world and life different from that of either your father's or mine. It is the only key that can do that, and only those who seek it earnestly and perseveringly will get anywhere in the white man's world. Education will open doors where none seem to exist. It'll make people talk to you, listen to you and help you; people who otherwise wouldn't bother. It will make you soar, like a bird lifting up into the endless blue sky, and leave poverty, hunger and suffering behind. It'll teach you to learn to embrace what's good and shun what's bad and evil. Above all, it'll make you a somebody in this world. It'll make you grow up to be a good and proud person. That's why I want you to go to school, child, so that education can do all that, and more, for you."

SUMMARIZE: State the theme of the preceding paragraph in a sentence.

A long, awkward silence followed, during which I reflected upon the significance of my mother's lengthy speech. I looked at my mother; she looked at me.

Finally, I asked, "How come you know so much about school, Mama? You didn't go to school, did you?"

"No, child," my mother replied. "Just like your father, I never went to school." For the second time that evening, a mere statement of fact had a thunderous impact on me. All the confusion I had about school seemed to leave my mind, like darkness giving way to light. And what had previously been a dark, yawning void in my mind was suddenly transformed into a beacon of light that began to grow larger and larger, until it had swallowed up, blotted out, all the blackness. That beacon of light seemed to reveal things and facts, which, though they must have always existed in me, I hadn't been aware of up until now.

"But unlike your father," my mother went on, "I've always wanted to go to school, but couldn't because my father, under the sway of tribal traditions, thought it unnecessary to educate females. That's why I so much want you to go, child, for if you do, I know that someday I too would come to go, old as I would be then. Promise me, therefore, that no matter what, you'll go back to school. And I, in turn, promise that I'll do everything in my power to keep you there."

With tears streaming down my cheeks and falling upon my mother's bosom, I promised her that I would go to school "forever." That night, at seven and a half years of my life, the battlelines in the family were drawn. My mother on the one side, illiterate but determined to have me drink, for better or for worse, from the well of knowledge. On the other side, my father, he too illiterate, yet determined to have me drink from the well of ignorance. Scarcely aware of the magnitude of the decision I was making or, rather, the decision which was being emotionally thrusted upon me, I chose to fight on my mother's side, and thus my destiny was forever altered.

Kaffir Boy   **465**

After Reading

Making Connections

Shaping Your Response

1. Write down questions that you would like to ask the adult Mark Mathabane.

2. At the end of the selection, Johannes observes "and thus my destiny was forever altered." Do you think that decisions about schooling are important enough to alter a person's destiny? Explain.

3. Which qualities of the characters in Mathabane's autobiography do you think the photographs that accompany this selection capture?

Analyzing the Autobiography

4. What details in this account indicate the conditions of poverty in this South African **setting?**

5. What is the significance of the encounter with the strange woman?

6. The **theme** of this group of selections is "Worth Fighting For?" In *Kaffir Boy,* who are the fighters, and what is each fighting for?

7. Why might people in Mathabane's culture have opposed getting a formal education? Before answering, you may want to reread the paragraph that begins at the bottom of page 464 ("He refused to go to school . . .").

Extending the Ideas

8. Judging from this excerpt and from information supplied on page 455, would you recommend Mathabane's autobiography to another teenager? Explain.

9. 👣 Words such as *Kaffir* reflect prejudice and lack of **communication** among cultural groups. Why do you think people use derogatory racial terms? What do you think is the best way to react to the use of such terms?

Literary Focus: Characterization

Mathabane's **characterization** of the strange woman encountered on the street is conveyed in a number of ways.

• What does the woman look like?

• Which of the woman's actions do you think reveals the most about her?

• Which of the woman's statements do you find the most memorable?

Vocabulary Study

Study the relationship of each pair of words in capital letters; then write the letter of another pair that has the same relationship.

austere
belligerent
cubicle
peruse
pretext

1. BELLIGERENT : PEACEFUL :: **a.** tiny : small **b.** sad : happy **c.** troubled : upset **d.** thrifty : sale

2. CUBICLE : SMALL :: **a.** theater : crowded **b.** classroom : school **c.** mansion : large **d.** auditorium : empty

3. AUSTERE : STERN :: **a.** fudge : candy **b.** delicious : tasteless **c.** sly : crafty **d.** nervous : calm

4. PRETEXT : EXCUSE :: **a.** pale : rosy **b.** friend : rival **c.** money : credit **d.** objective : goal

5. PERUSE : BOOK :: **a.** strum : guitar **b.** cover : wrap **c.** iron : fold **d.** expire : license

Expressing Your Ideas

Writing Choices

Writer's Notebook Update Mathabane characterizes people through their appearance, actions, and words. Use these three techniques to expand the descriptive words in your notebook into a character sketch of the person who made a school day memorable.

Mr. Mathabane's Neighborhood In this selection, Mathabane provides glimpses of the ghetto in which he lived. Now that apartheid has been abolished, the new government has hired you, a city planner, to make suggestions to improve this area. Write a description of the area and some suggestions for improvement. Organize your **report** under three headings: housing, vacant lots, and streets. You might illustrate your ideas with sketches or diagrams.

The Limits of Tyrants The following quotation by Frederick Douglass appears as a preface to *Kaffir Boy:* "The limits of tyrants are prescribed by the endurance of those whom they oppress." In a paragraph that could be used in a **book review,** explain what these words mean and how they are illustrated in Mathabane's work.

Other Options

Listen Up Write and deliver a brief **motivational speech** that Mark Mathabane might give to a youth group summarizing why he decided to attend and succeed at school.

After 1994 With a team, research what has happened in South Africa since Nelson Mandela was elected president in 1994. Present your findings in the form of a **chalk talk** or display, using visuals such as graphs, charts, and photographs.

Before Reading

Living Well. Living Good.

by Maya Angelou   USA

Maya Angelou
born 1928

She was three years old and on a train. On her wrist was a tag stating that she was Marguerite Johnson, traveling with her four-year-old brother to Stamps, Arkansas, from Long Beach, California, c/o Mrs. Annie Henderson, her grandmother. Before she was fifty, she would be known as Maya Angelou (mä′yä än′-jə lō) and have more than half a dozen successful careers: professional dancer, poet, screenwriter and director, singer, composer, civil rights worker, and college professor. Her greatest achievement may be five volumes of autobiography, from *I Know Why the Caged Bird Sings* (1970) to *Wouldn't Take Nothing for My Journey Now* (1993).

Building Background

Our Strength They are all about us, and their numbers are rapidly increasing. They cure us, they teach us, they file our letters. They fix our broken windows and our broken hearts. They buy stocks, sell shoes, cook meals, clean houses, babysit children, defend us in court, and make us attractive. They are the millions of Americans who, like the aunt Maya Angelou describes, earn their living by offering services, not by making goods. As Aunt Tee's story implies, they are America's strength and future.

Literary Focus

Irony Each of the three kinds of **irony** involves a contradiction between what appears to be and what actually is. If someone whom you've made angry says sarcastically, "Have a nice day," that's *verbal irony*. In *situational irony,* something happens that is the opposite of what you would expect to happen, as when a wealthy person goes bankrupt. In *dramatic irony,* you as reader or audience know something that the fictional characters do not. As you read the following selection, decide which of these kinds of irony is emphasized.

Writer's Notebook

Storytellers In this selection, Maya Angelou recalls the stories related by an elderly relative. Think of a story told by a relative or an old friend of your family. In your notebook, write down several key words or phrases that you could use to summarize this story.

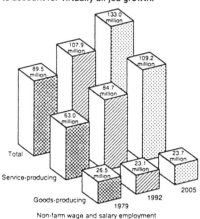

Service-producing industries will continue to account for virtually all job growth.

133.0 million

107.9 million

89.5 million

84.7 million

63.0 million

109.2 million

23.7 million

26.5 million

23.1 million

Total

Service-producing

Goods-producing

1979   1992   2005

Non-farm wage and salary employment

Source: Bureau of Labor Statistics

Living Well. Living Good.

Maya Angelou

Aunt Tee was a Los Angeles member of our extended family. She was seventy-nine when I met her, sinewy, strong, and the color of old lemons. She wore her coarse, straight hair, which was slightly streaked with gray, in a long braided rope across the top of her head. With her high cheekbones, old gold skin, and almond eyes, she looked more like an Indian chief than an old black woman. (Aunt Tee described herself and any favored member of her race as Negroes.

This detail from Archibald J. Motley, Jr.'s *Barbecue* shows lively figures enjoying their leisure during the 1930s. Is dining out part of your image of "living well"? Why or why not? ➤

Black was saved for those who had incurred[1] her disapproval.)

She had retired and lived alone in a dead, neat ground-floor apartment. Wax flowers and china figurines sat on elaborately embroidered and heavily starched doilies. Sofas and chairs were tautly upholstered. The only thing at ease in Aunt Tee's apartment was Aunt Tee.

I used to visit her often and perch on her uncomfortable sofa just to hear her stories. She was proud that after working thirty years as a maid, she spent the next thirty years as a live-in housekeeper, carrying the keys to rich houses and keeping meticulous[2] accounts.

"Living in lets the white folks know Negroes are as neat and clean as they are, sometimes more so. And it gives the Negro maid a chance to see white folks ain't no smarter than Negroes. Just luckier. Sometimes."

Aunt Tee told me that once she was housekeeper for a couple in Bel Air, California,[3] lived with them in a fourteen-room ranch house. There was a day maid who cleaned, and a gardener who daily tended the lush gardens. Aunt Tee oversaw the workers. When she had begun the job, she had cooked and served a light breakfast, a good lunch, and a full three- or four-course dinner to her employers and their guests. Aunt Tee said she watched them grow older and leaner. After a few years they stopped entertaining and ate dinner hardly seeing each other at the table. Finally, they sat in a dry silence as they ate evening meals of soft scrambled eggs, melba toast, and weak tea. Aunt Tee said she saw them growing old but didn't see herself aging at all.

She became the social maven. She started "keeping company" (her phrase) with a chauffeur down the street. Her best friend and her friend's husband worked in service[4] only a few blocks away.

On Saturdays Aunt Tee would cook a pot of pigs' feet, a pot of greens, fry chicken, make potato salad, and bake a banana pudding. Then, that evening, her friends—the chauffeur, the other housekeeper, and her husband—would come to Aunt Tee's commodious[5] live-in quarters. There the four would eat and drink, play records and dance. As the evening wore on, they would settle down to a serious game of bid whist.[6]

Naturally, during this revelry[7] jokes were told, fingers snapped, feet were patted, and there was a great deal of laughter.

Aunt Tee said that what occurred during every Saturday party startled her and her friends the first time it happened. They had been playing cards, and Aunt Tee, who had just won the bid, held a handful of trumps. She felt a cool breeze on her back and sat upright and turned around. Her employers had cracked her door open and beckoned to her. Aunt Tee, a little peeved, laid down her cards and went to the door. The couple backed away and asked her to come into the hall, and there they both spoke and won Aunt Tee's sympathy forever.

"Theresa, we don't mean to disturb you . . ." the man whispered, "but you all seem to be having such a good time. . . ."

The woman added, "We hear you and your friends laughing every Saturday night, and we'd just like to watch you. We don't want to bother you. We'll be quiet and just watch."

The man said, "If you'll just leave your door ajar, your friends don't need to know. We'll never make a sound." Aunt Tee said she saw no harm in agreeing, and she talked it over with

---

1. **incur** (in kėr′), *v.* bring on oneself.
2. **meticulous** (mə tik′yə ləs), *adj.* extremely or excessively careful about small details.
3. **Bel Air, California,** a wealthy section of Los Angeles.
4. **worked in service,** in the occupation or employment of a servant.
5. **commodious** (kə mō′dē əs), *adj.* having plenty of room.
6. **bid whist,** a card game somewhat like bridge.
7. **revelry** (rev′əl rē), *n.* boisterous merrymaking or festivity.

her company. They said it was OK with them, but it was sad that the employers owned the gracious house, the swimming pool, three cars, and numberless palm trees, but had no joy. Aunt Tee told me that laughter and relaxation had left the house; she agreed it was sad.

That story has stayed with me for nearly thirty years, and when a tale remains fresh in my mind, it almost always contains a lesson which will benefit me.

My dears, I draw the picture of the wealthy couple standing in a darkened hallway, peering into a lighted room where black servants were lifting their voices in merriment and comradery, and I realize that living well is an art which can be developed. Of course, you will need the basic talents to build upon: They are a love of life and ability to take great pleasure from small offerings, an assurance that the world owes you nothing and that every gift is exactly that, a gift. That people who may differ from you in political stance, sexual persuasion, and racial inheritance can be founts of fun, and if you are lucky, they can become even convivial[8] comrades.

Living life as art requires a readiness to forgive. I do not mean that you should suffer fools gladly, but rather remember your own shortcomings, and when you encounter another with flaws, don't be eager to righteously seal yourself

We don't want to bother you. We'll be quiet and just watch.

away from the offender forever. Take a few breaths and imagine yourself having just committed the action which has set you at odds.

Because of the routines we follow, we often forget that life is an ongoing adventure. We leave our homes for work, acting and even believing that we will reach our destinations with no unusual event startling us out of our set expectations. The truth is we know nothing, not where our cars will fail or when our buses will stall, whether our places of employment will be there when we arrive, or whether, in fact, we ourselves will arrive whole and alive at the end of our journeys. Life is pure adventure, and the sooner we realize that, the quicker we will be able to treat life as art: to bring all our energies to each encounter, to remain flexible enough to notice and admit when what we expected to happen did not happen. We need to remember that we are created creative and can invent new scenarios as frequently as they are needed.

Life seems to love the liver of it. Money and power can liberate only if they are used to do so. They can imprison and inhibit more finally than barred windows and iron chains.

---

8. **convivial** (kən viv′ē əl), *adj.* sociable.

After Reading

Making Connections

Shaping Your Response

1. Aunt Tee's favorite **proverb** belongs in a frame like the one above. With a partner, decide what this proverb might be.

2. Whose child would you rather be—Aunt Tee's or the wealthy couple's? Why?

3. Why do you think Aunt Tee is so proud of having been a live-in housekeeper?

Analyzing the Autobiography

4. Compare these two **settings**: Aunt Tee's apartment and the Bel Air house.

5. Do you find the **tone** of this selection friendly, preachy, or something else? Explain your choice.

6. 👣 Do you think that despite their cultural differences, the old couple and Aunt Tee **communicate** effectively? Why or why not?

Extending the Ideas

7. How is it possible to live both well and good?

8. Angelou ends by stating that "Money and power . . . can imprison and inhibit more finally than barred windows and iron chains." What examples can you think of to prove or disprove this statement?

Literary Focus: Irony

What **ironic** comment is the painter making about youth and beauty? Like this picture, the selection "Living Well. Living Good." presents an ironic situation that appears to be one thing but in reality is another. What **situational irony** is Maya Angelou revealing?

Vocabulary Study

On your paper, write the letter of the most appropriate answer to each item.

commodious
convivial
incur
meticulous
revelry

1. Which of the following would most likely be *commodious*?
   a. trees   **b.** food   **c.** automobiles   **d.** snow

2. In which job would it be most important to be *convivial?*
   a. accountant   **b.** research scientist   **c.** restaurant host   **d.** coal miner

3. You could be said to *incur* all of the following, with the exception of which item?
   a. anger   **b.** debt   **c.** disapproval   **d.** bad weather

4. If you are *meticulous,* you are ___ .
   a. careless   **b.** awkward   **c.** very careful   **d.** humorous

5. In which setting would you most likely find *revelry?*
   a. a funeral parlor   **b.** a wedding reception   **c.** a factory   **d.** a library

Expressing Your Ideas

Writing Choices

Writer's Notebook Update Before reading this selection, you wrote down key words or phrases from a story told by a relative or friend. Now, summarize that story in a paragraph.

Passing the Torch Aunt Tee has decided to retire. Write the **job description** she would leave for her successor.

Dream House Aunt Tee describes her Bel Air employers' house as being a fourteen-room ranch house. Imagine that you are a real-estate agent charged with listing the house for sale. Write a **listing sheet** describing some of the rooms and emphasizing any features that would appeal to a prospective buyer.

Other Options

Good Times and Bad Working in groups of two or three, find news stories from either television or newspapers that illustrate Angelou's belief that life is an "ongoing adventure." Make a **collage** of the headlines of these stories. If the story comes from television, make up your own headline.

Blues in the Night Divide into groups, one for each of the following decades: the '20s, '30s, '40s, and '50s. Find a **recording** of a popular song or two from that decade, one that Aunt Tee might have danced to. Play it in class, and ask classmates whether or not they think that music like this could be popular today.

Before Reading

from An American Childhood

by Annie Dillard USA

Annie Dillard
born 1945

"I grew up in Pittsburgh in the 1950s, in a house full of comedians, reading books," says Annie Dillard. A voracious reader and keen observer of nature, Dillard wrote, "The visible world turned me curious to books; the books propelled me reeling back to the world." In 1975, she published *Pilgrim at Tinker Creek*, a work which combines her "penchant for quirky facts" with meditations on both the natural and the spiritual worlds. The book won a Pulitzer prize, a rare achievement for a first work. Other works include her auto-biography, *An American Childhood,* from which the following excerpt is taken.

Building Background

Life Sentences In her book, *A Writing Life,* Annie Dillard muses about writers and the importance of childhood:

> It should surprise no one that the life of the writer—such as it is—is colorless to the point of sensory deprivation. Many writers do little else but sit in small rooms recalling the real world. This explains why so many books describe the author's childhood. A writer's childhood may well have been the occasion of his only firsthand experience.

Do you agree with Dillard's observation that childhood may be the "only firsthand experience"? What about growing older might make life's experiences seem less direct?

Literary Focus

Suspense In both fiction and nonfiction, the element of **suspense** impels us to read on. Will the detective find the murderer? Will the avalanche trap the skier? Will the good guys defeat the bad ones? In this selection from her autobiography, Dillard leads both readers and an unidentified man on a merry chase, using suspense to build interest.

Writer's Notebook

Is She a Ten? The incident Dillard describes occurred when she was seven. As you read the selection, rate qualities the young Dillard possesses on a scale of 1 (lowest) to 10 (highest).

Quality	Rating
Sheer Nerve	
Physical Endurance	
Imagination	
Sense of Fairness	

An American Childhood

Annie Dillard

Some boys taught me to play football. This was fine sport. You thought up a new strategy for every play and whispered it to the others. You went out for a pass, fooling everyone. Best, you got to throw yourself mightily at someone's running legs. Either you brought him down or you hit the ground flat out on your chin, with your arms empty before you. It was all or nothing. If you hesitated in fear, you would miss and get hurt: You would take a hard fall while the kid got away, or you would get kicked in the face while the kid got away. But if you flung yourself wholeheartedly at the back of his knees—if you gathered and joined body and soul and pointed them diving fearlessly—then you likely wouldn't get hurt, and you'd stop the ball. Your fate, and your team's score, depended on your concentration and courage. Nothing girls did could compare with it.

Boys welcomed me at baseball, too, for I had, through enthusiastic practice, what was weirdly known as a boy's arm. In winter, in the snow, there was neither baseball nor football, so the boys and I threw snow-

This photograph captures some of the excitement of a snowball fight. What qualities of nature might be conveyed by the looming shadow of a tree and pieces of snow spraying on impact? ▼

balls at passing cars. I got in trouble throwing snowballs, and have seldom been happier since.

On one weekday morning after Christmas, six inches of new snow had just fallen. We were standing up to our boot tops in snow on a front yard on trafficked Reynolds Street, waiting for cars. The cars traveled Reynolds Street slowly and evenly; they were targets all but wrapped in red ribbons, cream puffs. We couldn't miss.

I was seven; the boys were eight, nine, and ten. The oldest two Fahey boys were there—Mikey and Peter—polite blond boys who lived near me on Lloyd Street, and who already had four brothers and sisters. My parents approved Mikey and Peter Fahey. Chickie McBride was there, a tough kid, and Billy Paul and Mackie Kean too, from across Reynolds, where the boys grew up dark and furious, grew up skinny, knowing, and skilled. We had all drifted from our houses that morning looking for action, and had found it here on Reynolds Street.

It was cloudy but cold. The cars' tires laid behind them on the snowy street a complex trail of beige chunks like crenellated[1] castle walls. I had stepped on some earlier; they squeaked. We could have wished for more traffic. When a car came, we all popped it one. In the intervals between cars we reverted to the natural solitude of children.

I started making an iceball—a perfect iceball, from perfectly white snow, perfectly spherical, and squeezed perfectly translucent[2] so no snow remained all the way through. (The Fahey boys and I considered it unfair actually to throw an iceball at somebody, but it had been known to happen.)

I had just embarked[3] on the iceball project when we heard tire chains come clanking from afar. A black Buick was moving toward us down the street. We all spread out, banged together some regular snowballs, took aim, and, when the Buick drew nigh, fired.

A soft snowball hit the driver's windshield right before the driver's face. It made a smashed star with a hump in the middle.

Often, of course, we hit our target, but this time, the only time in all of life, the car pulled over and stopped. Its wide black door opened; a man got out of it, running. He didn't even close the car door.

He ran after us, and we ran away from him, up the snowy Reynolds sidewalk. At the corner, I looked back; incredibly, he was still after us. He was in city clothes: a suit and tie, street shoes. Any normal adult would have quit, having sprung us into flight and made his point. This man was gaining on us. He was a thin man, all action. All of a sudden, we were running for our lives.

Wordless, we split up. We were on our turf; we could lose ourselves in the neighborhood backyards, everyone for himself. I paused and considered. Everyone had vanished except Mikey Fahey, who was just rounding the corner of a yellow brick house. Poor Mikey, I trailed him. The driver of the Buick sensibly picked the two of us to follow. The man apparently had all day.

He chased Mikey and me around the yellow house and up a backyard path we knew by heart: under a low tree, up a bank, through a hedge, down some snowy steps, and across the grocery store's delivery driveway. We smashed through a gap in another hedge, entered a scruffy backyard and ran around its back porch and tight between houses to Edgerton Avenue; we ran across Edgerton to an alley and up our own sliding woodpile to the Halls' front yard; he kept coming. We ran up Lloyd Street and wound through mazy backyards toward the steep hilltop at Willard and Lang.

He chased us silently, block after block. He chased us silently over picket fences, through thorny hedges, between houses, around

---

1. **crenellated** (kren′l āt əd), *adj.* having squared-off notches at the top.
2. **translucent** (tran slü′snt), *adj.* letting light through without being transparent.
3. **embark** (em bärk′), *v.* set out.

garbage cans, and across streets. Every time I glanced back, choking for breath, I expected he would have quit. He must have been as breathless as we were. His jacket strained over his body. It was an immense discovery, pounding into my hot head with every sliding, joyous step, that this ordinary adult evidently knew what I thought only children who trained at football knew: that you have to fling yourself at what you're doing, you have to point yourself, forget yourself, aim, dive.

Mikey and I had nowhere to go, in our own neighborhood or out of it, but away from this man who was chasing us. He impelled[4] us forward; we compelled him to follow our route. The air was cold; every breath tore my throat. We kept running, block after block; we kept improvising,[5] backyard after backyard, running a frantic course and choosing it simultaneously, failing always to find small places or hard places to slow him down, and discovering always, exhilarated, dismayed, that only bare speed could save us—for he would never give up, this man—and we were losing speed.

He chased us through the backyard labyrinths[6] of ten blocks before he caught us by our jackets. He caught us and we all stopped.

We three stood staggering, half-blinded, coughing, in an obscure hilltop backyard: a man in his twenties, a boy, a girl. He had released our jackets, our pursuer, our captor, our hero: He knew we weren't going anywhere. We all played by the rules. Mikey and I unzipped our jackets. I pulled off my sopping mittens. Our tracks multiplied in the backyard's new snow. We had been breaking new snow all morning. We didn't look at each other. I was cherishing my excitement. The man's lower pants legs were wet; his cuffs were full of snow, and there was a prow of snow beneath them on his shoes and socks. Some trees bordered the little flat backyard, some messy winter trees. There was no one around: a clearing in a grove, and we the only players.

It was a long time before he could speak. I had some difficulty at first recalling why we were there. My lips felt swollen; I couldn't see out of the sides of my eyes; I kept coughing.

"You stupid kids," he began perfunctorily.[7]

We listened perfunctorily indeed, if we listened at all, for the chewing out was redundant,[8] a mere formality, and beside the point. The point was that he had chased us passionately without giving up, and so he had caught us. Now he came down to earth. I wanted the glory to last forever.

But how could the glory have lasted forever? We could have run through every backyard in North America until we got to Panama. But when he trapped us at the lip of the Panama Canal, what precisely could he have done to prolong the drama of the chase and cap its glory? I brooded about this for the next few years. He could only have fried Mikey Fahey and me in boiling oil, say, or dismembered us piecemeal, or staked us to anthills. None of which I really wanted, and none of which any adult was likely to do, even in the spirit of fun. He could only chew us out there in the Panamanian jungle, after months or years of exalting pursuit. He could only begin, "You stupid kids," and continue in his ordinary Pittsburgh accent with his normal righteous anger and the usual common sense.

If in that snowy backyard the driver of the black Buick had cut off our heads, Mikey's and mine, I could have died happy, for nothing has required so much of me since as being chased all over Pittsburgh in the middle of winter— running terrified, exhausted—by this sainted, skinny, furious red-headed man who wished to have a word with us. I don't know how he found his way back to his car.

---

4. **impel** (im pel′), *v.* cause to move forward.
5. **improvise** (im′prə vīz), *v.* make up on the spur of the moment.
6. **labyrinth** (lab′ə rinth′), *n.* a confusing, complicated passage or arrangement.
7. **perfunctorily** (pər fungk′tər ə lē), *adv.* mechanically; indifferently.
8. **redundant** (ri dun′dənt), *adj.* not needed; extra.

An American Childhood   **477**

After Reading

Making Connections

Shaping Your Response

1. Why do you think some children throw snowballs at cars?

2. As the girl's parent, what would be your response to this incident? Why?

3. Do you think the skinny man was overreacting, or was he justified in his passionate chase? Explain.

Analyzing the Autobiography

4. In the third paragraph, cars are described as "targets all but wrapped in red ribbons, cream puffs." What do these **metaphors** suggest?

5. Mention some interesting or unexpected **images** that Dillard uses.

6. How does her choice of activities and playmates help **characterize** the narrator?

7. In the last two paragraphs, how does **hyperbole**, or exaggeration, emphasize Dillard's delight in the chase?

Extending the Ideas

8. The driver, "a young man in his twenties," might have been a snowball thrower himself as a child. How would you account for his change of behavior and attitude?

9. What **theme** or lesson about life do you think this incident illustrates?

Literary Focus: Suspense

Dillard uses the following techniques to create suspense:

- *exaggeration:* "He could have fried Mikey Fahey and me in boiling oil."

- *powerful imagery:* ". . . every breath tore my throat."

- *repetition:* "We kept running, block after block. . . ."

- *accumulated details:* "He chased us silently over picket fences, through thorny hedges, between houses, around garbage cans, and across streets."

Find another example of each of these techniques in the selection.

Vocabulary Study

On your paper, write the word that best completes each sentence. You will not use all of the words.

embark
impel
improvise
labyrinth
perfunctorily
redundant
translucent

1. The narrator and her friends could easily ____ games on a snowy day.

2. Although they made ____ iceballs, they threw only soft snowballs at cars.

3. Why did the driver ____ on a chase, even though he wasn't dressed for it?

4. Mikey and the girl led the driver through a ____ of streets, alleys, and yards.

5. Once he caught them, the driver scolded them ____.

Expressing Your Ideas

Writing Choices

Writer's Notebook Update In your notebook, you rated some of the narrator's qualities. Add any other traits that you think characterize her. Then, focusing on these qualities, write a paragraph discussing whether or not she is someone you'd like for a kid sister.

Cliffhanger Hollywood once made short serials to be shown at Saturday matinees. Each episode ended suspensefully, with the hero or heroine in a tight spot—tied to the railroad tracks or hanging from a cliff. Write a **summary** of a scene in which a protagonist is in a dangerous situation. Use some of the techniques that Dillard uses to create suspense, as well as a few vocabulary words.

Other Options

Ditch 'Im Draw a **map** of the chase scene based on details of the story, or make a model of the neighborhood and point out where events occurred.

Zoom In Many movies include a memorable chase scene. With a partner, screen one such movie that would make appropriate viewing for the class. Get your teacher's permission to show at least the chase scene in class and afterward to describe in a **film chat** how techniques such as special effects, music, and camera shots are used to create suspense.

Speak One's Piece Once the driver catches Mikey and the narrator, he begins to talk to them. He starts, "You stupid kids. . . ." What do you think he says next? Be the driver and without swearing finish his angry **monologue**, acting it out for the class.

By Any Other Name

by Santha Rama Rau   India

Santha Rama Rau
born 1923

At the age of six, Santha Rama Rau (sän′thä rä′mä rou) left India when her father, a diplomat, was sent to England. When she returned to India ten years later, the first thing her grandmother said to her was, "My dear child, where in India will we find a husband tall enough for you?" At Wellesley College in Massachusetts, Rama Rau began writing *Home to India* (1945), a book about her rediscovery of India. Rama Rau's works, which range from novels, biographies, short stories, travel books, and autobiography to a cookbook, present the dual perspective of someone equally at home in the East and the West.

Building Background

Expanding Empire
The first English people to settle in India were traders interested in exporting spices and silk. As the picture suggests, local princes initially welcomed the English, along with the wealth and military power they represented. By 1860, however, England controlled India and made it a colony, part of the British Empire. The English established a judicial system and built factories, railroads, and—as the following selection indicates—schools.

Literary Focus

Stereotypes Broad generalized ideas about people and situations are called **stereotypes.** Real people are rarely one-dimensional or stereotypical. All blondes are not dizzy; all librarians are not prim; all used-car salesmen are not dishonest. As you read "By Any Other Name," be on the alert for stereotypes.

Writer's Notebook

First Impressions In your notebook, list one pleasant and one unpleasant association you have with school. Add some vivid images and details to describe each association.

By Any Other Name

Santha Rama Rau

This title comes from Shakespeare's tragedy, Romeo and Juliet. *When Juliet learns that Romeo is a Montague and, thus, an enemy of her family, she cries: "What's in a name? That which we call a rose by any other name would smell as sweet."*

At the Anglo-Indian[1] day school in Zorinabad[2] to which my sister and I were sent when she was eight and I was five and a half, they changed our names. On the first day of school, a hot, windless morning of a north Indian September, we stood in the head-mistress's study and she said, "Now you're the *new* girls. What are your names?"

My sister answered for us. "I am Premila, and she"—nodding in my direction—"is Santha."

The headmistress had been in India, I suppose, fifteen years or so, but she still smiled her helpless inability to cope with Indian names. Her rimless half-glasses glittered, and the precarious[3] bun on the top of her head trembled as she shook her head. "Oh, my dears, those are much too hard for me. Suppose we give you pretty English names. Wouldn't that be more jolly? Let's see, now—Pamela for you, I think." She shrugged in a baffled way at my sister. "That's as close as I can get. And for *you*," she said to me, "how about Cynthia? Isn't that nice?"

My sister was always less easily intimidated[4] than I was, and while she kept a stubborn silence, I said, "Thank you," in a very tiny voice.

We had been sent to that school because my father, among his responsibilities as an officer of the civil service, had a tour of duty to perform in the villages around that steamy little provin-cial town, where he had his headquarters at that time. He used to make his shorter inspection tours on horseback, and a week before, in the stale heat of a typically postmonsoon[5] day, we had waved goodby to him and a little proces-sion—an assistant, a secretary, two bearers, and the man to look after the bedding rolls and lug-gage. They rode away through our large garden, still bright green from the rains, and we turned back into the twilight of the house and the sound of fans whispering in every room.

Up to then, my mother had refused to send Premila to school in the British-run establish-ments of that time, because, she used to say, "you can bury a dog's tail for seven years and it still comes out curly, and you can take a Britisher away from his home for a lifetime and he still remains insular." The examinations and degrees from entirely Indian schools were not, in those days, considered valid. In my case, the question had never come up, and probably never would have come up if Mother's extraor-dinary good health had not broken down. For the first time in my life, she was not able to con-tinue the lessons she had been giving us every

---

1. **Anglo-Indian,** relating to people either of English birth who live in India, or of mixed English and Indian parentage.
2. **Zorinabad,** a city in northern India.
3. **precarious** (pri ker′ē əs), *adj.* not safe or secure; uncertain.
4. **intimidate** (in tim′ə dāt), *v.* frighten.
5. **postmonsoon,** a dry spell. From April to October, a seasonal wind called a monsoon brings rain to south-ern Asia.

morning. So our Hindi books were put away, the stories of the Lord Krishna[6] as a little boy were left in midair, and we were sent to the Anglo-Indian school.

The first day of school is still, when I think of it, a remarkable one. At that age, if one's name is changed, one develops a curious form of dual personality. I remember having a certain detached and disbelieving concern in the actions of "Cynthia," but certainly no responsibility. Accordingly, I followed the thin, erect back of the headmistress down the veranda to my classroom feeling, at most, a passing interest in what was going to happen to me in this strange, new atmosphere of School.

The building was Indian in design, with wide verandas opening onto a central courtyard, but Indian verandas are usually whitewashed, with stone floors. These, in the tradition of British schools, were painted dark brown and had matting on the floors. It gave a feeling of extra intensity to the heat.

I suppose there were about a dozen Indian children in the school—which contained perhaps forty children in all—and four of them were in my class. They were all sitting at the back of the room, and I went to join them. I sat next to a small, solemn girl who didn't smile at me. She had long, glossy-black braids and wore a cotton dress, but she still kept on her Indian jewelry—a gold chain around her neck, thin gold bracelets, and tiny ruby studs in her ears. Like most Indian children, she had a rim of black kohl[7] around her eyes. The cotton dress should have looked strange, but all I could think of was that I should ask my mother if I couldn't wear a dress to school, too, instead of my Indian clothes.

I can't remember too much about the proceedings in class that day, except for the beginning. The teacher pointed to me and asked me to stand up. "Now, dear, tell the class your name."

I said nothing.

"Come along," she said, frowning slightly. "What's your name, dear?"

"I don't know," I said finally.

The English children in the front of the class—there were about eight or ten of them—giggled and twisted around in their chairs to look at me. I sat down quickly and opened my eyes very wide, hoping in that way to dry them off. The little girl with the braids put out her hand and very lightly touched my arm. She still didn't smile.

Most of that morning I was rather bored. I looked briefly at the children's drawings pinned to the wall, and then concentrated on a lizard clinging to the ledge of the high, barred window behind the teacher's head. Occasionally it would shoot out its long yellow tongue for a fly, and then it would rest, with its eyes closed and its belly palpitating, as though it were swallowing several times quickly. The lessons were mostly concerned with reading and writing and simple numbers—things that my mother had already taught me—and I paid very little attention. The teacher wrote on the easel blackboard words like *bat* and *cat*, which seemed babyish to me; only *apple* was new and incomprehensible.

When it was time for the lunch recess, I followed the girl with the braids out onto the veranda. There the children from the other classes were assembled. I saw Premila at once and ran over to her, as she had charge of our lunchbox. The children were all opening packages and sitting down to eat sandwiches. Premila and I were the only ones who had Indian food—thin wheat chapatties,[8] some vegetable curry, and a bottle of buttermilk. Premila thrust half of it into my hand and whispered fiercely that I should go and sit with my class, because that was what the others seemed to be doing.

---

6. **Lord Krishna,** one of the most widely worshiped of the Hindu gods.
7. **kohl** (kōl), *n.* a metallic powder used to darken the eyelids and lashes.
8. **chapatty** (chə pä′tē), *n.* thin griddle cake of unleavened bread, eaten in northern India.

These Indian girls might be on their way to school. Explain how this photograph compares to the mental image you have of the sisters from descriptions in the story.

The enormous black eyes of the little Indian girl from my class looked at my food longingly, so I offered her some. But she only shook her head and plowed her way solemnly through her sandwiches.

I was very sleepy after lunch, because at home we always took a siesta. It was usually a pleasant time of day, with the bedroom darkened against the harsh afternoon sun, the drifting off into sleep with the sound of Mother's voice reading a story in one's mind, and, finally, the shrill, fussy voice of the ayah[9] waking one for tea.

At school, we rested for a short time on low, folding cots on the veranda, and then we were expected to play games. During the hot part of the afternoon we played indoors, and after the shadows had begun to lengthen and the slight breeze of the evening had come up we moved outside to the wide courtyard.

I had never really grasped the system of competitive games. At home, whenever we played tag or guessing games, I was always allowed to "win"—"because," Mother used to tell Premila, "she is the youngest, and we have to allow for that." I had often heard her say it, and it seemed quite reasonable to me, but the result was that I had no clear idea of what "winning" meant.

When we played twos-and-threes that afternoon at school, in accordance with my training, I let one of the small English boys catch me, but was naturally rather puzzled when the other children did not return the courtesy. I ran about

9. **ayah** (ä′yə), _n._ a native maid or nurse in India.

By Any Other Name   483

for what seemed like hours without ever catching anyone, until it was time for school to close. Much later I learned that my attitude was called "not being a good sport," and I stopped allowing myself to be caught, but it was not for years that I really learned the spirit of the thing.

When I saw our car come up to the school gate, I broke away from my classmates and rushed toward it yelling, "Ayah! Ayah!" It seemed like an eternity since I had seen her that morning—a wizened,[10] affectionate figure in

---

. . . friendship with the English or Anglo-Indian children was out of the question.

---

her white cotton sari, giving me dozens of urgent and useless instructions on how to be a good girl at school. Premila followed more sedately, and she told me on the way home never to do that again in front of the other children.

When we got home we went straight to Mother's high, white room to have tea with her, and I immediately climbed onto the bed and bounced gently up and down on the springs. Mother asked how we had liked our first day in school. I was so pleased to be home and to have left that peculiar Cynthia behind that I had nothing whatever to say about school, except to ask what *apple* meant. But Premila told Mother about the classes, and added that in her class they had weekly tests to see if they had learned their lessons well.

I asked, "What's a test?"

Premila said, "You're too small to have them. You won't have them in your class for donkey's years." She had learned the expression that day and was using it for the first time. We all laughed enormously at her wit. She also told Mother, in an aside, that we should take sandwiches to school the next day. Not, she said, that *she* minded. But they would be simpler for me to handle.

That whole lovely evening I didn't think about school at all. I sprinted barefoot across the lawns with my favorite playmate, the cook's son, to the stream at the end of the garden. We quarreled in our usual way, waded in the tepid[11] water under the lime trees, and waited for the night to bring out the smell of the jasmine. I listened with fascination to his stories of ghosts and demons, until I was too frightened to cross the garden alone in the semi-darkness. The ayah found me, shouted at the cook's son, scolded me, hurried me in to supper—it was an entirely usual, wonderful evening.

It was a week later, the day of Premila's first test, that our lives changed rather abruptly. I was sitting at the back of my class, in my usual inattentive way, only half listening to the teacher. I had started a rather guarded friendship with the girl with the braids, whose name turned out to be Nalini (Nancy, in school). The three other Indian children were already fast friends. Even at that age it was apparent to all of us that friendship with the English or Anglo-Indian children was out of the question. Occasionally, during the class, my new friend and I would draw pictures and show them to each other secretly.

The door opened sharply and Premila marched in. At first, the teacher smiled at her in a kindly and encouraging way and said, "Now, you're little Cynthia's sister?"

Premila didn't even look at her. She stood with her feet planted firmly apart and her shoulders rigid, and addressed herself directly to me. "Get up," she said. "We're going home."

I didn't know what had happened, but I was aware that it was a crisis of some sort. I rose obediently and started to walk toward my sister.

---

10. **wizened** (wiz′nd), *adj.* dried up; withered.
11. **tepid** (tep′id), *adj.* lukewarm.

"Bring your pencils and your notebook," she said.

I went back for them, and together we left the room. The teacher started to say something just as Premila closed the door, but we didn't wait to hear what it was.

In complete silence we left the school grounds and started to walk home. Then I asked Premila what the matter was. All she would say was "We're going home for good."

It was a very tiring walk for a child of five and a half, and I dragged along behind Premila with my pencils growing sticky in my hand. I can still remember looking at the dusty hedges, and the tangles of thorns in the ditches by the side of the road, smelling the faint fragrance from the eucalyptus trees and wondering whether we would ever reach home. Occasionally a horse-drawn tonga[12] passed us, and the women, in their pink or green silks, stared at Premila and me trudging along on the side of the road. A few coolies[13] and a line of women carrying baskets of vegetables on their heads smiled at us. But it was nearing the hottest time of day, and the road was almost deserted. I walked more and more slowly, and shouted to Premila, from time to time, "Wait for me!" with increasing peevishness.[14] She spoke to me only once, and that was to tell me to carry my notebook on my head, because of the sun.

When we got to our house the ayah was just taking a tray of lunch into Mother's room. She immediately started a long, worried questioning about what are you children doing back here at this hour of the day.

Mother looked very startled and very concerned, and asked Premila what had happened.

Premila said, "We had our test today, and She made me and the other Indians sit at the back of the room, with a desk between each one."

Mother said, "Why was that, darling?"

"She said it was because Indians cheat," Premila added. "So I don't think we should go back to that school."

Mother looked very distant, and was silent a long time. At last she said, "Of course not, darling." She sounded displeased.

We all shared the curry she was having for lunch, and afterward I was sent off to the beautifully familiar bedroom for my siesta. I could hear Mother and Premila talking through the open door.

Mother said, "Do you suppose she understood all that?"

Premila said, "I shouldn't think so. She's a baby."

Mother said, "Well, I hope it won't bother her."

Of course, they were both wrong. I understood it perfectly, and I remember it all very clearly. But I put it happily away, because it had all happened to a girl called Cynthia, and I never was really particularly interested in her.

---

12. **tonga** (ton′gə), *n.* a horse-drawn vehicle with two wheels, commonly used in India.
13. **cooly** (kü′lē), *n.* an unskilled, native laborer in China, India, and elsewhere.
14. **peevishness** (pē′vish nəs), *n.* irritability; crossness.

After Reading

Making Connections

Shaping Your Response

1. Do you think that it's possible for someone like Santha, who is not yet six years old, to understand prejudice? Why or why not?

2. In your opinion, was Premila's walking out of the school justified? Why or why not?

3. What would you have done if you had been the girls' mother?

Analyzing the Autobiography

4. What **inferences** can you make about the advantages to the sisters of attending a British-run school? the disadvantages?

5. Why do you think Santha tells the teacher she does not know her name?

6. Review the note about the title on page 481. Then explain how this **allusion** relates to this story.

7. Does this selection illustrate internal or external **conflict**—or both? Explain.

Extending the Ideas

8. 👣 Do you consider peaceful protest such as Premila's walking out of school an effective way to **communicate** opposition to prejudice? Explain. What historical examples can you find of peaceful protest?

9. In a Venn diagram, compare similarities and differences of the early school experiences of Mark Mathabane and Santha Rama Rau as described in their autobiographical excerpts.

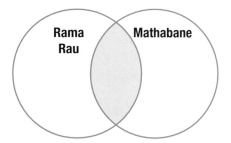

Literary Focus: Stereotype

In "By Any Other Name," the English officials at the school regard the Indian students as **stereotypes**.

- What general conclusion do the English teachers draw about Indian students?

- How might the headmistress's refusal to call Indian students by their given names be stereotypical?

Vocabulary Study

Match each numbered word with the letter of its synonym. Then pantomime two of these words for the class.

intimidate
peevishness
precarious
tepid
wizened

1. precarious
2. intimidate
3. wizened
4. tepid
5. peevishness

a. irritability
b. uncertain
c. frighten
d. withered
e. lukewarm

Expressing Your Ideas

Writing Choices

Writer's Notebook Update Review your notes about a pleasant and an unpleasant association with school. Did Rama Rau's account give you any additional ideas? For example, with time and distance, does it seem like it all happened to someone else? Write about one of your associations in a narrative paragraph.

What a Character! In "By Any Other Name," you have seen Santha and Premila in their relationships with each other at school, at home, with their mother, and with their nurse. Jot down notes about these relationships and use them as the basis for a **character sketch** of either sister.

Private Life When Premila explains why she and Santha have returned home, their mother is described as *concerned, worried, startled, distant, silent,* and *displeased*. Imagine you are Mother. Write a **diary entry** that explains your feelings.

Other Options

May I Have a Word? Santha's mother will have to talk with the headmistress. What do you think she will say? With a partner, work out an **improvisation** that takes place between the two women. Be prepared to act out the scene in class.

A Dressing Down What would the clothes that Santha wore to school have looked like? If she had a brother, what would he be wearing? **Research** the kind of clothes that upper-class Indian children might have worn in the 1920s. Find pictures or make drawings of those clothes.

Worth Fighting For?

What's in a Name?

Multicultural Connection
Names have tremendous power, as revealed in the selection by Santha Rama Rau. Have you ever thought about how your name might affect you? about the person you could be with an entirely different name?

THE
NAMING
OF CATS

T. S. ELIOT

The Naming of Cats is a difficult matter,
 It isn't just one of your holiday games;
You may think at first I'm as mad as a hatter
When I tell you, a cat must have three different names.
First of all, there's the name that the family use daily,
 Such as Peter, Augustus, Alonzo or James,
Such as Victor or Jonathan, George or Bill Bailey—
 All of them sensible everyday names.
There are fancier names if you think they sound sweeter,
 Some for the gentlemen, some for the dames:
Such as Plato, Admetus, Electra, Demeter—
 But all of them sensible everyday names.
But I tell you, a cat needs a name that's particular,
 A name that's peculiar, and more dignified,
Else how can he keep up his tail perpendicular,
 Or spread out his whiskers, or cherish his pride?
Of names of this kind, I can give you a quorum,
 Such as Munkustrap, Quaxo, or Coricopat,
Such as Bombalurina, or else Jellylorum—
 Names that never belong to more than one cat.
But above and beyond there's still one name left over,
 And that is the name that you never will guess;
The name that no human research can discover—
 But THE CAT HIMSELF KNOWS, and will never confess.
When you notice a cat in profound meditation,
 The reason, I tell you, is always the same:
His mind is engaged in a rapt contemplation
 Of the thought, of the thought, of the thought of
 his name:
   His ineffable effable
   Effanineffable
Deep and inscrutable singular Name.

Edward Gorey, *The Naming of Cats (detail)*, 1982, from the artist's
illustrations for *Old Possum's Book of Practical Cats*

NAMES

Some parents call their children by names that are also numbers. For example, the Japanese name Ichiko, the Spanish name Primo, and the Latin name Una all mean firstborn. A family in Michigan even named their sons One, Two, and Three. Their daughters were named First, Second, and Third.

In some African societies, babies get to try a name out before keeping it. Parents name their child and then observe his or her behavior over the next few months. If the baby seems happy, the parents keep the name they chose. If the baby seems fretful or difficult, the parents try a new name.

The government of France kept an official register of names approved for French children. If a child's name was not on the approved list, he or she may not have been allowed to join the army, marry, or get a driver's license.

The Puritans, among the first European settlers in America, sometimes chose names for their children that reflected their own religious concerns and values. Thus, Patience, Prudence, Chastity, Charity, Repentance, Sorry-for-Sin, and Sufferanna.

Like the ancient Romans, the Delaware Indians of Oklahoma keep their real name a secret. Outside their immediate family, people are known only by their nicknames. In this way, the Delaware keep the secrets of their identity safe from outsiders.

The names Anna, Ava, and Ede are examples of palindromes—words that are spelled the same backwards and forwards.

Many people can make anagrams of names by scrambling the letters to form new words—or even sentences—that describe their owners. For example, Florence Nightingale can be transformed into "Flit on, cheering angel."

The most common surname in the world is Chang; the most common surname in America is Smith. In New York City, in the 1980s, it was Cohen, which comes from a Hebrew word that means "prince" or "priest."

SMITH SMITH FOR PRESIDENT?

Harding Brewster and Percival Oder are both being considered for college president. Who do you think will get the job? If you guessed Brewster, you are probably right. College presidents and foundation heads are often men with what appears to be two last names. In fact, experts in psychonomics—the psychology of names—suggest that your name may affect your fate in other startling ways.

While some psychologists found that boys with popular names had higher self-esteem and aspirations than others, some researchers have found that people with less common first names, or with initials in place of first names, gained higher positions in business than people with common names. Women with plain names are reported to be promoted more often than other women. Researchers have found that college professors and West Point graduates often have unusual names. But then, so do criminals.

In general, people with unusual names tend to stand out, and people with plain or common names fit in. Both, however, find their own opportunities for popularity, respect, and success. So, what is the perfect name? It depends on who you really are—beneath the label.

Responding

1. Why do you think that Norma Jean Baker changed her name to Marilyn Monroe? What do you think are the chances of someone named, say, Herman Frump becoming a leading man in movies?

2. Research facts about names from other cultures—their significance and the manner in which they are bestowed.

3. Encourage school mates with unusual names to provide information on how they got them.

Reading Mini-Lesson

Connotation and Denotation

Close your eyes and think for a moment about the word *home*. What things do you associate with this word? In one dictionary, a definition of *home* is "place where a person or family lives," but if you're like most people, the word *home* evokes a series of other images—perhaps love, sisters, noise, food smells, or lots of shoes at the front door.

The dictionary definitions of a word are its *denotations.* The special meanings and associations that go beyond dictionary definitions are a word's *connotations.* Connotations come from people's individual or group experiences. For example, to different students, *breakfast* might be a roll on the run, a nourishing sit-down ritual, a school cafeteria meal, or memories of Grandma's blueberry muffins. Understanding denotation and connotation is important for getting the most from what you read.

Names, too, can have different connotations. In the article, "Smith, Smith for President?" (page 491), the author mentions the names Harding Brewster and Percival Oder. Which of these names would you consider more desirable for a male? What connotations do the names *Percival* and *Oder* have for you? How might these connotations negatively influence Percival Oder's chances for success?

Some authors give characters connotative names that reflect personality or physical traits. Readers of novels by Charles Dickens are familiar with the Murdstones, Mr. Bumble, Alfred Jingle, and the Gradgrinds. Public figures such as movie stars and wrestlers sometimes choose their names with an eye toward connotations.

Activity Options

1. Make a list of names that you think would be suitable for: a computer whiz, a sports fanatic, a studious person, an actor, a talkative person, and a miser.

2. Create an ad for a car, clothes, vacation, drink, or cosmetic. Use words with highly connotative associations suitable to the product. Consider words such as *luxury, elite, distinctive, power, rugged, soothing,* and *breathtaking.*

3. Think of a word that has many connotations for you. Then make a web like the example at the left.

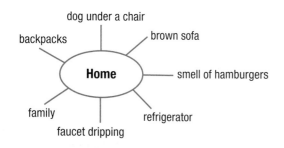

Writing Workshop

Standing Tall

Assignment In this part of the unit you've read about individuals and groups who stand up for something they believe in. Now write about a time in your life when you did the same.

WRITER'S BLUEPRINT

Product	An autobiographical incident
Purpose	To tell about a time you stood up for something you believed in
Audience	People who want to know more about you
Specs	As the writer of a successful paper, you should:

❑ Describe a memorable incident from your life when you decided to stand up for something you believed in.

❑ Tell what happened in chronological order, from start to finish, using the first-person ("I") point of view.

❑ Explain how you felt about what happened and what made the incident memorable for you.

❑ Finish by telling whether you succeeded in standing up for what you believed in and whether you'd behave the same way today, and why.

❑ Write in the active voice. Use dialogue where appropriate.

❑ Follow the rules of grammar, usage, spelling, and mechanics. Take care to use apostrophes correctly.

STEP **1** PREWRITING

Review characters in the literature. Create a chart like the one on the next page, showing how the characters in the selections you have read stood up for something they believed in.

Title and Character's Name	What Character Did and Why	Supporting Quote	What Character Stood Up For
"By Any Other Name" Premila	Premila, taking her little sister with her, left school because the teacher said that all Indians cheat.	"She said it was because Indians cheat," Premila added. "So I don't think we should go back to that school."	Dignity of her heritage; self-respect

OR . . .
In groups of four, have the group members each select one of the main characters and, acting as those characters, explain how they stood up for themselves. Take notes on the results.

OR . . .
Tape-record your description and listen to it when you make your writing plan.

OR . . .
Make a time line that shows your incident broken into individual events, from start to finish. Along the line, list each event and make notes about what happened and how you felt about it.

Choose an incident from your life. Recall incidents you have experienced, arguments you have had, or actions you have taken to support a strong personal belief. Look back at your literature chart for ideas. Make sure that for each incident on your list you can identify what it was you stood up for. Then select the incident you'll write about.

Describe the incident to a partner. Be sure to include details that explain what happened, and to describe how you stood up for yourself.

Try a quickwrite. Write for five minutes about what made the incident so memorable for you. The point of a quickwrite is to write down your ideas as fast as they come to you, so don't worry about developing full sentences or paragraphs right now. Check your quickwrite to make sure this really is the incident you'll want to write about.

Plan your essay. Look back at your prewriting activities as you develop your writing plan. Organize your notes into an informal outline like the one shown here.

Introduction
Time and place
Why I was there

Body
What happened first
How I felt about it
Lines of dialogue I might use
What happened next
How I felt about it
Lines of dialogue I might use
and so on

Conclusion
How well did I succeed in standing up for my beliefs?
Would I behave the same way today?
Why?

Ask a partner to review your plan.

✔ Have I written in first-person point of view?

✔ Have I narrated events in chronological order, from first to last?

✔ Have I explained why this incident was so memorable for me?

✔ Have I followed the Specs in the Writer's Blueprint?

Use any helpful comments from your partner to revise your plan.

STEP 2 DRAFTING

Before you write, look at your prewriting notes and writing plan and reread the Writer's Blueprint.

As you draft, concentrate on putting the ideas from your writing plan on paper; worry about spelling and punctuation mistakes later. Here are some drafting tips.

- Begin your paper with dialogue that creates an air of suspense: "You don't really believe that, do you?"

- Sustain the suspense. Let your readers discover what happened, as you did, as the incident unfolded.

- Write in the active voice. (See the Revising Strategy in Step 3 of this lesson.)

STEP 3 REVISING

Ask a partner to comment on your draft before you revise it. Exchange papers and respond to these statements:

✔ What you took a stand on was _____.

✔ This incident was memorable to you because _____.

✔ I could/could not follow the sequence of events because _____.

✔ This incident made you feel _____. I can tell because _____.

✔ You did/did not succeed in standing up for what you believe in because you say _____.

Revising Strategy

Writing in the Active Voice

In the **active voice,** the subject does something: *We planted the new tree* that afternoon. *Mrs. Gordon thanked us.*

In the **passive voice**, something is done to the subject: *The new tree was planted* by us that afternoon. *We were thanked* by Mrs. Gordon.

Which pair of sentences sounds more natural? Most writing, especially narrative writing, is in the active voice because the active voice sounds more natural and direct. Here are more examples:

Passive   The wallet was picked up by me from where it had fallen on the sidewalk.

Active   I picked up the wallet from where it had fallen on the sidewalk.

Passive   It was returned by me to its rightful owner.

Active   I returned it to its rightful owner.

Check your narrative to see that it moves along in the active voice. When you find sentences that sound awkward, it may be because they're in the passive voice and need to made active, as in the student model that follows.

STUDENT MODEL

Coach Paustion worked with me during the off season as well as during the season. *He noticed* ^My intense desire to excel ~~was noticed by him~~ and he went above and beyond the call of duty to help me. *My teammates* ~~I was~~ sometimes made fun of *me* ~~by my teammates~~ and teased *me* ^ about my size. However, thanks to the guidance of Coach Paustion, I had the confidence to stand up to them and show them I could make an important contribution to the team.

4 EDITING

Ask a partner to review your revised draft before you edit. When you edit, look for errors in grammar, usage, spelling, and mechanics. Look over each sentence to make sure you've used apostrophes correctly.

Editing Strategy

Using Apostrophes Correctly

Use apostrophes to form the possessives of nouns.

FOR REFERENCE
See the Language and Grammar Handbook at the back of the book for more information on using apostrophes correctly.

1. Add **'s** to form the possessive of most singular nouns (Alice**'s** courage, one class**'s** desks)
2. Add only an apostrophe to form the possessive of plural nouns ending in **s** (five whales**'** spouts, the kites**'** long tails).
3. Add **'s** to form the possessive of plural nouns that do not end in **s** (the children**'s** room, two deer**'s** tracks).

Use apostrophes to form contractions, showing where letters have been omitted.

do not = don't   let us = let's   there is = there's   it is = it's

But <u>do not</u> use apostrophes to form plurals (four desks, two pairs of jeans).

Notice how this writer corrected mistakes with the use of apostrophes.

> ○ Practice was always hard for me. The team's goal was supposed to be to work together, but it sometimes seemed like it was every player for
>
> ○ himself. I made good blocks, but that would only make the player I blocked angry, even though we were teammates. It wasn't long and I was
>
> ○ thinking about quitting.

STUDENT MODEL

5 PRESENTING

Consider these ideas for presenting your essay.

- Make a cover sheet with graphics to enhance your paper. Illustrate your topic by drawing a time line to picture the events.

- Read your papers aloud in a small student group. In a discussion, compare and contrast the different strategies people took in standing up for something they believed in. Which strategies seemed to work best?

- Dramatize your narrative. Turn it into a stage, radio, or video production. You might work with classmates to put your productions together into a program of autobiographical performances.

- Read your narrative to someone else who was involved in the incident and ask for their comments. How does their memory of things differ from yours?

6 LOOKING BACK

Self-evaluate. Look back at the Writer's Blueprint and give your paper a score for each item, from 6 (superior) to 1 (inadequate).

Reflect. Think about what you've learned from writing this paper as you write answers to these questions.

✔ Is there something that you believe in that you could or should stand up for now? How might you go about addressing this issue?

✔ Compare drafts. What kinds of mistakes did you catch at the editing stage? How did you do in terms of grammar, usage, mechanics, and spelling? Assess your strengths and weaknesses.

For Your Working Portfolio Add your narrative and reflection responses to your working portfolio.

Beyond Print

Visualizing

Writers use many strategies to help readers visualize a scene. Some writers accompany their text with maps, photos, or diagrams, but most of them rely on descriptive details. It's up to you to do the visualizing. Here are some tactics to help you do that—and to remember what you read. To form a mental picture of a scene, consider these points.

Location In the excerpt from *Kaffir Boy,* Mark Mathabane describes a school principal's office. Notice the arrangement of people and things.

"He was sitting behind a brown table upon which stood piles of dust and cobweb-covered books and papers. In one upper pocket of his jacket was arrayed a variety of pens and pencils; in the other nestled a lily-white handkerchief whose presence was more decorative than utilitarian. Alongside him stood a disproportionately portly black woman. . . ."

Motion In the excerpt from *An American Childhood,* Annie Dillard describes being chased. She uses several prepositions to help readers visualize the escaping children.

"He chased Mikey and me **around** the yellow house and **up** a backyard path we knew by heart: **under** a low tree, **up** a bank, **through** a hedge, **down** some snowy steps, and **across** the grocery store's delivery driveway."

Appearances (sizes, shapes, colors, and textures) In "By Any Other Name," Santha Rama Rau describes a classmate, largely through the use of adjectives.

"She had long, glossy-black braids and wore a cotton dress, but she still kept on her Indian jewelry—a gold chain around her neck, thin gold bracelets, and tiny ruby studs in her ears."

Activity Options

1. Review "By Any Other Name," and find other passages that mention size, shape, color, or texture.

2. Look back at your own writing to find parts that you could rewrite using one or more of the strategies that help readers visualize.

Part Two

Something of Value

A flower? a pet? a sunrise? a car? a beautiful object? freedom? What things do you hold dear? Make a mental list and then compare your "treasures" with those in the following selections.

Multicultural Connection **Perspective** involves seeing people, things, and events from diverse viewpoints. These viewpoints—shaped by history, heritage, culture, and experiences—cause people to place different values on things. As you read these selections, determine to what extent the backgrounds and experiences of the authors determine what they value.

Literature

Interdisciplinary Study Power and Horsepower

Writing Workshop Expository Writing

Beyond Print Media Literacy

Before Reading

One Perfect Rose by Dorothy Parker   USA

Daybreak in Alabama by Langston Hughes   USA

The Flying Cat by Naomi Shihab Nye   USA

Building Background

True Value The poems you are about to read describe different things that have value for the poets. Fill out a chart like the one below to describe something that has value in your life.

_____ has great value in my life.

I value it because

_____

_____ .

Qualities I associate with it are

_____ .

Other things that are important to me are

_____ .

Literary Focus

Tone The attitude of an author toward a subject and toward the reader is called **tone**. Try to determine the authors' attitudes toward their subjects in the following poems.

Writer's Notebook

Get the Picture? As you read each of the poem titles—"One Perfect Rose," "The Flying Cat," and "Daybreak in Alabama"—what images pop into your mind? Quickly sketch one of these images in your notebook. Then as you read the poem, jot down details that would help you add to or change your illustration.

Dorothy Parker
1893–1967

When told that solemn U.S. President Calvin Coolidge had died, Dorothy Parker asked, "How could they tell?" Such biting wit typifies Parker's verse and stories, which have delighted readers for many years. While working as a critic in New York in the 1920s, she was a member of the Algonquin Round Table, a witty and influential group of literary figures. The titles of some of Parker's books of poetry suggest the wry humor that she favored: *Enough Rope, Death and Taxes,* and *Not So Deep as a Well*. She later went to Hollywood where she worked as a screenwriter. She also taught English at Los Angeles State College, where she claimed, "The students read things and then they fight. It's called discussion."

Langston Hughes
1902–1967

Like his poems, Langston Hughes's novels, short stories, plays, and translations have given voice to the concerns and the changing roles of African Americans. When he was in second grade, he observed that "books began to happen to me, and I began to believe in nothing but books and the wonderful world in books." His poetry career was launched when his eighth-grade class in Lincoln, Illinois, voted him the Class Poet. "My classmates, knowing that a poem had to have rhythm, elected me unanimously—thinking, no doubt, that I had some, being a Negro." Hughes believed that "humor is a weapon . . . of no mean value against one's foes."

Naomi Shihab Nye
born 1952

Having published her first poem at age seven, Naomi Shihab Nye has long been a "quiet observer of the human condition." Her parents—a Palestinian father and an American mother—and the experiences she faced while living in the Middle East and San Antonio, Texas, during her high school years have contributed to Nye's multicultural perspective. In addition to writing several books of poetry, including *Different Ways to Pray* and *Hugging the Jukebox,* Nye, now living in Texas, has been a writer in residence, a teacher, a songwriter, and a world-wide traveler who promotes international goodwill through the arts.

One Perfect Rose

Dorothy Parker

A single flow'r he sent me, since we met.
    All tenderly his messenger he chose;
Deep-hearted, pure, with scented dew still wet—
    One perfect rose.

5 I knew the language of the floweret;
    "My fragile leaves," it said, "his heart enclose."
Love long has taken for his amulet[1]
    One perfect rose.

Why is it no one ever sent me yet
10   One perfect limousine, do you suppose?
Ah no, it's always just my luck to get
    One perfect rose.

---

1. **amulet** (am′yə lit), *n.* a small object worn as a magic charm against evil, disease, or bad luck.

Daybreak in Alabama

Langston Hughes

When I get to be a composer
I'm gonna write me some music about
Daybreak in Alabama
And I'm gonna put the purtiest songs in it
5 Rising out of the ground like a swamp mist
And falling out of heaven like soft dew.
I'm gonna put some tall tall trees in it
And the scent of pine needles
And the smell of red clay after rain
10 And long red necks
And poppy[1] colored faces
And big brown arms
And the field daisy eyes
Of black and white black white black people
15 And I'm gonna put white hands
And black hands and brown and yellow hands
And red clay earth hands in it
Touching everybody with kind fingers
And touching each other natural as dew
20 In that dawn of music when I
Get to be a composer
And write about daybreak
In Alabama.

---

1. poppy (pop′ē), *n.* a bright red.

Painted during the Depression by artist Aaron Douglass, *Song of the Towers* was one of a series of four large murals depicting significant episodes in African American history. What does this panel, which shows a jazz musician atop the cog of a machine gear, seem to be saying about the relationship between music and other aspects of modern life? ➤

The Flying Cat

Naomi Shihab Nye

Never, in all your career of worrying, did you imagine
what worries could occur concerning the flying cat.
You are traveling to a distant city.
The cat must travel in a small box with holes.

5   Will the baggage compartment be pressurized?[1]
Will a soldier's footlocker fall on the cat during take-off?
Will the cat freeze?

You ask these questions one by one, in different voices
over the phone. Sometimes you get an answer,
10 sometimes a click.
Now it's affecting everything you do.
At dinner you feel nauseous, like you're swallowing
at twenty thousand feet.
In dreams you wave fish-heads, but the cat has grown propellers,
15 the cat is spinning out of sight!

Will he faint when the plane lands?
Is the baggage compartment soundproofed?
Will the cat go deaf?

"Ma'am, if the cabin weren't pressurized, your cat would explode."
20 And spoken in a droll[2] impersonal tone, as if
the explosion of cats were another statistic![3]

Hugging the cat before departure, you realize again
the private language of pain. He purrs. He trusts you.
He knows little of planets or satellites,
25 black holes in space or the weightless rise of fear.

---

1. **pressurized** (presh′ə rīzd′), *adj.* having the
   atmospheric pressure inside (the cabin of an
   aircraft) kept at a normal level in spite of the altitude.
2. **droll** (drōl), *adj.* odd and amusing.
3. **statistic** (stə tis′tik), *n.* a numerical fact about
   people, the weather, business conditions, and so on
   in order to show their significance.

After Reading

Making Connections

Shaping Your Response

1. Explain which of the things these poets value comes closest to what you consider "Something of Value."

2. In your notebook, list several phrases or images from the poems that you find most memorable.

Analyzing the Poems

3. Judging from the author biographies and the poems included here, which poet do you think would make the best interviewee on a late-night talk show? Why?

4. What examples do you find of **hyperbole**, or exaggeration, in "The Flying Cat"?

5. Each of the three stanzas in "One Perfect Rose" ends with the words *one perfect rose.* Briefly explain how you think the speaker would vary her delivery each time she repeats the phrase.

6. Find **images** in "Daybreak in Alabama" that appeal to the senses of smell, sight, and touch.

7. Hughes jumbles together many images, uses the word *and* frequently, and rarely uses punctuation to slow a reader down. How does this style suit his **theme**?

8. Compare the **styles** of two of these poets. Note things such as **word choice, rhyme** and **rhythm, tone,** and **images**.

Extending the Ideas

9. The speaker in "Daybreak in Alabama" plans to make a musical statement about people of all colors getting along in the world. What songs do you know that make statements about cultural diversity and harmony? Check with your teacher to see if you could play them for the class and discuss their messages.

10. 🐾 In which of these poems do you feel the author's cultural background contributes significantly to his or her **perspective** on what is valuable? Describe this perspective.

Literary Focus: Tone

Almost every element in a poem can reveal the author's attitude, or **tone,** including diction, or word choice; imagery; syntax, or arrangement of words in sentences; and rhythm.

- From the box below choose one or more words to describe the tone in each poem. Add your own words, if necessary.

angry	idealistic	cynical	pleasing	frustrated
romantic	hopeful	sarcastic	humorous	worried

Vocabulary Study

Solve the riddles by writing on your paper a vocabulary word for each numbered item.

amulet
droll
poppy
pressurized
statistic

1. This can describe an aircraft's interior or the inside of a cast-iron cooker.

2. This refers to something odd or amusing.

3. Some people believe this can fend off evil or disease.

4. This is a numerical fact about things or people to show their significance.

5. This is a flower or a vibrant color.

Expressing Your Ideas

Writing Choices

Writer's Notebook Update How well does your original sketch suit the actual poem? Look back at the notes you jotted down as you read the poem, and decide how the sketch should be changed. If you like the sketch as is, add a few more details.

Pet Worries "Should I put Poopsie in the pet motel while I'm away, or should she come with me?" Many travelers have worried about what to do with pets when vacations or work call them away from home. Imagine you are a writer for an airlines travel magazine. Write an **article** describing pet owners' concerns about their pets that travel with them or remain at home and offering possible solutions to owners' problems.

Other Options

The Scent of Music How can a song smell like pine needles and red clay? Read "Daybreak in Alabama" again and work with a partner to decide what kind of music might suit this poem. Then bring a recording or, if possible, produce your own **musical interpretation** of this song for the class.

Getting It Down Pat Many poems, like songs, lend themselves to memorization because they have a regular rhythm. Choose one of the poems you have just read or any poem of your choice, and memorize it for a **poetry reading** to be performed for a group of classmates. Try to capture the tone of the poem in your voice.

Bumper Wisdom What are the most memorable bumper stickers you have seen? Why are they memorable? With a partner, brainstorm ideas for a **bumper sticker** about something you value. Quickwrite thoughts about these ideas. Then express them as bumper stickers.

Before Reading

Tuesday Siesta

by Gabriel García Márquez   Colombia

Gabriel García Márquez
born 1928

Gabriel García Márquez
(gäv′rē el′ gär sē′ə mär′kez)
was born in a coastal town in
Colombia that resembles the
magical town of Macondo,
where he sets much of his fiction. He was raised in part by
grandparents whose myths,
legends, and world full of
ghosts and "fantastic terrors"
served as inspiration for his
richly imaginative writing. His
best-known novel, *One
Hundred Years of Solitude,*
which has sold over eleven
million copies and been translated into more than thirty languages, illustrates magic
realism, a style that blends
incredible events with realistic
details. In 1982, he was
awarded the Nobel Prize for
literature.

Building Background

The sweltering setting of "Tuesday Siesta" is an unnamed, rural town
in Colombia—perhaps Aracataca, where García Márquez was born.

Fact Sheet Colombia	
Location	northwest corner of South America
Capital	Bogotá
Land area	440,000 square miles—about the size of Texas and California together
Language	Spanish
Climate	coastlands: tropical; highlands: moderate
Currency	1 peso = 100 centavos
Religion	about 98% Roman Catholic
Farm exports	coffee, bananas, sugar cane, tobacco
Minerals	emeralds, platinum, gold, iron, petroleum
Livestock	cattle

Literary Focus

Mood The title, "Tuesday Siesta," is the first clue to the story's
mood, its overall atmosphere or prevailing feeling. What atmosphere
do you associate with the word *siesta*? Throughout the story, phrases
like "oppressive sun" and "floating in the heat" help establish the
mood.

Writer's Notebook

The Little Things in Life "Tuesday Siesta" begins with a description
of a poor woman and her daughter as they travel on a train. Although
these people have no material goods, you will note during the course
of the story that they value nonmaterial things. During your reading,
list things that are meaningful in the mother's and daughter's lives. Be
prepared to make some inferences.

Tuesday Siesta

• Gabriel García Márquez •

▲ In this picture of a cemetery, María de Mater O'Neill uses
vivid color, flattened perspective, and varied patterns to
convey the energy that exists even in death. What details
can you find that indicate this is a cemetery?

The train emerged from the quivering tunnel of sandy rocks, began to cross the symmetrical, interminable[1] banana plantations, and the air became humid and they couldn't feel the sea breeze anymore. A stifling blast of smoke came in the car window. On the narrow road parallel to the railway there were oxcarts loaded with green bunches of bananas. Beyond the road, in uncultivated spaces set at odd intervals there were offices with electric fans, red-brick buildings, and residences with chairs and little white tables on the terraces among dusty palm trees and rosebushes. It was eleven in the morning, and the heat had not yet begun.

"You'd better close the window," the woman said. "Your hair will get full of soot."

The girl tried to, but the shade wouldn't move because of the rust.

They were the only passengers in the lone third-class car. Since the smoke of the locomotive kept coming through the window, the girl left her seat and put down the only things they had with them: a plastic sack with some things to eat and a bouquet of flowers wrapped in newspaper. She sat on the opposite seat, away from the window, facing her mother. They were both in severe and poor mourning clothes.

The girl was twelve years old, and it was the first time she'd ever been on a train. The woman seemed too old to be her mother, because of the blue veins on her eyelids and her small, soft, and shapeless body, in a dress cut like a cassock. She was riding with her spinal column braced firmly against the back of the seat, and held a peeling patent-leather handbag in her lap with both hands. She bore the conscientious serenity[2] of someone accustomed to poverty.

By twelve the heat had begun. The train stopped for ten minutes to take on water at a station where there was no town. Outside, in the mysterious silence of the plantations, the shadows seemed clean. But the still air inside the car smelled like untanned leather. The train did not pick up speed. It stopped at two identical towns with wooden houses painted bright colors. The woman's head nodded and she sank into sleep. The girl took off her shoes. Then she went to the washroom to put the bouquet of flowers in some water.

When she came back to her seat, her mother was waiting to eat. She gave her a piece of cheese, half a cornmeal pancake, and a cookie, and took an equal portion out of the plastic sack for herself. While they ate, the train crossed an iron bridge very slowly and passed a town just like the ones before, except that in this one there was a crowd in the plaza. A band was playing a lively tune under the oppressive[3] sun. At the other side of town the plantations ended in a plain which was cracked from the drought.

The woman stopped eating.

"Put on your shoes," she said.

The girl looked outside. She saw nothing but the deserted plain, where the train began to pick up speed again, but she put the last piece of cookie into the sack and quickly put on her shoes. The woman gave her a comb.

"Comb your hair," she said.

The train whistle began to blow while the girl was combing her hair. The woman dried the sweat from her neck and wiped the oil from her face with her fingers. When the girl stopped combing, the train was passing the outlying houses of a town larger but sadder than the earlier ones.

"If you feel like doing anything, do it now," said the woman. "Later, don't take a drink anywhere even if you're dying of thirst. Above all, no crying."

The girl nodded her head. A dry, burning

---

1. **interminable** (in tėr′mə nə bəl), *adj.* seemingly endless.
2. **serenity** (sə ren′ə tē), *n.* quiet; calmness.
3. **oppressive** (ə pres′iv), *adj.* hard to bear.

THE WOMAN SCRATCHED THE METAL GRATING ON THE DOOR WITH HER FINGERNAIL. . . .

wind came in the window, together with the locomotive's whistle and the clatter of the old cars. The woman folded the plastic bag with the rest of the food and put it in the handbag. For a moment a complete picture of the town, on that bright August Tuesday, shone in the window. The girl wrapped the flowers in the soaking-wet newspapers, moved a little farther away from the window and stared at her mother. She received a pleasant expression in return. The train began to whistle and slowed down. A moment later it stopped.

There was no one at the station. On the other side of the street, on the sidewalk shaded by the almond trees, only the pool hall was open. The town was floating in the heat. The woman and the girl got off the train and crossed the abandoned station—the tiles split apart by the grass growing up between—and over to the shady side of the street.

It was almost two. At that hour, weighted down by drowsiness, the town was taking a siesta. The stores, the town offices, the public school were closed at eleven, and didn't reopen until a little before four, when the train went back. Only the hotel across from the station, with its bar and pool hall, and the telegraph office at one side of the plaza stayed open. The houses, most of them built on the banana company's model, had their doors locked from inside and their blinds drawn. In some of them it was so hot that the residents ate lunch in the patio. Others leaned a chair against the wall, in the shade of the almond trees, and took their siesta right out in the street.

Keeping to the protective shade of the almond trees, the woman and the girl entered the town without disturbing the siesta. They went directly to the parish house. The woman scratched the metal grating on the door with her fingernail, waiting a moment, and scratched

again. An electric fan was humming inside. They did not hear the steps. They hardly heard the slight creaking of a door, and immediately a cautious voice, right next to the metal grating: "Who is it?" The woman tried to see through the grating.

"I need the priest," she said.

"He's sleeping now."

"It's an emergency," the woman insisted.

Her voice showed a calm determination.

The door was opened a little way, noiselessly, and a plump, older woman appeared, with very pale skin and hair the color of iron. Her eyes seemed too small behind her thick eyeglasses.

"Come in," she said, and opened the door all the way.

They entered a room permeated[4] with an old smell of flowers. The woman of the house led them to a wooden bench and signaled them to sit down. The girl did so, but her mother remained standing, absent-mindedly, with both hands clutching the handbag. No noise could be heard above the electric fan.

The woman of the house reappeared at the door at the far end of the room. "He says you should come back after three," she said in a very low voice. "He just lay down five minutes ago."

"The train leaves at three-thirty," said the woman.

It was a brief and self-assured reply, but her voice remained pleasant, full of undertones. The woman of the house smiled for the first time.

"All right," she said.

When the far door closed again, the woman sat down next to her daughter. The narrow waiting room was poor, neat, and clean. On the other side of the wooden railing which divided the room, there was a worktable, a plain one

_____

4. **permeated** (pėr′mē āt əd), *adj.* spread throughout; filled with.

with an oilcloth cover, and on top of the table a primitive typewriter next to a vase of flowers. The parish records were beyond. You could see that it was an office kept in order by a spinster.[5]

The far door opened and this time the priest appeared, cleaning his glasses with a handkerchief. Only when he put them on was it evident that he was the brother of the woman who had opened the door.

"How can I help you?" he asked.

"The keys to the cemetery," said the woman.

The girl was seated with the flowers in her lap and her feet crossed under the bench. The priest looked at her, then looked at the woman, and then through the wire mesh of the window at the bright, cloudless sky.

"In this heat," he said. "You could have waited until the sun went down."

The woman moved her head silently. The priest crossed to the other side of the railing, took out of the cabinet a notebook covered in oilcloth, a wooden penholder, and an inkwell, and sat down at the table. There was more than enough hair on his hands to account for what was missing on his head.

"Which grave are you going to visit?" he asked.

"Carlos Centeno's," said the woman.

"Who?"

"Carlos Centeno," the woman repeated.

The priest still did not understand.

"He's the thief who was killed here last week," said the woman in the same tone of voice. "I am his mother."

The priest scrutinized[6] her. She stared at him with quiet self-control, and the Father blushed. He lowered his head and began to write. As he filled the page, he asked the woman to identify herself, and she replied unhesitatingly, with precise details, as if she were reading them. The Father began to sweat. The girl unhooked the buckle of her left shoe, slipped her heel out of it, and rested it on the bench rail. She did the same with the right one.

It had all started the Monday of the previous week, at three in the morning, a few blocks from there. Rebecca, a lonely widow who lived in a house full of odds and ends, heard above the sound of the drizzling rain someone trying to force the front door from outside. She got up, rummaged[7] around in her closet for an ancient revolver that no one had fired since the days of Colonel Aureliano Buendía,[8] and went into the living room without turning on the lights. Orienting herself not so much by the noise at the lock as by a terror developed in her by twenty-eight years of loneliness, she fixed in her imagination not only the spot where the door was but also the exact height of the lock. She clutched the weapon with both hands, closed her eyes, and squeezed the trigger. It was the first time in her life that she had fired a gun. Immediately after the explosion, she could hear nothing except the murmur of the drizzle on the galvanized[9] roof. Then she heard a little metallic bump on the cement porch, and a very low voice, pleasant but terribly exhausted: "Ah, Mother." The man they found dead in front of the house in the morning, his nose blown to bits, wore a flannel shirt with colored stripes, everyday pants with a rope for a belt, and was barefoot. No one in town knew him.

"So his name was Carlos Centeno," murmured the Father when he finished writing.

"Centeno Ayala,"[10] said the woman. "He was my only boy."

The priest went back to the cabinet. Two big rusty keys hung on the inside of the door; the girl imagined, as her mother had when she was

---

5. **spinster** (spin′stər), *n.* an unmarried woman, especially an older woman.

6. **scrutinize** (skrüt′n īz), *v.* examine closely.

7. **rummage** (rum′ij), *v.* search in a disorderly way.

8. **Aureliano Buendía** (ou′rā lyä′nō bwän dē′ä).

9. **galvanized** (gal′və nīzd), *adj.* covered with a thin coating of zinc to prevent rust.

10. **Centeno Ayala** (cen tē′nō ä yä′lä). In Spanish-speaking countries, a person's first name and surname are customarily followed by his or her mother's maiden name. Thus, the young man's full name was Carlos Centeno Ayala.

a girl and as the priest himself must have imagined at some time, that they were Saint Peter's keys. He took them down, put them on the open notebook on the railing, and pointed with his forefinger to a place on the page he had just written, looking at the woman.

"Sign here."

The woman scribbled her name, holding the handbag under her arm. The girl picked up the flowers, came to the railing shuffling her feet, and watched her mother attentively.

The priest sighed.

"Didn't you ever try to get him on the right track?"

The woman answered when she finished signing.

"He was a very good man."

The priest looked first at the woman and then at the girl, and realized with a kind of pious amazement that they were not about to cry. The woman continued in the same tone:

"I told him never to steal anything that anyone needed to eat, and he minded me. On the other hand, before, when he used to box, he used to spend three days in bed, exhausted from being punched."

"All his teeth had to be pulled out," interrupted the girl.

"That's right," the woman agreed. "Every mouthful I ate those days tasted of the beatings my son got on Saturday nights."

"God's will is inscrutable,"[11] said the Father.

But he said it without much conviction, partly because experience had made him a little skeptical[12] and partly because of the heat. He suggested that they cover their heads to guard against sunstroke. Yawning, and now almost completely asleep, he gave them instructions about how to find Carlos Centeno's grave. When they came back, they didn't have to knock. They should put the key under the door; and in the same place, if they could, they should put an offering for the Church. The woman listened to his directions with great attention, but thanked him without smiling.

The Father had noticed that there was someone looking inside, his nose pressed against the metal grating, even before he opened the door to the street. Outside was a group of children. When the door was opened wide, the children scattered. Ordinarily, at that hour there was no one in the street. Now there were not only children. There were groups of people under the almond trees. The Father scanned the street swimming in the heat and then he understood. Softly, he closed the door again.

"Wait a moment," he said without looking at the woman.

His sister appeared at the far door with a black jacket over her nightshirt and her hair down over her shoulders. She looked silently at the Father.

"What was it?" he asked.

"The people have noticed," murmured his sister.

"You'd better go out by the door to the patio," said the Father.

"It's the same there," said his sister. "Everybody is at the windows."

The woman seemed not to have understood until then. She tried to look into the street through the metal grating. Then she took the bouquet of flowers from the girl and began to move toward the door. The girl followed her.

"Wait until the sun goes down," said the Father.

"You'll melt," said his sister, motionless at the back of the room. "Wait and I'll lend you a parasol."

"Thank you," replied the woman. "We're all right this way."

She took the girl by the hand and went into the street.

---

11. **inscrutable** (in skrü′tə bəl), *adj.* so mysterious or obscure that one cannot make out its meaning.
12. **skeptical** (skep′tə kəl), *adj.* doubtful.

After Reading

Making Connections

Shaping Your Response

1. In your opinion, would "Tuesday Siesta" make a good episode for a television series? Why or why not?

2. What do you think happens after the woman and her daughter leave the parish house?

3. If you could control the characters' fate, how would you change the events of the story?

Analyzing the Story

4. How does the **setting** help create the **mood** of the story?

5. What do you think the description of the mother "riding with her spinal column braced firmly against the back of the seat" suggests about her **character**?

6. Explain what qualities you **infer** the mother possesses as you read about the following.

   • her warning to her daughter as they get off the train;

   • her statements when the priest's housekeeper opens the door;

   • her actions at the end of the story.

7. At the **conclusion** of the story, the woman assures the priest, "We're all right this way." Do you think she will be able to maintain her dignity among the townspeople? Why or why not?

Extending the Ideas

8. What are your feelings about gun control? Does this story confirm or go against these feelings? Explain.

9. ☙ Review the things that are valued in these works by Parker, Nye, Hughes, and García Márquez. Then explain whether or not you think these people of different countries or cultures share similar **perspectives** about what is valuable.

Literary Focus: Mood

The atmosphere or general feeling the author conveys to the reader through setting, imagery, details, and descriptions is called **mood**. In "Tuesday Siesta," the use of mood helps evoke feelings of pity toward the characters and anger toward the social conditions that create such human suffering.

• Describe the mood of "Tuesday Siesta."

• Find five details, images, or phrases that help establish the mood.

Vocabulary Study

On your paper, match each numbered word with the letter of its definition.

galvanized
inscrutable
interminable
oppressive
permeated
rummage
scrutinize
serenity
skeptical
spinster

1. interminable
2. serenity
3. oppressive
4. permeated
5. scrutinize
6. rummage
7. galvanized
8. inscrutable
9. skeptical
10. spinster

a. an unmarried woman
b. coated with zinc
c. to watch closely
d. doubtful
e. burdensome
f. seemingly endless
g. to search haphazardly
h. spread throughout
i. not easily understood
j. calmness

Expressing Your Ideas

Writing Choices

Writer's Notebook Update Using your list of items that the mother and daughter value, write a paragraph about why they may have considered those things to be important. Support your ideas with examples from the story.

Looking for New Ideas? "Tuesday Siesta" was inspired by the author's boyhood memory of a woman and a small girl he had seen carrying an umbrella in the afternoon sun, and the comment someone made to him: "She's the mother of that thief." Think of a sight or a comment overheard—on the bus, in the cafeteria, in the street—that could inspire a story. Then write a story **summary**.

Travels with My Mother She has only one line of dialogue, but the daughter has many unspoken thoughts. Imagine what she's thinking as she returns home. Then describe a **dream** she might have about the day's events. Remember that dreams aren't always logical.

Other Options

Just the Facts, Ma'am Jot down ideas for a **fact sheet**, like the one on Colombia preceding this story, that lists at least eight facts about *your* town, area, or neighborhood. Write your fact sheet on a posterboard. Add a map of important sites.

Come to Sunny Colombia You are a travel agent investigating the possibility of conducting tours to Colombia. Research to find out if it's a place tourists would enjoy visiting. You might start with information provided in Before Reading and build from there. Then make a recommendation in a **memo** about whether or not to add Colombia to your tour sites.

Woman Shoots Night Visitor The town prosecutor has charged Rebecca with murder. Her attorney has claimed that she was merely defending herself. Hold a **trial** with a prosecution team, a defense team, and a judge. Let the class act as jury.

Before Reading

The Pillow Book by Sei Shōnagon Japan
Porsche by Bailey White USA

Sei Shōnagon
965–?

Sei Shōnagon (sī shō′nə gon), lady-in-waiting to an empress of Japan, recorded thoughts in a "pillow book" kept by her bedside. *The Pillow Book,* with its lively anecdotes and character sketches, is today considered one of the greatest works of Japanese literature.

Bailey White
born 1950

This first-grade teacher in Georgia is also a commentator on National Public Radio— interesting careers for some- one who, as a teenager, tried "to be not noticed." "Porsche" is an excerpt from White's book, *Mama Makes Up Her Mind . . . ,* a humorous account of an eccentric Southern family.

Building Background

Sei, Meet Bailey In the selections you are about to read, two women, writing over a thousand years apart, present lively, perceptive pictures of their respective cultures. Sei Shōnagon said of her writing, "I set about filling the notebooks with odd facts, stories from the past, and all sorts of other things, often including the most trivial material." But those "trivial" accounts of court life, etiquette, and nature provide a vivid and fascinating picture of Japanese culture.

Just as Sei Shōnagon's telling images provide clues to medieval Japan, Bailey White's description of her cluttered household and 1958 Porsche may provide people living in the 30th century with important insights about our culture. Her other works, such as the collection, *Sleeping at the Starlight Motel,* include daft characters (Red the Rat Man) and details of Americana (vignettes of the one-room schoolhouse and the flashes of human nature behind the "No Fishing" sign) that will entertain and inform generations to come.

Literary Focus

Imagery Concrete details that appeal to the five senses are called **images**. A writer uses images to give readers a sense of experiencing what they are reading. *The Pillow Book* and "Porsche" are memorable for their images. As you read these selections, list several images in your notebook that you find appealing.

Images	
The Pillow Book	Porsche

Writer's Notebook

Writing Inspirations How many times have you read something and thought to yourself, "Why didn't I think of that?" or "That reminds me of the time. . . ." Well, keep that pen handy as you read the following selections. Use your notebook as a portable "pillow book" to jot down any writing ideas that pop into your head.

from The Pillow Book

Sei Shōnagon

Things That Give a Pleasant Feeling

A set of well-executed pictures of women, accompanied by interesting texts.

The return journey from a festival, with a large number of escorts in attendance. The costumes of the women passengers spill out at the sides of the carriage, and, thanks to the skill of the ox-drivers, the carriages run smoothly along the road.

On a pretty sheet of white Michinoku paper someone has written a letter with a brush that would not seem capable of making such delicate strokes.

The sight of a boat as it glides downstream.

Well-blackened teeth.[1]

To throw equal numbers repeatedly in a game of dice.

Fine strands of silk that have been entwined.

A skilled Master of Divination performs a purification service[2] on a river bank.

A drink of water when one wakes up at night.

One is in a rather bored mood when a visitor arrives—a man with whom one's relations are neither too intimate nor too distant. He tells one what has been happening in society, things pleasant and disagreeable and strange; moving from one topic to another, he discusses matters both public and private—and all in so clear a fashion that there is no possibility of misunderstanding. This gives one a very pleasant feeling.

One has visited a shrine or a temple with the request that certain prayers be said on one's behalf. What a pleasure to hear the ritualist[3] or priest intone them in a better voice, and more fluently,[4] than one had expected!

This painting, done in the 1820s by Japanese artist Keisai Eisen, shows the teenage daughter of a well-to-do family fixing her hair and makeup. Based on the cultural **perspective** presented by Sei Shōnagon in her *Pillow Book*, why do you think this young woman is giving such attention to her appearance?

---

1. **well-blackened teeth**. In Sei Shōnagon's time, blackening the teeth was thought to help keep Japanese girls healthy and attractive.
2. **purification service,** the ritual cleansing of the body with water, performed before the beginning of any Japanese ceremony.
3. **ritualist** (rich′ü ə list), *n.* person who practices or advocates observance of the form or system of rites, or ceremonies.
4. **fluently** (flü′ənt lē), *adv.* speaking or writing easily and rapidly.

A Preacher Ought to Be Good-Looking

A preacher ought to be good-looking. For, if we are properly to understand his worthy sentiments, we must keep our eyes on him while he speaks; should we look away, we may forget to listen. Accordingly an ugly preacher may well be the source of sin. . . .

But I really must stop writing this kind of thing. If I were still young enough, I might risk the consequence of putting down such impieties,[5] but at my present stage of life I should be less flippant.[6]

Some people, on hearing that a priest is particularly venerable[7] and pious, rush off to the temple where he is preaching, determined to arrive before anyone else. They, too, are liable to bring a load of sin on themselves and would do better to stay away.

Elegant Things

A white coat worn over a violet waistcoat.
Duck eggs.
Shaved ice mixed with liana syrup and put in a new silver bowl.
A rosary of rock crystal.[8]
Snow on wisteria[9] or plum blossoms.
A pretty child eating strawberries.

Things That Have Lost Their Power

A large boat which is high and dry in a creek at ebb-tide.
A woman who has taken off her false locks to comb the short hair that remains.
A large tree that has been blown down in a gale and lies on its side with its roots in the air.
The retreating figure of a *sumo* wrestler who has been defeated in a match.
A man of no importance reprimanding[10] an attendant.
An old man who removes his hat, uncovering his scanty topknot.

---

5. **impiety** (im pī′ə tē), *n.* lack of respect.
6. **flippant** (flip′ənt), *adj.* disrespectful or pert in speech.
7. **venerable** (ven′ər ə bəl), *adj.* worthy of reverence or respect.
8. **rock crystal,** a colorless, transparent variety of quartz, often used for jewelry.
9. **wisteria** (wi ster′ē ə), *n.* a climbing shrub with large drooping clusters of flowers.
10. **reprimand** (rep′rə mand), *v.* criticize.

PORSCHE

BAILEY WHITE

Mama and I live in one of those houses where things accumulate. Something can get laid down on a table or in the seat of a broken chair and just stay there forever. There's my great-grandmother's coat she hung on a nail before she died, and an old cousin's unfinished model of the *Flying Cloud*. There's a couple of bamboo chinaberry-seed popguns from three generations back and six bottles of Maybloom Cream beginning to turn iridescent with the tops rusted on. There's a row of Mason jars with some spooky-looking mold growing inside, left over from an old dead aunt's experiments with lethal herbs, and a drop-seat viyella union suit folded up on top of the carburetor of a Model A Ford. After a while the things begin to interlock. I really don't think we could get the ship model out in one piece even if we tried.

When I was eight years old, it got to be too much for my father. I remember the day he left for good. "I can't take it anymore!" he wailed. "I'm stagnating here! That coat!" He clutched the top of his head. I looked at my great-grandmother's coat. "That coat has been hanging there for fifty years!" And he hurled himself out of the house, jumped into his little red Porsche, and scratched off in a swirl of dust.

I missed my father. "Why don't we move the coat?" I asked my mother. "Then maybe he'll come back."

"It's not just the coat, child," she told me. I looked around. There were my great-aunt Bertie's lavender satin wedding shoes perched on the seat of my Uncle Luten's unicycle, and Uncle Ralph's wall-eyed, hunchbacked, one-legged stuffed turkey on the library table. She was right. Even I could see it wasn't just the coat.

We never saw my father again, but we heard that he had driven that Porsche all the way to Hollywood, California, and made piles of money writing scripts for TV shows. Our neighbors told us they had actually seen his name on TV. We wouldn't know. We didn't have a TV set. Where would we have put it?

The years went by. Twenty years, thirty years. Then one fall my father died. His fourth wife, now his widow, called us on the phone. "He left you something," she said. "It should be there in a few days."

And a week later it arrived. It was my father's Porsche, the same one he had left us in—a 1958 Model 356 speedster, in original condition, complete with a wild-eyed driver whose hair stood straight up on end. Mama told him, "Just park it out behind the garden with those two tractors and that thing that might have been a lawnmower."

But he wouldn't do it. "Lady, you're crazy. You don't know what this is." He rubbed the car's fender with his shirttail. "You don't park a car like this out with the tractors."

We stood around and looked at it. Mama sighed. Then she went over and started pulling a section of screen off the side porch. We built a ramp, and the man drove the car up onto the porch. We drained the oil and gas out of it, put it up on blocks, and replaced the screen.

Now a man who says he belongs to the Porsche Club of America calls us up almost every night hoping to buy the car. We keep telling him no, no, no. Besides, that car has been in our house almost a year now. Even if he came all the way down here, I doubt he could get to it.

French sculptor Arman embedded sixty automobiles in concrete to create *Long Term Parking*, a project he worked on from 1975 to 1982. What **perspective** on the automobile in modern culture do you think is expressed by this work? ➤

After Reading

Making Connections

Shaping Your Response

1. Do you think the father in Bailey White's account had a right to leave? Why or why not?

2. What would you have done with the Porsche if it had been delivered to your house?

3. How relevant do you think Sei Shōnagon's observations are today—more than one thousand years after she wrote them?

4. List five items in your house about which a visitor might ask, "Why do you keep that thing?"

Analyzing the Selection

5. What three words would you use to describe the **narrator** of *The Pillow Book?* of "Porsche"?

6. Do you think the first-person **point of view** is more effective for these selections than third person would have been? Explain.

7. Why do you think the father sent the Porsche back to his ex-wife and daughter?

8. In your opinion, what does the Porsche **symbolize** for the father? for the mother and the narrator?

Extending the Ideas

9. 👣 Both writers mention things they value. What cultural insights into medieval Japan and modern America do these valued items provide?

Literary Focus

Images Details that stimulate the reader's senses or imagination and bring pictures to mind are called **images**. Both Bailey White and Sei Shōnagon evoke images from the world around them.

• List four concrete details in "Things That Give a Pleasant Feeling" that bring pictures to your mind.

• To which senses does "Elegant Things" appeal?

• In "Porsche," how does Bailey White help you visualize the accumulated clutter in the house?

Vocabulary Study

Study the relationship of the following pairs of words in capital letters; then choose another pair that has the same relationship.

fluently
impiety
reprimand
ritualist
wisteria

1. REPRIMAND : SCOLD :: **a.** annoy : bother **b.** listen : attention **c.** forget : remember **d.** accept : gift

2. RITUALIST : CEREMONY :: **a.** clown : laugh **b.** secretary : office **c.** athlete : trophy **d.** entertainer : performance

3. FLUENTLY : HALTINGLY :: **a.** quickly : swiftly **b.** happily : smilingly **c.** angrily : boldly **d.** gracefully : clumsily

4. SHRUB : WISTERIA :: **a.** book : magazine **b.** bacteria : antibiotic **c.** sport : basketball **d.** leaf : flower

5. IMPIETY : RESPECT :: **a.** disrespect : peace **b.** prayer : church **c.** blame : praise **d.** hatred : scorn

Expressing Your Ideas

Writing Choices

Writer's Notebook Update What kinds of writing ideas did the selections trigger? Choose one of the ideas you wrote down as you read the selections and expand it into a paragraph. Engage the reader's imagination by including vivid images.

Zuihitsu A type of occasional writings and random notes, such as *The Pillow Book,* is known in Japan as *zuihitsu.* Start your own *zuihitsu* of observations similar to Sei Shōnagon's. Share your work with a classmate.

Old Sneakers, Faded Celebrities Both people and things can lose their power. Reread Sei Shōnagon's "Things That Have Lost Their Power." Then write a **"has-been list"** of five people or things that were once popular, but now have little importance or value.

Other Options

Comedy Stage Like Sei Shōnagon and Bailey White, who closely observed their surroundings, stand-up comedians cast a humorous eye toward *their* world—personal experiences, public figures, news events—to find material for their routines. With a small group, conduct a **comedy workshop** in which you try out various comedic routines based on close observations of daily life.

Pillow Talk Make your own contemporary **pillow book**, based on "chapters" such as Things That I Like But Can't Afford, The Worst Things to Give Teenagers for Birthdays, Things That Represent Me, and so forth. List appropriate things under your heads and illustrate them.

Time Will Tell How will people one hundred years from now know about the things your generation treasures today? With a group, list things that could be put into a **time capsule** to inform future generations about What Really Matters to young people today.

Before Reading

Nobel Acceptance Speeches
by Albert Campus, France and Elie Wiesel, Romania/USA

Albert Camus
1913–1960

Albert Camus (kä mü′) captured the moral dilemma of World War II and the postwar era in his writings. Awarded the Nobel Prize for literature in 1957, Camus responded, "What else have I done but meditate on an idea I found in the streets of my time?"

Elie Wiesel
born 1928

In 1944, when Elie Wiesel (el′ē wē zel′) was fifteen, most of his family perished in an extermination camp in Auschwitz. His account, *Night*, documents the horrors of the Holocaust. He was awarded the Nobel Prize for peace in 1986.

Building Background

It's a "Dynamite" Award In 1888 a French newspaper mistakenly reported the death of Alfred Nobel, Swedish inventor of dynamite. Shaken by the premature obituary and its reference to "the dynamite king," Nobel established a prize to promote international peace, as well as awards in literature, physics, chemistry, economics, and physiology or medicine. Wiesel and Camus are only two of the authors represented in this book who have been awarded the prestigious Nobel Prize. With the exception of Wiesel, who won the peace prize, all the writers listed have won the prize for literature.

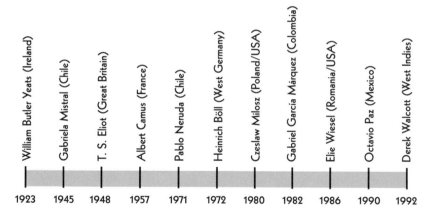

William Butler Yeats (Ireland)	Gabriela Mistral (Chile)	T. S. Eliot (Great Britain)	Albert Camus (France)	Pablo Neruda (Chile)	Heinrich Böll (West Germany)	Czeslaw Milosz (Poland/USA)	Gabriel García Márquez (Colombia)	Elie Wiesel (Romania/USA)	Octavio Paz (Mexico)	Derek Walcott (West Indies)
1923	1945	1948	1957	1971	1972	1980	1982	1986	1990	1992

Literary Focus

Style The manner in which writers use words to fit their ideas is called **style**. A writer's style is a combination of many techniques and devices that work together to express ideas. In the following acceptance speeches, note things such as **word choice, images,** and **rhythms.**

Writer's Notebook

Mixed Emotions In his speech, Albert Camus says that he and other artists are "obliged to understand rather than to judge." As you read both speeches, jot down other phrases that explain each writer's **perspectives** and view of his duty.

NOBEL ACCEPTANCE SPEECH
(1957)

ALBERT CAMUS

In receiving the distinction with which your free Academy has so generously honored me, my gratitude has been profound, particularly when I consider the extent to which this recompense[1] has surpassed my personal merits. Every man, and for stronger reasons, every artist, wants to be recognized. So do I. But I have not been able to learn of your decision without comparing its repercussions to what I really am. A man almost young, rich only in his doubts and with his work still in progress, accustomed to living in the solitude of work or in the retreats of friendship: how would he not feel a kind of panic at hearing the decree that transports him all of a sudden, alone and reduced to himself, to the center of a glaring light? And with what feelings could he accept this honor at a time when other writers in Europe, among them the very greatest, are condemned to silence, and even at a time when the country of his birth is going through unending misery?

I felt that shock and inner turmoil. In order to regain peace I have had, in short, to come to terms with a too generous fortune. And since I cannot live up to it by merely resting on my achievement, I have found nothing to support me but what has supported me through all my life, even in the most contrary circumstances: the idea that I have of my art and of the role of the writer. Let me only tell you, in a spirit of gratitude and friendship, as simply as I can, what this idea is.

For myself, I cannot live without my art. But I have never placed it above everything. If, on the other hand, I need it, it is because it cannot be separated from my fellow men, and it allows me to live, such as I am, on one level with them. It is a means of stirring the greatest number of people by offering them a privileged picture of common joys and sufferings. It obliges the artist not to keep himself apart; it subjects him to the most humble and the most universal truth. And often he who has chosen the fate of the artist because he felt himself to be different soon realizes that he can maintain neither his art nor his difference unless he admits that he is like the others. The artist forges himself to the others, midway between the beauty he cannot do without and the community he cannot tear himself away from. That is why true artists scorn nothing: they are obliged to understand rather than to judge. And if they have to take sides in this world, they can perhaps side only with that society in which, according to Nietzsche's[2] great words, not the judge but the creator will rule, whether he be a worker or an intellectual.

By the same token, the writer's role is not free from difficult duties. By definition he cannot put himself today in the service of those who make history; he is at the service of those who suffer it. Otherwise, he will be alone and deprived of his art. Not all the armies of tyranny with their millions of men will free him from his isolation, even and particularly if he falls into step with them. But the silence of an unknown prisoner, abandoned to humiliations at the other end of the world, is enough to draw the writer out of his exile, at least whenever, in the midst of the privileges of freedom, he manages not to forget that

---

1. **recompense** (rek′əm pens), *n.* reward.
2. **Nietzsche** (nē′chə), Friedrich Wilhelm, 1844–1900, German philosopher and writer.

silence, and to transmit it in order to make it resound by means of his art.

None of us is great enough for such a task. But in all circumstances of life, in obscurity or temporary fame, cast in the irons of tyranny or for a time free to express himself, the writer can win the heart of a living community that will justify him, on the one condition that he will accept to the limit of his abilities the two tasks that constitute the greatness of his craft: the service of truth and the service of liberty. Because his task is to unite the greatest possible number of people, his art must not compromise with lies and servitude which, wherever they rule, breed solitude. Whatever our personal weaknesses may be, the nobility of our craft will always be rooted in two commitments, difficult to maintain: the refusal to lie about what one knows and the resistance to oppression.

For more than twenty years of an insane history, hopelessly lost like all the men of my generation in the convulsions of time, I have been supported by one thing: by the hidden feeling that to write today was an honor because this activity was a commitment—and a commitment not only to write. Specifically, in view of my powers and my state of being, it was a commitment to bear, together with all those who were living through the same history, the misery and the hope we shared.

THEY HAVE HAD TO FORGE FOR THEMSELVES AN ART OF LIVING IN TIMES OF CATASTROPHE. . . .

torture and prisons—these men must today rear their sons and create their works in a world threatened by nuclear destruction. Nobody, I think, can ask them to be optimists. And I even think that we should understand—without ceasing to fight it—the error of those who in an excess of despair have asserted their right to dishonor and have rushed into the nihilism[3] of the era. But the fact remains that most of us, in my country and in Europe, have refused this nihilism and have engaged upon a quest for legitimacy. They have had to forge for themselves an art of living in times of catastrophe in order to be born a second time and to fight openly against the instinct of death at work in our history.

Each generation doubtless feels called upon to reform the world. Mine knows that it will not reform it, but its task is perhaps even greater. It consists in preventing the world from destroying itself. Heir to a corrupt history, in which are mingled fallen revolutions, technology gone mad, dead gods, and worn-out ideologies, where mediocre powers can destroy all yet no longer know how to convince, where intelligence has debased itself to become the servant of hatred and oppression, this generation starting from its own negations has had to re-establish, both within and without, a little of that which constitutes the dignity of life and death.

CLARIFY: In what sense does the writer bear the misery of others?

~

These men, who were born at the beginning of the First World War, who were twenty when Hitler came to power and the first revolutionary trials were beginning, who were then confronted as a completion of their education with the Spanish Civil War, the Second World War, the world of concentration camps, a Europe of

CONNECT: Do you think that the preceding sentence describes the present generation as well as Camus's? Explain.

~

In a world threatened by disintegration, in which our grand inquisitors run the risk of

---

3. **nihilism** (nī′ə liz′əm), entire rejection of the established beliefs in religion, morals, government, laws, and so forth.

hard to live with as it is elating. We must march toward these two goals, painfully but resolutely, certain in advance of our failings on so long a road. What writer would from now on in good conscience dare set himself up as a preacher of virtue? For myself, I must state once more that I am not of this kind. I have never been able to renounce the light, the pleasure of being, and the freedom in which I grew up. But although this nostalgia explains many of my errors and my faults, it has doubtless helped me toward a better understanding of my craft. It is helping me still to support unquestioningly all those silent men who sustain the life made for them in the world only through memory of the return of brief and free happiness.

Thus reduced to what I really am, to my limits and debts as well as to my difficult creed, I feel freer, in concluding, to comment upon the extent and the generosity of the honor you have just bestowed upon me, freer also to tell you that I would receive it as an homage[5] rendered to all those who, sharing in the same fight, have not received any privilege, but have on the contrary known misery and persecution. It remains for me to thank you from the bottom of my heart and to make before you publicly, as a personal sign of my gratitude, the same and ancient promise of faithfulness which every true artist repeats to himself in silence every day.

establishing forever the kingdom of death, it knows that it should, in an insane race against the clock, restore among the nations a peace that is not servitude, reconcile anew labor and culture, and remake with all men the Ark of the Covenant.[4] It is not certain that this generation will ever be able to accomplish this immense task, but already it is rising everywhere in the world to the double challenge of truth and liberty and, if necessary, knows how to die for it without hate. Wherever it is found, it deserves to be saluted and encouraged, particularly where it is sacrificing itself. In any event, certain of your complete approval, it is to this generation that I should like to pass on the honor that you have just given me.

At the same time, after having outlined the nobility of the writer's craft, I should have put him in his proper place. He has no other claims but those which he shares with his comrades in arms: vulnerable but obstinate, unjust but impassioned for justice, doing his work without shame or pride in view of everybody, not ceasing to be divided between sorrow and beauty, and devoted finally to drawing from his double existence the creations that he obstinately tries to erect in the destructive movement of history. Who after all this can expect from him complete solutions and high morals? Truth is mysterious, elusive, always to be conquered. Liberty is dangerous, as

---

4. **Ark of the Covenant,** literally, the chest containing the Ten Commandments. Here, Camus refers to the solemn promises made by God to human beings.
5. homage (hom′ij), *n.* dutiful respect.

NOBEL ACCEPTANCE SPEECH
(1986)

ELIE WIESEL

It is with a profound sense of humility that I accept the honor you have chosen to bestow upon me. I know: your choice transcends me. This both frightens and pleases me.

It frightens me because I wonder: do I have the right to represent the multitudes who have perished? Do I have the right to accept this great honor on their behalf? I do not. That would be presumptuous.[1] No one may speak for the dead, no one may interpret their mutilated dreams and visions.

It pleases me because I may say that this honor belongs to all the survivors and their children, and through us, to the Jewish people with whose destiny I have always identified.

I remember: it happened yesterday or eternities ago. A young Jewish boy discovered the kingdom of night. I remember his bewilderment, I remember his anguish.[2] It all happened so fast. The ghetto. The deportation. The sealed cattle car. The fiery altar upon which the history of our people and the future of mankind were meant to be sacrificed.

I remember: he asked his father: "Can this be true? This is the twentieth century, not the Middle Ages. Who would allow such crimes to be committed? How could the world remain silent?"

And now the boy is turning to me: "Tell me," he asks. "What have you done with my future? What have you done with your life?"

And I tell him that I have tried. That I have tried to keep memory alive, that I have tried to fight those who would forget. Because if we forget, we are guilty, we are accomplices.

And then I explained to him how naive we were, that the world did know and remain silent. And that is why I swore never to be silent whenever and wherever human beings endure suffering and humiliation. We must always take sides. Neutrality helps the oppressor, never the victim. Silence encourages the tormentor, never the tormented.

Sometimes we must interfere. When human lives are endangered, when human dignity is in jeopardy, national borders and sensitivities become irrelevant. Wherever men or women are persecuted because of their race, religion, or political views, that place must—at that moment—become the center of the universe.

Of course, since I am a Jew profoundly rooted in my people's memory and tradition, my first response is to Jewish fears, Jewish needs, Jewish crises. For I belong to a traumatized[3] generation, one that experienced the abandonment and solitude of our people. It would be unnatural for me not to make Jewish priorities my own: Israel, Soviet Jewry, Jews in Arab lands.

But there are others as important to me. Apartheid[4] is, in my view, as abhorrent as anti-Semitism. To me, Andrei Sakharov's isolation is as much of a disgrace as Iosif Begun's imprisonment. As is the denial of Solidarity and its leader

---

1. **presumptuous** (pri zump′chü əs), *adj.* acting without permission or right; bold.
2. **anguish** (ang′gwish) *n.* severe physical pain or mental suffering.
3. **traumatized** (trô′mé tīzd), *adj.* undergoing great shock.
4. **apartheid** (ə pärt′hāt), *n.* South Africa's former governmental policy of racial segregation.

Lech Walesa's right to dissent. And Nelson Mandela's interminable imprisonment.[5]

There is so much injustice and suffering crying out for our attention: victims of hunger, or racism and political persecution, writers and poets, prisoners in so many lands governed by the left and by the right. Human rights are being violated in every continent. More people are oppressed than free.

And then, too, there are the Palestinians[6] to whose plight I am sensitive but whose methods I deplore. Violence and terrorism are not the answer. Something must be done about their suffering, and soon. I trust Israel, for I have faith in the Jewish people. Let Israel be given a chance, let hatred and danger be removed from her horizons, and there will be peace in and around the Holy Land.

Yes, I have faith. Faith in God and even in His creation. Without it no action would be possible. And action is the only remedy to indifference: the most insidious[7] danger of all. Isn't this the meaning of Alfred Nobel's legacy? Wasn't his fear of war a shield against war?

There is much to be done, there is much that can be done. One person—a Raoul Wallenberg, an Albert Schweitzer,[8] one person of integrity, can make a difference, a difference of life and death. As long as one dissident[9] is in prison, our freedom will not be true. As long as one child is hungry, our lives will be filled with anguish and shame.

What all these victims need above all is to know that they are not alone; that we are not forgetting them, that when their voices are stifled we shall lend them ours, that while their freedom depends on ours, the quality of our freedom depends on theirs.

This is what I say to the young Jewish boy wondering what I have done with his years. It is in his name that I speak to you and that I express to you my deepest gratitude. No one is as capable of gratitude as one who has emerged from the kingdom of night.

We know that every moment is a moment of grace, every hour an offering; not to share them would mean to betray them. Our lives no longer belong to us alone; they belong to all those who need us desperately.

Thank you Chairman Aarvik. Thank you, members of the Nobel Committee. Thank you, people of Norway, for declaring on this singular occasion that our survival has meaning for mankind.

---

5. **Andrei Sakharov's . . . imprisonment**, references to leaders who were imprisoned or in forced isolation because of their resistance to government policies and their pursuit of human rights. These dissidents have all been freed since Wiesel's speech was delivered. Walesa and Mandela have since served as presidents of Poland and South Africa, respectively.

6. **Palestinians,** people who became refugees when Israel was created as a nation in 1948 or in later shifts of Israel's boundaries.

7. insidious (in sid′ē əs) *adj.* working secretly or subtly.

8. **Raoul Wallenberg . . . Albert Schweitzer.** Wallenberg, a Swedish diplomat who saved many Jews from the Holocaust by intervening with the Nazis, died in a Russian prison after World War II. Schweitzer, an Alsatian physician, philosopher, and missionary, was awarded the Nobel Peace Prize in 1952.

9. **dissident** (dis′ə dənt), *n.* person who disagrees or dissents.

After Reading

Making Connections

Shaping Your Response

1. Speaking of the Holocaust, Wiesel says, ". . . if we forget, we are guilty, we are accomplices." Do you agree? Explain.

2. What images from each speech do you find most memorable?

3. Camus says, "Each generation doubtless feels called upon to reform the world." Do you feel this observation applies to your generation? Why or why not?

Analyzing the Speeches

4. Who might you **infer** is the "young Jewish boy" mentioned in Wiesel's speech, and what is the "kingdom of night" he discovers in paragraph four?

5. How would you describe Wiesel's **tone** in this speech?

6. What does Camus consider his generation's responsibility in light of modern-day oppression?

Extending the Ideas

7. Compare Wiesel's view of the writer's mission to that of Camus.

8. 👣 Wiesel lived through the Holocaust; Camus experienced its horrors less directly. In what respects do you think experiencing the Holocaust would determine a person's **perspective** about life and values?

9. Near the end of his speech, Wiesel expresses his faith and asserts that "one person of integrity can make a difference." Do you agree? Why or why not?

Literary Focus: Style

The manner in which writers use words and sentences to fit their ideas is called **style**. Style involves choices on the part of the writer such as: from whose point of view? what tone? what mood? which words? what kind of imagery? whether or not to use figurative language?

• What do you think is the purpose of Wiesel's many **allusions** to historical figures?

• Which speech uses more **figurative language**? What are some examples of such language?

• What effect does Wiesel create by portraying things from a young boy's **point of view**?

Vocabulary Study

Choose the letter of the word that is most nearly the *opposite* of the italicized word.

anguish
homage
insidious
presumptuous
traumatized

1. *presumptuous* **a.** unexpected **b.** bold **c.** appropriate **d.** shy
2. *insidious* **a.** releasing **b.** questioning **c.** provoking **d.** obvious
3. *anguish* **a.** attention **b.** suffering **c.** rebellion **d.** comfort
4. *traumatized* **a.** shocked **b.** restless **c.** calm **d.** angry
5. *homage* **a.** duty **b.** disrespect **c.** celebration **d.** praise

Expressing Your Ideas

Writing Choices

Writer's Notebook Update Look back at your observations about how these Nobel Prize winners view their duties. Then use this information to explain which writers, if any, appearing in this book might share these views.

Up Close and Personal You can learn a lot about a writer who speaks from the heart, as both Wiesel and Camus do in their Nobel acceptance speeches. Refer to the notes in your notebook as you write a **character sketch** of each man based upon what you learned from his speech.

Congratulations! Image that you are a dear friend of either Wiesel or Camus, but you were unable to attend his acceptance ceremony in Stockholm. Send a **Fax** to your friend congratulating him on his well-deserved award and eloquent acceptance speech. Mention highlights of his speech.

Other Options

The Unknown Award Alfred Nobel might have planned the Nobel Prize because he wanted to be remembered as something other than the "dynamite king." For what would you want to be remembered after your death? Think of a new **award** promoting a cause that you believe in. Name the award and design a medallion, trophy, or ornament that will be distributed with it.

Find Out More In their acceptance speeches, Wiesel and Camus make allusions, or references to people, events, and ideas. Research one of these allusions—perhaps Nietzsche, Hitler, the Spanish Civil War, apartheid, or Nelson Mandela—and present an **oral report** to the class.

Bearing Witness Conduct an **interview** of someone who has survived the Holocaust. Include a question about how the experience has shaped this person's **perspectives** about what is important. You might ask for permission to record the interview and share it with the class.

Something of Value

Power and Horsepower

Big Cars as

Pop Culture Connection
The preceding group of selections examines things people value—from peace to Porsches. These next pages explore the Car Culture and how it reflects the connection between power and horsepower.

A disastrous flop when Ford brought it out in the mid-1950s, the Edsel's most notorious feature was its grille, which reminded one observer of "an Oldsmobile sucking a lemon."

The first mass-produced American automobile, Ford's Model T, had been an open car; by contrast, closed sedans, like this 1929 Willys Whippet, offered the luxury of privacy.

The American slang term "hot rod" dates from the late 1940s, the period when the fascination of young people with fast and often vividly painted automobiles blossomed.

Wheels

STATUS SYMBOLS

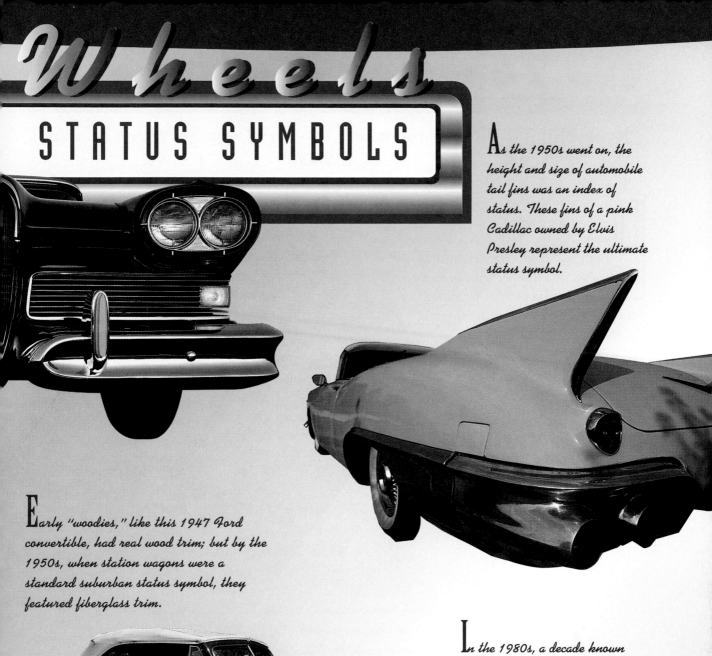

As the 1950s went on, the height and size of automobile tail fins was an index of status. These fins of a pink Cadillac owned by Elvis Presley represent the ultimate status symbol.

Early "woodies," like this 1947 Ford convertible, had real wood trim; but by the 1950s, when station wagons were a standard suburban status symbol, they featured fiberglass trim.

In the 1980s, a decade known for conspicuous consumption, an index of status was the size and luxury of one's stretch limo. This 71-foot-long Cadillac Eldorado has a swimming pool, a crystal chandelier, and 3 color TVs.

The Car Culture

"Everything in life is somewhere else, and you get there in a car!"

E. B. White

Power, mobility, speed, status! Cars have come to represent not only a means of transportation but the dreams, fantasies, and illusions of a society on-the-go. Today, due in large part to savvy marketing, competitive pricing, and a fast-paced lifestyle, the car has become essential to the American way of life.

Cars are a barometer of our history—the wars, the economics, the styles, the social climate. The market collapse of 1929 put the brakes on the era of the true luxury car, and World War II nearly halted the production of cars in general. After the war, when gasoline rationing ended and factories turned once more to building passenger cars instead of jeeps, tanks, and airplanes, there was a pent-up demand for new cars. The postwar prosperity of the 1950s and the Sputnik era of scientific advance both had their impact on car size, production, and design. (Note, for example, the rocket-like fins of Elvis Presley's car in the photo essay.) Smaller, more fuel-efficient cars came into vogue with the gas shortages of the 1970s

As concern grows about the environmental impact of fossil fuels, the future may belong to alternative vehicles, like this solar-powered General Motors Sunraycer.

and concerns about air pollution. Despite these adaptations, the car, as one observer put it, "reaches to the heart of the American self-image."

But the Car Culture is by no means an exclusively American phenomenon. Monarchs and politicians worldwide have equated power and horsepower. The Rolls-Royce was adopted in 1952 by Britain's Queen Elizabeth II and has been elevated to the status of the car of royalty in India, where one maharajah maintained a personal fleet of 22. VIP cars carry dignitaries and "wheeler-dealers" throughout the world, including a group of women in Togo, who are known throughout West Africa as the "Mercedes Ladies."

Cars—the ultimate monogram—serve as an extension of one's personality and a method of identification. The urge to personalize a car can have many outlets—custom paint jobs, knickknacks dangling from the rearview mirror, bumper stickers, and—the final word in personalizing—vanity license plates. And car fanciers collect anything

from hubcaps, hood ornaments, and dashboard nameplates to old cars themselves– faithfully restored and commanding astronomical prices. Even models that were originally unpopular (like the Edsel, whose grille one observer likened to an Oldsmobile sucking a lemon) are now chic.

Car makers and advertisers are well aware of the images a car projects. It's not by chance that cars have been named after mythic figures (Mercury and Saturn), wild animals (Jaguar and Cougar), or vaguely "futuristic" concepts (Acura, Windstar). Although cars may still carry the unmistakable aura of power, prestige, and prosperity—sometimes referred to as the P Factor—current image makers want to convey their practicality, efficiency, and endurance.

Are cars still status symbols, as we embark into the 21st century? To a degree, yes. But the popularity of the van, the jeep, and 4-wheel drive (and don't forget those Volkswagen "Bug" diehards) seems to suggest a reversal of the Mercedes mentality. Some Americans, sick of the expense and hassle of own-

As part of its rejection of middle-class values, the Counterculture of the 1960s and '70s embraced the reverse status represented by the economical and unglamorous Volkswagen.

ing a car and fighting long commutes, are no longer car owners. Increasingly, celebrities, heads of state, and the wealthy, to say nothing of bridal couples and prom-goers, now lease cars or hire a chauffeur-driven limousine to transport them. Perhaps the ultimate status symbol today is having a car you don't have to drive yourself!

Perhaps heralding a return of family values, the most popular automotive status symbols of the 1990s are minivans, like this Jeep Cherokee.

The Car Culture

The perennial classic status symbol among automobiles is the sports car, like this Mercedes Benz 300 SL.

Oh, Lord, won't you buy me a Mercedes-Benz?
My friends all drive Porsches, I must make amends,
Worked hard all my lifetime, no help from my friends,
So, Lord, won't you buy me a Mercedes-Benz?

Oh, Lord, won't you buy me a color T.V.?
Dialing For Dollars is trying to find me.
I wait for delivery each day until three,
So, Lord, won't you buy me a color T.V.?
~Janis Joplin

Responding

1. Analyze a car ad on TV or from a magazine. How does the ad use emotional appeal, language, and design to sell the product? (See Looking at Ads, page 542, for tips on evaluating ads.)

2. Choose three cars from the picture essay and explain what they suggest about power or status.

Writing Workshop

The Sum of My Parts

Assignment The authors of the selections in this part of the unit focus on things, great and small, that for one reason or another are of value to them. What are the things that hold value for you? Answer this question in an artful exploration.

WRITER'S BLUEPRINT

Product   A multimedia presentation

Purpose   To show people what is important to you

Audience   People who don't know you well

Specs   As the creator of a successful presentation, you should:

❏ Choose five or six things that are important to you and would say something about you to others. These may include objects, such as a bracelet or a basketball; places, such as your room or a lake; and living things, such as a plant or a pet.

❏ Present these items as part of a guided tour, an autobiographical narrative, or another method of your choice.

❏ Use a combination of visuals, writing, and speaking that will tell people who don't know you well why these items are important to you.

❏ Address your audience in a tone that's friendly and conversational, yet serious.

❏ When you speak, pronounce words clearly and speak loudly enough for everyone to hear.

❏ When you write, follow the rules of grammar, usage, spelling, and mechanics. Avoid run-on sentences.

Create a chart, like the one below, of a dozen things that you value highly. Fill in the first two columns. Then fold your paper so the second column is hidden. Exchange your chart with another group. In the third column have members of the other group note what they think the items show about you.

Item and description	What I think this item shows about me	What others think this item shows about me
stuffed unicorn; made of socks, sweet face, whimsical	I believe in imagination and fantasy.	sentimental; daydreamer; good imagination

Discuss your ideas. Meet with your group to discuss the items on your charts. Listen carefully to how others see you in relation to the items you value. Use their observations to expand your understanding of what the items mean to you.

Add relevant comments to your chart. Then answer this question: *If I were going to another country for a year, what would I take with me to introduce myself to the people I meet?* Choose a group of five or six items as the focus of your presentation.

Try a quickwrite. Write for five minutes about why the items you have chosen are important to you, how you feel about them, and what they say about you.

Plan your presentation. Use your prewriting materials to create a plan.

First, decide on the method you'll use to organize your presentation. Here are some ideas on method:
- a tour, with you as tour guide
- a museum exhibit, with you as museum guide
- an autobiographical narrative, with you as narrator
- another method of your choice

Then decide on the order in which you'll present the items. You might:
- proceed in order of importance, from least to most important
- proceed in time order, beginning with the oldest item
- use another method of your choice

OR . . .
Discuss your items with a partner or small group.

Decide how you'll present each item visually:
- present the item itself
- show pictures of it
- show symbols, perhaps a collage, to represent it
- another method of your choice

Decide how you'll write about each item:
- a description on a note card, as you'd find in a museum
- as part of a descriptive poem
- as an anecdote—an incident or event connected with the item
- another method of your choice

Finally, make detailed notes about each item. Explain:
- why the item is important to you
- how you feel about it
- what it says about you

STEP 2 DRAFTING

Before you draft the written part of the presentation, review your prewriting materials and the Writer's Blueprint.

As you draft, concentrate on getting your ideas down on paper. The following tips may help:

- Keep your description of each item short and to the point. Don't go into long, involved explanations that get away from the main points you're trying to make about the item. Stick to telling why it's important, how you feel about it, and what it says about you.

- Use a friendly, conversational tone in your draft. See the Revising Strategy in Step 3 for ideas on establishing tone.

STEP 3 REVISING

Ask a partner for comments on your draft before you revise it.

✔ Have I written about items that are important to me?

✔ Do I go beyond a simple description and communicate what my items say about me?

✔ Is the tone of my presentation friendly and conversational, yet serious?

Revising Strategy

Using the Appropriate Tone

For a highly personal presentation like this, you don't want to use an extremely formal tone:

> "Ladies and gentlemen, kindly allow me to present to you several items that hold much meaning. . . ."

However, you don't want to use an extremely chatty tone either:

> "Hey, guys, guess what? I cannot WAIT to show you all my cool stuff!"

Remember, you're aiming your presentation at an audience of people who don't know you well; so you'll want to aim somewhere in between the two extremes:

> "Here are some things that mean a lot to me. . . ."

Notice in the student model how the author made changes to alter the tone.

woke up bright and early
I ~~awakened at an unusually early hour~~ in the place. ~~I favor above~~ *best in the world*

~~all others~~, my room. ~~Presently,~~ I opened up my eyes to see sunshine
soft
through my peach curtains. The color soothed my eyes. My troll
made me smile
collection was to the right of me and their smiling faces ~~affected my~~
my favorite
~~mood favorably~~. I turned on my radio to hear a song ~~I knew~~ playing. I
was
~~seemed to be~~ in heaven.

STEP 4 EDITING

Ask a partner to review your revised draft before you edit. When you edit, look for errors in grammar, usage, spelling, and mechanics. Look closely for errors with run-ons.

Editing Strategy

Avoiding Run-ons

A run-on sentence results when two or more independent clauses are run together in a sentence without a conjunction or proper punctuation:

> I've had this stuffed animal since I was a baby I started collecting seashells when I was six.

Read what you've written out loud and listen for places where a natural pause should be—at the point where one thought ends and another begins. If you see you have two complete thoughts run together, make a correction:

> I've had this stuffed animal since I was a baby, but I started collecting seashells when I was six.

FOR REFERENCE
More information about avoiding run-ons can be found in the Language and Grammar Handbook at the back of this book.

STEP 5 PRESENTING

- If you're giving a guided tour, make a separate note card for each item. Jot down key words and phrases and arrange the cards in order.

- Videotape your items and narrate the tape. Make background music a part of the video as well.

COMPUTER TIP
Use a computer HyperCard program to organize a HyperText presentation that includes visuals, sound, and text. See the Beyond Print article on page 447 for ideas about multimedia presentations.

STEP 6 LOOKING BACK

Self-evaluate. Look back at the Writer's Blueprint and give your presentation a score for each point, from 6 (superior) to 1 (inadequate).

Reflect. Write answers to these questions.

✔ What have you learned about combining different modes of expression (written, oral, and visual) to convey information to an audience? Were you able to make them work well together? Why or why not?

✔ What new insights have you gained about yourself as a result of doing this assignment?

For Your Working Portfolio Add your presentation material and your reflection responses to your working portfolio.

Beyond Print

Looking at Ads

The people who make and market the products you buy or want to buy spend a lot of money on television, magazine, and newspaper advertising. Their target is *you,* and their goal is to sell. If you can become more aware of how you are being influenced through advertising, you may save some money. You will certainly be a wiser consumer.

Examine the Colt ad on the opposite page in light of the following advertising techniques.

Design

Composition What is in the background of the ad? How does this background, along with other details in the ad, serve to suggest that the car is a means to a fun getaway? Why do you think the car is headed up and forward? What purpose do the Japanese characters serve?

Color Different colors and textures create different moods. Bright and shiny colors often make things seem new, exciting, and desirable. Subdued colors create a sense of romance and well-being. Dark colors or shadows might be scary or sophisticated. Why might the car be red?

Advertising Techniques

Bandwagon *Bandwagon* appeal suggests you will be part of a popular trend if you buy a product. Note that the car is full of people going somewhere exciting. Why do you think the passengers aren't clearly shown?

Emotional Appeal Ads try to associate the product with something they assume you value. What about the image seems to imply that if you buy this product, you will be popular or happy or successful?

Language What buzz words and persuasive phrases can you find? What does "spirited" handling mean? What does the name Vista suggest?

Activity Option

Copy the chart on your paper. Rate the ad according to each design and technique factor on your chart. Use a five point scale, with five meaning the ad is highly persuasive and one meaning it is not persuasive. Then give the ad an overall rating based on its effectiveness.

Design	Advertising Techniques
Composition	Bandwagon
Color	Emotional Appeal
	Language
Overall Ad Rating	1 2 3 4 5

Four-wheel drive with room to 余裕.

It's the Colt Vista. The sleek new wagon with an ingenious capacity for both people and things. Designed and built by Mitsubishi in Japan.

And you'd be hard-pressed to find another wagon that offers you as much versatility.

Or fun. Or value.

With first class seating for seven passengers. And seats that fold forward and backwards to lay down more ways than those in any other small wagon.

So it'll accommodate just about any combination of family, friends and freight.

And with push-button four-wheel drive, Vista confidently moves all of the above through snow, mud and adversity on all fours. (A two-wheel drive version is also available.)

And if Vista's looks, utility and versatility aren't justification enough to consider one, wait till you drive one. The handling is precise and spirited. And its perfect size makes it perfectly easy to park and maneuver.

Colt is imported for Chrysler-Plymouth and Dodge dealers.

So try one on for size. And solve all of your transportation problems in one fell 極めて簡単.

優秀 Colt
It's all the Japanese you need to know.

Colts are built by Mitsubishi Motors Corp. and sold exclusively at Chrysler-Plymouth and Dodge dealers.

Multicultural Connections

Communication

Part One: Worth Fighting For? Cultural differences prevent effective communication between the narrator's parents in *Kaffir Boy* and between a British teacher and the young Indian students she stereotypes in "By Any Other Name."

■ What threats does education pose for South Africans who, like Mathabane's father, have tribal affiliations? Explain whether or not you think that some Americans have similar fears about education.

■ In each of these four autobiographical pieces, which of the following factors would you say causes miscommunication: age differences, language, culture, and social class?

Perspective

Part Two: Something of Value Perspective involves seeing people and events from a particular viewpoint. And that viewpoint, largely shaped by culture, determines what a person or a society values— from peace to pets to Porsches.

■ List ten things valued by characters or authors in this unit titled What Really Matters? Arrange them in the order that *you* would value them, with the most important being number 1. Then explain what this order reveals about you and your personal perspective.

■ A Nobel Prize is worth a great deal of money. Do you think it is ironic to award someone, such as Elie Wiesel or Albert Camus, who has enriched the world spiritually, with a gift that is now close to one million dollars? Suppose the prize were a gold watch, a poem, or a parade instead. From your perspective, what would the best prize be? Explain.

Activities

1. List ten things you value in order and explain what your choices reflect about you.

2. Work with a group to bring ads to class to display. Give an Ad Talk, explaining what these ads are designed to communicate and to whom (group, social class) they seem directed.

Independent and Group Projects

Art

Special Letters With a partner, explore calligraphy, the art of beautiful handwriting. Then choose five different sentences, phrases, or words from Unit 4 that reflect the theme of the unit, What Really Matters? Write this material in a calligraphic style, decorate your work with simple designs, and put on paper suitable to use as greeting cards.

Media

Commercial Values With your group, create a television commercial for an insurance company, stressing the need to insure "things of value." How will your creative team convince people that they should insure both material and nonmaterial things? Be prepared to present your commercial to the class.

Poll

Value Votes Brainstorm with classmates a list of things students consider important. Use this list to draw up a questionnaire to determine what things are most valued. Tally the results on a graph and share it with the class.

Demonstration

Display Case Your group is in charge of planning a new exhibit for the Natural History Museum. The topic you have been assigned is What Really Matters? Collect special things from your childhood as well as items that your parents, grandparents, and family friends value. (In some cases, you may have to substitute a photograph or drawing of a valued item.) Identify each item and its approximate date on a notecard. Put these items on display for the class and explain their significance.

Dialogue

A Literary Party Annie Dillard observes, ". . . you have to fling your-self at what you're doing. . . ." Imagine that five of the authors in this unit were to join Dillard at a party. In a group of six, with each student representing an author, prepare a dialogue that might follow from this statement. Base comments on what you have learned about these authors and their works.

A Place in the World

Connections
Part One, pages 550–595

Reflections
Part Two, pages 596–629

Culture Crossroads
Part Three, pages 630–671

Reading

a tornado of song...

making a fist

Words in poems do a big job, since they must convey word pictures, sound effects, and much more than mere dictionary meanings. In the poems you are about to read, for example, the devastating effects of love are variously described in terms of "first frost," "the fist clenched round my heart," and "a woman, turned to stone." As you read poetry, pay special attention to the words—their sounds and the visual images they convey. Here are some things to look for as you read.

SOUND

The sound of a word helps create an atmosphere and reinforce meaning. Note, for example, the harsh sound of "first frost" and the effect that would be lost if the poet had substituted a softer word such as *initial* for *first*. Note the soft sounds and rhythms that Gabriela Mistral chooses— bread baked "with anise seed and honey" and "sequined goldfish"—to lull her baby to sleep.

WORD CHOICE

Poets choose one word rather than another to convey special meanings. For example, the "splintering, breaking" cold described in "Those Winter Sundays" may remind some readers of cracking ice, and others of the splintering sound of chopping firewood. The father's cracked hands suggest a life of hard physical labor.

FORM

How are lines grouped on the page? Instead of paragraphs, lines in poetry are usually grouped in stanzas. Are these lines and stanzas of equal length? If not, try to figure out why they look as they do. For example, a short line may indicate emphasis or an abrupt shift. Long lines that run into each other may suggest overflowing emotion. Note punctuation and use it as a key to reading.

FIGURATIVE LANGUAGE

Poetry is based on figurative comparisons—language used in fresh, new ways. This imaginative use of language, although not literally true, suggests real similarities and insights. For example, Ruth Dallas's description of a mother who sews with a "grasshopper thimble" suggests the quickness and skill of her actions.

Poetry

...a tornado of song...

...a fish in a bowl...

TIPS

1
Read poetry aloud to enjoy the sounds and rhythms.

2
Try to get the overall meaning before zeroing in on details.

3
Visualize the images and figurative language.

4
See if the form provides any clues to the meaning.

5
Try to determine what the poet's purpose is— to entertain, to instruct, to create a mood, or something else.

...that smelled of rotting fish

...splintering, breaking cold...

"...a fish in a bowl."

first frost

first frost

First frost clinging

a tornado of song

making a fist

IMAGES

Poets rely on word pictures called *images* to help readers see, touch, feel, taste, and smell the things being described. Tía Chucha becomes an unforgettable character in Luis Rodriguez's poem from the moment she visits the family "in a tornado of song" with her perfume that smelled of rotting fish. As you read these poems, look for other images that make these characters real and memorable.

Two roads diverged in a wood, and I...

549

Part One

Connections

We find our own place in the world by connecting with others—through family ties and love, among other things.

 Multicultural Connection **Communication** is essential in establishing connections with others and with the world at large. Communicating with a member of another generation can be a special challenge.

Before Reading

A New Dress by Ruth Dallas   New Zealand
Those Winter Sundays by Robert Hayden   USA
Tía Chucha by Luis J. Rodriguez   USA

Building Background

Family Portraits Somewhere in your home probably sits an album of family photographs. As a child, you might have examined the pages, laughing at the funny clothes and old cars, puzzling over the identities of people who looked vaguely familiar. Poets, too, are creators of portraits, using words rather than a camera lens to create images.

Literary Focus

Figurative Language Words used outside of their literal, or usual, meanings are called **figurative language.** This type of language includes **figures of speech** such as the following: A **simile** is a stated comparison between two dissimilar things, using the words *like, as, appears, than,* or *seems:* "That hat looks like a bird cage." A **metaphor** is an implied comparison between two basically unlike things without a connective such as *like* or *as:* "His face was a map of suffering." **Personification** gives human qualities to nonhuman or nonliving things: "angry winds, flowers nodding their heads." **Hyperbole** is exaggeration for effect: "a street that winds on to infinity."

Restate the cartoon's caption in purely literal terms.

Writer's Notebook

Figure It Out As you read the following poems, jot down figurative language that helps you picture the people described.

"It didn't tug at my heart."

Drawing by Stan Hunt; © 1987 The New Yorker Magazine, Inc.

Ruth Dallas
born 1919

Ruth Dallas grew up at the southernmost tip of New Zealand's South Island, which she describes as a place "where the sheer magnitude of the sky and sea seemed to dwarf human beings to insignificance." As a child who couldn't find books about New Zealand children, she vowed that when she grew up, she would write about her native country. She has published novels for children, mostly about New Zealand pioneer life, as well as many poetry collections.

Robert Hayden
1913–1980

Born in Detroit and raised by foster parents, Robert Hayden went on to write poetry that both reflected and went beyond his African American heritage to reveal his compassion for all humanity. In 1976, he was named Consultant in Poetry to the Library of Congress. In the 1930s, he did research in African American history, a recurring subject in his poems. Hayden, who taught at both Fisk University and the University of Michigan, described himself as "a poet who teaches in order to earn a living so that he can write a poem or two now and then."

Luis J. Rodriguez
born 1954

In his autobiography, *Always Running: La Vida Loca—Gang Days in L.A.*, Luis Rodriguez recounts how he escaped gang life because of a caring counselor and his own increasing love of writing. A survivor who profited from contact with the Chicano movement of the 1960s, Rodriguez now spends time working as a peace arbiter with gangs and conducting poetry workshops for the homeless. He considers the job of a writer "a heroic and necessary task." His printing company is called Tía Chucha Press, after a beloved aunt.

A New Dress

Ruth Dallas

I don't want a new dress, I said.
My mother plucked from her mouth ninety-nine pins.
I suppose there are plenty, she said, *girls of ten
Who would be glad to have a new dress.*

5 Snip-snip. Snip-snip. The cold scissors
Ate quickly as my white rabbit round my arm.

She won't speak to me if I have a new dress!
My feet rattled on the kitchen floor.

How can I fit you if you won't stand still?

10 My tears made a map of Australia
On the sofa cushion; from the hot center
My friend's eyes flashed, fierce as embers.[1]
She would not speak to me, perhaps never again.
She would paralyze me with one piercing look.

15 *I'd rather have my friend than a new dress!*

My mother wouldn't understand, my grownup mother
Whose grasshopper thimble winked at the sun
And whose laughter was made by small waves
Rearranging seashells on Australia's shore.

---

1. **ember** (em′bər), *n.* ashes in which there is still some fire.

Those Winter Sundays

Robert Hayden

Sundays too my father got up early
and put his clothes on in the blueblack cold,
then with cracked hands that ached
from labor in the weekday weather made
5 banked fires blaze. No one ever thanked him.

I'd wake and hear the cold splintering, breaking.
When the rooms were warm, he'd call,
and slowly I would rise and dress,
fearing the chronic[1] angers of that house,

10 Speaking indifferently to him,
who had driven out the cold
and polished my good shoes as well.
What did I know, what did I know
of love's austere[2] and lonely offices?

---

1. **chronic** (kron′ik), *adj.* never stopping.
2. **austere** (ô stir′), *adj.* stern in manner or appearance;
   harsh.

This oil painting by Frank Joseph Dillon was completed
in 1933, during the Depression. Why might the artist
have painted the backs instead of the fronts of houses?
Do you think the figure with the sack lives in one of the
houses or is just passing by? ➤

Tía Chucha

by Luis J. Rodriguez

Every few years
Tía Chucha would visit the family
in a tornado of song
and open us up
5   as if we were an overripe avocado.
She was a dumpy, black-haired
creature of upheaval,
who often came unannounced
with a bag of presents
10 including home-made perfumes and
        colognes
that smelled something like
rotting fish
on a hot day at the tuna cannery.

They said she was crazy.
15 Oh sure, she once ran out naked
to catch the postman
with a letter that didn't belong to us.
I mean, she had this annoying habit
of boarding city buses
20 and singing at the top of her voice
(one bus driver even refused to go on
until she got off).
But crazy?

To me, she was the wisp
25 of the wind's freedom,
a music-maker
who once tried to teach me guitar
but ended up singing
and singing,
30 me listening,
and her singing
until I put the instrument down
and watched the clock
click the lesson time away.

35 I didn't learn guitar,
but I learned something
about her craving
for the new, the unbroken
. . . so she could break it.
40 Periodically she banished
herself from the family
and was the better for it.

I secretly admired Tía Chucha.
She was always quick with a story,
45 another "*Pepito*" joke,
or a hand-written lyric
that she would produce
regardless of the occasion.

She was a despot[1]
50 of desire;
uncontainable
as a splash of water
on a varnished table.

I wanted to remove
55 the layers
of unnatural seeing
the way Tía Chucha beheld
the world, with first eyes,
like an infant
60 who can discern
the elixir[2]
within milk.

I wanted to be
one of the prizes
65 she stuffed into
her rumpled bag.

1. **despot** (des′pət), *n*. ruler having unlimited power.
2. **elixir** (i lik′sər), *n*. medicine with curing powers.

After Reading

Making Connections

Shaping Your
Response

1. Which poetic portrait of a family member do you find most vivid? Draw this character in your notebook.

2. Which poem reminds you of a childhood incident of your own? Explain.

3. Which main character in these poems would you prefer having as a parent? Why?

Analyzing the Poems

4. What **inferences** can you make about the attitudes of the three speakers toward their family members? Cite lines to support your opinion.

5. What do you think causes the change of **tone** in the last two lines of "Those Winter Sundays"?

6. In "A New Dress," how is the phrase "my grownup mother" a clue to the **theme** of the poem?

7. What examples of surprising **images** did you find in "Tía Chucha"?

8. What phrase in each poem do you think best **characterizes** the subject? Explain your choices.

Extending the Ideas

9. 🐾 Do you think that **communication** between parents and children changes once those children become teenagers? Explain.

10. Recently, newspapers and television have focused on the plight of the American family. What seems to be causing its disintegration? What remedies would you suggest?

Literary Focus: Figurative Language

Answer the following questions about **figurative language**:

- Considering the time of day mentioned, how can cold be blueblack, as described in line 2 of "Those Winter Sundays"?

- In line 17 of "A New Dress," what does the **metaphor** "grass–hopper thimble" suggest about the mother's actions?

- How does Dallas use **hyperbole** (exaggeration) and **personification** (giving human qualities to nonhuman things) to make her poem lively?

- Which figures of speech in "Tía Chucha" do you find most memorable?

Vocabulary Study

On your paper, write the letter of the vocabulary word from the list that best completes each sentence.

austere
chronic
despot
elixir
ember

1. If you were a *despot*, your subjects would most likely react to you with ____.   **a.** laughter   **b.** fear   **c.** sympathy   **d.** joy

2. A *chronic* offender would offend ____.

   a. all the time   **b.** occasionally   **c.** rarely   **d.** never

3. You would expect the effects of an *elixir* to be ____.

   a. painful   **b.** loud   **c.** beneficial   **d.** destructive

4. You would most likely find an *ember* in a ____.

   a. bathroom   **b.** closet   **c.** car   **d.** fireplace

5. If you had an *austere* appearance, strangers would most likely ____ you.
   a. smile at   **b.** shout at   **c.** lecture   **d.** avoid

Expressing Your Ideas

Writing Choices

Writer's Notebook Update Review the figurative language you found in each poem. Make a chart that shows each figure of speech along with its meaning.

Figure of Speech	Meaning

Family Photos Look through a family photo album, noting details and characteristics of family members and settings. If you don't know some of these people personally, imagine what they would be like. Then write **captions** for several of these pictures, using figurative language.

All in the Family Every family has at least one colorful member who stands out because of his or her actions, dress, or attitudes. Write a **character sketch** of this family member showing that person's uniqueness as well as your feelings about him or her.

Point of View Respond to the ideas in one of the poems you have just read by writing your own **poem** from the point of view of one of the main characters.

Other Options

Clothes Encounters It is not uncommon for a teenager and a parent, guardian, or school official to have a difference of opinion about clothes, hair styles, or something else connected with fashion. Draw a **cartoon** that captures your differing opinions.

Talk Radio Your group will simulate a radio talk show in which listeners call in with comments on the state of the American family. One student will act as host and other group members will be the callers. Make a **recording** of the on-air comments and the host's responses, serious or humorous. Play the tape in class.

Before Reading

Girls Can We Educate We Dads? by James Berry West Indies

If You'll Only Go to Sleep by Gabriela Mistral Chile

Mi Prima Agueda by Ramón López Velarde Mexico

Building Background

Between Generations What goes on between generations? There may be a close bond, such as between mother and infant. There may be a special connection, such as between a favorite relative and a young person. Or there may be friction—for example, that between parent and child when they hold different opinions and beliefs. A lack of understanding between adults and young adults, such as that conveyed in the poem by James Berry that you are about to read, is sometimes referred to as the **"generation gap."**

Literary Focus

Diction Writers' choices of words, determined by their subject, audience, and desired effect, is called **diction.** An important element in a writer's style, diction can be described as *casual* or *formal* (bugged/vexed), *old-fashioned* or *contemporary* (steed/horse), *general* or *specific* (dog/golden retriever). When you read a poem, think about why the poet chose those particular words.

This cartoon serves as a reminder that word choice depends on the setting, the speaker, and the occasion.

Writer's Notebook

Not To Tattoo Make a list of comments— "That's not music; that's noise!" "But everyone has pierced ears!"—that suggest some current generation gaps.

"He's, like, 'To be or not to be,' and I'm, like, 'Get a life.'"

Drawing by Lorenz; © 1995 The New Yorker Magazine, Inc.

James Berry
born 1925

"It's the function of writers and poets," James Berry once wrote, "to bring in the left-out side of the human family." A Jamaican living in England, Berry felt very much a part of that left-out family. He began writing while working in British schools, having noted that the school libraries had few books about children with either an African or Caribbean heritage. Berry's background is evident in his short stories and poetry, where he often uses the Creole language spoken in Jamaica to capture the character of his island's people.

Gabriela Mistral
1889–1957

Gabriela Mistral (mē sträl′) is the pen name of Lucila Godoy, who feared she might lose her teaching job if she published under her own name. After the suicide of her fiancé in 1909, she devoted herself to teaching, writing, and raising the child of her half-brother. Although she first gained renown as an educator, Mistral later became a diplomat, serving in Brazil, Mexico, Italy, and the United States. She often writes of love—physical, maternal, and spiritual. In 1945, she received the Nobel Prize for literature.

Ramón López Velarde
1888–1921

The oldest of nine children, Ramón López Velarde (bə lär′dā) published his first poetry in 1905, despite his father's strong objections to a literary career. Although he earned his law degree, he continued to write for various literary magazines. After moving to Mexico City, Velarde worked as both a government official and a professor of literature. Four days after his thirty-third birthday and just as he was beginning to be recognized for his poetry, Velarde died of pneumonia. Today he is considered the father of modern Mexican poetry.

Girls
Can We Educate We
Dads?

James Berry

Listn the male chauvinist[1] in mi dad—
a girl walkin night street mus be bad.
He dohn sey, the world's a free place
for a girl to keep her unmolested[2] space.
5 Instead he sey—a girl is a girl.

He sey a girl walkin swingin hips about
call boys to look and shout.
He dohn sey, if a girl have style
she wahn to sey, look
10 I okay from top to foot.
Instead he sey—a girl is a girl.

Listn the male chauvinist in mi dad—
a girl too laughy-laughy look too glad-glad
jus like a girl too looky-looky roun
15 will get a pretty satan at her side.
He dohn sey—a girl full of go
dohn wahn stifle[3] talent comin on show.
Instead he sey—a girl is a girl.

---

1. **chauvinist** (shō′və nist), *n.* person excessively
   enthusiastic about his or her sex, race, or group.
2. **unmolested** (un mə lest′əd), *adj.* undisturbed.
3. **stifle** (stī′fəl) *v.* keep back; stop.

If You'll Only Go to Sleep

Gabriela Mistral

The crimson rose
Plucked yesterday,
the fire and cinnamon
of the carnation,

5 the bread I baked
with anise seed and honey,
and the goldfish
flaming in its bowl.

All these are yours,
10 baby born of woman,
if you'll only
go to sleep.
A rose, I say!
And a carnation!
15 Fruit, I say!
And honey!

And a sequined goldfish,
and still more I'll give you
if you'll only sleep
20 till morning.

Canción de cuna (Cradle Song) by Colombian artist Beatriz González is constructed of metal laminate and painted with enamel. Does the flat perspective make the mother-child relationship seem more personal, or less so, than other works of art on the same subject? If the crib were used for a baby, would you consider this art wasted or not? ▼

Mi Prima Agueda

A Jesús Villalpando

Ramón López Velarde

Mi madrina invitaba a mi prima Agueda
a que pasara el día con nosotros,
y mi prima llegaba
con un contradictorio
5 prestigio de almidón y de temible
luto ceremonioso.

Agueda aparecía, resonante
de almidón, y sus ojos
verdes y sus mejillas rubicundas
10 me protegían contra el pavoroso
luto. . . .
        Yo era rapaz
y conocía la O por lo redondo,
y Agueda que tejía
mansa y perseverante en el sonoro
15 corredor, me causaba
calofríos ignotos. . . .

(Creo que hasta la debo la costumbre
heroicamente insana de hablar solo.)

A la hora de comer, en la penumbra
20 quieta del refectorio,
me iba embelesando un quebradizo
sonar intermitente de vajilla
y el timbre caricioso
de la voz de mi prima.
               Agueda era
25 (luto, pupilas verdes y mejillas
rubicundas) un cesto policromo
de manzanas y uvas
en el ébano de un armario añoso.

The Art of Translation

The translator, no less than the original poet, must deal with words and meanings sensitively and imaginatively. A translator of poetry is in effect a poet, re-creating the poem in the new language so that it approximates (not duplicates) the effect of the original. Many elements of poetry may cause problems for a less-than-skillful translator. Consider, for example, the challenge of translating figurative language. The translation must not only be true to the meaning of the first language, but it must capture the emotions and associations of the words beyond their literal meanings.

    Consider this analogy: a translator must get both the *words* (meaning) and the *tune* (spirit) right. To carry the comparison further, the translator must get the *rhythm* accurate, as well. Words must be chosen for their sound effects as well as their meanings in order to create the mood of the original. Here is a poem by Ramón López Velarde in its original Spanish, followed on the next page by two translations. Examine how the translators interpret words differently.

My Cousin Agatha

To Jesús Villalpando

translated by Cheli Durán

My godmother used to ask my cousin
    Agatha
to spend the day with us,
and my cousin used to arrive
wrapped in a contradictory magic
5 of starch and odious[1] ritual
mourning.

Agatha entered, rustling
starch, and her green eyes
and warm red cheeks
10 protected me from the dreadful
black. . . .
          I was only a child
who knew the O by its roundness,
and Agatha, who knitted
mildly, persistently, in the echoing
    corridor,
15 sent little unknown shivers
up my spine.

(I think I owe her, too, my crazy
but heroic habit of talking alone.)

At dinner, in the restful twilight
20 of the dining room,
I was slowly bewitched by the brittle
intermittent ring of plates,
and the lilt that was like a caress
in my cousin's voice.
            Agatha was
25 (rosy cheeks, green eyes, black mourning)
a polychrome basket of colors,
crammed with apples and grapes,
on the ebony of an old cupboard.

---

1. **odious** (ō′dē əs), *adj.* hateful; offensive.

My Cousin Agueda

translated by Willis Knapp Jones

My godmother often invited my cousin
    Agueda
To come and spend the day.
My cousin used to arrive
Appearing in a mixed-up way,
5 Suggesting starch and fearful
Mourning of a funereal[1] day.

Agueda would appear rustling
With starch, and with her eyes green.
And her rosy cheeks
10 Protecting me against the mourning
That I'd seen.

I was a kid
And knew nothing at all,
And Agueda, who was moving
15 Tamely and persistently in the hall,
With her rustling brought excitement
About which I knew nothing at all.

(I even think she is responsible
For my mad habit of talking to myself.)

20 At the dinner hour in the quiet
Shadows of the dining room,
How delightful the fragile
Intermittent rattle of the dishes
And the affectionate tone
25 Of the voice of my cousin
            Agueda.
(in her black mourning, her green eyes, and
Pink cheeks) was a many colored basket
Of apples and green grapes
On the ebony of our ancestral sideboard.

---

1. **funereal** (fyü nir′ē əl), *adj.* gloomy.

▲ ☙ This 1990 untitled work by Peruvian photographer Jeanette Ortiz Osorio is a photograph combined with a painted filter. Which English or Spanish words in the poem **communicate** the same mood as this mixed media portrait?

After Reading

Making Connections

Shaping Your Response

1. Think of a musical piece that could accompany each poem. Explain your choices.

2. Which pair of characters in these poems bears the closest similarity to people in your own family? Explain the resemblance.

3. In your opinion, is a stubborn father, a crying baby, or an older cousin important enough to be the subject of a poem? Why or why not?

Analyzing the Poems

4. Which lines in each stanza of Berry's poem express the girl's **point of view?** Which lines express the father's viewpoint?

5. What **stereotypes** about girls appear in Berry's poem?

6. What words create the **mood** of "If You'll Only Go to Sleep"?

7. In lines 12–13 of "My Cousin Agueda," which translation do you think better suggests the speaker's age? Explain.

Extending the Ideas

8. The dad in Berry's poem is guilty of **stereotyping** girls. What current stereotypes of girls, boys, and teenagers have you noticed? How do you think they came to exist?

9. Compare Tía Chucha and Cousin Agueda.

10. 👁 Do you think that **communication** would be improved if U.S. textbooks included more works in languages other than English? Why or why not?

Literary Focus: Diction

Examine the **diction** in these three poems by discussing the following questions.

- What do you think is meant by the phrases "full of go" and "dohn wahn stifle . . . show" in lines 16–17 of Berry's poem?

- Why might Mistral mention a "crimson red" rose instead of merely a red one? the "fire and cinnamon" instead of the "smell" of a carnation?

- Which version of lines 7–11 of the three poems on pages 563–564 creates the most vivid image for you? Why?

- Imagine that Berry had chosen to write his poem in standard English. What would be gained or lost, in your opinion?

Vocabulary Study

For each numbered item, write on your paper a vocabulary word to complete the sentence.

chauvinist
funereal
odious
stifle
unmolested

1. The father in Berry's poem could not ____ his criticism of the girl's behavior.

2. The girl values her freedom and guards her ____ space.

3. Anyone who stereotypes either sex can be called a ____.

4. The effects of stereotyping can be ____.

5. The lively tone of Berry's poem would certainly not be described as ____.

Expressing Your Ideas

Writing Choices

Writer's Notebook Update Look over comments you made before reading these poems. What issues do these comments raise? Choose one issue that seems to be universal and discuss it in your notebook.

Say What? Write a **translation** of the Berry poem, using words that seem parallel to those Berry chooses. After reading your version aloud in class, decide what the poem has gained or lost. Alternatively, if you speak a language other than English, translate one of the poems in this unit into that language. In class, discuss the difficulties in trying to **communicate** from one language to another.

Rock-a-bye Baby The word *lullaby* comes from the words *lull,* to soothe, and *bye-bye,* sleep. Write a **lullaby** that employs the soft and liquid sounds created by the consonants *l, m, n,* and *r* and by long vowels.

In Your Own Words Write a **poem** in everyday language that expresses your ideas about communicating with someone from another generation. Your word choice could include slang and idioms.

Other Options

Who Gives a Rap? With a partner, divide the lines of the Berry poem and give an **oral reading** that captures both the rhythm of the language and the attitudes of the two voices. You might cast your reading as a rap.

Seeing Eye to Eye Make a collage of words and images to suggest that generations can communicate effectively. Cut or duplicate appropriate images from magazines, and include song lyrics, ads, bumper stickers, proverbs, and your own quotes. Arrange your material on a piece of heavy paper that could be made into a **greeting card** and sent to someone special you know that belongs to another generation.

Before Reading

First Frost by Andrei Voznesensky   Russia

For Anne Gregory by William Butler Yeats   Ireland

The Fist by Derek Walcott   Trinidad

The Stone by Wilfrid Wilson Gibson   Great Britain

Building Background

Shapes of Love As old as scraps of Egyptian poetry, as new as today's popular love songs, love fascinates, infuriates, bewilders, and, occasionally, amuses us. What aspects of love do the following quotations suggest? What other things do you associate with love?

"By heaven, I do love, and it hath taught me to rhyme, and to be melancholy."   *William Shakespeare*

"Love, and a cough, cannot be hid."   *George Herbert*

"Love's like the measles—all the worse when it comes late in life."

Douglas Jerrold

"Love is much nicer to be in than an automobile accident, a tight girdle, a higher tax bracket or a holding pattern over Philadelphia."

Judith Viorst

"Love conquers all things except poverty and toothache." *Mae West*

Literary Focus

Rhythm The term **rhythm** refers to a pattern of stressed and unstressed syllables, or beats. Regular rhythm is like the beat of a waltz or a march. "The Stone," which you are about to read, has rhythm that is generally regular. In the following lines from this poem, stressed syllables are marked ´; unstressed syllables are marked ˘.

> I went to break the news to her:
> And I could hear my own heart beat
> With dread of what my lips might say;
> But some poor fool had sped before; . . .

Writer's Notebook

Loved and Lost Quickwrite your response to the following observation: " 'Tis better to have loved and lost, / Than never to have loved at all." Keep your ideas in mind as you read the following poems.

Andrei Voznesensky
born 1933

Andrei Voznesensky (än'drā väz nə sen'skē) studied architecture in Moscow, but gave up this career after his drawings were destroyed in a fire. His poetry, which is marked by musical sounds, imaginative twists in meaning, and occasional wry humor, became known in Russia during the "thaw" of the 1960s, when Soviet writers enjoyed a period of freedom of expression. An advocate of *glasnost,* or greater openness in the former Soviet Union, Voznesensky works for continued freedom of expression in Russia today.

William Butler Yeats
1865–1939

Though he was a mediocre student, William Butler Yeats listened avidly to the Irish folk tales his sailor uncles told. Because his father was an artist, Yeats studied art, but at twenty-one he quit art school and devoted himself to writing. In the 1890s, his works were influenced by his study of Irish folklore, a study that led him to support the Irish revolt against England and to write plays for Ireland's national theater. In 1923, Yeats received the Nobel Prize for literature.

Derek Walcott
born 1930

Growing up on the West Indian island of St. Lucia, Derek Walcott was both biracial and bilingual, speaking Creole at home and English at school. A major theme in his work is "the dichotomy between black and white, subject and ruler, Caribbean and Western civilization." His complicated feelings about his mixed ancestry and allegiances are expressed in one of his poems: ". . . either I'm a nobody or a nation." Walcott's rich blend of folk and formal language, includes chants, jokes, and fables. Awarded the Nobel Prize for literature in 1992, he is considered one of the great modern masters of the English language.

Wilfrid Wilson Gibson
1878–1962

By the time he was fifty, W. W. Gibson had published more than twenty-two books of poetry. His first poems were influenced by Tennyson, especially his narrative poems about King Arthur and his knights. By 1910, however, Gibson began writing poems about the dreams, fears, and hopes of common humanity—the farmers and laborers he had known as a child.

First Frost

Andrei Voznesensky

A girl is freezing in a telephone booth,
huddled in her flimsy coat,
her face stained by tears
and smeared with lipstick.

5 She breathes on her thin little fingers.
Fingers like ice. Glass beads in her ears.

She has to beat her way back alone
down the icy street.

First frost. A beginning of losses.
10 The first frost of telephone phrases.

It is the start of winter glittering on her cheek,
the first frost of having been hurt.

◄ Do you think the photographer, Burt Glinn, was more
interested in communicating a mood or depicting a person
in this photograph? Is there anything in the photo that
reveals the girl's nationality, or could she be from one of
several cultures?

For Anne Gregory

William Butler Yeats

"Never shall a young man,
Thrown into despair
By those great honey-colored
ramparts[1] at your ear,
5 Love you for yourself alone
And not your yellow hair."

"But I can get a hair-dye
And set such color there,
Brown, or black, or carrot,
10 That young men in despair
May love me for myself alone
And not my yellow hair."

"I heard an old religious man
But yesternight declare
15 That he had found a text to prove
That only God, my dear,
Could love you for yourself alone
And not your yellow hair."

---

1. **rampart** (ram′pärt), *n.* a mound of earth used to help defend a fort. Yeats uses the word to refer to coils of hair at the ears.

The Fist

Derek Walcott

The fist clenched round my heart
loosens a little, and I gasp
brightness; but it tightens
again. When have I ever not loved
5 the pain of love? But this has moved

past love to mania.[1] This has the strong
clench of the madman, this is
gripping the ledge of unreason, before
plunging howling into the abyss.[2]

10 Hold hard then, heart. This way at least you live.

---

1. **mania** (mā′nē ə), *n.* a kind of mental disorder characterized by great excitement, elation, and uncontrolled, often violent, activity.
2. **abyss** (ə bis′), *n.* bottomless or very great depth; chasm.

The Stone

Wilfrid Wilson Gibson

"And will you cut a stone for him,
To set above his head?
And will you cut a stone for him—
A stone for him?" she said.

5 Three days before, a splintered rock
Had struck her lover dead—
Had struck him in the quarry[1] dead,
Where careless of the warning call,
He loitered,[2] while the shot was fired—
10 A lively stripling, brave and tall,
And sure of all his heart desired . . .
A flash, a shock,
A rumbling fall . . .
And, broken 'neath the broken rock,
15 A lifeless heap, with face of clay,
And still as any stone he lay,
With eyes that saw the end of all.

I went to break the news to her:
And I could hear my own heart beat
20 With dread of what my lips might say;
But some poor fool had sped before;
And, flinging wide her father's door,
Had blurted out the news to her,
Had struck her lover dead for her,
25 Had struck the girl's heart dead in her,
Had struck life, lifeless, at a word,
And dropped it at her feet:

Then hurried on his witless way,
Scarce knowing she had heard.
30 And when I came, she stood alone—
A woman, turned to stone:
And, though no word at all she said,
I knew that all was known.

Because her heart was dead,
35 She did not sigh nor moan.
His mother wept:
She could not weep.
Her lover slept:
She could not sleep.
40 Three days, three nights,
She did not stir:
Three days, three nights,
Were one to her,
Who never closed her eyes
45 From sunset to sunrise,
From dawn to evenfall—
Her tearless, staring eyes,
That, seeing naught,[3] saw all.

(Continued)

---

1. **quarry** (kwôr′ē), *n.* place where stone, slate, etc., is
   dug, cut, or blasted out for use in building.
2. **loiter** (loi′tər), *v.* lingered idly or aimlessly.
3. **naught** (nôt), *n.* nothing.

This photograph by Franz Altschuler shows the delicate effects
that can be achieved by a master stonemason. What effect is
achieved by having the figure gaze downward? by having
patterns and a stern face in the background? ➤

The fourth night when I came from work,
50 I found her at my door.
"And will you cut a stone for him?"
She said: and spoke no more:
But followed me, as I went in,
And sank upon a chair;
55 And fixed her grey eyes on my face,
With still, unseeing stare.
And, as she waited patiently,
I could not bear to feel
Those still, grey eyes that followed me,
60 Those eyes that plucked the heart from me,
Those eyes that sucked the breath from me
And curdled the warm blood in me,
Those eyes that cut me to the bone,
And pierced my marrow[4] like cold steel.

65 And so I rose, and sought a stone;
And cut it, smooth and square:
And, as I worked, she sat and watched,
Beside me, in her chair.
Night after night, by candlelight,
70 I cut her lover's name:
Night after night, so still and white,
And like a ghost she came;
And sat beside me, in her chair,
And watched with eyes aflame.
75 She eyed each stroke,

And hardly stirred:
She never spoke
A single word:
And not a sound or murmur broke
80 The quiet, save the mallet-stroke.

With still eyes ever on my hands,
With eyes that seemed to burn my hands,
My wincing, overwearied hands,
She watched, with bloodless lips apart,
85 And silent, indrawn breath:
And every stroke my chisel cut,
Death cut still deeper in her heart:
The two of us were chiselling,
Together, I and death.

90 And when at length the job was done,
And I had laid the mallet by,
As if, at last, her peace were won,
She breathed his name; and, with a sigh,
Passed slowly through the open door;
95 And never crossed my threshold more.

Next night I labored late, alone,
To cut her name upon the stone.

---

4. **marrow** (mar′ō), *n.* the inmost or essential part.

After Reading

Making Connections

1. Describe how the people and situations in these poems make you feel.

Poem	Feelings

2. Do you think many people today love someone for reasons other than their "self alone"? Explain.

3. Poets write more often about lost love than about fulfilled love. Why do you think this is true?

4. How would you **characterize** the woman in "The Stone"?

5. In what way is Gibson's title both literal and **figurative**?

6. From the **imagery** of Walcott's poem, describe how the speaker feels.

7. How does Yeats use **hyperbole**, or exaggeration, in "For Anne Gregory" for humorous effect?

8. How would you describe the **tone** of each poem?

9. These poems include a number of **sound devices**. Find examples of repetition (both of consonant sounds and of words and phrases).

10. With the help of your classmates, make a list of current love songs. Divide them into two groups: fulfilled, happy love and unfulfilled, painful love. Make some generalizations about the messages in current love songs.

11. Do you think that the portrayal of romantic love in the media is realistic? In answering, think about ads, TV programs, and movies that include romantic relationships.

Literary Focus: Rhythm

Rhythm refers to the pattern of stressed and unstressed syllables in a line of poetry. Poetry that lacks a regular pattern of stresses and sounds more like everyday speech is called **free verse.**

- Which of the four poems in this group have regular rhythm? Which are free verse?

- The speaker in "The Stone" describes a woman in mourning. The speaker of "The Fist" is "gripping the edge of unreason." Do you find the rhythm of each poem suitable to its speaker? Explain.

Vocabulary Study

On your paper, next to each number write the letter of the pair of words that has the same relationship as the original pair.

abyss
loiter
marrow
naught
quarry

1. BONE : MARROW ::   **a.** vein : blood   **b.** speech : applause   **c.** hatchet : blood   **d.** frying pan : bacon

2. LOITER : LEAVE ::   **a.** banana : slip   **b.** laugh : giggle   **c.** cup : saucer   **d.** passive : active

3. QUARRY : STONE ::   **a.** eagle : prey   **b.** mine : ore   **c.** barn : stable   **d.** envelope : stamp

4. ABYSS : BOTTOMLESS DEPTH ::   **a.** moon : sun   **b.** mountain : valley   **c.** boat : island   **d.** creek : stream

5. NAUGHT : NOTHING ::   **a.** never : seldom   **b.** frequent: always   **c.** fortunate : lucky   **d.** silent : shy

Expressing Your Ideas _____

Writing Choices

Writer's Notebook Update Now that you have read these four poems, review your thoughts about having loved and lost. Write a sentence for each poem, explaining how you think the speaker or main character would respond to this quotation.

Bravo or Bah! Humbug! A newspaper editorial doesn't have to be about a burning issue or a national or international problem. As editor of your school newspaper, write an **editorial** about Valentine's Day, explaining whether or not it's a tradition you want to preserve.

Other Options

Love Triangle You work as an artist in an advertising agency. Your new client, the American Association of Candy Manufacturers, wants to replace the traditional Valentine heart. Make a **diagram** of the new shape of love. Beneath the diagram, write a caption explaining why this is a suitable representation.

Lovemobile Prepare a **mobile** featuring different views of love. You might include pictures, small items, cards, captions, fabric, quotations from poems you have just read—anything that represents for you a facet of love. Present your mobile to the class along with appropriate background music.

Heart to Heart Present your own image to suggest love, using a computer program, clay, origami, freehand—or anything else at your disposal.

Before Reading

The Other by Judith Ortiz Cofer   USA
To Julia de Burgos by Julia de Burgos   Puerto Rico
We Are Many by Pablo Neruda   Chile

Building Background

Who Am I? In wood, in marble, in paint, and in words, creators of portraits attempt to establish the identity of their subjects. Often they try to capture the complexities of a person—the different personalities within. What can you guess about the girl in this picture? Keep this painting in mind when you read the following poems about identity.

Literary Focus

Speaker Each of the three poems that follow has a **speaker**, an "I" who presents information in the first person. This "I" is not necessarily the poet, but rather the imaginary voice assumed by the poet. As you read these poems, try to identify the speaker and the speaker's tone. Both are strong clues to the meaning of each poem.

Writer's Notebook

Private "I's" You can't tell a book by its cover. Nevertheless, we tend to make judgments based on people's appearances. Have you ever thought about all those exciting people living inside their plain wrappings? Quickwrite an example of someone, from literature or real life, with a misleading appearance.

Judith Ortiz Cofer
born 1952

Judith Ortiz Cofer (ôr tēz′ kō′fər) once wrote, "My family is one of the main topics of my poetry; the ones left behind on the island of Puerto Rico, and the ones who came to the United States. In tracing their lives, I discover more about mine." As a Spanish speaker, Cofer's greatest challenge was to master English "enough to teach it and—the ultimate goal—to write poetry in it." She reached that goal before she was forty, publishing several books of poetry, a memoir titled *Silent Dancing,* a play, a book of essays, and an acclaimed novel, *The Line of the Sun.*

Julia de Burgos
1917–1953

Like Cofer, Julia de Burgos was born in Puerto Rico, the oldest of thirteen children. Her father, a farmer, often fired her imagination with tales about Napoleon and Don Quixote. When the time came for her to go to school, neighbors paid her tuition. Although a fervent nationalist, de Burgos left Puerto Rico and spent her final years as an exile in Cuba and New York.

Pablo Neruda
1904–1973

When he began publishing poetry in his teens, Ricardo Neftalí Reyes took the pen name Pablo Neruda (pä′blō nə rü′dä). An early teacher and fellow Chilean poet, Gabriela Mistral, gave him books and encouraged him to write—just as he later encouraged Julia de Burgos. Neruda became a diplomat and remained active in politics, while continuing to write. His early poems tend to be political, while his later poetry looks with humor at everyday things such as socks and watermelon, which in his words, represent "the world of objects at rest." In 1971, he received the Nobel Prize for literature.

THE OTHER

JUDITH ORTIZ COFER

A sloe-eyed[1] dark woman shadows me.
In the morning she sings
Spanish love songs in a high
falsetto,[2] filling my shower stall
5   with echoes.
She is by my side
in front of the mirror as I slip
into my tailored skirt and she
into her red cotton dress.
10 She shakes out her black mane as I
run a comb through my closely cropped[3] cap.
Her mouth is like a red bull's eye
daring me.
Everywhere I go I must
15 make room for her; she crowds me
in elevators where others wonder
at all the space I need.
At night her weight tips my bed, and
it is her wild dreams that run rampant[4]
20 through my head exhausting me. Her heartbeats,
like dozens of spiders carrying the poison
of her restlessness,
drag their countless legs
over my bare flesh.

---

1. **sloe-eyed** (slō′īd), *adj.* having very dark eyes.
2. **falsetto** (fôl set′ō), *n.* an artificially high-pitched
   voice, especially in a man.
3. **cropped** (kropt), *adj.* cut short; clipped.
4. **rampant** (ram′pənt), *adj.* growing without any limits.

TO JULIA DE BURGOS

JULIA DE BURGOS

The word is out that I am your enemy
        that in my poetry I am giving you away.

        They lie, Julia de Burgos. They lie, Julia de Burgos.
    That voice that rises in my poems is not yours: it is my voice;
5   you are the covering and I the essence;[1]
    and between us lies the deepest chasm.

        You are the frigid[2] doll of social falsehood,
    and I, the virile[3] sparkle of human truth.

        You are honey of courtly hypocrisy,[4] not I;
10 I bare my heart in all my poems.

        You are selfish, like your world, not I;
    I gamble everything to be what I am.

        You are but the grave lady, ladylike;
    not I; I am life, and strength, and I am woman.

15   You belong to your husband, your master, not I;
    I belong to no one or to everyone, because to all, to all
    I give myself in pure feelings and in my thoughts.

        You curl your hair, and paint your face, not I;
    I am curled by the wind, painted by the sun.

20   You are lady of the house, resigned and meek,
    tied to the prejudices of men, not I;
    smelling the horizons of the justice of God.
    I am Rocinante,[5] running headlong.

---

1. **essence** (es′ns), *n.* that which makes a thing what it is;
   important feature or features.
2. **frigid** (frij′id), *adj.* cold in feeling or manner.
3. **virile** (vir′əl), *adj.* vigorous, forceful.
4. **hypocrisy** (hi pok′rə sē), *n.* pretense.
5. **Rocinante** (rō sē nän′tā), the broken-down but spirited
   horse of Don Quixote (dōn kē hō′tā) in the classic Spanish
   novel, *Don Quixote de la Mancha*, by Miguel de Cervantes.

Oil on copper is the medium for Frida Kahlo's 1942 work titled *Portrait of Marucha Lavin.* What things in the portrait **communicate** clues to the culture and character of the woman depicted? ➤

WE ARE MANY

PABLO NERUDA

Of the many men who I am, who we are,
I can't find a single one;
they disappear among my clothes,
they have left for another city.

5 When everything seems to be set
to show me off as intelligent,
the fool I always keep hidden
takes over all that I say.

At other times, I'm asleep
10 among distinguished people,
and when I look for my brave self,
a coward unknown to me
rushes to cover my skeleton
with a thousand fine excuses.

15 When a decent house catches fire,
instead of the fireman I summon,
an arsonist bursts on the scene,
and that's me. What can I do?
What can I do to distinguish myself?
20 How can I pull myself together?

All the books I read
are full of dazzling heroes,
always sure of themselves.
I die with envy of them:

25 and in films full of wind and bullets,
I goggle[1] at the cowboys,
I even admire the horses.

But when I call for a hero,
out comes my lazy old self;
30 so I never know who I am,
nor how many I am or will be.
I'd love to be able to touch a bell
and summon the real me,
because if I really need myself,
35 I mustn't disappear.

While I am writing, I am far away;
and when I come back, I've gone.

I would like to know if others
go through the same things that I do,
40 have as many selves as I have,
and see themselves similarly;
and when I have exhausted this problem,
I am going to study so hard
that when I explain myself,
45 I will be talking geography.

---

1. **goggle** (gog′əl), *v.* stare with bulging eyes.

◄ Diana Ong's work is titled *Parts Equal the Whole III*. Do you
think the title of Neruda's poem would have been just as
suitable for the picture? Explain.

After Reading

Making Connections

Shaping Your
Response

1. Do the people in these poems reveal serious personality problems, or do you think "split personalities" of this kind are typical of people in general? Explain.

2. Julia de Burgos says, ". . . you are the covering and I the essence." How would you distinguish people's covering from their essence?

3. If you could be any one of these **speakers** or alter egos, whom would you choose and why?

4. How do you think each of these three speakers would answer the question, "Who Am I?"

Analyzing the Poems

5. State a **theme** that these three poems have in common.

6. All but one of the stanzas in Neruda's poem are four to eight lines. What clues does the two-line stanza (lines 36-37) provide about the **character** of the speaker?

7. Choose three examples of **figurative language** or **imagery** from these poems that you think are effective and explain why you like them.

8. Do you find the **tone** of these poems similar? Explain.

9. How does the **allusion** to Rocinante help characterize Julia de Burgos?

Extending the Ideas

10. Many entertainment celebrities or political figures hire image makers—public relations specialists who create an image for their clients. Discuss whether public figures today have, as Neruda worries, lost the ability to "summon the real me."

11. In books, TV shows, and movies there are often characters who present a double image or a false front. Work with a group to present some of these stories to the class. Encourage the class to discuss why these posers, dreamers, and deceivers make such interesting reading and viewing.

Literary Focus: Speaker

Answer the following questions about the **speakers**—the imaginary voices the poets have chosen to "tell" the poems.

- In Cofer's poem, how does the "sloe-eyed woman" differ from the speaker?

- Is the speaker in "To Julia de Burgos" like or unlike the speaker in Cofer's poem? Explain.

- Choose five words to characterize the speaker in "We Are Many."

Vocabulary Study

cropped
essence
falsetto
frigid
hypocrisy
rampant
virile

Write five different sentences that might be found in a fortune cookie, answering the question, "Who am I?" Use at least one of the vocabulary words in each sentence.

Expressing Your Ideas

Writing Choices

Writer's Notebook Update Review your quickwrite. Then write a brief poem with your described person acting as speaker and telling about his or her secret self.

An Arsonist Bursts on the Scene Choose one of the following lines from these poems as the title of a best-selling novel: *The Fool I Always Keep Hidden; I Goggle at the Cowboys; She Crowds Me in Elevators; The Word Is Out That I Am Your Enemy; I Will Be Talking Geography.* You have been asked to write a paragraph that praises or pans this novel. Use your imagination to write a rousing **review**!

Petite Grandma Out-muscles Burglar Sometimes people say or do things that seem "out of character." In a **news story** that might appear in the *National Wow,* describe a person who has acted or done something out of character. Conclude by trying to account for the person's behavior.

Other Options

Another Angle Look again at the picture on page 577. Draw a **picture** of yourself in a similar style that reflects different aspects of your personality.

Personality Splits The speakers of the three poems in this section are to appear on a popular television **talk show**, discussing their secret selves. What will they say? How will the audience react? What will the host or hostess say or do? As a group, present a segment from the show in class.

Getting to Know You At the first campfire of the season, you must introduce yourself to the other campers. Deliver a one- to two-minute **speech of introduction**. Use one of the following topics or one of your own. Remember, your introduction doesn't have to be serious.

- "No one would think that I. . . ."
- "An experience I wish I hadn't had is. . . ."
- "No one knows I'm good at. . . ."

Connections

It's All Family

History Connection
Many of the poems in this group explore the relationships between family members. The following pages offer a comparison between a colonial family and contemporary TV families.

"Reading" a Family Portrait

by Caroline Sloat

Joseph Lauriston Moore was eleven years old when he and his family were painted by Erastus Salisbury Field in Ware, Massachusetts, just a few miles down the road from where Old Sturbridge Village is located today. Family records have provided us with some information about the Moores, but the portrait painted a century and a half ago tells its own story in a way no written record could.

The Moore family was smaller than many in Ware at that time. In fact, the two children standing beside the mother were cousins and had only recently come to live with the family after their own mother had died in 1838. The boy, Frederick Babbit Cook (standing far left), was four years old, and the girl, Louisa Ellen, was two. Joseph's younger brother, George Francis (center, next to father), was also four. Little Louisa Ellen is wearing a white dress, but everyone else is dressed in black, perhaps in mourning over a relative's death.

Unlike the Moores' dark clothes, however, the furnishings in the portrait are bright and cheerful. The carpet design is bright red and green on a light background, and extends from wall to wall as was the fashion. The green shutters are closed. Perhaps the artist painted them that way so that he could include an additional color, or the shutters may actually have been closed to keep the summer sun from fading the carpet.

Mr. Moore is sitting casually on the fancy Hitchcock-type chair so that we can see a part of the bright stenciled decoration. The wood in both the looking glass and the square-topped work table beneath it is decorated in a fashionable style called graining.

Joseph's suit resembles the one his father is wearing. His white shirt is tied with a black neck cloth, whose ribbons are left hanging from the bow–unlike his father's bow which is tied. Young Joseph's jacket is also like his father's but cut short in a manner worn by boys of his age. Four-year-old Frederick, while old enough to handle a pocket knife to whittle

a stick, wears a long, loose coat called a surtout. Louisa Ellen is wearing pantalettes and a long dress.

Mrs. Almira Moore has arranged her hair elaborately for the portrait, with a tortoise shell comb stuck into a bun at the back of her head. The corkscrew curls on either side of her face, adding a touch of elegance, may well have been store bought. Needle in hand, Mrs. Moore looks as if she is so busy sewing that she could not stop even for her portrait. She probably made clothes for the entire family, including the embroidered collar she is wearing. Her choice to wear the collar and to include the sewing items tells us that she wanted the portrait to show her as an expert needlewoman.

Joseph's father belonged to the group of tradesmen and craftsmen called artisans who were beginning to set up their shops in New England town centers. He made silk hats in the winter, probably working at home, and traveled to neighboring towns as a dentist in the summer.

Like his mother, Joseph Lauriston holds an object meant to tell us something about who he is—a schoolbook he probably used in a one-room school with students ranging in age from four to nineteen, all working at different levels.

The Industrial Revolution changed Ware just as it changed many other New England towns, altering the lives of the people who lived there. But when Erastus Salisbury Field painted the Moore family portrait, he captured a history for us to enjoy.

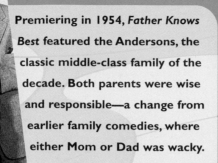

Premiering in 1954, *Father Knows Best* featured the Andersons, the classic middle-class family of the decade. Both parents were wise and responsible—a change from earlier family comedies, where either Mom or Dad was wacky.

The Cleavers of *Leave It to Beaver* were another model family like the Andersons. What was new here was presenting domestic life from the perspective of young Theodore "Beaver" Cleaver, seven years old when the series began in 1957.

TV Families

The Brady Bunch, which premiered in 1969, featured the populous Bradys, one of the last of the idealized television families that were staples of '50s and '60s situation comedies.

The Jetsons was a cartoon from the early '60s about a middle-class family of the future. Yet it was a look backward in its stereotypes: goofy Dad, ditzy Mom, airhead teenage daughter, nerdy son.

The Cosby Show, which premiered in 1984, introduced the Huxtables, another affluent television family. The big difference was that they were black.

Premiering in 1988, Roseanne broke new ground in television situation comedy by featuring a working-class family, the Connors, and a foul-mouthed Mom who was a long way from June Cleaver.

The '90s cartoon series titled The Simpsons, set in a fictional community called Springfield, introduced bizarre, sometimes irreverent characters and keen social satire.

Responding

1. With a team, research what a New England family living 150 years ago ate, read, and did for entertainment. Present your findings to the class.

2. Write a description of one of the TV families pictured – or another TV family of your choice – that would provide insights into contemporary families for readers 150 years from now.

3. Do you think TV presents an accurate portrayal of modern families? Why or why not?

Writing Workshop

Not-So-Ancient History

Assignment You have read about family life in different countries and generations. Now work in a small group to put together a picture of life as it was lived in another time not so long ago.

WRITER'S BLUEPRINT

Product   An illustrated interview
Purpose   To show what life was like for a teenager in the recent past
Audience   Family and friends of your subject
Specs   As the creators of a successful project, your group should:

❏ Choose someone over fifty whom one of you knows well and who is willing to be interviewed. Interview your subject about life when he or she was a teenager, using questions you've worked out in advance.

❏ Gather appropriate visuals, such as photographs and home movies of your subject as a teenager, and magazine pictures, newspaper headlines, phonograph records, and movie posters from the period.

❏ Write a brief introduction giving a few basic facts about your subject. Then write up your interview, using the most interesting and informative parts and omitting the rest. Use a question-answer or narrative format. Make sure your readers can visualize your subject.

❏ Conclude by commenting on whether you would have preferred to be a teenager now or when your subject was a teenager, and why.

❏ Assemble your written and illustrative materials in the most effective way you can.

❏ Follow the rules of grammar, usage, spelling, and mechanics. Take special care to avoid spelling mistakes with homophones and to punctuate direct quotations correctly.

Brainstorm a list of subjects. In your group, list possible subjects for this project. The subject should be over fifty, known personally by at least one member of the group, and willing to work with you. Consider family members, neighbors, or acquaintances who like to talk about the past.

As a group, choose a person you would like to interview. Contact this person right away and be sure he or she is willing to participate.

Do research on the years when your subject was a teenager. Use newspapers and magazines from the period. Use your research to make a time line of historical events that took place during your subject's teenage years and use it to help prepare your list of questions for the interview.

Plan the interview. Working in your group, develop the questions you'll be asking when you interview your subject. Prepare questions like these:

- **General questions:** *What were teenagers like then?*

- **Specific questions**, about details of the general question: *Describe how the teenagers you went around with dressed and wore their hair.*

- **Follow-up questions** to expand on the information in the specific questions: *Did you have cliques and in-groups at your school like we have now? What were they like?*

- **Historical questions:** *Where were you when you heard that John F. Kennedy had been shot? How did you react?*

> **OR . . .**
> Ask your subject about what sorts of questions he or she would like to be asked about his or her life as a teenager.

Divide up the tasks—interviewing, gathering visuals, writing the introduction, body, and conclusion—among group members. Or you might work closely as a group on all these tasks. A successful group project needs careful planning, dedication, and cooperation from everyone.

Interview your subject. See the Beyond Print article on page 595 for information on planning and conducting a successful interview.

Gather visual materials. Locate photos or home movies of your subject that your group could borrow for the presentation. Gather pictures from magazines, movie posters, music, artifacts, and other items that present a picture of the period when your subject was a teenager.

Make an inventory of important facts about your subject and about the historical period. Include where and when your subject was born, anecdotes he or she told you, personality traits, and a physical description. Include facts about what life was like when your subject was a teenager. Look back at your inventory and star the points you want to focus on when you write.

STEP 2 DRAFTING

Before you draft, decide whether you will write up the interview in **question-answer format:**
Q: Was high school all work, or was there fun too?
A: "Well, let me think. . . ."

or in **narrative format:**
Mr. Watson told us more about crewcuts. Then we asked him to tell us more about how students looked then.

"Well," he said, raising his coffee cup halfway to his mouth and pausing, "I suppose nowadays those pants with the little buckles on the back look pretty silly, but back then. . . ."

If you decide on a narrative format, read about using direct quotes and paraphrases in the Revising Strategy in Step 3 of this lesson.

As you draft, carefully pick out the best parts of the interview—the most informative and interesting—and delete the rest. You might do this as a group.

STEP 3 REVISING

Ask another group to comment on your draft before you revise it. Use this checklist as a guide.

✔ Does the introduction state enough basic facts about the subject to give the reader a good idea of who the subject is?

✔ Does the interview use direct quotes and paraphrases effectively?

Revising Strategy

Quoting Directly and Paraphrasing

A **direct quote** states the speaker's exact words:

> "No, in those days I didn't think much about styles. I was conservative, I guess you'd say."

A **paraphrase** is a summary of what was said:

> Mr. Watson said that his own clothing styles were conservative.

Paraphrase when you want to conserve space or when you want to express ideas more clearly or concisely than your subject may have stated them.

A narrative format consists of a mixture of direct quotes, paraphrases, and description:

> Mr. Watson raised a hand to his forehead. "I remember the time we sailed around the whole lake. It took us all day," he said, smiling. "Were we ever sore!" He explained that his boat had lost a vital part along the way that made steering difficult. "We zigged and zagged all over. . . ."

Notice how this writer paraphrased part of the interview.

I asked what kinds of peer pressure Cynthia Roberts faced
that teenagers didn't experience peer pressure because all the
during her teenage years. She replied, "~~They didn't have peer~~
parents in the neighborhood took a role in keeping them out of
~~pressure back then because everyone's parents were alike. Any one~~
trouble.
~~of them could chastise you. If you got caught doing something you~~

~~shouldn't be doing, they could yell at you and if they took you~~

~~home you'd get yelled at again, so there was no peer pressure.~~

Ask another group to review your revised draft before you edit. When you edit, look for errors in grammar, usage, spelling, and mechanics. Make sure you have spelled homophones correctly.

Editing Strategy

Spelling Homophones Correctly

Homophones are words that sound alike and are spelled similarly, but do not have the same meaning. You can avoid misspelling these words in your writing by connecting their meanings with their spellings in companion sentences. For example:

it's, its: <u>It's</u> (it is) fun to remember my first car, a convertible. It lost <u>its</u> muffler on a bumpy road.

your, you're: <u>Your</u> question seems strange. <u>You're</u> the first one to ask it.

> **COMPUTER TIP**
> A spell checker won't catch a homophone mistake, like substituting *it's* for *its*. Proofread your writing carefully for spelling, whether you have a spell checker or not.

STEP 5 PRESENTING

Integrate your materials. Put the visual materials you have gathered with the introduction and interview you've written up. Arrange and rearrange your materials to get them in the order that most effectively tells your subject's story. Here are some ideas:

- If you taped the interview, play portions of it during your presentation, so the class can hear your subject's actual voice.

- Give a copy of the project to your subject.

STEP 6 LOOKING BACK

Self-evaluate. Look back at the Writer's Blueprint and give your paper a score for each item, from 6 (superior) to 1 (inadequate).

Reflect. Write answers to these questions.

✔ What three things stand out to you most about the differences between being a teenager then and now?

✔ Did you learn anything surprising or memorable—either about the times or the person—from your interview?

For Your Working Portfolio Add a copy of your group's project and your reflection responses to your working portfolio.

Beyond Print

Conducting an Interview

Books and media are great ways to get information, but occasionally you will want to get it straight from a person! In an interview, you can choose just the right person—a recent immigrant, a Vietnam veteran, a day-care worker—and personally design your questions to get the information you need. Imagine you are interviewing an immigrant. Determine if you will need a translator. Consider asking questions like these.

1. What is unique about your background?

2. What were the most difficult adjustments you had to make?

3. What family customs and celebrations do you still observe?

4. What connections do you still maintain with your old country?

Listening Tips

You've chosen a person to interview, set up the time and place, jotted down questions, and arrived on time with a tape recorder or pencil and paper. Now what? Here are some tips for effective listening.

- **Focus your attention on what the speaker says, not on how he or she says it.** People may speak in different dialects or accents, at different rates, and at different decibels. Try to ignore the verbal habits of the speaker, and concentrate on what is being said.

- **Maintain eye contact and watch your posture.** Focus on the speaker, don't slouch, and don't fiddle with pen or paper.

- **Be patient.** Allow time for your interviewee to recall events or to find the right words. Ask another question only after you have gotten a complete answer to the previous one.

Activity Options

1. Review the interview on page 260. What are three additional questions you might ask Tamara Camp about analyzing evidence?

2. Think of someone you'd like to interview. Write four questions you would ask.

Part Two

Reflections

Finding your place in the world requires careful reflection and informed decisions about where you're going and how to get there.

🐾 **Multicultural Connection** **Choice** is often influenced by the cultural values of the society or smaller groups in which we live. We must learn to make informed choices that both reflect cultural insights and overcome cultural restraints.

Before Reading

Sunday Morning by Oscar Peñaranda USA
Some Keep the Sabbath by Emily Dickinson USA

Oscar Peñaranda
born 1944

Born in the Philippines, Oscar Peñaranda (pen yə rän′də) teaches high school in California. He identifies the site of "Sunday Morning" as China Beach in San Francisco, "where they shooed the Chinese to live, in tents and shanties."

Emily Dickinson
1830–1886

"How can you print a piece of your own soul?" So said Emily Dickinson, whose brilliant unconventional, and intensely personal poems indeed revealed an unusual soul.

Building Background

Sundays and Special Days For Jews, Saturday, the Sabbath, is a holy day of rest, worship services, and special meals. Orthodox Jews do not work, travel, or carry money on the Sabbath. On Fridays, Muslims, who practice Islam, are expected to attend noon prayers at a mosque. For practicing Christians, Sunday has traditionally been a day of prayer and rest. Yet with the 7-day work week, 24-hour convenience stores, and "Sunday Special" sales, Sunday has lost some of its traditional associations. Nevertheless, certain communities still have "blue laws" that control activities such as liquor sales on Sundays. Do you think there should be legal measures to set Sundays apart from other days? Why or why not?

Literary Focus

Assonance The repetition of vowel sounds followed by different consonant sounds in stressed syllables or words is called **assonance** (made/pale; hit/miss). Assonance is one of several sound devices that poets use to reinforce meaning and unify ideas.

Writer's Notebook

> **REFLECTION**
> an idea or remark resulting from careful thinking

Taking a Careful Look Make a list of the places where you go to reflect. Then examine the list and write down the qualities or characteristics that draw you to those places. As you read the two poems that follow, record descriptions of the places in which the speakers like to reflect.

Sunday Morning

(for my elders)

Oscar Peñaranda

Here I am again
sitting alone in my car
nostrils and mouth sucking wafts[1]
of wind rushing through open side windows
5 on a cliff hanging over the bay there is
music from the radio

That green monster of a gelatin sea
hisses white tongues of foam kneeling
to lick the shore serenading the lone
10 oak tree
atop the jagged crags[2] of rocks there
is music there also

they drown the chimes of distant chapel bells

come, take my hand
15 roll up your sleeves
and bare your chests before the naked sun

but

what I want to know is where
they ever got the barbaric[3] gall
20 to call me
an unbeliever

this is how I pray

---

1. **waft** (waft), *n.* breath or puff of air, wind, or scent.
2. **crag** (krag), *n.* steep, rugged rock or cliff rising above others.
3. **barbaric** (bär bar′ik), *adj.* not civilized; coarse.

Would *Sunday Morning* be a good title for this photograph by Ansel Adams? Explain why it would make an appropriate title, or provide another title and tell why you think it would be better. ➤

Some Keep the Sabbath

Emily Dickinson

Some keep the Sabbath going to Church—
I keep it, staying at Home—
With a Bobolink for a Chorister—
And an Orchard, for a Dome—

5 Some keep the Sabbath in Surplice[1]—
I just wear my Wings—
And instead of tolling the Bell, for Church,
Our little Sexton[2]—sings.

God preaches, a noted Clergyman—
10 And the sermon is never long,
So instead of getting to Heaven, at last—
I'm going, all along.

---

1. **surplice** (sėr′plis), *n.* a broad-sleeved, white gown or
vestment worn by members of the clergy and choir
singers.
2. **sexton** (sek′stən), *n.* person who takes care of a
church building.

After Reading

Making Connections

Shaping Your Response

1. With which speaker in the poems would you prefer to spend a Sunday? Why?

2. Do you think the speakers in these poems would agree on how to spend a Sunday? Why or why not?

3. Do these two works fit your idea of what a poem should be? Explain.

Analyzing the Poems

4. Do you think these poems share a common **theme**? Explain.

5. What **image**, or word picture, do you have of the sea in "Sunday Morning"?

6. How does the speaker's **tone** change in "Sunday Morning," starting in line 17?

7. How do you interpret the final two lines of Dickinson's poem?

Extending the Ideas

8. When the first volume of Dickinson's poems was published in 1890, an editor "smoothed rhymes, regularized meter, and substituted 'sensible' metaphors." If you were reprinting "Some Keep the Sabbath," which appears here in its original form, would you want to make any changes? Explain.

9. Dickinson explained that poetry had the power to make her feel "as if the top of my head were taken off." What do you think she meant? What effect do you think a good poem should have on readers?

Literary Focus: Assonance

The repetition of similar vowel sounds followed by different consonant sounds, usually in stressed syllables, is called **assonance**. Assonance differs from rhyme, in which both vowel and consonant sounds are similar. For example, *wild* and *child* are rhyming words; *mild* and *white* illustrate assonance. Like other sound devices, assonance helps create a unified effect and can reinforce meaning.

- What long vowel sound appearing in line 2 is repeated throughout the first two stanzas of "Sunday Morning"?

- How does this sound suggest the speaker's feeling of excitement and freedom?

Vocabulary Study

Write the letter of the word that is *least* closely related in meaning to the first word.

barbaric
crag
sexton
surplice
waft

1. *crag*   **a.** gully   **b.** cliff   **c.** peak
2. *waft*   **a.** gale   **b.** whiff   **c.** puff
3. *barbaric*   **a.** coarse   **b.** cultured   **c.** uncivilized
4. *surplice*   **a.** robe   **b.** undershirt   **c.** vestment
5. *sexton*   **a.** singer   **b.** caretaker   **c.** church custodian

Expressing Your Ideas

Writing Choices

Writer's Notebook Update In your notebook, compare the places where the speakers of the poems reflect with the places where you like to reflect.

Reflections of My Mind Use either of these "Sunday" poems as a model to write a **poem** about a time and place in which you reflect. Try to use assonance to help convey a mood.

Literary Self-Portrait An author once wrote to Emily Dickinson asking for her photograph. He received the following written reply: "I have no portrait, now, but am small, like the Wren, and my Hair is bold, like the Chestnut Bur, and my eyes, like the Sherry in the Glass, that the Guest leaves." Reflect on your image in a mirror. Then write a **description** of your own appearance in Dickinson's style, using some figurative language and—if you wish—unconventional capitalization.

Other Options

Daily Reflections In *The Meaning of Culture*, John Cowper Powys wrote, "Without long, lovely moments spent in day-dreams life becomes an iron-ribbed, sterile puffing machine." With a partner or a small group make up your own observations about life that will cause a reader to reflect. Then use a computer program to make a **monthly calendar** of the sayings, or copy the sayings and statements by hand onto a ready-made calendar.

Stamp of Approval
The United States Postal Service issued this commemorative stamp in honor of Emily Dickinson. What poet would you like to honor with a commemorative stamp? Remember that writers of song lyrics can be considered poets too. Nominate your candidate in a **persuasive speech**—complete with a poster-size mock-up of your stamp design.

Dance a Poem Convey the mood and images of "Sunday Morning" in **dance** form. You might want to use props such as scarves, a fan, or bells to help achieve a desired effect.

Before Reading

Ceremony by Leslie Marmon Silko   USA   **from** Ecclesiastes, the Bible

A Story by Czeslaw Milosz   Poland/USA

The Road Not Taken by Robert Frost   USA

Building Background

And That Has Made All the Difference What has made a difference in shaping your life? Perhaps it is your heritage, your religion, your family or close friends, your interests and activities, your environment, or an event or decision. With a group, brainstorm things in your own lives and in the lives of historical figures that have determined events, shaped outcomes, and "made all the difference."

Literary Focus

Symbol Something concrete, such as an object, a person, a place, or an event, that represents something abstract, such as an idea, a quality, a concept, or a

Symbol	Thing Represented
skull and crossbones	poison

condition, is called a **symbol**. Some of the symbols pictured below have particular cultural significance. Work with a partner to add other symbols, completing a chart such as the one started here.

Writer's Notebook

Life Lines When you finish watching a movie or a television show or reading an article, you may remember a certain line that has special meaning for you. The poems you are about to read deal with special things—traditions, decisions, and insights—that have made a difference. After you have read the poems, jot down what you think is the most significant line in each.

Leslie Marmon Silko
born 1948

Leslie Marmon Silko's 1977 novel, *Ceremony*, which demonstrates her gift of storytelling and depicts life on an Indian reservation, helped establish her as an important Native American voice in literature. Raised in the Laguna Pueblo in New Mexico, she was introduced to a rich oral tradition at an early age. One critic has called Silko "without question . . . the most accomplished Indian writer of her generation." She is associated with the University of Albuquerque and is an assistant professor of English at the University of Arizona, Tucson. Silko observes that in order to recognize "the power of what we share, we must understand how different we are, too."

Czeslaw Milosz
born 1911

Nobel Prize laureate Czeslaw Milosz (ches′lô mē′wosh), who was born in Lithuania and raised in Poland, became a leader of the new poetry movement in Poland during the 1930s and worked for the Polish Resistance during World War II. His writings of a tragic past affirm the value of human life. One critic says "Milosz is eloquent in his call for a literature grounded in moral, as well as esthetic, values." Milosz, who now lives in the United States, tells aspiring poets to "read good poetry." He explains, "I have been taught by history, if you are completely cornered, if you have no way out except to give vent to your moral indignation, then you write poems."

Robert Frost
1874–1963

Robert Frost observed about literature: "You learn first to know what you see and to put fresh words to it," a process he termed "sights and insights." After getting married and graduating from Harvard, Frost struggled for years to get his poetry published. Discouraged, he moved with his family to England where, three days after receiving Frost's manuscript, a publisher agreed to release his work. When Frost returned to the United States, he was already famous for his fresh, original poetry. Asked to define the process of writing poetry, Frost explained that a "definition of poetry is dawn—that it's something dawning on you while you're writing it."

These Mimbres bowls have been ceremonially "killed" by having a hole made at the base before being placed in a grave. What does this custom suggest about the role of art in Mimbres culture? ➤

CEREMONY

LESLIE MARMON SILKO

I will tell you something about stories,
[he said]
They aren't just entertainment.
Don't be fooled.
5   They are all we have, you see,
all we have to fight off
illness and death.

You don't have anything
if you don't have the stories.

10   Their evil is mighty
but it can't stand up to our stories.
So they try to destroy the stories
let the stories be confused or forgotten.
They would like that
15   They would be happy
Because we would be defenseless then.

He rubbed his belly.
I keep them here
[he said]
20   Here, put your hand on it
See, it is moving.
There is life here
for the people.

And in the belly of this story
25   the rituals and the ceremony
are still growing.

A STORY

CZESLAW MILOSZ

Now I will tell Meader's story; I have a moral in view.
He was pestered by a grizzly so bold and malicious[1]
That he used to snatch caribou meat from the eaves of the cabin.
Not only that. He ignored men and was unafraid of fire.
5 One night he started battering the door
And broke the window with his paw, so they curled up
With their shotguns beside them, and waited for the dawn.
He came back in the evening, and Meader shot him at close range,
Under the left shoulder blade. Then it was jump and run,
10 A real storm of a run: A grizzly, Meader says,
Even when he's been hit in the heart, will keep running
Until he falls down. Later, Meader found him
By following the trail—and then he understood
What lay behind the bear's odd behavior:
15 Half of the beast's jaw was eaten away by an abscess,[2] and caries.
Toothache, for years. An ache without comprehensible[3] reason,
Which often drives us to senseless action
And gives us blind courage. We have nothing to lose,
20 We come out of the forest, and not always with the hope
That we will be cured by some dentist from heaven.

---

1. **malicious** (mə lish′əs), *adj.* showing ill will; spiteful.
2. **abscess** (ab′ses), *n.* pus resulting from infected tissues of the body.
3. **comprehensible** (kom′pri hen′sə bəl), *adj.* understandable.

THE ROAD NOT TAKEN

ROBERT FROST

Two roads diverged[1] in a yellow wood,
And sorry I could not travel both
And be one traveler, long I stood
And looked down one as far as I could
5 To where it bent in the undergrowth;

Then took the other, as just as fair,
And having perhaps the better claim,
Because it was grassy and wanted wear;
Though as for that, the passing there
10 Had worn them really about the same,

And both that morning equally lay
In leaves no step had trodden black.
Oh! I kept the first for another day!
Yet knowing how way leads on to way,
15 I doubted if I should ever come back.

I shall be telling this with a sigh
Somewhere ages and ages hence:
Two roads diverged in a wood, and I—
I took the one less traveled by,
20 And that has made all the difference.

---

1. **diverge** (də vėrj′), *v.* move or lie in different
   directions from the same point.

ECCLESIASTES

THE BIBLE

To every thing there is a season, and a time to every purpose
    under the heaven.
A time to be born, and a time to die: a time to plant, and a time
    to pluck[1] up that which is planted:
A time to kill, and a time to heal: a time to break down, and a
    time to build up:
A time to weep, and a time to laugh: a time to mourn, and a time
    to dance:
5 A time to cast away stones, and a time to gather stones together:
    a time to embrace, and a time to refrain from embracing:
A time to get, and a time to lose: a time to keep and a time to cast
    away:
A time to rend,[2] and a time to sew: a time to keep silence, and a time to speak:
A time to love, and a time to hate: a time of war, and a time of peace.

---

1. **pluck** (pluk), *v.* pull or tug.
2. **rend** (rend), *v.* tear or pull apart.

This detail of a mandala, or symbolic circle, from a ceiling
painting of an Indian palace depicts the cycle of seasons. How
does this picture reinforce the message of Ecclesiastes? ➤

After Reading

Making Connections

Shaping Your Response

1. What music or style of music would you choose as background for an oral reading of each poem?

2. Work with classmates to pose for a tableau, or frozen picture, that captures a scene or a mood from one of the poems. Ask other classmates to guess which poem your tableau represents.

3. In your notebook, write a word or phrase to describe your thoughts about each poem.

Analyzing the Poems

4. Now that you know Leslie Silko grew up on a Pueblo Indian reservation in New Mexico, **infer** what you think the stories in "Ceremony" are about.

5. What do you think the **moral** of "A Story" is?

6. Describe the **personification** of the bear in lines 17-21 of "A Story."

7. How would you describe the **tone** of "The Road Not Taken"?

8. How does the **repetition** in the excerpt from Ecclesiastes reinforce the **theme** of the poem?

Extending the Ideas

9. What insights could the ending of "A Story" provide for certain professionals such as counselors and social workers who work with troubled people?

10. To what degree do you think the **choices** people make are determined by their cultural values and backgrounds? In answering, focus on a major decision—marriage, career, lifestyle—and try to think through the steps you would take in making choices.

Literary Focus: Symbol

Literary **symbols**—concrete things that represent abstractions—allow readers to make associations and arrive at meaning. For example, in "A Poison Tree" by William Blake on page 288, the effects of hatred are represented by a tree that bears poison fruit.

• In your opinion, what do the diverging roads in "The Road Not Taken" symbolize?

• The passage from Ecclesiastes was made into a song titled "Turn! Turn! Turn!" What do you think the circular motion suggested by the title might symbolize about life?

• What do you think the bear's ache, which drives him to senseless action, suggests?

Vocabulary Study

Word analogy tests require you to understand the relationship between word pairs. For example, rend : mend :: separate : unite. Study the relationship of the following pairs of words in capital letters; then choose another pair that has the same relationship.

abscess
comprehensible
diverge
malicious
pluck

1. COMPREHENSIBLE : UNDERSTANDABLE :: **a.** visible : hidden **b.** jolly : ridiculous **c.** reluctant : hesitant **d.** athletic : fast

2. GARDEN : PLUCK :: **a.** mall : shop **b.** chicken : feathers **c.** weed : flower **d.** kitchen : dishes

3. MALICIOUS : SPITEFUL :: **a.** big : frightening **b.** valuable : rare **c.** illiterate : ignorant **d.** happy : joyous

4. DIVERGE : MERGE :: **a.** rip : mend **b.** eat : digest **c.** cheat : swindle **d.** hide : conceal

5. INFECTION : ABSCESS :: **a.** sore : wound **b.** virus : cold **c.** brook : flow **d.** joke : smile

Expressing Your Ideas

Writing Choices

Writer's Notebook Update Take a look at the favorite lines you copied down. Then in your notebook, explain why each line stands out in your mind.

Passing the Baton Leslie Marmon Silko tells of the importance that stories play in passing on the traditions, customs, rituals, and beliefs of Native Americans. How will future generations of your family learn about their heritage? Share the importance of one of your traditions or customs in a **poem**.

Dear Gabby How do you make difficult decisions? Why not ask "Dear Gabby" in her **advice column**? Write two questions that deal with making tough choices. Then exchange questions with a partner and answer the questions as "Dear Gabby" might in her advice column.

Other Options

Pass the Torch Find out about the customs, beliefs, activities, foods, and types of clothing that have been passed in your family from generation to generation. As a class, collect information and artifacts that reveal heritage. Display this information at a **Heritage Fest** and invite other classes to view the display.

Music for All Seasons In the 1960s, musician Pete Seeger adapted the words from Ecclesiastes into a song titled "Turn! Turn! Turn!" Play a **recording** of Seeger's song for the class and pantomime the words.

Words to Live By You can spread your own "words of wisdom." What pointers about life do you want to share with a friend, classmate, or a younger brother or sister? Write at least five brief messages about life and compile them in a **booklet** entitled "Five Things That Can Make All the Difference." Illustrate your messages.

Before Reading

This Is a Photograph of Me by Margaret Atwood   Canada

Water Picture by May Swenson   USA

Six Haiku by Matsuo Bashō and Yosa Buson   Japan

Building Background

Snapshots The poems that follow highlight the beauty and mysteries of nature. As you read each poem, you will notice that the descriptions have a photographic quality, almost as if the writer had taken a snapshot of the scene and translated it into words.

Just as there are photographic qualities in poems, there are poetic elements in photographs. Examine the photograph on pages 654-655. Work with a partner to look at elements of the picture and describe them, filling out a chart like the one here. Save your chart for later use.

Elements of Photograph	Examples
Main focal point	
Background details	
Mood	
Point of view	

Literary Focus

Simile A figure of speech involving a direct comparison between two unlike things and using words such as *like* and *as* is called a **simile**: "Her laugh was like running water." Writers use similes to draw attention to similar qualities or feelings that two unlike people, places, or things share.

Writer's Notebook

Details Big and Small Jot down details in the following poems that would make an interesting picture. Then select one detail and illustrate it in your notebook.

Margaret Atwood
born 1939

Margaret Atwood—known for her novels, short stories, television plays, children's books, critical works, and poetry—considers it an advantage that she did not attend a full year of school until she was in eighth grade. Born in Ottawa, Canada, she grew up in the Quebec bush as well as in Ottawa, Sault Ste. Marie, and Toronto. She was an avid reader of children's classics and comic books. When asked why she writes, she replied, "Why does the sun shine?. . . It's a human activity. I think the real question is, Why doesn't everyone?" Atwood often writes as a Canadian and a woman, creating characters searching for identity and freedom amid political and sexual oppression.

May Swenson
1919–1989

May Swenson wrote that the poetic experience is "based in a craving to get through the curtains of things as they *appear*, to things as they *are*, and then into the larger, wilder space of things as they *are becoming.*" Swenson was born in Logan, Utah, and earned a degree from the University of Utah. She worked as a reporter for a Salt Lake City newspaper before going to New York City to hold a variety of jobs, including editor, reviewer, teacher, and poet-in-residence. Swenson's poems play with language, twisting words in magical ways.

Matsuo Bashō
1644–1694

Bashō, considered the greatest of all writers of haiku, was born into a family of samurai—men of the warrior class—at a time of peace and stability in Japan. At eight, he was taken into the service of a nobleman's son. By nine, he had written his first verses. Though he wrote for most of his life, he did not reach the peak of his ability until his last ten years. Some of Bashō's poems are infused with a religious mysticism, but most are simple descriptions of everyday scenes and real events.

Yosa Buson
1715–1783

Buson, considered second only to Bashō as a writer of haiku, is equally famous as a painter. His subject matter displays a great appreciation of the ever-changing world. Born Taniguchi Buson, he later took the name Yosa in honor of a region near Kyoto known for its scenic beauty.

This Is a Photograph of Me

Margaret Atwood

It was taken some time ago.
At first it seems to be
a smeared
print: blurred lines and grey flecks
5 blended with the paper;

then, as you scan
it, you see in the left-hand corner
a thing that is like a branch: part of a tree
(balsam or spruce) emerging
10 and, to the right, halfway up
what ought to be a gentle
slope, a small frame house.

In the background there is a lake,
and beyond that, some low hills.

15 (The photograph was taken
the day after I drowned.

I am in the lake, in the center
of the picture, just under the surface.

It is difficult to say where
20 precisely, or to say
how large or small I am:
the effect of water
on light is a distortion[1]

but if you look long enough,
25 eventually
you will be able to see me.)

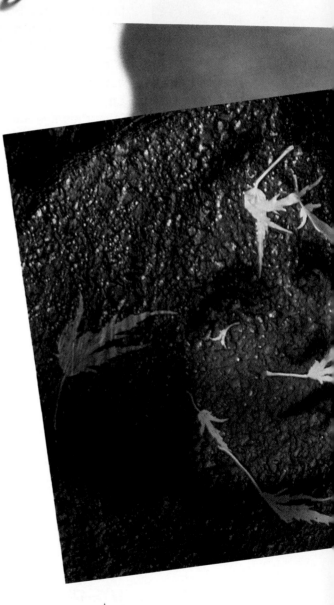

▲ Do you think this is an appropriate image
for Atwood's poem? What details suggest
that the subject is submerged in water?

---

1. **distortion** (dis tôr′shən), *n.* twisting out of shape.

Water Picture

May Swenson

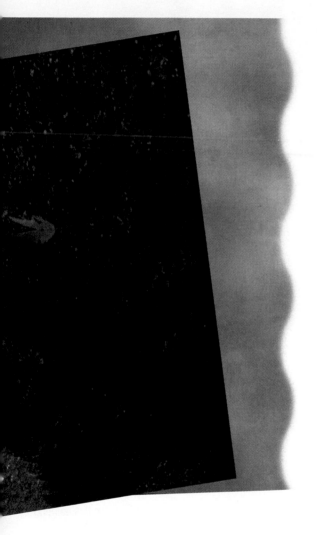

In the pond in the park
all things are doubled:
Long buildings hang and
wriggle gently. Chimneys
5 are bent legs bouncing
on clouds below. A flag
wags like a fishhook
down there in the sky.

The arched stone bridge
10 is an eye, with underlid
in the water. In its lens
dip crinkled heads with hats
that don't fall off. Dogs go by,
barking on their backs.
15 A baby, taken to feed the
ducks, dangles upside-down,
a pink balloon for a buoy.

Treetops deploy[1] a haze of
cherry bloom for roots,
20 where birds coast belly-up
in the glass bowl of a hill;
from its bottom a bunch
of peanut-munching children
is suspended by their
25 sneakers, waveringly.[2]

A swan, with twin necks
forming the figure three,
steers between two dimpled
towers doubled. Fondly
30 hissing, she kisses herself,
and all the scene is troubled:
water-windows splinter,
tree-limbs tangle, the bridge
folds like a fan.

---

1. **deploy** (di ploi′), *v.* spread out in a planned or
   strategic position.
2. **waveringly** (wā′vər ing lē), *adv.* unsteadily.

Six Haiku

Matsuo Bashō

Spring:
A hill without a name
Veiled in morning mist.

On a bare branch
A rook[1] roosts:
Autumn dusk.

Clouds now and then
Giving men relief
From moon-viewing.

Yosa Buson

Spring rain:
In our sedan
Your soft whispers.

Mosquito-buzz
Whenever honeysuckle
Petals fall.

Sudden shower:
Grasping the grass-blades
A shoal[2] of sparrows.

▲ *Cherry Blossom*, attributed to Hasegawa Kyūzō, who lived in Japan in the 1500s, depicts a cherry tree exploding with blossoms set against glittering golden clouds. What is the main impression this painting leaves with you?

---

1. **rook** (ru̇k), *n.* a bird that resembles the crow.
2. **shoal** (shōl), *n.* a large number.

After Reading

Making Connections

Shaping Your
Response

1. Why do you think the selections in this group are considered poems, although they lack **rhyme** and regular **rhythm**?

2. Choose a detail from one of these poems that would make an interesting photograph. Then explain whether you would "shoot" in black or white, close-up or from a distance, in sharp focus or soft focus.

3. Which poem would you want to read aloud to a younger brother or sister? Why?

Analyzing the Poems

4. From what perspective does the reader see things in "Water Picture"?

5. Explain the **image** of the swan "with twin necks forming the figure three" in Swenson's poem.

6. What causes the scene to be "troubled" in the final stanza?

7. What do you think the drowned figure might represent, or **symbolize,** in "This Is a Photograph of Me"? Refer to the end of Atwood's biography on page 613 for possible clues.

8. What season other than spring and fall is represented in these **haiku**? How can you tell?

Extending the Ideas

9. Which of these poets do you think could best describe some outdoor scenes from your neighborhood? Pick one such scene and explain how this poet might describe it.

Literary Focus: Simile

A **simile**—a comparison between two unlike things using the words *like* or *as*—adds vividness and impact to an image. Be careful not to confuse similes with metaphors, in which two things are directly compared without using *like* or *as*: "Chimneys are bent legs."

- Identify two similes in "Water Picture."

- What qualities or feelings are being compared in each simile you identified?

Vocabulary Study

deploy
distortion
rook
shoal
waveringly

Draw a word picture to represent one of the listed words. You might capture a quality of the word or an impression the word suggests. An example has been done for *rook.*

Expressing Your Ideas

Writing Choices

Writer's Notebook Update Look at your drawing and the list of details in your notebook, as well as the items in your chart from Building Background. Let one of these activities trigger an idea for your own poem.

It's How You Look At It Both May Swenson and Margaret Atwood present things from unusual perspectives. Choose an unusual perspective of your own to describe an object in a **riddle**. To obtain a different perspective, you may want to view the object through colored glasses, in a distorted mirror, in water, or upside down. Ask a classmate to guess what you are describing.

You Too Can Haiku Haiku, a poetic form that originated in Japan, often describe nature. Some haiku consist of three lines containing seventeen syllables—five syllables in the first line, seven in the second line, and five in the third line. Others, like those on page 616, have a looser structure. Write a **haiku** describing a familiar scene from nature.

Other Options

Fantastic Folds Scenes from these poems—especially the haiku—lend themselves to **origami**, the art of paper folding. With origami paper, an instruction book, or a classmate familiar with this form of art, make a figure based on an image from these poems.

Mural, Mural on the Wall With a partner or a small group of students, create a **mural** of images from the poems in this group. You might expand on drawings from your notebooks. Post your mural on a wall or bulletin board in your classroom.

Snappy Shots With a partner choose scenes and objects in your community that you find especially picturesque or unique. Take at least ten photographic slides of these things. Make up a brief poetic caption for each slide. Then present a **slide show** to the class, reading each caption with its picture on screen.

Reflections

The Eye and the Lens

Career Connection
A skilled photographer takes great care to compose and present images to convey particular meanings. Photographer Wade Patton has definite ideas of how he wants other people to see a building or a dog or a teepee.

No Headdresses or Horses
Wade Patton
Rapid City, South Dakota

When Wade Patton, a Native American photographer, was seven, he started taking pictures of relatives with a cheap Kodak camera and old-style flash bulbs. He bought his first real camera when he took a photography course while earning a B.A. degree in fine arts from Black Hills State University in Spearfish, South Dakota. For a year and a half after graduating, he worked as a fashion photographer. About his current work as a freelance photographer, he says, "I'm doing Native American people now. Although perhaps less glamorous than fashion photography, the photography I'm doing now is an art form."

"I start out with a general idea of what I want to do and how I want other people to see a building or a dog or a teepee. I take a picture of the object. Usually it's part of a familiar scene on the reservation. I blow it up to sixteen by twenty inches. Then I take other pictures and cut out just the parts I want and affix those to the big photograph.

"For example, the religious aspect of Native American life is dominant. It is very important.

I found the steeple of a church on the reservation peering through the leaves of a tree and I took a picture and enlarged it. The steeple was shiny and silvery. I wanted to show that it was on the reservation, so I went to a powwow and took pictures, especially of men and boys dancing. The leaves and trees in front of the church were dark, but light came through them. And when I affixed the dancers on the picture of the steeple, the fringe on the dancers' clothes made them blend into the trees. It was a picture full of contrasts. You had to look hard—stare at the picture—to see the people. Being able to create a certain effect is what I find challenging about photography.

"I've done painting, but photography is more spontaneous. I try to have a deeper meaning in my work, but I have a lot of artistic energy, and I need to see the results soon. I do a lot of black and white because I think it is more real and conveys more meaning than color. There aren't so many elements to deal with. Reservation life has a contrast and starkness, which I think black and white highlights.

"My purpose in photography is to convey a point of view. I want to get away from the headdresses and the horses against the sky. I want to show real reservation life. Through montages, which combine aspects of drawing and painting with photography, I can do this. For me, photography can give the viewer an actual rendition of surroundings. A writer describes, but the reader then must imagine. Photography has more real feeling for me than words."

Responding
How do you feel about a place in school, such as the cafeteria or the gym? Brainstorm with a partner how you might photograph this place to convey your feelings. For example, what kind of light, color, and details would you choose?

INTERDISCIPLINARY STUDY

Photography Connection
The poets represented in this group offer verbal snapshots—memorable images captured in words. Following are an essay that favors the human eye over the camera lens and photographs displaying special effects achieved by a camera.

The Cerebral

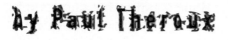

By Paul Theroux

I t is my good fortune that I've never owned a camera. Once, when I was in Italy, I saw about three dozen doves spill out of the eaves of an old cathedral. It was lovely, the sort of thing that makes people say if only I had a camera! I didn't have a camera with me and have spent the past two-and-a-half years trying to find the words to express that sudden deluge of white doves. This is a good exercise—especially good because I still can't express it. When I'm able to express it I'll know I've made the grade as a writer.

And recently I was driving through Kenya with a friend of mine. It was dusk, an explosion of red shot with gold, and the setting sun and the red air seemed to be pressing the acacias flat. Then we saw a giraffe! Then two, three, four—about ten of the lanky things standing still, the silhouettes of their knobby heads protruding into the red air.

I brought the car to a halt and my friend unsheathed his camera and cocked it. He snapped and snapped while I backed up. I was so busy looking at the giraffes that I zigzagged the car all over the road and finally into a shallow ditch.

The giraffes moved slowly among the trees like tired dancers. I wanted them to gallop. Once you've seen a giraffe galloping—they gallop as if they're about to come apart any second, yet somehow all their flapping limbs stay miraculously attached—you know that survival has something to do with speed, no matter how grotesque, double-bellied and gawky the beast may be.

My friend continued to fire his camera into the sunset, and pretty soon all the giraffes had either loped away or had camouflaged themselves in the trees. Both of us, rendered speechless by beauty, nodded and we continued along the road.

Snapshot

After a while my friend told me that we should have stayed longer with the giraffes. Why? Because he didn't get a good look at them.

"See," he explained calmly, "if you take a picture of things—especially moving things like giraffes—you don't really see them." He said he would have had trouble explaining what the giraffes looked like except that he had seen some in the Chicago Zoo. I could only agree and I told him about my Italian dove episode.

The next day, when we saw another herd of giraffes, he pushed his camera aside and we both sat there—it was blazing Kenyan noon— and watched the giraffes placidly munching leaves and glancing at us, pursing their lips in our direction.

No camera is like no hands, a feat of skill. And if you know that sooner or later you will have to explain it all, without benefit of slides or album, to your large family, then as soon as you see something you start searching the view for clues and rummaging through your lexical baggage for the right phrases. Otherwise, what's the use? And when you see something like a galloping giraffe which you can't capture on film you are thrown back on the English language like a cowboy's grizzled sidekick against a cactus. You hope for the sake of posterity and spectators that you can rise unscratched with a blossom. . . .

Ignoring cameras is also good for the eyes. I have often sat staring at something wide-eyed, feeling a fabulous clicking in my skull, snapping everything in sight and, occasionally, things that aren't in sight. Afterwards, strenuously gesturing and leaping out of my seat, I have described these phenomena to my friends.

This is also good exercise. What I have told may not always have been the pictorial truth—a camera may easily have seen something different. But when you see a sunset or a giraffe or a child eating a melting ice-cream cone there is a chemical reaction inside you. If you really stand as innocent as you can, something of the movement, entering through your eyes, gets into your body where it continues to rearrange your senses. Also— and for a writer this bit of information is priceless—a picture is worth only a thousand or so words.

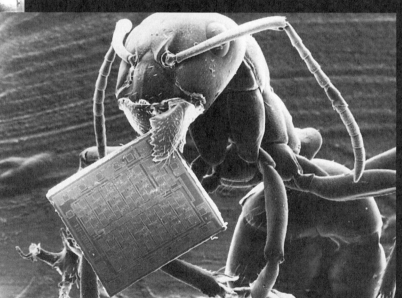

© The Harold E. Edgerton 1992 Trust, courtesy of Palm Press, Inc.

(top left) Image of the skull and spinal column using a magnetic resonance imaging (MRI) scanner; **(above)** Stop-time photograph of a .30 caliber bullet slicing through a playing card; **(left)** A photomicrograph of an ant grasping a micro-chip; **(below)** Stroboscopic photo of a jogger.

How does each of these images exceed the limits of the human eye?

Responding

Study the photographs on this page. Then work with a partner to search your "lexical baggage" for the right phrases to describe one of these images in some detail. Work to develop this "verbal snapshot" into a poem.

Reading Mini-Lesson

Compare and Contrast

Writers use comparison and contrast to show how things are alike or different. In his article, "The Cerebral Snapshot" (page 620), Paul Theroux describes an incident with a photographer in Kenya that made him aware of similarities and differences between the eyes and a camera. He makes a comparison: "I have often sat staring at something wide-eyed, feeling a fabulous clicking in my skull, snapping everything in sight and, occasionally, things that aren't in sight."

Theroux observes that eyesight combined with human perception provides the viewer a degree of insight a camera cannot provide. You could record Theroux's ideas on a comparison-contrast chart like this:

Camera	Eyesight
records images	records images
provides physical images	provides mental images
viewer relies on camera	viewer relies on own words and memories

What is being compared and contrasted in the following paragraph?

Buying a dog is a big decision. Once you're sure that you can provide adequate care, you must decide what dog is best for you. If you are on a tight budget or live in an apartment, keep in mind that large dogs, such as mastiffs and St. Bernards, require a great deal of food, space, and exercise. If you're in the market for a small dog, you might look for certain kinds of poodles, terriers, and spaniels. If size makes no difference to you, think about other considerations such as price, upkeep, temperament, and compatibility.

Activity Options

1. Make a comparison-contrast chart to record information from the paragraph on dogs.

2. Work with a group to collect the covers of different magazines. Choose two images to compare and contrast.

Writing Workshop

Verbal Snapshots

Assignment The writers in this part of the unit have re-created special moments in time, freezing them in verbal snapshots. Now create your own verbal snapshot.

WRITER'S BLUEPRINT

Product	A verbal snapshot
Purpose	To re-create a memorable place through vivid description
Audience	Students in an art class
Specs	As the writer of a successful paper, you should:

❑ Imagine that an art teacher has asked you to prepare a verbal snapshot for her students to respond to through painting or drawing.

❑ Choose a place that is special for you. It could be indoors or outdoors, but it must be a place you can describe in great sensory detail. Examples: a basketball arena during a game, a place where your family took a memorable vacation, a secret hiding place you had as a child.

❑ Write a vivid description of this place. Guide your reader by using spatial organization.

❑ Show, not tell. Let the reader know why this place is memorable for you, but don't explain this directly. Let the sensory details you emphasize do the telling for you.

❑ Follow the rules of grammar, usage, spelling, and mechanics.

STEP 1  PREWRITING

Examine the photographs in this part as a warm-up exercise. Use the chart that follows as a guide. The example in the chart is based on the Ansel Adams photograph on page 599. Notice that the details in the second column include size, shape, location, and make-up of the items.

Items	Sensory Details
mountains	tall; rising behind town; snow-covered; tall trees; majestic
buildings	steep roofs; wooden; small; part of a mining town

Find the place you want to describe. Look through family photo albums, read journal entries, take a tour of your surroundings, and talk to your family and friends to get ideas.

Plan your paper. Follow these steps.

- First, read the Beyond Print articles on visualizing (page 499) and on looking at photographs (pages 628–629).

- Then draw the scene. Include as many descriptive details as possible.

- Finally, look back at your chart and drawing and make your writing plan.

Keep these ideas in mind as you make your plan:

- Take the reader on a guided tour.

- Arrange the details in spatial order, from left to right, right to left, up to down, down to up, near to far, or far to near.

OR . . .
Describe your scene on a tape recorder as though you were giving directions to guide your listener through unfamiliar territory.

STEP 2 DRAFTING

Before you draft, review your chart, drawing, writing plan, and any other notes. Then reread the Writer's Blueprint.

As you draft, consider these drafting tips.

- Show—don't tell—the reader why this place is memorable. (See the Revising Strategy in Step 3 of this lesson.)

- Write as though you were watching a scene in a movie, with each shot framed and edited as the camera moves from one view to the next. (See the Beyond Print article on pages 62–63.)

- Use direction words and phrases to make transitions as you move through the scene: *to the left, on the right, in front, behind, beyond, down, up, at the back, farthest, over, under,* and so on.

Ask a partner to comment on your draft before you revise it.

✔ Did I describe the place vividly with sensory details?

✔ Did I show, not tell, why this place is memorable to me?

Revising Strategy

Showing, Not Telling

Don't just tell your readers why this place is memorable. Telling is a secondhand way of doing things. Show your readers why this place is memorable to you by having them experience it the way you experienced it, in full sensory detail.

Telling   The ocean waves come up to the shore near the oak tree.

Showing   "That green monster of a gelatin sea / hisses white tongues of foam kneeling / to lick the shore serenading the lone / oak tree," from "Sunday Morning" by Oscar Peñaranda

Reread each paragraph to make sure that you "show" some aspect of the snapshot. If you find a paragraph that "tells" rather than "shows," revise it by rewriting from a photographer's perspective, as in the model below.

STUDENT MODEL

When I was twelve I went to my first football game. We arrived early on game day and had a cookout in the parking lot. Then it was time for the game. ~~When we got into the stadium it was a mess and it smelled~~ *Inside the stadium the floor was sticky and there was garbage everywhere. I was assaulted by the smell of cigars, and the wild* ~~awful. I didn't like the crowds either.~~ *crowd pushed me around like a pinball.* Luckily we soon found our seats.

Ask a partner to review your revised draft before you edit. As you edit, try reading each line backwards, a word at a time, to spot careless spelling errors.

Editing Strategy

Avoiding Careless Spelling Errors

We all make careless spelling errors—misspelling short, simple words we actually *do* know how to spell. Often, we end up writing the right letters, but in the wrong order:

Teh crowd cheered **fro** the team.

Or we write one familiar word when we mean another:

Than we moved **threw** the forest to the stream.

Or we leave out letters or add extra ones:

I didn't **rember** this place **untill** I saw an old family movie.

Because these kinds of words are so simple and so familiar, we often don't see them as we've written them. When you proofread for spelling, *look* at each word, no matter how simple or familiar.

STEP 5 PRESENTING

- Read your verbal snapshot to students in a real art class and have them draw the scene.

- Take a photograph of your memorable place and put it together with your verbal snapshot to make a greeting card to send to someone.

STEP 6 LOOKING BACK

Self-evaluate. Look back at the Writer's Blueprint and give your paper a score for each item, from 6 (superior) to 1 (inadequate).

Reflect. Think about what you have learned from writing this verbal snapshot as you write answers to these questions.

✔ How has writing this description changed the way you think of your special place?

✔ How did your writing plan work? Was it helpful? Explain what you might have done differently.

For Your Working Portfolio Add your paper and reflection responses to your working portfolio.

Beyond Print

Looking at Photographs: It's a Snap!

Looking at a photograph is much like looking at a painting or a piece of sculpture. First of all, you determine what the subject is. Then you examine details more closely and try to understand the techniques used to create the work. By this point, you are probably able to make some inferences about the photographer's purpose. Finally, you have a basis to make a judgment about this work.

Although you might think that the painter creates something from a blank canvas while a photographer can only *record* things, photographers are creators too, with a great deal of control over their subject matter. How to frame a subject? How to arrange details? What things or moods to emphasize through camera angles and techniques? How to use light and shadow? The photographer asks these and many other questions before shooting.

Here are some questions that you might ask yourself when viewing a photograph.

- What is the subject of the photograph?

- What is the photographer's vantage point? For example, the camera might be at close range, or the photograph might be an aerial shot like the one featured on the opposite page.

- Why might a photographer have chosen to shoot the image in color or in black-and-white? Do you think that the photograph on the opposite page would have been more dramatic, or less so, in color? Why?

- If a title is provided, how does it add to your understanding of the photograph?

- What do you notice about light and shadow? shapes? textures?

- Is the photographer more interested in creating a mood? portraying a person? depicting an event? capturing an emotion? something else?

- What is it about the photograph that does or does not appeal to you?

Activity Options

1. Study this photograph by André Kertész, titled *Shadows of the Eiffel Tower,* and jot down the answers to some of the questions on the opposite page. Compare your answers to those of your classmates.

2. Apply these viewing tips to another photograph from a magazine or from this book.

Part Three

Culture Crossroads

The world has become smaller, with cultures bumping together in amazing ways. Whether we consider such contacts collisions or opportunities for enrichment is crucial in the development of a multicultural world.

 Multicultural Connection **Interactions** between people of different backgrounds require a recognition of common qualities, a respect of differences, and a willingness to arrive at understandings and compromises.

Literature

Interdisciplinary Study Culture Quilt

Writing Workshop Expository Writing

Beyond Print Technology

Before Reading

Woman from America Bessie Head South Africa

Bessie Head
1937–1986

Born of racially mixed parentage, Bessie Head was raised by foster parents. After teaching in South African primary schools, she worked as a reporter in Johannesburg and Cape Town. In an effort to flee apartheid (ə pär′tāt), she settled in Botswana, a south central African country. Ironically, she suffered discrimination as a refugee in her new land. Head writes about political and sexual oppression, exile, personal identity, and the conflict between old and new ways. Just as she was becoming recognized as a prominent literary voice, Head died of hepatitis.

Building Background

Culture Collisions Although amazing social changes have occurred recently all over the world, probably nowhere have they happened more dramatically than in Africa, with the ending of colonial rule. Villages and traditional societies have been thrust into a modern fast-paced world of technology. Since the ending of **apartheid,** South Africa's former policy of racial discrimination, in 1991, there is a new sense of power and hope, although nonwhites still face much unofficial discrimination—in education, jobs, housing, and even in social and sports activities. Given this context, the two women you are about to encounter represent two very different ways of life: the rebellious, independent newcomer versus the narrator—imbued with tribal values and fearful of authority.

Literary Focus

Setting The time and place in which a narrative occurs is called its **setting**. In this essay, Head provides information about contemporary life in a small African village. As you read, jot down details about this setting in a chart such as the one started here.

African Bush
a village mud hut

Writer's Notebook

All-American What is an American? Do Americans have certain characteristics that readily identify them? In a group, brainstorm characteristics—clothing, behavior, musical tastes, personality traits—that non-Americans might regard as particularly American. In your notebook, list these characteristics.

WOMAN from AMERICA

Bessie Head

This woman from America married a man of our village and left her country to come and live with him here. She descended on us like an avalanche. People are divided into two camps: those who feel a fascinated love and those who fear a new thing.

Some people keep hoping she will go away one day, but already her big strong stride has worn the pathways of the village flat. She is everywhere about because she is a woman, resolved and unshakable in herself. To make matters worse or more disturbing she comes from the west side of America, somewhere near California. I gather from her conversation that people from the West are stranger than most people.

People of the West of America must be the most oddly beautiful people in the world; at least this woman from the West is the most oddly beautiful person I have ever seen. Every cross-current of the earth seems to have stopped in her and blended into an amazing harmony. She has a big dash of Africa, a dash of Germany, some Cherokee and heaven knows what else. Her feet are big and her body is as tall and straight and strong as a mountain tree. Her neck curves up high and her thick black hair cascades[1] down her back like a wild and tormented stream. I cannot understand her eyes though, except that they are big, black, and startled like those of a wild free buck racing against the wind. Often they cloud over with a deep, intense, brooding[2] look.

It takes a great deal of courage to become friends with a woman like that. Like everyone here, I am timid and subdued.[3] Authority, everything can subdue me; not because I like it that way but because authority carries the weight of an age pressing down on life. It is terrible then to associate with a person who can shout authority down. Her shouting matches with authority are the terror and sensation of the village. It has come down to this. Either the woman is unreasonable or authority is unreasonable, and everyone in his heart would like to admit that authority is unreasonable. In reality, the rule is: If authority does not like you, then you are the outcast and humanity associates with you at their peril.[4] So try always to be on the right side of authority, for the sake of peace, and please avoid the outcast. I do not say it will be like this forever. The whole world is crashing and interchanging itself and even remote bush villages in Africa are not to be left out!

It was inevitable though that this woman and I should be friends. I have an overwhelming curiosity that I cannot keep within bounds. I passed by the house for almost a month, but one cannot crash in on people. Then one day a dog they own had puppies, and my small son chased one of the puppies into the yard and I chased after him. Then one of the puppies became his and there had to be discussions about the puppy, the desert heat, and the state of the world and as a result of curiosity an avalanche of wealth has descended on my life. My small hut-house is full of short notes written in a wide sprawling hand. I have kept them all because they are a statement of human generosity and the wild carefree laugh of a woman who is as busy as women the world over about things women always entangle themselves in—a man, a home . . . Like this. . . .

"Have you an onion to spare? It's very quiet here this morning and I'm all fagged out from sweeping and cleaning

---

1. **cascade** (ka skād′), *v.* fall or pour.
2. **brooding** (brü′ding), *adj.* worried.
3. **subdued** (səb düd′), *adj.* toned down.
4. **peril** (per′əl), *n.* danger.

the yard, shaking blankets, cooking, fetching water, bathing children, and there's still the floor inside to sweep and dishes to wash . . . it's endless!"

Sometimes too, conversations get all tangled up and the African night creeps all about and the candles are not lit and the conversation gets more entangled, intense; and the children fall asleep on the floor dazed by it all.

She is a new kind of American or even maybe will be a new kind of African. There isn't anyone here who does not admire her. To come from a world of chicken, hamburgers, TV, escalators, and whatnot to a village mud hut and a life so tough, where the most you can afford to eat is ground millet[5] and boiled meat. Sometimes you cannot afford to eat at all. Always you have to trudge miles for a bucket of water and carry it home on your head. And to do all this with loud, ringing, sprawling laughter?

Black people in America care about Africa, and she has come here on her own as an expression of that love and concern. Through her, too, one is filled with wonder for a country that breeds individuals about whom, without and within, rushes the wind of freedom. I have to make myself clear, though. She is a different person who has taken by force what America will not give black people.

The woman from America loves both Africa and America, independently. She can take what she wants from both and say, "Dammit." It is a most strenuous and difficult thing to do.

---

5. **millet** (mil′it), *n.* a food grain.

This dressmaker's sign by Nana Eln's Afro Art, photographed in Ghana in 1978, depicts clothes fashionable at the time. How is this sign alike and different from contemporary fashion ads in the United States? ➤

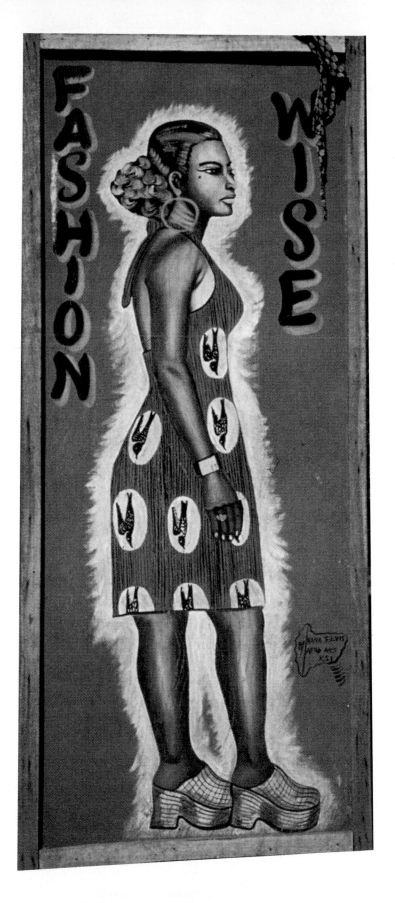

After Reading

Making Connections

Shaping Your
Response

1. Do you agree with Head's observation that America ". . . breeds individuals about whom, without and within, rushes the wind of freedom"? Explain.

2. Do you think that the American will change the villagers or the villagers will change the American? Explain.

3. 🐾 In what ways do the woman from America and the narrator represent **interractions** in the modern world, which "is crashing and interchanging itself"?

Analyzing the Essay

4. Do you think that there are any **stereotypes** about Americans suggested in this essay? Explain.

5. Choose a **figure of speech** in the first three paragraphs and explain how it enriches Head's portrayal of the American.

6. What do you think Head means by the following: "She is a different person who has taken by force what America will not give black people"?

7. 🐾 Explain how the **interactions** in this selection illustrate the theme Culture Crossroads.

Extending the Ideas

8. Explain whether or not you agree with Head's observation, ". . . everyone in his heart would like to admit that authority is unreasonable."

9. Immigration laws and policy have been debated and revised throughout the history of the United States. Explain what restrictions, if any, you think the U.S. government should impose on immigration.

Literary Focus: Setting

Head includes a number of specific details about **setting**, the time and place in which the narrative occurs. Review details about setting in your chart. Then explain which elements you think would be difficult for an American to adjust to.

Vocabulary Study

Word analogy tests require you to understand the relationship between a pair of words and then to choose another pair with the same relationship. Analogies reflect relationships such as the following: antonyms *(impotent : powerful);* item and process *(bread : knead);* synonyms *(beg : implore).*

Number your paper from 1–5; then write the letter of the pair of words that best completes the analogy.

brooding
cascade
millet
peril
subdued

1. CASCADE : FALL :: **a.** attack : assault **b.** run : trickle **c.** remember : forget **d.** lift : drop

2. MILLET : GRIND :: **a.** carrot : orange **b.** potato : mash **c.** butter : margarine **d.** cabbage : coleslaw

3. BROODING : WORRYING :: **a.** wondering : forgetting **b.** annoying : irritating **c.** celebrating : anniversary **d.** ignoring : abusing

4. SUBDUED : EXCITED :: **a.** abused : ignored **b.** satisfied : pleased **c.** designed : colored **d.** steady : nervous

5. PERIL : SAFETY :: **a.** accident : misfortune **b.** weakness : strength **c.** adult : grown-up **d.** pour : pitcher

Expressing Your Ideas

Writing Choices

Writer's Notebook Update Reread your list of characteristics associated with Americans. In your notebook, identify why Americans are associated with these qualities. If you consider any of these characteristics stereotypical, briefly explain why they do not represent most Americans and how you think the stereotypes came about.

Go Home, Yankee! The villagers are not pleased with the new American resident. On their behalf, write a **letter of complaint** to an official in the capital about her.

The African Queen Delighted to have a friend in the village, the American writes an enthusiastic **character sketch** of the narrator in her journal. What do you think she would say?

Other Options

Musical Interlude Find recordings of African music—by Ladysmith Black Mambazo, Miriam Makeba, or another South African folk singer or group. Present a class **concert**, explaining the kinds of instruments used and/or the messages the songs contain.

Read A-Head Read one of Bessie Head's books, such as her collected essays, sketches, and stories in two books titled *Tales of Tenderness and Power* and *A Women Alone;* her collection of interviews and stories titled *Scrowe: Village of the Rain Wind;* or her short story collection titled *The Collector of Treasures.* Give the class an **oral critique** of the book.

Before Reading

Rain Music   Longhang Nguyen   USA

Longhang Nguyen
born 1970

Longhang Nguyen (long häng we′ən) emigrated from Vietnam to the United States in 1979. For two years her father looked after her brother and her while he attended school to reobtain his veterinary license. At the end of this time, his wife rejoined the family. Today, Nguyen lives in San Francisco where she is studying medicine. Nguyen says that "Rain Music," which you are about to read, illustrates that "love is a complex of emotions. There aren't straightforward or universal answers to its questions."

Building Background

Vietnam Until the past century, Vietnam was an agricultural society built on tradition and strong family ties, with extended families living in rural areas. In the past century, however, especially since the Vietnam War of the '60s and '70s, families were broken up by military duties and death, many people fled to cities, close family ties were severed, and people learned Western customs. Since the end of the Vietnam War (U.S. ground troops left in 1973 and South Vietnam surrendered to North Vietnam in 1975), over a million people have left the country, with the largest number moving to the U.S. Among these immigrants were Longhang Nguyen and her family. Her story, "Rain Music," will have special significance if you remember that according to Vietnamese tradition, parents choose their children's marriage partners.

Literary Focus

Conflict When cultures clash, **conflict** results. As you read "Rain Music," note both the internal conflicts within Linh and the external conflicts that involve society.

Writer's Notebook

Head Over Heart Young people are sometimes accused of acting impulsively, according to emotion rather than reason. In your notebook, record key impressions about an instance when you acted reasonably in an emotional situation.

Rain Music

Longhang Nguyen

*L*inh and I grew up penned in the same yard, so our sibling rivalry did not last very long. By third grade we had stopped physically assaulting one another and reached a permanent truce. At that time her hair was long and flowing, brushed daily by my mother as Linh closed her eyes and counted each stroke. It always felt like cool satin when I yanked it, her head jerking backward, mimicking[1] the motion of my arm. In actuality, she was very kind and I was not too violent, so we became intimate friends. I have not had any trouble from her since.

She is the red rose of the family and I am the green thorn. We have both decided that we are beautiful, so she tells me, but I believe she is also very beautiful outside in face and gesture. I always pout when I accuse her of being a selfish firstborn, picking, stealing the best of our parents' genes and leaving me the rejected remainder. She has wide, almond-shaped eyes like black, pearl-black reflecting pools with brown-colored flecks swirling beneath the surface, light honey-color skin and even, velvet-smooth cheeks. Her nose is just slightly upturned, her lips rosebud shaped, her chin small and delicate. Her hair still looks and feels the same now as in third grade. The vision, taken together as a whole, is breathtaking. There is something about it, a wistful,[2] dandelion, orchidlike kind of beauty that feels like notes in a chord being played separately, finger by finger, harmonizing back and forth. I marvel even now.

My mother and father have polished her until she shines. She graduated summa cum laude[3] from the College of Chemistry at Cal and double majored in Ethnic Studies. However, my parents don't count the latter. She is now a fourth-year student at UCSF[4] preparing to enter the surgical residency program next

---

1. **mimicking** (mim′ik), *adj.* making fun of by imitating.
2. **wistful** (wist′fəl), *adj.* longing; yearning.
3. **summa cum laude** (sùm′ə kùm lou′də), with highest honors.
4. **UCSF,** University of California at San Francisco.

fall. My parents are bursting at the seams, gorged with devouring so much blessedness and good fortune.

"Will your daughter become a surgeon?" our relatives ask.

"It's possible," my father says, beaming.

"She is friends with this young man in her class. He's tall, distinguished-looking, loyal and respectful to his parents, hard-working but generous. He was even born in Vietnam! But he came over here with his family in 1975. He went to Harvard"—my mother pauses to let the relatives gasp in unison—"on a full scholarship!" she smiles modestly, then lowers her eyes.

"A possible son-in-law?" they ask.

She shrugs and sighs. "That is up to God."

Linh hasn't told my parents about David. She met him five years ago during her final year at Cal. That semester they were in three classes together: a choral class, an Afro-American literature class, and a creative writing class. They became good friends.

David is a writer. His subjects are ordinary preoccupations[5] of other writers: his mother, the father he has never seen or known, the friends of his childhood. Some of them are dead now. The others are spread out across the country. One is a construction worker in St. Louis. Another is a teacher in Baton Rouge. The third is a journalist in Washington, D.C. They write to him once in a while or call him. Linh hasn't met any of them, but she knows them all.

After David feverishly completes a story, Linh cooks him dinner. Afterward, she tucks him into bed and sits nearby in the wicker chair, legs drawn up and hugged tightly to her chest, to watch him while he sleeps. His soft, black curls rest against the white of the pillow, his closed eyelids and long lashes flutter minutely[6] while he dreams, his breath whistles through the evenness of his teeth as the cover grazes the dark honey of his skin.

They always have a good time together, and he makes her laugh in many different ways, wherever they happen to be. He always gets close to finishing her off during a tennis set, but then she cries out that he has cheated and treated her unfairly and he has to start over again. He never wins. Sometimes they sing together, his clear resonant tenor melding with her flutelike, crystalline soprano. Then they have tea.

I know all about David. She won't stop talking about him, but I know less about Thanh, the Vietnamese friend at UCSF. I know he's nice but that's all. She woke me up this morning at ten thirty and said, "It's a bright, beautiful, Saturday morning. Let's go and have a picnic."

"No, no," I mumbled hazily in my sleep. "Take David. Leave me alone."

"I don't want to take David. I want to spend quality time with you, my darling sister. Get up, you piece of mutton. Toast on the table in five minutes and we're leaving in half an hour."

"Oh, lord," I groaned, "I'm being punished for sins from past lives."

We arrived at the park at twelve, lugged our ample picnic hamper heavily laden with cheese, fruits, sandwiches, ice, and bottles of juice from the car, and trudged into the heart of the lightly shaded, green forest. When I opened the basket and took out the butter, she started to talk.

"David kissed me last night. . . ."

"He what?"

". . . or I kissed him. It just happened. I guess. He invited me to dinner, promised to cook a sumptuous Cajun[7] feast with Vietnamese

---

5. **preoccupation** (prē ok′yə pā′shən), *n.* thing that absorbs or engrosses.

6. **minutely** (mī nūt′lē), *adv.* in a small way or a detailed manner.

7. **Cajun** (kā′jən), descending from the French who came to Louisiana from Acadia in Canada.

Although Diana Ong's style is informal and her figures roughly sketched in *School Days*, she communicates precise impressions. Choose three words about school you think are suggested in this picture. What similarities and differences do you find between this and another Ong picture that appears on page 582? ➤

desserts. *Bánh flanc*,[8] you know. My favorite." She plucked a blade of grass from its roots and twisted it back and forth, watching a streak of feeble, yellow sun play on its linear edges. "I expected it to be a celebration. He'd just finished his first novel, not quite a love story, he says, and he wanted me read it." She spoke more softly. "When I arrived, he had set tiny blossoms in water dishes throughout the apartment. It smelled wonderful. The food was delicious, everything so lovely, so tranquil I didn't know where to begin. After dinner he led me into the living room.

"'Rain music,' he said. 'It's for you.' After the last note on the piano had stopped to echo, he turned toward me and kissed me for a long, long time. I didn't know what I was doing. I just couldn't stop. I didn't breathe. When he let me go, I kept thinking of his hands and fingers, seeing them fly over the ivory keys like little Russian men dancing in their black fur hats and noticing how his brown was different from mine. I was raging inside, screaming in my head, 'Why can't his fingers be brown like mine, be my brown? Why is his hair curly, not straight like mine?' I saw brown pigments[9] run across my eyes, all different colored browns. Those pigments keep us apart. How do I stand there and tell this man who writes me music and whose hands burn my cheeks that I can't be who he wants me to be?"

"But he doesn't want to change you."

"No, I can't be who he thinks I am. He's a starving writer. He can't give me anything, just himself. And he doesn't even know that I'm using him. He doesn't even know." She choked on her tears, swallowed, and cried quietly, hugging her knees, until exhausted. The leaves rustled softly while I waited.

After a while she grew calm, her eyes gazing steadily at the flashing water of the stream below. "I love Thanh. I would never hurt him for anything. Throughout the four years at UCSF, he has been so patient, so kind, so dedicated to medicine for its own good, not for just its technology, even though he's brilliant and understands these details completely. He's so perfect for me, just perfect. It's like he stepped out of my story and came to life. We speak the same language and share the same past. Everything. And Mom and Dad, they've done so much for us. Now they think they've won the lottery from God for being good all their life."

"But how do you feel about Thanh? How does he make you feel?"

"He will be my lifelong friend. He'll make a wonderful father. That's what a husband should be. Our children will know the culture and customs of our homeland. They'll speak Vietnamese and English, just like us."

"And how does David make you feel?" I tugged at her gently.

She bowed her head for a long while reflecting. Then she softly murmured, "It's just not possible."

"But why? I don't understand."

The picnic basket remained quite full. Neither of us was hungry. It threatened to rain as we packed up to go home. On the drive back, we were silent. I watched the windshield wipers swing back and forth, clearing rain cascading down the front window.

---

8. *bánh flanc,* a sweet egg and milk dessert.
9. **pigment** (pig′mənt), *n.* natural substance that colors skin tissue.

After Reading

Making Connections

Shaping Your Response

1. Whom do you think Linh should marry? Explain.

2. If you had a friend in Linh's predicament, what would you say to her?

3. To what degree, if any, do you think parents should be able to determine their child's choice of a marriage partner?

Analyzing the Story

4. 👆 Although Linh says that "pigments" prevent her from marrying David, what other cultural factors influence her choice of a husband?

5. The narrator says of Linh, "My mother and father have polished her until she shines." What does this **figurative language** reveal about their treatment of her?

6. If Linh is the **protagonist** of this story, who or what do you think is the **antagonist**?

7. What do you think the rain of the title and of the last paragraph represents, or **symbolizes**?

Extending the Ideas

8. Does this story reinforce any **stereotypes** about Asians? about African Americans? Explain.

9. If you were choosing a husband or wife, what are the five most important characteristics you would look for?

Literary Focus: Conflict

Answer the following questions about the various **conflicts** in "Rain Music."

- What evidence can you find that David, too, may have experienced conflicts?

- What external conflicts is Linh trying to avoid?

- What conflict is implied by the observation regarding Linh's double major of Chemistry and Ethnic Studies that her parents "don't count the latter"?

Vocabulary Study

Use context clues to help you choose the word that best completes each sentence.

mimic
minutely
pigment
preoccupation
wistful

1. Like many younger sisters, the narrator fears she cannot copy, or ____, Linh's success.

2. Linh says that ____ is what keeps her and David apart, but their differences go beyond skin color.

3. The narrator feels ____ as she yearns to be like her beautiful, talented sister.

4. Linh examines David's face ____, noting every detail as he sleeps.

5. Linh's ____ with her Vietnamese heritage will absorb her the rest of her life.

Expressing Your Ideas

Writing Choices

Writer's Notebook Update Review your impressions about a time you acted reasonably in an emotional situation. Write a paragraph explaining the situation, your response, and your feelings about it now.

Box Office Smash Imagine the story were continued. Briefly describe two possible **extended endings**. Then explain which ending you think would be more popular at the box office if the story were made into a movie.

Sisters Linh wants you, her sister, to help her decide what to do about her dilemma. Instead of giving direct advice, put your thoughts into the form of a **fable**. Like those in traditional fables, the characters should be animals; the ending should contain a moral.

Other Options

TV Newcomer It is your job to write **promotional material** for "Rain Music," which has been expanded into a weekly TV program. Name the show, design an identifying logo, and write a paragraph that captures highlights and entices prospective viewers.

Speaking Up Conduct an **interview** of someone who has emigrated from Vietnam to the U.S. since the 1970s. Beforehand, work with a group to write questions, including those about traditions, values, and family. Alternatively, you may want to invite a Vietnamese immigrant to come and speak to the class.

Your Own Rain Music With a partner, brainstorm appropriate **background music** for this story. You might consider something already on disk or CD, or you may want to write and perform your own composition. Bring this music to class and play it as background while selected passages are read aloud.

Before Reading

My Father Writes to My Mother   Assia Djebar Algeria

Assia Djebar
born 1936

Assia Djebar (ä sē′ə jə bär′) is both a writer and a noted film maker who uses film to reach those who cannot read, especially Islamic women, who are frequently given little or no formal education. When in her twenties, she won acclaim for her first four novels, the first of which, *The Mischief,* she wrote during the 1956 student uprising in France. Six years later, she published *Children of the New World,* an account of the Algerian war of independence from France. Her feminist leanings, along with her eloquent pleas for equality and empathy, distinguish her works. Drawing on the cultures of France and Algeria, she presents to westerners the dilemmas many Muslim women face in trying to emerge from "behind the veil."

Building Background

Words from the Koran Many Muslim customs are derived from teachings of the **Koran,** Islam's book of revelations. Below are quotations from two of its chapters, or *suras.* Think about how these standards of behavior would affect relationships between husbands and wives.

> Men have authority over women because God has made the one superior to the other, and because they spend their wealth to maintain them. Good women are obedient. ("Women")
>
> Enjoin believing women to turn their eyes away from temptation and to preserve their chastity; to cover their adornments (except such as are normally displayed); to draw their veils over their bosoms and not to reveal their finery. . . . And let them not stamp their feet when walking so as to reveal their hidden trinkets. ("Light")

Literary Focus

Character The English novelist E. M. Forster classified fictional characters as either *static* (unchanged by events) or *active* (affected by events). Using this definition, make a chart such as the one below listing at least six characters from selections in this book under the appropriate head. Then, as you read "My Father Writes to My Mother," decide whether the mother is a static or an active character.

Static	Active

Writer's Notebook

Are They Really? Quickwrite your impressions of these words from the Koran: "Good women are obedient."

My Father Writes to My Mother

Assia Djebar

Whenever my mother spoke of my father, she, in common with all the women in her town, simply used the personal pronoun in Arabic corresponding to "him." Thus, every time she used a verb in the third person singular which didn't have a noun subject, she was naturally referring to her husband. This form of speech was characteristic of every married woman, from fifteen to sixty, with the proviso[1] that in later years, if the husband had undertaken the pilgrimage to Mecca, he could be given the title of "Hajj."[2]

Everybody, children and adults, especially girls and women, since all important conversations took place among the womenfolk, learnt very quickly to adapt to this rule whereby a husband and wife must never be referred to by name.

After she had been married a few years, my mother gradually learnt a little French. She was able to exchange a few halting words with the wives of my father's colleagues who had, for the most part, come from France and, like us, lived with their families in the little block of flats set aside for the village teachers.

I don't know exactly when my mother began to say, "*My husband* has come, *my husband* has gone out . . . I'll ask *my husband*," etc. Although my mother did make rapid progress in the language, in spite of taking it up fairly late in life, I can still hear the evident awkwardness in her voice betrayed by her labored phraseology, her slow and deliberate enunciation at that time. Nevertheless, I can sense how much it cost her modesty to refer to my father directly in this way.

It was as if a floodgate had opened within

1. proviso (prə vī′zō), *n.* any provision or stipulation.
2. **hajj** (haj); more commonly *hajji* (haj′ē).

her, perhaps in her relationship with her husband. Years later, during the summers we spent in her native town, when chatting in Arabic with her sisters or cousins, my mother would refer to him quite naturally by his first name, even with a touch of superiority. What a daring innovation! Yes, quite unhesitatingly—I was going to say, unequivocally[3]—in any case, without any of the usual euphemisms[4] and verbal circumlocutions.[5] When her aunts and elderly female relations were present, she would once more use the traditional formalities, out of respect for them; such freedom of language would have appeared insolent and incongruous to the ears of the pious old ladies.

QUESTION: What questions about this culture and its customs would you like to ask?

Years went by. As my mother's ability to speak French improved, while I was still a child of no more than twelve, I came to realize an irrefutable[6] fact: namely that, in the face of all these womenfolk, my parents formed a couple. One thing was an even greater source of pride in me: when my mother referred to any of the day-to-day incidents of our village life—which in our city relatives' eyes was very backward—the tall figure of my father—my childhood hero—seemed to pop up in the midst of all these women engaged in idle chit-chat on the age-old patios to which they were confined.

My father, no one except my father; none of the other women ever saw fit to refer to their menfolk, their masters who spent the day outside the house and returned home in the evening, taciturn,[7] with eyes on the ground. The nameless uncles, cousins, relatives by marriage, were for us an unidentifiable collection of individuals to all of whom their spouses alluded impartially in the masculine gender.

With the exception of my father . . . My mother, with lowered eyes, would calmly pronounce his name "Tahar"—which, I learned very early, meant "The Pure"—and even when a suspicion of a smile flickered across the other women's faces or they looked half ill at ease, half indulgent, I thought that a rare distinction lit up my mother's face.

These harem conversations ran their imperceptible[8] course: my ears only caught those phrases which singled my mother out above the rest. Because she always made a point of bringing my father's name into these exchanges, he became for me still purer than his given name betokened.[9]

One day something occurred which was a portent[10] that their relationship would never be the same again—a commonplace enough event in any other society, but which was unusual to say the least with us: in the course of an exceptionally long journey away from home (to a neighboring province, I think), my father wrote to my mother—yes, to my mother!

He sent her a postcard, with a short greeting written diagonally across it in his large, legible handwriting, something like "Best wishes from this distant region" or possibly, "I am having a good journey and getting to know an unfamiliar region," etc. and he signed it simply with his first name. I am sure that, at the time, he himself would not have dared add any more intimate formula above his signature, such as "I am thinking of you," or even less, "Yours affectionately." But, on the half of the card reserved for the address of the recipient, he had written "Madame" followed by his own surname, with the possible addition—but here I'm not sure—

---

3. **unequivocally** (un′i kwiv′ə kəl ē), *adv.* clearly.
4. **euphemism** (yü′fə miz′əm), *n.* use of a mild or indirect expression instead of a harsh, direct one.
5. **circumlocution** (sėr′kəm lō kyü′shən), *n.* the use of many words instead of a few.
6. **irrefutable** (i ref′yə tə bəl), *adj.* undeniable.
7. **taciturn** (tas′ə tėrn′), *adj.* silent.
8. **imperceptible** (im′pər sep′tə bəl), *adj.* gradual.
9. **betoken** (bi tō′kən), *v.* indicate.
10. **portent** (pôr′tent), *n.* sign.

"and children," that is to say we three, of whom I, then about ten years old, was the eldest. . . .

The radical change in customs was apparent for all to see: my father had quite brazenly[11] written his wife's name, in his own handwriting, on a postcard which was going to travel from one town to another, which was going to be exposed to so many masculine eyes, including eventually our village postman—a Muslim postman to boot—and, what is more, he had dared to refer to her in the western manner as "Madame So-and-So . . . ," whereas, no local man, poor or rich, ever referred to his wife and children in any other way than by the vague periphrasis: "the household."

CLARIFY: Why was sending the postcard considered "western" and daring?

So, my father had "written" to my mother. When she visited her family she mentioned this postcard, in the simplest possible words and tone of voice, to be sure. She was about to describe her husband's four or five days' absence from the village, explaining the practical problems this had posed: my father having to order the provisions just before he left, so that the shopkeepers could deliver them every morning; she was going to explain how hard it was for a city woman to be isolated in a village with very young children and cut off in this way. . . . But the other women had interrupted, exclaiming, in the face of this new reality, this almost incredible detail:

"He wrote to you, *to you?*"

"He wrote his wife's name and the postman must have read it? Shame! . . ."

"He could at least have addressed the card to his son, for the principle of the thing, even if his son is only seven or eight!"

CLARIFY: What would have been the purpose of addressing the postcard to his son?

My mother did not reply. She was probably pleased, flattered even, but she said nothing. Perhaps she was suddenly ill at ease, or blushing from embarrassment; yes, her husband had written to her, in person! . . . The eldest child, the only one who might have been able to read the card, was her daughter: so, daughter or wife, where was the difference as far as the addressee was concerned?

"I must remind you that I've learned to read French now!"

This postcard was, in fact, a most daring manifestation of affection. Her modesty suffered at that very moment that she spoke of it. Yet, it came second to her pride as a wife, which was secretly flattered.

The murmured exchanges of these segregated women struck a faint chord with me, as a little girl with observing eyes. And so, for the first time, I seem to have some intuition of the possible happiness, the mystery in the union of a man and a woman.

My father had dared "to write" to my mother. Both of them referred to each other by name, which was tantamount[12] to declaring openly their love for each other, my father by writing to her, my mother by quoting my father henceforward without false shame in all her conversations.

---

11. brazenly (brāʹzn lē), *adv.* boldly.
12. tantamount (tanʹtə mount), *adj.* equal; equivalent.

After Reading

Making Connections

Shaping Your Response

1. In your notebook, write three words to describe the father and mother's relationship.

2. Whose actions in this selection do you think are the more daring—those of the mother or the father? Explain.

3. Judging from her biography on page 643, what lasting effects might this episode described in her autobiographical sketch have had on the young narrator?

Analyzing the Autobiography

4. How does the **setting** help to explain the significance of the letter?

5. What **conflicts** does this selection exhibit? Are they internal, external, or both?

6. In referring to her husband in the traditional way when she visited her older relatives, do you think the mother was being hypocritical or thoughtful? Explain.

7. Choose the phrase that best summarizes a **theme** of this selection—or state a theme of your own:

   a. the advantage of knowing two languages

   b. the power of love to free us

   c. the tyranny of tradition

Extending the Ideas

8. ☀ The selections by Djebar, Nguyen, and Head deal with women's **interactions** and reactions to cultural traditions. Which characters do you consider "liberated" from sexist cultural restraints? Explain.

9. What one behavior currently expected of American females or males would you most like to change? Why?

Literary Focus: Characterization

Characters can be static (unchanged) or active (changed) by people and events surrounding them. Review the chart you made in your notebook about static and active characters. All evidence in Djebar's narrative points to the fact that her mother is an active character. Write a paragraph comparing Djebar's mother to another active character from your chart.

Vocabulary Study

On your paper, match the numbered word with the letter of its synonym.

betoken
brazenly
euphemism
imperceptible
irrefutable
portent
proviso
tantamount
taciturn
unequivocally

1. brazenly
2. tantamount
3. portent
4. euphemism
5. taciturn
6. unequivocally
7. betoken
8. irrefutable
9. proviso
10. imperceptible

a. stipulation
b. silent
c. equivalent
d. indicate
e. clearly
f. undeniable
g. mild saying
h. gradual
i. boldly
j. sign

Expressing Your Ideas

Writing Choices

Writer's Notebook Update Look at the quickwrite you did before reading this selection. How do you think people in a Muslim country would respond to your ideas? In another quickwrite, describe this response.

As the Roles Turn TV programs reveal a great deal about husband-wife roles in the United States. Watch several weekly programs and record your observations about couples. Write up your observations in a **media report.**

Heart-to-Heart The mother's friends are deeply concerned about her behavior. Write a **dialogue** in which they try to persuade her to return to the old ways.

A Male Perspective As he wrote and addressed the postcard, the father must have thought about the traditions he was breaking and the feelings he had for his wife. Capture his thoughts in an **interior monologue**, expressing ideas in the jumbled, unpunctuated way that thoughts tend to bounce into the mind.

Other Options

From Behind the Veil Muslim women, along with women throughout the world, spoke out for equality in the 1990s. With a group, do research on literature, conferences, and protests in the past decade in which women have sought equality. Find also copies of the laws that they were protesting and legislation they have promoted. Report your findings to the class as a **TV documentary**.

Love, Sweet Love Talk to a couple who has been married since before you were born. Find out how they met, what they initially thought about each other, how they solved any problems that occurred, and how their relationship has changed over the years. Record the **interview** and play it in class.

Before Reading

Legal Alien by Pat Mora   USA   **I Am Not with Those** by Anna Akhmatova Russia

For the White Poets Who Would Be Indian by Wendy Rose USA

Jerusalem by Yehuda Amichai Israel   **Dos Patrias/Two Countries** by José Martí Cuba

Building Background

Pulling Up Stakes Throughout history, people have been on the move—leaving family, friends, and the countries of their birth. What prompted them to do so? Examine the following chart, adding categories if necessary. Cite examples of people or groups who fit each category. If possible, determine which category fits your own family.

Reasons to Emigrate	Emigrants
War	
Religious intolerance	
Racial injustice	
Famine	
Political oppression	
Inadequate education	
Lack of economic opportunities	

Literary Focus

Allusion   An **allusion** is a reference to a person, event, or place, real or fictitious, or to a work of art. For example, you might refer to someone with a mysterious smile as a Mona Lisa or someone with a bad attitude as a Scrooge. In literature, allusions serve to enhance meaning, beauty, or mood.

Writer's Notebook

Out of the Loop It doesn't take a move to a new country to make someone feel like an outsider. In your notebook, describe a time when you felt alienated or alone and explain what, if anything, you did to overcome the feeling.

Pat Mora
born 1942

Pat Mora says, "I write, in part, because Hispanic perspectives need to be part of our literary heritage." Active in efforts to conserve Mexican American culture, Mora has published several books for children as well as a collection of essays and several volumes of poetry.

Wendy Rose
born 1948

Wendy Rose grew up in Oakland, California, the daughter of a Hopi father and an Anglo-Miwok mother. An artist, editor, and anthropologist, as well as a poet, Rose says, "For everything in this universe, there is a song to accompany its existence; writing is another way of singing these songs."

Anna Akhmatova
1889–1966

Anna Gorenko, who adopted the pen name Akhmatova (uk mät′ə və, äk′mə tō′və), suffered greatly at the hands of Soviet authorities: for years she was forbidden to publish, her husband was executed for his opposition to the government, and her son was sent to the labor camps. Nevertheless, she remained in the Soviet Union, leaving an impressive legacy as a poet and a human being.

Yehuda Amichai
born 1924

During World War II, Yehuda Amichai (yə hü′də ä′mi kī) served in the British army's Jewish Brigade in Egypt. In the Arab-Israeli war of 1948, he joined the Israeli defense forces. Afterwards, he completed his education and began writing short stories, radio plays, novels, and poetry. Amichai's poetry, written in Hebrew, is characterized by clarity and everyday language.

José Martí
1853–1895

José Martí (hō sā′ mär tē′) was a leader in the revolution against Spanish rule in 1895. Exiled from Cuba for his political activities, he lived from 1881 to 1895 in New York City, writing works that made him famous throughout Latin America. Martí's death in a skirmish with Spanish forces right after returning to Cuba in 1895 made him a national hero.

LEGAL ALIEN

Pat Mora

Bi-lingual,[1] Bi-cultural,[2]
able to slip from "How's life?"
to *"Me'stan volviendo loca,"*[3]
able to sit in a paneled office
5 drafting memos in smooth English,
able to order in fluent Spanish
at a Mexican restaurant,
American but hyphenated,
viewed by Anglos as perhaps exotic,
10 perhaps inferior, definitely different,
viewed by Mexicans as alien,
(their eyes say, "You may speak
Spanish but you're not like me")
an American to Mexicans
15 a Mexican to Americans
a handy token
sliding back and forth
between the fringes of both worlds
by smiling
20 by masking the discomfort
of being pre-judged
Bi-laterally.[4]

---

1. **bi-lingual** (bī ling′gwəl), *adj.* able to speak another
   language as well or almost as well as one's own.
   (Note that *bilingual, bicultural,* and *bilaterally* are
   usually written with no hyphen.)
2. **bi-cultural** (bī kul′chər əl), *adj.* having distinct cultures existing side by side.
3. ***Me'stan volviendo loca.*** They're driving me crazy.
   [Spanish]
4. **bi-laterally** (bī lat′ər əl ē), *adv.* on two sides.

FOR THE WHITE POETS WHO WOULD BE INDIAN

Wendy Rose

just once
just long enough
to snap up the words
fish-hooked
5 from our tongues.
You think of us now
when you kneel
on the earth,
turn holy
10 in a temporary tourism
of our souls.
With words
you paint your faces.
chew your doeskin,
15 touch breast to tree
as if sharing a mother
were all it takes,
could bring
instant and primal[1]
20 of knowledge.
You think of us only
when your voice
wants for roots,
when you have sat back
25 on your heels
and become primitive.
You finish your poem
and go back.

---

1. **primal** (prī′məl), *adj.* fundamental.

I Am Not with Those

Anna Akhmatova

I am not with those who left their land
For enemies to tear apart.
No heed[1] I pay to their gross flattery,
My songs I will not give to them.

5 But I feel pity for the exiled,
As for prisoners or the sick.
Obscure is your road, O wanderer,
Bitter the taste of alien corn.

But here, in the dense fumes of the fire
10 Destroying what's left of one's youth,
Not a single solitary blow
Did we try to deflect[2] from ourselves.

And we know that in the final count
Each hour will have its reckoning . . .
15 But the world knows no people more tearless,
More proud, more simple than we.

---

1. **heed** (hēd), *n.* attention.
2. **deflect** (di flekt′), *v.* bend or turn aside.

▲ In *Portrait of Anna Akhmatova,* Nathan Altman uses triangular shapes, including the subject's knees and V-shaped neckline, to create a three-dimensional pattern. What effect do the icy blue cubes in the background have on your impression of the subject?

Jerusalem

Yehuda Amichai

On a roof in the Old City
laundry hanging in the late afternoon sunlight:
the white sheet of a woman who is my enemy,
the towel of a man who is my enemy,
5 to wipe off the sweat of his brow.

In the sky of the Old City
a kite.
At the other end of the string,
a child
10 I can't see
because of the wall.

We have put up many flags,
they have put up many flags.
To make us think that they're happy.
15 To make them think that we're happy.

This photograph was taken near the Damascus Gate
in East Jerusalem. Here an Arab boy flies a kite that
resembles the Palestinian flag. Has the photographer
chiefly captured an emotion? depicted an event?
made a political statement? something else? ➤

Dos Patrias

José Martí

Dos patrias tengo yo: Cuba y la noche.
¿O son una las dos? No bien retira
su majestad el Sol, con largos velos
y un clavel en la mano, silenciosa
5 Cuba cual viuda triste me aparece.
¡Yo sé cuál es ese clavel sangriento
que en la mano le tiembla! Está vacío
mi pecho, destrozado está y vacío
en donde estaba el corazón. Ya es hora
10 de empezar a morir. La noche es buena
para decir adiós. La luz estorba
y la palabra humana. El universo
habla mejor que el hombre.
                    Cual bandera
que invita a batallar, la llama roja
15 de la vela flamea. Las ventanas
abro, ya estrecho en mí. Muda, rompiendo
las hojas del clavel, como una nube
que enturbia el cielo, Cuba, viuda, pasa. . . .

Two Countries

translated by Elinor Randall

I have two countries: Cuba and the night.
Or are both one? No sooner does the sun
Withdraw its majesty, than Cuba,
With long veils and holding a carnation,
5 Appears as a sad and silent widow.
I know about that bloodstained carnation
That trembles in her hand! My breast
Is empty, destroyed and empty
Where the heart lay. Now is the time
10 To commence dying. Night is a good time
To say farewell. Light is a hindrance
As is the human word. The universe
Talks better than man.
                    Like a flag
That calls to battle, the candle's
15 Red flame flutters. I feel a closeness
And open windows. Crushing the
            carnation's
Petals silently, widowed Cuba passes by
Like a cloud that dims the heavens. . . .

After Reading

Making Connections

Shaping Your Response

1. What do you think of when you hear the term "Culture Crossroads"? Does the term have positive or negative associations for you?

2. If you could invite one of these poets to speak to your class, whom would you choose and what topics would you most want to hear about?

Analyzing the Poems

3. What do you think Mora means by "American but hyphenated"?

4. Explain both the **denotation** and the **connotation** of the word *token* in line 16 of Mora's poem.

5. What do you think the **figurative** phrase "temporary tourism of our souls" means in Rose's poem?

6. How does Akhmatova feel toward each of these three groups: those who left their land; the exiled; those who stayed?

7. In Amichai's poem, how might both the wall and the flags be **symbolic**?

8. In what ways does Martí **personify**, or give human characteristics to, Cuba?

Extending the Ideas

9. Identify the conflicting cultures and **interactions** in each of these five poems.

Literary Focus: Allusion

In order to understand the biblical **allusion** in lines 7 and 8 of Akhmatova's poem, you may need some background. In the Bible, Ruth was a young Moabite widow who wanted to follow her mother-in-law Naomi to Bethlehem. Naomi begged her to remain with her own people, but Ruth insisted on leaving, saying, ". . . whither thou goest, I will go. . . ." In Judah, Ruth worked in the fields gathering grain.

- How does this allusion to Ruth help express Akhmatova's pity for exiled people?

- How does the description of the *alien* (strange, disagreeable) corn reinforce the poet's attitude?

Vocabulary Study

On your paper, write the word that best completes each sentence next to its number. You will not use all the words.

bicultural
bilaterally
bilingual
deflect
heed
primal

1. A treaty signed ____ between Cuba and Spain might have satisfied José Martí's desire for Cuban independence.

2. Wendy Rose confirms that ____ knowledge is too fundamental to be quickly acquired.

3. Anna Akhmatova asks her country to pay more ____ to its suffering people.

4. Pat Mora says that ____ people are not always widely accepted just because they speak two languages.

5. How might Yehuda Amichai ____ the criticism that writing in Hebrew limits the audience for his work?

Expressing Your Ideas

Writing Choices

Writer's Notebook Update Review your description of being an outsider. Find or add words that express your feelings. Then list words or phrases that might describe the feelings of those who, in the same situation, were insiders.

Strangers in a Strange Land You are president of International Club, a school organization that brings together people of different cultures. In this capacity, write a **proposal** to your school administration suggesting ways to make people aware of the cultural diversity of the student body and the positive aspects of such diversity.

Bilingual Insights Students who speak Spanish can read "Dos Patrias" aloud and indicate on the board word pairs in both languages *(la noche/night; silenciosa/silent; morir/dying)* to help convey the different sounds and shades of meaning words have in different languages.

Other Options

American Mosaic As a class project, make a poster-sized **Culture Crossroads Chart** that represents the members of your class. In each quadrant, labeled National Origins, Languages, Religions, and one other category of your choosing, indicate the contributions of your classmates to the cultural mix that is the United States.

Pieces of America Using words and phrases from these poems and other poems in this book, make a **verbal collage** representing many facets of the United States and its people. Illustrate your verbal collage with pictures.

In Memoriam Washington, D.C., is a city of monuments: older ones like those honoring George Washington, as well as recent memorials such as the Holocaust Museum and the Vietnam Veterans Memorial. Design a **sketch** or **blueprint** for a monument or memorial that celebrates the multiplicity of peoples who have created the United States.

Culture Crossroads

Culture Quilt

Multicultural Connection

A walk down almost any street serves as a reminder that ours is a society of cultural mixes. Whether these cultures blend or clash depends on the amount of respect and understanding each group has for the other.

IT'S HARD TO SMILE
K. CONNIE KANG

A crowd gathers on a Brooklyn street, listening to an African American speak out on the boycott of Korean businesses.

Early in 1990, several African American groups began a boycott of a grocery store owned by Korean immigrants in the Flatbush section of Brooklyn. The African Americans charged that an incident in which a Haitian woman had allegedly been mistreated by one of the store's owners reflected the general lack of respect with which the Koreans treated their black customers. Later in 1990, African Americans began another boycott of a Korean-owned grocery. The second protest soon ended, but the original dispute was still unsettled when the following editorial, by K. Connie Kang, an Asian American journalist, appeared in The New York Times on September 8, 1990. The "Confucian culture" mentioned by Kang is the code of social conduct based on the writings of the Chinese philosopher Confucius (551-479 B.C.). Emphasizing familial duty and respect for tradition, Confucianism has had an enormous impact on Asian civilization.

One of the two black-led boycotts of Korean grocers in Brooklyn ended last week, but the original, eight-month boycott continues. It is no longer a community affair, but a national concern.

As an Asian American, I was jolted at the beginning of the boycott, which allegedly began with an assault on a customer by a store employee, by a comment from a black resident: "The Koreans are a very rude people. They don't understand you have to smile."

Would she have reacted differently had she known smiling at strangers just isn't part of the Korean culture? Would it have made a difference had she known Koreans are just as "unfriendly" to their own because they equate being solicitous to being insincere? The Korean demeanor is the absence of a demeanor. Koreans have a name for it: *mu-pyo-jung*. It means "lack of expression."

Koreans who travel or live abroad are often concerned that this trait causes misunderstanding. Before the 1988 Seoul Olympics, South Korean officials launched a television and radio campaign urging citizens to greet visitors with a friendly smile. Some tried but found it difficult. As one housewife told me: "It's hard to smile at strangers when you're not used to it. It seems so phony."

Though it may be difficult for most Americans to tell Koreans apart from Japanese and Chinese, who have been in this country much longer, the contrast between Koreans and their Asian neighbors is striking. Having suffered invasions and a long period of colonization by Japan in this century, Koreans have had to fight for their lives to retain their language and culture. Koreans are feisty. They certainly don't fit the subservient or docile Asian stereotype.

And Koreans live by *cheong*—a concept that has no Western translation. *Cheong* is love, respect, affinity and loyalty rolled into one. *Cheong* comes only with time, and only betrayal can end it. For a people who live by this ethos [the characteristic attitudes of a group], a mechanical smile is hard to produce.

In America's inner cities, newcomers from Korea do business where no one else will, and where frustration levels are high. . . . Culturally and socially, the newcomers are ill equipped to run businesses in America's inner cities. But because they, like other Asian immigrants, are denied mainstream jobs, they pool their resources and start mom-and-pop stores.

Inner-city African Americans wonder how these newcomers, who can hardly speak English, have the money to run their own businesses when they themselves can't even get a small loan from a bank. They have little hope of escaping the poverty cycle,

yet they see new arrivals living in better neighborhoods and driving better cars.

What they don't see are the 16-hour days and the deep sacrifices made for their children. They don't see the contributions of family and friends, and the informal money-lending system called *kye* that Koreans use instead of banks.

All immigrants go through an "American passage" that requires cultural insight on both sides. Koreans, like other Asians who live in the U.S., mustn't forget that they are indebted to blacks for the social gains won by their civil rights struggle.

Asian Americans must also remember that while the Confucian culture has taught us how to be good parents, sons and daughters and how to behave with people we know, it has not prepared us for living in a democracy. The Confucian ethos lacks the social conscience that makes democracy work. It isn't enough that we educate our children; we need to think of other people's children too.

One of the boycotted grocers told me this had been a painful but valuable experience: "We Koreans must learn to participate in this society," he said. "When this is over, I'm going to reach out. I want to give part-time work to black youths."

By working together, maybe we can do privately what institutions can't. With Asian American drive and African American political experience, we can make it work not only in New York but in Los Angeles, San Francisco, Oakland and Chicago.

CULTURE QUILT

An Amazonian
Indian poses with
his motorcycle.

*Two thousand
Iranian Muslim
women, wearing
the Islamic veil,
participate in track
events at the 100th
Anniversary of
the International
Olympic Committee
in 1994.*

Interdisciplinary Study   **661**

Two Mennonite women
and a cross-country skater
get acquainted.

Mickey Mouse and a friend
offer tourists opportunities
for souvenir photographs
in Mongolia.

Responding

1. Do you think that K. Connie Kang
presents both sides fairly? Explain.

2. According to this article, what
values are emphasized by Confucian
culture versus democracy? Do
you think these values can be
reconciled?

3. Illustrate, photograph, or describe
a culture blend you have observed
in your area, in a magazine, or in
the media.

Writing Workshop

Cultured Questions

Assignment You have read about different cultures. Now research a topic about culture that intrigues you.

WRITER'S BLUEPRINT

Product   A personalized research report

Purpose   To explore intriguing questions you have about culture

Audience   You, your teacher, classmates, and friends

Specs   As the writer of a successful report, you should:

❏ Select an intriguing question you have about culture for the topic of your report.

❏ Begin your report by telling the reader why this topic intrigues you, what you already know—or think you know—about it, and what you would like to find out. Use the first-person ("I") point of view.

❏ Next, test your knowledge by researching your topic. Investigate any useful resources you can think of: books, magazines, online sources, videotapes, museums. Try to get at an interview with at least one firsthand source.

❏ Continue your report by narrating the story of your research. Tell what you discovered and where and how you discovered it. Mention any problems you encountered along the way and how you went about solving them.

❏ End your report by comparing and contrasting what you knew—or thought you knew—before your research with what you discovered later on. Draw conclusions from what you learned. Did your research provide a definitive answer to the original question, or did it raise new questions?

❏ Follow the rules of grammar for correct usage, spelling, and mechanics. Make sure that the facts you present are based on reliable sources that you have documented in a Works Cited list.

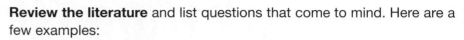
Review the literature and list questions that come to mind. Here are a few examples:

- What is it like to be an outcast in another culture? What makes you an outcast? What injustices do you suffer?

- How do dating and courting customs differ from one culture to another?

- Why would men refer to their wives and family only as "the house-hold"? Don't the wives and children have names?

Add to your list of questions about culture and choose the one that will serve as the topic of your report. Work with a small group, brainstorming ideas. The questions don't have to be from the literature. Perhaps you have a question about your own cultural heritage, or about the heritage of a classmate. Since you'll be spending a lot of time on this paper, make sure the question you choose is genuinely meaningful to you.

Try a quickwrite. Write for five minutes. Explain what your question is, why you want to know about it, and how you plan to gather information. Share your quickwrite with your group. Perhaps they can help you refine your question or give you more ideas about gathering information.

Chart your knowledge. Write down what you already know, what you assume, and what you imagine about the topic, using a chart like the one shown. Also, note what you would like to find out. Remember to write in the first-person ("I") point of view.

How are women's roles changing in the Middle East?

What I Know	What I Assume	What I Imagine	What I Would Like to Find Out
I know that women must wear veils and long robes any time they leave the house.	I assume the women's lives are still controlled by men and that they have no rights.	I imagine that women and girls stay at home and don't have an opportunity to shop, go to school, or get jobs.	Have there been any changes lately in women's lives in the Middle East?

OR . . .

Discuss your question with the group and ask for comments.

Research your topic. Visit the library, museums, and other community institutions to find sources of useful information. Try to get an interview with at least one firsthand source: an expert who knows something about your topic.

For each source, make a **source card** that lists the information you'll need for your Works Cited list. Give each source card a separate number. Record relevant information on **note cards**. Include the source name and number and the appropriate page numbers. See the examples that follow.

Source Card

1

Schwartz, Melvin, and John R. O'Connor.

Exploring a Changing World.

Englewood Cliffs:

Globe Book Company, 1988.

Note Card

Exploring a Changing World   1

Saudi Arabian women follow rules laid down by the government; rules are part of the Islamic faith; Islamic faith allows women to own property and money separate from their husbands.

p. 424

Plan your report. Organize the information from your notes into a plan like this one:

Your topic
Why it intrigues you
What you already know about it
What you assume or imagine about it
What you would like to find out

Your research experience
The steps you took
Problems and how you handled them
What you discovered

What you already knew compared/contrasted with what you discovered
Similarities
Differences
Conclusions

OR . . .
Use a tape recorder to record your research experience first. Then, take notes from the tape and put them into the plan.

Before you draft, look over your notes and writing plan and reread the Writer's Blueprint.

As you draft, concentrate on putting the ideas from your report plan on paper. Try these drafting tips to help you get started.

- Begin your report with an intriguing question, fact, anecdote, or other attention-getting device. See the Revising Strategy in Step 3.

- Narrate the story of your research experience as if you were taking a journey. Use words like *embark, destination, stops,* and *side trips.*

- For the third section, include personal insights that you discovered about the research process as well as about the topic itself.

Notice how this student includes personal insights about the research experience.

> The people I talked to felt that over time, society has become more tolerant of diversity. However, current events reported in the newspaper and magazines told a different story. Why would this discrepancy exist? Maybe individual people are ready to accept differences in others but this isn't always reflected in the news.

Compile a Works Cited list. Use your source cards. See the Editing Strategy in Step 4 of this lesson.

STEP 3 REVISING

Ask a partner to comment on your draft before you revise it. Use this checklist as a guide.

✔ Did I narrate my information search in a way that will not just inform but engage my reader?

✔ Did I compare and contrast what I knew and what I discovered later on?

✔ Did I begin the paper with an intriguing opening?

Revising Strategy

Writing an Intriguing Opening

Since this is about a topic that intrigues you, you should open your paper in a way that intrigues the reader. When you revise, experiment with different types of openings to get the reader as involved as you are. Try one of these opening ideas:

- Pose a provocative question: "Why can't people accept each other's differences?"

- Relate an anecdote—an incident that you were involved in—that shows how you became interested in your topic: "The first time I realized there was such a thing as prejudice was the morning I. . . ."

- Write a short, lively question-answer dialogue about what you would like to discover about your topic, as if you were talking with yourself.

Notice how the writer in the student model revised her opening to turn it into a question-answer dialogue.

○   *Why can't people accept each other's differences?*
     ~~People have a hard time accepting each other's differences.~~

     Throughout history there have been cultural differences between

○   people and it seems there has also been prejudice. But people are
                      Where do these biases come from?
     born without prejudices. ~~These biases must come from somewhere.~~

○   The people you grow up around influence the way you think and do

     things, so you think that's the only right way.

STEP **4** EDITING

Ask a partner to review your revised draft before you edit. When you edit, look for errors in grammar, usage, spelling, and mechanics. Make sure the research sources are cited correctly in the Works Cited list.

Editing Strategy

Works Cited Form

The Works Cited list is the last page of your report. All the sources you cited in your report are listed on this page. Here are examples of how to cite three different kinds of sources.

For a book with more than one author:
Schwartz, Melvin, and John R. O'Connor. *Exploring a Changing World.* Englewood Cliffs: Globe Book Company, 1988.

For a periodical:
Clarke, John I. "Islamic Populations: Limited Demographic Transitions." *Geography*, vol. 70 (1985), 118–128.

For a general reference book:
"Saudi Arabia." *The New Encyclopedia Britannica*. 1979 ed.

Your teacher might ask you to use **footnotes** to acknowledge sources of information within the text of your report. Find out which style of footnotes your teacher prefers. Then, be consistent.

STEP 5 PRESENTING

- Condense your paper into a five- or ten-minute oral presentation and share your questions and discoveries with the class.

- Include a map or time line to go along with the second part of your report. See the Computer Tip.

STEP 6 LOOKING BACK

Self-evaluate. Look back at the Writer's Blueprint and give your paper a score for each item, from 6 (superior) to 1 (inadequate).

Reflect. How was writing a personalized research report different from writing a standard research report?

For Your Working Portfolio Add your report and reflection responses to your working portfolio.

Beyond Print

Computer Terms

CD-ROM, Compact Disc Read Only Memory. This disc, which looks similar to an audio CD, is readable only with a computer that has a CD-ROM player and is used to store information such as text, sound, pictures, and movies.

Database, an organized collection of information, especially one in electronic form that can be accessed by computer software.

Internet, a series of computer servers connected together around the world.

Network, two or more computers connected together by cables, allowing them to communicate with each other.

Server, a computer that operates a network.

Electronic Research

As you prepare for any research project, review what electronic tools are available and how to make the best use of these tools. With modern technology at your fingertips, you can spend less research time tracking down materials and more time analyzing and sorting information. In your school, local library, or home, you may find these resources:

- A *magazine or newspaper index* stored on a CD-ROM. Many of these databases contain summaries or the full text of material in periodicals.

- *Reference materials* such as dictionaries, atlases, and almanacs on CD-ROM. Entire encyclopedias can be written onto a single CD-ROM!

- *Online services* connect you with other computers, giving you access to encyclopedias, magazines, reviews, interviews, and subject-specific databases. Using online services, librarians can search other libraries for books, articles, or other material necessary for your research. An important online database is the Internet, which can be accessed through government or educational institutions, as well as by individuals who buy membership in a consumer online service. With so much information at your fingertips, the biggest challenge is narrowing your search. Keep these things in mind:

- **Enter information accurately.** The computer can't read your mind, and it is extremely literal! If you are searching for an author, for example, be sure to spell the author's name correctly.

- **If you are searching by subject, try several different key words.** Don't quit if the first word you try doesn't turn up much. If you are researching apartheid in South Africa, the information you want may be filed under South Africa, Johannesburg, apartheid, Nelson Mandela, or any number of other key words. Keep trying!

Activity Options

1. Ask your librarian for a tour of the library's electronic research resources.

2. Work with a partner to create a list of key words on a particular subject, and use these words to collect information.

Multicultural Connections

Communication

Part One: Connections Both culture and individual personalities determine the way we communicate. This group of poems reflects on the ways we reach out to communicate and connect—with family, with lovers, and with ourselves. Some poems provide poignant reminders of the pain of miscommunication and loss.

■ Choose three poems that deal with a lack of communication. Explain what is preventing communication in each case.

Choice

Part Two: Reflections Choice is often influenced by the cultural values of the society in which we live. But despite the different ceremonies, values, and directions we choose, there is a common life cycle that encompasses and reconciles various choices, as we are reminded in Ecclesiastes.

■ Do you think the message in Ecclesiastes suggests that people have a great deal of choice, or little choice, in determining their lives? Explain.

Interactions

Part Three: Culture Crossroads The cross-cultural interactions represented in this group of selections show that cultural mixes can have both positive and negative results.

■ Which selections in this group illustrate the positive effects of cross-cultural interactions? Which, the negative effects?

Activities

1. Examine your neighborhood, the Yellow Pages, or your school to find examples of cultures interacting. You might focus on bilingual signs and conversations, or music, foods, or clothing styles that reflect cultural combinations. Prepare a video, a poster, or an oral report to share with the class.

2. Ask a student who has immigrated to the U.S. to explain some of the main problems he or she has had with communication. Try to provide some solutions for preventing future problems.

Independent and Group Projects

Media

Literary Quest You and your group are writers for a TV quiz show titled *A Place in the World*. It is your job to devise twenty questions for the category, Literature and Authors from Around the World, based on the biographies and works of authors represented in this unit. Have a group member act as host, and invite class members to be contestants.

Art

Multicultural Mixes Find photographs, articles, and quotations that show the influence of one culture on another (for example, elderly people attending rap or rock concerts). Use this material to make your own Interdisciplinary Study, like the one that begins on page 659. Write several questions to elicit student response to your words and images.

Oral Presentation

Book Talk You are a librarian who hosts a weekly program called *Book Talk* on cable TV. Prepare a two-minute sampler of the works in this unit and present the talk to the class. Remember, your job is to attract readers.

Translations

Many Tongues Several of the poems in this unit appear in their original language and in their English translations. Class members who are native speakers or students of a language other than English can provide translations of other poems in this unit. Studying the same word or phrase in various languages can spark a discussion about the skill and artistry required of a translator, as well as the complexities of a language.

Research

Take Off The Ministry of Tourism in one of the countries represented by selections in this unit has asked your ad agency to write copy and provide pictures for a travel brochure. In a group, decide what to include and how to present it. Display your brochure for the class.

POWER PLAYS

The Cost of Winning
Pages 676–799

READING A
SHAKESPEAREAN
PLAY

Some of the words may seem outdated; the sentences may look difficult. But reading Shakespearean drama is not much different from reading any play—so long as you read actively and become familiar with Shakespeare's richly unique language. Here are some tools to enrich your reading and make it easier.

READ THE SCENE SUMMARY

Take advantage of the scene summaries immediately preceding each scene. They tell you what to expect and provide the highlights. You might also reread these summaries later to clarify action you missed or details you overlooked.

READ THE SCENE STRAIGHT THROUGH

Read initially to find out what happens—and pay attention to the stage directions. Once you have a general idea of the action and the relationships of the characters, you can reread, focusing on more specific details.

USE THE MARGINAL NOTES

When you read closely and need help, refer to the notes in the margins. They define unfamiliar words, clarify allusions, explain word play, and provide pronunciations which may come in handy when you read aloud. The marginal questions marked with black boxes are especially valuable as reading tools to help you clarify, question, summarize, predict, evaluate, and make connections.

Think About the Characters

Focus on the major characters. What do these characters reveal in their conversations? What do others say about them? What conflicts or alliances do they have with others? What motivates and troubles them? What makes them "ring true"? Think also about why minor characters appear. To add humor? To introduce tension? To clarify situations or provide background?

Rearrange Inverted Sentences

English sentences typically begin with a subject followed by a verb. Shakespeare often changes that order. For example, in the first scene of *Julius Caesar*, Flavius says to Marullus, "Go you down that way towards the Capitol." Rearranged, this sentence would read: "You go down that way. . . ."

Be Alert for Word Omissions

In the preceding example, the line continues with these words: "This way will I." Modernized, this would read "I will go this way."

Interpret Figurative Language

Shakespeare often uses figurative language to convey important ideas. Ask yourself what the comparison is and what it suggests. For example, Cassius says about Caesar,

"He were no lion, were not Romans hinds." Since a hind is a female deer, Cassius implies that Caesar's strength is due to the Roman citizens' cowardice (that is, "If the Romans weren't cowards, Caesar wouldn't be in power").

Recognize Blank Verse

Most of the characters in *Julius Caesar* speak in blank verse (also called iambic pentameter), a form of unrhymed poetry in which each line has ten syllables—five unstressed alternating with five stressed. This rhythm pattern can be shown like this, with ´ indicating stressed words and syllables and ‿ indicating those that are unstressed.

And why/should Cae/sar be/a ty/rant then?

As you read, notice that a line of blank verse can be divided among two or more characters. Note also that, depending on his purpose, Shakespeare may vary the rhythm in this form, or abandon it altogether for prose.

Read Passages Aloud

Plays were meant to be *said*, not *read*. Read aloud to yourself or with a friend. Read for sense, using punctuation as clues. Once you determine the character's attitude and purpose in speaking, you should find just the right tone of voice.

These are some tools. But the best way to understand and enjoy a Shakespearean play is to see it in action. So rent a film (the 1953 production of *Julius Caesar* starring Marlon Brando, from which some of the photographs in this book are taken, would be a good place to begin); see a play; or put on your own classroom production. You'll be surprised to learn how modern the situations, themes, and even the language can seem!

"SPEAK, HANDS, FOR ME!"

The Cost of Winning

Power, land, wealth—all have their appeal. But is winning always worth it? The characters in these selections give up a great deal of what is human in their pursuits of power. And the cost? Respect, reputation, maybe life itself.

Multicultural Connection **Change** can be good for a society, but it can also devastate a social order. Read about people who try to make drastic changes in their lives or the lives of others.

Before Reading

Julius Caesar

by William Shakespeare   Great Britain

William Shakespeare
1564–1616

William Shakespeare grew up in a middle-class family in Stratford-upon-Avon, a small town north of London. He attended grammar school until he was fourteen, and by age eighteen he was married to Anne Hathaway. Their first child was born in 1583, followed two years later by twins. At school, Shakespeare may first have read Plutarch's *Lives of the Noble Greeks and Romans,* his chief source for *Julius Caesar.* No one knows why or when Shakespeare left Stratford for London, but by 1592 he was an actor; by 1602, he was a prolific dramatist and part owner of the Globe Theater. In 1611, he retired to Stratford, respected and wealthy. He died on April 16, 1616, the anniversary of his baptism.

Building Background

Power Struggle For many years Julius Caesar struggled with Pompey (pom′pē), once his ally, for control of Rome and its territories. Eventually war broke out between them and in 48 B.C. Caesar, a superb military leader, defeated Pompey, who fled to Egypt for safety and was murdered there. When Pompey's two sons took up the war, Caesar defeated them too. Returning to Rome, Caesar was named dictator, a title that gave him absolute authority for life. Many Romans became suspicious of Caesar's power, fearing that his desire to become king would put an end to their republic. Still other Romans were angry that Caesar celebrated a public triumph over Pompey's sons, who were not foreigners but Romans like themselves. The action of Shakespeare's *Julius Caesar* begins on the day Caesar has selected to celebrate his triumphant return to the city.

Literary Focus

Plot A series of related events that present and resolve a conflict is called **plot**. Watch for ways in which Shakespeare advances plot through action and dialogue. Reproduce the plot diagram in your notebook that appears on page 65, and add plot elements to the diagram as you read. The beginning of the play, or the **exposition**, introduces the viewers or readers to the background, characters, and setting. The first incident begins the **conflict**.

Writer's Notebook

Caesar As you read this play, fill out a chart like the one below, listing and illustrating Caesar's character traits, based both on what he says and does and on how others speak of him.

Character Trait	Illustration
suspicious	"Cassius . . . thinks too much."

Source

Shakespeare drew on Plutarch's *Lives of the Noble Greeks and Romans*, translated from Latin by Sir Thomas North, for most of the material in the play. "The Life of Caesar" gave him much of the basic plot; "The Life of Brutus" provided characterization, especially of Brutus and Cassius; and "The Life of Mark Antony" gave him information about Antony, as well as the idea for another tragedy, *Antony and Cleopatra*, written in 1606.

Major Characters

Julius Caesar (100 B.C.–44 B.C.) was a great conqueror and politician. He gained territory for Rome and frequently sent money back to the city to be used for public works or to help the common people. Although he was given the honor of ruling Rome as long as he lived, many suspected that he wanted to set up a monarchy so that power would pass to his heirs. Caesar was married to Calpurnia, but thus far she had borne no children.

Marcus Brutus (85 B.C.–44 B.C.) was a descendant of Lucius Junius Brutus, who had driven out the Tarquin kings and made Rome a republic. Marcus Brutus was a quiet idealist who enjoyed reading and study. At one time, he had supported Pompey, one of Caesar's chief rivals for power, and had fought with him against Caesar. After Pompey's defeat Caesar pardoned Brutus, and the two resumed their friendship. Though Brutus liked Caesar, he feared Caesar's ambition. Brutus was married to Portia, whose father had killed himself rather than submit to Caesar's rule.

Caius Cassius (? B.C.–42 B.C.) was a thin, quick-tempered, practical man with a grudge against Caesar. Like Brutus, he had supported Pompey in the war against Caesar. After Brutus was pardoned, Caesar also pardoned Cassius, who was Brutus's brother-in-law.

Mark Antony (83 B.C.–30 B.C.) was a young man notorious for his wild living. He had fought under Caesar and supported Caesar's ambitious schemes. A holder of various public offices, including that of tribune, Antony understood the instability of the commoners and how a speaker could sway their emotions.

JULIUS CAESAR

WILLIAM SHAKESPEARE

CHARACTERS

JULIUS CAESAR
CALPURNIA, *Caesar's wife*
MARK ANTONY
OCTAVIUS CAESAR } *triumvirs¹ after Caesar's death*
LEPIDUS
MARCUS BRUTUS
PORTIA, *Brutus's wife*
CAIUS CASSIUS
CASCA
DECIUS BRUTUS
CINNA } *conspirators with Brutus*
METELLUS CIMBER
TREBONIUS
CAIUS LIGARIUS
CICERO
PUBLIUS } *senators*
POPILIUS LENA
FLAVIUS } *tribunes² of the people*
MARULLUS
SOOTHSAYER
ARTEMIDORUS, *a teacher of rhetoric*
CINNA, *a poet*
Another POET
LUCILIUS
TITINIUS
MESSALA } *officers and soldiers in the army of Brutus and Cassius*
YOUNG CATO
VOLUMNIUS
VARRO

CLAUDIUS
CLITUS
DARDANIUS } *officers and soldiers in the army of Brutus and Cassius*
LABEO
FLAVIUS
PINDARUS, *Cassius's servant*
LUCIUS } *Brutus's servants*
STRATO
Caesar's SERVANT
Antony's SERVANT
Octavius's SERVANT
CARPENTER
COBBLER
Five PLEBEIANS
Three SOLDIERS *in Brutus's army*
Two SOLDIERS *in Antony's army*
MESSENGER
GHOST *of Caesar*
Senators, Plebians, Officers, Soldiers , and Attendants

---

1. **triumvirs** (trī um′vərz), three officials who jointly ruled Rome, from the Latin *trium virorum,* "of three men."
2. **tribunes,** elected officials who served as spokesmen for the commoners and protected them from the government if necessary.

ACT ONE

Summary *When the tribunes Flavius and Marullus encounter a crowd of commoners gathered to celebrate Caesar's victory over Pompey's sons, Marullus angrily scolds them for forgetting their former allegiance to Pompey. The two men disperse the crowd, then exit, vowing to remove any decorations on Caesar's public statues.*

A street in Rome. The COMMONERS, *dressed in holiday garments for the Feast of Lupercalia and talking excitedly, look to the right, the direction from which* CAESAR's *procession will appear. Offstage shouts and cheers send* COMMONERS *scurrying for vantage points.* FLAVIUS *and* MARULLUS *enter.*

FLAVIUS. Hence! Home, you idle creatures, get you home!
   Is this a holiday? What, know you not,
   Being mechanical, you ought not walk
   Upon a laboring without the sign
5 Of your profession? Speak, what trade art thou?
CARPENTER. Why, sir, a carpenter.
MARULLUS. Where is thy leather apron and thy rule?
   What dost thou with thy best apparel on?
   You, sir, what trade are you?
10 **COBBLER.** Truly, sir, in respect of a fine workman, I am but, as you
   would say, a cobbler.
MARULLUS. But what trade art thou? Answer me directly.
COBBLER. A trade, sir, that I hope I may use with a safe conscience,
   which is indeed, sir, a mender of bad soles.
15 **FLAVIUS.** What trade, thou knave? Thou naughty knave, what trade?
COBBLER. Nay, I beseech you, sir, be not out with me. Yet if you be out,
   sir, I can mend you.
FLAVIUS. What mean'st thou by that? Mend me, thou saucy fellow?
COBBLER. Why, sir, cobble you.
20 **FLAVIUS.** Thou art a cobbler, art thou?
COBBLER. Truly, sir, all that I live by is with the awl. I meddle with no
   tradesman's matters nor women's matters, but withal I am indeed,
   sir, a surgeon to old shoes. When they are in great danger, I recover
   them. As proper men as ever trod upon neat's leather have gone
25 upon my handiwork.
FLAVIUS. But wherefore art not in thy shop today? Why dost thou lead
   these men about the streets?
COBBLER. Truly, sir, to wear out their shoes, to get myself into more
   work. But indeed, sir, we make holiday to see Caesar and to rejoice
30 in his triumph.

3 mechanical, workingmen.

3–5 you ought not . . . profession, a reference to a law of Shakespeare's time requiring workers to wear their laboring clothes and carry the tools of their profession.

11 cobbler. In Shakespeare's time this word meant not only a shoe mender but also a clumsy worker. This explains Marullus's question.

16 be not . . . me, a pun. To be out meant both "out of temper" as well as "having worn-out soles."

22 withal, yet. Another pun, on both "all" and "with awl" (a shoemaker's tool).
24 neat's leather, cowhide.

The Armorer's Shop was painted in 1866 by Sir Lawrence Alma-Tadema, known for his attention to historical and archaeological detail. To what point is your eye immediately directed? What do you think the armorer is saying? ▼

MARULLUS. Wherefore rejoice? What conquest brings he home?
What tributaries follow him to Rome
To grace in captive bonds his chariot wheels?
You blocks, you stones, you worse than senseless things!
35 O you hard hearts, you cruel men of Rome,
Knew you not Pompey? Many a time and oft
Have you climbed up to walls and battlements,
To towers and windows, yea, to chimney tops,
Your infants in your arms, and there have sat
40 The livelong day, with patient expectation,
To see great Pompey pass the streets of Rome.
And when you saw his chariot but appear,
Have you not made an universal shout,
That Tiber trembled underneath her banks
45 To hear the replication of your sounds
Made in her concave shores?
And do you now put on your best attire?
And do you now cull out a holiday?
And do you now strew flowers in his way
50 That comes in triumph over Pompey's blood?
Begone!
Run to your houses, fall upon your knees,
Pray to the gods to intermit the plague
That needs must light on this ingratitude.
55 **FLAVIUS.** Go, go, good countrymen, and for this fault
Assemble all the poor men of your sort;
Draw them to Tiber banks, and weep your tears
Into the channel, till the lowest stream
Do kiss the most exalted shores of all.
(All the COMMONERS *exit.)*
60 See whe'er their basest mettle be not moved.
They vanish tongue-tied in their guiltiness.
Go you down that way towards the Capitol;
This way will I. Disrobe the images
If you do find them decked with ceremonies.
65 **MARULLUS.** May we do so?
You know it is the Feast of Lupercal.
FLAVIUS. It is no matter. Let no images
Be hung with Caesar's trophies. I'll about
And drive away the vulgar from the streets;
70 So do you too, where you perceive them thick.
These growing feathers plucked from Caesar's wing
Will make him fly an ordinary pitch,
Who else would soar above the view of men
And keep us all in <u>servile</u> fearfulness. *(The* TRIBUNES *exit.)*

32 tributaries, captives who must pay tribute (ransom) to Rome for their freedom.

36 Knew . . . Pompey? The fickle mob had once cheered Pompey as they now cheer his enemy, Caesar.
37–38 battlements . . . chimney tops. Ancient Rome had neither battlements nor chimney tops. Such an error, deliberate or otherwise, is called an *anachronism* (ə-nak′rə niz′əm). Look for others as you read.
44 Tiber, the river that runs through Rome.
45 replication, echo.

50 Pompey's blood, Pompey's sons.

53 intermit, withhold.

55 Characters from upper social levels, like Marullus and Flavius, speak in *blank verse* (see page 675); commoners speak prose. What other indication is there that the tribunes outrank the commoners?
57–59 weep your tears . . . of all, weep enough tears to bring the lowest water line up to the highest.
63 Disrobe the images . . . ceremonies. Take down any decorations adorning Caesar's statues.
66 Feast of Lupercal, celebrated on February 15 in honor of Lupercus, god of fertility.
71 These growing feathers, Caesar's new followers.
74 servile (sèr′vəl), *adj.* like that of a slave.

Summary *When Caesar and his entourage enter, a soothsayer warns him of the ides (īdz), the 15th, of March. Caesar dismisses the warning and moves on, and Cassius and Brutus remain. Cassius attempts to enlist Brutus in the conspiracy against Caesar. Later, Casca reports that Antony offered Caesar a crown three times, and when Caesar refused it, the crowd cheered. Cassius and Brutus agree to meet the next day.*

A public place in Rome. The COMMONERS *crowd in to await* CAESAR's *arrival.* SOLDIERS *march on to control the crowd. After a trumpet flourish,* CAESAR *enters, accompanied by* ANTONY, CALPURNIA, PORTIA, DECIUS, CICERO, BRUTUS, CASSIUS, *and* CASCA; FLAVIUS *and* MARULLUS *enter. As the* COMMONERS *cheer and bow to* CAESAR, *a* SOOTHSAYER *edges toward* CAESAR.

CAESAR. Calpurnia!

CASCA. Peace, ho! Caesar speaks.

CAESAR. Calpurnia!

CALPURNIA. Here, my lord.

CAESAR. Stand you directly in Antonio's way
When he doth run his course. Antonio!

5 **ANTONY.** Caesar, my lord?

CAESAR. Forget not, in your speed, Antonio,
To touch Calpurnia; for our elders say
The barren, touched in this holy chase,
Shake off their sterile curse.

ANTONY. I shall remember.

10 When Caesar says "Do this," it is performed.

CAESAR. Set on, and leave no ceremony out. *(Sound of trumpets.)*

SOOTHSAYER. Caesar!

CAESAR. Ha? Who calls?

CASCA. Bid every noise be still. Peace yet again!
(The music ceases.)

15 **CAESAR.** Who is it in the press that calls on me?
I hear a tongue shriller than all the music
Cry "Caesar!" Speak. Caesar is turned to hear.

SOOTHSAYER. Beware the ides of March.

CAESAR. What man is that?

BRUTUS. A soothsayer bids you beware the ides of March.

20 **CAESAR.** Set him before me. Let me see his face.

CASSIUS. Fellow, come from the throng. *(The* SOOTHSAYER *comes forward.)* Look upon Caesar.

CAESAR. What sayst thou to me now? Speak once again.

SOOTHSAYER. Beware the ides of March.

---

soothsayer, person who claims to foretell events.

4 when he doth run his course. During the Lupercalia, groups watched priest-celebrants who ran a specified course, striking people in their way with goatskin thongs. Women desiring children purposely sought to be struck as a cure for infertility. Antony, as one of the priests, will be one of the young nobles making the run through the streets.
■ What traits does Caesar have in common with other leaders you have known or observed?

15 press, throng, crowd.

18 the ides of March. It fell one month after the feast of Lupercal.

CAESAR. He is a dreamer. Let us leave him. Pass.
(*All exit except* BRUTUS *and* CASSIUS.)

25 **CASSIUS.** Will you go see the order of the course?

BRUTUS. Not I.

CASSIUS. I pray you, do.

BRUTUS. I am not gamesome. I do lack some part
    Of that quick spirit that is in Antony.
30   Let me not hinder, Cassius, your desires;
    I'll leave you.

CASSIUS. Brutus, I do observe you now of late.
    I have not from your eyes that gentleness
    And show of love as I was wont to have.
35   You bear too stubborn and too strange a hand
    Over your friend that loves you.

BRUTUS.   Cassius,
    Be not deceived. If I have veiled my look,
    I turn the trouble of my countenance
    Merely upon myself. Vexèd I am
40   Of late with passions of some difference,
    Conceptions only proper to myself,
    Which give some soil, perhaps, to my behaviors.
    But let not therefore my good friends be grieved—
    Among which number, Cassius, be you one—
45   Nor construe any further my neglect
    Than that poor Brutus, with himself at war,
    Forgets the shows of love to other men.

CASSIUS. Then, Brutus, I have much mistook your passion,
    By means whereof this breast of mine hath buried
50   Thoughts of great value, worthy cogitations.
    Tell me, good Brutus, can you see your face?

BRUTUS. No, Cassius, for the eye sees not itself
    But by reflection, by some other things.
(*He moves downstage;* CASSIUS *follows.*)

CASSIUS. 'Tis just.
55   And it is very much lamented, Brutus,
    That you have no such mirrors as will turn
    Your hidden worthiness into your eye,
    That you might see your shadow. I have heard
    Where many of the best respect in Rome,
60   Except immortal Caesar, speaking of Brutus
    And groaning underneath this age's yoke,
    Have wished that noble Brutus had his eyes.

BRUTUS. Into what dangers would you lead me, Cassius,
    That you would have me seek into myself
65   For that which is not in me?

---

28 gamesome, fond of sports, merry.
29 quick spirit, liveliness, responsiveness.

34 as I was wont to have, that I customarily had.
35 stubborn, rough.

38 countenance (koun′tə-nəns), expression of the face.
38–39 I turn the trouble . . . upon myself. Brutus's facial expression masks troubled thoughts, not any change of attitude toward Cassius.
42 soil, blemish.
■ How does Cassius describe Brutus's unusual behavior, and what is Brutus's response?
48–50 Then . . . worthy cogitations. Here Cassius hints at the thoughts (cogitations) locked in his own breast and begins sounding out Brutus to see whether he has the same thoughts and, thus, will join with the conspirators.

58 shadow, image, reflection.
59 best respect, highest repute and station (class).

CASSIUS. Therefore, good Brutus, be prepared to hear;
    And since you know you cannot see yourself
    So well as by reflection, I, your glass,
    Will modestly discover to yourself
70 That of yourself which you yet know not of.
    And be not jealous on me, gentle Brutus.
    Were I a common laughter, or did use
    To stale with ordinary oaths my love
    To every new protester; if you know
75 That I do fawn on men and hug them hard
    And after scandal them, or if you know
    That I profess myself in banqueting
    To all the rout, then hold me dangerous.
    (Sound of trumpets and a shout.)
BRUTUS. What means this shouting? I do fear the people
80 Choose Caesar for their king.
CASSIUS.   Ay, do you fear it?
    Then must I think you would not have it so.
BRUTUS. I would not, Cassius, yet I love him well.
    But wherefore do you hold me here so long?
    What is it that you would impart to me?
85 If it be aught toward the general good,
    Set honor in one eye and death i' th' other
    And I will look on both indifferently;
    For let the gods so speed me as I love
    The name of honor more than I fear death.
90 **CASSIUS.** I know that virtue to be in you, Brutus,
    As well as I do know your outward favor.
    Well, honor is the subject of my story.
    I cannot tell what you and other men
    Think of this life; but, for my single self,
95 I had as lief not be as live to be
    In awe of such a thing as I myself.
    I was born free as Caesar, so were you;
    We both have fed as well, and we can both
    Endure the winter's cold as well as he.
100 For once, upon a raw and gusty day,
    The troubled Tiber chafing with her shores,
    Caesar said to me, "Dar'st thou, Cassius, now
    Leap in with me into this angry flood
    And swim to yonder point?" Upon the word,
105 Accoutred as I was, I plungèd in
    And bade him follow; so indeed he did.
    The torrent roared, and we did buffet it
    With lusty sinews, throwing it aside

71 jealous on, suspicious of.
72–74 common laughter . . . protester, a laughing-stock or one who cheapens his friendship with oaths to everyone who declares (protests) friendship.

78 the rout, the mob; worthless people.

■ Cassius pounces on Brutus's use of the word *fear.* What might this suggest about Cassius's feelings toward Caesar?

84 impart, communicate; tell.
85–87 If it be . . . indifferently. If what Cassius has in mind is for the public welfare and is honorable, Brutus will do it, even if it means death.

91 favor, appearance.

95 lief, willingly.

105 accoutred (ə kü′tərd), **as I was.** The statement implies that Cassius was fully dressed.

And stemming it with hearts of controversy.
110　But ere we could arrive the point proposed,
　　　Caesar cried, "Help me, Cassius, or I sink!"
　　　Ay, as Aeneas, our great ancestor,
　　　Did from the flames of Troy upon his shoulder
　　　The old Anchises bear, so from the waves of Tiber
115　Did I the tirèd Caesar. And this man
　　　Is now become a god, and Cassius is
　　　A wretched creature and must bend his body
　　　If Caesar carelessly but nod on him.
　　　He had a fever when he was in Spain,
120　And when the fit was on him I did mark
　　　How he did shake. 'Tis true, this god did shake.
　　　His coward lips did from their color fly,
　　　And that same eye whose bend doth awe the world
　　　Did lose his luster. I did hear him groan.
125　Ay, and that tongue of his that bade the Romans
　　　Mark him and write his speeches in their books,
　　　Alas, it cried, "Give me some drink, Titinius,"
　　　As a sick girl. Ye gods, it doth amaze me
　　　A man of such a feeble temper should
130　So get the start of the majestic world
　　　And bear the palm alone.
　　　(Shouts and the sound of trumpets.)
　　　BRUTUS *(turning his head upstage).* Another general shout?
　　　　I do believe that these applauses are
　　　　For some new honors that are heaped on Caesar.
135　**CASSIUS.** Why, man, he doth bestride the narrow world
　　　Like a Colossus, and we petty men
　　　Walk under his huge legs and peep about
　　　To find ourselves dishonorable graves.
　　　Men at some time are masters of their fates.
140　The fault, dear Brutus, is not in our stars,
　　　But in ourselves, that we are underlings.
　　　"Brutus" and "Caesar." What should be in that "Caesar"?
　　　Why should that name be sounded more than yours?
　　　Write them together, yours is as fair a name;
145　Sound them, it doth become the mouth as well;
　　　Weigh them, it is as heavy; conjure with 'em,
　　　"Brutus" will start a spirit as soon as "Caesar."
　　　Now, in the names of all the gods at once,
　　　Upon what meat doth this our Caesar feed
150　That he is grown so great? Age, thou art shamed!
　　　Rome, thou has lost the breed of noble bloods!
　　　When went there by an age since the great flood

112–114 as Aeneas (i nē′əs) **. . . Anchises** (an kī′sēz) **bear.** Aeneas carried his aged father Anchises out of Troy as it was falling to the Greeks. After wandering for years, he settled near the banks of the Tiber River and his descendants founded Rome.
■ *Lines 100–131.* Why do you think Cassius draws Brutus's attention to Caesar's physical weaknesses?
122 His coward lips . . . fly. His lips became white.
123 bend, glance.
124 his, its, in modern usage.

129 a man . . . feeble temper, weak constitution. The Romans worshiped strength; here Cassius paints Caesar as a weakling.
131 the palm, the victor's prize, a palm leaf.

136 like a Colossus (kə-los′əs). The Colossus, a 100-foot-high bronze statue of Helios, the sun god, stood astride the entrance to the harbor at the island of Rhodes. According to legend, it was so enormous that ships could pass between its legs.

147 start a spirit, call forth a ghost from the spirit world

■ *Lines 135–161.* What impact do you think these arguments of Cassius will have on Brutus?

But it was famed with more than with one man?
When could they say, till now, that talked of Rome,
155   That her wide walks encompassed but one man?
Now is it Rome indeed, and room enough,
When there is in it but one only man.
O, you and I have heard our fathers say
There was a Brutus once that would have brooked
160   Th' eternal devil to keep his state in Rome
As easily as a king.
  BRUTUS. That you do love me, I am nothing jealous.
What you would work me to, I have some aim.

156 Rome . . . room, a
pun, since in Shakespeare's
time the two words were
pronounced alike.
Shakespeare's audience
delighted in such word play.

A film of *Julius Caesar* was produced in 1953 by John Houseman and directed by
Joseph Mankiewicz. The cast included the following: *Mark Antony* (Marlon Brando),
Brutus (James Mason), *Cassius* (John Gielgud), *Julius Caesar* (Louis Calhern),
Casca (Edmond O'Brien), *Calpurnia* (Greer Garson), and *Portia* (Deborah Kerr). ▼

How I have thought of this and of these times
165 I shall recount hereafter. For this present,
I would not, so with love I might entreat you,
Be any further moved. What you have said
I will consider; what you have to say
I will with patience hear, and find a time
170 Both meet to hear and answer such high things.
Till then, my noble friend, chew upon this.
Brutus had rather be a villager
Than to repute himself a son of Rome
Under these hard conditions as this time
175 Is like to lay upon us.

CASSIUS. I am glad that my weak words
Have struck but this much show of fire from Brutus.

(CAESAR *and his followers reenter at left and start across the stage,* ANTONY
on CAESAR*'s left,* CASCA *following at rear.*)

BRUTUS. The games are done, and Caesar is returning.

CASSIUS. As they pass by, pluck Casca by the sleeve,
180 And he will, after his sour fashion, tell you
What hath proceeded worthy note today.

BRUTUS. I will do so. But look you, Cassius,
The angry spot doth glow on Caesar's brow,
And all the rest look like a chidden train.
185 Calpurnia's cheek is pale, and Cicero
Looks with such ferret and such fiery eyes
As we have seen him in the Capitol,
Being crossed in conference by some senators.

CASSIUS. Casca will tell us what the matter is.

(CAESAR *stops before he reaches center stage and looks speculatively at*
CASSIUS.)

190 **CAESAR.** Antonio!

ANTONY. Caesar?

CAESAR. Let me have men about me that are fat,
Sleek-headed men, and such as sleep o' nights.
Yond Cassius has a lean and hungry look.
195 He thinks too much. Such men are dangerous.

ANTONY. Fear him not, Caesar, he's not dangerous.
He is a noble Roman, and well given.

CAESAR. Would he were fatter! But I fear him not.
Yet if my name were liable to fear,
200 I do not know the man I should avoid
So soon as that spare Cassius. He reads much,
He is a great observer, and he looks
Quite through the deeds of men. He loves no plays,
As thou dost, Antony; he hears no music.

184 like a chidden train, like followers who were harshly scolded (chided or chidden).
186 such ferret . . . eyes, red and angry-looking eyes, like a weasel's.

■ Do you agree with Caesar's reasons for calling Cassius dangerous?

197 given, disposed; having a favorable nature.

204 hears no music. In Shakespeare's time, this was regarded as a sign of a treacherous nature.

205 Seldom he smiles, and smiles in such a sort
As if he mocked himself and scorned his spirit
That could be moved to smile at anything.
Such men as he be never at heart's ease
Whiles they behold a greater than themselves,
210 And therefore are they very dangerous.
I rather tell thee what is to be feared
Than what I fear, for always I am Caesar.
Come on my right hand, for this ear is deaf,
And tell me truly what thou think'st of him.
(ANTONY *steps to* CAESAR's *right. The trumpets sound and the procession,
with* CASCA *still at rear, moves slowly out at right. When* CASCA *reaches cen-
ter stage, he is detained by* BRUTUS *and* CASSIUS.)

215 **CASCA.** You pulled me by the cloak. Would you speak with me?
BRUTUS. Ay, Casca. Tell us what hath chanced today,
That Caesar looks so sad.
CASCA. Why, you were with him, were you not?
BRUTUS. I should not then ask Casca what had chanced.
220 **CASCA.** Why, there was a crown offered him; and, being offered him,
he put it by with the back of his hand, thus, and then the
people fell a-shouting.
BRUTUS. What was the second noise for?
CASCA. Why, for that too.
225 **CASSIUS.** They shouted thrice. What was the last cry for?
CASCA. Why, for that too.
BRUTUS. Was the crown offered him thrice?
CASCA. Ay, marry, was't, and he put it by thrice, every time gentler than
other, and at every putting-by mine honest neighbors shouted.
230 **CASSIUS.** Who offered him the crown?
CASCA. Why, Antony.
BRUTUS. Tell us the manner of it, gentle Casca.
CASCA. I can as well be hanged as tell the manner of it. It was mere
foolery; I did not mark it. I saw Mark Antony offer him a crown
235 yet 'twas not a crown neither 'twas one of these coronets—and, as
I told you, he put it by once; but for all that, to my thinking, he
would fain have had it. Then he offered it to him again; then he
put it by again; but to my thinking he was very loath to lay his fingers off it. And then he offered it the third time. He put it the
240 third time by, and still as he refused it the rabblement hooted and
clapped their chapped hands, and threw up their sweaty
nightcaps, and uttered such a deal of stinking breath because
Caesar refused the crown that it had almost choked Caesar, for he
swooned and fell down at it. And for mine own part I durst not
245 laugh for fear of opening my lips and receiving the bad air.
CASSIUS. But soft, I pray you. What, did Caesar swoon?

■ What insight into Caesar's character does this speech give?

217 **sad,** serious.

228 **marry,** a mild exclamation or oath. Originally, "by the Virgin Mary."

242 **nightcaps,** a scornful allusion to the felt cap worn by the commoners on festival days.
244 **durst,** dared.
■ Based on Casca's description, how do you think the commoners felt about Caesar's being offered a crown?

CASCA. He fell down in the marketplace, and foamed at mouth, and was speechless.

BRUTUS. 'Tis very like. He hath the falling sickness.

250 **CASSIUS.** No, Caesar hath it not, but you and I,
And honest Casca, we have the falling sickness.

CASCA. I know not what you mean by that, but I am sure Caesar fell down. If the tag-rag people did not clap him and hiss him, accord–ing as he pleased and displeased them, as they use to do the
255 players in the theater, I am no true man.

BRUTUS. What said he when he came unto himself?

CASCA. Marry, before he fell down, when he perceived the common herd was glad he refused the crown, he plucked me ope his dou–blet and offered them his throat to cut. An I had been a man of
260 any occupation, if I would not have taken him at a word, I would I might go to hell among the rogues. And so he fell. When he came to himself again, he said if he had done or said anything amiss, he desired their worships to think it was his infirmity. Three or four wenches where I stood cried, "Alas, good soul!" and forgave him
265 with all their hearts. But there's no heed to be taken of them; if Caesar had stabbed their mothers they would have done no less.

BRUTUS. And after that, he came thus sad away?

CASCA. Ay.

CASSIUS. Did Cicero say anything?

270 **CASCA.** Ay, he spoke Greek.

CASSIUS. To what effect?

CASCA. Nay, an I tell you that, I'll ne'er look you i' the face again. But those that understood him smiled at one another and shook their heads; but, for mine own part, it was Greek to me. I could tell
275 you more news too. Marullus and Flavius, for pulling scarves off Caesar's images, are put to silence. Fare you well. There was more foolery yet, if I could remember it.

CASSIUS. Will you sup with me tonight, Casca?

CASCA. No, I am promised forth.

280 **CASSIUS.** Will you dine with me tomorrow?

CASCA. Ay, if I be alive, and your mind hold, and your dinner worth the eating.

CASSIUS. Good. I will expect you.

CASCA. Do so. Farewell both. (CASCA *exits.*)

285 **BRUTUS.** What a blunt fellow is this grown to be!
He was quick mettle when he went to school.

CASSIUS. So is he now in execution
Of any bold or noble enterprise,
However he puts on this tardy form.
290 This rudeness is a sauce to his good wit,
Which gives men stomach to digest his words

249 falling sickness, epilepsy. Note how Cassius, in the next few lines, uses the words figuratively, suggesting a similarity between "falling" and failing to take action.

258–259 doublet, a man's close-fitting jacket. Doublets were not worn until about the 1400s; hence, another anachronism.
259 an, if.
■ What question would you ask Casca about his account of the events?

274 . . . it was Greek to me, a saying popular even today when a person is unable to understand something.
276 put to silence, deprived of their rank as tribunes, a position that permitted them to speak for the people.

286 mettle (met′l), *n.* spirit; courage. *Quick mettle* means "of a lively and spirited temperament."
289 tardy form, appearance of sluggishness.
290 wit, intellect.

With better appetite.

BRUTUS. And so it is. For this time I will leave you.
Tomorrow, if you please to speak with me,
295   I will come home to you; or, if you will,
Come home to me, and I will wait for you.

CASSIUS. I will do so. Till then, think of the world.
(BRUTUS *exits.*)
Well, Brutus, thou art noble. Yet I see
Thy honorable mettle may be wrought
300   From that it is disposed. Therefore it is meet
That noble minds keep ever with their likes;
For who so firm that cannot be seduced?
Caesar doth bear me hard, but he loves Brutus.
If I were Brutus now, and he were Cassius,
305   He should not humor me. I will this night
In several hands in at his windows throw,
As if they came from several citizens,
Writings, all tending to the great opinion
That Rome holds of his name, wherein obscurely
310   Caesar's ambition shall be glancèd at.
And after this let Caesar seat him sure,
For we will shake him, or worse days endure. (CASSIUS *exits.*)

299–300 Thy honorable . . . disposed, your spirit can be turned from its natural inclination.
300 meet (mēt), *adj.* fitting; appropriate.
303 Caesar . . . hard, Caesar bears me a grudge.
305 humor me, win me over to his opinions.
306 in several hands, in different handwritings.
310 glancèd at, hinted at.
■ Explain in your own words what Cassius is saying in this, the play's first soliloquy.

SCENE 3

Summary *Cassius persuades a frightened Casca to join the conspiracy, then instructs Cinna, another conspirator, to place letters condemning Caesar where Brutus will find them. Cassius and Casca plan a visit to Brutus later that evening.*

A street in Rome. A stormy night. Eve of the ides of March. Thunder and lightning. CICERO *enters at left;* CASCA, *his sword drawn, enters at right.*

CICERO. Good even, Casca. Brought you Caesar home?
Why are you breathless? And why stare you so?

CASCA. Are not you moved, when all the sway of earth
Shakes like a thing unfirm? O Cicero,
5   I have seen tempests when the scolding winds
Have rived the knotty oaks, and I have seen
Th' ambitious ocean swell and rage and foam
To be exalted with the threatening clouds;
But never till tonight, never till now,
10   Did I go through a tempest dropping fire.
(*More thunder, then a scream;* CASCA *darts behind a pillar.*)
Either there is a civil strife in heaven,
Or else the world, too saucy with the gods,

1 even, evening.

3 sway, established order.

8 exalted with, raised to the level of.

12 saucy, showing lack of respect; rude.

Incenses them to send destruction.

CICERO. Why, saw you anything more wonderful?

15 **CASCA.** A common slave—you know him well by sight—
Held up his left hand, which did flame and burn
Like twenty torches joined, and yet his hand,
Not sensible of fire, remained unscorched.
Besides—I ha' not since put up my sword—
20 Against the Capitol I met a lion,
Who glazed upon me and went surly by
Without annoying me. And there were drawn
Upon a heap a hundred ghastly women,
Transformèd with their fear, who swore they saw
25 Men all in fire walk up and down the streets.
And yesterday the bird of night did sit
Even at noonday upon the marketplace,
Hooting and shrieking. When these prodigies
Do so conjointly meet, let not men say,
30 "These are their reasons, they are natural,"
For I believe they are portentous things
Unto the climate that they point upon.

CICERO. Indeed, it is a strange-disposèd time.
But men may construe things after their fashion,
35 Clean from the purpose of the things themselves.
Comes Caesar to the Capitol tomorrow?

CASCA. He doth; for he did bid Antonio
Send word to you he would be there tomorrow.

CICERO. Good night then, Casca. This disturbèd sky
40 Is not to walk in.

CASCA. Farewell, Cicero.

(CICERO *exits at right. There is another flash of lightning and* CASCA *retreats further upstage, taking shelter under a balcony.* CASSIUS *enters at left.*)

CASSIUS. Who's there?

CASCA. A Roman.

CASSIUS. Casca, by your voice.

CASCA. Your ear is good. Cassius, what night is this!

CASSIUS. A very pleasing night to honest men.

CASCA. Who ever knew the heavens menace so?

45 **CASSIUS.** Those that have known the earth so full of faults.
For my part, I have walked about the streets,
Submitting me unto the perilous night,
And thus unbracèd, Casca, as you see,
Have bared my bosom to the thunder-stone;
50 And when the cross blue lightning seemed to open
The breast of heaven, I did present myself
Even in the aim and very flash of it.

18 **not sensible of fire**, not feeling the fire.

20 **against**, opposite; nearby.
21 **glazed**, peered, stared.

■ What unusual sights has Casca seen?

28–32 **When these prodigies . . . upon.** Though some may try to explain these marvels (prodigies) as natural, Casca regards them as omens (portentous things) foretelling disaster for Rome.

43 **what night**, what a night!

47 **perilous** (per′ə ləs), *adj.* dangerous.
48 **thus unbracèd.** Cassius unlaces (unbraces) his garment at the neck, exposing his chest to the thunderbolts (thunder-stones).
50 **cross**, forked, jagged.
■ What films have you seen in which weather reinforces mood?

CASCA. But wherefore did you so much tempt the heavens?
  It is the part of men to fear and tremble
55 When the most mighty gods by tokens send
  Such dreadful heralds to astonish us.
CASSIUS. You are dull, Casca, and those sparks of life
  That should be in a Roman you do want,
  Or else you use not. You look pale, and gaze,
60 And put on fear, and cast yourself in wonder,
  To see the strange impatience of the heavens.
  But if you would consider the true cause
  Why all these fires, why all these gliding ghosts,
  Why birds and beasts from quality and kind,
65 Why old men, fools, and children calculate,
  Why all these things change from their ordinance,
  Their natures, and preformèd faculties,
  To monstrous quality—why, you shall find
  That heaven hath infused them with these spirits
70 To make them instruments of fear and warning
  Unto some monstrous state.
  Now could I, Casca, name to thee a man
  Most like this dreadful night,
  That thunders, lightens, opens graves, and roars
75 As doth the lion in the Capitol—
  A man no mightier than thyself or me
  In personal action, yet prodigious grown
  And fearful, as these strange eruptions are.
CASCA. 'Tis Caesar that you mean, is it not, Cassius?
80 **CASSIUS.** Let it be who it is. For Romans now
  Have thews and limbs like to their ancestors;
  But, woe the while, our fathers' minds are dead,
  And we are governed with our mothers' spirits.
  Our yoke and sufferance show us womanish.
85 **CASCA.** Indeed, they say the senators tomorrow
  Mean to establish Caesar as a king,
  And he shall wear his crown by sea and land
  In every place save here in Italy.
CASSIUS. I know where I will wear this dagger then;
90 Cassius from bondage will deliver Cassius.
  Therein, ye gods, you make the weak most strong;
  Therein, ye gods, you tyrants do defeat.
  Nor stony tower, nor walls of beaten brass,
  Nor airless dungeon, nor strong links of iron,
95 Can be retentive to the strength of spirit;
  But life, being weary of these worldly bars,
  Never lacks power to dismiss itself.

65 calculate, prophesy.
66 ordinance, established nature; accustomed ways.
67 preformèd faculties, innate or inborn mental powers or capabilities.

■ How does Cassius use emotional appeal to influence Casca?

77 prodigious (prə dij′əs), *adj.* very great or huge; ominous.

82 woe the while, alas for the age.

92 therein, in the ability to commit suicide.

If I know this, know all the world besides,
That part of tyranny that I do bear
100 I can shake off at pleasure.

(Thunder still.)

CASCA.   So can I.
So every bondman in his own hand bears
The power to cancel his captivity.

CASSIUS. And why should Caesar be a tyrant then?
Poor man, I know he would not be a wolf
105 But that he sees the Romans are but sheep;
He were no lion, were not Romans hinds.
Those that with haste will make a mighty fire
Begin it with weak straws. What trash is Rome,
What rubbish and what offal, when it serves
110 For the base matter to illuminate
So vile a thing as Caesar! But, O grief,
Where hast thou led me? I perhaps speak this
Before a willing bondman; then I know
My answer must be made. But I am armed,
115 And dangers are to me indifferent.

CASCA. You speak to Casca, and to such a man
That is no fleering telltale. Hold. My hand.
Be factious for redress of all these griefs,
And I will set this foot of mine as far
120 As who goes farthest. *(They shake hands.)*

CASSIUS.   There's a bargain made.
Now know you, Casca, I have moved already
Some certain of the noblest-minded Romans
To undergo with me an enterprise
Of honorable-dangerous consequence;
125 And I do know by this they stay for me
In Pompey's porch. For now, this fearful night,
There is no stir or walking in the streets,
And the complexion of the element
In favor's like the work we have in hand,
130 Most bloody, fiery, and most terrible.

(CINNA enters.)

CASCA. Stand close awhile, for here comes one in haste.

CASSIUS. 'Tis Cinna; I do know him by his gait.
He is a friend. Cinna, where haste you so?

CINNA. To find out you. Who's that? Metellus Cimber?

135 **CASSIUS.** No, it is Casca, one incorporate
To our attempts. Am I not stayed for, Cinna?

CINNA. I am glad on 't. What a fearful night is this!
There's two or three of us have seen strange sights.

---

106 he were . . . hinds. He would be no lion if Romans were not submissive like deer. (A hind is a female deer.)

117 fleering, deceitful, fawning.
118 Be factious . . . griefs, be ready to join the faction (group) to right the grievances Romans have suffered at Caesar's hands.
■ Do you think Casca has made the right decision in joining the conspiracy?

125–126 stay . . . porch, wait for me on the porch of Pompey's theater.

128–129 the element . . . favor's, the sky is in appearance.

131 close, concealed.

135–136 one incorporate . . . attempts, one who knows our plans and is in sympathy with them.

CASSIUS. Am I not stayed for? Tell me.

140 **CINNA.** Yes, you are. O Cassius, if you could
But win the noble Brutus to our party—

CASSIUS. Be you content. Good Cinna, take this paper,
(Giving papers.)
And look you lay it in the praetor's chair,
Where Brutus may but find it. And throw this

145 In at his window. Set this up with wax
Upon old Brutus's statue. All this done,
Repair to Pompey's porch, where you shall find us.
Is Decius Brutus and Trebonius there?

CINNA. All but Metellus Cimber, and he's gone

150 To seek you at your house. Well, I will hie,
And so bestow these papers as you bade me.
(CINNA exits.)

CASSIUS. That done, repair to Pompey's theater.
Come Casca, you and I will yet ere day
See Brutus at his house. Three parts of him

155 Is ours already, and the man entire
Upon the next encounter yields him ours.

CASCA. O, he sits high in all the people's hearts;
And that which would appear offense in us,
His countenance, like richest alchemy,

160 Will change to virtue and to worthiness.

CASSIUS. Him and his worth, and our great need of him,
You have right well conceited. Let us go,
For it is after midnight, and ere day
We will awake him and be sure of him.
(They exit.)

143 in the praetor's chair.
Brutus at this time was a
praetor (prē′tər), a Roman
judge or magistrate.
146 old Brutus's, Lucius
Junius Brutus's. Brutus was
reputed to be his
descendent.

150 hie, go quickly.

**154–155 Three parts . . .
ours.** Brutus is three-quarters
persuaded to join the
conspirators; when they next
meet with him, they
undoubtedly will win him
over completely.

162 conceited, grasped.
■ Whom do you think
Brutus will support—Caesar
or the conspirators?

Act 1

After Reading

Making Connections

Shaping Your Response

1. Do you think Caesar has the qualities of an effective politician? Why or why not?

2. What advice would you give him?

3. For a television production, what actor would you choose to play Caesar? Antony? Cassius? Brutus? Casca? Explain your casting choices.

Analyzing the Play

4. **Characterize** Caesar as he appears in the opening lines of scene 2.

5. 👣 How do the contrasting opinions that characters express about Caesar in this act reflect social **change** at this point in Roman history?

6. What can you **infer** is the reason for the mention of such things as his deafness and his "falling sickness"?

7. Do you think the presence of the crowd influences Caesar's response to the Soothsayer's warning? Explain.

8. What can you **infer** will be the main **conflict** in the play?

9. Which side do you think Brutus will join? Why?

10. What do you think the strange events seen by Cassius and Casca **foreshadow**?

Extending the Ideas

11. Do you think that a modern crowd would be as emotional and as swayed by speeches as the Roman commoners seem to be? Explain, citing specific examples.

12. 👣 Before Caesar was declared dictator for life, Romans had enjoyed a republican government for over four centuries. What kinds of drastic **changes** do you think a dictatorship would cause in *your* country?

Literary Focus: Plot

Look at the plot diagram you copied in your notebook. Under the diagram, briefly describe the background and the situation as the play opens. Then jot down a few sentences describing the incidents that have set the plot in motion in act 1.

Vocabulary Study

On your paper, write the word that best fits each numbered description.

meet
mettle
perilous
prodigious
servile

1. ____ describes a person who acts like a slave.
2. ____ describes something dangerous.
3. ____ denotes something large or vast.
4. ____ refers to something that is appropriate.
5. ____ denotes courage and spirit.

Expressing Your Ideas

Writing Choices

Writer's Notebook Update Look over the entries you made about Caesar in your chart. Compare the traits you listed with those listed by other members of your class. Are you in agreement? Try to sum up his character in a sentence or two.

Roman Holiday Caesar has hired a public relations expert to spruce up his image. Submit five **tips** for upgrading Caesar's popularity rating. Use a few vocabulary words to enliven your writing.

Ancient Chronicle Imagine that you are a reporter in ancient Rome. Your assignment is to write an **article** about Caesar's rejection of the crown. Decide whether your article will be objective—a straight news story—or a human interest feature that includes imaginative details such as Calpurnia's reaction, Casca's opinions, and so forth.

Blank Check Jot down your impressions of one of the characters appearing in this act. Then recast your impressions in **blank verse**— the verse form Shakespeare usually employs. Refer to the description of blank verse on page 675 if you need to review its features.

Other Options

In the Spotlight Choose a speech from act 1 to deliver in a dramatic reading. After rehearsing it, give an **oral interpretation** before the class, complete with costume or props, if you wish.

Times Roman Do some research about life in ancient Rome—the clothes, customs, living quarters, entertainment, and so on. Make drawings or photocopy pictures, provide captions, and present your information and **visual display** to classmates.

Caesar Song Select a musical piece that you consider fit for a king whose rule is in jeopardy. Make arrangements to play this music for the class and explain why you think this piece is appropriate.

ACT TWO

SCENE 1

Summary *Alone, Brutus weighs the arguments for joining the conspiracy. His servant Lucius brings him one of Cassius's "letters." Cassius and five other conspirators enter. Brutus becomes a conspirator but opposes three ideas: swearing an oath, including Cicero in the conspiracy, and killing Mark Antony. Portia, Brutus's wife, begs her husband to reveal why he is troubled. Brutus refuses and, accompanied by Caius Ligarius, leaves for the Capitol.*

BRUTUS's *orchard, between midnight and 3:00 A.M., the ides of March.* BRUTUS, *who has been awake most of the night, is seated on a small bench. As the scene develops, he alternates between sitting and walking back and forth.*

BRUTUS. What, Lucius, ho!
    I cannot by the progress of the stars
    Give guess how near to day. Lucius, I say!
    I would it were my fault to sleep so soundly.
5   When, Lucius, when? Awake, I say! What, Lucius!
(LUCIUS *appears, rubbing his eyes.*)
LUCIUS. Called you, my lord?
BRUTUS. Get me a taper in my study, Lucius.
    When it is lighted, come and call me here.
LUCIUS. I will, my lord.
(*As* LUCIUS *withdraws,* BRUTUS *resumes his restless pacing.*)
10 **BRUTUS.** It must be by his death. And for my part
    I know no personal cause to spurn at him,
    But for the general. He would be crowned.
    How that might change his nature, there's the question.
    It is the bright day that brings forth the adder,
15   And that craves wary walking. Crown him that,
    And then I grant we put a sting in him
    That at his will he may do danger with.
    Th' abuse of greatness is when it disjoins
    Remorse from power. And to speak truth of Caesar,
20   I have not known when his affections swayed
    More than his reason. But 'tis a common proof
    That lowliness is young ambition's ladder,
    Whereto the climber-upward turns his face;
    But when he once attains the upmost round
25   He then unto the ladder turns his back,
    Looks in the clouds, scorning the base degrees
    By which he did ascend. So Caesar may.

■ Why do you think Brutus is so wakeful?

7 taper, candle.

10 his, Caesar's.
11–12 I know no personal . . . general. Though Brutus has no personal reason for striking at (spurning) Caesar, he nevertheless feels he should do so for the public (general) good.
15 craves, requires.

20 affections, passions (as opposed to reason).

Then, lest he may, prevent. And since the quarrel
Will bear no color for the thing he is,
30   Fashion it thus: that what he is, augmented,
Would run to these and these extremities.
And therefore think him as a serpent's egg
Which, hatched, would, as his kind, grow mischievous;
And kill him in the shell.

(LUCIUS, *yawning, enters carrying a letter—a small scroll.*)

35   **LUCIUS.** The taper burneth in your closet, sir.
Searching the window for a flint, I found
This paper, thus sealed up, and I am sure
It did not lie there when I went to bed.

(Gives him the letter.)

BRUTUS. Get you to bed again. It is not day.
40   Is not tomorrow, boy, the ides of March?

LUCIUS. I know not, sir.

BRUTUS. Look in the calendar and bring me word.

LUCIUS. I will, sir. (LUCIUS *exits.*)

BRUTUS. The exhalations whizzing in the air
45   Give so much light that I may read by them.

(Opens the letter and reads.)

"Brutus, thou sleep'st. Awake, and see thyself!
Shall Rome, et cetera? Speak, strike, redress!"
"Brutus, thou sleep'st. Awake!"
Such instigations have been often dropped
50   Where I have took them up.
"Shall Rome et cetera?" Thus must I piece it out.
Shall Rome stand under one man's awe? What, Rome?
My ancestors did from the streets of Rome
The Tarquin drive, when he was called a king.
55   "Speak, strike, redress!" Am I entreated
To speak and strike? O Rome, I make thee promise,
If the redress will follow, thou receivest
Thy full petition at the hand of Brutus.

(LUCIUS *enters.*)

LUCIUS. Sir, March is wasted fifteen days.

(Knock within.)

60   **BRUTUS.** 'Tis good. Go to the gate; somebody knocks.

(LUCIUS *exits.*)

Since Cassius first did whet me against Caesar,
I have not slept.
Between the acting of a dreadful thing
And the first motion, all the interim is
65   Like a phantasma or a hideous dream.
The genius and the mortal instruments

---

28 prevent, he must be prevented.

30 augmented, increased.

33 as his kind, according to his nature.
■ What reasons does Brutus consider for assassinating Caesar?

35 closet, private chamber, room.

44 exhalations, meteors, which were thought to be caused by vapors exhaled into the atmosphere.

49 instigations, urgings on; stirrings up.

54 The Tarquin, Tarquinius Superbus (sù pėrb′əs), the last Roman king.

61 whet, make keen or eager; stimulate.

64 motion, proposal.
66 the genius . . . instruments, the soul and the body.

Are then in council; and the state of man,
Like to a little kingdom, suffers then
The nature of an insurrection.

(LUCIUS *enters.*)

70 **LUCIUS.** Sir, 'tis your brother Cassius at the door,
Who doth desire to see you.

BRUTUS.   Is he alone?

LUCIUS. No, sir. There are more with him.

BRUTUS.   Do you know them?

LUCIUS. No sir. Their hats are plucked about their ears,
And half their faces buried in their cloaks,

75 That by no means I may discover them
By any mark of favor.

BRUTUS.   Let 'em enter.

(LUCIUS *exits.*)

They are the faction. O conspiracy,
Sham'st thou to show thy dangerous brow by night,
When evils are most free? O, then by day

80 Where wilt thou find a cavern dark enough
To mask thy monstrous visage? Seek none, conspiracy!
Hide it in smiles and affability;
For if thou put thy native semblance on,
Not Erebus itself were dim enough

85 To hide thee from prevention.

(LUCIUS *ushers in the* CONSPIRATORS—CASSIUS, CASCA, DECIUS, CINNA,
METELLUS CIMBER *and* TREBONIUS—*and then exits.*)

CASSIUS. I think we are too bold upon your rest.
Good morrow, Brutus. Do we trouble you?

BRUTUS. I have been up this hour, awake all night.
Know I these men that come along with you?

90 **CASSIUS.** Yes, every man of them, and no man here
But honors you; and every one doth wish
You had but that opinion of yourself
Which every noble Roman bears of you.
This is Trebonius.

BRUTUS.   He is welcome hither.

95 **CASSIUS.** This, Decius Brutus.

BRUTUS.   He is welcome too.

CASSIUS. This, Casca; this, Cinna; and this, Metellus Cimber.

BRUTUS. They are all welcome.
What watchful cares do interpose themselves
Betwixt your eyes and night?

100 **CASSIUS.** Shall I entreat a word?

(BRUTUS *and* CASSIUS *whisper.*)

70 brother, actually brother-in-law; Cassius was married to Brutus's sister.

76 any mark of favor, any features by which they can be recognized.

83–85 for if thou . . . prevention. If the conspirators walk about wearing their natural appearance, not even Erebus (er′ə bəs) would be dark enough to keep them from detection. In Greek mythology, Erebus was a dark, gloomy place through which the dead passed en route to Hades.

■ Given his statements in lines 77–85, do you think Brutus will join the conspiracy? Explain.

98 interpose, come or be between other things.

DECIUS. Here lies the east. Doth not the day break here?

CASCA. No.

CINNA. O, pardon, sir, it doth; and yon gray lines
That fret the clouds are messengers of day.

105 **CASCA.** You shall confess that you are both deceived.
Here, as I point my sword, the sun arises,
Which is a great way growing on the south,
Weighing the youthful season of the year.
Some two months hence, up higher toward the north
110 He first presents his fire; and the high east
Stands, as the Capitol, directly here.

BRUTUS *(coming forward).* Give me your hands all over, one by one.

CASSIUS. And let us swear our resolution.

BRUTUS. No, not an oath. If not the face of men,
115 The sufferance of our souls, the time's abuse—
If these be motives weak, break off betimes,
And every man hence to his idle bed;
So let high-sighted tyranny range on
Till each man drop by lottery. But if these,
120 As I am sure they do, bear fire enough
To kindle cowards and to steel with valor
The melting spirits of women, then, countrymen,
What need we any spur but our own cause
To prick us to redress? What other bond
125 Than secret Romans that have spoke the word
And will not palter? And what other oath
Than honesty to honesty engaged
That this shall be or we will fall for it?
Swear priests and cowards and men cautelous,
130 Old feeble carrions, and such suffering souls
That welcome wrongs; unto bad causes swear
Such creatures as men doubt. But do not stain
The even virtue of our enterprise,
Nor th' insuppressive mettle of our spirits,
135 To think that or our cause or our performance
Did need an oath, when every drop of blood
That every Roman bears—and nobly bears—
Is guilty of a several bastardy
If he do break the smallest particle
140 Of any promise that hath passed from him.

CASSIUS. But what of Cicero? Shall we sound him?
I think he will stand very strong with us.

CASCA. Let us not leave him out.

CINNA. No, by no means.

METELLUS. O, let us have him, for his silver hairs

114–119 If not the face . . . by lottery. If the wrongs the conspirators see about them are not sufficient to bind them to firm purpose, then let each man go his own way, become a weakling, and die when it suits a tyrant's whims.

119 these, that is, these injustices just cited.

126 palter, use trickery.

129 cautelous, deceitful.

135 or . . . or, either . . . or. To maintain a ten-syllable line, Shakespeare often uses "or . . . or" or "nor . . . nor."

This Roman coin, showing a liberty cap and two daggers, commemorates the assassination of Caesar. The inscription reads "The Ides of March." What does such an artifact suggest about Roman attitudes toward political violence? ▼

145 Will purchase us a good opinion
And buy men's voices to commend our deeds.
It shall be said his judgment ruled our hands;
Our youths and wildness shall no whit appear,
But all be buried in his gravity.

150 **BRUTUS.** O, name him not. Let us not break with him,
For he will never follow anything
That other men begin.

CASSIUS. Then leave him out.

CASCA. Indeed he is not fit.

155 **DECIUS.** Shall no man else be touched but only Caesar?

CASSIUS. Decius, well urged. I think it is not meet
Mark Antony, so well beloved of Caesar,
Should outlive Caesar. We shall find of him
A shrewd contriver; and you know his means,

160 If he improve them, may well stretch so far
As to annoy us all. Which to prevent,
Let Antony and Caesar fall together.

BRUTUS. Our course will seem too bloody, Caius Cassius,
To cut the head off and then hack the limbs,

165 Like wrath in death and envy afterwards;
For Antony is but a limb of Caesar.
Let's be sacrificers, but not butchers, Caius.
We all stand up against the spirit of Caesar,
And in the spirit of men there is no blood

170 O, that we then could come by Caesar's spirit
And not dismember Caesar! But, alas,
Caesar must bleed for it. And, gentle friends,
Let's kill him boldly, but not wrathfully;
Let's carve him as a dish fit for the gods,

175 Not hew him as a carcass fit for hounds.
And let our hearts, as subtle masters do,
Stir up their servants to an act of rage
And after seem to chide 'em. This shall make
Our purpose necessary, and not envious;

180 Which so appearing to the common eyes,
We shall be called purgers, not murderers.
And for Mark Antony, think not of him;
For he can do no more than Caesar's arm
When Caesar's head is off.

CASSIUS.   Yet I fear him,

185 For in the engrafted love he bears to Caesar—

BRUTUS. Alas, good Cassius, do not think of him.
If he love Caesar, all that he can do
Is to himself—take thought and die for Caesar.

---

150 break with, confide in.

160 improve, exploit; make good use of.
161 annoy, injure.

■ Do you think Brutus has erred in opposing the killing of Antony?

172 gentle, noble.

177 their servants, that is, our hands.

188–189 take thought . . . should, despair and die for Caesar, and that would be too much for him to do; hence, it is unlikely.

And that were much he should, for he is given
190 To sports, to wildness, and much company.
TREBONIUS. There is no fear in him. Let him not die,
For he will live, and laugh at this hereafter.
(Clock strikes.)
BRUTUS. Peace! Count the clock.
CASSIUS.   The clock hath stricken three.
TREBONIUS. 'Tis time to part.
CASSIUS.   But it is doubtful yet
195 Whether Caesar will come forth today or no;
For he is superstitious grown of late,
Quite from the main opinion he held once
Of fantasy, of dreams, and ceremonies.
It may be these apparent prodigies,
200 The unaccustomed terror of this night,
And the persuasion of his augurers
May hold him from the Capitol today.
DECIUS. Never fear that. If he be so resolved,
I can o'ersway him; for he loves to hear
205 That unicorns may be betrayed with trees,
And bears with glasses, elephants with holes,
Lions with toils, and men with flatterers;
But when I tell him he hates flatterers,
He says he does, being then most flattered.
210 Let me work;
For I can give his humor the true bent,
And I will bring him to the Capitol.
CASSIUS. Nay, we will all of us be there to fetch him.
BRUTUS. By the eighth hour. Is that the uttermost?
215 **CINNA.** Be that the uttermost, and fail not then.
METELLUS. Caius Ligarius doth bear Caesar hard,
Who rated him for speaking well of Pompey.
I wonder none of you have thought of him.
BRUTUS. Now, good Metellus, go along by him.
220 He loves me well, and I have given him reasons;
Send him but hither, and I'll fashion him.
CASSIUS. The morning comes upon 's. We'll leave you, Brutus.
And, friends, disperse yourselves; but all remember
What you have said, and show yourselves true Romans.
225 **BRUTUS.** Good gentlemen, look fresh and merrily;
Let not our looks put on our purposes,
But bear it as our Roman actors do,
With untired spirits and formal constancy.
And so good morrow to you every one.
(The CONSPIRATORS *exit.)*

191 There is no fear in him. There is no reason to fear Antony.

193 Count the clock, one of the most famous anachronisms in the play; yet Shakespeare needed some way of conveying to his audience what time it was.

197 quite from the main opinion, contrary to the strong opinion.

201 augurers, priests who predicted the future by reading signs. Sometimes spelled *augurs.*
■ In Cassius's view (lines 194–202), what might prevent Caesar from going to the Capitol?
205–207 That unicorns . . . toils, methods thought effective for capturing animals. When the hunter stepped behind a tree, a charging unicorn would trap himself by driving his horn into the tree. A bear, given a mirror, would be so fascinated by its image that it became easy prey. Elephants were captured in pits; lions were sometimes rendered helpless by nets (toils).
216–217 bear Caesar hard. . . rated him. Caius bears a grudge toward Caesar who had angrily scolded (berated) him.

226 put on, wear in open view; that is, betray.

230 Boy! Lucius! Fast asleep? It is no matter.
Enjoy the honey-heavy dew of slumber.
Thou hast no figures nor no fantasies
Which busy care draws in the brains of men;
Therefore thou sleep'st so sound.

(PORTIA *enters.*)

PORTIA.   Brutus, my lord!

235 **BRUTUS.** Portia, what mean you? Wherefore rise you now?
It is not for your health thus to commit
Your weak condition to the raw cold morning.

PORTIA. Nor for yours neither. You've ungently, Brutus,
Stole from my bed. And yesternight, at supper,
240 You suddenly arose, and walked about
Musing and sighing, with your arms across,
And when I asked you what the matter was,
You stared upon me with ungentle looks.
I urged you further; then you scratched your head
245 And too impatiently stamped with your foot.
Yet I insisted, yet you answered not,
But with an angry wafture of your hand
Gave sign for me to leave you. So I did,
Fearing to strengthen that impatience
250 Which seemed too much enkindled, and withal
Hoping it was but an effect of humor,
Which sometimes hath his hour with every man.
It will not let you eat, nor talk, nor sleep,
And could it work so much upon your shape
255 As it hath much prevailed on your condition,
I should not know you Brutus. Dear my lord,
Make me acquainted with your cause of grief.

BRUTUS. I am not well in health, and that is all.

PORTIA. Brutus is wise, and were he not in health
260 He would embrace the means to come by it.

BRUTUS. Why, so I do. Good Portia, go to bed.

PORTIA. Is Brutus sick? And is it physical
To walk unbracèd and suck up the humors
Of the dank morning? What, is Brutus sick,
265 And will he steal out of his wholesome bed
To dare the vile contagion of the night,
And tempt the rheumy and unpurgèd air
To add unto his sickness? No, my Brutus,
You have some sick offense within your mind,
270 Which by the right and virtue of my place
I ought to know of. (*She kneels.*) And upon my knees
I charm you, by my once-commended beauty,

232 **figures**, imaginings.

241 **across**, folded.

■ What does Portia's thumbnail description of Brutus indicate about his state of mind?

262 **physical**, healthful.
263 **humors**, damps, mists.

267 **the rheumy . . . air**, air that causes colds because it has not yet been purified (purged) by the sun.

272 **charm**, conjure.

By all your vows of love, and that great vow
Which did incorporate and make us one,
275 That you unfold to me, your self, your half,
Why you are heavy, and what men tonight
Have had resort to you; for here have been
Some six or seven, who did hide their faces
Even from darkness.

BRUTUS.   Kneel not, gentle Portia.
(He raises her.)

280 **PORTIA.** I should not need if you were gentle Brutus.
Within the bond of marriage, tell me, Brutus,
Is it excepted I should know no secrets
That appertain to you? Am I your self
But as it were in sort or limitation,
285 To keep with you at meals, comfort your bed,
And talk to you sometimes? Dwell I but in the suburbs
Of your good pleasure? If it be no more,
Portia is Brutus's harlot, not his wife.

BRUTUS. You are my true and honorable wife,
290 As dear to me as are the ruddy drops
That visit my sad heart.

PORTIA. If this were true, then should I know this secret.
I grant I am a woman, but withal
A woman that Lord Brutus took to wife.
295 I grant I am a woman, but withal
A woman well reputed, Cato's daughter.
Think you I am no stronger than my sex,
Being so fathered and so husbanded?
Tell me your counsels, I will not disclose 'em.
300 I have made strong proof of my constancy,
Giving myself a voluntary wound
Here, in the thigh. Can I bear that with patience,
And not my husband's secrets?

BRUTUS.   O ye gods,
Render me worthy of this noble wife!
(Knock within.)
305 Hark, hark, one knocks. Portia, go in awhile,
And by and by thy bosom shall partake
The secrets of my heart.
All my engagements I will construe to thee,
All the charactery of my sad brows.
310 Leave me with haste. (PORTIA *exits.*) Lucius, who's that knocks?
(LUCIUS and CAIUS LIGARIUS, who is wearing a kerchief, enter.)
LUCIUS. Here is a sick man that would speak with you.

282–283 Is it excepted . . . you? Portia asked if an exception was made in the marriage vows so that she would have no legal right to inquire into affairs pertaining to Brutus.
286 suburbs, periphery, outskirts.

298 being so fathered. Portia's father, Cato, had killed himself rather than submit to Caesar's tyranny. He was Brutus's uncle as well as his father-in-law.
■ What question do you think the actress playing Portia in this scene might ask of her director?

309 charactery, handwriting; i.e., lines of worry on his face.

BRUTUS. Caius Ligarius, that Metellus spake of.
　　Boy, stand aside. (LUCIUS *exits.*)
　　Caius Ligarius, how?
LIGARIUS. Vouchsafe good morrow from a feeble tongue.
315　**BRUTUS.** O, what a time have you chose out, brave Caius,
　　To wear a kerchief! Would you were not sick!
LIGARIUS. I am not sick, if Brutus have in hand
　　Any exploit worthy the name of honor.
BRUTUS. Such an exploit have I in hand, Ligarius,
320　Had you a healthful ear to hear of it.
LIGARIUS. By all the gods that Romans bow before,
　　I here discard my sickness! Soul of Rome!
(He throws off his kerchief.)
　　Brave son, derived from honorable loins!
　　Thou like an exorcist hast conjured up
325　My mortifièd spirit. Now bid me run,
　　And I will strive with things impossible,
　　Yea, get the better of them. What's to do?
BRUTUS. A piece of work that will make sick men whole.
LIGARIUS. But are not some whole that we must make sick?
330　**BRUTUS.** That must we also. What it is, my Caius,
　　I shall unfold to thee as we are going
　　To whom it must be done.
LIGARIUS.　　　　　　　Set on your foot,
　　And with a heart new-fired I follow you
　　To do I know not what; but it sufficeth
　　That Brutus leads me on. *(Thunder.)*
335　**BRUTUS.**　　　　　　Follow me, then. *(They exit.)*

313 how? how are you?
314 vouchsafe, agree or deign (to accept).

■ What dramatic effect might Shakespeare have been trying to achieve by establishing Caius Ligarius's illness?

324–325 conjured . . . spirit, brought to life my deadened spirit.

Summary *Calpurnia, Caesar's wife, begs Caesar not to go to the Capitol. At first he laughs at her fears but eventually agrees to remain at home. Decius enters, flatters Caesar, and succeeds in changing Caesar's mind. The conspirators enter, then Mark Antony, and all set off for the Capitol.*

Caesar's House. Wearing a dressing-gown, CAESAR *enters at right. Speaking to himself, he crosses left where his street robe is draped across a chair.*

CAESAR. Nor heaven nor earth have been at peace tonight.
Thrice hath Calpurnia in her sleep cried out,
"Help, ho, they murder Caesar!" *(Calling.)* Who's within? *(He claps.)*

(A SERVANT *enters.)*

SERVANT. My lord?

5 **CAESAR.** Go bid the priests do present sacrifice
And bring me their opinions of success.

SERVANT. I will, my lord.

(He exits through a rear door as CALPURNIA, *in night clothes, enters at right.)*

CALPURNIA. What mean you, Caesar? Think you to walk forth?
You shall not stir out of your house today.

10 **CAESAR.** Caesar shall forth. The things that threatened me
Ne'er looked but on my back. When they shall see
The face of Caesar, they are vanishèd.

CALPURNIA. Caesar, I never stood on ceremonies,
Yet now they fright me. There is one within,

15 Besides the things that we have heard and seen,
Recounts most horrid sights seen by the watch.
A lioness hath whelpèd in the streets,
And graves have yawned and yielded up their dead.
Fierce fiery warriors fight upon the clouds

20 In ranks and squadrons and right form of war,
Which drizzled blood upon the Capitol.
The noise of battle hurtled in the air;
Horses did neigh, and dying men did groan,
And ghosts did shriek and squeal about the streets.

25 O Caesar, these things are beyond all use,
And I do fear them.

CAESAR.   What can be avoided
Whose end is purposed by the mighty gods?
Yet Caesar shall go forth; for these predictions
Are to the world in general as to Caesar.

30 **CALPURNIA.** When beggars die there are no comets seen;
The heavens themselves blaze forth the death of princes.

CAESAR. Cowards die many times before their deaths;

---

1 Nor . . . nor, neither . . . nor.

5–6 Go bid the priests . . . success. By killing a bird and examining its entrails, the priest-augurers predicted the future. Caesar commands the augurers to sacrifice a bird and to report the result (opinions of success).

14 one within, probably a servant.

20 right form, regular formations.

25 use, normal experience; that is, supernatural.
26–27 What can be . . . gods? Note Caesar's fatalism, a belief that fate controls everything that happens.

The valiant never taste of death but once.
Of all the wonders that I yet have heard,
35   It seems to me most strange that men should fear,
Seeing that death, a necessary end,
Will come when it will come.

(A SERVANT *enters.)*

                                    What say the augurers?

SERVANT. They would not have you to stir forth today.
Plucking the entrails of an offering forth,
40   They could not find a heart within the beast.

CAESAR. The gods do this in shame of cowardice.
Caesar should be a beast without a heart
If he should stay at home today for fear.
No, Caesar shall not. Danger knows full well
45   That Caesar is more dangerous than he.
We are two lions littered in one day,   **46 we**, Caesar and danger.
And I the elder and more terrible;
And Caesar shall go forth.

CALPURNIA.   Alas, my lord,
Your wisdom is consumed in confidence.
50   Do not go forth today! Call it my fear
That keeps you in the house, and not your own.
We'll send Mark Antony to the Senate House,
And he shall say you are not well today.
Let me, upon my knee, prevail in this. *(She kneels.)*

55   **CAESAR.** Mark Antony shall say I am not well,
And for thy humor I will stay at home. *(He raises her.)*   **56 humor**, whim.

*(*DECIUS *enters.)*

Here's Decius Brutus. He shall tell them so.

DECIUS. Caesar, all hail! Good morrow, worthy Caesar.
I come to fetch you to the Senate House.

60   **CAESAR.** And you are come in very happy time   **60 happy**, opportune.
To bear my greeting to the senators
And tell them that I will not come today.
Cannot is false, and that I dare not, falser;
I will not come today. Tell them so, Decius.

CALPURNIA. Say he is sick.

65   **CAESAR.**   Shall Caesar send a lie?
Have I in conquest stretched mine arm so far
To be afeared to tell graybeards the truth?
Decius, go tell them Caesar will not come.

DECIUS. Most mighty Caesar, let me know some cause,
70   Lest I be laughed at when I tell them so.

CAESAR. The cause is in my will. I will not come.

That is enough to satisfy the Senate.
But for your private satisfaction,
Because I love you, I will let you know.
75 Calpurnia here, my wife, stays me at home.
She dreamt tonight she saw my statue,
Which like a fountain with an hundred spouts
Did run pure blood; and many lusty Romans
Came smiling and did bathe their hands in it.
80 And these does she apply for warnings and portents
Of evils imminent, and on her knee
Hath begged that I will stay at home today.
DECIUS. This dream is all amiss interpreted;
It was a vision fair and fortunate.
85 Your statue spouting blood in many pipes,
In which so many smiling Romans bathed,
Signifies that from you great Rome shall suck
Reviving blood, and that great men shall press
For tinctures, stains, relics, and cognizance.
90 This by Calpurnia's dream is signified.

76–79 She dreamt . . . hands in it. These lines foreshadow future events. Keep them in mind as you read further.

80 apply for, interpret as.

89 cognizance (kog′nə-zəns), heraldic emblems worn by a nobleman's followers.

CAESAR. And this way have you well expounded it.

DECIUS. I have, when you have heard what I can say;
And know it now. The Senate have concluded
To give this day a crown to mighty Caesar.
95 If you shall send them word you will not come,
Their minds may change. Besides, it were a mock
Apt to be rendered for someone to say
"Break up the Senate till another time
When Caesar's wife shall meet with better dreams."
100 If Caesar hide himself, shall they not whisper
"Lo, Caesar is afraid"?
Pardon me, Caesar, for my dear dear love
To you proceeding bids me tell you this,
And reason to my love is liable.

105 **CAESAR.** How foolish do your fears seem now, Calpurnia!
I am ashamèd I did yield to them.
Give me my robe, for I will go.
(BRUTUS, LIGARIUS, METELLUS, CASCA, TREBONIUS, CINNA, *and*
PUBLIUS *enter.*)
And look where Publius is come to fetch me.

PUBLIUS. Good morrow, Caesar.

CAESAR.   Welcome, Publius.
110 What, Brutus, are you stirred so early too?
Good morrow, Casca. Caius Ligarius,
Caesar was ne'er so much your enemy
As that same ague which hath made you lean.
What is 't o'clock?

BRUTUS.   Caesar, 'tis strucken eight.

115 **CAESAR.** I thank you for your pains and courtesy.
(ANTONY *enters.*)
See, Antony, that revels long o' nights,
Is notwithstanding up. Good morrow, Antony.

ANTONY. So to most noble Caesar.

CAESAR (*to a* SERVANT). Bid them prepare within.
(SERVANT *exits.*)
120 I am to blame to be thus waited for.
Now, Cinna. Now, Metellus. What, Trebonius,
I have an hour's talk in store for you;
Remember that you call on me today.
Be near me, that I may remember you.

125 **TREBONIUS.** Caesar, I will. (*Aside.*) And so near will I be
That your best friends shall wish I had been further.

CAESAR. Good friends, go in and taste some wine with me,
And we, like friends, will straightway go together.

BRUTUS (*aside*). That every like is not the same, O Caesar,

96–97 a mock . . . rendered,
witty remark that someone
would be apt to make.

**102–104 my dear dear love
. . . liable,** love bids me
speak frankly and prudence
(reason) must bow to my
affection for you.

■ In reinterpreting
Calpurnia's dream, what
incentives does Decius give
Caesar to go to the Capitol?

113 ague (āʹgyü), *n.* fever.

119 prepare within, set out
refreshments in another
room.

130 The heart of Brutus yearns to think upon!

(CAESAR, *followed by the others, exits; a worried* CALPURNIA *waits a moment, then exits.*)

129–130 that every . . . think upon. Brutus's heart grieves that everyone who appears to be a friend is not a friend.

SCENE 3

Summary *Artemidorus, a teacher of rhetoric, reads a paper which he intends to present to Caesar.*

A street near the Capitol. Morning of the ides of March. ARTEMIDORUS *enters at left, reading from a paper.*

ARTEMIDORUS. "Caesar, beware of Brutus; take heed of Cassius; come not near Casca; have an eye to Cinna; trust not Trebonius; mark well Metellus Cimber; Decius Brutus loves thee not; thou has wronged Caius Ligarius. There is but one mind in all these men,
5   and it is bent against Caesar. If thou beest not immortal, look about you. Security gives way to conspiracy. The mighty gods defend thee! Thy lover,

                    Artemidorus."

Here will I stand till Caesar pass along,
10   And as a suitor will I give him this.
My heart laments that virtue cannot live
Out of the teeth of emulation.
If thou read this, O Caesar, thou mayest live;
If not, the Fates with traitors do contrive. *(He exits.)*

6 Security . . . conspiracy, overconfidence eases the way for conspirators.
7 lover, often used by Shakespeare to mean "friend."
10 suitor, petitioner.
12 emulation, copying or imitating in order to equal or excel the achievements or qualities of an admired person.
14 contrive, conspire.
■ If you were Artemidorus, would you reveal what you know about the conspiracy? Why or why not?

SCENE 4

Summary *An anxious Portia sends her servant Lucius to the Capitol for news, then talks briefly to the Soothsayer, who intends to warn Caesar a second time.*

A street outside the house of BRUTUS. *The ides of March.* PORTIA *enters followed by* LUCIUS.

PORTIA. I prithee, boy, run to the Senate House.
Stay not to answer me, but get thee gone.
Why dost thou stay?
LUCIUS.   To know my errand, madam.
PORTIA. I would have had thee there and here again
5   Ere I can tell thee what thou shouldst do there.
(Aside.) O constancy, be strong upon my side;
Set a huge mountain 'tween my heart and tongue!
I have a man's mind, but a woman's might.
How hard it is for women to keep counsel!

1 prithee, pray thee; request of you.

6 constancy, self-control.

9 to keep counsel, to keep a secret.

Art thou here yet?

10 **LUCIUS.**   Madam, what should I do?
Run to the Capitol, and nothing else?
And so return to you, and nothing else?
PORTIA. Yes, bring me word, boy, if thy lord look well,
For he went sickly forth; and take good note
15 What Caesar doth, what suitors press to him.
Hark, boy, what noise is that?
LUCIUS. I hear none, madam.
PORTIA. Prithee, listen well.
I heard a bustling rumor, like a fray,
20 And the wind bring it from the Capitol.
LUCIUS. Sooth, madam, I hear nothing.
(The SOOTHSAYER *enters.)*
PORTIA. Come hither, fellow. Which way hast thou been?
SOOTHSAYER. At mine own house, good lady.
PORTIA. What is 't o'clock?
SOOTHSAYER.   About the ninth hour, lady.
25 **PORTIA.** Is Caesar yet gone to the Capitol?
SOOTHSAYER. Madam, not yet. I go to take my stand,
To see him pass on to the Capitol.
PORTIA. Thou has some suit to Caesar, hast thou not?
SOOTHSAYER. That I have, lady, if it will please Caesar
30 To be so good to Caesar as to hear me:
I shall beseech him to befriend himself.
PORTIA. Why, know'st thou any harms intended towards him?
SOOTHSAYER. None that I know will be, much that I fear may
chance.
Good morrow to you. Here the street is narrow.
35 The throng that follows Caesar at the heels,
Of senators, of praetors, common suitors,
Will crowd a feeble man almost to death.
I'll get me to a place more void, and there
Speak to great Caesar as he comes along. *(He exits.)*
40 **PORTIA.** I must go in. Ay me, how weak a thing
The heart of woman is! O Brutus,
The heavens speed thee in thine enterprise!
Sure, the boy heard me. Brutus hath a suit
That Caesar will not grant. O, I grow faint.
45 Run, Lucius, and commend me to my lord;
Say I am merry. Come to me again
And bring me word what he doth say to thee.
*(*LUCIUS *runs off at right;* PORTIA *exits into house.)*

■ What might account for Portia's state of mind?

19 bustling rumor, like a fray, confused sound, like fighting.

21 Sooth, truly.

38 void, empty; less crowded.

■ What could prevent the conspirators from accomplishing their goal?

After Reading

Making Connections

1. Do you think that Cassius has been unwise in giving in to Brutus's demand to spare Antony? Explain.

2. Given these qualities—loyalty, honor, insight, independence—who, in your opinion, is the better wife, Portia or Calpurnia? Explain.

3. In your notebook, write three adjectives you think best describe Brutus's character.

4. ☜ Given his personality, do you think it is easy or difficult for Brutus to endure this period of political and cultural **change?** Explain.

5. In line 14 of scene 1, Brutus introduces the **image** of an adder. With what other words or phrases in this soliloquy does Shakespeare develop this **metaphor**? What point is Brutus making?

6. On the basis of Brutus's short **soliloquies**, what do you think most motivates him to join the conspiracy to assassinate Caesar?

7. In scene 1, what is the difference in **connotation** between the words in each pair: "sacrificers, but not butchers" (line 167) and "purgers, not murderers" (line 181)?

8. Describe the relationship between Brutus and Portia as revealed in their **dialogue.**

9. How does Decius demonstrate his understanding of Caesar's **character**?

10. How do scenes 1 and 2 advance the action of the **plot**?

11. Mention some elements that contribute to the **suspense** of the play.

12. Speculate on why Artemidorus's lines in scene 3 are not written in **blank verse.**

13. What details lead you to **infer** that Portia has learned Brutus's secret?

14. Do you think *Julius Caesar* has the components of a bestselling modern thriller? Why or why not?

ACT THREE

Summary *With the conspirators, Caesar goes to the Capitol. He encounters but ignores the Soothsayer and Artemidorus. The conspirators stab Caesar and Mark Antony flees. Brutus then promises to explain to the people the reasons for Caesar's death, after which Antony will be allowed to deliver Caesar's funeral oration. Antony returns, pretending friendship. Later, alone, Antony vows vengeance with the help of Octavius, who is camped near Rome.*

Rome. Before the Capitol. ARTEMIDORUS *and the* SOOTHSAYER *enter at left among a crowd of well-wishers.* CAESAR *enters at right, followed by* ANTONY, BRUTUS, CASSIUS, CASCA, DECIUS, METELLUS CIMBER, TREBONIUS, CINNA, LEPIDUS, POPILIUS, PUBLIUS, *and others.* CAESAR *approaches the* SOOTHSAYER *and speaks defiantly.*

CAESAR *(to the* SOOTHSAYER*).* The ides of March are come.

SOOTHSAYER. Ay, Caesar, but not gone.

(ARTEMIDORUS *approaches and presents his paper to* CAESAR.)

ARTEMIDORUS. Hail, Caesar! Read this schedule.

DECIUS. Trebonius doth desire you to o'erread,

5   At your best leisure, this his humble suit.

ARTEMIDORUS. O Caesar, read mine first, for mine's a suit
    That touches Caesar nearer. Read it, great Caesar.

CAESAR. What touches us ourself shall be last served.

ARTEMIDORUS. Delay not, Caesar, read it instantly.

CAESAR. What, is the fellow mad?

10 **PUBLIUS.**   Sirrah, give place.

CASSIUS. What, urge you your petitions in the street?
    Come to the Capitol.

(*All but the* SOOTHSAYER *and* ARTEMIDORUS *enter the Senate-house where, downstage and to the left, a prominent statue of Pompey stands.*)

POPILIUS. *(to* CASSIUS*).* I wish your enterprise today may thrive.

CASSIUS. What enterprise, Popilius?

15 **POPILIUS** *(to* CASSIUS*).* Fare you well. (*He advances to* CAESAR.)

BRUTUS. What said Popilius Lena?

CASSIUS. He wished today our enterprise might thrive.
    I fear our purpose is discovered.

BRUTUS. Look how he makes to Caesar. Mark him.

(POPILIUS *speaks apart to* CAESAR.)

20 **CASSIUS.** Casca, be sudden, for we fear prevention.
    Brutus, what shall be done? If this be known,
    Cassius or Caesar never shall turn back,
    For I will slay myself.

---

3 schedule, document.

10 sirrah (sir′ə), a form of address used for servants or inferiors.
■ Why do you think both Cassius and Decius force Artemidorus aside?

19 makes to Caesar, advances toward Caesar.

BRUTUS.   Cassius, be constant.
    Popilius Lena speaks not of our purposes;

25   For look, he smiles, and Caesar doth not change.
    (ANTONY *and* TREBONIUS *move away from* CAESAR *and the others.*)

CASSIUS. Trebonius knows his time, for look you, Brutus,
    He draws Mark Antony out of the way.

DECIUS. Where is Metellus Cimber? Let him go
    And presently prefer his suit to Caesar.

30   **BRUTUS.** He is addressed. Press near and second him.

CINNA. Casca, you are the first that rears your hand.
    (BRUTUS, CASSIUS, CASCA, DECIUS, *and* CINNA *move toward* CAESAR.)

CAESAR. Are we all ready? What is now amiss
    That Caesar and his Senate must redress?

METELLUS *(kneeling).* Most high, most mighty, and most <u>puissant</u>
      Caesar,

35   Metellus Cimber throws before thy seat
    An humble heart—

CAESAR.   I must prevent thee, Cimber.
    These couchings and these lowly courtesies
    Might fire the blood of ordinary men,
    And turn preordinance and first decree

40   Into the law of children. Be not fond
    To think that Caesar bears such rebel blood
    That will be thawed from the true quality
    With that which melteth fools—I mean, sweet words,
    Low-crookèd curtsies, and base spaniel fawning.

45   Thy brother by decree is banishèd.
    If thou dost bend and pray and fawn for him,
    I spurn thee like a cur out of my way.
    Know, Caesar doth not wrong, nor without cause
    Will he be satisfied.

50   **METELLUS.** Is there no voice more worthy than my own
    To sound more sweetly in great Caesar's ear
    For the repealing of my banished brother?

BRUTUS *(kneeling).* I kiss thy hand, but not in flattery, Caesar,
    Desiring thee that Publius Cimber may

55   Have an immediate freedom of repeal.

CAESAR. What, Brutus?

CASSIUS *(kneeling).*   Pardon, Caesar! Caesar, pardon!
    As low as to thy foot doth Cassius fall,
    To beg enfranchisement for Publius Cimber.

CAESAR. I could be well moved, if I were as you;

60   If I could pray to move, prayers would move me.
    But I am constant as the northern star,
    Of whose true-fixed and resting quality

■ Why does Trebonius draw Antony aside?

29 presently prefer his suit, immediately present his petition (suit).
30 addressed, ready.

34 puissant (pyü′ə sənt), *adj.* powerful.

37 couchings, kneelings.

39–40 and turn . . . children, and turn matters already firmly decided into laws to be changed just as children change rules in their games.

45 Thy brother, Publius Cimber, who had earlier incurred Caesar's wrath.

52 repealing, recall, return.

58 enfranchisement (en-fran′chīz mənt), liberation; that is, he asks that Publius Cimber be allowed to return to Rome as a citizen with full rights (franchises).

There is no fellow in the firmament.
The skies are painted with unnumbered sparks;
65   They are all fire and every one doth shine;
But there's but one in all doth hold his place.
So in the world: 'tis furnished well with men,
And men are flesh and blood, and apprehensive;
Yet in the number I do know but one
70   That unassailable holds on his rank,
Unshaked of motion. And that I am he,
Let me a little show it even in this—
That I was constant Cimber should be banished,
And constant do remain to keep him so.
CINNA (*kneeling*). O Caesar—
75   **CAESAR.**   Hence! Wilt thou lift up Olympus?
DECIUS (*kneeling*). Great Caesar—
CAESAR.   Doth not Brutus <u>bootless</u> kneel?
CASCA. Speak, hands, for me!
(*The other* CONSPIRATORS, *daggers in hand, surge forward, and all but* BRU-
TUS *stab* CASEAR. CAESAR *tries to ward off the blows until he sees* BRUTUS*'s
uplifted dagger, then covers his face with his cloak and submits.*)
CAESAR (*as* BRUTUS *stabs him*). Et tu, Brutè? Then fall, Caesar! (*Dies.*)
CINNA. Liberty! Freedom! Tyranny is dead!
80   Run hence, proclaim, cry it about the streets.
CASSIUS. Some to the common pulpits, and cry out
    "Liberty, freedom and enfranchisement!"
(*As the* CONSPIRATORS *move down left and stand together, the crowd, includ-
ing* ARTEMIDORUS *and the* SOOTHSAYER, *momentarily stands stunned, then
flees in panic.*)
BRUTUS. People and senators, be not affrighted.
    Fly not; stand still. Ambition's debt is paid.
CASCA. Go to the pulpit, Brutus.
85   **DECIUS.**   And Cassius too.
BRUTUS. Where's Publius?
CINNA. Here, quite confounded with this mutiny.
METELLUS. Stand fast together, lest some friend of Caesar's
    Should chance—
90   **BRUTUS.** Talk not of standing. Publius, good cheer.
    There is no harm intended to your person,
    Nor to no Roman else. So tell them, Publius.
CASSIUS. And leave us, Publius, lest that the people,
    Rushing on us, should do your age some mischief.
95   **BRUTUS.** Do so, and let no man abide this deed
    But we the doers. (*Everyone exits but the* CONSPIRATORS.)
(TREBONIUS *enters.*)
CASSIUS. Where is Antony?

63 fellow, equal.

68 apprehensive, capable of reason.

70 unassailable (un ə sāl′ə-bəl), *adj.* not able to be attacked (with violent blows, hostile words, arguments, or abuse).

■ How does this allusion to Olympus (a mountain in Greece and the home of the gods), as well as the content of his speeches in lines 36–49 and 59–74, show Caesar's egotism?

77 bootless (būt′lis), *adv.* in vain.

78 Et tu, Brutè (brū′tā) "And you, Brutus!" [*Latin*]. The betrayal overwhelms Caesar.

81 common pulpits, elevated areas where public debates were held.

■ What other famous political leaders can you name who have been assassinated because of principle rather than madness or private vengeance?

86 Publius, an elderly senator too astounded to flee.

95 abide this deed, answer for this deed.

TREBONIUS.   Fled to his house amazed.
    Men, wives, and children stare, cry out, and run
    As it were doomsday.
BRUTUS.   Fates, we will know your pleasures.
100 That we shall die, we know; 'tis but the time,
    And drawing days out, that men stand upon.
CASCA. Why, he that cuts off twenty years of life
    Cuts off so many years of fearing death.
BRUTUS. Grant that, and then is death a benefit.
105 So are we Caesar's friends, that have abridged
    His time of fearing death. Stoop, Romans, stoop,
    And let us bathe our hands in Caesar's blood

99 Fates, the three goddesses who were thought to control human destinies.
101 stand upon, attach importance to.

Up to the elbows and besmear our swords.
Then walk we forth even to the marketplace,
110 And, waving our red weapons o'er our heads,
Let's all cry "Peace, freedom, and liberty!"

CASSIUS. Stoop, then, and wash. *(They bathe their hands and weapons.)*
How many ages hence
Shall this our lofty scene be acted over
In states unborn and accents yet unknown!

115 **BRUTUS.** How many times shall Caesar bleed in sport,
That now on Pompey's basis lies along
No worthier than the dust!

CASSIUS. So oft as that shall be,
So often shall the knot of us be called
120 The men that gave their country liberty.

DECIUS. What, shall we forth?

CASSIUS.   Ay, every man away.
Brutus shall lead, and we will grace his heels
With the most boldest and best hearts of Rome.

(SERVANT enters.)

BRUTUS. Soft, who comes here? A friend of Antony's.

125 **SERVANT** *(kneeling).* Thus, Brutus, did my master bid me kneel;
Thus did Mark Antony bid me fall down,
And, being prostrate, thus he bade me say:
"Brutus is noble, wise, valiant, and honest;
Caesar was mighty, bold, royal, and loving.
130 Say I love Brutus and I honor him;
Say I feared Caesar, honored him, and loved him.
If Brutus will vouchsafe that Antony
May safely come to him and be resolved
How Caesar hath deserved to lie in death,
135 Mark Antony shall not love Caesar dead
So well as Brutus living, but will follow
The fortunes and affairs of noble Brutus
Thorough the hazards of this untrod state
With all true faith." So says my master Antony.

140 **BRUTUS.** Thy master is a wise and valiant Roman;
I never thought him worse.
Tell him, so please him come unto this place,
He shall be satisfied and, by my honor,
Depart untouched.

SERVANT.   I'll fetch him presently.

(SERVANT exits.)

145 **BRUTUS.** I know that we shall have him well to friend.

CASSIUS. I wish we may. But yet have I a mind
That fears him much, and my misgiving still

■ What actions do the conspirators take immediately following the stabbing of Caesar and prior to the entrance of Antony's servant? Where has this been foreshadowed?

116 on Pompey's . . . along, at the foot of Pompey's statue Caesar lies prostrate.

122 grace his heels, do honor to (by following closely).

133 be resolved, receive an explanation of.

138 untrod state, new and unfamiliar state of affairs; the image can be compared to a field unmarked by footsteps (untrod).

■ What question would you ask Brutus at this point in the play?

Falls shrewdly to the purpose.

(ANTONY *enters.*)

BRUTUS. But here comes Antony. Welcome, Mark Antony.

150 **ANTONY.** O mighty Caesar! Dost thou lie so low?
Are all thy conquests, glories, triumphs, spoils,
Shrunk to this little measure? Fare thee well.
I know not, gentlemen, what you intend,
Who else must be let blood, who else is rank;

155 If I myself, there is no hour so fit
As Caesar's death's hour, nor no instrument
Of half that worth as those your swords, made rich
With the most noble blood of all this world.
I do beseech ye, if you bear me hard,

160 Now, whilst your purpled hands do reek and smoke,
Fulfill your pleasure. Live a thousand years,
I shall not find myself so apt to die;
No place will please me so, no mean of death,
As here by Caesar, and by you cut off,

165 The choice and master spirits of this age.

BRUTUS. O Antony! Beg not your death of us.
Though now we must appear bloody and cruel,
As by our hands and this our present act
You see we do, yet see you but our hands

170 And this the bleeding business they have done.
Our hearts you see not. They are pitiful;
And pity to the general wrong of Rome—
As fire drives out fire, so pity pity—
Hath done this deed on Caesar. For your part,

175 To you our swords have leaden points, Mark Antony.
Our arms in strength of malice, and our hearts
Of brothers' temper, do receive you in
With all kind love, good thoughts, and reverence.

CASSIUS. Your voice shall be as strong as any man's

180 In the disposing of new dignities.

BRUTUS. Only be patient till we have appeased
The multitude, beside themselves with fear,
And then we will deliver you the cause
Why I, that did love Caesar when I struck him,
Have thus proceeded.

185 **ANTONY.**   I doubt not of your wisdom.
Let each man render me his bloody hand.

(*He shakes hands with the* CONSPIRATORS.)

First, Marcus Brutus, will I shake with you;
Next, Caius Cassius, do I take your hand;
Now, Decius Brutus, yours; now yours, Metellus;

154 who else . . . rank, who else must be killed.

161–162 Live . . . die. [If I should] live a thousand years, I would not find myself so ready (apt) to die.
163 mean, means or method.

173 so pity pity, so pity for the wrongs Rome has endured from Caesar over-shadows pity for his death.

180 dignities, new government positions.
■ What is the difference between what Cassius offers Antony and what Brutus has offered him?

190   Yours, Cinna; and, my valiant Casca, yours;
        Though last, not least in love, yours, good Trebonius.
        Gentlemen all—alas, what shall I say?
        My credit now stands on such slippery ground
        That one of two bad ways you must conceit me,
195   Either a coward or a flatterer.
        That I did love thee, Caesar, O, 'tis true!
        If then thy spirit look upon us now,
        Shall it not grieve thee dearer than thy death
        To see thy Antony making his peace,
200   Shaking the bloody fingers of thy foes—
        Most noble!—in the presence of thy corpse?
        Had I as many eyes as thou has wounds,
        Weeping as fast as they stream forth thy blood,
        It would become me better than to close
205   In terms of friendship with thine enemies.
        Pardon me, Julius! Here wast thou bayed, brave hart,
        Here didst thou fall, and here thy hunters stand,
        Signed in thy spoil and crimsoned in thy lethe.
        O world, thou wast the forest to this hart,
210   And this indeed, O world, the heart of thee!
        How like a deer, strucken by many princes,
        Dost thou here lie!
    CASSIUS. Mark Antony—
    ANTONY.   Pardon me, Caius Cassius.
        The enemies of Caesar shall say this;
215   Then in a friend it is cold modesty.
    CASSIUS. I blame you not for praising Caesar so,
        But what compact mean you to have with us?
        Will you be pricked in number of our friends,
        Or shall we on and not depend on you?
220 **ANTONY.** Therefore I took your hands, but was indeed
        Swayed from the point by looking down on Caesar.
        Friends am I with you all, and love you all,
        Upon this hope, that you shall give me reasons
        Why and wherein Caesar was dangerous.
225 **BRUTUS.** Or else were this a savage spectacle.
        Our reasons are so full of good regard
        That were you, Antony, the son of Caesar,
        You should be satisfied.
    ANTONY.   That's all I seek,
        And am moreover suitor that I may
230   Produce his body to the marketplace,
        And in the pulpit, as becomes a friend,
        Speak in the order of his funeral.

---

194 conceit, think, judge.

204 close, come to an agreement.

206 hart. Here and in lines 209–210, Antony puns on *hart* ("stag," as in deer) and *heart*.

208 lethe (lē′thē), death.
196–212 That I did love . . . lie. In this, as in his preceding speech, Antony cleverly alternates between placating the conspirators and revealing his feelings about Caesar's death.
215 modesty, moderation.

218 pricked in number, marked off on a list.

226 good regard, merit.

232 order, ceremony.

BRUTUS. You shall, Mark Antony.

CASSIUS.   Brutus, a word with you.

    (aside to BRUTUS*).* You know not what you do. Do not consent

235   That Antony speak in his funeral.

    Know you how much the people may be moved

    By that which he will utter?

BRUTUS *(aside to* CASSIUS*).*   By your pardon:

    I will myself into the pulpit first

    And show the reason of our Caesar's death.

240   What Antony shall speak, I will protest

    He speaks by leave and by permission,

    And that we are contented Caesar shall

    Have all true rites and lawful ceremonies.

    It shall advantage more than do us wrong.

245 **CASSIUS** *(aside to* BRUTUS*).* I know not what may fall. I like it not.

BRUTUS. Mark Antony, here, take you Caesar's body.

    You shall not in your funeral speech blame us,

    But speak all good you can devise of Caesar,

    And say you do 't by our permission.

250   Else shall you not have any hand at all

    About his funeral. And you shall speak

    In the same pulpit whereto I am going,

    After my speech is ended.

ANTONY.   Be it so.

    I do desire no more.

255 **BRUTUS.** Prepare the body then, and follow us.

    (All exit except ANTONY*.)*

ANTONY. O, pardon me, thou bleeding piece of earth,

    That I am meek and gentle with these butchers!

    Thou art the ruins of the noblest man

    That ever livèd in the tide of times.

260   Woe to the hand that shed this costly blood!

    Over thy wounds now do I prophesy—

    Which, like dumb mouths, do ope their ruby lips

    To beg the voice and utterance of my tongue—

    A curse shall light upon the limbs of men;

265   Domestic fury and fierce civil strife

    Shall cumber all the parts of Italy;

    Blood and destruction shall be so in use

    And dreadful objects so familiar

    That mothers shall but smile when they behold

270   Their infants quartered with the hands of war,

    All pity choked with custom of fell deeds;

    And Caesar's spirit, ranging for revenge,

    With Ate by his side come hot from hell,

240 protest, announce.

■ *Lines 225–253.* In what respect has Brutus made another error in judgment? Keep these lines in mind as you read scene 2, to see whether Antony obeys Brutus's directions when speaking to the commoners.

259 tide of times, course of all history.

268 objects, sights.
271 with custom of fell deeds, with the familiarity of cruel (fell) deeds.
273 Ate (ā′tē), Greek goddess of discord and moral chaos.

Shall in these confines with a monarch's voice
275　Cry havoc and let slip the dogs of war,
That this foul deed shall smell above the earth
With carrion men, groaning for burial.
(OCTAVIUS'S SERVANT *enters.*)
You serve Octavius Caesar, do you not?
SERVANT. I do, Mark Antony.
280　**ANTONY.** Caesar did write for him to come to Rome.
SERVANT. He did receive his letters, and is coming,
And bid me say to you by word of mouth—
O Caesar! *(Seeing the body.)*
ANTONY. Thy heart is big. Get thee apart and weep.
285　Passion, I see, is catching, for mine eyes,
Seeing those beads of sorrow stand in thine,
Began to water. Is thy master coming?
SERVANT. He lies tonight within seven leagues of Rome.
ANTONY. Post back with speed and tell him what hath chanced.
290　Here is a mourning Rome, a dangerous Rome,
No Rome of safety for Octavius yet;
Hie hence and tell him so. Yet stay awhile;
Thou shalt not back till I have borne this corpse
Into the marketplace. There shall I try,
295　In my oration, how the people take
The cruel issue of these bloody men,
According to the which thou shalt discourse
To young Octavius of the state of things.
Lend me your hand.
(ANTONY *and the* SERVANT *carry off Caesar's body.*)

SCENE 2

Summary *After Brutus explains why Caesar had to be killed, the mob cheers him. Antony's oration arouses in the mob both gratitude toward Caesar, who has left them a generous bequest, and anger against the conspirators. A servant announces that Octavius has ridden into the city, and Brutus and Cassius have fled.*

Rome. The Forum. BRUTUS *and* CASSIUS *enter at left. Indignant* CITIZENS *clamor for an explanation of* CAESAR's *assassination.*

PLEBEIANS. We will be satisfied! Let us be satisfied!
BRUTUS. Then follow me, and give me audience, friends.
Cassius, go you into the other street
And part the numbers.
5　Those that will hear me speak, let 'em stay here;
Those that will follow Cassius, go with him;

---

275 cry havoc . . . let slip the dogs of war, give a command to sack, pillage, and slaughter (which could be given only by a king) and unleash fire, sword, and famine.
■ What does Antony promise in this soliloquy (lines 256–277)?

288 He lies . . . Rome. With the news that Caesar's grandnephew Octavius is within seven leagues (twenty miles) of Rome, Antony's side is strengthened. As Caesar's adopted son and heir, Octavius would attract Caesar's supporters.
294 try, test.
296 issue, deed.
297 discourse (dis kôrs′), *v.* talk, converse.
■ Do you think that Antony will be effective in his speech before the citizens? Why or why not?

1 We . . . satisfied. Note how throughout this scene the commoners are easily swayed to support first one side, then the other.
4 part the numbers, divide the crowd.

And public reasons shall be renderèd
Of Caesar's death.
(BRUTUS *ascends a speaker's platform.*)

FIRST PLEBEIAN. I will hear Brutus speak.

SECOND PLEBEIAN. I will hear Cassius, and compare their reasons
10   When severally we hear them renderèd.
(CASSIUS *moves off at right, accompanied by various* CITIZENS.)

THIRD PLEBEIAN. The noble Brutus is ascended. Silence!

BRUTUS. Be patient till the last.

Romans, countrymen, and lovers, hear me for my cause, and be
silent that you may hear. Believe me for mine honor, and have
15   respect to mine honor, that you may believe. <u>Censure</u> me in your
wisdom, and awake your senses, that you may the better judge. If
there be any in this assembly, any dear friend of Caesar's, to him I
say that Brutus's love to Caesar was no less than his. If then that
friend demand why Brutus rose against Caesar, this is my answer:
20   not that I loved Caesar less, but that I loved Rome more. Had
you rather Caesar were living and die all slaves, than that Caesar
were dead, to live all free men? As Caesar loved me, I weep for him;
as he was fortunate, I rejoice at it; as he was valiant, I honor him;
but, as he was ambitious, I slew him. There is tears for his love; joy
25   for his fortune; honor for his valor; and death for his ambition.
Who is here so base that would be a bondman? If any, speak, for
him have I offended. Who is here so rude that would not be a
Roman? If any, speak, for him have I offended. Who is here so vile
that will not love his country? If any, speak, for him have I
30   offended. I pause for a reply.

ALL. None, Brutus, none!

BRUTUS. Then none have I offended. I have done no more to Caesar
than you shall do to Brutus. The question of his death is enrolled
in the Capitol, his glory not extenuated wherein he was worthy,
35   nor his offenses enforced for which he suffered death.
(MARK ANTONY *and others enter with* CAESAR*'s body.*)

Here comes his body, mourned by Mark Antony, who, though he
had no hand in his death, shall receive the benefit of his dying, a
place in the commonwealth, as which of you shall not? With this I
depart, that, as I slew my best lover for the good of Rome, I have
40   the same dagger for myself when it shall please my country to
need my death.

ALL. Live, Brutus, live, live! (BRUTUS *comes down.*)

FIRST PLEBEIAN. Bring him with triumph home unto his house.

SECOND PLEBEIAN. Give him a statue with his ancestors.

THIRD PLEBEIAN. Let him be Caesar.

45 **FOURTH PLEBEIAN.** Caesar's better parts

---

10 **severally,** separately.

13 **lovers,** friends.

15 **censure,** (sen′shər), *v.*
express disapproval of;
blame.
16 **senses,** intellectual
powers.
■ What does Brutus mean
by "not that I loved Caesar
less, but that I loved Rome
more"?

27 **rude,** barbarous.

33–35 **The question . . .
enforced.** The reason for
Caesar's death is recorded;
his fame is not minimized,
nor his crime exaggerated.

Shall be crowned in Brutus.

FIRST PLEBEIAN. We'll bring him to his house with shouts and
    clamors.

BRUTUS. My countrymen—

SECOND PLEBEIAN.   Peace, silence! Brutus speaks.

FIRST PLEBEIAN. Peace, ho!

50 **BRUTUS.** Good countrymen, let me depart alone,
    And, for my sake, stay here with Antony.
    Do grace to Caesar's corpse, and grace his speech
    Tending to Caesar's glories, which Mark Antony,
    By our permission, is allowed to make.

55   I do entreat you, not a man depart,
    Save I alone, till Antony have spoke. *(Exits.)*

FIRST PLEBEIAN. Stay, ho, and let us hear Mark Antony.

THIRD PLEBEIAN. Let him go up into the public chair.
    We'll hear him. Noble Antony, go up.

60 **ANTONY.** For Brutus's sake I am beholding to you.

*(ANTONY ascends the platform. His ATTENDANTS place CAESAR's body below
him and near the crowd.)*

FOURTH PLEBEIAN. What does he say of Brutus?

THIRD PLEBEIAN. He says, for Brutus's sake
    He finds himself beholding to us all.

FOURTH PLEBEIAN. 'Twere best he speak no harm of Brutus here.

FIRST PLEBEIAN. This Caesar was a tyrant.

65 **THIRD PLEBEIAN.**   Nay, that's certain.
    We are blest that Rome is rid of him.

SECOND PLEBEIAN. Peace! Let us hear what Antony can say.

ANTONY. You gentle Romans—

ALL.   Peace, ho! Let us hear him.

ANTONY. Friends, Romans, countrymen, lend me your ears.

70   I come to bury Caesar, not to praise him.
    The evil that men do lives after them;
    The good is oft interrèd with their bones.
    So let it be with Caesar. The noble Brutus
    Hath told you Caesar was ambitious.

75   If it were so, it was a grievous fault,
    And grievously hath Caesar answered it.
    Here, under leave of Brutus and the rest—
    For Brutus is an honorable man,
    So are they all, all honorable men—

80   Come I to speak in Caesar's funeral.
    He was my friend, faithful and just to me;
    But Brutus says he was ambitious,
    And Brutus is an honorable man.
    He hath brought many captives home to Rome,

52 Do grace . . . speech,
show respect to Caesar's
corpse, and listen
courteously to Antony's
speech.

■ How do you think
Antony's oration will differ
from Brutus's oration?

72 inter (in tėr′), *v.* bury.

75 grievous (grē′vəs), *adj.*
causing great pain or
suffering.

**78 Brutus is an honorable
man.** The crowd's anger at
words against Brutus makes
Antony quick to express his
admiration for the man—and
for the other conspirators.

84 He, Caesar.

85 Whose ransoms did the general coffers fill.
Did this in Caesar seem ambitious?
When that the poor have cried, Caesar hath wept;
Ambition should be made of sterner stuff.
Yet Brutus says he was ambitious,
90 And Brutus is an honorable man.
You all did see that on the Lupercal
I thrice presented him a kingly crown,
Which he did thrice refuse. Was this ambition?
Yet Brutus says he was ambitious
95 And sure he is an honorable man.
I speak not to disprove what Brutus spoke,
But here I am to speak what I do know.
You all did love him once, not without cause.
What cause withholds you then to mourn for him?
100 O judgment! Thou art fled to brutish beasts,
And men have lost their reason. Bear with me;
My heart is in the coffin there with Caesar,
And I must pause till it come back to me.

FIRST PLEBEIAN. Methinks there is much reason in his sayings.
105 **SECOND PLEBEIAN.** If thou consider rightly of the matter,

85 the general coffers fill, Caesar gave the ransom money to the city; he hadn't kept it for himself.

91–93 Lupercal . . . ambition. Compare this explanation of Caesar's reaction with Casca's view in act one, scene 2.

Caesar has had great wrong.

THIRD PLEBEIAN. Has he, masters?
I fear there will a worse come in his place.

FOURTH PLEBEIAN. Marked ye his words? He would not take the
    crown,
Therefore 'tis certain he was not ambitious.

110 **FIRST PLEBEIAN.** If it be found so, some will dear abide it.

SECOND PLEBEIAN. Poor soul, his eyes are red as fire with weeping.

THIRD PLEBEIAN. There's not a nobler man in Rome than Antony.

FOURTH PLEBEIAN. Now mark him. He begins again to speak.

ANTONY. But yesterday the word of Caesar might
115   Have stood against the world. Now lies he there,
And none so poor to do him reverence.
O masters! If I were disposed to stir
Your hearts and minds to mutiny and rage,
I should do Brutus wrong, and Cassius wrong,
120   Who, you all know, are honorable men.
I will not do them wrong; I rather choose
To wrong the dead, to wrong myself and you,
Than I will wrong such honorable men.
But here's a parchment with the seal of Caesar.
125   I found it in his closet; 'tis his will. *(He shows the will.)*
Let but the commons hear this testament—
Which, pardon me, I do not mean to read—
And they would go and kiss dead Caesar's wounds
And dip their napkins in his sacred blood,
130   Yea, beg a hair of him for memory,
And dying, mention it within their wills,
Bequeathing it as a rich legacy
Unto their issue.

FOURTH PLEBEIAN. We'll hear the will! Read it, Mark Antony.

135 **ALL.** The will, the will! We will hear Caesar's will.

ANTONY. Have patience, gentle friends: I must not read it.
It is not meet you know how Caesar loved you.
You are not wood, you are not stones, but men;
And being men, hearing the will of Caesar,
140   It will inflame you, it will make you mad.
'Tis good you know not that you are his heirs,
For if you should, O, what would come of it?

FOURTH PLEBEIAN. Read the will! We'll hear it, Antony.
You shall read us the will, Caesar's will.

145 **ANTONY.** Will you be patient? Will you stay awhile?
I have o'ershot myself to tell you of it.
I fear I wrong the honorable men
Whose daggers have stabbed Caesar; I do fear it.

110 dear abide it, pay a heavy penalty for.
■ Do you think that Antony's tears are genuine? Are they effective?

116 and none . . . reverence, not even the lowliest Roman is poorer (lower in estate) than Caesar now.

125 closet, study; private chamber.

129 napkins, handkerchiefs.

132 bequeath (bi kwēŦH′), *v.* give or leave (money or property) by a will; **legacy** (leg′ə sē), *n.* something handed down in a will.
■ What might be behind Antony's refusal to read the will?

146 I have o'ershot myself, I have said more than I intended—or so Antony pretends.

FOURTH PLEBEIAN. They were traitors. "Honorable men"!

150 **ALL.** The will! The testament!

SECOND PLEBEIAN. They were villains, murderers. The will! Read
the will!

ANTONY. You will compel me then to read the will?
Then make a ring about the corpse of Caesar
And let me show you him that made the will.

155 Shall I descend? And will you give me leave?

ALL. Come down.

SECOND PLEBEIAN. Descend.

THIRD PLEBEIAN. You shall have leave.

(ANTONY *comes down. They gather around* CAESAR.)

FOURTH PLEBEIAN. A ring; stand round.

160 **FIRST PLEBEIAN.** Stand from the hearse. Stand from the body.

SECOND PLEBEIAN. Room for Antony, most noble Antony!

ANTONY. Nay, press not so upon me. Stand far off.

ALL. Stand back! Room! Bear back!

ANTONY. If you have tears, prepare to shed them now.

165 You all do know this mantle. I remember
The first time ever Caesar put it on;
'Twas on a summer's evening in his tent,
That day he overcame the Nervii.
Look, in this place ran Cassius' dagger through.

170 See what a rent the envious Casca made.
Through this the well-belovèd Brutus stabbed,
And as he plucked his cursèd steel away,
Mark how the blood of Caesar followed it,
As rushing out of doors to be resolved

175 If Brutus so unkindly knocked or no;
For Brutus, as you know, was Caesar's angel.
Judge, O you gods, how dearly Caesar loved him!
This was the most unkindest cut of all;
For when the noble Caesar saw him stab,

180 Ingratitude, more strong than traitors' arms,
Quite vanquished him. Then burst his mighty heart,
And in his mantle muffling up his face,
Even at the base of Pompey's statue,
Which all the while ran blood, great Caesar fell.

185 O, what a fall was there, my countrymen!
Then I, and you, and all of us fell down,
Whilst bloody treason flourished over us.
O, now you weep, and I perceive you feel
The dint of pity. These are gracious drops.

190 Kind souls, what weep you when you but behold
Our Caesar's vesture wounded? Look you here,

---

160 hearse, bier (coffin stand).

168 Nervii (nẻr′vē ī), a Celtic tribe whom Caesar defeated.
170 rent (rent), *n.* tear; torn place.
■ Since Antony could not have known which conspirator was responsible for which wound, why do you think he associates various cuts in Caesar's cloak with individual conspirators?

189 dint, effect.
191 Caesar's vesture wounded, Caesar's clothing (vesture) cut.

Here is himself, marred as you see with traitors.
(He lifts CAESAR'*s mantle.)*

FIRST PLEBEIAN. O piteous spectacle!

SECOND PLEBEIAN. O noble Caesar!

195 **THIRD PLEBEIAN.** O woeful day!

FOURTH PLEBEIAN. O traitors, villains!

FIRST PLEBEIAN. O most bloody sight!

SECOND PLEBEIAN. We will be revenged.

ALL. Revenge! About! Seek! Burn! Fire! Kill! Slay! Let not a traitor
200 live!

ANTONY. Stay, countrymen.

FIRST PLEBEIAN. Peace there! Hear the noble Antony.

SECOND PLEBEIAN. We'll hear him, we'll follow him, we'll die with
him!

205 **ANTONY.** Good friends, sweet friends, let me not stir you up
To such a sudden flood of mutiny.
They that have done this deed are honorable.
What private griefs they have, alas, I know not,
That made them do it. They are wise and honorable,
210 And will no doubt with reasons answer you.
I come not, friends, to steal away your hearts.
I am no orator, as Brutus is,
But, as you know me all, a plain blunt man
That love my friend, and that they know full well
215 That gave me public leave to speak of him.
For I have neither wit, nor words, nor worth,
Action, nor utterance, nor the power of speech
To stir men's blood. I only speak right on.
I tell you that which you yourselves do know,
220 Show you sweet Caesar's wounds, poor poor dumb mouths,
And bid them speak for me. But were I Brutus,
And Brutus Antony, there were an Antony
Would ruffle up your spirits and put a tongue
In every wound of Caesar that should move
225 The stones of Rome to rise and mutiny.

ALL. We'll mutiny!

FIRST PLEBEIAN. We'll burn the house of Brutus!

THIRD PLEBEIAN. Away, then! Come, seek the conspirators.

ANTONY. Yet hear me, countrymen. Yet hear me speak.

230 **ALL.** Peace, ho! Hear Antony, most noble Antony!

ANTONY. Why, friends, you go to do you know not what.
Wherein hath Caesar thus deserved your loves?
Alas, you know not. I must tell you then:
You have forgot the will I told you of.

235 **ALL.** Most true. The will! Let's stay and hear the will.

■ What is Antony's purpose
in showing the body?

208 private griefs, personal
reasons.
■ *Lines 205–225.* How does
this speech relate to
Antony's soliloquy near the
end of scene 1 (lines
256–277)?

ANTONY. Here is the will, and under Caesar's seal.
  To every Roman citizen he gives,
  To every several man, seventy-five drachmas.

SECOND PLEBEIAN. Most noble Caesar! We'll revenge his death.

240 **THIRD PLEBEIAN.** O royal Caesar!

ANTONY. Hear me with patience.

ALL. Peace, ho!

ANTONY. Moreover, he hath left you all his walks,
  His private arbors, and new-planted orchards,
245   On this side Tiber; he hath left them you,
  And to your heirs forever—common pleasures,
  To walk abroad and recreate yourselves.
  Here was a Caesar! When comes such another?

FIRST PLEBEIAN. Never, never! Come, away, away!
250   We'll burn his body in the holy place
  And with the brands fire the traitors' houses.
  Take up the body.

SECOND PLEBEIAN. Go fetch fire!

THIRD PLEBEIAN. Pluck down benches!

FOURTH PLEBEIAN. Pluck down forms, windows,
255   anything! (PLEBIANS *exit with the body.*)

ANTONY. Now let it work. Mischief, thou art afoot.
  Take thou what course thou wilt.
  (OCTAVIUS's *servant enters.*)   How now, fellow?

SERVANT. Sir, Octavius is already come to Rome.

ANTONY. Where is he?

260 **SERVANT.** He and Lepidus are at Caesar's house.

ANTONY. And thither will I straight to visit him.
  He comes upon a wish. Fortune is merry,
  And in this mood will give us anything.

SERVANT. I heard him say Brutus and Cassius
265   Are rid like madmen through the gates of Rome.

ANTONY. Belike they had some notice of the people,
  How I had moved them. Bring me to Octavius.
  (ANTONY *leads his* ATTENDANTS *and the* SERVANT *out at left.*)

238 seventy-five drachmas
(drak′mə), Although
experts estimate this amount
as being worth anywhere
from $10 to $100, it
represented a substantial
bequest.

245 on this side Tiber, on
this side of the Tiber, Rome's
river. Shakespeare shortened
the phrase to maintain the
rhythm of this speech.

254 forms, public benches.

265 are rid, have ridden.
■ In your notebook write
any questions you have
about the events of the play
to this point.

SCENE 3

Summary *Mistaken for Cinna the conspirator, Cinna the poet is attacked by the mob. The mob then moves off to find the conspirators or to burn their houses.*

Rome. A street near the Forum. CINNA *enters followed by a group of angry and suspicious* CITIZENS.

CINNA. I dreamt tonight that I did feast with Caesar,
    And things unluckily charge my fantasy.
    I have no will to wander forth of doors,
    Yet something leads me forth.

5 FIRST PLEBEIAN. What is your name?

SECOND PLEBEIAN. Whither are you going?

THIRD PLEBEIAN. Where do you dwell?

FOURTH PLEBEIAN. Are you a married man or a bachelor?

SECOND PLEBEIAN. Answer every man directly.

10 FIRST PLEBEIAN. Ay, and briefly.

FOURTH PLEBEIAN. Ay, and wisely.

THIRD PLEBEIAN. Ay, and truly, you were best.

CINNA. What is my name? Whither am I going? Where do I dwell? Am
    I a married man or a bachelor? Then to answer every man directly
15   and briefly, wisely and truly: wisely I say, I am a bachelor.

SECOND PLEBEIAN. That's as much as to say they are fools that
    marry. You'll bear me a bang for that, I fear. Proceed directly.

CINNA. Directly, I am going to Caesar's funeral.

FIRST PLEBEIAN. As a friend or an enemy?

20 CINNA. As a friend.

SECOND PLEBEIAN. That matter is answered directly.

FOURTH PLEBEIAN. For your dwelling—briefly.

CINNA. Briefly, I dwell by the Capitol.

THIRD PLEBEIAN. Your name, sir, truly.

25 CINNA. Truly, my name is Cinna.

FIRST PLEBEIAN. Tear him to pieces! He's a conspirator!

CINNA. I am Cinna the poet, I am Cinna the poet!

FOURTH PLEBEIAN. Tear him for his bad verses, tear him for his bad
    verses!

30 CINNA. I am not Cinna the conspirator.

FOURTH PLEBEIAN. It is no matter, his name's Cinna.
    Pluck but his name out of his heart, and turn him going.

THIRD PLEBEIAN. Tear him, tear him! Come, brands, ho, firebrands!
    To Brutus's, to Cassius's; burn all! Some to Decius's house, and
35   some to Casca's; some to Ligarius's. Away go!

(*All the* PLEBEIANS *exit, dragging off* CINNA.)

1 **tonight**, last night.

17 **bear me a bang**, get a
beating.

■ What does this scene show
about the nature of the commoners?

After Reading

Making Connections

Shaping Your Response

1. If you were a soldier, would you prefer to serve under Brutus, Antony, or Cassius? Why?

2. For a radio presentation of *Julius Caesar,* what sound effects would you need for scene 1?

3. If you were directing this play for television or stage, would you have the murder take place on or off camera or stage? Explain.

Analyzing the Play

4. From which of Antony's lines in scene 1 should the conspirators **infer** that he is not to be trusted?

5. What trait in Brutus's **character** leads him to misjudge Antony so consistently?

6. Explain what is being compared in the hart **metaphor** (scene 1, lines 206–212), and whether you think the metaphor is appropriate for Caesar.

7. A **soliloquy** is a speech made by an actor to himself or herself when alone on the stage. It reveals the character's thoughts and feelings to the audience, but not to other characters in the play. What do you think is the purpose of Antony's soliloquy in scene 1, lines 256-277?

8. Which lines in Antony's funeral oration do you think an actor would express in an **ironic** tone? Why?

9. One purpose of scene 3 is to provide comic relief. Yet it shows a murderous mob setting upon an innocent victim. In your judgment, is this scene really humorous? necessary? Explain.

Extending the Ideas

10. 🐾 Caesar considered himself a defender of the common people. Do you think that a dictator can have the interests of the group at heart? Why or why not?

11. In the opening of his funeral oration, Antony observes that "The evil that men do lives after them; / The good is oft interrèd with their bones." Using such modern examples as John F. Kennedy, Christa McAuliffe, Elvis Presley, Malcolm X, or others, discuss whether you agree or disagree with this observation.

Literary Focus: Plot

On the plot chart in your notebook under **rising action**, list the events that point toward Caesar's assassination. The **climax** occurs when the central problem of the plot must be resolved. It also signals a change in the fortune of the main character. Write what you think the climax is.

Vocabulary Study

Tell whether the following word pairs are synonyms, antonyms, or neither by writing *S, A,* or *N* on your paper.

bequeath
bootless
censure
discourse
grievous
inter
legacy
puissant
rent
unassailable

1. grievous: causing pain
2. discourse: talk
3. bequeath: inherit
4. unassailable: ambitious
5. censure: praise
6. puissant: weak
7. bootless: poor
8. rent: torn place
9. inter: dig up
10. legacy: dagger

Expressing Your Ideas

Writing Choices

Writer's Notebook Update Write an obituary for Caesar that mentions some of the traits you included in your chart.

Eyewitness Assume that you are Lucius and write a **letter** to a friend telling what you have witnessed, overheard, and participated in from midnight to mid-morning of the ides of March.

Et Tu Write a short **dialogue** that ends "Et tu, Brutè!" Alternatively, you might draw an original cartoon based on these words.

"Et tu, Baxter?"

Drawing by Robert Mankoff; © 1987
The New Yorker Magazine, Inc.

Other Options

Home Sweet Home Assume that you are the set designer for a stage production of *Julius Caesar.* Research the kind of house and garden that Brutus, a wealthy Roman, would have had. Then draw or construct a **model** of your set.

I, Antony Analyze the lines in Mark Antony's oration for clues to tone and gestures. Then memorize lines from the speech, or the entire speech. Enhance your delivery with stage props or costumes, if you wish, and **act out** the oration for the class.

The Globe Theater

London Bridge teems with pedestrians and men on horseback; boats large and small move along the Thames River carrying eager spectators toward a dock on the south bank. Their destination? The octagonal, three-story Globe Theater, where a flag flies atop the building to indicate that a performance will take place this afternoon.

As the spectators enter through the double wooden doors, they begin to separate according to class. The groundlings (apprentices and the lower class) crowd into the round Yard, or pit area, where they will stand during the performance. Middle class folks move to the bench areas in the roofed galleries. Nobles take their places in special boxes. Vendors hawk both food and drink. The mood of the nearly 3,000 spectators is festive—and in the pit, even rowdy. As the audience begins to settle down in anticipation of the play, what do they see?

From a few surviving maps, carpenters' contracts, and written descriptions, we can put together the following picture of the Globe. The main acting area, the Platform, extended well into the Yard so that the spectators almost surrounded the actors. At the back was the Study, a curtained room used for interior scenes. At either side were large Permanent Doors, similar to the street doors of Elizabethan townhouses. These were the main stage entrances. In the floor of the Platform were several trap doors. Imagine smoke and fog rising and falling to announce the appearance of Caesar's ghost.

On the second level was another curtained room, the Chamber, typically used for domestic scenes. In front of this was a narrow balcony called the Tarras (ter′is). Often the Tarras and the Platform would be used together, with the Tarras representing a hill, the wall of a town, or a gallery from which observers watched the action below. On the third level, was a narrow musicians' gallery. Above it was a canopied roof supported by two large stage posts that rose from the Platform. Above the canopy were

the Huts that housed a pulley system for lowering objects supposed to appear from midair. Sound effects such as thunder or battle alarums (sounds of fighting) also came from the Huts. This entire three-story structure was known as the Tiring House. It was the Globe's permanent set.

Shakespeare quiets his audience by beginning *Julius Caesar* with the noise and bustle of excited crowds. There is little scenery. In later scenes, a bed, a table, a bench, or a chair suggests the setting. Often, a trumpet or a line or two of dialogue is enough to alert the audience to a change of scene.

The first Globe Theater, completed in 1599, burned to the ground in 1613. The second Globe, which was built immediately afterward, stood until 1644. Today, many Shakespearean-style theaters have been built—in Chichester, England; in Stratford, Canada; and in Minneapolis, Minnesota. A full-scale replica of the Globe has been recently completed as part of a Shakespearean complex in London, close to the site of the original Globe Theater.

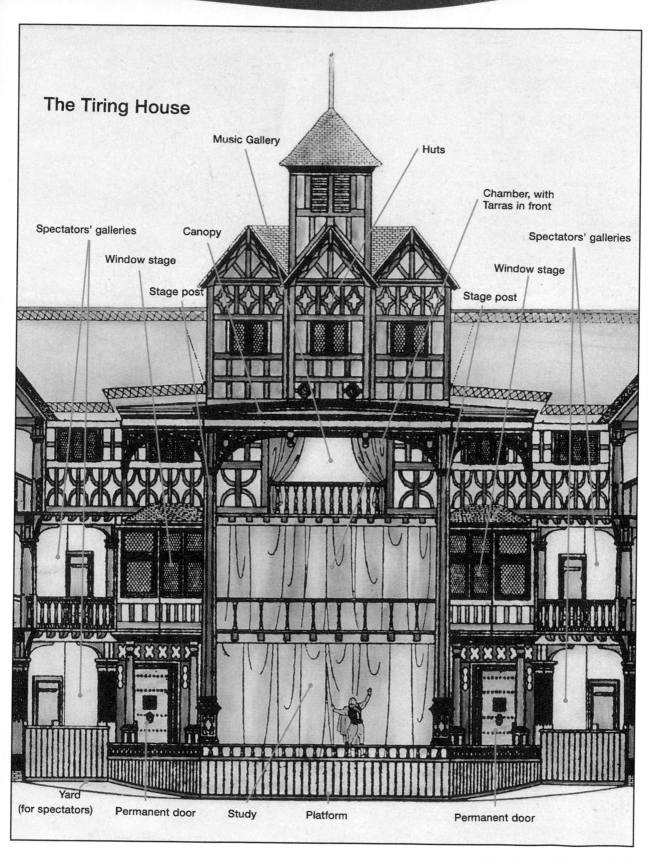

The Tiring House

Music Gallery

Huts

Chamber, with Tarras in front

Spectators' galleries

Canopy

Spectators' galleries

Window stage

Window stage

Stage post

Stage post

Spectators' galleries

Yard (for spectators)

Permanent door

Study

Platform

Permanent door

ACT FOUR

SCENE 1

Summary *Brutus and Cassius have fled to Greece and Asia Minor. After his civil war against Octavius, Antony has joined forces with Octavius and Lepidus. This triumvirate meets to condemn those Romans who might be opposed to them. After Antony sends Lepidus to get a copy of Caesar's will, he and Octavius agree that war against Brutus and Cassius is imminent.*

A house in Rome. One year after Caesar's assassination. Seated around a table, ANTONY, OCTAVIUS, *and* LEPIDUS *are closely examining a wax tablet and making plans to crush their opposition.*

ANTONY. These many, then shall die. Their names are pricked.
OCTAVIUS. Your brother too must die. Consent you, Lepidus?
LEPIDUS. I do consent—
OCTAVIUS.   Prick him down, Antony.
LEPIDUS. Upon condition Publius shall not live,
5   Who is your sister's son, Mark Antony.
ANTONY (*picking up the stylus*). He shall not live. Look, with a spot I
      damn him.
    But Lepidus, go you to Caesar's house.
    Fetch the will hither, and we shall determine
    How to cut off some charge in legacies.
10 **LEPIDUS.** What, shall I find you here?
OCTAVIUS. Or here or at the Capitol. (LEPIDUS *leaves by a rear door.*)
ANTONY. This is a slight, unmeritable man,
    Meet to be sent on errands. Is it fit,
    The threefold world divided, he should stand
    One of the three to share it?
15 **OCTAVIUS.**   So you thought him,
    And took his voice who should be pricked to die
    In our black sentence and proscription.
ANTONY. Octavius, I have seen more days than you;
    And though we lay these honors on this man
20   To ease ourselves of divers slanderous loads,
    He shall but bear them as the ass bears gold,
    To groan and sweat under the business,
    Either led or driven as we point the way;
    And having brought our treasure where we will,
25   Then take we down his load, and turn him off,
    Like to the empty ass, to shake his ears
    And graze in commons.
OCTAVIUS.   You may do your will;
    But he's a tried and valiant soldier.

---

1 These many . . . pricked, many Roman citizens are marked for death.

6 stylus, a pointed instrument for writing.
6 with a spot I damn him, with my mark (with the stylus) I condemn him to death.
8–9 we shall determine . . . legacies. Antony wishes to find a way to reduce the amount Caesar has bequeathed each Roman.
■ In the first fifteen lines of this scene, what three questionable activities has Antony been involved in? What, if anything, in earlier acts has foreshadowed Antony's behavior?
16–17 took his voice . . . proscription, accepted his statements about who should be marked for death or banishment (proscription).
20 divers (dī′vərz) **slanderous loads,** various false charges.

27 commons, public pastures.

ANTONY. So is my horse, Octavius, and for that
30 I do appoint him store of provender.
    It is a creature that I teach to fight,
    To wind, to stop, to run directly on,
    His corporal motion governed by my spirit.
    And in some taste is Lepidus but so.
35 He must be taught, and trained, and bid go forth—
    A barren-spirited fellow, one that feeds
    On objects, arts, and imitations,
    Which, out of use and staled by other men,
    Begin his fashion. Do not talk of him
40 But as a property. And now, Octavius,
    Listen great things. Brutus and Cassius
    Are levying powers. We must straight make head.

30 appoint . . . provender, provide him with food.
33 corporal, of the body; bodily.
37 objects, arts, and imitations, wonders and things that are artificial and fashionable.
■ What do you predict will ultimately happen to Lepidus?
41–42 Brutus and Cassius . . . head. Brutus and Cassius have been gathering forces (powers); so must Antony and his associates.

Therefore let our alliance be combined,
Our best friends made, our means stretched;

45 And let us presently go sit in council
How covert matters may be best disclosed
And open perils surest answerèd.

OCTAVIUS. Let us do so, for we are at the stake
And bayed about with many enemies;

50 And some that smile have in their hearts, I fear,
Millions of mischiefs.

(ANTONY *and* OCTAVIUS *exit.*)

SCENE 2

Summary *Lucilius, one of Brutus's officers, alerts Brutus that Cassius is near. He also verifies Brutus's suspicion that Cassius has changed. Preceded by his servant Pindarus, Cassius enters to find an angry Brutus.*

BRUTUS's *tent at Sardis, a city in Asia Minor. Several months later.* LUCIUS, BRUTUS's *servant, enters from the left, followed by* BRUTUS *and several* SOLDIERS. LUCILIUS *and* TITINIUS, *friends of* BRUTUS, *enter at the right, accompanied by* CASSIUS's *servant* PINDARUS.

BRUTUS. Stand, ho!
LUCILIUS. Give the word, ho, and stand!
BRUTUS. What now, Lucilius, is Cassius near?
LUCILIUS. He is at hand, and Pindarus is come

5   To do you salutation from his master.
BRUTUS. He greets me well. Your master, Pindarus,
In his own change, or by ill officers,
Hath given me some worthy cause to wish
Things done undone; but if he be at hand
I shall be satisfied.

10 **PINDARUS.**   I do not doubt
But that my noble master will appear
Such as he is, full of regard and honor.
BRUTUS. He is not doubted. A word, Lucilius.
(BRUTUS *and* LUCILIUS *speak apart.*)
How he received you let me be resolved.

15 **LUCILIUS.** With courtesy and with respect enough,
But not with such familiar instances
Nor with such free and friendly conference
As he hath used of old.
BRUTUS.   Thou hast described
A hot friend cooling. Ever note, Lucilius:

20 When love begins to sicken and decay

---

45 sit in council, discuss.
46–47 how covert . . . answerèd, how hidden (covert) dangers may be discovered, and dangers already known be met most securely.
48–49 we are at the stake . . . enemies, we are tied to a stake (like a bear in the sport of bear baiting), while enemies bark (bay) like dogs about to attack us.

1–2 Stand . . . stand! Halt! Pass the word (to Cassius's soldiers) to halt.

5 to do you salutation, to bring you greeting.

7 in his own . . . officers, by his own change of heart or by bad advice from troublemakers.

10 be satisfied, have things explained to my satisfaction.

13–14 A word . . . resolved. Not content with Pindarus's assurance of Cassius's loyalty, Brutus asks Lucilius, his own man, for a further report.

It useth an enforcèd ceremony.
There are no tricks in plain and simple faith.
But hollow men, like horses hot at hand,
Make gallant show and promise of their mettle;
(*Martial music within.*)
25 But when they should endure the bloody spur,
They fall their crests and like deceitful jades
Sink in the trial. Comes his army on?
LUCILIUS. They mean this night in Sardis to be quartered.
The greater part, the horse in general,
Are come with Cassius.
(CASSIUS *enters with some of his soldiers.*)
30 **BRUTUS.**   Hark, he is arrived.
March gently on to meet him.
CASSIUS. Stand, ho!
BRUTUS. Stand, ho! Speak the word along.
FIRST SOLDIER. Stand!
35 **SECOND SOLDIER.** Stand!
THIRD SOLDIER. Stand!
CASSIUS. Most noble brother, you have done me wrong.
BRUTUS. Judge me, you gods! Wrong I mine enemies?
And if not so, how should I wrong a brother?
40 **CASSIUS.** Brutus, this sober form of yours hides wrongs;
And when you do them—
BRUTUS.   Cassius, be content;
Speak your griefs softly. I do know you well.
Before the eyes of both our armies here,
Which should perceive nothing but love from us,
45 Let us not wrangle. Bid them move away.
Then in my tent, Cassius, enlarge your griefs,
And I will give you audience.
CASSIUS.   Pindarus,
Bid our commanders lead their charges off
A little from this ground.
50 **BRUTUS.** Lucius, do you the like, and let no man
Come to our tent till we have done our conference.
Let Lucilius and Titinius guard our door.
(BRUTUS *watches as his* SOLDIERS *follow* LUCILIUS *off at left.*)

21 enforcèd ceremony, forced politeness.
23 hollow, insincere.

26 jades, worthless horses.
■ How has the relationship between Brutus and Cassius changed?
29 the horse in general, all the cavalry.

40 sober form, dignified manner.

■ Is Brutus wise in insisting that he and Cassius meet in private? Why?

Summary *Brutus reprimands Cassius for defending an officer who took bribes and for being too greedy. Their argument heats up when Brutus accuses Cassius of dishonoring their cause. Distressed, Cassius offers Brutus his life. Brutus then reveals that Portia has killed herself. Titinius and Messala, another officer, enter. The men discuss strategy for the upcoming battle against Antony and Octavius's forces on the plains of Philippi. As Brutus prepares for bed, he is visited by the sudden appearance of the ghost of Caesar who promises that he will see Brutus again at Philippi.*

Within BRUTUS's *tent. Immediately following.* LUCIUS *and* TITINIUS *guard the entrance to* BRUTUS's *tent.* BRUTUS *and* CASSIUS *stand facing each other.* CASSIUS *is very angry.*

CASSIUS. That you have wronged me doth appear in this.
  You have condemned and noted Lucius Pella
  For taking bribes here of the Sardians,
  Wherein my letters, praying on his side,
5 Because I knew the man, was slighted off.
BRUTUS. You wronged yourself to write in such a case.
CASSIUS. In such a time as this it is not meet
  That every nice offense should bear his comment.
BRUTUS. Let me tell you, Cassius, you yourself
10 Are much condemned to have an itching palm,
  To sell and mart your offices for gold
  To undeservers.
CASSIUS.   I an itching palm?
  You know that you are Brutus that speaks this,
  Or, by the gods, this speech were else your last.
15 **BRUTUS.** The name of Cassius honors this corruption,
  And chastisement doth therefore hide his head.
CASSIUS. Chastisement?
BRUTUS. Remember March, the ides of March remember.
  Did not great Julius bleed for justice' sake?
20 What villain touched his body that did stab
  And not for justice? What, shall one of us,
  That struck the foremost man of all this world
  But for supporting robbers, shall we now
  Contaminate our fingers with base bribes,
25 And sell the mighty space of our large honors
  For so much trash as may be graspèd thus?
  I had rather be a dog and bay the moon
  Than such a Roman.
CASSIUS.   Brutus, bait not me.
  I'll not endure it. You forget yourself

2 noted, publicly disgraced.

3 for taking . . . Sardians. Brutus had publicly accused Lucius Pella of embezzling public money and, finding him guilty, had condemned him.

8 that every . . . comment, that every trivial (nice) offense should be criticized.
10 condemned to have an itching palm, accused of being greedy for money.
11 mart, traffic in.
■ What do you still need to know to understand why Brutus and Cassius are so angry with one another?
15–16 The name of Cassius . . . head. Because Cassius, a man of influence, approves of these dishonest practices, legal authority is afraid to act.
22–23 that struck . . . robbers, who killed Caesar for protecting dishonest public figures.

30 To hedge me in. I am a soldier, I,
   Older in practice, abler than yourself
   To make conditions.

BRUTUS. Go to! You are not, Cassius.

CASSIUS. I am.

35 **BRUTUS.** I say you are not.

CASSIUS. Urge me no more; I shall forget myself.
   Have mind upon your health. Tempt me no farther.

BRUTUS. Away, slight man!

CASSIUS. Is't possible?

BRUTUS.   Hear me, for I will speak.

40 Must I give way and room to your rash choler?
   Shall I be frighted when a madman stares?

CASSIUS. O ye gods, ye gods! Must I endure all this?

BRUTUS. All this? Ay, more. Fret till your proud heart break.
   Go show your slaves how choleric you are
45 And make your bondmen tremble. Must I budge?
   Must I observe you? Must I stand and crouch
   Under your testy humor? By the gods,
   You shall digest the venom of your spleen
   Though it do split you; for, from this day forth,
50 I'll use you for my mirth, yea, for my laughter,
   When you are waspish.

CASSIUS.   Is it come to this?

BRUTUS. You say you are a better soldier.
   Let it appear so; make your vaunting true,
   And it shall please me well. For mine own part,
55 I shall be glad to learn of noble men.

CASSIUS. You wrong me every way! You wrong me, Brutus.
   I said an elder soldier, not a better.
   Did I say "better"?

BRUTUS.   If you did, I care not.

CASSIUS. When Caesar lived he durst not thus have moved me.

60 **BRUTUS.** Peace, peace! You durst not so have tempted him.

CASSIUS. I durst not?

BRUTUS. No.

CASSIUS. What, durst not tempt him?

BRUTUS.   For your life you durst not.

CASSIUS. Do not presume too much upon my love,
65 I may do that I shall be sorry for.

BRUTUS. You have done that you should be sorry for.
   There is no terror, Cassius, in your threats,
   For I am armed so strong in honesty
   That they pass by me as the idle wind,
70 Which I respect not. I did send to you

---

30 hedge me in, interfere with me.

32 to make conditions, manage affairs; that is, about the behavior of such men as Pella and for the appointment of officers.

■ In lines 33–58 Brutus and Cassius resort to childish argument and name-calling. How should the actors playing their parts deliver the lines?

40 rash choler (kol′ər), wrathful temperament.

47 testy, easily irritated; impatient.

59 moved, angered.

70 respect not, pay no attention to.

For certain sums of gold, which you denied me;
For I can raise no money by vile means.
By heaven, I had rather coin my heart
And drop my blood for drachmas than to wring
75 From the hard hands of peasants their vile trash
By any indirection. I did send
To you for gold to pay my legions,
Which you denied me. Was that done like Cassius?
Should I have answered Caius Cassius so?
80 When Marcus Brutus grows so covetous
To lock such rascal counters from his friends,
Be ready, gods, with all your thunderbolts;
Dash him to pieces!

CASSIUS.   I denied you not.
BRUTUS.   You did.
CASSIUS. I did not. He was but a fool
85 That brought my answer back. Brutus hath rived my heart.
A friend should bear his friend's infirmities,
But Brutus makes mine greater than they are.
BRUTUS. I do not, till you practice them on me.
CASSIUS. You love me not.
BRUTUS.   I do not like your faults.
90 **CASSIUS.** A friendly eye could never see such faults.
BRUTUS. A flatterer's would not, though they do appear
As huge as high Olympus.
CASSIUS. Come, Antony, and young Octavius, come,
Revenge yourselves alone on Cassius;
95 For Cassius is aweary of the world,
Hated by one he loves, braved by his brother,
Checked like a bondman, all his faults observed,
Set in a notebook, learned and conned by rote
To cast into my teeth. O, I could weep
100 My spirit from mine eyes! There is my dagger,
(offering his unsheathed dagger)
And here my naked breast; within, a heart
Dearer than Pluto's mine, richer than gold.
If that thou be'st a Roman, take it forth.
I, that denied thee gold, will give my heart.
105 Strike, as thou didst at Caesar; for I know,
When thou didst hate him worst, thou loved'st him better
Than ever thou loved'st Cassius.
BRUTUS.   Sheathe your dagger.
Be angry when you will, it shall have scope;
Do what you will, dishonor shall be humor.
110 O Cassius, you are yokèd with a lamb

76 indirection, devious or unjust means.

80 covetous, desiring things that belong to others.
81 rascal counters, worthless coins.
■ What subjects does Brutus touch on in lines 66–83?

85 rived, split; broken.

97 checked, rebuked.
98 conned by rote, memorized until letter-perfect.

102 Pluto's mine. Pluto, the god of the underworld, is here confused with Plutus, the Greek god of riches.

109 dishonor shall be humor, that is, I'll regard your corruption as something to be humored.

That carries anger as the flint bears fire,
Who, much enforcèd, shows a hasty spark
And straight is cold again.

CASSIUS.   Hath Cassius lived
To be but mirth and laughter to his Brutus
115   When grief and blood ill-tempered vexeth him?

BRUTUS. When I spoke that, I was ill-tempered too.

CASSIUS. Do you confess so much? Give me your hand.

BRUTUS. And my heart too.   *(They embrace.)*

CASSIUS.   O Brutus!

BRUTUS.   What's the matter?

CASSIUS. Have not you love enough to bear with me,
120   When that rash humor which my mother gave me
Makes me forgetful?

BRUTUS.   Yes, Cassius, and from henceforth,
When you are overearnest with your Brutus,
He'll think your mother chides, and leave you so.

(A POET *enters, followed by* LUCIUS, TITINIUS, *and* LUCILIUS.*)*

POET. Let me go in to see the generals!
125   There is some grudge between 'em; 'tis not meet
They be alone.

LUCILIUS.   You shall not come to them.

POET. Nothing but death shall stay me.

CASSIUS. How now? What's the matter?

POET. For shame, you generals! What do you mean?
130   Love and be friends, as two such men should be;
For I have seen more years, I'm sure, than ye.

CASSIUS. Ha, ha, how vilely doth this cynic rhyme!

BRUTUS. Get you hence, sirrah. Saucy fellow, hence!

CASSIUS. Bear with him, Brutus. 'Tis his fashion.

135 **BRUTUS.** I'll know his humor when he knows his time.
What should the wars do with these jigging fools?
Companion, hence!

CASSIUS.   Away, away, begone!

*(*POET *exits.)*

BRUTUS. Lucilius and Titinius, bid the commanders
Prepare to lodge their companies tonight.

140 **CASSIUS.** And come yourselves, and bring Messala with you
Immediately to us. (LUCILIUS *and* TITINIUS *exit.)*

BRUTUS *(to* LUCIUS *within)*. Lucius, a bowl of wine.

CASSIUS. I did not think you could have been so angry.

BRUTUS. O Cassius, I am sick of many griefs.

CASSIUS. Of your philosophy you make no use
145   If you give place to accidental evils.

BRUTUS. No man bears sorrow better. Portia is dead.

■ How does Cassius manage to sidestep responsibility for his behavior?

123 **leave you so**, let it go at that.

135 **I'll know his humor . . . time**. I'll indulge his eccentric behavior when he knows the proper time for it.
■ What question would you like to ask Shakespeare about this short episode with the poet?

144 **Of your philosophy . . . use**. Brutus was a Stoic (stō′ik). Believers in this philosophy thought that people should rise above emotional upsets and be unmoved by any of life's happenings.

CASSIUS. Ha? Portia?

BRUTUS. She is dead.

CASSIUS. How scaped I killing when I crossed you so?

150　　O insupportable and touching loss!

　　Upon what sickness?

BRUTUS.　　　　　　　　Impatient of my absence,

　　And grief that young Octavius with Mark Antony

　　Have made themselves so strong—for with her death

　　That tidings came—with this she fell distract

155　　And, her attendants absent, swallowed fire.

CASSIUS. And died so?

BRUTUS.　　　　　　Even so.

CASSIUS.　　　　　　　　　O ye immortal gods!

(LUCIUS *pours a bowl of wine for* CASSIUS. *As he does,* BRUTUS *greets*
TITINIUS, *who has reentered at left.* TITINIUS *is accompanied by* MESSALA, *a
friend of* BRUTUS.)

BRUTUS. Speak no more of her. Give me a bowl of wine.

　　In this I bury all unkindness, Cassius. *(Drinks.)*

CASSIUS. My heart is thirsty for that noble pledge.

160　　Fill, Lucius, till the wine o'erswell the cup;

　　I cannot drink too much of Brutus's love.

(He drinks. LUCIUS *exits.)*

(TITINIUS *and* MESSALA *enter.*)

BRUTUS. Come in, Titinius. Welcome, good Messala.

　　Now sit we close about this taper here

　　And call in question our necessities.　*(They sit.)*

CASSIUS. Portia, art thou gone?

165　**BRUTUS.**　　　　　　　　No more, I pray you.

　　Messala, I have here receivèd letters

　　That young Octavius and Mark Antony

　　Come down upon us with a mighty power,

　　Bending their expedition toward Philippi.

(He shows letters.)

170　**MESSALA.** Myself have letters of the selfsame tenor.

BRUTUS. With what addition?

MESSALA. That by proscription and bills of outlawry

　　Octavius, Antony, and Lepidus

　　Have put to death an hundred senators.

175　**BRUTUS.** Therein our letters do not well agree;

　　Mine speak of seventy senators that died

　　By their proscriptions, Cicero being one.

CASSIUS. Cicero one?

MESSALA.　　　　　Cicero is dead,

　　And by that order of proscription.

180　　Had you your letters from your wife, my lord?

---

150 insupportable, unbearable; intolerable.

155 swallowed fire.
According to Plutarch,
Portia "took hot burning
coals and cast them in her
mouth, and kept her mouth
so close that she choked herself."
■ Which of her lines in act
2, scene 1 foreshadow
Portia's ability to bring about
such a painful death?

**164　call in question our
necessities**, discuss our problems.

169 Philippi (fə lip′ī), a city
in ancient Macedonia, now
part of Greece.
170　of the selfsame tenor,
bearing the same tidings.
172 bills of outlawry, public
notices declaring certain
persons no longer protected
by Roman law. As enemies of
the state they could be
killed.

BRUTUS. No, Messala.

MESSALA. Nor nothing in your letters writ of her?

BRUTUS. Nothing, Messala.

MESSALA.   That, methinks, is strange.

BRUTUS. Why ask you? Hear you aught of her in yours?

185 **MESSALA.** No, my lord.

BRUTUS. Now, as you are a Roman, tell me true.

MESSALA. Then like a Roman bear the truth I tell,
    For certain she is dead, and by strange manner.

BRUTUS. Why, farewell, Portia. We must die, Messala.

190   With meditating that she must die once,
    I have the patience to endure it now.

MESSALA. Even so great men great losses should endure.

CASSIUS. I have as much of this in art as you,
    But yet my nature could not bear it so.

195 **BRUTUS.** Well, to our work alive. What do you think
    Of marching to Philippi presently?

CASSIUS. I do not think it good.

BRUTUS.   Your reason?

CASSIUS.   This it is:
    'Tis better that the enemy seek us.
    So shall he waste his means, weary his soldiers,

200   Doing himself offense, whilst we, lying still,
    Are full of rest, defense, and nimbleness.

BRUTUS. Good reasons must of force give place to better.
    The people twixt Philippi and this ground
    Do stand but in a forced affection,

205   For they have grudged us contribution.
    The enemy, marching along by them,
    By them shall make a fuller number up,
    Come on refreshed, new-added, and encouraged;
    From which advantage shall we cut him off

210   If at Philippi we do face him there,
    These people at our back.

CASSIUS.   Hear me, good brother—

BRUTUS. Under your pardon. You must note besides
    That we have tried the utmost of our friends;
    Our legions are brim full, our cause is ripe.

215   The enemy increaseth every day;
    We, at the height, are ready to decline.
    There is a tide in the affairs of men
    Which, taken at the flood, leads on to fortune;
    Omitted, all the voyage of their life

220   Is bound in shallows and in miseries.
    On such a full sea are we now afloat,

■ Some scholars think this retelling of the news of Portia's death was the episode Shakespeare actually wanted to use in the play, but that he forgot to take out the earlier episode dealing with it. Others argue that the earlier episode provides a perfect reason for Brutus's uncharacteristic emotional tirade and that he shows his stoicism as he listens to Messala bring up the subject again.

193 art, that is, the acquired wisdom of stoical fortitude.

196 presently, immediately.

208 new-added, reinforced.

■ In lines 202–223. Brutus persuades the others to go to Philippi. What do you predict will happen to his and Cassius's forces? Why?

And we must take the current when it serves
Or lose our ventures.
CASSIUS.   Then, with your will, go on.
We'll along ourselves and meet them at Philippi.
225 BRUTUS. The deep of night is crept upon our talk,
And nature must obey necessity,
Which we will niggard with a little rest.
There is no more to say.
CASSIUS.   No more. Good night.
Early tomorrow will we rise and hence.
230 BRUTUS. Lucius! (LUCIUS *enters.*) My gown. (LUCIUS *exits.*)
    Farewell, good Messala.
Good night, Titinius. Noble, noble Cassius,
Good night and good repose.
CASSIUS.   Oh my dear brother!
This was an ill beginning of the night.
Never come such division 'tween our souls!
235 Let it not, Brutus.
(LUCIUS *enters with the gown.*)
BRUTUS. Everything is well.
CASSIUS. Good night, my lord.
BRUTUS. Good night, good brother.
TITINIUS, MESSALA. Good night, Lord Brutus.
240 BRUTUS. Farewell, everyone.
(CASSIUS, TITINIUS *and* MESSALA *exit right.* LUCIUS *unfolds his master's night robe.*)
    Give me the gown. Where is thy instrument?
LUCIUS. Here in the tent.
BRUTUS.   What, thou speak'st drowsily?
Poor knave, I blame thee not; thou art o'erwatched.
Call Claudius and some other of my men;
245 I'll have them sleep on cushions in my tent.
LUCIUS. Varro and Claudius!
(VARRO *and* CLAUDIUS *enter at left and cross toward* BRUTUS.)
VARRO. Calls my lord?
BRUTUS. I pray you, sirs, lie in my tent and sleep.
    It may be I shall raise you by and by
250 On business to my brother Cassius.
VARRO. So please you, we will stand and watch your pleasure.
BRUTUS. I will not have it so. Lie down, good sirs.
    It may be I shall otherwise bethink me.
(VARRO *and* CLAUDIUS *lie down.*)
    Look, Lucius, here's the book I sought for so;
255 I put it in the pocket of my gown.
LUCIUS. I was sure your lordship did not give it me.

227 we will niggard, we will satisfy somewhat.

241 thy instrument, your lute.

243 Poor knave . . . o'erwatched, Poor lad, I don't blame you; you are exhausted.

Flemish artist Peter Paul Rubens (1577–1640) painted this bust of Julius Caesar wearing a crown of olive leaves. Does this representation show a Caesar with the weaknesses Cassius describes or the Caesar who conquered Gaul?

BRUTUS. Bear with me, good boy, I am much forgetful.
Canst thou hold up thy heavy eyes awhile
And touch thy instrument a strain or two?
LUCIUS. Ay, my lord, an 't please you.
260 **BRUTUS.**   It does, my boy.
I trouble thee too much, but thou art willing.
LUCIUS. It is my duty, sir.
BRUTUS. I should not urge thy duty past thy might;
I know young bloods look for a time of rest.
265 **LUCIUS.** I have slept, my lord, already.
BRUTUS. It was well done, and thou shalt sleep again;
I will not hold thee long. If I do live,
I will be good to thee.
(*Music, and a song.* LUCIUS *falls asleep.*)
This is a sleepy tune. O murderous slumber,
270 Layest thou thy leaden mace upon my boy,
That plays thee music? Gentle knave, good night;
I will not do thee so much wrong to wake thee.
If thou dost nod, thou break'st thy instrument;

260 an 't, if it.
■ Do you think a modern general would calm himself before a battle by reading or listening to music?

270 thy leaden mace. Morpheus (môr′phē əs), the Greek god of dreams, carried a leaden club, or mace, with which he cast the spell of slumber.

I'll take it from thee. And, good boy, good night.

(He removes LUCIUS *'s instrument, and begins to read.)*

275   Let me see, let me see; is not the leaf turned down
Where I left reading? Here it is, I think.

(The GHOST OF CAESAR *slowly ascends through an upstage trap door.)*

How ill this taper burns! Ha! Who comes here?
I think it is the weakness of mine eyes
That shapes this monstrous apparition.

280   It comes upon me. Art thou any thing?
Art thou some god, some angel, or some devil,
That mak'st my blood cold and my hair to stare?
Speak to me what thou art.

GHOST. Thy evil spirit, Brutus.

BRUTUS.   Why com'st thou?

285   **GHOST.** To tell thee thou shalt see me at Philippi.

BRUTUS. Well; then I shall see thee again?

GHOST. Ay, at Philippi.

BRUTUS. Why, I will see thee at Philippi, then. (GHOST *exits.*)
Now I have taken heart, thou vanishest.

290   Ill spirit, I would hold more talk with thee.
Boy, Lucius! Varro! Claudius! Sirs, awake!
Claudius!

LUCIUS.   The strings, my lord, are false.

BRUTUS. He thinks he still is at his instrument.
Lucius, awake!

295   **LUCIUS.** My lord?

BRUTUS. Didst thou dream, Lucius, that thou so criedst out?

LUCIUS. My lord, I do not know that I did cry.

BRUTUS. Yes, that thou didst. Didst thou see anything?

LUCIUS. Nothing, my lord.

300   **BRUTUS.** Sleep again, Lucius. Sirrah Claudius!
(To VARRO.) Fellow thou, awake!

VARRO.   My lord?

(They get up.)

CLAUDIUS.   My lord?

BRUTUS. Why did you so cry out, sirs, in your sleep?

VARRO, CLAUDIUS. Did we, my lord?

BRUTUS.   Ay. Saw you anything?

VARRO. No, my lord, I saw nothing.

CLAUDIUS.   Nor I, my lord.

305   **BRUTUS.** Go and commend me to my brother Cassius.
Bid him set on his powers betimes before,
And we will follow.

VARRO, CLAUDIUS.   It shall be done, my lord.

(VARRO and CLAUDIUS *exit at right, leaving* BRUTUS *and* LUCIUS *on stage.)*

---

275 the leaf turned down, an anachronism. Roman books were in the form of scrolls; there were no pages to turn down.

■ Do you think Brutus has responded appropriately to the ghost? Why or why not?

292 false, out of tune.

306 set on . . . before, advance his troops early in the morning, before me.

After Reading

Making Connections

Shaping Your Response

1. Do you find Antony ruthless? Why or why not?

2. Why do you think Shakespeare includes the report of Portia's death?

3. Given their actions so far, where would you place Mark Antony, Brutus, and Cassius on the following scale of morality?

immoral   moral

Analyzing the Play

4. When Cassius first arrives outside Brutus's tent, is the conduct of each man consistent with what you have learned of his **character**? Explain.

5. What do the events in scenes 1 and 2 **foreshadow** about the future of the triumvirate? of Brutus and Cassius?

6. In scene 3, lines 43–51, what is **ironic** about Brutus's accusation that Cassius is bad-tempered?

7. What undesirable traits does Brutus reveal during his argument with Cassius?

8. What do you think the appearance of Caesar's ghost might **foreshadow**?

Extending the Ideas

9. *Julius Caesar* is very much a play about politics. Do you think world political leaders today are motivated mostly by a desire for power, a desire to make government better, or something else? Explain.

10. If Brutus, Antony, Cassius, Caesar, Cicero, Portia, and Calpurnia were in the United States government today, what posts would each seem best suited for? (Consider positions in all three branches of government.)

Expressing Your Ideas

Writing Choice

Spirits on Stage This is only one of several plays in which Shakespeare included ghosts. Explain why you think he included this supernatural element. Then describe what special effects a director could use to make the ghost's appearance a dramatic feature of the play. Write several paragraphs that could appear in a **stage bill**.

ACT FIVE

SCENE 1

Summary *The opposing generals meet and exchange taunts and insults. Antony and Octavius return to their armies. To Messala, Cassius reveals that this is his birthday, and that he is concerned about some bad omens. Cassius and Brutus bid farewell to one another. Cassius vows suicide rather than be captured. Brutus seems to reject the idea of suicide.*

The plains of Philippi. Early morning, the day of the battle. Offstage battle sounds. OCTAVIUS *enters, followed by* ANTONY *and a few* OFFICERS.

OCTAVIUS. Now, Antony, our hopes are answerèd.
   You said the enemy would not come down,
   But keep the hills and upper regions.
   It proves not so. Their battles are at hand;
5 They mean to warn us at Philippi here,
   Answering before we do demand of them.
ANTONY. Tut, I am in their bosoms, and I know
   Wherefore they do it. They could be content
   To visit other places, and come down
10 With fearful bravery, thinking by this face
   To fasten in our thoughts that they have courage;
   But 'tis not so.

(A MESSENGER *enters.)*

MESSENGER.   Prepare you, generals.
   The enemy comes on in gallant show.
   Their bloody sign of battle is hung out,
15 And something to be done immediately.
ANTONY. Octavius, lead your battle softly on
   Upon the left hand of the even field.
OCTAVIUS. Upon the right hand, I. Keep thou the left.
ANTONY. Why do you cross me in this exigent?
20 **OCTAVIUS.** I do not cross you, but I will do so.

(Drum. BRUTUS, CASSIUS, *and their army enter;*
LUCILIUS, TITINIUS, MESSALA, *and others enter.)*

BRUTUS. They stand and would have parley.
CASSIUS. Stand fast, Titinius. We must out and talk.
OCTAVIUS. Mark Antony, shall we give sign of battle?
ANTONY. No, Caesar, we will answer on their charge.
25 Make forth. The generals would have some words.
OCTAVIUS *(to his officers).* Stir not until the signal.

(The two sides advance toward one another.)

BRUTUS. Words before blows. Is it so, countrymen?
OCTAVIUS. Not that we love words better, as you do.

4 battles, armies.

5 warn, challenge.

7 bosoms, secret councils.
8-9 They could . . . places, they would prefer to be elsewhere.

14 bloody sign, red flag.

19 exigent (ek′sə jənt), *n.* critical moment.
■ How has the relationship between Antony and Octavius changed since act 4, scene 1?

24 answer . . . charge, respond when they attack us. Notice that Antony is addressing Octavius by the title Caesar.
25 Make forth, march forward.

BRUTUS. Good words are better than bad strokes, Octavius.

30 **ANTONY.** In your bad strokes, Brutus, you give good words.
Witness the hole you made in Caesar's heart,
Crying "Long live! Hail, Caesar!"

CASSIUS.   Antony,
The posture of your blows are yet unknown;
But for your words, they rob the Hybla bees,

35 And leave them honeyless.

ANTONY. Not stingless too?

BRUTUS. O, yes, and soundless too.
For you have stolen their buzzing, Antony,
And very wisely threat before you sting.

40 **ANTONY.** Villains! You did not so when your vile daggers
Hacked one another in the sides of Caesar.
You showed your teeth like apes, and fawned like hounds,
And bowed like bondmen, kissing Caesar's feet,
Whilst damnèd Casca, like a cur, behind,

45 Struck Caesar on the neck. O you flatterers!

CASSIUS. Flatterers? Now, Brutus, thank yourself!
This tongue had not offended so today
If Cassius might have ruled.

OCTAVIUS. Come, come, the cause. If arguing make us sweat,

50 The proof of it will turn to redder drops.
Look, *(He draws.)*
I draw a sword against conspirators.
When think you that the sword goes up again?
Never, till Caesar's three-and-thirty wounds

55 Be well avenged, or till another Caesar
Have added slaughter to the sword of traitors.

BRUTUS. Caesar, thou canst not die by traitors' hands,
Unless thou bring'st them with thee.

OCTAVIUS.   So I hope.
I was not born to die on Brutus's sword.

60 **BRUTUS.** O, if thou wert the noblest of thy strain,
Young man, thou couldst not die more honorable.

CASSIUS. A peevish schoolboy, worthless of such honor,
Joined with a masker and a reveler!

ANTONY. Old Cassius still.

OCTAVIUS.   Come, Antony, away!

65 Defiance, traitors, hurl we in your teeth.
If you dare fight today, come to the field;
If not, when you have stomachs.

(OCTAVIUS, ANTONY, and army exits.)

CASSIUS. Why, now, blow wind, swell billow and swim bark!
The storm is up, and all is on the hazard.

---

34 Hybla (hī′blə) **bees**, bees from Hybla, an area in ancient Sicily famous for its honey.

40 You did not so, you did not give warning.

42 fawn (fôn), *v.* try to get favor or notice by slavish acts.

■ What is Cassius referring to in lines 46-48?

60 strain, lineage.

62 schoolboy . . . reveler. Octavius was nineteen at the time of Caesar's assassination; Antony was known as a playboy.

BRUTUS. Ho, Lucilius! Hark, a word with you. 70
LUCILIUS *(stands forth).* My lord?
(BRUTUS *and* LUCILIUS *converse apart.*)
CASSIUS. Messala!
MESSALA *(stands forth).* What says my general?
CASSIUS. Messala,

This is my birthday; as this very day 75
Was Cassius born. Give me thy hand, Messala.
Be thou my witness that against my will,
As Pompey was, am I compelled to set
Upon one battle all our liberties.
You know that I held Epicurus strong 80
And his opinion. Now I change my mind
And partly credit things that do <u>presage</u>.
Coming from Sardis, on our former ensign
Two mighty eagles fell, and there they perched,
Goring and feeding from our soldiers' hands, 85
Who to Philippi here <u>consorted</u> us.
This morning are they <u>fled away</u> and gone,
And in their steads do ravens, crows, and kites
Fly o'er our heads and downward look on us
As we were sickly prey. Their shadows seem 90
A canopy most fatal, under which
Our army lies, ready to give up the ghost.
MESSALA. Believe not so.
CASSIUS.   I but believe it partly,
For I am fresh of spirit and resolved
To meet all perils very constantly. 95
BRUTUS. Even so, Lucilius. *(He rejoins* CASSIUS.*)*
CASSIUS.   Now, most noble Brutus,
The gods today stand friendly, that we may,
Lovers in peace, lead on our days to age!
But since the affairs of men rest still incertain,
Let's reason with the worst that may befall. 100
If we do lose this battle, then is this
The very last time we shall speak together.
What are you then determinèd to do?
BRUTUS. Even by the rule of that philosophy
By which I did blame Cato for the death 105
Which he did give himself—I know not how,
But I do find it cowardly and vile,
For fear of what might fall, so to prevent
The time of life—arming myself with patience
To stay the providence of some high powers 110
That govern us below.

---

80 Epicurus (ep′ə kyùr′əs), Greek philosopher who did not believe in omens or superstitions.
82 presage (pri sāj′), *v.* predict.
83–84 on our former ensign . . . fell, on the foremost or forwardmost standard two eagles swooped down.
86 consort (kən sôrt′), *v.* accompany.
■ What reasons does Cassius give for being pessimistic about the outcome of the battle?

96–98 Now . . . days to age! Cassius hopes that the gods will be on their side so the two will end their days as friends in peaceful times.

104–106 Even by . . . give himself. Stoicism, the philosophy Brutus follows, does not favor suicide; thus Brutus blames his father-in-law Cato for killing himself.
108–109 prevent the time of life, cut short one's own life by suicide.
110–111 to stay . . . below, to await (stay) a normal death to be sent when the gods so decree.

CASSIUS.   Then, if we lose this battle,
You are contented to be led in triumph
Thorough the streets of Rome?
BRUTUS. No, Cassius, no. Think not, thou noble Roman,
115   That ever Brutus will go bound to Rome;
He bears too great a mind. But this same day
Must end that work the ides of March begun.
And whether we shall meet again I know not;
Therefore our everlasting farewell take.
120   Forever and forever farewell, Cassius!
If we do meet again, why, we shall smile;
If not, why then this parting was well made.
CASSIUS. Forever and forever farewell, Brutus!
If we do meet again, we'll smile indeed;
125   If not, 'tis true this parting was well made.
BRUTUS. Why, then, lead on. O, that a man might know
The end of this day's business ere it come!
But it sufficeth that the day will end,
And then the end is known. Come, ho, away!
(They exit.)

SCENE 2

Summary *Brutus sends Messala with orders for Cassius.*

The field of battle. Mid-morning. BRUTUS *and* MESSALA *enter at left.*

BRUTUS. Ride, ride, Messala, ride, and give these bills
Unto the legions on the other side.
(He hands him written orders. Loud trumpets and drum beats.)
Let them set on at once; for I perceive
But cold demeanor in Octavio's wing,
5   And sudden push gives them the overthrow.
Ride, ride, Messala! Let them all come down.
(They exit separately.)

SCENE 3

Summary *Cassius sends Titinius to find out whose troops he sees. When Pindarus mistakenly reports that Titinius has been captured, Cassius orders Pindarus to kill him. Titinius returns wearing a crown of victory. Finding Cassius dead, Titinius kills himself.*

A hill in another part of the battlefield. Mid-afternoon. Several SOLDIERS,

■ Lines 94–125 show that
Brutus and Cassius have set
aside their earlier quarrel.
What do the lines reveal
about their characters in the
face of danger?

1 bills, orders.
2 side, wing; that is,
Cassius's wing.

4 demeanor (di mē′nər), *n.*
behavior; manner. Brutus
sees signs of faltering in
Octavius's men.
6 come down, come down
from the hills where they
have been awaiting the
battle.

■ What do you think is
Brutus's message to Cassius?

weary from the fighting, enter at right and fall exhausted. As offstage trumpets sound, CASSIUS *and* TITINIUS *enter at right and climb to the top of the shorter of two hills.* CASSIUS, *carrying a broken standard, speaks angrily.*

CASSIUS. O, look, Titinius, look, the villains fly!
　　Myself have to mine own turned enemy.
　　This ensign here of mine was turning back;
　　I slew the coward and did take it from him.

5　**TITINIUS.** O Cassius, Brutus gave the word too early,
　　Who, having some advantage on Octavius,
　　Took it too eagerly. His soldiers fell to spoil,
　　Whilst we by Antony are all enclosed. (PINDARUS *enters.*)

PINDARUS. Fly further off, my lord, fly further off!
10　Mark Antony is in your tents, my lord.
　　Fly therefore, noble Cassius, fly far off.

CASSIUS. This hill is far enough. Look, look, Titinius.
　　Are those my tents where I perceive the fire?

TITINIUS. They are, my lord.

CASSIUS. 　　　　　　　　Titinius, if thou lovest me,
15　Mount thou my horse, and hide thy spurs in him
　　Till he have brought thee up to yonder troops
　　And here again, that I may rest assured
　　Whether yond troops are friend or enemy.

TITINIUS. I will be here again even with a thought. (*Exits.*)

20　**CASSIUS.** Go, Pindarus, get higher on that hill.
　　My sight was ever thick. Regard Titinius,
　　And tell me what thou not'st about the field.
　　(*Pointing to the higher hill.*)
　　(PINDARUS *ascends the hill.*)
　　This day I breathèd first. Time is come round,
　　And where I did begin, there shall I end.
25　My life is run his compass. Sirrah, what news?

PINDARUS (*above*). O my lord!

CASSIUS. What news?

PINDARUS (*above*). Titinius is enclosed round about
　　With horsemen, that make to him on the spur,
30　Yet he spurs on. Now they are almost on him.
　　Now, Titinius! Now some light. O, he
　　Lights too. He's ta'en (*Shout.*) And hark! They shout for joy.

CASSIUS. Come down, behold no more.
　　O coward that I am, to live so long
35　To see my best friend ta'en before my face. (PINDARUS *descends and rejoins* CASSIUS.)
　　Come hither, sirrah.
　　In Parthia did I take thee prisoner,

---

1 the villains fly. Cassius's own troops are fleeing.
2–4 Myself . . . from him. Cassius killed one of his own men, a cowardly ensign, and took the standard (flag) he now holds.
7 fell to spoil, began looting Octavius's camp.
■ Is it Cassius's or Brutus's fault that Cassius's men have been encircled by Antony's forces? Explain.

17–18 that I may . . . enemy. Cassius wonders if the approaching horsemen belong to his or Brutus's army, or to Antony's.
19 even . . . thought, as quick as thought.
21 My sight . . . thick, my eyesight is imperfect, dim.
23–24 This day . . . end, I shall die on the same day I was born.

31 light, alight; dismount.

37 Parthia, an ancient country, now Iran.

And then I swore thee, saving of thy life,
That whatsoever I did bid thee do
40   Thou shouldst attempt it. Come now, keep thine oath;
Now be a freeman, and with this good sword,
That ran through Caesar's bowels, search this bosom.
Stand not to answer. Here, take thou the hilts,
And when my face is covered, as 'tis now,
45   Guide thou the sword. (PINDARUS *does so.*) Caesar, thou
        art revenged,
Even with the sword that killed thee.
(He dies.)
PINDARUS. So, I am free, yet would not so have been,
Durst I have done my will. O Cassius!
Far from this country Pindarus shall run,
50   Where never Roman shall take note of him.
(PINDARUS, *leaving* CASSIUS*'s sword behind, hastens left and exits.* TITINIUS, *with* MESSALA, *reenters at right. On his head* TITINIUS *wears a victory garland.*)
MESSALA. It is but change, Titinius; for Octavius
Is overthrown by noble Brutus's power,
As Cassius's legions are by Antony.
TITINIUS. These tidings will well comfort Cassius.
MESSALA. Where did you leave him?
55 **TITINIUS.**   All disconsolate,
With Pindarus his bondman, on this hill.
MESSALA. Is not that he that lies upon the ground?
TITINIUS. He lies not like the living. O my heart!
MESSALA. Is not that he?
TITINIUS.   No, this was he, Messala,
60   But Cassius is no more. O setting sun,
As in thy red rays thou dost sink to night,
So in his red blood Cassius's day is set.
The sun of Rome is set. Our day is gone;
Clouds, dews, and dangers come; our deeds are done.
65   Mistrust of my success hath done this deed.
MESSALA. Mistrust of good success hath done this deed.
O hateful Error, Melancholy's child,
Why dost thou show to the apt thoughts of men
The things that are not? O Error, soon conceived,
70   Thou never com'st unto a happy birth,
But kill'st the mother that engendered thee.
TITINIUS. What, Pindarus! Where art thou, Pindarus?
MESSALA. Seek him, Titinius, whilst I go to meet
The noble Brutus, thrusting this report

▲ Portrait sculptures, such as this marble head of Mark Antony, were very popular in ancient Rome and provide a good idea of how the Romans looked. What does their concern about preserving such accurate likenesses suggest about the cultural values of the ancient Romans?

41–42 now be . . . bosom. Cassius will give Pindarus his freedom if Pindarus will kill Cassius. It was a custom in ancient warfare to avoid the shame of captivity at all costs, even death, to preserve military honor.
■ Do you think that Brutus will commit suicide, too? Why or why not?
51 but change, an exchange of advantage.
55 disconsolate (dis kon′sə-lit), *adj.* without hope, unhappy.
63 sun of Rome. (Note pun on son.)
68–69 Why dost thou . . . not? Why do people so readily accept things as true when they are really not?

75 Into his ears. I may say "thrusting" it,
For piercing steel and darts envenomèd
Shall be as welcome to the ears of Brutus
As tidings of this sight.

TITINIUS.   Hie you, Messala,
And I will seek for Pindarus the while.
(MESSALA *exits.*)
80 Why didst thou send me forth, brave Cassius?
Did I not meet thy friends? And did not they
Put on my brows this wreath of victory
And bid me give it thee? Didst thou not hear their shouts?
Alas, thou hast misconstrued everything.
85 But, hold thee, take this garland on thy brow.
(*He places the garland on* CASSIUS's *brow.*)
Thy Brutus bid me give it thee, and I
Will do his bidding. Brutus, come apace
And see how I regarded Caius Cassius.
By your leave, gods! This is a Roman's part.
90 Come, Cassius's sword, and find Titinius's heart.
(*He stabs himself and dies.*)
(*Trumpets.* BRUTUS, MESSALA, YOUNG CATO, STRATO, VOLUMNIUS,
LUCILIUS, LABEO, *and* FLAVIUS *enter.*)
BRUTUS. Where, where, Messala, doth his body lie?
MESSALA. Lo, yonder, and Titinius mourning it.
BRUTUS. Titinius's face is upward.
CATO.   He is slain.
BRUTUS. O Julius Caesar, thou art mighty yet!
95 Thy spirit walks abroad and turns our swords
In our own proper entrails. (*Low drumbeats.*)
CATO.   Brave Titinius!
Look whe'er he have not crowned dead Cassius.
BRUTUS. Are yet two Romans living such as these?
The last of all the Romans, fare thee well!
100 It is impossible that ever Rome
Should breed thy fellow. Friends, I owe more tears
To this dead man than you shall see me pay.
I shall find time, Cassius, I shall find time.
Come, therefore, and to Thasos send his body.
105 His funerals shall not be in our camp,
Lest it discomfort us. Lucilius, come,
And come, young Cato, let us to the field.
Labeo and Flavius, set our battles on.
'Tis three o'clock, and, Romans, yet ere night
110 We shall try fortune in a second fight. (*They exit with the bodies.*)

81 thy friends, Brutus's man Messala and his army.

84 misconstrue (mis′kən-strü′), *v.* misunderstand; misinterpret.

89 This is a Roman's part. The Romans prided themselves on being freemen. To avoid capture, Titinius also commits suicide.
■ How has Shakespeare emphasized the power of Caesar, even beyond the grave?

104 Thasos (thä′sôs), an island in the Aegean Sea, near Philippi.

Summary *The tides of war swing back to Antony and Octavius. A captured Lucilius pretends to be Brutus and tells Antony that Brutus will not be taken alive.*

Another part of the battlefield. Late afternoon. BRUTUS, *exhausted, runs on from right, sword in hand, followed by* MESSALA, YOUNG CATO, LUCILIUS, *and* FLAVIUS.

BRUTUS. Yet, countrymen, O, yet hold up your heads!
(*He exits, followed by* MESSALA *and* FLAVIUS.)

CATO. What bastard doth not? Who will go with me?
    I will proclaim my name about the field:
    I am the son of Marcus Cato, ho!
5   A foe to tyrants, and my country's friend.
    I am the son of Marcus Cato, ho!
(SOLDIERS *enter and fight.*)

LUCILIUS. And I am Brutus, Marcus Brutus I!
    Brutus, my country's friend! Know me for Brutus!
(YOUNG CATO *is slain by* ANTONY's *men.*)
    O young and noble Cato, art thou down?
10   Why, now thou diest as bravely as Titinius,
    And mayst be honored, being Cato's son.

FIRST SOLDIER (*capturing* LUCILIUS). Yield, or thou diest.

LUCILIUS (*offering money*).   Only I yield to die.
    There is so much that thou wilt kill me straight;
    Kill Brutus, and be honored in his death.

15 **FIRST SOLDIER.** We must not. A noble prisoner!

SECOND SOLDIER. Room, ho! Tell Antony, Brutus is ta'en.
(ANTONY *enters.*)

FIRST SOLDIER. I'll tell the news. Here comes the General.
    Brutus is ta'en, Brutus is ta'en, my lord.

ANTONY. Where is he?

20 **LUCILIUS.** Safe, Antony, Brutus is safe enough.
    I dare assure thee that no enemy
    Shall ever take alive the noble Brutus.
    The gods defend him from so great a shame!
    When you do find him, or alive or dead,
25   He will be found like Brutus, like himself.

ANTONY (*to* FIRST SOLDIER). This is not Brutus, friend, but,
     I assure you,
    A prize no less in worth. Keep this man safe;
    Give him all kindness. I had rather have
    Such men my friends than enemies. Go on,
30   And see whe'er Brutus be alive or dead;

2 what . . . doth not? Who is so base or low-born that he would not (hold up his head)?

■ Why might Lucilius be claiming to be Brutus?

12 only I . . . die, I surrender only to die immediately.

And bring us word unto Octavius's tent
How everything is chanced.
(SOLDIERS *lead* LUCILIUS *off left;* ANTONY *exits right.*)

■ What questions about the events of this act do you still have?

SCENE 5

Summary *With Strato's help, Brutus kills himself. The victorious Antony and Octavius promise that all soldiers will receive the proper burial rites.*

Another part of the battlefield. Early evening. VOLUMNIUS, *carrying a lighted torch, enters at left, followed by* BRUTUS, CLITUS, DARDANIUS, *and* STRATO. *Overcome with fatigue and a sense of defeat, they sit, leaning against a large rock placed downstage center.*

BRUTUS. Come, poor remains of friends, rest on this rock.
(He sits.)
CLITUS. Statilius showed the torchlight, but, my lord,
   He came not back. He is or ta'en or slain.
BRUTUS. Sit thee down, Clitus. Slaying is the word.
5   It is a deed in fashion. Hark thee, Clitus. *(He whispers.)*
CLITUS. What, I, my lord? No, not for all the world.
BRUTUS. Peace then. No words.
CLITUS.   I'll rather kill myself.
BRUTUS. Hark thee, Dardanius. *(He whispers.)*
DARDANIUS.   Shall I do such a deed?
(DARDANIUS *and* CLITUS *move away from* BRUTUS.)
CLITUS. O Dardanius!
10 **DARDANIUS.** O Clitus!
CLITUS. What ill request did Brutus make to thee?
DARDANIUS. To kill him, Clitus. Look, he meditates.
CLITUS. Now is that noble vessel full of grief,
   That it runs over even at his eyes.
15 **BRUTUS.** Come hither, good Volumnius. List a word.
VOLUMNIUS. What says my lord?
BRUTUS.   Why, this, Volumnius.
   The ghost of Caesar hath appeared to me
   Two several times by night—at Sardis once,
   And this last night here in Philippi fields.
   I know my hour is come.
20 **VOLUMNIUS.**   Not so, my lord.
BRUTUS. Nay, I am sure it is, Volumnius.
   Thou seest the world, Volumnius, how it goes;
   Our enemies have beat us to the pit. *(Low trumpets and drums.)*
   It is more worthy to leap in ourselves
25   Than tarry till they push us. Good Volumnius,
   Thou know'st that we two went to school together.

2–3 **Statilius** (stə til′ē əs) . . . **slain**. A scout named Statilius has gone to see if Cassius's camp is still occupied; he signals back but is captured and slain.

23 **beat us . . . pit**, driven us to a trap (for wild animals; also a grave).

Julius Caesar—Act Five, Scene 5   **759**

Even for that, our love of old, I prithee,
Hold thou my sword hilts whilst I run on it.
VOLUMNIUS. That's not an office for a friend, my lord.
(Drums still.)
30 **CLITUS.** Fly, fly, my lord! There is no tarrying here.
BRUTUS. Farewell to you, and you, and you, Volumnius.
    Strato, thou hast been all this while asleep;
    Farewell to thee too, Strato. Countrymen,
    My heart doth joy that yet in all my life
35 I found no man but he was true to me.
    I shall have glory by this losing day
    More than Octavius and Mark Antony
    By this vile conquest shall attain unto.
    So fare you well at once, for Brutus's tongue
40 Hath almost ended his life's history.
    Night hangs upon my eyes; my bones would rest,
    That have but labored to attain this hour.
(Trumpets. Cry within, "Fly, fly, fly!")
CLITUS. Fly, my lord, fly!
BRUTUS.   Hence, I will follow.
(CLITUS, DARDANIUS, and VOLUMNIUS exit.)
    I prithee, Strato, stay thou by thy lord.
45 Thou art a fellow of a good respect;
    Thy life hath had some smatch of honor in it.
    Hold then my sword, and turn away thy face,
    While I do run upon it. Wilt thou, Strato?
STRATO. Give me your hand first. Fare you well, my lord.
50 **BRUTUS.** Farewell, good Strato. *(He runs on his sword.)*
                        Caesar, now be still.
    I killed not thee with half so good a will. *(Dies.)*
*(Trumpets sound retreat within. ANTONY, OCTAVIUS and the army
enter with MESSALA and LUCILIUS as prisoners.)*
OCTAVIUS. What man is that?
MESSALA. My master's man. Strato, where is thy master?
STRATO. Free from the bondage you are in, Messala.
55 The conquerors can but make a fire of him,
    For Brutus only overcame himself,
    And no man else hath honor by his death.
LUCILIUS. So Brutus should be found. I thank thee, Brutus,
    That thou hast proved Lucilius's saying true.
60 **OCTAVIUS.** All that served Brutus, I will entertain them.
    Fellow, wilt thou bestow thy time with me?
STRATO. Ay, if Messala will prefer me to you.
OCTAVIUS. Do so, good Messala.
MESSALA. How died my master, Strato?

■ Explain Brutus's attitude
toward his life and death in
this speech.

46 smatch, taste; touch.

55 The conquerors . . . him,
a reference to the Roman
custom of burning the dead.
57 no man . . . death, no
one can claim the honor of
defeating him in combat.
59 Lucilius's . . . true.
Lucilius had said that
Brutus's enemies would
never take him alive.
60 I will . . . them. I will take
all of Brutus's servants and
soldiers and make them my
own.
62 prefer, recommend.

Julius Caesar—Act Five, Scene 5 **761**

65 **STRATO.** I held the sword, and he did run on it.

MESSALA. Octavius, then take him to follow thee,
That did the latest service to my master.

ANTONY. This was the noblest Roman of them all.
All the conspirators save only he

70 Did that they did in envy of great Caesar;
He only in a general honest thought
And common good to all made one of them.
His life was gentle, and the elements
So mixed in him that Nature might stand up

75 And say to all the world, "This was a man!"

OCTAVIUS. According to his virtue let us use him,
With all respect and rites of burial.
Within my tent his bones tonight shall lie,
Most like a soldier, ordered honorably.

80 So call the field to rest, and let's away
To part the glories of this happy day.
(All exit with BRUTUS's *body.)*

72 made one of them, joined them.
73 elements. The ancients believed that people were made of four basic elements—earth, air, fire, and water. Antony says they were mixed in Brutus in ideal proportions.

■ What question would you ask Antony about his assessment (lines 68–75) of Brutus?
81 part the glories, share the honors.

After Reading

Making Connections

1. How did you feel about Cassius's death? Did you have the same feeling about the death of Brutus? Explain.

2. Some scholars say Caesar's tragic flaw is ambition. What might Brutus's flaw be?

3. In literature, characters are frequently used as **foils**; that is, the traits of one point up by contrast the traits of another. How is Antony a foil for Octavius? for Brutus?

4. In scene 1, lines 40–45, what attitude is conveyed in the **similes** Antony uses?

5. In terms of **plot**, what dramatic purposes does the short scene 2 serve?

6. How is Cassius's manner of death in keeping with his **character**?

7. What qualities do his soldiers show in their refusal to kill Brutus?

8. In bidding his friends farewell, Brutus says, "I found no man but he was true to me." Do you find Brutus's remark **ironic**? Why or why not?

9. 👆 Do you find Brutus's suicide in keeping with his character, or is his act dictated by his culture? Explain.

10. Do you think Antony's remarks over Brutus's body are sincere? Explain.

11. Who would you say are the real winners in this play? Who are the losers?

12. Although ambition is sometimes considered a positive quality, it can become a negative one. In your opinion, when does ambition cross the line and become destructive?

Literary Focus: Plot

The fifth act of a Shakespearean drama always contains the **falling action** and the **resolution.** On your plot diagram, list at least one example of how Brutus's fortune changes. Then write a description of how Shakespeare resolves the plot.

Vocabulary Study

consort
demeanor
disconsolate
fawn
misconstrue
presage

Using five of the listed words, write one of the following.

- a plot summary of *Julius Caesar*
- a commercial using propaganda to endorse a product that has "snob appeal"
- a news item about a crime or scandal

Expressing Your Ideas

Writing Choices

Writer's Notebook Update In act 2, scene 2, Brutus dismisses Antony as "but a limb of Caesar." After Caesar's death, however, Antony, along with Octavius, surprises the conspirators. In your notebook, give reasons to explain why Caesar or Antony is the better leader.

War Hero Caesar's fame grew out of his military victories over tribes in the Roman province of Gaul—which included what are today France, Belgium, and Switzerland, as well as parts of Holland and Germany. Read the following poem aloud to make sense of the "words." Then write a **translation** of the poem. (Hint: Vercingetorix was a leader defeated by Caesar.)

> Caesar cari dona militari orgi versus Belgae,
>
> Helvetii, Germani, Venetii, Britanni—iunemit.
>
> "Romis glorius," sed Caesar, "Nomen me impunit!"
>
> Meni tridit—Vercingetorix, forin stans—
>
> Caesar noctim sili fors ticinis nec aut.
>
> Ab ludi, nervi felo, Caius Julius, iubet.
>
> from *Inklings* by Maurice Sagoff

Heroic Status A tragic hero is a noble character who, through some flaw in character, causes his or her own downfall. Write an **explanation** of whether or not Caesar measures up to this description of a tragic hero.

Other Options

✋ **Breaking the Pattern** In Shakespeare's day, it was believed that a monarch had a God-given right to rule. Anything that disrupted a stable and orderly reign caused chaos, which affected the entire social order. Given this cultural view of power, do you think assassination and the drastic political **changes** that result from this act were more devastating, or less so, than in our society? Hold a **debate** on the subject.

A Banner Day Design a **standard** to be carried by the armies of either the conspirators or the triumvirate. Be prepared to explain your choice of design.

Making Fun-nies Of A comic book publisher has hired you to draw colored illustrations for *Julius Caesar.* Do a **plot strip** for one of the scenes, complete with dialogue captions and any background information you think is necessary.

Caesar Sampler Work with a group to create a **performance** for another class, a sampler of the best of *Julius Caesar*— soliloquies, short scenes, action sequences, anything that will give an audience a taste of the play. Provide background information whenever necessary.

Before Reading

The Balek Scales

by Heinrich Böll   Germany

Heinrich Böll
1917–1985

A reluctant soldier, Heinrich Böll (hīn′riH bōl) served with the German army from 1939 to 1945 and spent the last part of World War II in an American prison camp. After the war, he worked in his brother's cabinet shop while attending Cologne University. By 1951, he had published two novels about his war experiences. In 1972, for his perceptive and ironic short stories and novels, Böll won the Nobel Prize for literature. An active defender of freedom, he donated part of his prize money to aid writers imprisoned for their beliefs.

Building Background

Seeking Justice Although "The Balek Scales" is fiction, the situation it depicts is based on history. In the 1800s, much of eastern Europe was made up of many small states, mostly controlled by wealthy landowners who dominated every aspect of village and peasant life. Many of the impoverished peasants, who were totally dependent on these aristocrats for their livelihood, eventually fled Europe for America. In this story, Böll portrays the wealthy Balek family and the results of a peasant boy's attempt to obtain justice.

Literary Focus

Theme An underlying meaning of a work is called its **theme.** You have already learned that a theme is not always directly stated but must often be inferred. One technique for discovering theme in a short story is to note one or two words, ideas, or motifs that recur within the narrative. You will notice that throughout "The Balek Scales," especially in the final three paragraphs, an important word appears repeatedly. Look for it, and use it as a key to identify the theme of the story.

Writer's Notebook

It's Your World Böll's story takes place in another country and another century—a setting he skillfully re-creates through descriptions of food, the countryside, work, and other aspects of that society. Assume that someone one hundred years from now will read about your world. Make a list of details that you think are most revealing of your life, culture, surroundings, and society. You might use a chart like the one below.

Food	Entertainment	Clothing	Transportation	Other

The Balek Scales

Heinrich Böll

Where my grandfather came from, most of the people lived by working in the flax sheds. For five generations they had been breathing in the dust which rose from the crushed flax[1] stalks, letting themselves be killed off by slow degrees, a race of long-suffering, cheerful people who ate goat cheese, potatoes, and now and then a rabbit; in the evening they would sit at home spinning and knitting; they sang, drank mint tea, and were happy. During the day they would carry the flax stalks to the antiquated machines, with no protection from the dust and at the mercy of the heat which came pouring out of the drying kilns.[2] Each cottage contained only one bed, standing against the wall like a closet and reserved for the parents, while the children slept all round the room on benches. In the morning the room would be filled with the odor of thin soup; on Sundays there was stew, and on feast days the children's faces would light up with pleasure as they watched the black acorn coffee turning paler and paler from the milk their smiling mother poured into their coffee mugs.

The parents went off early to the flax sheds, the housework was left to the children: they would sweep the room, tidy up, wash the dishes, and peel the potatoes, precious pale-yellow fruit, whose thin peel had to be produced afterwards to <u>dispel</u>[3] any suspicion of extravagance or carelessness.

As soon as the children were out of school they had to go off into the woods and, depending on the season, gather mushrooms and

---

1. **flax** (flaks), *n.* a plant that can be crushed, dried, and spun into thread for weaving into linen.
2. **kiln** (kil, kiln), *n.* furnace or oven for burning, baking, or drying.
3. **dispel** (dis pel′), *v.* drive away.

▲ American artist George Tooker painted *Market* in 1949. Which figure is dominant and how did the artist achieve this? What can you tell from the facial expressions?

herbs: woodruff and thyme, caraway, mint, and foxglove, and in summer, when they had brought in the hay from their meager[4] fields, they gathered hayflowers. A kilo[5] of hayflowers was worth one pfennig,[6] and they were sold by the apothecaries[7] in town for twenty pfennigs a kilo to highly strung ladies. The mushrooms were highly prized: they fetched twenty pfennigs a kilo and were sold in the shops in town for one mark twenty. The children would crawl deep into the green darkness of the forest during the autumn when dampness drove the mushrooms out of the soil, and almost every family had its own places where it gathered mushrooms, places which were handed down in whispers from generation to generation.

The woods belonged to the Baleks, as well as the flax sheds, and in my grandfather's village the Baleks had a chateau,[8] and the wife of the head of the family had a little room next to the dairy, where mushrooms, herbs, and hayflowers were weighed and paid for. There on the table stood the great Balek scales, an old-fashioned, ornate, bronze-gilt contraption, which my grandfather's grandparents had already faced when they were children, their grubby hands holding their little baskets of mushrooms, their paper bags of hayflowers, breathlessly watching the number of weights Frau Balek had to throw on the scale before the swinging pointer came to rest exactly over the black line, that thin line of justice which had to be redrawn every year. Then Frau Balek would take the big book covered in brown leather, write down the weight, and pay out the money, pfennigs or ten-pfennig pieces and, very, very occasionally, a mark. And when my grandfather was a child, there was a big glass jar of lemon drops standing there, the kind that cost one mark a kilo, and when Frau Balek—whichever one happened to be presiding over the little room—was in a good mood, she would put her hand into this jar and give each child a lemon drop, and the children's faces would light up with pleasure, the way they used to when on feast days their mother poured milk into their coffee mugs, milk that made the coffee turn paler and paler until it was as pale as the flaxen pigtails of the little girls.

One of the laws imposed by the Baleks on the village was: no one was permitted to have any scales in the house. The law was so ancient that nobody gave a thought as to when and how it had arisen, and it had to be obeyed, for anyone who broke it was dismissed from the flax sheds, he could not sell his mushrooms or his thyme or his hayflowers, and the power of the Baleks was so far-reaching that no one in the neighboring villages would give him work either, or buy his forest herbs. But since the days when my grandfather's parents had gone out as small children to gather mushrooms and sell them in order that they might season the meat of the rich people of Prague[9] or be baked into game pies, it had never occurred to anyone to break this law: flour could be measured in cups, eggs could be counted, what they had spun could be measured by the yard, and besides, the old-fashioned, bronze-gilt, ornate Balek scales did not look as if there was anything wrong with them, and five generations had entrusted the swinging black pointer with what they had gone out as eager children to gather from the woods.

True, there were some among these quiet people who flouted the law, poachers bent on making more money in one night than they could earn in a whole month in the flax sheds, but even these people apparently never thought of buying scales or making their own. My grandfather was the first person bold enough to test

---

4. **meager** (mē′gər), *adj.* scanty.
5. **kilo** (kē′lō, kil′ō), *n.* one thousand grams; the equivalent of 2.2 lbs.
6. **pfennig** (pfen′ig), *n.* Just as a penny is worth 1/100th of a dollar, a pfennig was worth 1/100th of a mark.
7. **apothecary** (ə poth′ə ker′ē), *n.* druggist.
8. **chateau** (sha tō′), *n.* a large country house.
9. **Prague** (präg), the capital and largest city of Czechoslovakia, now the Czech Republic. At the time of the story, it was located in the Austro-Hungarian Empire.

the justice of the Baleks, the family who lived in the chateau and drove two carriages, who always maintained one boy from the village while he studied theology[10] at the seminary in Prague, the family with whom the priest played tarok[11] every Wednesday, on whom the local reeve,[12] in his carriage emblazoned with the imperial coat of arms, made an annual New Year's Day call, and on whom the emperor conferred a title on the first day of the year 1900.

My grandfather was hard-working and smart: he crawled farther into the woods than the children of his clan had crawled before him, he penetrated as far as the thicket where, according to legend, Bilgan the Giant was supposed to dwell, guarding a treasure. But my grandfather was not afraid of Bilgan: he worked his way deep into the thicket, even when he was quite little, and brought out great quantities of mushrooms; he even found truffles,[13] for which Frau Balek paid thirty pfennigs a pound. Everything my grandfather took to the Baleks he entered on the back of a torn-off calendar page: every pound of mushrooms, every gram of thyme, and on the right-hand side, in his childish handwriting, he entered the amount he received for each item; he scrawled in every pfennig, from the age of seven to the age of twelve, and by the time he was twelve, the year 1900 had arrived, and because the Baleks had been raised to the aristocracy by the emperor, they gave every family in the village a quarter of a pound of real coffee, the Brazilian kind; there was also free beer and tobacco for the men, and at the chateau there was a great banquet; many carriages stood in the avenue of poplars leading from the entrance gates to the chateau.

But the day before the banquet the coffee was distributed in the little room which had housed the Balek scales for almost a hundred years, and the Balek family was now called Balek von Bilgan because, according to legend, Bilgan the Giant used to have a great castle on the site of the present Balek estate.

My grandfather often used to tell me how he went there after school to fetch the coffee for four families: the Cechs, the Weidlers, the Vohlas, and his own, the Brüchers. It was the afternoon of New Year's Eve: there were the front rooms to be decorated, the baking to be done, and the families did not want to spare four boys and have each of them go all the way to the chateau to bring back a quarter of a pound of coffee.

And so my grandfather sat on the narrow, wooden bench in the little room while Gertrud the maid counted out the wrapped four-ounce packages of coffee, four of them, and he looked at the scales and saw that the pound weight was still lying on the left-hand scale; Frau Balek von Bilgan was busy with preparations for the banquet. And when Gertrud was about to put her hand into the jar with the lemon drops to give my grandfather one, she discovered it was empty: it was refilled once a year, and held one kilo of the kind that cost a mark.

Gertrud laughed and said: "Wait here while I get the new lot," and my grandfather waited with the four four-ounce packages which had been wrapped and sealed in the factory, facing the scales on which someone had left the pound weight, and my grandfather took the four packages of coffee, put them on the empty scale, and his heart thudded as he watched the black finger of justice come to rest on the left of the black line: the scale with the pound weight stayed down, and the pound of coffee remained up in the air; his heart thudded more than if he had been lying behind a bush in the forest waiting for Bilgan the Giant, and he felt in his pocket for the pebbles he always carried with him so he could use his catapult to shoot the

---

10. **theology** (thē ol′ə jē), *n.* study of religion and religious beliefs.
11. **tarok** (tar′ək), a card game played in central Europe.
12. **reeve** (rēv), *n.* the chief official of a town or district.
13. **truffle** (truf′əl), *n.* an edible fungus that resembles a mushroom and is considered a delicacy.

The Balek Scales   **769**

sparrows which pecked away at his mother's cabbage plants—he had to put three, four, five pebbles beside the packages of coffee before the scale with the pound weight rose and the pointer at last came to rest over the black line. My grandfather took the coffee from the scale, wrapped the five pebbles in his kerchief, and when Gertrud came back with the big kilo bag of lemon drops, which had to last for another whole year in order to make the children's faces light up with pleasure, when Gertrud let the lemon drops rattle into the glass jar, the pale little fellow was still standing there, and nothing seemed to have changed. My grandfather only took three of the packages, then Gertrud looked in startled surprise at the white-faced child, who threw the lemon drop onto the floor, ground it under his heel, and said: "I want to see Frau Balek."

"Balek von Bilgan, if you please," said Gertrud.

"All right, Frau Balek von Bilgan," but Gertrud only laughed at him, and he walked back to the village in the dark, took the Cechs, the Weidlers, and the Vohlas their coffee, and said he had to go and see the priest.

Instead he went out into the dark night with his five pebbles in his kerchief. He had to walk a long way before he found someone who had scales, who was permitted to have them; no one in the villages of Blaugau and Bernau had any, he knew that, and he went straight through them till, after two hours' walking, he reached the little town of Dielheim, where Honig the apothecary lived. From Honig's house came the smell of fresh pancakes, and Honig's breath, when he opened the door to the half-frozen boy, already smelled of punch, there was a moist cigar between his narrow lips, and he clasped the boy's cold hands firmly for a moment, saying: "What's the matter, has your father's lung got worse?"

"No, I haven't come for medicine, I wanted—" My grandfather undid his kerchief, took out the five pebbles, held them out to Honig, and said: "I wanted to have these weighed." He glanced anxiously into Honig's face, but when Honig said nothing and did not get angry, or even ask him anything, my grandfather said: "It is the amount that is short of justice," and now, as he went into the warm room, my grandfather realized how wet his feet were. The snow had soaked through his cheap shoes, and in the forest the branches had showered him with snow, which was now melting, and he was tired and hungry and suddenly began to cry because he thought of the quantities of mushrooms, the herbs, the flowers, which had been weighed on the scales which were short five pebbles' worth of justice. And when Honig, shaking his head and holding the five pebbles, called his wife, my grandfather thought of the generations of his parents, his grandparents, who had all had to have their mushrooms, their flowers, weighed on the scales, and he was overwhelmed by a great wave of injustice, and began to sob louder than ever, and, without waiting to be asked, he sat down on a chair, ignoring the pancakes, the cup of hot coffee which nice, plump Frau Honig put in front of him, and did not stop crying till Honig himself came out from the shop at the back and, rattling the pebbles in his hand, said in a low voice to his wife: "Fifty-five grams, exactly."

My grandfather walked the two hours home through the forest, got a beating at home, said nothing, not a single word, when he was asked about the coffee, spent the whole evening doing sums on the piece of paper on which he had written down everything he had sold to Frau Balek, and when midnight struck, and the cannon could be heard from the chateau, and the whole village rang with shouting and laughter and the noise of rattles, when the family kissed and embraced all round, he said into the New Year's silence: "The Baleks owe me eighteen marks and thirty-two pfennigs." And again he thought of all the children there were in the village, of his brother Fritz who had gathered so many mushrooms, of his sister Ludmilla; he thought of the many hundreds of children who had all gathered mushrooms for the Baleks, and herbs and flowers, and this time he did not cry but told his parents and brothers and sisters of his discovery.

When the Baleks von Bilgan went to High Mass on New Year's Day, their new coat of arms—a giant crouching under a fir tree—already emblazoned in blue and gold on their carriage, they saw the hard, pale faces of the people all staring at them. They had expected garlands in the village, a song in their honor, cheers, and hurrahs, but the village was completely deserted as they drove through it, and in church the pale faces of the people were turned toward them, mute[14] and hostile, and when the priest mounted the pulpit to deliver his New Year's sermon, he sensed the chill in those otherwise quiet and peaceful faces, and he stumbled painfully through his sermon and went back to the altar drenched in sweat. And as the Baleks von Bilgan left the church after Mass, they walked through a lane of mute, pale faces. But young Frau Balek von Bilgan stopped in front of the children's pews, sought out my grandfather's face, pale little Franz Brücher, and asked him, right there in the church: "Why didn't you take the coffee for your mother?" And my grandfather stood up and said: "Because you owe me as much money as five kilos of coffee would cost." And he pulled the five pebbles from his pocket, held them out to the young woman, and said: "This much, fifty-five grams, is short in every pound of your justice"; and before the woman could say anything, the men and women in the church lifted up their voices and sang: "The justice of this earth, O Lord, hath put Thee to death. . . ."

While the Baleks were at church, Wilhelm Vohla, the poacher, had broken into the little room, stolen the scales and the big, fat, leather-bound book in which had been entered every kilo of mushrooms, every kilo of hayflowers, everything bought by the Baleks in the village, and all afternoon of that New Year's Day the men of the village sat in my great-grandparents' front room and calculated, calculated one tenth of everything that had been bought—but when they had calculated many thousands of talers and had still not come to an end, the reeve's gendarmes arrived, made their way into my great-grandfather's front room, shooting and stabbing as they came, and removed the scales and the book by force. My grandfather's little sister Ludmilla lost her life, a few men were wounded, and one of the gendarmes was stabbed to death by Wilhelm Vohla the poacher.

Our village was not the only one to rebel: Blaugau and Bernau did, too, and for almost a week no work was done in the flax sheds. But a great many gendarmes appeared, and the men and women were threatened with prison, and the Baleks forced the priest to display the scales publicly in the school and demonstrate that the finger of justice swung to and fro accurately. And the men and women went back to the flax sheds—but no one went to the school to watch the priest: he stood there all alone, helpless and forlorn with his weights, scales, and packages of coffee.

And the children went back to gathering mushrooms, to gathering thyme, flowers, and foxglove, but every Sunday, as soon as the Baleks entered the church, the hymn was struck up: "The justice of this earth, O Lord, hath put Thee to death," until the reeve ordered it proclaimed in every village that the singing of this hymn was forbidden.

My grandfather's parents had to leave the village and the new grave of their little daughter; they became basket weavers, but did not stay long anywhere because it pained them to see how everywhere the finger of justice swung falsely. They walked along behind their cart, which crept slowly over the country roads, taking their thin goat with them, and passers-by could sometimes hear a voice from the cart singing: "The justice of this earth, O Lord, hath put Thee to death." And those who wanted to listen could hear the tale of the Baleks von Bilgan, whose justice lacked a tenth part. But there were few who listened.

---

14. **mute** (myūt), *adj.* silent.

After Reading

Making Connections

Shaping Your Response

1. Do you think this would have been a better story if justice had been obtained at the end? Explain.

2. What three words would you choose to describe Franz Brücher, the **narrator**'s grandfather?

Analyzing the Story

3. Böll's story is filled with **local color,** details that convey the feeling of rural Middle Europe a good many years ago. What specific details produce that feeling?

4. Where does the **climax** appear in this story?

5. Why do you think the Baleks did not admit their guilt?

6. How does the hymn relate to the **theme** of the story?

7. Do you feel the villagers would have been better off not knowing about the false scales? Why or why not?

Extending the Ideas

8. As representatives of a socially, politically, and economically elite class, the Balek family gets away with a terrible injustice. Does this happen today in the United States? Explain.

9. What marks the difference between social classes today? education? wealth? luck? talent? race? Explain.

10. 👋 What do you think it takes to **change** a class system like the one described in the story?

Literary Focus: Theme

Explain whether or not each of the following statements is an appropriate expression of a **theme** of "The Balek Scales."

- "Might makes right."
- "A little child shall lead them."
- "A penny saved is a penny earned."
- "Justice delayed is justice denied."
- "No use crying over spilt milk."

Vocabulary Study

Determine the relationship between the first pair of capitalized words. Then write the letter of the pair of words with a similar relationship to complete the analogy.

chateau
dispel
meager
mute
theology

1. MEAGER : AMPLE :: **a.** hungry : starving **b.** humid : warm
   c. timid : courageous **d.** precise : accurate

2. CHATEAU : COTTAGE :: **a.** yacht : canoe **b.** tree : oak
   c. shoe : sock **d.** tailor : thread

3. THEOLOGY : RELIGION :: **a.** church : synagogue **b.** dollar : dime
   c. botany : plants **d.** kitten : purr

4. MUTE : SILENT :: **a.** sharp : blunt **b.** loyal : dog
   c. clumsy : agile **d.** plain : simple

5. DISPEL : DRIVE AWAY :: **a.** permit : forbid **b.** scatter : leaves
   c. combine : mix **d.** distribute : gather

Expressing Your Ideas

Writing Choices

Writer's Notebook Update Review your list of details that reveal your life, surroundings, and society. Use this information to write the opening of a story. Start your story the way Böll starts his: "Where ____ [insert your name] came from, most of the people. . . ."

Read All About It! People or organizations often buy space in a newspaper to air their grievances. As Franz, combine words with pictures to create an **ad** that tells the world what the Balek family has done.

Family Discussion The young Frau Balek has discovered that the weights used to balance the family scales are inaccurate. Write a **dialogue** in which she tries to persuade her mother-in-law to exchange them for accurate ones.

Other Options

Family Symbol The Balek's coat of arms is described as a "giant crouching under a fir tree." Draw either what you think it actually looked like, or draw the coat of arms that you think the Baleks should have had.

Knock and Mock Political cartoons are visual as well as verbal satires. Create a **political cartoon** that focuses on the major event of "The Balek Scales" and reveals its injustice. Add a caption.

Where Upon a Time From hints in the narrative, the events in this story take place during the time of the Austro-Hungarian empire. Find or draw a **map** of the boundaries of that empire, locating and labeling its capital. Then decide where the villages mentioned in the story are located and show what events in the story happen in each.

Before Reading

How Much Land Does a Man Need?

by Leo Tolstoy   Russia

Leo Tolstoy
1828–1910

One night, at the age of 82, Leo Tolstoy, a wealthy Russian count and world-famous writer, dressed in peasant clothes, fled his estate, and set out on a religious pilgrimage. He died while on the journey, in search of a peace that had eluded him throughout his long life. Despite the advantages of his birth and the great successes in his life, Tolstoy was tormented by a sense of failure. At different times he sought escape in idealistic schemes of reform on his estate, in sprees of compulsive gambling, in military service, in family life, and in creative efforts. But at the end of his life, he was still searching.

Building Background

A Hunger for Land Because of poor soil, frequent drought, and a short growing season, farming was difficult in much of Russia. Throughout most of the country's history, mainly because of the distribution of rainfall, Russia had one bad harvest out of every three. To make matters worse, Russian peasants were inefficient farmers who exhausted the fertility of the soil and then sought more land. This hunger for land drove Russia to expand east and south, seizing the grazing lands of the nomadic peoples of Central Asia, such as those of the Bashkirs mentioned in Tolstoy's story.

Literary Focus

Parable A **parable** is a brief narrative that illustrates a moral or philosophical teaching. The New Testament uses parables such as the Prodigal Son or the Good Samaritan to stress the value of forgiveness and compassion; the Greek philosopher Plato used his Parable of the Cave to express his view that our senses reveal only a shadowy glimpse of reality to us.

Writer's Notebook

Pahom's Progress? In each of the nine sections of this story, events occur that have an important effect on the protagonist and the development of his character. After you read each section, jot down notes for the following chart. The first one is done for you.

Section	Significant Event	Effect on Pahom
1	Visit of sister-in-law from town	Dissatisfaction with land he owns
2		
3		

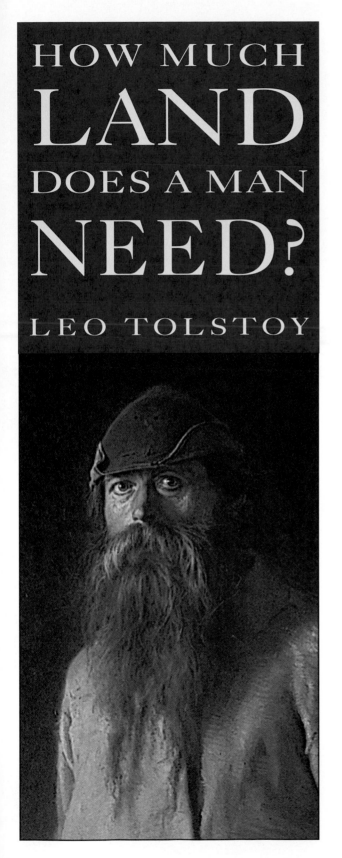

HOW MUCH LAND DOES A MAN NEED?

LEO TOLSTOY

1

An elder sister came to visit her younger sister in the country. The elder was married to a shopkeeper in town, the younger to a peasant in the village. As the sisters sat over their tea talking, the elder began to boast of the advantages of town life, saying how comfortably they lived there, how well they dressed, what fine clothes her children wore, what good things they ate and drank, and how she went to the theater, promenades, and entertainments.

The younger sister was piqued, and in turn disparaged[1] the life of a shopkeeper, and stood up for that of a peasant.

"I wouldn't change my way of life for yours," said she. "We may live roughly, but at least we're free from worry. You live in better style than we do, but though you often earn more than you need, you're very likely to lose all you have. You know the proverb, 'Loss and gain are brothers twain.' It often happens that people who're wealthy one day are begging their bread the next. Our way is safer. Though a peasant's life is not a rich one, it's long. We'll never grow rich, but we'll always have enough to eat."

The elder sister said sneeringly:

"Enough? Yes, if you like to share with the pigs and the calves! What do you know of elegance or manners! However much your good man may slave, you'll die as you live—in a dung heap—and your children the same."

"Well, what of that?" replied the younger sister. "Of course our work is rough and hard. But on the other hand, it's sure,

---

1. disparage (dis par′ij), v. belittle; discredit.

◀ *Forester* by Russian artist Ivan N. Kramskoi (1837–1887) was painted in 1874. All successful portraits reveal something of the inner person. What can you tell about this man?

and we need not bow to anyone. But you, in your towns, are surrounded by temptations; today all may be right, but tomorrow the Evil One may tempt your husband with cards, wine, or women, and all will go to ruin. Don't such things happen often enough?"

Pahom, the master of the house, was lying on the top of the stove[2] and he listened to the women's chatter.

"It is perfectly true," thought he. "Busy as we are from childhood tilling mother earth, we peasants have no time to let any nonsense settle in our heads. Our only trouble is that we haven't land enough. If I had plenty of land I shouldn't fear the Devil himself!"

The women finished their tea, chatted a while about dress, and then cleared away the tea things and lay down to sleep.

But the Devil had been sitting behind the stove and had heard all that had been said. He was pleased that the peasant's wife had led her husband into boasting and that he had said that if he had plenty of land he would not fear the Devil himself.

"All right," thought the Devil. "We'll have a tussle. I'll give you land enough; and by means of the land I'll get you into my power."

CONNECT: What other stories do you recall in which power or money is acquired through an arrangement with the Devil?

2

Close to the village there lived a lady, a small landowner who had an estate of about three hundred acres. She had always lived on good terms with the peasants until she engaged as her manager an old soldier, who took to burdening the people with fines. However careful Pahom tried to be, it happened again and again that now a horse of his got among the lady's oats, now a cow strayed into her garden, now his calves found their way into her meadows—and he always had to pay a fine.

Pahom paid up, but grumbled, and, going home in a temper, was rough with his family. All through that summer Pahom had much trouble because of this manager, and he was actually glad when winter came and the cattle had to be stabled. Though he grudged the fodder when they could no longer graze on the pasture land, at least he was free from anxiety about them.

In the winter the news got about that the lady was going to sell her land and that the keeper of the inn on the high road was bargaining for it. When the peasants heard this they were very much alarmed.

"Well," thought they, "if the innkeeper gets the land, he'll worry us with fines worse than the lady's manager. We all depend on that estate."

So the peasants went on behalf of their village council and asked the lady not to sell the land to the innkeeper, offering her a better price for it themselves. The lady agreed to let them have it. Then the peasants tried to arrange for the village council to buy the whole estate, so that it might be held by them all in common. They met twice to discuss it, but could not settle the matter; the Evil One sowed discord[3] among them and they could not agree. So they decided to buy the land individually, each according to his means; and the lady agreed to this plan as she had to the other.

Presently Pahom heard that a neighbor of his was buying fifty acres, and that the lady had consented to accept one half in cash and to wait a year for the other half. Pahom felt envious.

"Look at that," thought he, "the land is all being sold, and I'll get none of it." So he spoke to his wife.

"Other people are buying," said he, "and we must also buy twenty acres or so. Life is becom-

---

2. **lying . . . stove.** In Russian cottages, flat-topped stoves were large enough for people to lie on.

3. **discord** (dis′kôrd), *n.* disagreement.

ing impossible. That manager is simply crushing us with his fines."

So they put their heads together and considered how they could manage to buy it. They had one hundred rubles laid by. They sold a colt and one half of their bees, hired out one of their sons as a farm hand and took his wages in advance, borrowed the rest from a brother-in-law, and so scraped together half the purchase money.

Having done this, Pahom chose a farm of forty acres, some of it wooded, and went to the lady to bargain for it. They came to an agreement, and he shook hands with her upon it and paid her a deposit in advance. Then they went to town and signed the deeds, he paying half the price down, and undertaking to pay the remainder within two years.

So now Pahom had land of his own. He borrowed seed and sowed it on the land he had bought. The harvest was a good one, and within a year he had managed to pay off his debts both to the lady and to his brother-in-law. So he became a landowner, plowing and sowing his own land, making hay on his own land, cutting his own trees, and feeding his cattle on his own pasture. When he went out to plow his fields, or to look at his growing corn, or at his grass meadows, his heart would fill with joy. The grass that grew and the flowers that bloomed there seemed to him unlike any that grew elsewhere. Formerly, when he had passed by that land, it had appeared the same as any other land, but now it seemed quite different.

3

So Pahom was well contented, and everything would have been right if the neighboring peasants would only not have trespassed on his wheatfields and meadows. He appealed to them most civilly, but they still went on: now the herdsmen would let the village cows stray into his meadows, then horses from the night pasture would get among his corn. Pahom turned them out again and again, and forgave their owners, and for a long time he forbore to prosecute anyone. But at last he lost patience and complained to the District Court. He knew it was the peasants' want of land, and no evil intent on their part, that caused the trouble, but he thought:

"I can't go on overlooking it, or they'll destroy all I have. They must be taught a lesson."

So he had them up, gave them one lesson, and then another, and two or three of the peasants were fined. After a time Pahom's neighbors began to bear him a grudge for this, and would now and then let their cattle on to his land on purpose. One peasant even got into Pahom's wood at night and cut down five young lime trees for their bark. Pahom, passing through the wood one day, noticed something white. He came nearer and saw the stripped trunks lying on the ground, and close by stood the stumps where the trees had been. Pahom was furious.

"If he'd only cut one here and there it would have been bad enough," thought Pahom, "but the rascal has actually cut down a whole clump. If I could only find out who did this, I'd get even with him."

He racked his brains as to who it could be. Finally he decided: "It must be Simon—no one else could have done it." So he went to Simon's homestead to have a look around, but he found nothing and only had an angry scene. However, he now felt more certain than ever that Simon had done it, and he lodged a complaint. Simon was summoned. The case was tried, and retried, and at the end of it all Simon was acquitted, there being no evidence against him. Pahom felt still more aggrieved, and let his anger loose upon the Elders and the Judges.

"You let thieves grease your palms," said he. "If you were honest folk yourselves you wouldn't let a thief go free."

So Pahom quarreled with the judges and with his neighbors. Threats to burn his hut began to be uttered. So though Pahom had more land, his place in the community was much worse than before.

About this time a rumor got about that many people were moving to new parts.

"There's no need for me to leave my land," thought Pahom. "But some of the others may leave our village and then there'd be more room for us. I'd take over their land myself and make my estates somewhat bigger. I could then live more at ease. As it is, I'm still too cramped to be comfortable."

One day Pahom was sitting at home when a peasant, passing through the village, happened to drop in. He was allowed to stay the night, and supper was given him. Pahom had a talk with this peasant and asked him where he came from. The stranger answered that he came from beyond the Volga,[4] where he had been working. One word led to another, and the man went on to say that many people were settling in those parts. He told how some people from his village had settled there. They had joined the community there and had had twenty-five acres per man granted them. The land was so good, he said, that the rye sown on it grew as high as a horse, and so thick that five cuts of a sickle made a sheaf. One peasant, he said, had brought nothing with him but his bare hands, and now he had six horses and two cows of his own.

Pahom's heart kindled with desire.

"Why should I suffer in this narrow hole if one can live so well elsewhere?" he thought. "I'll sell my land and my homestead here, and with the money I'll start afresh over there and get everything new. In this crowded place one is always having trouble. But I must first go and find out all about it myself."

Toward summer he got ready and started out. He went down the Volga on a steamer to Samara, then walked another three hundred miles on foot, and at last reached the place. It was just as the stranger had said. The peasants had plenty of land: every man had twenty-five acres of communal[5] land given him for his use and anyone who had money could buy, besides, at a ruble and a half an acre, as much good freehold land[6] as he wanted.

Having found out all he wished to know, Pahom returned home as autumn came on, and began selling off his belongings. He sold his land at a profit, sold his homestead and all his cattle, and withdrew from membership in the village. He only waited till the spring, and then started with his family for the new settlement.

4

As soon as Pahom and his family reached their new abode, he applied for admission into the council of a large village. He stood treat to the Elders and obtained the necessary documents. Five shares of communal land were given him for his own and his sons' use: that is to say—125 acres (not all together, but in different fields) besides the use of the communal pasture. Pahom put up the buildings he needed and bought cattle. Of the communal land alone he had three times as much as at his former home, and the land was good wheat land. He was ten times better off than he had been. He had plenty of arable[7] land and pasturage, and could keep as many head of cattle as he liked.

At first, in the bustle of building and settling down, Pahom was pleased with it all, but when he got used to it he began to think that even here he hadn't enough land. The first year he sowed wheat on his share of the communal land and had a good crop. He wanted to go on sowing wheat, but had not enough communal land for the purpose, and what he had already used was not available, for in those parts wheat is sown only

---

4. **Volga**, river in western Russia.
5. communal (kə myü′nl), *adj.* owned jointly by all.
6. **freehold land.** In legal terms, freehold land is land held or owned free and clear. In many countries a person can own a house, but the land that it sits on is merely leased for a period of time—usually 100 years. Such a house would be called a leasehold.
7. arable (ar′ə bəl), *adj.* suitable for producing crops.

on virgin soil or on fallow land. It is sown for one or two years, and then the land lies fallow till it is again overgrown with steppe[8] grass. There were many who wanted such land, and there was not enough for all, so that people quarreled about it. Those who were better off wanted it for growing wheat, and those who were poor wanted it to let to dealers, so that they might raise money to pay their taxes. Pahom wanted to sow more wheat, so he rented land from a dealer for a year. He sowed much wheat and had a fine crop, but the land was too far from the village—the wheat had to be carted more than ten miles. After a time Pahom noticed that some peasant dealers were living on separate farms and were growing wealthy, and he thought:

"If I were to buy some freehold land and have a homestead on it, it would be a different thing altogether. Then it would all be fine and close together."

The question of buying freehold land recurred to him again and again.

He went on in the same way for three years, renting land and sowing wheat. The seasons turned out well and the crops were good, so that he began to lay by money. He might have gone on living contentedly, but he grew tired of having to rent other people's land every year and having to scramble for it. Wherever there was good land to be had, the peasants would rush for it and it was taken up at once, so that unless you were sharp about it, you got none. It happened in the third year that he and a dealer together rented a piece of pasture land from some peasants, and they had already plowed it up, when there was some dispute and the peasants went to law about it, and things fell out so that the labor was all lost.

"If it were my own land," thought Pahom, "I should be independent, and there wouldn't be all this unpleasantness."

So Pahom began looking out for land which he could buy, and he came across a peasant who had bought thirteen hundred acres, but having got into difficulties was willing to sell again cheap.

Pahom bargained and haggled with him, and at last they settled the price at fifteen hundred rubles, part in cash and part to be paid later. They had all but clinched the matter when a passing dealer happened to stop at Pahom's one day to get feed for his horses. He drank tea with Pahom, and they had a talk. The dealer said that he was just returning from the land of the Bashkirs,[9] far away, where he had bought thirteen thousand acres of land, all for a thousand rubles. Pahom questioned him further, and the dealer said:

"All one has to do is to make friends with the chiefs. I gave away about one hundred rubles' worth of silk robes and carpets, besides a case of tea, and I gave wine to those who would drink it; and I got the land for less than three kopecks an acre." And he showed Pahom the title deed, saying:

"The land lies near a river, and the whole steppe is virgin soil."

Pahom plied him with questions, and the dealer said:

"There's more land there than you could cover if you walked a year, and it all belongs to the Bashkirs. They're as simple as sheep, and land can be got almost for nothing."

"There, now," thought Pahom, "with my one thousand rubles, why should I get only thirteen hundred acres, and saddle myself with a debt besides? If I take it out there, I can get more than ten times as much for my money."

5

Pahom inquired how to get to the place, and as soon as the grain dealer had left him, he prepared to go there himself. He left his wife to look after the homestead, and started on his journey, taking his hired man with him. They stopped at a town on their way and bought a case of tea, some wine, and other presents, as the grain dealer had advised.

---

8. **steppe,** vast, treeless plains.
9. **Bashkirs,** nomadic people living in central Asia.

▲ *The Mowers* (1887) was painted by Grigori G. Myasoyedov. Explain whether you would describe the mood of the picture as gloomy, sentimental, happy, or something else.

On and on they went until they had gone more than three hundred miles, and on the seventh day they came to a place where the Bashkirs had pitched their round tents. It was all just as the dealer had said. The people lived on the steppe, by a river, in felt-covered tents. They neither tilled the ground nor ate bread. Their cattle and horses grazed in herds on the steppe. The colts were tethered behind the tents, and the mares were driven to them twice a day. The mares were milked, and from the milk kumiss[10] was made. It was the women who prepared the kumiss, and they also made cheese. As far as the men were concerned, drinking kumiss and tea, eating mutton, and playing on their pipes was all they cared about. They were all stout and merry, and all the summer long they never thought of doing any work. They were quite ignorant, and knew no Russian, but were good-natured enough.

As soon as they saw Pahom, they came out of their tents and gathered around the visitor. An interpreter was found, and Pahom told them he had come about some land. The Bashkirs seemed very glad; they took Pahom and led him into one of the best tents, where they made him sit on some down cushions placed on a carpet, while they sat around him. They gave him some tea and kumiss, and had a sheep killed, and gave him mutton to eat. Pahom took presents out of his cart and distributed them among the Bashkirs, and divided the tea amongst them. The Bashkirs were delighted. They talked a great deal among themselves and then told the interpreter what to say.

"They wish to tell you," said the interpreter, "that they like you and that it's our custom to do all we can to please a guest and to repay him for his gifts. You have given us presents, now tell us which of the things we possess please you best, that we may present them to you."

"What pleases me best here," answered Pahom, "is your land. Our land is crowded and

_____

10. **kumiss,** fermented mare's or camel's milk.

the soil is worn out, but you have plenty of land, and it is good land. I never saw the likes of it."

The interpreter told the Bashkirs what Pahom had said. They talked among themselves for a while. Pahom could not understand what they were saying, but saw that they were much amused and heard them shout and laugh. Then they were silent and looked at Pahom while the interpreter said:

"They wish me to tell you that in return for your presents they will gladly give you as much land as you want. You have only to point it out with your hand and it is yours."

The Bashkirs talked again for a while and began to dispute. Pahom asked what they were disputing about, and the interpreter told him that some of them thought they ought to ask their chief about the land and not act in his absence, while others thought there was no need to wait for his return.

6

While the Bashkirs were disputing, a man in a large fox-fur cap appeared on the scene. They all became silent and rose to their feet. The interpreter said: "This is our chief himself."

Pahom immediately fetched the best dressing gown and five pounds of tea, and offered these to the chief. The chief accepted them and seated himself in the place of honor. The Bashkirs at once began telling him something. The chief listened for a while, then made a sign with his head for them to be silent, and addressing himself to Pahom, said in Russian:

"Well, so be it. Choose whatever piece of land you like; we have plenty of it."

"How can I take as much as I like?" thought Pahom. "I must get a deed to make it secure, or else they may say: 'It is yours,' and afterward may take it away again."

"Thank you for your kind words," he said aloud. "You have much land, and I only want a little. But I should like to be sure which portion is mine. Could it not be measured and made over to me? Life and death are in God's hands.

You good people give it to me, but your children might wish to take it back again."

"You are quite right," said the chief. "We will make it over to you."

"I heard that a dealer had been here," continued Pahom, "and that you gave him a little land, too, and signed title deeds to that effect. I should like to have it done in the same way."

The chief understood.

"Yes," replied he, "that can be done quite easily. We have a scribe, and we will go to town with you and have the deed properly sealed."

"And what will be the price?" asked Pahom.

"Our price is always the same: one thousand rubles a day."

Pahom did not understand.

"A day? What measure is that? How many acres would that be?"

"We do not know how to reckon it out," said the chief. "We sell it by the day. As much as you can go around on your feet in a day is yours, and the price is one thousand rubles a day."

Pahom was surprised.

"But in a day you can get around a large tract of land," he said.

The chief laughed.

"It will all be yours!" said he. "But there is one condition: If you don't return on the same day to the spot whence you started, your money is lost."

PREDICT: Why do you think the Bashkirs are so generous with land?

"But how am I to mark the way that I have gone?"

"Why, we shall go to any spot you like and stay there. You must start from that spot and make your round, taking a spade with you. Wherever you think necessary, make a mark. At every turning, dig a hole and pile up the turf; then afterward we will go around with a plow from hole to hole. You may make as large a circuit as you please, but before the sun sets you must return to the place you started from. All the land you cover will be yours."

Pahom was delighted. It was decided to start early next morning. They talked a while, and after drinking some more kumiss and eating some more mutton, they had tea again, and then the night came on. They gave Pahom a feather bed to sleep on, and the Bashkirs dispersed[11] for the night, promising to assemble the next morning at daybreak and ride out before sunrise to the appointed spot.

7

Pahom lay on the feather bed, but could not sleep. He kept thinking about the land.

"What a large tract I'll mark off!" thought he, "I can easily do thirty-five miles in a day. The days are long now, and within a circuit of thirty-five miles what a lot of land there will be! I'll sell the poorer land or let it to peasants, but I'll pick out the best and farm it myself. I'll buy two ox teams and hire two more laborers. About a hundred and fifty acres shall be plowland, and I'll pasture cattle on the rest."

Pahom lay awake all night and dozed off only just before dawn. Hardly were his eyes closed when he had a dream. He thought he was lying in that same tent and heard somebody chuckling outside. He wondered who it could be, and rose and went out, and he saw the Bashkir chief sitting in front of the tent holding his sides and rolling about with laughter. Going nearer to the chief, Pahom asked, "What are you laughing at?" But he saw that it was no longer the chief but the grain dealer who had recently stopped at his house and had told him about the land. Just as Pahom was going to ask: "Have you been here long?" he saw that it was not the dealer, but the peasant who had come up from the Volga long ago to Pahom's old home. Then he saw that it was not the peasant either, but the Devil himself with hoofs and horns, sitting there and chuckling, and before him lay a man, prostrate on the ground, barefooted, with only trousers and a shirt on. And Pahom dreamed that he looked more attentively to see what sort of man it was lying there, and he saw that the man was dead, and that it was himself. Horror-struck, he awoke.

"What things one dreams about!" thought he.

Looking around he saw through the open door that the dawn was breaking.

"It's time to wake them up," thought he. "We ought to be starting."

He got up, roused his man (who was sleeping in his cart), bade him harness, and went to call the Bashkirs.

"It's time to go to the steppe to measure the land," he said.

The Bashkirs rose and assembled, and the chief came, too. Then they began drinking kumiss again, and offered Pahom some tea, but he would not wait.

"If we are to go, let's go. It's high time," said he.

8

The Bashkirs got ready and they all started: some mounted on horses and some in carts. Pahom drove in his own small cart with his servant and took a spade with him. When they reached the steppe, the red dawn was beginning to kindle. They ascended a hillock (called by the Bashkirs a *shikhan*) and, dismounting from their carts and their horses, gathered in one spot. The chief came to Pahom and, stretching out his arm toward the plain:

"See," said he, "all this, as far as your eye can reach, is ours. You may have any part of it you like."

Pahom's eyes glistened; it was all virgin soil, as flat as the palm of your hand, as black as the seed of a poppy, and in the hollows different kinds of grasses grew breast-high.

The chief took off his fox-fur cap, placed it on the ground, and said:

"This will be the mark. Start from here, and return here again. All the land you go around shall be yours."

---

11. **disperse** (dis pėrs'), *v.* go off in different directions.

Pahom took out his money and put it on the cap. Then he took off his outer coat, remaining in his sleeveless undercoat. He unfastened his girdle[12] and tied it tight below his stomach, put a little bag of bread into the breast of his coat, and, tying a flask of water to his girdle, he drew up the tops of his boots, took the spade from his man, and stood ready to start. He considered for some moments which way he had better go—it was tempting everywhere.

"No matter," he concluded, "I'll go toward the rising sun."

He turned his face to the east, stretched himself, and waited for the sun to appear above the rim.

"I must lose no time," he thought, "and it's easier walking while it's still cool."

The sun's rays had hardly flashed above the horizon when Pahom, carrying the spade over his shoulder, went down into the steppe.

Pahom started walking neither slowly nor quickly. After having gone a thousand yards he stopped, dug a hole, and placed pieces of turf one on another to make it more visible. Then he went on; and now that he had walked off his stiffness he quickened his pace. After a while he dug another hole.

Pahom looked back. The hillock could be distinctly seen in the sunlight, with the people on it, and the glittering iron rims of the cartwheels. At a rough guess Pahom concluded that he had walked three miles. It was growing warmer; he took off his undercoat, slung it across his shoulder, and went on again. It had grown quite warm now; he looked at the sun—it was time to think of breakfast.

"The first shift is done, but there are four in a day, and it's too soon yet to turn. But I'll just take off my boots," said he to himself.

He sat down, took off his boots, stuck them into his girdle, and went on. It was easy walking now.

"I'll go on for another three miles," thought he, "and then turn to the left. This spot is so fine that it would be a pity to lose it. The further one goes, the better the land seems."

He went straight on for a while, and when he looked around, the hillock was scarcely visible and the people on it looked like black ants, and he could just see something glistening there in the sun.

"Ah," thought Pahom, "I have gone far enough in this direction; it's time to turn. Besides, I'm in a regular sweat, and very thirsty."

He stopped, dug a large hole, and heaped up pieces of turf. Next he untied his flask, had a drink, and then turned sharply to the left. He went on and on; the grass was high, and it was very hot.

Pahom began to grow tired; he looked at the sun and saw that it was noon.

"Well," he thought, "I must have a rest."

He sat down, and ate some bread and drank some water; but he did not lie down, thinking that if he did he might fall asleep. After sitting a little while, he went on again. At first he walked easily, the food had strengthened him; but it had become terribly hot and he felt sleepy. Still he went on, thinking: "An hour to suffer, a lifetime to live."

He went a long way in this direction also, and was about to turn to the left again, when he perceived a damp hollow; "It would be a pity to leave that out," he thought. "Flax would do well there." So he went on past the hollow and dug a hole on the other side of it before he made a sharp turn. Pahom looked toward the hillock. The heat made the air hazy; it seemed to be quivering, and through the haze the people on the hillock could scarcely be seen.

"Ah," thought Pahom, "I have made the sides too long; I must make this one shorter." And he went along the third side, stepping faster. He looked at the sun: it was nearly halfway to the horizon, and he had not yet done two miles of the third side of the square. He was still ten miles from the goal.

---

12. **girdle** (gėr′dl), *n.* belt worn around the waist.

"No," he thought, "though it will make my land lopsided, I must hurry back in a straight line now. I might go too far, and as it is I have a great deal of land."

So Pahom hurriedly dug a hole and turned straight toward the hillock.

9

Pahom went straight toward the hillock, but he now walked with difficulty. He was exhausted from the heat, his bare feet were cut and bruised, and his legs began to fail. He longed to rest, but it was impossible if he meant to get back before sunset. The sun waits for no man, and it was sinking lower and lower.

"Oh, Lord," he thought, "If only I have not blundered trying for too much! What if I am too late?"

He looked toward the hillock and at the sun. He was still far from his goal, and the sun was already near the rim of the sky.

Pahom walked on and on; it was very hard walking but he went quicker and quicker. He pressed on, but was still far from the place. He began running, threw away his coat, his boots, his flask, and his cap, and kept only the spade which he used as a support.

"What am I to do?" he thought again. "I've grasped too much and ruined the whole affair. I can't get there before the sun sets."

And this fear made him still more breathless. Pahom kept on running; his soaking shirt and trousers stuck to him, and his mouth was parched. His breast was working like a black-smith's bellows, his heart was beating like a hammer, and his legs were giving way as if they did not belong to him. Pahom was seized with terror lest he should die of the strain.

Though afraid of death, he could not stop.

"After having run all that way they will call me a fool if I stop now," thought he.

And he ran on and on, and drew near and heard the Bashkirs yelling and shouting to him, and their cries inflamed his heart still more. He gathered his last strength and ran on.

The sun was close to the rim of the sky and, cloaked in mist, looked large, and red as blood. Now, yes, now, it was about to set! The sun was quite low, but he was also quite near his goal. Pahom could already see the people on the hillock waving their arms to make him hurry. He could see the fox-fur cap on the ground and the money in it, and the chief sitting on the ground holding his sides. And Pahom remembered his dream.

"There's plenty of land," thought he, "but will God let me live on it? I have lost my life, I have lost my life! Never will I reach that spot!"

Pahom looked at the sun, which had reached the earth: one side of it had already disappeared. With all his remaining strength he rushed on, bending his body forward so that his legs could hardly follow fast enough to keep him from falling. Just as he reached the hillock it suddenly grew dark. He looked up—the sun had already set!

He gave a cry: "All my labor has been in vain," thought he, and was about to stop, but he heard the Bashkirs still shouting and remembered that though to him, from below, the sun seemed to have set, they on the hillock could still see it. He took a long breath and ran up the hillock. It was still light there. He reached the top and saw the cap. Before it sat the chief, laughing and holding his sides. Again Pahom remembered his dream, and he uttered a cry: his legs gave way beneath him, he fell forward and reached the cap with his hands.

"Ah, that's a fine fellow!" exclaimed the chief. "He has gained much land!"

Pahom's servant came running up and tried to raise him, but he saw that blood was flowing from his mouth. Pahom was dead.

The Bashkirs clicked their tongues to show their pity.

His servant picked up the spade and dug a grave long enough for Pahom to lie in, and buried him in it.

Six feet from his head to his heels was all he needed.

After Reading

Making Connections

Shaping Your Response

1. Three lifestyles are described in this story—that of the town-dweller, the peasant, and the steppe nomad. Explain which seems the most desirable to you.

2. Do you think this parable, or lesson, is relevant to life today in the U.S.? Explain.

Analyzing the Story

3. Tolstoy introduces the Devil into a largely realistic narrative. Do you think the story would be better without this supernatural element? Why or why not?

4. In section 3, what is **ironic** about Pahom's treatment of his neighbors?

5. What is **symbolic** about Pahom's journey from one place to another? about the fox fur hat the Bashkir chief wears?

6. What does Pahom's insistence on a title deed from the Bashkirs contribute to his **characterization**?

7. List the events in the story that **foreshadow** the ending.

8. How does the wife's **proverb,** "Loss and gain are brothers twain," illustrate a **theme** of this story?

Extending the Ideas

9. In the last two centuries many nomadic groups, such as the peoples of Central Asia and the Plains Indians of the American West, have been forced to face enormous cultural **change.** Discuss some of the social problems these groups have experienced in adjusting to change.

Literary Focus: Parable

A **parable** is a brief narrative that concretely illustrates an abstract moral or philosophical teaching.

- How would you sum up the lesson of this story?

- How do the **title** and final sentence use **irony** to illustrate this lesson?

Vocabulary Study

On your paper write the listed vocabulary word that best completes each sentence below.

arable
communal
discord
disparage
disperse

1. Wherever he went, Pahom stirred up ____.
2. Pahom's sister-in-law tried to ____ the life of her country sister.
3. Pahom became dissatisfied with ____ land because he longed to have his own homestead.
4. Pahom was delighted to find that the land of the Bashkirs was so rich and ____.
5. The Bashkirs promised Pahom all the land he could cover by sunset; then they decided to ____ for the night.

Expressing Your Ideas

Writing Choices

Writer's Notebook Update Review the notes you kept for the chart. In your notebook, respond to the following statement: Pahom's reasons for wanting more and more land changed as he grew older.

A Victim of Circumstances? Do human beings have free will? Are the things that happen to people the result of their own actions or of outside forces? Is Pahom a victim of circumstances? Write an **essay** in which you discuss these issues, citing as evidence details from the story.

Listen My Children Bashkir parents now tell the story of Pahom as a warning to their children. Write a **folk tale** about Pahom from the Bashkir point of view. End with a brief statement of the moral.

Grin and Bear It Pahom says to himself, "An hour to suffer, a lifetime to live." Write an **autobiographical sketch** that illustrates the truth of that idea as it applies to some event in your own life. Incorporate the saying into your sketch.

Other Options

In Common By 1886, when he wrote this story, Tolstoy had concluded that the ownership of private property was evil. What arguments might support or refute Tolstoy's view? Present a **debate** on the following premise: It is evil to own property.

Show-and-Tell Acquiring land is only one example of the human desire to collect and own. People collect coins, plates, dolls, hubcaps, whatever. Bring to class an example of something that you collect. Present a **collector's guide** showing your objects and explaining how your collection came about.

Home Is Where the Hearth Is A Russian peasant's home typically consisted of one room. One side of the room included a large stove, with fireplace and ovens below and a flat, tiled surface above for sleeping. One corner contained the family's religious icons. The family, sitting on benches, ate at a plank table. They stored their clothes in large wooden trunks. Draw a **picture** or make a **three-dimensional model** of the interior of a typical Russian cottage.

The Cost of Winning

Image Makers

Media Connection

The selections in this unit deal with power, the people who have it, and the impressions they make on others. The following pages examine how favorable impressions are created and maintained by image makers.

A trained actor, President Reagan was extraordinarily successful in the role of a kind of "super-salesman" of the policies of his administration. But although one of Reagan's nicknames – "the Great Communicator" – suggested a positive view of the phenomenon of his continuing popularity, another one – "the Teflon President" – expressed a more critical attitude.

THE TEFLON PRESIDENT

An excerpt from *The Press and The Presidency*
John Tebbel and Sarah Miles Watt

THE TEFLON PRESIDENT

As the first actor ever to occupy the White House, he found himself in command of a formidable propaganda machine that had been building steadily since the Kennedy administration, and with each advance in technology, had become a still more powerful instrument in the hands of a President who knew how to use it. To it Reagan brought the fundamental skills peculiar to the actor's craft, particularly the ability to suspend disbelief, as in the theater, and make illusion seem like reality. Since the vast panoply of the White House had been designed to do just that, the joining of the two was an epic conjunction – an actor working in a studio dwarfing in power if not in size the sound stages of Hollywood, and whose audience was an entire nation.

To manipulate this machine and make it work effectively, Reagan possessed an ideal combination of qualities. He was highly popular, as both the Roosevelts and Eisenhower had been, and he had the acquired ability, which no previous President had enjoyed, to create a character the whole country could enjoy–amiable, wisecracking, pointedly nonintellectual, embodying the virtues Carter talked about without agonizing over them. Nor did he have the negative qualities that had destroyed other presidents. He was not a tortured, introspective, complicated sufferer, as Johnson, Nixon, and Carter had been, but, as he sincerely believed, a plain, simple, eternally optimistic man of the people (albeit rich himself and living in the world of the rich and privileged) of a sort the Democrats had always talked about being. Such a man had never before emerged as a Republican.

Until recently, the White House had taken the public pulse by carefully scanning and analyzing what was printed and broadcast by the media. Reagan, however, now made use of the sophisticated new polling techniques available to him. Using funds from the Republican National Committee, he hired a firm called Decision Making Information, directed by an eminent plotter named Richard Wirthlin, to carry out the most comprehensive (and expensive) poll taking on a continous basis ever done for a President. What Wirthlin's figures showed became an important part of White House political strategy and sometimes influenced the President's decisions.

[White House aide David] Gergen was valuable in these operations because he, too, had been a successful poll taker, founder and editor of *Public Opinion,* a periodical devoted to that arcane art.

There were those who believed that some of this was wasted motion. [White House correspondent for *Time,* Laurence] I. Barrett, for example, considered it a myth that Wirthlin's figures gave Reagan an extraordinary power to shape public perceptions. If that were true, he pointed out, Reagan should have been relatively free from criticism, which was far from the case, and the process should also have insulated him from the political effects of bad news, which was also not the case. What helped the President more was not statistics but his amazing popularity. No matter how bad the news might be, none of it stuck to the presidential image – "the Teflon President," as his critics called him. The public simply refused to associate Reagan with the results of his policies, unless those results were good.

Responding

1. How important do you think the following are in a presidential candidate: acting skills, good looks, intelligence, money, youth? Work with a group to create a description of the ideal presidential candidate.

2. With a partner, research polling techniques used in presidential campaigns. Report on these techniques and their value.

3. Think of a slogan that could have enhanced Caesar's image.

Career Connection

Image maker Diego Muñoz paints a "portrait" of a political candidate. But before the paint dries, he may touch up or play down features, in order to create the most effective image for his client.

CREATING AN IMAGE
in Three Easy Steps

Image maker Diego Muñoz studied political science in college and works as a political consultant in the state of New York for both candidates and issues. He considers a political image a portrait rather than a mask and works to present that portrait to the public.

For Muñoz, the creation of an image is easy as one, two, three:

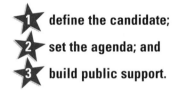

1 **define the candidate;**

2 **set the agenda; and**

3 **build public support.**

He goes on to explain. "To define the candidate, I develop a detailed portrait of what that person believes in and stands for. The more detailed the list of principles is, the better it will be later in the campaign when negatives crop up–and they always do. Prioritize the list. Have a clear idea of what the candidate wants to accomplish.

"The second step–setting the agenda–involves deciding on a time frame for the campaign and then developing your strategy. First, evaluate your resources. How much money does the campaign have to spend? How many volunteers? What media exposure can you get? Do you have the telephones, computers, and supplies that you'll need? Are there lawyers who will help the candidate follow the campaign and election laws and defend against possible election law suits? Form alliances with organizations that would like to see your candidate elected. Once you've identified and contacted your resources, work out a time line for the use of those resources. "Use that time line to build public support, the third step. Educate the public on the issues and the candidate. Identify the audience that you are trying to reach. What people are likely to vote for your candidate if they know what he or she stands for? Where do they live? Go to them. Pass out leaflets. Send faxes. Drive around in cars with bullhorns. Use the media and community meetings.

Diego Muñoz, Image Maker

"The campaign is underway, but your problems aren't over yet! Negative information that can hurt your candidate's image may be made public. You can address the criticism by adjusting, downplaying, or highlighting aspects of the candidate's portrait. You might even turn a negative into a positive. Another way to counter a negative is with a negative, but I don't like to run a "smear campaign." I prefer to work with the people who have raised negative issues and to develop a collaboration that is beneficial to us all.

"And there, in three steps, you have the foundation of any campaign. Now jump on the roller coaster and ride it out to election day."

Responding

If you were campaign manager for a friend running for class office, how would you use or adapt the steps that Diego Muñoz mentions? How would you build support?

Reading Mini-Lesson

Propaganda

Wherever you look in books, TV, radio, music, magazines, or newspapers, you can find propaganda—attempts to persuade you to adopt someone's opinions or beliefs. Propaganda isn't always bad. Any persuasive appeals to use seat belts or to exercise more, for example, are worthwhile. But propaganda can be used to manipulate you into doing or thinking something unawares. Use the following criteria to evaluate information, ads, articles, speeches, and comments.

Is information relevant? "Vote for Bob Billings for President—family man, pillar of the community, decorated war veteran, and founder of Micro-Chips, the leading exporter of minicomputers." Although these attributes suggest basic decency, stability, bravery, and initiative—important qualities—they do not qualify this man as a national leader. Nevertheless, such qualities often affect the way people vote. Information about Billings's job experience and political views bear more directly on his suitability for public office.

What is fact? What is opinion? Watch out for words and phrases like *clearly*, *everybody knows,* and *without question.* Examine the rest of the statement. Is it a fact that expansion of an airport will improve a community or that building a low-income high-rise will ruin the area?

Beware of oversimplification. Simplifying complicated issues is a common propaganda device. Slogans, bumper stickers, and use of stereotypes are all simplifications. "More jobs with Jacobs" makes a promise that may be hard to deliver.

Watch out for loaded words. Be on the lookout for words designed to appeal to your emotions. In "The Teflon President" (page 788), Ronald Reagan is spoken of as a "trained actor," a "super-salesman" and "pointedly nonintellectual." These three attributes contributed to Reagan's popularity, according to the article. But these phrases are also designed to affect your feelings about Reagan and his sincerity. What effect do you think they are intended to have?

Activity Option

Collect all unsolicited mail that your family receives asking for money for one week and analyze the persuasive appeals and propaganda.

Writing Workshop

Making Caesar Over

Assignment Things might have turned out differently for Julius Caesar if, like some modern politicians, he'd hired a public relations specialist to reshape his public image. Imagine that he's hired you to do the job.

WRITER'S BLUEPRINT

Product	A persuasive essay and speech
Purpose	To improve Caesar's public image and refute criticism
Audience	The people of Rome
Specs	To create a successful persuasive essay and speech, you should:

❏ Imagine that you are Caesar's public relations specialist and write an essay that characterizes the emperor as a strong, wise, considerate, capable leader. To accomplish this, turn things upside down by recasting Caesar's negative points as positive points, as well as emphasizing his strong points.

❏ Begin your essay in a dramatic way. Establish a bond with your audience. Strike a tone of authority by using persuasive techniques.

❏ Neutralize the opposition by acknowledging and then disposing of potential criticisms.

❏ Finish with an emotional conclusion that appeals to the patriotism and nationalistic pride of your audience.

❏ Make note cards from your essay and use them to deliver a persuasive speech.

❏ Follow the rules of grammar, usage, spelling, and mechanics. Pay special attention to comparative and superlative forms of adjectives and adverbs.

Chart Caesar's character. In a group, review the play and create a chart, like the one shown, of Caesar's words and actions that reveal his positive and negative character traits.

Caesar's Comments or Actions	Quote from the Play	What Caesar Is Trying to Do	What This Reveals About Him: Positive	What This Reveals About Him: Negative
Tells Antony that Cassius is a dangerous man but that he, Caesar, is above such fear.	"I rather tell thee what is to be feared/ Than what I fear, for always I am Caesar." act 1, scene 2	To make his enemy, Cassius, look dangerous and make himself look powerful	—Self-confident, believes in himself	—manipulative —arrogant, too sure of himself

STUDENT MODEL

Negative point:

manipulative—tries to make his enemy, Cassius, look dangerous

Recast as positive point:

helpful—looking out for Antony's welfare, just as he always looks out for the people's welfare

◄ **Recast Caesar's character.** On a note card, jot down each negative point from your chart along with ideas about how you might recast it as a positive point.

Address potential criticisms. On the flip side of each note card, jot down potential criticisms of this recasting and a positive response for each criticism. ▼

STUDENT MODEL

Potential Criticism:

But Caesar is being dishonest in trying to make Cassius look dangerous

Positive Response:

Caesar is not being dishonest; he's being cautious and fatherly, as a leader who is looking out for the welfare of his people must be.

Quickwrite an emotional appeal to the citizens of Rome, based on the arguments on your note cards. Use both reasonable-sounding arguments ("Caesar must deal firmly with his enemies, for his enemies are our enemies") and emotional appeals ("Caesar is our father and we are his children!").

Examine the funeral speeches delivered by Brutus and Mark Antony. Look for how Shakespeare uses persuasive devices, such as rhetorical questions and repetition of key words. (See the Revising Strategy in Step 3 of this lesson.) Then examine the Interdisciplinary Study on image makers on pages 787–789 for more examples of how to reshape someone's public image.

Plan your essay. Use your note cards as a guide. Organize your notes into a plan similar to the one shown here. The examples in parentheses might give you some ideas.

OR . . .
Get together with a partner or small group and together, discuss how you could reshape Caesar's public image.

Introduction

- Dramatic opening ("Are we all gathered here at the Coliseum to bite the hand of Caesar, the mighty hand that feeds us?")

- Establish bond with audience ("No, we've all of us gathered here for a far more sensible reason than that. . . .")

Body

- Build on Caesar's personal strengths ("Here is a man who is intimately acquainted with our deepest fears and desires.")

- Recast negative points in a positive light ("Here is a man who is not harsh and vindictive but firm and realistic.")

- Neutralize potential criticisms ("To all those who would say that Caesar is out for revenge, I would say. . . .")

Conclusion

- Emotional appeal to patriotism ("Is our nation to be less than the mightiest nation on earth? Then, I ask you, how can Rome be led by any but the mightiest of leaders?")

  DRAFTING

Before you draft, review your writing plan and reread the Writer's Blueprint.

As you draft, concentrate on getting the ideas down on paper. See the drafting tips on the next page.

- Use persuasive devices, such as rhetorical questions and repetition of key words, to get your points across. See the Revising Strategy in Step 3 of this lesson. See also the lesson on Propaganda on page 790.

- Spend more time addressing Caesar's strengths than defending his weaknesses, since his strengths are what you want the audience to remember.

- As you discredit Caesar's enemies, write as if you respected them ("But these fine, goodhearted people do not know what they do").

STEP 3 REVISING

Ask a partner to comment on your draft before you revise it. Use this checklist as a guide.

✔ Did I show Caesar as a strong, capable, considerate leader?

✔ Did I refute possible criticisms of him?

✔ Did I use persuasive devices, such as rhetorical questions and the repetition of key words?

Revising Strategy

LITERARY SOURCE
" . . . Who is here so base that would be a bondman? . . . Who is here so rude that would not be a Roman? . . . Who is here so vile that will not love his country?"
from *Julius Caesar* by William Shakespeare

Using Persuasive Devices

Rhetorical questions are asked to emphasize a point and push readers in the direction the writer wants them to go. No real answers are expected to rhetorical questions, such as those in the Literary Source, except the obvious "Yes" the writer assumes.

Repetition of a word or phrase is used to create a sense of rhythm and emphasis, as in the repetition of "Who is here" in the Literary Source.

In their funeral speeches, Brutus and Mark Antony use both rhetorical questions and repetition as persuasive devices. As you revise your essay, look back at these speeches for ideas on using these persuasive devices.

4 EDITING

Ask a partner to review your revised draft before you edit. When you edit, look for errors in grammar, usage, spelling, and mechanics. Look over each sentence to make sure you have used modifiers correctly.

Editing Strategy

Comparative and Superlative Forms of Modifiers

Take care to form the comparative and superlative forms of adjectives and adverbs correctly. Most of the time, use *-er* or *-est:*
prettier, stronger, greenest, soonest

For some longer words, use *more* or *most* instead:
more corrupt, most carelessly

Never use *more* and *-er* or *most* and *-est* together:

Don't write:	**more dangerouser**
Write:	**more dangerous**
Don't write:	**most latest**
Write:	**latest**

FOR REFERENCE
See the Language and Grammar Handbook in the back of this text for more information on comparative and superlative forms of modifiers.

When you edit, check to see that you formed comparative and superlative forms of adjectives and adverbs correctly. Notice how this student model has been corrected for the use of comparative and superlative forms.

Caesar is also the most generous~~est~~ of all his peers. He goes out of his way to thank Brutus and Cassius for their pain and courtesy and blames himself for keeping others waiting. He also invited his friends to share his wine. Caesar is *more* modest~~er~~ than other rulers and doesn't care for flattery. He only wishes to serve his people to the best of his ability.

STUDENT MODEL

STEP 5 PRESENTING

Prepare your speech. Make new note cards to capture the main points of your essay, paragraph by paragraph. Jot down key words and phrases from your essay to remind you of what you'll want to say.

Practice your speech. Look at the Beyond Print article on page 797 for tips on delivering a speech. Then ask a small group to listen and comment as you practice your speech. Use this checklist as a guide.

✔ Did I use persuasive techniques?

✔ Did I include rational and emotional appeals?

✔ Did I present a convincing case for Caesar?

✔ Was my delivery effective?

Consider these ideas for presenting your speech to an audience.

• Create a campaign poster about Caesar to use as a visual aid when you give your speech.

• Present your speech as part of a mock political rally in your classroom.

STEP 6 LOOKING BACK

Self-evaluate. What grade would you give your essay and speech? Look back at the Writer's Blueprint and give yourself a score for each item, from 6 (superior) to 1 (inadequate).

Reflect. Think about what you have learned in organizing and presenting this speech as you write answers to these questions.

✔ How difficult was it for you to create a convincing picture of someone by contradicting the facts? Why?

✔ Do you feel your real strength lies in writing or speaking? Why?

For Your Working Portfolio Add your persuasive essay, note cards, and reflection responses to your working portfolio.

Beyond Print

Speaking Up

A successful speech requires preparation and practice. Effective speeches don't just happen. And even the smoothest speakers must work to make their speeches sound lively and effortless. Though you may experience some nervousness (nearly everyone does), there are ways to reduce your anxiety. Here are some pointers on how to make your audience pay attention to what you have to say.

Rehearse. If you're well prepared, you'll be more self-assured. Rehearse your speech aloud several times, perhaps recording it, and try out different gestures, pauses, or tones of voice. This helps you become familiar with your material. If you're using visuals, rehearse with them.

Get organized. If you spend the first minute or so in front of an audience shuffling your notes or locating your materials, you might lose their attention before you begin. Get everything in order before you stand up to deliver your speech.

Try to relax. Take several deep breaths as you wait for your audience to become quiet and ready to listen. Deep breathing will help calm you.

Maintain good posture. Good posture will help you project your voice. Stand straight and on both feet, keeping your shoulders back and your head up. If you are behind a desk, don't lean on it.

Look at your audience. Talk *to* your listeners, not *at* them. If you are speaking from notes, look at them only briefly, making your points as you look at different members of the audience.

Speak up. Speak in a normal voice, but try to project it to the back of the room. Remember to speak slowly, enunciate clearly, and pronounce words correctly. (For example, say *have to,* not *hafta; going to,* not *gonna.)* Rehearse in front of a family member, or videotape yourself.

Activity Option

Prepare a three-minute speech on some aspect of winning or power. Use persuasive techniques to sway your audience.

Multicultural Connections

Change

The Cost of Winning Change creates challenges by introducing new dimensions to cultural situations. People respond both by clinging to existing cultural patterns and by changing traditions to fit new situations. In this way, new cultures are created, by deliberate acts of people and by the simple fact that change is bound to occur.

■ Kinds of change may include political, social, and economic—or a combination of the three. Discuss the long-range changes that would have occurred if the Baleks had acknowledged the injustice they had committed over the years, fixed their scales, and made restitution.

■ An abrupt change of government, such as Caesar's dictatorship after centuries of a republic, was bound to cause social turmoil. Why, then, was Caesar nevertheless popular with many of the common people?

■ Consider how owning a large tract of land could change the life of a peasant like Pahom. In what ways would he become more independent? How could this threaten the existing social system?

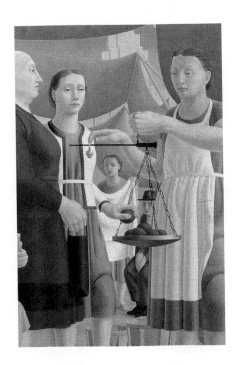

Activities

Work in small groups on the following activities.

1. Brainstorm a list of ten people you feel have had a leading role in changing the world. Rank these change-makers from 1 to 10, with 1 being the person you feel has effected the greatest changes. Prepare a picture gallery of change-makers with an illustration and caption for each person. Present your gallery to the class and explain your choices and rankings.

2. Think of a tradition in your circle of friends, family, school, or community that has changed, or is threatening to change. What is causing the change? Who favors it? Who opposes it? What, if anything, will this change mean to you?

3. Make a time line indicating major changes in clothing fashions during the past five decades in the U.S. Explain how different social and cultural influences affected these changes.

Independent and Group Projects

Poem

Power Poem Using a variety of computer fonts or display type, reproduce words, phrases, and lines from each of the selections in this unit that say something about power. Arrange the lines to create a "found poem" about power.

Game

Are You Game? Getting ideas from *Julius Caesar* and the two stories from this unit, think of a computer game that could be titled *Power Plays.* Identify the first and last levels of the game. Write a description of this game and draw an illustration that could appear on the game's box.

Discussion

The Cost of Winning In a group of five, plan a TV talk show, with one student playing the host and the others playing Julius Caesar, Mark Antony, a representative of the Balek family, and Pahom. The topic of the show is power—its advantages and disadvantages. Devise three questions to use as the basis for this group discussion. Put on your talk show for the class.

Media

Power Surge Work with a partner to analyze current TV programs, magazines, and movies, including the ads, noting their portrayal of power. Consider questions such as these: With what is power equated? Is power used or misused? Is power generally equated with a particular sex, social class, or personal quality? Analyze your information, make some generalizations about power as represented in the media, and give a report to the class.

Glossaries, Handbooks, and Indexes

Glossary of Vocabulary Words

a hat	o hot	ü rule	
ā age	ō open	ch child	ə { a in about
ä far	ô order, all	ng long	e in taken
e let	oi oil	sh she	i in pencil
ē equal	ou out	th thin	o in lemon
ė term	u cup	ᴛʜ then	u in circus
i it	u̇ put	zh measure	
ī ice			

A

abscess (ab′ses), *n.* pus resulting from infected tissues of the body.

abyss (ə bis′), *n.* bottomless or very great depth.

acquittal (ə kwit′l), *n.* discharge; release.

adlib (ad lib′), *v.* make up words or music as one goes along; improvise.

advertent (əd vėrt′nt), *adj.* alert.

advocate (ad′və kāt), *v.* support.

albeit (ôl bē′it), *conj.* even though; although.

aloft (ə lôft′), *adj.* in the air.

aloof (ə lüf′), *adj.* unsympathetic; reserved.

amulet (am′yə lit), *n.* a small object worn as a magic charm against evil, disease, or bad luck.

anguish (ang′gwish) *n.* severe physical pain or mental suffering.

antimacassar (an′ti mə kas′ər), *n.* a small covering to protect the back or arms of a chair, sofa, etc., against soiling.

aperture (ap′ər chər), *n.* an opening; hole.

aphorism (af′ə riz′əm), *n.* brief statement expressing a truth.

aplomb (ə plom′), *n.* assurance; poise.

appalled (ə pôld′), *adj.* shocked; dismayed.

apprehension (ap′ri hen′shən), *n.* fear.

arable (ar′ə bəl), *adj.* suitable for producing crops which require plowing and tillage.

arpeggio (är pej′ē ō), *n.* the sounding of the individual notes of a chord.

assail (ə sāl′), *v.* bother; trouble.

atrophy (at′rə fē), *v.* waste away.

attribute (ə trib′yüt), *v.* think of as caused by.

audaciously (ô dā′shəs lē), *adv.* courageously taking risks; daringly.

audible (ô′də bəl), *adj.* that can be heard; loud enough to be heard.

austere (ô stir′), *adj.* stern in manner or appearance.

avaricious (av′ə rish′əs), *adj.* greedy for wealth.

B

balefully (bāl′fə lē), *adv.* destructively or threateningly.

barbaric (bär bar′ik), *adj.* not civilized; coarse.

belligerent (bə lij′ər ənt), *adj.* fond of fights.

bequeath (bi kwēᴛʜ′), *v.* give or leave (money or property) by a will.

bereaved (bi rēvd′), *adj.* deprived ruthlessly; robbed.

beseeching (bē sēch′ing), *adj.* asking earnestly; begging.

bestow (bi stō′), *v.* give (something) as a gift.

betoken (bi tō′kən), *v.* indicate.

bickering (bik′ər ing), *n.* petty, noisy quarreling.

bicultural (bī kul′chər əl), *adj.* having distinct cultures existing side by side.

bifocals (bī fō′kəlz), *n.* pair of glasses having two focuses.

bigot (big′ət), *n.* intolerant person.

bilaterally (bī lat′ər əl ē), *adv.* on two sides.

bilingual (bī ling′gwəl), *adj.* able to speak another language as well or almost as well as one's own.

blandly (bland′lē), *adv.* in a smoothly agreeable, polite manner.

blasphemy (blas′fə mē), *n.* abuse or contempt for God or sacred things.

blight (blīt), *n.* disease, or anything that causes destruction or ruin.

bootless (büt′lis), *adj.* in vain; useless.

brazenly (brā′zn lē), *adv.* boldly.

brooding (brü′ding), *adj.* worried.

C

calabash (kal′ə bash), *n.* a gourdlike fruit whose dried shell is used to make bottles, bowls, drums, pipes, and rattles.

candid (kan′did), *adj.* frank and sincere.

capricious (kə prish′əs), *adj.* changeable.

carnage (kär′nij), *n.* slaughter of a great number of people.

cascade (ka skād′), *v.* fall or pour.

castellated (kas′tl ā′tid), *adj.* built like a castle with turrets and battlements.

cataclysm (kat′ə kliz′əm), *n.* any violent change or upheaval.

censure (sen′shər), *v.* express disapproval of; blame.

chateau or **château** (sha tō′), *n.* a large country house.

chauvinist (shō′və nist), *n.* person excessively enthusiastic about his or her sex, race, or group.

chronic (kron′ik), *adj.* never stopping.

commodious (kə mō′dē əs), *adj.* having plenty of room.

communal (kə myü′nl), *adj.* owned jointly by all.

compact (kom′pakt), *n.* 1 agreement or contract. 2 a small case containing face powder or rouge.

compensation (kom′pən sā′shən), *n.* something given to make up for a loss or injury.

complacent (kəm plā′snt), *adj.* self-satisfied.

composure (kəm pō′zhər), *n.* calmness; quietness.

comprehensible (kom′pri hen′sə bəl), *adj.* able to be understood.

confiscated (kon′fə skāt əd), *adj.* seized; taken.

conjecture (kən jek′chər), *v.* guess; admit without sufficient evidence.

conniving (kə nī′ving), *adj.* giving aid to wrongdoing by not telling of it or by helping it secretly.

consort (kən sôrt′), *v.* accompany.

contagious (kən tā′jəs), *adj.* spreading by direct or indirect contact; catching.

contemplate (kon′təm plāt). *v.* gaze at; think about.

contort (kən tôrt′), *v.* twist or bend out of shape.

contrition (kən trish′ən), *n.* guilt.

convivial (kən viv′ē əl), *adj.* sociable.

countenance (koun′tə nəns), *n.* face.

crag (krag), *n.* steep, rugged rock or cliff rising above others.

cropped (kropt), *adj.* cut short; clipped.

crucial (krü′shəl), *adj.* very important or decisive.

cubicle (kyü′bə kəl), *n.* a very small room or compartment.

D

daunt (dônt), *v.* overcome with fear; frighten.

dauntless (dônt′lis), *adj.* brave.

dawdle (dô′dl), *v.* waste time; loiter.

debauchery (di bô′chər ē), *n.* corruption.

decorum (di kôr′əm), *n.* proper behavior; good taste in conduct, speech, or dress.

defilement (di fīl′mənt), *n.* destruction of the purity or cleanness of (anything sacred); desecration.

deflect (di flekt′), *v.* bend or turn aside.

degrading (di grā′ding), *adj.* dishonorable.

dejectedly (di jek′tid lē), *adv.* sadly.

demeanor (di mē′nər), *n.* behavior; manner.

denizen (den′ə zən), *n.* inhabitant or occupant of a place or region.

deploy (di ploi′), *v.* spread out in a planned or strategic position.

despise (di spīz′), *v.* feel hatred or scorn for.

despot (des′pət), *n.* ruler having unlimited power.

devastate (dev′ə stāt′), *v.* make desolate; destroy.

devastation (dev′ə stā′shən), *n.* waste; destruction.

device (di vīs′), *n.* plan, scheme, or trick.

diagram (dī′ə gram), *n.* sketch showing an outline or general scheme of something with its various parts.

dilemma (də lem′ə), *n.* difficult choice.

disconsolate (dis kon′sə lit), *adj.* without hope; unhappy.

discord (dis′kôrd), *n.* disagreement of opinions and aims; dissension.

discordant (dis kôrd′nt), *adj.* not in harmony.

discourse (dis kôrs′), *v.* talk, converse.

disdain (dis dān′), *n.* scorn.

disparage (dis par′ij), *v.* belittle; discredit.

dispel (dis pel′), *v.* drive away.

disperse (dis pėrs′), *v.* go off in different directions.

dissembled (di sem′bəld), *adj.* hidden; disguised.

distortion (dis tôr′shən), *n.* twisting out of shape.

distraction (dis trak′shən), *n.* disturbance of thought.

diverge (də vėrj′), *v.* move or lie in different directions from the same point.

doggedly (dô′gid lē), *adv.* not giving up; stubbornly.

dolefully (dōl′fəl lē), *adv.* mournfully.

droll (drōl), *adj.* odd and amusing.

dubious (dü′bē əs), *adj.* filled with or being in doubt; uncertain.

duly (dü′lē), *adv.* rightly; suitably.

E

ecstatic (ek stat′ik), *adj.* feeling great joy.

edict (ē′dikt), *n.* decree or law proclaimed by a king or other ruler on his or her sole authority.

elapse (i laps′), *v.* slip away; pass.

elixir (i lik′sər), *n.* medicine with special curing powers.

emanate (em′ə nāt′), *v.* come forth; spread out.

embark (em bärk′), *v.* set out.

embellishment (em bel′ish mənt), *n.* decoration; adornment.

ember (em′bər), *n.* ashes in which there is still some fire.

en masse (en mas′), in a group; all together. *[French]*

enhance (en hans′), *v.* add to; heighten.

ensue (en sü′), *v.* follow.

entice (en tīs′), *v.* tempt; lure.

entranced (en transd′), *adj.* delighted; charmed.

entreatingly (en trēt′ing lē), *adv.* in a begging or praying manner.

eradicable (i rad′ə kə bəl), *adj.* that can be gotten rid of or destroyed.

essence (es′ns), *n.* that which makes a thing what it is; important feature or features.

euphemism (yü′fə miz′əm), *n.* use of a mild or indirect expression instead of a harsh, direct one.

expiation (ek′spē ā′shən), *n.* atonement.

exploitation (ek′sploi tā′shən), *n.* selfish or unfair use.

F

falsetto (fôl set′ō), *n.* an artificially high-pitched voice, especially in a man.

fawn (fôn), *v.* try to get favor or notice by slavish acts.

fiasco (fē as′kō), *n.* a complete or ridiculous failure; humiliating breakdown.

flagrant (flā′grənt), *adj.* glaringly offensive; outrageous.

flout (flout), *v.* treat with contempt or scorn.

fluently (flü′ənt lē), *adv.* speaking or writing easily and rapidly.

forcefully (fôrs′fəl lē), *adv.* powerfully.

frenzied (fren′zēd), *adj.* greatly excited; frantic.

friction (frik′shən), *n.* a rubbing of one object against another; a clash.

frigid (frij′id), *adj.* cold in feeling or manner.

funereal (fyü nir′ē əl), *adj.* gloomy.

furtive (fėr′tiv), *adj.* done quickly and with stealth to avoid being noticed; sly.

futile (fyü′tl), *adj.* not successful; useless.

G

galvanized (gal′və nīzd), *adj.* covered with a thin coating of zinc to prevent rust.

garrulity (gə rü′lə tē), *n.* wordiness.

glaze (glāz), *v.* become smooth, glassy, or glossy.

gratifying (grat′ə fī ing), *adj.* satisfying; pleasing.

grievance (grē′vəns), *n.* a cause for complaint.

grievous (grē′vəs), *adj.* causing great pain or suffering.

grimace (grə mās′, grim′is), *n.* a twisting of the face; ugly or funny smile.

guile (gīl), *n.* sly trick; cunning.

H

haphazard (hap′haz′ərd), *adj.* not planned; random.

hapless (hap′lis), *adj.* unlucky; unfortunate.

heed (hēd), *n.* careful attention.

homage (hom′ij), *n.* dutiful respect.

husbanded (huz′bənd əd), *adj.* managed carefully; saved.

hypocrisy (hi pok′rə sē), *n.* pretense.

I

ignoble (ig nō′bəl), *adj.* not of noble birth or position; without honor; humble.

imminent (im′ə nənt), *adj.* about to occur.

impale (im pāl′), *v.* pierce through with something pointed.

impel (im pel′), *v.* cause to move forward.

imperceptible (im′pər sep′tə bəl), *adj.* gradual.

imperiously (im pir′ē əs lē), *adv.* haughtily or arrogantly.

impersonate (im pėr′sə nāt), *v.* pretend to be.

imperturbably (im′pər tėr′bə blē), *adv.* calmly.

impiety (im pī′ə tē), *n.* lack of respect.

implicit (im plis′it), *adj.* meant, but not clearly expressed or distinctly stated; implied.

impotence (im′pə təns), *n.* helplessness.

impotent (im′pə tənt), *adj.* powerless; helpless.

improvise (im′prə vīz), *v.* make up on the spur of the moment.

impunity (im pyü′nə tē), *n.* freedom from injury, punishment, or other bad consequences.

incandescent (in′kən des′nt), *adj.* shining brightly; brilliant.

incredulous (in krej′ə ləs), *adj.* doubting; skeptical.

incur (in kėr′), *v.* bring on oneself.

indifferently (in dif′ər ənt lē), *adv.* in a manner that shows little interest.

indiscreet (in′dis krēt′), *adj.* not wise; foolish.

inexorable (in ek′sər ə bəl), *adj.* relentless, unyielding.

infamy (in′fə mē), *n.* a very bad reputation; public disgrace.

inimical (in im′ə kəl), *adj.* unfavorable.

initiative (i nish′ē ə tiv), *n.* active part in taking the first steps in any undertaking; lead.

insatiable (in sā′shə bəl), *adj.* that cannot be satisfied; greedy.

inscrutable (in skrü′tə bəl), *adj.* so mysterious or obscure that one cannot make out its meaning.

insidious (in sid′ē əs), *adj.* working secretly or subtly.

insignificant (in′sig nif′ə kənt), *adj.* unimportant; trivial.

insurrection (in′sə rek′shən), *n.* a rising against established authority; revolt.

inter (in tėr′), *v.* bury.

interminable (in tėr′mə nə bəl), *adj.* seemingly endless.

intimidate (in tim′ə dāt), *v.* 1 frighten. 2 influence or force by fear.

intolerant (in tol′ər ənt), *adj.* unwilling to let others do or believe as they want.

irrefutable (i ref′yə tə bəl), *adj.* undeniable.

irreproachable (ir′i prō′chə bəl), *adj.* free from blame; faultless.

J

jauntily (jôn′tē lē), *adv.* in an easy and lively way.

jeopardy (jep′ər dē), *n.* risk; danger.

jest (jest), *n.* something said to cause laughter; joke.

K

kittled (kit′ld), *adj.* born.

L

labyrinth (lab′ə rinth′), *n.* a confusing, complicated passage or arrangement.

legacy (leg′ə sē), *n.* something handed down in a will.

lethargy (leth′ər jē), *n.* lack of energy; inactivity.

liaison (lē′ā zon′), *n.* connection between military units, branches of a service, etc., to secure proper cooperation.

lineage (lin′ē ij), *n.* descent in a direct line from a common ancestor.

listlessly (list′lis lē), *adv.* seemingly too tired to care about anything.

loathsome (lōтн′səm), *adj.* disgusting.

loiter (loi′tər), *v.* linger idly or aimlessly.

lull (lul), *n.* period of less noise or violence; brief calm.

luminous (lü′mə nəs) *adj.* full of light; shining.

lustrous (lus′trəs), *adj.* shining; glossy.

M

malicious (mə lish′əs), *adj.* showing ill will; spiteful.

maligned (mä līnd′), *adj.* spoken against; slandered.

marrow (mar′ō), *n.* the inmost or essential part.

meager (mē′gər), *adj.* scanty.

meet (mēt), *adj.* fitting; appropriate.

mêlée (mā′lā), *n.* confused fight.

menace (men′is), *n.* threat.

mesmerizing (mez′mə rī′zing), *adj.* hypnotic.

meticulous (mə tik′yə ləs), *adj.* extremely or excessively careful about small details.

mettle (met′l), *n.* spirit, courage.

millet (mil′it), *n.* a cereal grass cultivated as a food grain.

mimic (mim′ik), *v.* make fun of by imitating.

minutely (mī nüt′lē), *adv.* in a small way or detailed manner.

misconstrue (mis′kən strü′), *v.* misunderstand; misinterpret.

monopoly (mə nop′ə lē), *n.* the exclusive possession or control of something.

motif (mō tēf′), *n.* a distinctive figure or pattern in a design, painting, etc.

muse (myüz), *v.* say thoughtfully.

muster (mus′tər), *v.* gather together.

mute (myüt), *adj.* silent.

mutilated (myü′tl āt′əd), *adj.* cut, torn, or broken off a limb or other important part of; maimed.

myriad (mir′ē əd), *n.* a great number.

N

naïve (nä ēv′), *adj.* simple in nature; like a child.

naught (nôt), *n.* nothing.

nonentity (non en′tə tē), *n.* a person or thing of little or no importance.

O

odious (ō′dē əs), *adj.* hateful; offensive.

officious (ə fish′əs), *adj.* too ready to offer services.

onslaught (ôn′slôt′), *n.* a vigorous attack.

oppressive (ə pres′iv), *adj.* hard to bear.

P

pandemonium (pan′də mō′nē əm), *n.* wild disorder.

passé (pa sā′), *adj.* old, stale. *[French]*

peevishness (pē′vish nəs), *n.* irritability; crossness.

perfunctorily (pər fungk′tər ə lē), *adv.* mechanically; indifferently.

peril (per′əl), *n.* danger.

perilous (per′ə ləs), *adj.* dangerous.

permeated (pėr′mē āt əd), *adj.* spread throughout; filled with.

peruse (pə rüz′), *v.* read, especially thoroughly and carefully.

perversity (pər vėr′sə tē), *n.* quality of being contrary and willful.

pigment (pig′mənt), *n.* natural substance that colors skin tissue.

piqued (pēkd), *adj.* aroused; stirred up.

plausible (plô′zə bəl), *adj.* appearing true, reasonable, or fair.

plight (plīt), *n.* 1 condition or situation, usually bad. 2 a solemn promise or pledge.

pluck (pluk), *v.* pull or tug.

poached (pōchd), *adj.* cooked by simmering in a liquid.

poppy (pop′ē), *n.* a bright red.

portent (pôr′tent), *n.* sign.

precarious (pri ker′ē əs), *adj.* not safe or secure; uncertain.

precedence (pres′ə dəns), *n.* higher position or rank; great importance.

preoccupation (prē ok′yə pā′shən), *n.* thing that absorbs or engrosses.

prerogative (pri rog′ə tiv), *n.* right or privilege that nobody else has.

presage (pri sāj′), *v.* predict.

pressurized (presh′ə rīzd′), *adj.* having the atmospheric pressure inside (the cabin of an aircraft) kept at a normal level in spite of the altitude.

presumptuous (pri zump′chü əs), *adj.* acting without permission or right; bold.

pretext (prē′tekst), *n.* a false reason concealing the real reason; misleading excuse.

primal (prī′məl), *adj.* fundamental.

prodigious (prə dij′əs), *adj.* very great; huge.

prodigy (prod′ə jē), *n.* person endowed with amazing brilliance or talent, especially a remarkably talented child.

profoundly (prə found′lē), *adv.* going more deeply than what is easily understood.

proletarian (prō′lə ter′ē ən), *n.* someone belonging to the proletariat, the lowest class in economic and social status, including all unskilled laborers.

promontory (prom′ən tôr′ē), *n.* high point of land extending from the coast.

propriety (prə prī′ə tē), *n.* proper behavior.

prosaic (prō zā′ik), *adj.* ordinary; not exciting.

prostrate (pros′trāt), *adj.* lying flat with face downward.

proverbial (prə vėr′bē əl), *adj.* relating to proverbs; commonly spoken of.

proviso (prə vī′zō), *n.* any provision or stipulation.

prowess (prou′is), *n.* bravery; skill.

puissant (pyü′ə sənt), *adj.* powerful.

pungent (pun′jənt), *adj.* sharply affecting the organs of taste and smell.

Q

quagmire (kwag′mīr′), *n.* soft, muddy ground.

quarry (kwôr′ē), *n.* 1 animal chased in a hunt; prey. 2 place where stone, slate, etc., is dug, cut, or blasted out for use in building.

R

rampant (ram′pənt), *adj.* growing without any limits.

rapport (ra pôr′, ra pôrt′), *n.* agreement; connection.

rebuke (ri byük′), *v.* express disapproval of.

recount (ri kount′), *v.* tell in detail.

redundant (ri dun′dənt), *adj.* not needed; extra.

refracted (ri frak′təd), *adj.* bent (a ray of light, waves, etc.) from a straight course.

rejuvenate (ri jü′və nāt), *v.* make young or vigorous again; renew.

rent (rent), *n.* tear; torn place.

reprimand (rep′rə mand), *v.* criticize.

reproach (ri prōch′), *n.* blame or disapproval.

resplendent (ri splen′dənt), *adj.* very bright; splendid.

retaliation (ri tal′ē ā′shən), *n.* paying back wrong.

reticence (ret′ə sens), *n.* tendency to be silent or say little.

revelry (rev′əl rē), *n.* boisterous merrymaking or festivity.

reverberate (ri vėr′bər āt′), *v.* echo back.

reverie (rev′ər ē), *n.* dreamy thoughts, especially of pleasant things.

ribald (rib′əld), *adj.* offensive in speech; obscene.

rite (rīt), *n.* solemn ceremony.

ritualist (rich′ü ə list), *n.* person who practices or advocates observance of the form or system of rites, or ceremonies.

rock crystal, a colorless, transparent variety of quartz, often used for jewelry, ornaments, etc.

rook (rùk), *n.* a bird that resembles the crow.

rout (rout), *n.* a complete defeat.

rubicund (rü′bə kund), *adj.* reddish; ruddy.

rudiment (rü′də mənt), *n.* part to be learned first; beginning.

rummage (rum′ij), *v.* search in a disorderly way.

rune (rün), *n.* inscription or letter.

ruse (rüz), *n.* scheme or device to mislead others; trick.

S

sacrilege (sak′rə lij), *n.* an intentional injury or disrespectful treatment of anyone or anything sacred.

sadist (sā′dist, sad′ist), *n.* person displaying cruel tendencies.

sagacious (sə gā′shəs), *adj.* wise in a keen, practical way; shrewd.

scribe (skrīb), *n.* writer; author.

scrutinize (skrüt′n īz), *v.* examine closely.

serenity (sə ren′ə tē), *n.* quiet; calmness.

servile (sėr′vəl), *adj.* like that of a slave.

sexton (sek′stən), *n.* person who takes care of a church building.

shard (shärd), *n.* broken piece.

sheepishly (shē′pish lē), *adv.* awkwardly bashful or embarrassed.

sheer (shir), *adj.* unmixed with anything else; complete.

shillelagh (shə lā′lē), *n.* a club used in fights.

shoal (shōl), *n.* a large number.

shrewd (shrüd), *adj.* clever; keen.

shrine (shrīn), *n.* place of worship.

simulated (sim′yə lāt əd), *adj.* fake; pretend.

skeptical (skep′tə kəl), *adj.* doubtful.

sordid (sôr′did), *adj.* filthy, contemptible.

soulful (sōl′fəl), *adj.* full of feeling; deeply emotional or passionate.

sovereignty (sov′rən tē), *n.* supreme power or authority.

spinster (spin′stər), *n.* an unmarried woman, especially an older woman.

sporadic (spə rad′ik), *adj.* appearing or happening at intervals in time; occasional.

spur (spėr), *n.* 1 ridge sticking out from or smaller than the main body of a mountain or mountain range. 2 a spiked instrument worn on a rider's heel for urging a horse on.

staidness (stād′nes), *n.* the condition of having a settled, quiet character.

statistic (stə tis′tik), *n.* a numerical fact about people, the weather, business conditions, etc., in order to show their significance.

steward (stü′ərd), *n.* a person employed on a ship to look after passengers.

stifle (stī′fəl), *v.* keep back; stop.

subdued (səb düd′), *adj.* suppressed; toned down.

subside (səb sīd′), *v.* die down.

subversive (səb vėr′siv), *adj.* tending to overthrow; causing ruin.

superficial (sü′pər fish′əl), *adj.* concerned with or understanding only what is on the surface; shallow.

supplication (sup′lə kā′shən), *n.* a humble and earnest prayer.

surplice (sėr′plis), *n.* a broad-sleeved, white gown or vestment worn by members of the clergy and choir singers.

surreptitiously (sėr′əp tish′əs lē), *adv.* secretly, deceptively.

T

taciturn (tas′ə tėrn′), *adj.* silent.

taint (tānt), *n.* a stain or spot.

talisman (tal′is mən, tal′iz mən), *n.* stone, ring, etc., engraved with figures or characters supposed to have magic power; charm.

tantamount (tan′tə mount), *adj.* equal; equivalent.

tempered (tem′pərd), *adj.* softened or moderated.

tenaciously (ti nā′shəs lē), *adv.* stubbornly.

tentative (ten′tə tiv), *adj.* hesitating.

tepid (tep′id), *adj.* lukewarm.

theology (thē ol′ə jē), *n.* study of religion and religious beliefs.

throng (thrông), *n.* a crowd; multitude.

translucent (tran slü′snt), *adj.* letting light through without being transparent.

traumatized (trô′mə tīzd), *adj.* undergoing great shock.

tribulation (trib′yə lā′shən), *n.* great trouble; severe trial.

tumultuous (tü mul′chü əs), *adj.* very noisy or disorderly.

turbot (tėr′bət, tėr′bō), *n.* a European fish, much valued as food.

turbulent (tėr′byə lənt), *adj.* filled with commotion; violent.

U

ulterior (ul tir′ē ər), *adj.* beyond what is seen or expressed; hidden.

unassailable (un ə sāl′ə bəl), *adj.* not able to be attacked (with violent blows, hostile words, arguments, or abuse).

uncanny (un kan′ē), *adj.* something that is strange and mysterious.

Glossary of Vocabulary Words   **809**

unequivocally (un/i kwiv/ə kəl ē), *adv.* clearly.

unfledged (un flejd/), *adj.* inexperienced.

unmolested (un mə lest/əd), *adj.* undisturbed.

unscathed (un skāᴛHd/), *adj.* not harmed.

unshakable (un shā/kə bl), *adj.* undisturbed; not able to be upset.

usurp (yü zėrp/), *v.* seize by force.

usury (yü/zhər ē), *n.* the lending of money at an unusually high or unlawful rate of interest.

V

virile (vir/əl), *adj.* vigorous; forceful.

visceral (vis/ər əl), *adj.* arising from instinct or strong feelings; not intellectual or rational.

viscous (vis/kəs), *adj.* thick like heavy syrup; sticky.

vixen (vik/sən), *n.* a female fox.

vociferousness (vō sif/ər əs nəs), *n.* noisiness; shouting.

W

waft (waft), *n.* breath or puff of air, wind, scent, etc.

waveringly (wā/vər ing lē), *adv.* unsteadily.

wily (wī/lē), *adj.* crafty; sly.

wisteria (wi ster/ē ə), *n.* a climbing shrub of the pea family with large drooping clusters of purple, blue, or white flowers.

wistful (wist/fəl), *adj.* longing; yearning.

wizened (wiz/nd), *adj.* dried up; withered.

wont (wunt), *adj.* accustomed.

wrath (rath), *n.* very great anger; rage.

Z

zeal (zēl), *n.* eager desire or effort; earnest enthusiasm.

Glossary of Literary Terms

Words in small capital letters within entries refer to other entries in the Glossary of Literary Terms.

A

alliteration (ə lit′ə rā′shən), the REPETITION of consonant sounds at the beginnings of words or within words, particularly in accented syllables. It can be used to reinforce meaning, unify thought, or create a musical effect. "The setting sun silhouettes a sailboat" is an example of alliteration.

allusion (ə lü′zhən), a brief reference to a person, event, or place, real or fictitious, or to a work of art. A writer who describes a shortage or something that is missing with the words "The cupboard is bare" is alluding to the nursery rhyme "Old Mother Hubbard."

analogy (ə nal′ə jē), a literal comparison made between two items, situations, or ideas that are somewhat alike but unlike in most respects. Frequently an unfamiliar or complex object or idea will be compared to a familiar or simpler one in order to explain the first.

antagonist (an tag′ə nist), a character in a story or play who opposes the chief character, or PROTAGONIST.

assonance (as′n əns), the REPETITION of similar vowel sounds followed by different consonant sounds in stressed syllables or words. It is sometimes used instead of RHYME. *Made* and *played* are examples of rhyme; *made* and *pale* are examples of assonance.

autobiography, story of all or part of a person's life written by the person who lived it. *Kaffir Boy* (page 456) is an autobiography.

B

ballad, a NARRATIVE passed on in the oral tradition. It often makes use of REPETITION and DIALOGUE.

biography, an account of a person's life written by someone else.

blank verse, unrhymed verse written in IAMBIC PENTAMETER—that is, ten-syllable lines with five unstressed syllables alternating with five stressed syllables. The following blank-verse lines are spoken by Julius Caesar. Note that the stressed syllables are marked ′ and the unstressed syllables are marked ˘.

Have I in conquest stretched mine arm so far,
To be afeard to tell graybeards the truth?

See also page 675.

C

characterization, the methods authors use to acquaint a reader with their characters. We may learn about characters through their DIALOGUE and actions, or through what others say about them.

climax, the decisive point in a story or play when the central problem of the PLOT must be resolved in one way or another. Not every story or play has a dramatic climax. Sometimes a character may simply resolve a problem in his or her mind. At times there is no resolution of the plot; the climax then comes when a character realizes that a resolution is impossible.

comedy, a play written primarily to amuse the audience. In addition to arousing laughter, comic writing often appeals to the intellect.

conflict, struggle between two opposing forces. The four basic kinds of conflict are: (1) a person against another person; (2) a person against nature; (3) a person against society; and (4) two elements within a person struggling for mastery. More than one kind of conflict can be present in a work. In *Red Azalea,* page 145, Anchee Min experiences several kinds of conflict: struggling within herself, with Secretary Chain, and with the principles of the Cultural Revolution.

connotation, the emotional associations surrounding a word or phrase, as opposed to its literal meaning or DENOTATION. Some connotations are fairly universal, others quite personal.
See also page 492.

consonance (kon′sə nəns), the repetition of similar or identical consonant sounds that are preceded by different vowel sounds. The *m* sound is repeated in the following lines.

> The moan of doves in immemorial elms,
> And murmuring of innumerable bees.
> Alfred, Lord Tennyson

couplet, a pair of rhyming lines with the same METER.

D

denotation, the strict, literal meaning of a word.
See also CONNOTATION.

dialect, a form of speech that is characteristic of a particular region or class, differing from the standard language in pronunciation, vocabulary, and grammatical form. The mother in "Two Kinds" (page 19) speaks in dialect.

dialogue, conversation between two or more people in a literary work. Dialogue can help develop the CHARACTERIZATION of those speaking and those spoken about, create MOOD, advance PLOT, and develop THEME.

diction, writers' choices of words, determined by their subject, audience, and desired effect. Diction may be casual or formal, simple or complex, old-fashioned or modern.

dimeter (dim′ə tər), line of VERSE having two metrical feet.

drama, a literary genre in verse or prose, written to be acted, that tells a story through the speech and actions of the characters; a play. *Julius Caesar* (page 679) is an example of drama.
See also pages 184–185.

E

end rhyme, the rhyming of words at the ends of lines of POETRY.
See also INTERNAL RHYME *and* RHYME.

essay, a brief prose composition that presents a personal viewpoint. "Woman from America" (page 632) is an essay that expresses the views of Bessie Head.

exposition, the beginning of a work of FICTION, particularly a play, in which the author sets the atmosphere and TONE, explains the SETTING, introduces the characters, and provides the reader with any other information needed to understand the PLOT.

extended metaphor, a figure of speech that compares two things throughout an entire work or a great part of it. It is more common in poetry than in prose.
See also METAPHOR.

F

fable, a brief TALE, in which the characters often are animals, told to point out a MORAL truth. "The Fox and the Woodcutter" (page 287) is one of many fables by Aesop.

falling action, the RESOLUTION of a dramatic PLOT, which takes place after the CLIMAX.

fantasy/science fiction. Both fantasy and science fiction are literary works set wholly or partly in an unreal world. Often, at least one character is unlike a human being. Frequently the PLOT concerns events that cannot be explained by current science. For example, Poe's classic story, "The Masque of the Red Death (page 95)," is a fantasy.

farce, comedy that involves improbable situations, exaggerated characters, and slapstick action. Farce relies on fast pacing, exaggeration, and physical action, and often includes mistaken identity and deception. *The Flying Doctor* by Molière (page 270) is a farce.

fiction, a type of literature drawn from the imagination of the author, that tells about imaginary people and events. NOVELS, SHORT STORIES, and many plays are fiction.

figurative language, language used in a nonliteral way to express a suitable relationship between essentially unlike things. SIMILE and METAPHOR are both examples of figurative language.

flashback, interruption of a NARRATIVE to show events that happened before that particular point in time.

folk literature, a type of literature that has been passed orally from generation to generation and written down only after centuries. The authors of folk literature, such as epics, LEGENDS, and the like, are unknown.

foot, in VERSE, a group of syllables usually consisting of one accented syllable and all unaccented syllables associated with it, as in the following lines by Robert Herrick. (Note that each foot is shown within slanted lines.)

> Then be/not coy,/but use/your time,/
> And, while/ye may,/go marry;/

foreshadowing, a hint given to the reader of what is to come.

free verse, a type of POETRY that differs from conventional VERSE in being free from a fixed pattern of METER and RHYME, but that uses RHYTHM and other devices.

G

genre (zhän rə), a form or type of literary work. For example, the NOVEL, SHORT STORY, DRAMA, and poem are all genres.

H

haiku (hī′kü), a brief poem of three lines that often consist of five syllables, seven syllables, and five syllables, respectively. Haiku often describe scenes in nature. Haiku poems appear on page 616.

hero, the central character in a NOVEL, SHORT STORY, DRAMA, or other work of FICTION. When the central character is a female, she is often called a heroine. The term *hero,* however, can be used to refer to both males and females.

historical fiction, fiction set in a time other than that in which it is written. The excerpt from *The Once and Future King* (page 365) is historical fiction based on Arthurian LEGEND.

hyperbole (hī pėr′bə lē), a figure of speech involving great exaggeration. The effect may be satiric or comic.

I

iambic pentameter, a line consisting of five two-syllable metrical feet—that is, five unstressed syllables alternating with five stressed syllables.
See also BLANK VERSE.

idiom, an expression whose meaning cannot be understood from the ordinary meaning of the words in it. For example, to "hold your tongue" or to "be all ears" are idioms.

imagery, sensory details that provide vividness in a literary work and tend to arouse emotions or feelings in a reader.

inference, a reasonable conclusion about the behavior of a character or the meaning of an event drawn from the limited information presented by the author.

internal rhyme, rhyming words or accented syllables within a line which may or may not have a rhyme at the end of the line as well.

inversion, reversal of the usual order of the parts of a sentence, primarily for emphasis or to achieve a certain RHYTHM or RHYME. Inversion is sometimes called *anastrophe* (ə nas′trə fē). The following line from *Julius Caesar* illustrates inversion:

> Go you down that way towards the Capitol.

irony, the term used to describe a contrast between what is expected, or what appears to be, and what really is. In *verbal irony,* the actual meaning of a statement is different from (often the opposite of) what the statement literally says. *Irony of situation* refers to an occurrence that is contrary to what is expected. *Dramatic irony* refers to a situation in which events or facts not known to a character on stage or in a fictional work are known to the audience or reader.

L

legend, a story handed down from the past, often associated with some period in the history of a people. A legend differs from a MYTH in having some historical truth and often less of the supernatural. Malory's *Le Morte d'Arthur* and other Arthurian TALES are based on legends of King Arthur and the Knights of the Round Table.
See also page 337.

Glossary of Literary Terms   **813**

light verse, short poems written chiefly to amuse or entertain. "One Perfect Rose" (page 503) is an example of light verse.

lyric, a poem, usually short, that expresses some basic emotion or state of mind. A lyric usually creates a single impression and is highly personal. It may be rhymed or unrhymed. "If You'll Only Go to Sleep" (page 562) is a lyric.

M

metaphor (met′ə fôr), a figure of speech that involves an implied comparison between two different things. "His eyes are dark pools" is a metaphor.

meter, the pattern of stressed and unstressed syllables in POETRY.

mood, the overall atmosphere or prevailing feeling within a work of art. Words such as *peaceful, gloomy, mysterious,* and *expectant* can be used to describe mood.

moral, the lesson or teaching in a FABLE or story.

motivation, the process of presenting a convincing cause for the actions of a character in a dramatic or fictional work in order to justify those actions. Motivation usually involves a combination of external events and the character's personality traits. The mother's actions in "Tuesday Siesta" (page 510) are motivated by her love for her son and her desire to see him properly buried.

mystery, a work of fiction that contains a puzzling problem or an event not explained until the end, so as to keep the reader in suspense.

myth, a traditional story connected with the religion or beliefs of a people, usually attempting to account for something in nature. In ancient Greek myths, for example, lightning was depicted as thunderbolts cast down from Mount Olympus by the god Zeus. A myth has less historical background than a LEGEND.

N

narrative, a story or an account of an event or a series of events. A narrative may be true or fictional.

narrator, the teller of a story. The narrator may be a character in the story or someone outside the story.
See also POINT OF VIEW.

nonfiction, literature about real people and events, rather than imaginary ones. Nonfiction includes history, AUTOBIOGRAPHY, BIOGRAPHY, ESSAY, and article.
See also pages 452–453.

novel, a long work of NARRATIVE prose FICTION dealing with characters, situations, and settings that imitate those of real life. A novelette is a short novel. A similar type of work, the novella, is longer than a short story but not as long as a novel.

O

onomatopoeia (on′ə mä′tə pē′ə), a word or words used in such a way that the sound imitates the sound of the thing described. Words such as *crack, gurgle,* and *swoosh* are onomatopoetic. The following lines from "William and Helen" by Sir Walter Scott illustrate onomatopoeia:

> Tramp! tramp! along the land they rode,
> Splash! Splash! along the sea.

P

parable, a brief fictional work that concretely illustrates an abstract idea or teaches some lesson or truth. It differs from a FABLE in that the characters in it are generally people rather than animals. "How Much Land Does a Man Need?" (page 775) can be considered a parable.

paradox, a statement, person, or situation that seems at first to be self-contradictory but that has a valid meaning. In *Antigone,* Teiresias, the blind seer, is a paradox.

pentameter (pen tam′ə tər), a metrical line of five feet.
See also IAMBIC PENTAMETER.

persona (pėr sō′nə), the mask or voice of the author or the author's creation in a particular work.
See also NARRATOR *and* POINT OF VIEW.

personification (pėr son′ə fə kā′shən), the representation of abstractions, ideas, or inanimate objects as living things or as human beings by endowing them with human qualities. In "Sunday Morning" (page 598) , the sun is described as "naked" and the sea as a "green monster." Personification is one kind of FIGURATIVE LANGUAGE.

play *See* DRAMA.

plot, a series of happenings in a literary work. The word is used to refer to the action as it is organized around a CONFLICT and builds through complication to a CLIMAX followed by the RESOLUTION. A plot diagram appears on page 65.

poetry, a literary GENRE that creates an emotional response by the imaginative use of words patterned to produce a desired effect through RHYTHM, sound, and meaning. Poetry may be rhymed or unrhymed. Among the many forms of poetry are the LYRIC, SONNET, and BALLAD. Most of the selections in Unit 5 are poems.

point of view, the relation between the teller of the story and the characters in it. The teller, or NARRATOR, may be a character in the story, in which case it is told from the *first-person* point of view. A writer who describes, in the *third person,* the thoughts and actions of any or all of the characters as the need arises is said to use the *omniscient* (om nish′ənt) point of view. A writer who, in the third person, follows along with one character and tends to view events from that character's perspective is said to use a *limited omniscient* point of view. An author who describes only what can be seen, like a newspaper reporter, is said to use the *dramatic* point of view.
    See also NARRATOR *and* PERSONA.

prologue, section that precedes the main body of a work and serves as an introduction.

protagonist (prō tag′ə nist), the leading character in a literary work.

proverb, a brief, traditional saying that contains popular wisdom. An Ashanti proverb states, "No one tests the depth of a river with both feet."

psalm, (säm, sälm), a song or poem in praise of God. The term is most often applied to the hymns in the Book of Psalms of the Bible.

pun, a play on words; a humorous use of a word where it can have different meanings, or of two or more words with the same or nearly the same sound but different meanings. In the opening scene of *Julius Caesar,* a cobbler puns on words such as *sole* and *soul.*

Q

quatrain (kwôt′rān), verse STANZA of four lines. This stanza may take many forms, according to line lengths and rhyme patterns.

R

realism, a way of representing life that emphasizes ordinary people in everyday experiences.

repetition, a poetic device in which a sound, word, or phrase is repeated for emphasis or effect.

resolution (rez′ə lü′shən), the part of a PLOT following the CLIMAX in which the complications of the plot are resolved or settled.

rhyme, exact repetition of sounds in at least the final accented syllables of two or more words. For example, William Blake wrote in "A Poison Tree" (page 288):
> I was angry with my *friend;/*I told my wrath, my wrath did *end.*

rhyme scheme, any pattern of rhyme in a STANZA.

rhythm (riᴛʜ′əm), the arrangement of stressed and unstressed sounds in speech and writing. Rhythm in poetry may be regular or irregular.

rising action, the part of a dramatic plot that leads up to the CLIMAX. In rising action, the complication caused by the CONFLICT of opposing forces is developed.

romance, a long NARRATIVE in poetry or prose that originated in the medieval period. Its main elements are adventure, love, and magic. There are elements of the romance in the LEGENDS of Arthur.

romanticism, a way of representing life that, unlike REALISM, tends to portray the uncommon. The material selected often deals with extraordinary people in unusual SETTINGS having unusual experiences. In romantic literature there often is a stress on past times and an emphasis on nature.

S

satire, a technique in writing that employs wit to ridicule a subject, usually some social institution or human weakness, with the purpose of pointing out problems in society or inspiring reform. In "The Censors" (page 30), Luisa Valenzuela satirizes both government censorship and people who succumb to it.

scansion (skan′shən), the marking off of lines of poetry into feet.

> *See also* RHYTHM.

science fiction *See* FANTASY.

setting, the time (both time of day or season and period in history) and place in which the action of a NARRATIVE occurs. The setting may be suggested through DIALOGUE and action, or it may be described by the narrator or one of the other characters. Setting contributes strongly to the MOOD or atmosphere and plausibility of a work. For example, the heat and poverty of the setting of "Tuesday Siesta" (page 510) contribute to a mood of oppressiveness and futility.

short story, a prose NARRATIVE that is shorter than a novel and that generally describes just one event or a tightly constructed series of events. Although brief, a short story must have a beginning, a middle, and an end.

> *See also pages 2–3.*

simile (sim′ə lē), a figure of speech involving a comparison using a word such as *like* or *as:* "Her hair looked like spun gold."

slant rhyme, rhyme in which the vowel sounds are not quite identical, as in these lines: Gather friends and gather *foods.* Count your blessings, share your *goods.*

soliloquy (sə lil′ə kwē), a dramatic convention that allows a CHARACTER alone on stage to speak his or her thoughts aloud. If someone else is on stage but cannot hear the character's words, the speech becomes an *aside.*

sonnet, a LYRIC poem with a traditional form of fourteen IAMBIC PENTAMETER lines and one of a variety of RHYME SCHEMES.

sound devices, the choice and arrangement of words to please the ear and suit meaning. RHYME, RHYTHM, ASSONANCE, ONOMATOPOEIA, and ALLITERATION are examples of sound devices.

speaker, the imaginary voice a poet chooses to "tell" a poem. This "I," who presents information in the first person, is not necessarily the poet.

speech, a literary composition written to be given as a public talk. A speech may be formal or informal in style, and the topic usually depends on the intended audience. The Nobel speeches of Albert Camus and Elie Wiesel appear on pages 525–529.

stage directions, directions given by the author of a play to indicate the action, costumes, SETTING, arrangement of the stage, and other instructions to the actors and director of the DRAMA. Stage directions are usually written in italics. For example, in *Twelve Angry Men* (page 228), we are introduced to the jury room, which is *a large, bare, unpleasant-looking room* full of men *who are ill at ease.*

stanza, a group of lines that are set off and form a division in a poem.

stereotype (ster′ē ə tīp′), a conventional character, PLOT, or SETTING that possesses little or no individuality or complexity. Inspector Moronoff in "The Chameleon" (page 283) is a stereotype of a politician who acts according to his own best interests.

style, the distinctive handling of language by an author. It is part of an author's special way of choosing words, shaping sentences, and expressing thoughts.

suspense, the methods an author uses to maintain readers' interest, and the resulting MOOD of anxious uncertainty in many interesting stories. In her excerpt from *An American Childhood* (page 475), Annie Dillard builds suspense as she describes a chase.

symbol, a person, place, event, or object that has meaning in itself but also suggests other meanings as well. The flag, for example, is a symbol for patriotism.

T

tale, a spoken or written NARRATIVE, usually less complicated than a SHORT STORY.

theme, an underlying meaning of a literary work. A single work may have several themes. A theme may be directly stated but more often is implied.

tone, an author's attitude toward the subject of his or her literary work and toward the reader.

tragedy, dramatic or narrative writing in which the main character suffers disaster after a serious and significant struggle but faces his or her downfall in such a way as to attain heroic stature. The play *Julius Caesar* is considered a tragedy because of the fate that befalls the overly ambitious Caesar.

trimeter (trim′ə tər), line of VERSE having three metrical feet.

V

verse, in its most general sense, a synonym for poetry. Verse also may be used to refer to poetry carefully composed as to RHYTHM and RHYME SCHEME, but of inferior literary value.

Language and Grammar Handbook

Are you sometimes confused when your teacher returns papers with comments such as, "Incorrect subject-verb agreement," or "Unclear antecedent for your pronoun"? This Handbook will help you respond to such comments as you edit your writing and also provide answers to questions that arise about language during peer- and self-evaluation.

The Handbook is alphabetically arranged with each entry explaining a term or concept. For example, if you can't remember when to use *accept* and *except,* look up the entry **accept, except** and you'll find an explanation of the meaning of each word and a sentence (many from selections in this book) using each word.

accept, except The similarity in sound causes these words to be confused. *Accept* means "to take or receive; consent to receive; say yes to." It is always a verb. *Except* is most commonly used as a preposition meaning "but."

◆ It is with a profound sense of humility that I accept the honor you have chosen to bestow upon me.
    from "Nobel Acceptance Speech" by Elie Wiesel

◆ Everyone broke into a nervous laugh, except me.
    from *Kaffir Boy* by Mark Mathabane

active and passive voice A verb is said to be in the active voice when its subject is the doer of the action, and in the passive voice when its subject is the receiver of the action. A passive verb is a form of the verb *be* plus the past participle of the verb: *is* written, *had been* written, *will be* written, and so on.

ACTIVE: The teacher prepared the class for the exam.
PASSIVE: The class was prepared for the exam by the teacher.

Active verbs are more natural, direct, and forceful than passive verbs. Passive verbs are useful and effective, however, when the doer of the action is unknown, unimportant, or obvious, or when special emphasis is wanted for the receiver of the action:

◆ My name was constantly mentioned by the school authority. . . .
    from *Red Azalea* by Anchee Min

◆ The power of his eyes was considerably enhanced by their position. . . .
    from "An Astrologer's Day" by R. K. Narayan

adjective Adjectives are modifiers that describe nouns and pronouns and make their meaning more exact. Adjectives tell *what kind, which one,* or *how many.*

What kind:	*white* rose	*fast* car	*tall* building
Which one:	*this* book	*that* movie	*those* shirts
How many:	*three* days	*few* customers	*many* runners

See also **comparative forms of adjectives and adverbs.**

adverb Adverbs modify verbs, adjectives, or other adverbs. They tell *how, when,* or *where* about verbs.

How:	carefully	rapidly	bravely
When:	later	now	yesterday
Where:	there	near	outside

See also **comparative forms of adjectives and adverbs.**

affect, effect *Affect* is a verb. It is most frequently used to mean "to influence." *Effect* is mainly used as a noun meaning "result" or "consequence."

◆ The weather always affects my allergies.
◆ Your dirty tricks will have no more effect on me!
   from *Red Azalea* by Anchee Min

In formal English, *effect* is also used as a verb meaning "to bring about or make happen."

◆ Sir Modred . . . laid siege to the Tower, but despite his large army, siege engines, and guns, was unable to effect a breach.
   from "The Death of King Arthur" by Sir Thomas Malory

agreement

1. subject-verb agreement When the subject and verb of a sentence are both singular or both plural, they agree in number. This is called subject-verb agreement. Usually, singular verbs in the present tense end in *s.* Plural verbs do not have the *s* ending.

Michael drives. (singular subject; singular verb)
Kate and Michael drive. (plural subject; plural verb)

Pronouns generally follow the same rule. However, *I* and *you* always take plural verbs.

	Singular	Plural
1st person	I drive	we drive
2nd person	you drive	you drive
3rd person	he/she/it drives	they drive

Changes also occur with the verb *to be* in both the present and past tense.

Present Tense		Past Tense	
I am	we are	I was	we were
you are	you are	you were	you were
he/she/it is	they are	he/she/it was	they were

a. Most compound subjects joined by *and* or *both . . . and* are plural and are followed by plural verbs.

- A sofa and a chair were in front of the fireplace.

b. A compound subject joined by *or, either . . . or,* or *neither . . . nor* is followed by a verb that agrees in number with the closer subject.

- Neither Maria nor her relatives live there anymore.

- Neither her relatives nor Maria lives there anymore.

Problems arise when it isn't obvious what the subject is. The following rules should help you with some of the most troublesome situations.

c. Phrases or clauses coming between the subject and the verb do not affect the subject-verb agreement.

- A variety of trades and occupations was represented all along its way. . . .
  from "An Astrologer's Day" by R. K. Narayan

- . . . the freedom, maybe even the life, of both sender and receiver is in jeopardy.
  from "Nobel Acceptance Speech" by Albert Camus

d. Singular verbs are used with singular indefinite pronouns—*each, every, either, neither, anyone, anybody, one, everyone, everybody, someone, somebody, nobody, no one.*

- Neither of us was hungry.
  from "Rain Music" by Longhang Nguyen

e. Plural indefinite pronouns take plural verbs. They are *both, few, many,* and *several.*

◆ Both of these authors write science fiction.
  [s above "Both", v above "write"]

f. The indefinite pronouns *all, any, most, none,* and *some* can be either singular or plural depending on their meaning in a sentence.

<u>Singular</u>	<u>Plural</u>
All of the journey *was* exciting.	*All* of the travelers *were* hungry.
Most of the voyage *was* calm.	*Most* of the inns *were* full.
None of the menu *was* in English.	*None* of the chairs *were* empty.

g. The verb agrees with the subject regardless of the number of the predicate complement (after a form of a linking verb).

◆ The greatest problem was the mosquitoes.
  [s above "problem", v above "was"]

◆ Mosquitoes were the biggest problem.
  [s above "Mosquitoes", v above "were"]

h. Unusual word order does not affect agreement; the verb generally agrees with the subject, whether the subject follows or precedes it.

◆ . . . and there flows a ruddier light through the blood-colored panes . . . .
  [v above "flows", s above "light"]
  from "The Masque of the Red Death" by Edgar Allan Poe

In informal English, you may often hear sentences like "There's a book and some paper for you on my desk." *There's* is a contraction for "There is." Technically, since the subject is *a book and some paper,* the verb should be plural and the sentence should begin, "There are. . . ." Since this may sound strange, you may want to revise the sentence to something like "A book and some paper are on my desk." Be especially careful of sentences beginning with *There;* be sure the verb agrees with the subject.

◆ There are no secrets in here!
  [v above "are", s above "secrets"]
  from *Twelve Angry Men* by Reginald Rose

◆ There was a flutter of excitement, everybody reaching for plates. . . .
  [v above "was", s above "flutter"]
  from "Dip in the Pool" by Roald Dahl

2. Pronoun-antecedent agreement An *antecedent* is a word, clause, or phrase to which a pronoun refers. The pronoun agrees with its antecedent in person, number, and gender.

◆ The girl took off her shoes. Then she went to the washroom to put the bouquet of flowers in some water.
  [a above "girl", p above "her", p above "she"]
  from "Tuesday Siesta" by Gabriel García Márquez

Language and Grammar Handbook   **821**

a. Singular pronouns are generally used to refer to the indefinite pronouns *one, anyone, each, either, neither, everybody, everyone, somebody, someone, nobody,* and *no one.*

◆ Neither of the women could practice her tennis.

◆ Everybody brought his ticket to the gate.

The second sentence poses problems. It is clearly plural in meaning, and *everybody* may not refer to men only. To avoid the latter problem, you could write "Everybody brought his or her ticket to the gate." This solution is clumsy and wordy, though. Sometimes it is best to revise:

◆ The students brought their tickets to the gate.

This sentence is now clear and nonsexist.

among, between *Among* implies more than two persons, places, or things. *Between* usually refers to two, followed either by a plural or by two expressions joined by *and*—not by *or.*

◆ All these years . . . she thought she understood them. But now she discovered that she was a stranger among them.
  from "The Rain Came" by Grace Ogot

◆ Between semesters, James hiked fifty miles.
◆ Sam couldn't decide between the fish sandwich and the pasta.

See also **between you and me.**

apostrophe (') An apostrophe is used in possessive words, both singular and plural, and in contractions. It is also used to form the plurals of letters and numbers.

Jeffrey's jacket	A's and B's	won't
women's basketball	6's and 7's	wasn't

It may be used to indicate places in words in which certain sounds or letters are omitted.

◆ "Where are we going, Gran'ma?" I said. . . .
  from *Kaffir Boy* by Mark Mathabane

appositive An *appositive* is a word or word group that follows another word or word group and identifies or explains it more fully. It is usually set off by commas or dashes.

◆ The latest heartache for Dutchmen was an edict making it a crime to sing the "Wilhelmus," our national anthem.
  from "The Secret Room" by Corrie ten Boom

◆ The library staffed two assistants—Rachel and Ben.

If, however, the appositive is used to specify a particular person or thing, it is not set off.

◆ Moronoff recognizes the man as Grunkin the goldsmith.
from "The Chameleon" by Anton Chekhov

awkward writing A general term (abbreviated *awk*) sometimes used in theme correcting to indicate such faults as inappropriate word choice, unnecessary repetition, clumsy phrasing, confusing word order, or any other weakness or expression that makes reading difficult and obscures meaning.

Many writers have found that reading their first drafts aloud helps them detect clumsy or unclear phrasing in their work. Once identified, awkward construction can almost always be improved by rethinking and rewording.

B

bad, badly In formal English and in writing, *bad* (the adjective) is used to modify a noun or pronoun and is used after a linking verb. *Badly* (the adverb) modifies a verb.

◆ She felt bad about hurting his feelings. (Adjective used with linking verb *felt*)
◆ The game was played badly. (Adverb modifying a verb)

between you and me After **prepositions** such as *between,* use the objective form of the personal pronouns: *between you and **me**, between you and **her**, between you and **him**, between you and **us**, between you and **them**.*

HINT: To check yourself, realize that you would never say "between we." You would say "between us," *us* being the objective form of the pronoun *we.*

◆ The misunderstanding is between you and her.
◆ Was the agreement between you and them?
◆ Here between us, the white light blazed and the blade shivered.
from *The Hollow Hills* by Mary Stewart

borrow, lend To *borrow* means to "get something from someone else with the understanding that it will be returned." To *lend* means to "let another have or use something temporarily."

◆ I borrowed a pen from Dad; he borrowed my calculator.
◆ Carlos offered to lend me his video.

Borrow is often followed by *from*—never by *off* or *off of*.

bring, take To *bring* means to "carry something toward." To *take* means to "carry something away."

◆ "Bring him back two weeks from today."
from *Kaffir Boy* by Mark Mathabane

◆ I rubbed the old silk against my skin, then wrapped them in tissue and decided to take them home with me.
from "Two Kinds" by Amy Tan

Language and Grammar Handbook **823**

C capitalization

1. Capitalize all proper nouns and adjectives.

Proper Nouns	Proper Adjectives
Canada	Canadian
China	Chinese
Victoria	Victorian

2. Capitalize people's names and titles.

General Powell	Bishop Clark
Justice Ginsburg	Dr. Fernandez
Ms. Sarah Stoner	Grandma
Uncle Jack	Senator Hanrahan

3. Capitalize the names of ethnic groups, languages, religions, revered persons, deities, religious bodies, buildings, and writings. Also capitalize any adjectives made from these names.

Indo-European	Buddha
German	Catholicism
Islam	Allah
Grace Lutheran Church	the Bible

NOTE: Do not capitalize directions of the compass or adjectives that indicate direction: Front Street runs north and south. The weather map showed showers in the northwest.

4. Capitalize geographical names (except for articles and prepositions) and any adjectives made from these names.

Australia	the Red Arrow Highway
Gila River	Danish pastry
Straits of Mackinac	Spanish rice
the Rockies	Southern accent
Arctic Circle	Gettysburg
Tampa Bay	Zion National Park

NOTE: Earth, sun, and moon are not capitalized unless used with the names of other planets: Is Venus closer to the Sun than Saturn? The earth revolves around the sun.

5. Capitalize the names of structures, organizations, and bodies in the universe.

the Capitol	the House of Representatives
Carnegie Hall	the United Way
the Eiffel Tower	Neptune
the Cubs	the Milky Way

6. Capitalize the names of historical events, times, and documents.

the Hundred Years' War	the Elizabethan Period
the Treaty of Versailles	the Emancipation Proclamation

NOTE: Do not capitalize the names of the seasons.

NOTE: Some modern poets do not begin each line with a capital letter.

7. Capitalize the names of months, days, holidays, and time abbreviations.

February   Sunday

Thanksgiving   A.M. P.M.

8. Capitalize the first letters in sentences, lines of poetry, and direct quotations.

◆ If thou shouldst never see my face again,
  Pray for my soul. More things are wrought by prayer
  Than this world dreams of.
  from *Idylls of the King* by Alfred, Lord Tennyson

◆ The announcer said, "It will be cloudy and windy."

9. Capitalize certain parts of letters and outlines.

Dear Mrs. Moore,   Sincerely yours,

I. Early types of automobiles
   A. Gasoline powered
      1. Haynes
      2. Ford
      3. Other makes
   B. Steam powered
   C. Electric cars

10. Capitalize the first, last, and all other important words in titles.
See also **italics.**

book	Dickens's *Great Expectations*
newspaper	story in the *Washington Post*
play and movie	starred in *Showboat*
television series	liked *Murphy Brown*
short story	read "The Monkey's Paw"
music (long)	saw *The Pirates of Penzance*
music (short)	sang "Swing Low, Sweet Chariot"
work of art	Winslow Homer's *Breezing Up*
magazine	*Seventeen* magazine

clause A clause is a group of words that has a subject and a verb. A clause is independent when it can stand alone and make sense. A dependent clause has a subject and a verb, but when it stands alone it is incomplete, and the reader is left wondering about the meaning.

Independent Clause	Dependent Clause
s v	s v
Bailey White wrote *Mama Makes Up Her Mind*.	Since Bailey White wrote *Mama Makes Up Her Mind*.

colon (:) A colon is often used to explain or clarify what has preceded it.

◆ That was one thing the occupation had done for Holland: churches were packed.
 from "The Secret Room" by Corrie ten Boom

A colon is also used after phrases that introduce a list or quotation.

◆ When he prepared for his hike, he packed the following items: a map, extra batteries, and a flashlight.

◆ One old man said: "Our son is a good man. . . ."
 from "The Voter" by Chinua Achebe

comma (,) Commas are used to show a pause or separation between words and word groups in sentences, to avoid confusion in sentences, and to separate items in addresses, in dialogue, and in figures.

1. Use commas between items in a series. Words, phrases, and clauses in a series are separated by commas.

◆ He knows that they examine, sniff, feel, and read between the lines of each and every letter. . . .
 from "The Censors" by Luisa Valenzuela

2. Use a comma after certain introductory words and groups of words such as clauses and prepositional phrases of five words or more.

◆ When my mother began dropping hints that I would soon be going to school, I vowed never to go. . . .
 from *Kaffir Boy* by Mark Mathabane

◆ During the absence of King Arthur from Britain, Sir Modred had decided to usurp the throne.
 from "The Death of King Arthur" by Sir Thomas Malory

3. Use a comma to set off nouns of direct address. The name or title by which persons (or animals) are addressed is called a noun of direct address.

◆ "Did you give him anything for it, Father?" inquired Mrs. White. . . .
 from "The Monkey's Paw" by W. W. Jacobs

◆ Sire, is it your will that Arthur shall succeed to the throne. . . ?
 from "The Coronation of Arthur" by Sir Thomas Malory

4. Use commas to set off interrupting elements and appositives. Any phrase or clause that interrupts the flow of a sentence is often set off by commas. Parenthetical expressions like *of course, after all, to be sure, on the other hand, I suppose,* and *as you know;* and words like *yes, no, oh,* and *well* are all set off by commas.

NOTE: If the items in a series are all separated by a word like *and,* no comma is necessary: Rain and wind and sleet all hampered the rescue.

♦ The average woman of twenty, it has been estimated, could expect about twelve years of childbearing. . . .
> from "Youth and Chivalry" by Barbara Tuchman

♦ The reporter, on the other hand, was determined to snatch her from death.
> from "And of Clay Are We Created" by Isabel Allende

5. Use a comma before a coordinating conjunction *(and, but, for, or, nor, yet, so)* in a compound sentence.

♦ Both men spoke with the bitterness of possible defeat before them, for each knew that it might be long before his men would seek him out or find him. . . .
> from "The Interlopers" by Saki

♦ She was exhausted, but the path was still winding.
> from "The Rain Came" by Grace Ogot

♦ The girl was twelve years old, and it was the first time she'd ever been on a train.
> from "Tuesday Siesta" by Gabriel García Márquez

6. Use a comma after a dependent clause that begins a sentence. Do not use a comma before a dependent clause that follows the independent clause.

♦ Though night had scarcely come and the heat was great, we gathered at the fire to see each other's faces. . . .
> from "The Boar Hunt" by José Vasconcelos

♦ Occasionally we had to stop firing because the frequent shooting heated the barrels of our rifles.
> from "The Boar Hunt" by José Vasconcelos

7. Use a comma to separate items in an address. The number and street are considered one item. The state and Zip Code are also considered one item. Use a comma after the Zip Code if it is within a sentence.

Diane Wong	Todd's address is 721 N. Buckeye,
5341 Palm Dr.	Columbus, OH 73215, but I don't
Messa, AZ 85210	have his phone number.

8. Use a comma to separate numerals greater than three digits.

900,321	4,500

9. Use commas in punctuating dialogue. *See* **dialogue.**

Comma splice *See* **run-on sentence.**

comparative forms of adjectives and adverbs To show a greater degree of the quality or characteristic named by an adjective or adverb, *-er* or *-est* is added to the word, or *more* or *most* is put before it.

Positive: Ron is quiet.

Comparative: Ron is quieter than Allen.

Superlative: Ron is the quietest person in the class.

More and *most* are generally used with longer adjectives and adverbs, and with all adverbs ending in *-ly.*

Positive: The movie was peculiar.

Comparative: The second movie was more peculiar than the first.

Superlative: The movie was the most peculiar one I have ever seen.

◆ Jan is more likely than Pat to enter the marathon.

The *comparative* forms are usually used in comparing two things or people, and the *superlative* in comparing more than two.

◆ Kim is the fastest runner on the team.
◆ Sarita is the taller of the two sisters.

Writers sometimes have trouble phrasing comparisons so that a reader can see immediately what things are being compared.

Faulty: The seats in the auditorium are better than the theater. [Seats are being compared to a theater.]

Corrected: The seats in the auditorium are better than those in the theater. *See also* **modifiers.**

conjunction A conjunction is a word that links one part of a sentence to another. It can join words, phrases, or entire sentences.

D

dash (—) A dash is used to indicate a sudden break or change of thought.

◆ By the time the last man had spoken it was possible—without great loss of dignity—to pick up the things from the floor.
from "The Voter" by Chinua Achebe

dialogue Dialogue is often used to enliven many types of writing. Notice the paragraphing and punctuation of the following passage.

◆ "Tell me," he said, coming straight to the point, "what did you think of the auction last night?"
"Auction?" she asked, frowning. "Auction? What auction?"
from "Dip in the Pool" by Roald Dahl

See also **quotation marks.**

direct address *See* **comma 3.**

E

ellipsis (. . .)   An ellipsis is used to indicate that words (or sentences or paragraphs) have been omitted. An ellipsis consists of three dots, but if the omitted portion would have completed the sentence, a fourth dot is added for the period.

> Next, to establish peace and order in the counties near London. . . .
> from "The Coronation of Arthur" by Sir Thomas Malory

exclamation point (!)   An exclamation mark is used at the end of an exclamatory sentence—one that shows excitement or strong emotion. Exclamation points can also be used with strong interjections.

F

fragment *See* **sentence fragment.**

G

gerund   A verb form usually ending in *-ing* that is used as a noun. In the sentence following, *going* is the object of the preposition *by.*

> ◆ It was unexplored underbrush into which we could enter only by going down the river in a canoe.
> from "The Boar Hunt" by José Vasconcelos

A gerund used as the object of a preposition should be related to the subject. Otherwise the phrase will dangle.

> Dangling: After driving one block, the tire was flat.
> Corrected: After driving one block, she noticed the tire was flat.

good, well   *Good* is used as an adjective to modify a noun or pronoun. Do not use it to modify a verb. *Well* is usually used as an adverb to modify a verb.

> ◆ Her teacher commented that she had written a good paper.
> ◆ Kathleen behaved well when, some months later, her fiancé was reported missing, presumed killed.
> from "The Demon Lover" by Elizabeth Bowen

> ◆ "Dear Sister," she began, followed by a little time-buying cough and throat clearing. "We are all well here."
> from "The Need to Say It" by Patricia Hampl

HINT: When you are referring to health, use *well* if the meaning is "not ill."

If the meaning is "pleasant" or "in good spirits," use *good:*

◆ I feel really good today!

hopefully This is often used to mean "it is hoped," or "I hope," as in the sentence, "Hopefully she will be able to console herself." However, in formal writing, avoid this usage and write the sentence as follows:

◆ They hoped she would, in a year or two, console herself. . . .
   from "The Demon Lover" by Elizabeth Bowen

however Words like *however, moreover, nevertheless,* and *consequently,* (known as conjunctive adverbs) require special punctuation. If the word comes within a clause, it is generally set off by commas.

◆ The man, however, was gazing in idle reverie at the city's skyline growing ever more beautiful. . . .
   from "He—y, Come on Ou—t!" by Shinichi Hoshi

If the conjunctive adverb separates two independent clauses, a semicolon is used preceding the word.

◆ I like sports; however, I seldom have time to be on a team.

infinitive An infinitive is the simple form of the verb, usually preceded by *to.* Infinitives are used as nouns, adjectives, or adverbs. In the following passage, each infinitive acts as an adjective.

◆ A time to weep, and a time to laugh: a time to mourn, and a time to dance. . . .
   from Ecclesiastes

interjection An interjection is a word or phrase used to express strong emotion.

Ouch! Stay off my foot.
Yes! I was accepted.
Oh, no, the show is sold out!

NOTE: In handwritten or non-computer writing, use underlining to indicate italics.

italics Italic type is used to indicate titles of whole works such as books, magazines, newspapers, plays, films, and so on. It is also used to indicate foreign words and phrases.

◆ ". . . there's still a table by the bay window, if *madame* and *monsieur* would like to enjoy the view."
   from "The Other Wife" by Colette

NOTE: In formal English, the correct way to respond to a question such as, "Who's there?" is "It is I." This sounds too formal in some situations, however. While it is not correct to say, "It's them," "It's him," "It's us," or "It's her," "It's me" is generally accepted as standard usage.

its, it's *Its* is the possessive form of the personal pronoun *it; it's* is the contraction meaning "it is."

◆ He brought the lamp close and tilted it at the money . . . to make sure he had not mistaken its value.
   from "The Voter" by Chinua Achebe

◆ Juan knows there won't be a problem with the letter's contents, that it's irreproachable, harmless.
   from "The Censors" by Luisa Valenzuela

lay, lie This verb pair presents problems because, in addition to the similarity between the words, the past tense of *lie* is *lay.* The verb *lay,* means "to put or place something somewhere."

Present	Past	Past Participle
lay	laid	(has) laid

The principal parts of the verb *lie,* which means "to rest," "to be at rest," or "to be in a reclining position," are the following.

Present	Past	Past Participle
lie	lay	(has) lain

Notice how the verbs are used in the following sentences.

◆ "Our cattle lie dying in the fields," they reported. "Soon it will be our children and then ourselves." (The cattle are in a reclining position.)
   from "The Rain Came" by Grace Ogot

◆ "I will lay down my life, if necessary, and the life of my household, to save this tribe from the hands of the enemy." (I will put down my life.)
   from "The Rain Came" by Grace Ogot

◆ America was where all my mother's hopes lay. (Where all my mother's hopes rested.)
   from "Two Kinds" by Amy Tan

◆ But his sickness grew worse, and after he had lain speechless for three days and three nights Merlin summoned the nobles. . . . (He had been in a reclining position.)
   from "The Coronation of Arthur" by Sir Thomas Malory

NOTE: *Lied* refers only to not telling the truth: Many people thought he *lied* on the witness stand.

lead, led The present tense of this verb rhymes with *seed;* the past tense (and past participle) is spelled *led* and rhymes with *red.*

◆ I forgot what I was supposed to do—to lead the crowd to shout the slogans—until Secretary Chain came to remind me of my duty.
   from *Red Azalea* by Anchee Min

◆ I led my schoolmates in collecting pennies. We wanted to donate the pennies to the starving children in America.
   from *Red Azalea* by Anchee Min

HINT: Remember that *lose* often means the opposite of *gain.* Each word has just four letters.

lose, loose *Lose* (to lose one's way, to lose a watch) is a verb; *loose* (to come loose, loose-fitting) is an adjective.

◆ As Oganda opened the gate a child, a young child, broke loose from the crowd and ran toward her.
   from "The Rain Came" by Grace Ogot

◆ In marking the path to the landing, we were careful not to lose ourselves in the thicket.
   from "The Boar Hunt" by José Vasconcelos

M

modifier A modifier is a word or group of words that restrict, limit, or make more exact the meaning of other words. The modifiers of nouns and pronouns are usually adjectives, participles, adjective phrases, and adjective clauses. The modifiers of verbs, adjectives, and adverbs are adverbs, adverb phrases, and adverb clauses. In the following examples, the italicized words modify the words that directly follow them.

◆ The *seventh* apartment was *closely* shrouded in *black velvet* tapestries. . . .
   from "The Masque of the Red Death" by Edgar Allan Poe

HINT: When trying to decide which pronoun to use, remember that you would not say "Myself is going to the game." You would say *I.*

myself (and himself, herself, and so on) Be careful not to use *myself* and the other reflexive and intensive pronouns when you simply need to use the personal pronoun *I* or its objective form *me.*

Incorrect: John and myself are going to the game.
Correct: John and I are going to the game.

Incorrect: Chidi told Laura and myself a funny story.
Correct: Chidi told Laura and me a funny story.

N

none, no one When *none* tells how many, a plural verb is generally used, unless the idea of "not a single one" is to be emphasized, as in the following example.

◆ . . . Oganda fought desperately to find another exit. . . .
   But there was none.
   from "The Rain Came" by Grace Ogot

No one is singular and is often used for emphasis.

◆ For some time they had predicted that the heat of the eruption could detach the eternal ice from the slopes of the volcano, but no one heeded their warnings.
from "And of Clay Are We Created" by Isabel Allende

See also **agreement 1f.**

noun A noun is a word that names a person, place, thing, or idea. Most nouns are made plural by adding -*s* or -*es* to the singular. When you are unsure about a plural form, check a dictionary.

P

parallel construction Items in a sentence that are of equal importance should be expressed in parallel (or similar) forms. These can take the form of noun phrases, verb phrases, infinitive phrases, and prepositional phrases.

◆ We sang at the top of our lungs, sang our oneness, our hope, our love for Queen and country.
from "The Secret Room" by Corrie ten Boom

◆ The boy would learn to ride, to fight, and to hawk . . . to play chess and backgammon, to sing and dance, play an instrument, and compose. . . .
from "Youth and Chivalry" by Barbara Tuchman

parentheses ( ) Parentheses are used to enclose words that interrupt or add explanation to a sentence. They are also used to enclose references to page numbers, chapters, or dates. Punctuation marks that belong to the sentence come after the parentheses, not before.

◆ I allowed myself a descriptive aria on the beauty of Minnesota winters (for the benefit of my California reader who might need some background material on the subject of ice hockey).
from "The Need to Say It" by Patricia Hampl

◆ Langston Hughes (1902–1967) was part of the Harlem Renaissance.

participle A participle is a verb form used in forming various tenses of verbs. The present participle ends in -*ing:* growing. The past participle usually ends in -*ed, -t, -d, -en,* or -*n:* scared, kept, said, risen, blown.

I am thinking.   We were running.   Leaves have blown away.

Participles are also used as adjectives, modifying nouns and pronouns.

◆ The purser looked at the anxious frowning face of Mr. Botibol and he smiled. . . .
from "Dip in the Pool" by Roald Dahl

possessive case The possessive case is formed in various ways. For singular nouns and indefinite pronouns, add an apostrophe and *s.*

  my sister's car   someone's shoe   everybody's grade

For plural nouns ending in an *s,* add only an apostrophe.

  the doctors' offices   the babies' pool   the churches' members

However, if the plural is irregular and does not end in *s,* add an apostrophe and then an *s.*

NOTE: Apostrophes are not used with personal pronouns to show possession.

> ◆ . . . even when a suspicion of a smile flickered across the other women's faces . . . I thought that a rare distinction lit up my mother's face.
> from "My Father Writes to My Mother" by Assia Djebar

prepositions Prepositions are words such as *about, between, during, from, of, over, until,* and *with* that show the relationship between a noun or pronoun and some other word in a sentence.

prepositional phrase Prepositional phrases are groups of words that begin with a preposition and end with a noun or pronoun. These phrases act as modifiers and create vivid pictures for the reader. Notice the three prepositional phrases in the following sentence.

> ◆ This woman from America married a man of our village and left her country to come and live with him here.
> from "Woman from America" by Bessie Head

pronoun Subject pronouns are used as subjects of sentences. Object pronouns can be used as direct objects, indirect objects, or objects of prepositions.

When a pronoun is used as the subject of a sentence, the pronoun is in the nominative case and is called a subject pronoun: *He* and *I* met at the movies.

Subject Pronouns

Singular	I	you	he, she, it
Plural	we	you	they

When a pronoun is used as an object, the pronoun is in the objective case and is called an object pronoun: The coach asked *me* and *him* to arrive early.

HINT: When you are uncertain about whether to use a subject pronoun or an object pronoun in a sentence, take out the first pronoun to test the sentence. (You wouldn't say "The coach asked *he* to arrive early.")

Object Pronouns

Singular	me	you	him, her, it
Plural	us	you	them

See also **agreement 2** *for pronoun-antecedent agreement.*

Q

quotation marks (" ") Quotation marks enclose a speaker's exact words. They are also used to enclose some titles. When you use someone's exact words in your writing, use the following rules:

1. Enclose all quoted words within quotation marks.

◆ Anchee Min wrote, "I stood up and felt dizzy."

2. The first word of a direct quotation begins with a capital letter.
When a quotation is broken into two parts, use two sets of quotation marks. Use one capital letter if the quote is one sentence. Use two capital letters if it is two sentences.

◆ "You'd better close the window," the woman said. "Your hair will get full of soot."
  from "Tuesday Siesta" by Gabriel García Márquez

3. Use a comma between the words that introduce the speaker and the words that are quoted. Place the end punctuation or the comma that ends the quotation inside the quotation marks. Put question marks and exclamation points inside the quotation marks only if they are a part of the quotation. Begin a new paragraph each time the speaker changes.

◆ "Come along," she said, frowning slightly. "What's your name, dear?"
  "I don't know," I said finally.
  from "By Any Other Name" by Santha Rama Rau

When a quoted passage is made up of more than one paragraph, opening quotation marks are put at the beginning of each paragraph, but closing marks are put only at the end of the last paragraph. *See also* **dialogue.**

R

raise, rise Use *raise* to mean "lift"; use *rise* to mean "get up."

Present	Past	Past Participle	Present Participle
raise	raised	had raised	is raising
rise	rose	had risen	is rising

◆ Then he sank trembling into a chair as the old woman, with burning eyes, walked to the window and raised the blind.
  from "The Monkey's Paw" by W. W. Jacobs

◆ I rose obediently and started to walk toward my sister.
  from "By Any Other Name" by Santha Rama Rau

reflexive pronouns Reflexive pronouns reflect the action of the verb back to the subject. An intensive pronoun adds emphasis to the noun or pronoun just named.

◆ That woman must be talking to herself. [reflexive]
◆ Merlin prophesied that they could be checked only by the presence of the king himself on the battlefield. . . . [intensive]
  from "The Coronation of Arthur" by Sir Thomas Malory

run-on sentence A run-on sentence occurs when there is only a comma (known as a comma splice) or no punctuation between two independent clauses. Separate the clauses into two complete sentences, join them with a semicolon, or join them with a comma and a coordinating conjunction.

Run-on: The man bought his groceries then he went to the party.
Run-on: The man bought his groceries, then he went to the party.
Correct: The man bought his groceries. Then he went to the party.
Correct: The man bought his groceries; then he went to the party.
Correct: The man bought his groceries, and then he went to the party.

Sometimes, in narrative writing, authors choose to use run-ons for effect, such as in the following passage.

◆ She sat, she brooded, she stared out the window.
  from "The Need to Say It" by Patricia Hampl

See also **stringy sentences.**

S

semicolon (;) Use this punctuation mark to separate the two parts of a compound sentence when they are not joined by a comma and a conjunction.

◆ In the day he made his speeches; at night his stalwarts conducted their whispering campaign.
  from "The Voter" by Chinua Achebe

sentence fragment A fragment often occurs when one sentence is finished, but another thought occurs to the writer. That thought is written and punctuated as a complete sentence, even though it may be missing a subject, verb, or both.

Fragment: I love reading mysteries. *Especially on cold evenings.*
Correct: I love reading mysteries, especially on cold evenings.

As with run-ons, fragments are sometimes used by writers for effect.

◆ I was never forgiven. Even after twenty-some years. After the Revolution was over.

    from *Red Azalea* by Anchee Min

sit, set Use *sit* to mean "to sit down"; use *set* to mean "to put something somewhere."

Present	Past	Past Participle	Present Participle
sit	sat	had sat	is sitting
set	set	had set	is setting

◆ Who is that sitting next to Diego?
◆ Laura set the sandwiches on the counter.

stringy sentences A stringy sentence is one in which several independent clauses are strung together with *and.* Since all the ideas seem to be treated equally, a reader may have difficulty seeing how they are related. Correct a stringy sentence by breaking it into individual sentences or changing some of the independent clauses into subordinate clauses or phrases.

Stringy sentence: I went to the library to find a book about Henry VIII for my research paper and then I met Martin and he wanted me to help him find a newspaper article on microfilm and when the library closed I still didn't have my book and my paper was overdue.

Corrected: When I went to the library to find a book about Henry VIII for my research paper, I met Martin. He wanted me to help him find a newspaper article on microfilm. Consequently, when the library closed, I still didn't have my book, and my paper was overdue.

Corrected: I met Martin when I went to the library to find a book about Henry VIII for my research paper. Since Martin wanted me to help him find a newspaper article on microfilm, the library closed before I could get my book. As a result, my paper was overdue.

T

their, there, they're *Their* is a possessive, *there* is an introductory word or adverb of place, and *they're* is the contraction for "they are."

HINT: Remember that *there* has the word *here* in it; these two words are related in that they can both be indicators of place.

- ◆ The blinding midday heat had forced the people into their huts.
  from "The Rain Came" by Grace Ogot
- ◆ There were sharp pains, and sudden dizziness, and then profuse bleeding. . . .
  from "The Masque of the Red Death" by Edgar Allan Poe
- ◆ Those cards have to be accounted for in a dozen ways. They're checked and double-checked.
  from "The Secret Room" by Corrie ten Boom

to, too, two *To* is a preposition that means "toward, in that direction" or is used in the infinitive form of the verb, as in "to follow" or "to run." *Too* means "also" or "more than enough." *Two* means "more than one."

- ◆ To take two tests in one day is too much.

V

verb A verb is a word that tells about an action or a state of being. The form or tense of the verb tells whether the action occurred in the past, is occurring in the present, or will occur in the future.

verb shifts in tense Use the same tense to show two or more actions that occur at the same time.

Incorrect: Marla arrives *(present)* early and parked *(past)* her bike.
Correct: Marla arrived *(past)* early and parked *(past)* her bike.

When the verb in the main clause is in the present tense, the verb in the subordinate clause is in whatever tense expresses the meaning intended.

- ◆ Jeremy *thinks* that the popcorn *was* too salty.
- ◆ Anna *believes* that she *passed* the test.

W

who, whom *Who* is used as a subject; *whom* is used as a direct object or the object of a preposition.

- ◆ Auntie Lindo's daughter, Waverly, who was about my age, was standing farther down the wall about five feet away.
  from "Two Kinds" by Amy Tan
- ◆ Danielle couldn't decide whom she would ask for a ride.
- ◆ Give the leftovers to whomever you wish.

who's, whose *Who's* is a contraction meaning "who is." *Whose* is a possessive.

- ◆ Who's the fellow in the straw hat?
- ◆ Whose gym bag is in my locker?

would of This expression is often used mistakenly because it sounds like *would've,* the contraction for *would have.* In formal writing, write out *would have,* and you won't be confused.

- ◆ I would have called, but Dad was on the phone.

Incorrect: If I would have had more time, I could make my paper better.

Correct: If I had more time, I could make my paper better.

Correct: If I had had more time, I could have made my paper better.

NOTE: In sentences beginning with the phrase "If (I) had" or when referring to a wish in the past, use the verb *had*—not *would have had.*

your, you're *Your* is the possessive form of the personal pronoun *you; you're* is a contraction meaning "you are."

- ◆ The woman added, "We hear you and your friends laughing every Saturday night. . . ."
  from "Living Well. Living Good." by Maya Angelou

- ◆ You're too small to have them.
  from "By Any Other Name" by Santha Rama Rau

Index of Skills and Strategies

Literary Genres, Terms, and Techniques

Alliteration, 168, 414, 811
Allusion, 225, 355, 357, 368, 369, 380, 486, 530, 584, 650, 657, 811
Antagonist, 189, 225, 238, 263, 641, 811
Analogy, 811
Antagonist, 811
Assonance, 597, 600, 601, 811
Autobiography, 452, 811
Ballad, 811
Biography/autobiography, 452, 455, 811
Blank verse, 675, 697, 713, 811
Cast of characters, 185
Character, 2, 17, 27, 33, 41, 48, 75, 77, 84, 112, 120–121, 153, 168, 174, 189, 211, 225, 238, 240, 254, 262, 263, 269, 279, 289, 301, 307, 347, 414, 426, 435, 442, 452, 455, 478, 479, 487, 493, 515, 557, 575, 584, 643, 648, 675, 696, 713, 732, 749, 763, 772, 785, 811
Climax, 2, 65, 120, 254, 301, 732, 772, 811
Comedy, 811
Commedia dell'arte, 269
Conclusion, 515
Conflict, 2, 15, 65, 75, 101, 112, 120, 133, 143, 153, 194, 254, 263, 301, 332, 436, 486, 636, 641, 648, 675, 677, 696, 811
Connotation, 160, 370, 380, 387, 492, 657, 713, 812
Consonance, 812
Couplet, 812
Denotation, 370, 380, 492, 657, 812
Dialect, 812
Dialogue, 28, 86, 92, 125, 142, 262, 675, 713, 812
Diction, 122, 339, 507, 524, 549, 559, 566, 567, 812
Dimeter, 812
Drama, 184–185, 187–188, 674–675, 812. See also Greek drama.

End rhyme, 812
Essay, 56–61, 174–178, 442–446, 453, 812
Exposition, 677, 812
Extended metaphor, 812
Fable, 135, 153, 171, 642, 812
Falling action, 763, 812
Fantasy, 160
Fantasy/science fiction, 812
Farce, 269, 279, 812
Fiction, 812
Figurative language, 339, 522, 530, 548, 551, 557, 558, 575, 584, 634, 641, 657, 675, 812
Flashback, 77, 84, 133, 261, 813
Foil, 381, 763
Folk literature, 813
Folk tale, 786
Foot, 813
Foreshadowing, 133, 309, 318, 347, 380, 696, 749, 785, 813
Free verse, 575, 813
Genre, 813. Overviews, 2–3, 184–185, 336–337, 452–453, 548–549, 674–675
Greek drama, 184–185
Haiku, 617, 813
Hero, 337, 438–439, 813
Historical fiction, 813
Humor, 41, 211, 289, 523, 575, 675, 732
Hyperbole, 368, 478, 507, 551, 557, 575, 813
Iambic pentameter, 813
Idiom, 416, 426, 567, 813
Imagery, 92, 168, 347, 355, 368, 380, 405, 428, 435, 478, 507, 517, 522, 524, 530, 549. 557, 575, 584, 600, 617, 713, 813
Inference, 92, 153, 155, 160, 168, 426, 515, 557, 696, 713, 813
Internal rhyme, 813
Inverted sentences, 675, 813
Irony, 101, 127, 133, 160, 175, 178, 225, 246, 368, 405, 468, 472, 732, 749, 763, 785, 813
Legend, 336–337, 339, 813
Light verse, 814

Literary criticism, 85, 280
Local color, 772
Lyric, 814
Marginal notes, 184, 674
Metaphor, 407, 414, 415, 478, 551, 557, 713, 732, 814
Meter, 814
Mood, 3, 73, 84, 85, 86, 94, 101, 133, 134, 141, 168, 181, 211, 292–293, 301, 311, 339, 347, 414, 426, 509, 515, 565, 566, 601, 814
Moral, 133, 135, 141, 414, 610, 814
Motivation, 814
Mystery, 814
Myth, 93, 814
Narrator, 3, 43, 48, 303, 307, 348, 405, 522, 577, 584, 772, 814
Nonfiction, 452–453, 814
Novel, 814
Onomatopoeia, 168, 339, 814
Parable, 774, 785, 814
Paradox, 380, 405, 814
Pentameter, 814
Persona, 814
Personification, 141, 225, 551, 557, 610, 657, 814
Play. See drama.
Plot, 2, 65, 75, 84, 86, 92, 120, 141, 161, 269, 291, 301, 452, 677, 696, 713, 732, 763, 815
Poetry, 154, 162, 168, 501, 548–549, 551, 559, 568, 577, 597, 612, 617, 675, 815.
See also Blank verse, Free verse, Haiku, Lyric, Sonnet.
Point of view, 3, 43, 48, 63, 84, 307, 330, 393, 395, 405, 453, 522, 530, 558, 566, 617, 786, 815
Prologue, 815
Protagonist, 189, 225, 238, 263, 641, 815
Proverb, 35, 41, 172, 435, 472, 785, 815
Psalm, 815
Pun, 301, 302, 680, 815
Quatrain, 815

Writing Forms, Modes, and Processes

369, 370, 381, 395, 406, 407,
415, 416, 427, 428, 437, 455,
467, 468, 473, 474, 479, 480,
487, 501, 508, 509, 516, 517,
523, 524, 531, 551, 558, 559,
567, 568, 576, 577, 585, 597,
601, 602, 611, 612, 618, 631,
635, 636, 642, 643, 649, 650,
658, 697, 733, 749, 764, 765,
773, 774, 786

Writing Process. *See* Writing
Workshops, 56, 119, 174, 262,
324, 386, 442, 493, 537, 590,
624, 663, 791

Reading/Thinking Strategies

Bias and propaganda, 542–543,
787–789, 790

Cause and effect, 15, 27, 33, 75,
84, 141, 168, 176, 179, 180,
246, 254, 301, 355, 380, 405,
436, 466, 478, 486, 641, 648,
696, 713, 732, 798

Clarify, xxiii, 15, 31, 41, 92, 97, 99,
112, 133, 141, 153, 160, 162,
180, 195, 202, 205, 211, 214,
215, 225, 238, 254, 261, 284,
289, 301, 307, 349, 368, 380,
398, 402, 405, 414, 426, 436,
464, 466, 472, 478, 486, 491,
507, 515, 522, 526, 530, 544,
566, 575, 584, 600, 610, 617,
634, 641, 643, 648, 657, 670,
674, 772, 785, 790

Comparison/contrast, 33, 44, 48,
50–51, 61, 65, 84, 129, 133,
141, 153, 160, 166–167, 181,
193, 211, 220, 225, 279, 284,
289, 301, 307, 318, 347, 355,
368, 407, 414, 426, 436, 437,
448, 472, 486, 507, 515, 522,
530, 544, 566, 575, 584, 600,
617, 623, 648, 713, 732, 749,
763, 772, 785

Comprehension. *See* Cause and
effect, Comparison/contrast,
Details, Drawing conclusions,
Fact and opinion, Main idea,
Visualizing.

Connect, xxiii, 5, 33, 41, 42, 48,
52, 75, 84, 92, 101, 112, 133,
141, 153, 160, 164, 175–176,
180, 189, 205, 211, 220, 225,
254, 279, 289, 307, 318, 322,
332, 347, 354, 355, 368, 370,
380, 401, 405, 414, 436, 439,
459, 478, 486, 492, 507, 515,
522, 526, 530, 557, 566, 575,
584, 600, 610, 634, 650, 657,
674, 696, 713, 732, 749, 772,
778, 790

Details, 15, 33, 41, 55, 84, 85, 92,
101, 113, 133, 138, 141, 161,
175, 195, 198, 211, 226, 238,
254, 272, 279, 289, 301, 318,
347, 349, 355, 356, 368, 405,
414, 436, 466, 472, 478, 479,
499, 515, 522, 530, 544, 557,
566, 584, 600, 617, 634, 641,
648, 674, 713, 749, 772, 785

Drawing conclusions, 15, 33, 41,
52, 56, 84, 92, 96, 101, 112,
160, 162, 210, 211, 225, 234,
238, 246, 254, 279, 289, 301,
307, 309, 340, 380, 405, 414,
436, 466, 478, 486, 515, 522,
542, 575, 584, 610, 634, 662,
713, 732, 763, 798

Evaluate, xxiii, 15, 27, 33, 37, 40,
41, 75, 92, 101, 112, 118, 133,
153, 180, 207, 211, 223, 238,
246, 259, 279, 286, 291, 301,
307, 318, 322, 333, 347, 353,
380, 387, 399, 405, 426, 453,
466, 472, 478, 486, 507, 515,
522, 530, 557, 566, 584, 589,
600, 602, 617, 634, 641, 648,
657, 674, 696, 713, 732, 749,
662, 772, 778, 790

Fact and opinion, 246, 279, 318,
355, 453

Images, 92, 102, 279, 355, 368,
405, 436, 478, 499, 507, 515,
517, 522, 530, 557, 600, 610,
657, 713, 732, 813

Inferring, 15, 27, 33, 41, 48, 75,
84, 88-89, 92, 112, 153, 155,
160, 162, 168, 192, 211, 225,
238, 254, 272, 279, 289, 301,
307, 309, 318, 347, 368, 380,

405, 414, 426, 436, 466, 472,
478, 486, 515, 530, 557, 576,
584, 600, 610, 617, 641, 657,
696, 713, 732, 763, 772

Main idea, 55, 75, 84, 113, 141,
194, 279, 289, 416, 453, 472,
478, 557, 584, 610, 641, 670,
674, 732

Personal response, 5, 15, 33, 35, 48,
75, 92, 112, 133, 153, 168, 180,
211, 225, 238, 246, 289, 307,
318, 322, 347, 355, 368, 405,
414, 426, 436, 466, 472, 478,
486, 507, 522, 530, 557, 575,
597, 600, 634, 641, 648, 657,
696, 732, 749, 763, 772, 785

Predict, xxiii, 5, 48, 77, 84, 127,
135, 149, 198, 204, 217, 225,
246, 286, 291, 318, 332, 380,
436, 507, 515, 584, 634, 674,
696, 749, 781

Prereading. *See* Previewing.

Previewing, 5, 17, 29, 35, 43, 65,
86, 94, 103, 127, 135, 143, 155,
162, 189, 227, 269, 281, 291,
303, 309, 339, 349, 357, 370,
395, 407, 416, 428, 455, 468,
474, 480, 501, 509, 517, 524,
551, 559, 568, 577, 597, 602,
612, 631, 636, 643, 650, 677

Question, xxiii, 15, 48, 75, 84, 112,
141, 147, 153, 200, 209, 217,
225, 254, 281, 405, 426, 441,
466, 522, 584, 587, 597, 600,
674, 785, 790

Reader response. *See* Personal
response.

Reading Mini-Lessons
finding main idea and supporting details, 55
chronology and time lines, 261
classifying, 441
connotation and denotation,
492
compare and contrast, 623
propaganda, 790

Sequence, 48, 84, 92, 141, 161,
168, 198, 211, 222, 225, 254,
261, 368, 380, 414, 426, 436,
466, 478, 515, 600, 696, 713,
749, 763, 772, 785

■

Vocabulary and Study Skills

■

Grammar, Usage, Mechanics, and Spelling

■

Speaking, Listening, and Viewing

Index of Fine Art and Artists

Index of Authors and Titles

Acknowledgments

continued from iv

118 From *Innumeracy* by John Allen Paulos. Copyright © 1988 by John Allen Paulos. Reprinted by permission of Hill and Wang, a division of Farrar, Straus & Giroux, Inc.

136 "The Boar Hunt" by José Vasconcelos, trans. by Paul Waldorf from *The Muse in Mexico: A Mid-Century Miscellany,* Supplement to the Texas Quarterly, Vol. II. Reprinted by permission of University of Texas Press.

145 From *Red Azalea* by Anchee Min. Copyright © 1994 by Anchee Min. Reprinted by permission of Pantheon Books, a division of Random House, Inc.

156 "He—y, Come on Ou—t!" by Shinichi Hoshi, translated by Stanleigh H. Jones, Jr. Reprinted by permission of the author.

164 "Flash Cards" from *Grace Notes* by Rita Dove. Copyright © 1989 by Rita Dove. Reprinted by permission of W. W. Norton & Company, Inc.

165 "In Memory of Richi" from *Sonnets to Human Beings and Other Selected Works* by Carmen Tafolla. Copyright © 1992 by Carmen Tafolla. Reprinted by permission of the author.

166 "The Rabbit" by Edna St. Vincent Millay from *Collected Poems.* Copyright 1939, © 1967 by Edna St. Vincent Millay and Norma Millay Ellis. Reprinted by permission of Elizabeth Barnett, Literary Executor.

170 "The Elephant in the Dark House" from *Rumi, Poet and Mystic* translated by Reynold A. Nicholson. Reprinted by permission of George, Allen and Unwin, an imprint of HarperCollins Publishers Limited.

171 "Thought For a Sunshiny Morning" by Dorothy Parker from *The Portable Dorothy Parker* by Dorothy Parker. Introduction by Brendan Gill. Copyright 1928, renewed © 1956 by Dorothy Parker. Reprinted by permission of Viking Penguin, a division of Penguin Books USA Inc.

191 *Antigone* from *The Theban Plays* by Sophocles, translated by E. F. Watling. Copyright 1947 E. F. Watling. Reprinted by permission of Penguin Books Ltd.

228 *Twelve Angry Men* by Reginald Rose. Copyright © 1956, renewed 1984 Reginald Rose. Reprinted by permission of International Creative Management, Inc.

256 "We the Jurors" from "Do You Swear That You Will Well and Truly Try . . .?" by Barbara Holland, *Smithsonian,* March 1995, Vol. 25, #12. Reprinted by permission of the author.

270 Adapted from *The Flying Doctor* from *One-Act Comedies of Moliére,* translated by Albert Bermel. Copyright © 1962, 1963, 1964, 1975 by Albert Bermel.

Reprinted by permission of Applause Theatre Books, 211 W. 71st St., New York, NY 10023.

283 "The Chameleon" from *Chekhov: The Early Stories, 1883–1888* translated by Patrick Miles and Harvey Pitcher. Copyright © 1982 by Patrick Miles and Harvey Pitcher. Reprinted by permission of John Murray Publishers, Ltd.

287 "The Fox and the Woodcutter" from *Aesop's Fables,* trans. by Dennison B. Hull. Copyright © 1960 The University of Chicago Press. Reprinted by permission of The University of Chicago Press.

292 Adapted from "Dip in the Pool" by Roald Dahl from *Someone Like You* by Roald Dahl. Copyright 1948 by Roald Dahl. Reprinted by permission of the author and the Watkins/Loomis Agency.

305 From "The Need To Say It" by Patricia Hampl. Copyright © 1991 by Patricia Hampl. Originally published in *The Writer on Her Work* edited by Janet Sternberg. Published by W. W. Norton. Reprinted by permission of Rhoda Weyr Agency, NY.

310 This work originally appeared as *Crossroads* by Carlos Solórzano in *Selected Latin American One-Act Plays,* Francesca Colecchia and Julio Matas, eds. and trans. Published in 1973 by the University of Pittsburgh Press. Reprinted by permission of the Publisher.

317 "Two Bodies" from *Selected Poems* by Octavio Paz. Copyright © 1973 by Octavio Paz and Muriel Rukeyser. Reprinted by permission of New Directions Publishing Corp.

340, 371 From *Le Morte d'Arthur* by Sir Thomas Malory, translated by Keith Baines. Translation copyright © 1962 by Keith Baines, renewed © 1990 by Francesca Evans. Introduction © 1962 by Robert Graves, renewed © 1990 by Beryl Graves. Reprinted by permission of Dutton Signet, a division of Penguin Books USA Inc.

344 From *The Hollow Hills* by Mary Stewart. Copyright © 1977 by Mary Stewart. Reprinted by permission of William Morrow & Company, Inc. and Hodder & Stoughton Ltd.

350 "Youth and Chivalry" from *A Distant Mirror* by Barbara Tuchman. Copyright © 1978 by Barbara W. Tuchman. Reprinted by permission of Alfred A. Knopf, Inc.

358 "The Tale of Sir Launcelot du Lake" by Sir Thomas Malory, translated by Keith Baines. Translation copyright © 1962 by Keith Baines, renewed © 1990 by Francesca Evans. Introduction © 1962 by Robert Graves, renewed © 1990 by Beryl Graves. Reprinted by permission of Dutton Signet, a division of Penguin Books USA Inc.

365 From *The Once and Future King* by T. H. White. Reprinted by permission of David Higham Associates.

384–385 "Bus Chivalry" from *Miss Manners' Guide to Excruciatingly Correct Behavior* by Judith Martin. Copyright © 1979, 1980, 1981, 1982 by United Features Syndicates, Inc. Reprinted by permission of Scribner, a Division of Simon & Schuster Inc.

384 From *Math for Smarty Pants* by Marilyn Burns. Copyright © 1982 by Yolla Bolly Press. Reprinted by permission of Little, Brown and Company.

385 "The Knight" from *Collected Early Poems: 1950–1970* by Adrienne Rich. Copyright © 1993 by Adrienne Rich. Copyright © 1967, 1963, 1962, 1961, 1960, 1959, 1958, 1957, 1956, 1955, 1954, 1953, 1952, 1951 by Adrienne Rich. Copyright © 1984, 1975, 1971, 1969, 1966 by W. W. Norton & Company, Inc. Reprinted by permission of W. W. Norton & Company, Inc.

396 "And of Clay Are We Created" from *The Stories of Eva Luna* by Isabel Allende, translated from the Spanish by Margaret Sayers Peden. Copyright © 1989 by Isabel Allende. English translation copyright © 1991 by Macmillan Publishing Company. Reprinted by permission of Scribner, an imprint of Simon & Schuster, Inc.

409 "A Soldier of Urbina" from *Jorge Luis Borges Selected Poems* 1923–1967 by Jorge Luis Borges. Copyright © 1968, 1969, 1970, 1971, 1972 by Jorge Luis Borges, Emece Editores, S. A. and Normal Thomas Di Giovanni. Reprinted by permission of Delacorte Press/Seymour Lawrence, a division of Bantam Doubleday Dell Publishing Group, Inc.

411 "Lineage" from *This is My Century: New and Collected Poems* by Margaret Walker Alexander. Reprinted by permission of The University of Georgia Press.

411 "The Gift" from *Rose* by Li-Young Lee. Copyright © 1986 by Li-Young Lee. Reprinted by permission of BOA Editions, Ltd., 92 Park Ave., Brockport, NY 14420.

412 "Turning Pro" from *New and Collected Poems* by Ishmael Reed. Copyright © 1988 by Ishmael Reed. Reprinted by permission of Ellis J. Freedman.

417 "The Secret Room" from *The Hiding Place* by Corrie ten Boom with John and Elizabeth Sherrill. Copyright © 1971 by Corrie ten Boom and John and Elizabeth Sherrill. Reprinted by permission of Chosen Books.

429 "The Street of the Cañon" from *Mexican Village* by Josefina Niggli. Copyright 1945 by The University of North Carolina Press. Reprinted by permission of the publisher.

437 From "Heroic Possibilities" by Michael Dorris, *Teaching Tolerance,* Spring 1995, Vol. 4, No. 1, pp. 13–14. Copyright © 1995 Southern Poverty Law Center. Reprinted by permission of Teaching Tolerance.

456 Adapted from *Kaffir Boy* by Mark Mathabane. Copyright © 1986 by Mark Mathabane. Reprinted by permission of Simon & Schuster, Inc.

469 "Living Well. Living Good." from *Wouldn't Take Nothing For My Journey Now* by Maya Angelou. Copyright © 1993 by Maya Angelou. Reprinted by permission of Random House Inc.

475 Excerpt from *An American Childhood* by Annie Dillard. Copyright © 1987 by Annie Dillard. Reprinted with permission of HarperCollins Publishers, Inc.

481 "By Any Other Name" from *Gifts of Passage* by Santha Rama Rau. Originally appeared in *The New Yorker.* Copyright 1951 by Vasanthi Rama Rau Bowers. Copyright renewed. Reprinted by permission of HarperCollins Publishers, Inc.

488 "The Naming of Cats" from *Old Possum's Book of Practical Cats.* Copyright 1939 by T. S. Eliot and renewed © 1967 by Esme Valerie Eliot. Reprinted by permission of Harcourt Brace & Company and Faber and Faber Limited, London.

489 Illustration from *Old Possum's Book of Practical Cats* by T. S. Eliot. Illustration copyright © 1982 by Edward Gorey. Reprinted by permission of Harcourt Brace & Company.

503 "One Perfect Rose" by Dorothy Parker from *The Portable Dorothy Parker* by Dorothy Parker. Introduction by Brendan Gill. Copyright 1929 renewed © 1957 by Dorothy Parker. Reprinted by permission of Viking Penguin, a division of Penguin Books USA Inc.

504 "Daybreak in Alabama" from *Selected Poems* by Langston Hughes. Copyright 1948 by Alfred A. Knopf, Inc. and renewed © 1976 by the Executors of the Estate of Langston Hughes. Reprinted by permission of the publisher.

506 "The Flying Cat" from *Hugging the Jukebox* by Naomi Shihab Nye. Copyright © 1982 Naomi Shihab Nye. Reprinted by permission of the author.

510 "Tuesday Siesta" from *No One Writes to the Colonel* by Gabriel García Márquez. Copyright © 1968 in the English translation by Harper & Row, Publishers, Inc. Reprinted by permission of HarperCollins Publishers, Inc.

518 "A Preacher Ought to Be Good-Looking" from *The Pillow Book of Sei Shōnagon,* trans. by Ivan Morris. Copyright © 1967 by Columbia University Press. Reprinted with permission of the publisher.

518 "Elegant Things" from *The Pillow Book of Sei Shōnagon,* trans. by Ivan Morris. Copyright © 1967 by Columbia University Press. Reprinted with permission of the publisher.

Acknowledgments **853**

518 "Things That Give A Good Feeling" from *The Pillow Book of Sei Shōnagon,* trans. by Ivan Morris. Copyright © 1967 by Columbia University Press. Reprinted with permission of the publisher.

518 "Things That Have Lost Their Power" from *The Pillow Book of Sei Shōnagon,* trans. by Ivan Morris. Copyright © 1967 by Columbia University Press. Reprinted with permission of the publisher.

520 "Porsche" from *Mama Makes up Her Mind: and Other Dangers of Southern Living* by Bailey White, pp. 19–21. Copyright © 1993 by Bailey White. Reprinted by permission of Addison-Wesley Publishing Company, Inc.

536 Lyrics from "Mercedes Benz" by Janis Joplin, Michael McClure and Bobby Neuwirth. Copyright © 1970 Strong Arm Music. Reprinted by permission. All Rights Reserved.

553 "A New Dress" by Ruth Dallas from *Collected Poems.* Copyright © 1987 by John McIndoe Publishers. Reprinted by permission of the University of Otago Press, New Zealand.

554 "Those Winter Sundays" from *Angle of Ascent: New and Selected Poems* by Robert Hayden. Copyright © 1966 by Robert Hayden. Reprinted by permission of Liveright Publishing Corporation.

556 "Tía Chucha" from *The Concrete River* by Luis Rodriguez. Copyright © 1991 by Luis J. Rodriguez. Reprinted by permission of Curbstone Press.

561 "Girls Can We Educate We Dads?" from *When I Dance.* Copyright © 1991, 1988 by James Berry. Reprinted by permission of Harcourt Brace & Company and Penguin Books Ltd.

562 "If You'll Only Go To Sleep" from *The Collected Poems of Gabriela Mistral* by Doris Dana. Copyright © 1961, 1964, 1970, 1971 by Doris Dana. Reprinted by arrangement with Doris Dana, c/o Joan Daves Agency as agent for the proprietor.

563 "Mi prima Agueda" from *Poesias Completas Y El Minutero* by Ramón López Velarde, edited by Antonio Castro Leal, 3/E, 1963. Reprinted by permission of Editorial Porrua S. A., Mexico.

564 From "My Cousin Agatha" (orig.: "Mi prima Agueda") by Ramón López Velarde from *The Yellow Canary Whose Eye Is So Black,* edited and translated by Cheli Durán. Copyright © 1977 by Cheli Durán Ryan. Reprinted by permission of Simon & Schuster Books for Young Readers, an imprint of Simon & Schuster Children's Publishing Division.

564 "My Cousin Agueda" by Ramón López Velarde from *Spanish-American Literature in Translation,* translated by Willis Knapp Jones. Copyright © 1963 by Frederick Ungar Publishing Company, Inc. Reprinted by permission of the publisher.

570 "First Frost" from *Antiworlds and the Fifth Ace: Poetry* by Andrei Voznesensky, edited by Patricia Blake and Max Hayward. Copyright © 1966, 1967 by Basic Books, Inc. Copyright © 1963 by Encounter Ltd. Copyright renewed. Reprinted by permission of Basic Books, a division of HarperCollins Publishers, Inc.

571 "For Anne Gregory" by W. B. Yeats from *The Poems of W. B. Yeats: A New Edition,* edited by Richard J. Finneran. Copyright 1933 by Macmillan Publishing Company, renewed © 1961 by Bertha Georgia Yeats. Reprinted by permission of Simon & Schuster, Inc.

571 "The Fist" from *Collected Poems 1948–1984* by Derek Walcott. Copyright © 1986 by Derek Walcott. Reprinted by permission of Farrar, Straus & Giroux, Inc.

572 "The Stone" from *Collected Poems* by W. W. Gibson. Reprinted by permission of Mr. Michael Gibson and Macmillan General Books, London.

579 "The Other" by Judith Ortiz Cofer from *Reaching for the Mainland* appearing in *Triple Crown,* 1987. Reprinted by permission of Bilingual Press/Editorial Bilingüe, Arizona State University, Tempe, AZ.

580 "To Julia de Burgos" by Julia de Burgos, translated by Maria Arrillaga, 1971. Reprinted by permission of Maria Consuelo Saez Burgos.

583 "We Are Many" from *Five Decades: Poems 1925–1970* by Pablo Neruda, translated by Ben Belitt. Copyright © 1961, 1969, 1972, 1974 by Ben Belitt. Reprinted by permission of Grove/Atlantic, Inc.

586 Abridgement of "Reading a Family Portrait" by Caroline Sloat. Copyright © 1982 by Caroline Sloat. Reprinted by permission of the author

598 "Sunday Morning" by Oscar Peñaranda. Copyright © 1969 by Oscar Peñaranda. Reprinted by permission of the author.

605 "Ceremony" by Leslie Marmon Silko. Copyright © 1981 by Leslie Marmon Silko. Reprinted by permission of Wylie, Aitken & Stone, Inc.

606 "A Story" from *The Collected Poems* 1931–1987 by Czeslaw Milosz. Translated by Renata Gorczynski and Robert Pinsky. Copyright © 1988 by Czeslaw Milosz Royalties, Inc. First published by The Ecco Press in 1988. Reprinted by permission of The Ecco Press.

607 "The Road Not Taken" by Robert Frost from *The Poetry of Robert Frost* edited by Edward Connery Lathem. Published in 1969 by Henry Holt and Co., Inc. Reprinted by permission of Henry Holt and Co., Inc.

608 *The Holy Bible.* Cleveland: The World Publishing Co.

614 "This is a Photograph of Me" from *The Circle Game* by Margaret Atwood, House of Anansi Press, Toronto, 1978. Reprinted with the permission of Stoddart Publishing Co., Limited, Don Mills, Ontario, Canada.

615 "Water Picture" from *The Complete Poems to Solve* by May Swenson. Copyright © 1966 by May Swenson. Copyright © 1993 by The Literary Estate of May Swenson. Originally appeared in *The New Yorker*. Reprinted by permission of Simon & Schuster Books for Young Readers, an imprint of Simon & Schuster Children's Publishing Division.

616 "On a Bare Branch," "Clouds Now and Then" and "Spring" by Matsuo Bashō from *The Penguin Book of Japanese Verse* translated by Geoffrey Bownas and Anthony Thwaite. Copyright © 1964 Geoffrey Bownas and Anthony Thwaite. Reprinted by permission of Penguin Books Ltd., England.

616 "Spring Rain," "Mosquito Buzz" and "Sudden Shower" by Yosa Buson from *The Penguin Book of Japanese Verse* translated by Geoffrey Bownas and Anthony Thwaite. Copyright © 1964 Geoffrey Bownas and Anthony Thwaite. Reprinted by permission of Penguin Books Ltd., England.

620 From "The Cerebral Snapshot" from *Sunrise with Seamonsters* by Paul Theroux. Copyright © 1985 by Cape Cod Scriveners. All rights reserved. Reprinted by permission of Houghton Mifflin Co.

632 "The Woman from America" by Bessie Head. Reprinted by permission of John Johnson Ltd.

637 Adapted from "Rain Music" by Longhang Nguyen. Copyright © 1992 by Longhang Nguyen. Reprinted by permission of the author.

644 "My Father Writes to My Mother" by Assia Djebar. Reprinted by permission of Quartet Books Ltd.

652 "For the White Poets Who Would Be Indian" from *Bone Dance: New and Selected Poems 1965–1993* by Wendy Rose. Copyright © 1994 by Wendy Rose. Reprinted by permission of Malki Museum Press.

652 "Legal Alien" by Pat Mora from *Chants,* 1985. Reprinted by permission of Arte Publico Press, University of Houston.

653 "I am not with those who left their land . . ." by Anna Akhmatova, translated by Peter Norman from *The Akhmatova Journals: Volume One 1938–1941* by Lydia Chukovskaya. Copyright © 1994 by Lydia Chukovskaya. Reprinted by permission of Farrar, Straus & Giroux, Inc.

654 "Jerusalem" from *The Selected Poetry of Yehuda Amichai* by Yehuda Amichai. Edited and translated by Chana Bloch and Stephen Mitchell. English translation copyright © 1986 by Chana Bloch and Stephen Mitchell. Reprinted by permission of HarperCollins Publishers, Inc.

656 "Dos Patrias" and "Two Countries" by José Martí from *José Martí: Major Poems.* Translated by Elinor Randall, edited by Philip S. Foner. Copyright © 1982 by Holmes & Meier Publishers, Inc. Reprinted by permission of the publisher, Holmes & Meier, New York.

659 "It's Hard to Smile" from "Koreans Have a Reason Not to Smile" by Connie Kang, *The New York Times,* September 8, 1990. Copyright © 1990 by The New York Times Company. Reprinted by permission.

764 "Caesar's Commentaries on the Gallic Wars" from *Shrinklits* by Maurice Sagoff. All rights reserved. Reprinted by permission of Workman Publishing Company, Inc.

766 "The Balek Scales" from *18 Stories* by Heinrich Böll, trans. by Leila Vennewitz. Copyright © 1966 by Heinrich Böll. Reprinted by arrangement with Verlag Kiepenheuer & Witsch, c/o Joan Daves Agency as agent for the proprietor and by permission of Leila Vennewitz.

775 "How Much Land Does a Man Need?" from *Twenty-three Tales* by Leo Tolstoy, translated by Louise and Aylmer Maude, 1906. Reprinted by permission of Oxford University Press, Oxford.

788 John Tebbel and Sarah Miles Watts, *The Press and the Presidency.* New York: Oxford University Press, 1985, pp. 535–36, 541.

Acknowledgments

Illustration

Unless otherwise acknowledged, all photographs are the property of Scott, Foresman and Company. Page abbreviations are as follows: (t)top, (c)center, (b)bottom, (l)left, (r)right, (INS)inset.

Cover (detail) and Frontispiece *The Afterglow in Egypt* by William Holman Hunt, 1834. Southampton City Art Gallery.

vii, xxxii–1 Antonio Ruiz, *The Bicycle Race*, 1938(detail). Philadelphia Museum of Art; Purchased by Nebinger Fund.

ix Roman mosaic of tragic and comic masks, Scala/Art Resource

xi Sir Frank Dicksee, *La Belle Dame Sans Merci,* Bridgeman/Art Resource

xiii Tsing-Fang Chen, *Human Achievement,* Lucia Gallery, New York City/Superstock, Inc.

xv Boris Kustodiev, *The Fair*, 1908/Scala/Art Resource

xviii Jean-Leon Gerome, *Death of Caesar*, 1859, The Walters Art Gallery, Baltimore

xxiv Photo Reunion des Musées Nationaux

1, 4, 50, 56, 62 (icon) Normand Cousineau/SIS

1, 64, 114, 119, 125 (icon) Husain Haqqash, *Akbar Hunting a Tiger Near Gwalior*, From the Akbar-Nama, By Courtesy of the Board of Trustees of the Victoria and Albert Museum, London/Bridgeman Art Library, London/Superstock, Inc.

1, 126, 170, 174, 179 (icon) Wheel of Fortune tarot card, The Pierpont Morgan Library/Art Resource

2 Private Collection. Photo: Jeffrey Ploskonka

3(t) From the collection of Nancy Berliner

3(b) Stuart Handler Family Collection, Evanston, Illinois/Photo: P.P.O.W.

5 Jill Krementz

10–11 Stuart Handler Family Collection, Evanston, Illinois/Photo: P.P.O.W.

17(l) Photo by Robert Foothorap

17(r) Sidney Harris

18–19 © Service photographique, Ville de Nice, © 1995 Succession H. Matisse, Paris/Artists Rights Society (ARS), New York

25 From the collection of Nancy Berliner

29(t) Layle Silbert

29(b) Drawing by Lorenz; ©1977 New Yorker Magazine, Inc.

31 Collection Nelly and Guido Di Tella, Buenos Aires/Museum of Modern Art, Oxford

35 Don Hamerman

37 Collection IWALEWA-Haus-INV.Nr. 14106

43 Corbis-Bettmann Archive

44 Tate Gallery, London/Art Resource

50(l) Scala/Art Resource

50(r) Cynthia Johnson/Time Magazine

51(tl) Steve Schapiro/Gamma-Liaison

51(tr) Suolang Loubu/Xinhua/Gamma-Liaison

51(br) Copyright British Museum

53 Copyright British Museum

63 Everett Collection, Inc.

65 Granger Collection, New York

68 National Portrait Gallery, London/Superstock, Inc.

77 Culver Pictures Inc.

78 Aarhus Kunstmuseum

86 AP/Wide World

88 British Library, MS OR 5259 fols 56v-57r

93 Reprinted with permission of Four Winds Press, an imprint of Macmillan Publishing Company from *Calendar Art* written and illustrated by Leonard Everett Fisher. ©1987 Leonard Everett Fisher.

94 Poe ms. Manuscripts Department, Lilly Library, Indiana University, Bloomington

96 Giraudon/Art Resource

105 Courtesy of Herbert Cole/Photo by unknown photographer

110 Private Collection. Photo: Jeffrey Ploskonka

114 Photofest

115(t inset, b) UPI/Corbis-Bettmann

115(br) Superstock, Inc.

115(bl) UPI/Corbis-Bettmann

127 Viking Press

129 Bridgeman/Art Resource/© 1996 C. Hercovici, Brussels/Artists Rights Society (ARS), New York

135 AP/Wide World

138 Neg. No. 323730 Painting by George Catlin, Courtesy Department Library Services, American Museum of Natural History

143(l) Emily Da

143(r) UPI/Corbis-Bettmann

144 From *Prop Art: Over 1000 Contemporary Political Posters* by Gary Yanker. Darien House, New York, distributed by New York Graphic Society, 1972. Copyright ©1972 by Gary Yanker.

334–335 Sir Frank Dicksee, *La Belle Dame Sans Merci* (detail), Bridgeman/Art Resource

335, 338, 382, 386, 392 (icon) Pierpont Morgan Library/Art Resource

335, 394, 437, 442, 447 (icon) Kasimir Malevich, *The Mower*, Russian State Museum, St.Petersburg /A.Burkatousky/Superstock, Inc.

336 Bridgeman/Art Resource

337 Giraudon/Art Resource

339 Courtesy William Morrow, photo by Mark Gerson

340 Courtesy of Sotheby's

345 Giraudon/Art Resource

349 © Randi Hendrix

351 The Bodleian Library, Oxford, MS. Douce 383, fol. 16r

356 Y Swyddfa Gymreig/Welsh Office

357 AP/Wide World

361 Bridgeman/Art Resource

366–367 The Pierpont Morgan Library/Art Resource

370 National Portrait Gallery, London

373 Bridgeman/Art Resource

381 E. Hugo

382(tl) National Museum of African Art, Eliot Elisofon Photographic Archives, Smithsonian Institution (GHSA89(6335)

382(bl) Skinsness

382-383(c) Pete Dancs/Tony Stone Images

382 Pierpont Morgan Library/Art Resource

383(t) Photofest

383(bl) Giraudon/Art Resource

383(br) Superstock, Inc.

384(t) K. Marine

384(b) K. Marine

385 K. Marine

393 Bridgeman/Art Resource

395 AP/Wide World

397 The Menil Collection, Houston, Gift of Philippa and Heiner Friedrich. Photo by Paul Hester, Houston

403 The Metropolitan Museum of Art, Hilson Fund, Inc. Gift, 1990 (1990.188)

407 Reprinted with special permission of North America Syndicate

408(t) Organization of American States

408(tc) University of Georgia Press

408(bc) B. O. A. Editions, Ltd., photo by Arthur Furst

408(b) ©1990 Jay Blakesberg

410 The Evans Tibbs Collection

413 Courtesy of Leo Jensen

416 Courtesy Archives of The Billy Graham Center, Wheaton, IL

419 Courtesy Archives of The Billy Graham Center, Wheaton, IL

422 Courtesy Archives of The Billy Graham Center, Wheaton, IL

428 Gary V. Fields

431 Private Collection. Courtesy of Sotheby's, New York

437(icon) Kasimir Malevich, *The Mower,* Russian State Museum, St.Petersburg/A.Burkatousky/ Superstock, Inc.

438(l) Granger Collection, New York

438(c) Hamburg Museum

438(r) Giraudon/Art Resource

438–439(background) British Library

439(l) Granger Collection, New York

439(c) Culver Pictures Inc.

439(r) Ancient Art & Architecture Collection/Ronald Sheridan Photo-Library

440 Courtesy Emilia Askari

448 Sir Frank Dicksee, *La Belle Dame Sans Merci* (detail), Bridgeman/Art Resource

449 The Evans Tibbs Collection

450–451 Tsing-Fang Chen, *Human Achievement*, (detail) Lucia Gallery, New York City/Superstock, Inc.

452 From *An American Childhood* by Annie Dillard. Copyright ©1987 by Annie Dillard, All rights reserved. Harper & Row Publishers, Inc., New York

453 Reprinted with the permission of Simon & Schuster from *Kaffir Boy* by Mark Mathabane. Copyright ©1986 by Mark Mathabane.

455(l) Gail Mathabane

455(r) South Light/ Gamma Liaison

456 David Turnley/Black Star

463 David Turnley/Black Star

468(l) AP/Wide World Photos

468(r) United States Bureau of Labor Statistics

469 Howard University Gallery of Art, Washington, D.C.

474 Rollie McKenna

475 Corbis-Bettmann Archive

480(l) UPI/Corbis-Bettmann

480(r) British Library

483 Superstock, Inc.

489 From *Old Possum's Book of Practical Cats* by T. S. Eliot. Drawings by Edward Gorey, Harcourt Brace Jovanovich Publishers. Copyright 1939 by T. S. Eliot. Copyright renewed ©1967 by Esme Valerie Eliot. Illustrations copyright ©1982 by Edward Gorey.

502(t) Viking Press

502(c) UPI/Corbis-Bettmann

502(b) Michael Nye

505 Art and Artifacts Division, Schomberg Center for Research in Black Culture, The New York Public Library, Astor, Lenox and Tilden Foundations

506 Oleg Tselkov, *With Cat*, 1993, oil on canvas, 51" x 38", Courtesy of The Sloane Gallery/ Contemporary Russian Art, Denver, Colorado

509 AP/Wide World

510 El pequeño cementerio de Culebra, by María de Mater O'Neill. ©1990 María de Mater O'Neill. Oils crayons, oils on linen. 64" x 94". Photograph by John Betancourt. Collection of Iliana Fonts.

517 Spencer Jarnigan

518 Copyright British Museum

521 The Sculpture Park at Le Monciel, Jouy-en Josas, France

524(t) Ricki Rosen

524(b) Hulton Deutsch Collection Ltd.

527 Roger-Viollet

532-533(t) David LeBon/Tony Stone Images

532(b) Superstock, Inc.

533(t) Superstock, Inc.

533(c) Superstock, Inc.

533-534(b) Keith Bernstein/FSP/Gamma Liaison

534(t) Courtesy, General Motors Corporation

534-535 E. Hugo

535(b) Martyn Goddard/Tony Stone Images

536 John Turner/Tony Stone Images

544 David Turnley/Black Star

545 Tsing-Fang Chen, *Human Achievement*, (detail) Lucia Gallery, New York City/Superstock, Inc.

546-547 Boris Kustodiev, *The Fair*, (detail), 1908/Scala/Art Resource

547, 550, 586, 590, 595, 596, 619, 624, 628, 630, 659, 663, 664, (icons) Superstock, Inc.

548–549 AP/Wide World

551 Drawing by Stan Hunt; ©1987 The New Yorker Magazine, Inc.

552(t) Courtesy of University of Otago Press

554-555 Collection Leontine D. Scott

559 Drawing by Lorenz; ©1995 The New Yorker Magazine, Inc.

560(t) Courtesy Harcourt Brace & Company

560(b) Organization of American States

562 Galerie Garces Velasquez, Bogata

565 Jeanette Ortiz Osorio

569(t) AP/Wide World

569(c) Royal Photographic Society, Bath

569(b) Evan Richman/Reuters/Corbis-Bettmann

570 Burt Glinn/Magnum Photos

573 Franz Altschuler

577 Christie's, London/Superstock, Inc./©1995 Artists Rights Society(ARS), New York/SPADEM, Paris

578(t) Courtesy of Arte Publico Press

578(b) AP/Wide World

581 Reproduced by authorization of the Instituto Nacional de Bellas Artes y Literatura, Mexico City

582 Superstock, Inc.

587 Gift of Maxim Karolik for the M. and M. Karolik Collection of American Paintings, 1815–1865. Courtesy, Museum of Fine Arts, Boston

588(t) Kobal Collection

588(c) Everett Collection, Inc.

588(bl) Kobal Collection

588(br) Everett Collection, Inc.

589(tl) Photofest

589(tr) Everett Collection, Inc.

589(b) Photofest

597(t) Courtesy of Oscar Peñaranda

597(b) Trustees of Amherst College

599 Ansel Adams, *Silverton Colorado*, c. 1951. Photograph by Ansel Adams, Copyright ©1993 by the Trustees of the Ansel Adams Publishing Trust. All Rights Reserved.

603(c) UPI/Corbis-Bettmann

603(t) ©1981 Linda Fry Poverman

603(b) Dartmouth College

604 Jerry Jacka

609 Roloff Beny

613(t) Laurence Acland

613(c) UPI/Corbis-Bettmann

613(b) Collection Kimiko and John Powers. Photo: Fogg Art Museum, Harvard University

614-615 Robert Amft

616 Chishaku-in temple, Kyoto/I.S.E.I., Tokyo, Japan

619 Courtesy, Wade Patton

620-621 Mitch Reardon/Tony Stone Images

622(tl) Howard Sochurek/Stock Market

622(tr) The Harold E. Edgerton 1992 Trust, courtesy of Palm Press, Inc.

622(c) North American Philips Corporation

629 André Kertész, American, 1894–1985, *Shadows of the Eiffel Tower* (view looking down from tower to people underneath), silver gelatin print, 1929. 16.5 x 21.9 cm, Julien Levy Collection, Special Photography Acquisition Fund, 1979.77, photograph ©1994 The Art Institute of Chicago. All Rights Reserved.

631 Courtesy Heineman Publishers, Oxford, England. Photo: Michael Uaha

633 Christine Kristen

636 Courtesy of Longhang Nguyen

639 Superstock, Inc.

643 Courtesy of Quartet Books Limited

644 Isabel Cutler/Gamma Liaison

651(t) Courtesy of Arte Público Press

651(tc) Pat Wolk

651(c) RIA-Novosti/Sovfoto

651(bc) Layle Silbert

651(b) Corbis-Bettmann Archive

653 Scala/Art Resource

654-655 Esais Baitel/Gamma Liaison

659(all) AP/Wide World

660(all) AP/Wide World

661(t) Farnood/Sipa Press

661(b) Ricardo Beliel/GLMR/Gamma Liaison

662(t) Michael Dwyer/Stock Boston

662(b) Leong Ka Tai/Material World

670(t) Reproduced by authorization of the Instituto Nacional de Bellas Artes y Literatura, Mexico City

670(b) Jeanette Ortiz Osorio

671 Roloff Beny

672–673 Jean-Leon Gerome, *Death of Caesar,* 1859 (detail), The Walters Art Gallery, Baltimore

673, 676, 787, 791, 797(icon) Christie's, London/Superstock, Inc.

674–675 Museum of Modern Art, Film Stills Archive

677 National Portrait Gallery, London

681 Courtesy of Sotheby's

687 Museum of Modern Art, Film Stills Archive

733 Drawing by Robert Mankoff; ©1987 The New Yorker Magazine, Inc.

734(t) Copyright British Museum

735 Scale drawing by Irwin Smith from *Shakespeare's Globe Playhouse: A Modern Reconstruction in Text and Scale Drawings* by Irwin Smith. Charles Scribner's Sons, New York, 1956. Hand colored by Cheryl Kucharzak

737 Photofest

747 Christie's, London/Superstock, Inc.

756 Ancient Art & Architecture Collection/Ronald Sheridan Photo-Library

765 McGraw Hill

767 Collection John P. Axelrod. Photo: Marisa del Ray Gallery

774 Granger Collection, New York

775 Tass/Sovfoto

780 Novosti/Sovfoto

787 Pete Souza/The White House

788 Pete Souza/The White House

789 Courtesy Diego Muñoz

798 Collection John P. Axelrod. Photo: Marisa del Ray Gallery